42.

Economics for Today

ISSUES AND APPLICATIONS

Mark Lovewell, B.A., M.A.
Ryerson Polytechnic University
Toronto, Ontario

Brian Lorimer, B.A.
Lorne Park Secondary School
Mississauga, Ontario

McGRAW-HILL RYERSON LIMITED
Toronto Montreal New York Auckland Bogotá Caracas
Lisbon London Madrid Mexico Milan New Delhi
San Juan Singapore Sydney Tokyo

This book is dedicated to Patricia and David Lovewell, for proving by their example that economics cannot explain everything, and to Kathleen and Barry Lorimer, whose fifty years of marriage is a tribute to itself.

Economics for Today
Issues and Applications

ISBN 0-07-551527-X

1 2 3 4 5 6 7 8 9 10 QP 4 3 2 1 0 9 8 7 6 5

Printed and bound in Canada

Readers wishing additional information on data provided through the co-operation of Statistics Canada may obtain copies of related publications by mail from:
Publications Sales, Statistics Canada, Ottawa, Ontario, K1A 0T6, by calling (613) 951-7277 or toll-free 800-267-6677. Readers may also facsimile their orders by dialing (613) 951-1584.

Canadian Cataloguing in Publication Data

Lovewell, Mark A.
    Economics for today: issues and applications

Includes index.
ISBN 0-07-551527-X

1. Economics. 2. Canada — Economic conditions.
I. Lorimer, Brian. II. Title

HB171.5.L68 1995   330   C94-932676-3

PUBLISHER: Andrea Crozier
ASSOCIATE EDITORS: Brenda Hutchinson/Laura Edlund
SUPERVISING EDITOR: Nancy Christoffer
PERMISSIONS EDITORS: Tina Dell/Jacqueline Donovan
PRODUCTION EDITOR: Claudia Kutchukian
COVER AND INTERIOR DESIGN: Brant Cowie/ArtPlus Limited
ELECTRONIC PAGE MAKEUP: Valerie Bateman/ArtPlus Limited
TECHNICAL ILLUSTRATIONS: Donna Guilfoyle/ArtPlus Limited
COVER ILLUSTRATION AND COMMISSIONED ART: Harvey Chan

This book was manufactured in Canada using acid-free and recycled paper.

Contents

Introduction

Our aim in *Economics for Today: Issues and Applications* is to provide an economics text geared to today's student. The result, we believe, is an easy-to-use learning tool that combines theory and application in a relevant and appealing way. To help stimulate effective learning, *Economics for Today* explores real-world economics, emphasizes skills, and facilitates study.

Real-World Economics

Economics is part of daily life—in the choices we make, in the decisions of communities, governments, and businesses, and in the media. While developing the theoretical framework of economics, *Economics for Today* offers real-world examples and explores current economic issues. Articles, editorials, essays, interviews, and cartoons stimulate critical thinking, research, application, and more. By providing a balanced and wide range of perspectives, these elements encourage students to evaluate and debate economic issues for themselves. **Sidelines** deal with current economic issues, such as the growth of a multimedia empire, one student's bid for a labour union, international finance in Canada, and the merits of growth versus development. **Developing Interpretation Skills** also address such issues—for example, the trend toward part-time employment, the debate over government debt, and the potential limits of worldwide economic growth—and provide activities that encourage evaluation and research. Within each chapter, **Advancing Economic Thought** details the ideas of an influential thinker of either the past or the present. So, for example, Adam Smith's defence of private markets, Karl Marx's theory of capitalist exploitation, and Thomas Malthus' treatment of population growth are featured, as well as Nuala Beck's analysis of the "new economy," Hazel Henderson's environmental and economic ideals, and Muhammad Yunus' grassroots banking scheme practised in Bangladesh. In addition, each chapter includes several points for discussion called **Thinking About Economics**, which help students to interpret and extend the concepts they are learning through a question-and-answer format.

Emphasis on Skills

Application is the key to effective learning. So that students have ample opportunity to apply the knowledge they acquire, this text emphasizes skills throughout. As an initial review and a resource to return to for direction and hints, the **Skills Resource** focuses on using visual materials and the basics of critical thinking, research, and ways of presenting findings. For example, this resource reviews interpreting and creating tables and graphs; it guides students in evaluating their own work or that of others to see that it is precise, logical, and considered; it illustrates economic forecasting; it lists possible resources; and, it supports essay-writing and debating.

Each chapter's **Skills Focus** identifies the learning outcomes to give students a sense of the ways they will use their new knowledge in the chapter activities. In addition to the activities provided in **Developing Interpretation Skills,** end-of-chapter activities entitled **Developing Application and Analysis Skills** engage the students in analyzing economic problems and applying economic theory. Within these activities, tables, graphs, and opinion pieces help students extend their learning to contemporary situations and issues.

Study Aids

So that *Economics for Today* invites and engages students, we have taken care to write in a clear and readable style, include quotations and cartoons for reflection and discussion, and use an appealing design. At the same time, we have provided a variety of features to make this text user-friendly. Every chapter begins with a **Chapter Focus**, which introduces the content students are to learn. Then, each **Brief Review** summarizes key ideas, while margin notes define key terms highlighted in the text. These terms are listed at the end of each chapter under the heading **Key Concepts** for review and are defined again in a central **Glossary** at the end of the book for easy reference. Because interpreting graphs is a challenge for many students, virtually all graphs are paired with tables so that it is possible to see at a glance how they are plotted. This technique not only makes graphs easier to interpret, it also helps students to better appreciate the usefulness of visual aids in presenting economic information. Lastly, an **Index** helps students access the text in a variety of ways.

Ancillaries

Teaching and testing aids have been developed for use with the text. They include the **Teacher's Resource** and a **Computer Test Bank**. The **Teacher's Resource** incorporates instructional strategies, lesson plans, evaluation/assessment suggestions, and complete solutions to all in-text questions. Also featured is a unit linking **Economics for Today** to E-STAT (CD-ROM), which is published and updated annually by Statistics Canada. E-STAT lesson plans and assignments integrate the use of the text with approximately 300,000 Canadian economic time series statistics available on E-STAT. The **Computer Test Bank** (provided in MS-DOS and Macintosh versions) provides over 1200 questions in various formats focusing on interpretation, analysis, and application skills. Answers to all test bank questions are included.

Acknowledgements

We owe a great debt to our publisher, Andrea Crozier, and to our editors—Laura Edlund, Brenda Hutchinson, and Claudia Kutchukian—as well as Nancy Christoffer, Tina Dell, Jacqueline Donovan, and ArtPlus for their innumerable contributions in casting this book in its final form. We are also grateful to reviewers of the book for their useful suggestions and criticisms. These include G.S. Murray Ault, Rideau High School, Ottawa; Laura Gini, Vaughan Secondary School, Thornhill; T.L. Seymour, Riverdale Collegiate Institute, Toronto; Sam Stajfer, Sir Frederick Banting Secondary School, London; and, Jamie Whitaker, Western Technical Commercial School, Toronto.

Past and present members of Ryerson's Economics Department have provided encouragement: Tom Barbiero, Ingrid Bryan, Harry Pope, Eric Wright, and Gus Zaks in particular. Steve Hammerschmidt also deserves thanks for his valuable work as a research assistant. Will Glass-Husain provided the inspiration for the system dynamics components of this text. Finally, we would like to express our special debt to Marina Vitkin and Linda and Michael Lorimer. Without their support and good-humoured endurance, writing this book would not have been possible.

Skills Resource

*E*conomics for Today requires that you interpret, analyze, and apply information. Use this general resource first to review the skills you will need, and then—as you venture further into *Economics for Today*—for direction and helpful hints.

Visual Materials

Because visual materials can present complex information at a glance, they are often used in economics. Whether you are interpreting or creating visual materials, keep the following advice in mind.

Tables

Tables present *related* information in **columns** (groups of information presented vertically) and **rows** (horizontal lines of information). A **heading** usually appears at the top of each column to describe the information presented; check the column heading to ensure you understand what information is being presented. Tables are "read" left to right—giving the **independent variable** first, at the left. When reading or creating complex tables, use a grid to help you line up information. Double-check at each stage any calculations you must make. Label your table for easy reference and to summarize the relationship it presents. Note that some tables are called **schedules** when they present, for example, the demand and/or supply information for a product.

Often you will need to examine tables for relationships and trends. Consider the following table. In the left column, the numbers are increasing; in the right column, the numbers are decreasing. Based on the hypothetical information in the table, we can say that as the price of compact disks goes up, the quantity sold goes down.

Sales of Compact Disks	
Price per CD ($)	**CDs Sold (no. of CDs)**
4	16
8	12
12	8
16	4

Now consider this table. It shows that, between 1983 and 1992, global sales of compact disks and cassettes have increased, while sales of long-playing records have decreased.

Manufacturers' Shipments per Year (millions of units)			
Year	**Cassettes**	**Long-Playing Records**	**Compact Disks**
1983	250	200	0
1992	375	0	400

Especially when interpreting and analyzing tables that have many columns and rows, you might find it easiest to look at the trend in each column, then start examining the possible relationships among columns and the trends they demonstrate.

Graphs

Related information also can be presented on a graph. Note on the following example how the horizontal line—called the **x-axis**—and the vertical line—called the **y-axis**—form an L-shape to meet at a **point of origin**. The range of values for one variable is indicated on each axis, and each axis is labelled, including the **units**. To graph correctly, the **scale** must be consistent—for example, if the height of the first square on the grid equals $2, the height of each subsequent square must also equal $2. In economics, the **independent variable** is usually plotted on the y-axis. In our example, using the price to give the **y co-ordinate** and CDs sold to give the **x co-ordinate**, we can plot the points shown. Joining the points together gives a **curve**. The term "curve" is used even for a straight line.

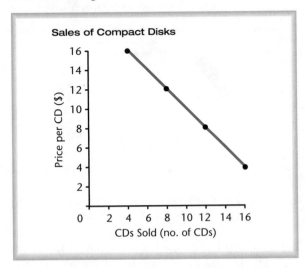

The resulting curve shows the relationship of the two variables. Note that a graph can relate more than two factors. For example, a third factor—the costs to the CD manufacturer—could be added if the graph's y-axis were changed to represent general dollar amounts.

Curves can depict a variety of relationships and are described in *Economics for Today* in particular ways. For example, the curve that illustrates prices and CDs sold shows that as price decreases, the quantity sold increases. In the text, we describe this as having a **negative (downward) slope** ("downward" because graphs, like tables, are "read" left to right and the curve slopes downward to the right). If, in contrast, quantity sold increases as price increases, the slope would be described as having a **positive (upward) slope**.

The **slope of a curve** demonstrates another aspect of the relationship—for example, whether

the decline in CD sales is the same as the increase in price. In this case it is, and our graph demonstrates this by showing a curve at a 45-degree angle. Other relationships will be represented by curves that we describe as **horizontal, flattened, steep**, and **vertical**. Note, however, that the slope of the curve depends on the scale used on the x- and y-axes. Take the CD example again. If the scale of the y-axis is reduced or increased, the slope seems to change. By calculating the slope and expressing it numerically, you will be able to overcome this problem.

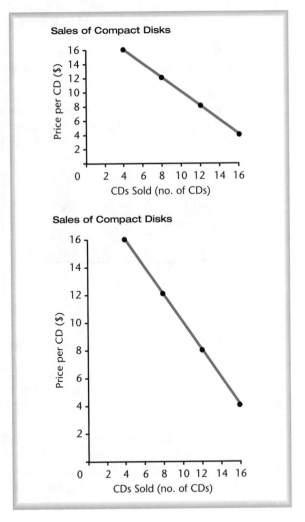

When asked to *draw* or *create* a graph, develop and label the graph precisely based on the information given. If instead you are asked to *sketch* a graph, develop a graph with labelled axes and a curve demonstrating the relationship of the variables. When "reading" or developing graphs, use a grid for precision. Label the x- and y-axes carefully, remembering to note units of measurement. Title your graphs for easy reference and to summarize the relationship shown.

Note that, depending on the information, graphs can take a variety of forms. For example, the information about sales of cassettes, long-playing records, and compact disks could be presented in a **bar graph**. The same basic principles of graphing apply. When various types of information are shown, as in the graph below, a legend must be included to identify the different types of bars.

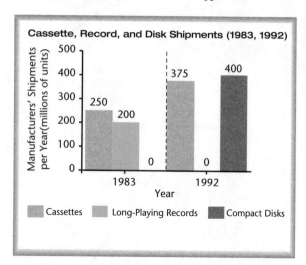

When interpreting any graph, consider these questions: What are the variables? What trends are evident? What relationships are suggested? Why? Particularly in macroeconomics, you might also ask: What additional factors could have caused this result (for example, a sudden downturn in the economy)? What is the context for this information (for example, expansionary years)? Why?

Flow Diagrams

Flow diagrams are a useful way of depicting causes and effects. For example, throughout the text we use flow diagrams to demonstrate the flow of resources and incomes in markets. **Causal loops** are a particular type of flow diagram. The following example illustrates how interest on a bank account balance will increase the balance, which, in turn, will increase the interest.[1]

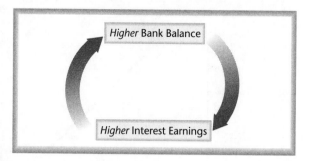

When you interpret flow diagrams, note the direction of the arrows and whether the result is "higher" or "lower." When you create flow diagrams, first clarify the starting point—that is, the initial action—and then the resulting actions. Label your diagram carefully and check it against the relationship it is to demonstrate.

Cartoons

Cartoons, particularly editorial cartoons, often comment on economic and political events and issues, and the personalities involved. When interpreting a cartoon, identify any characters and search for clues concerning time and place. Look for further clues in any caption. What is the issue or event? What is the context? What is the cartoonist's perspective? Examine newspapers and business publications to see how the editorial cartoon relates to its context—that is, the news and editorials of the day.

The Basics of Critical Thinking

Information, ideas, and opinions abound. Whether you are interpreting and analyzing the work of others or developing your own observations, opinions, and arguments, you must use critical thinking skills. Critical thinking involves precise meaning, logic, and consideration of values and perspectives. Evaluate your work and that of others against these basics.

Precise

The rule "Say what you mean and mean what you say" can be applied to all subjects and topics. Keep in mind these questions: What don't I understand? Can I paraphrase this? What really is the point? What might confuse the audience? Where is the meaning clear? Where is it murky?

With few exceptions, economic terms—such as "rent" and "aggregate demand"—have precise meanings. This is also true of other disciplines. For the few terms in economics that are ambiguous— such as "income equity" and "full employment"— the meaning should be clarified. See that a writer is using the terminology precisely or defines the term in the writing. In your own work, use the standard definition that is appropriate to the subject or discipline. If the meaning might be unclear, clarify it.

Statistics can be a particular trouble-spot. With every statistic you use or come across, ask yourself the following: What information is this giving? What definitions are used? What is the basis of this information (for example, a broad study, or a small sample)? How is this relevant to the discussion? How have the numbers been treated? What other factors should be taken into account? What relationships can I see?

See that a statistic means what you think it does, and use it precisely. For example:

- A **measure** differs from an **indicator**. For example, the *measure* of Gross Domestic Product *indicates* living standards. The *measure* of body temperature *indicates* physical health.
- **Average** differs from **median**. An average is the sum of all the values divided by the number of values. The median is the middle value in any group of values. For three hourly wages

(of $5, $10, and $30), the average wage is $15, but the median wage is $10.
- **Nominal** figures differ from **real** figures. Nominal dollar values, for example, make no adjustments for changes in prices over the years. However, real figures are adjusted using a **base year**, which gives a point of comparison.
- **Percentages** sometimes cause confusion. If you are to calculate the percentage difference between two numbers, determine what is the base from which the percentage is calculated, then divide the difference between the two numbers by the base number and multiply by 100 percent. For example, if a price increases from $1 to $3, it has risen by 200 percent $[((\$3 - \$1) \div \$1) \times 100\%]$. In this case, $1 is the base number. If, on the other hand, a price decreases from $3 to $1, the base number is now $3. The percentage fall in price is therefore 67 percent $[((\$1 - \$3) \div \$3) \times 100\%]$.
- Many statistics are **rounded**—for example, to the nearest whole number or nearest thousand.

Logical

Logical arguments move from one point to the next in a reasonable and orderly way. Reasons should support each point, and the points should follow some order, often a cause-and-effect order. The **scientific method**, which we outline in Chapter 1, gives one model for a logical approach. In the case of a written or spoken argument, we should be able to answer the following questions: What points does the author make? How does the author support each point? How do the points connect and are the connections valid? What is the main point or conclusion?

Read your own work and that of others carefully for the following problems:

- **Personal arguments.** A personal argument attacks an opponent rather than the opponent's reasoning. Personal arguments often appear when economic issues are debated in the political arena. For example, a government's expansionary fiscal policy might be disparaged as being the work of "doctrinaire socialists" rather than being criticized on its own merits.

- **False analogy**. Arguments can often be supported with analogies, or comparisons between two different things. For example, the flow of incomes and spending in an economy is sometimes likened to a circular flow of water. However, one extension of this analogy—that the flow of incomes and spending in an economy would stop unless propelled by some outside force—is false. Each analogy must be checked against the facts.

- **False causation**. Simply because two trends take place at the same time does not mean one trend is causing the other. For example, a trend toward more students staying in school and a trend toward more part-time jobs does not mean that the first necessarily causes the second, or vice versa. In each case, examine the situation to see how the factors are related, if at all.

- **Fallacy of composition**. What is true for one component of a group—say, an individual—is not necessarily true for the group as a whole. For example, just because higher savings benefit an individual household does not mean that they help the entire economy. Examine each generalization carefully.

Considered

Our experiences and background have implications for how we see the world; they inform our perspectives. Because many of the issues explored in *Economics for Today* deal with how we think things "ought" to be, they bring up questions of values—for example, how you value extra leisure time against more possessions. The key to critical thinking is recognizing and examining our perspectives (including our assumptions) and considering the perspectives of others. A blinkered view of the world—one that doesn't consider the perspectives of others—makes for a poor, unbalanced argument.

Examine your own work and that of others carefully for the following:

- **Opinions.** Are any opinions stated clearly, explained, and supported? Are any not stated but apparent? Remember that opinions are not the sign of dubious critical thinking. In fact, explicit opinions are preferable to unexamined perspectives in most cases.

- **Statement of specific assumptions**. If assumptions are not clearly identified, can they be inferred? Are the stated assumptions overly simplistic or irrelevant? For example, in an argument about product demand it is too simplistic to assume that the price of a product stays constant, while detailed assumptions concerning how a product is supplied are irrelevant.

- **Emotional or loaded language**. While emotional language may suit some persuasive arguments (for example, political speeches, letters to the editor, advertising), it can mask lack of evidence, presumptions, and a biased view. Loaded language—which usually lays blame—is especially common in the popular media. If you are faced with loaded language, try to decide whether an argument would be equally effective without it. Also keep in mind that loaded language does not always signify that an argument is unreasonable, and that arguments expressed in reasonable language can also be ill-considered.

- **Imprecise statements, distortions of fact, or faulty logic**. Double-check for misrepresentations, imprecise use, errors in logic, and so on in your reading.

Finally, ask yourself whether alternative perspectives have been considered and addressed. If not, why not? Keep in mind that arguments supporting the current state of things are not necessarily more objective than those that do not.

To summarize the basics of critical thinking, consider the task of **forecasting**. Suppose you are asked to use a current economic statistic that is in the news to try to forecast future values. To make a prediction concerning the prime interest rate, for example, you must define precisely the problem and terminology, decide which factors affecting interest rates will be most crucial in the near future, and try to weigh the importance of each of these factors in affecting the statistic's current value. Look to economic theory and economists for help; consult newspapers and magazines to see how closely your own hypothesis corresponds to the opinions of professional economic forecasters. Develop an argument, which you will support and check carefully for errors in logic—for example, what factors cause what. Then, present your forecast and evidence precisely, logically, and having considered a range of perspectives. Later, you will likely want to evaluate your forecast against what actually happened. Because forecasting is an extremely difficult task, consider yourself successful if you predicted the same direction of change.

Research

When you research a topic—for example, to write a research paper—first define your topic and your task carefully so that you do not waste time as you gather information. If your research takes you in a different direction from what you had planned, check with your teacher.

Use a range of sources. By doing so, you are more likely to be able to see your topic from different angles, address the relevant factors, and access the best sources. Evaluate your sources against one another using the basics of critical thinking.

Credit all your sources, both to recognize the debt you owe to others and to allow readers to refer to the sources themselves. As you collect information, note what is a direct quotation, what is a paraphrase, and what is a summary, and note the exact source. For example:

- for articles—author's name, article title, newspaper or magazine title, date of issue, and page number(s)

- for books—author's name, book title, place of publication, publishing company, year of publication, and page number(s)
- for television sources—television station, program name, date and time of airing
- for CD-ROM (Compact Disk–Read Only Memory) material—author's name, title of article/text portion, date, newspaper/magazine/encyclopedia title, edition, and CD-ROM title

Depending on your topic, you might do primary research, secondary research, or a combination of both. **Primary research**, in such forms as interviews and surveys, involves you in gathering "raw" information. **Secondary research**, which is based on the work of others, allows you to acquaint yourself with a range of opinions and to use data that would be difficult or impossible to collect on your own.

Valuable Sources

The research sources immediately available to you are likely newspapers (specifically their business sections), newsmagazines (such as *Maclean's*), business newspapers (such as *The Financial Post*), business magazines (such as *The Globe and Mail Report on Business Magazine, Forbes, The Economist*), and any collections of news clippings at your library. Some sources, such as *Maclean's*, may be available to you on CD-ROM, while others may be indexed on CD-ROM (for example, within the Canadian Business and Current Affairs Index and the Canadian Index). Alternatively, most libraries have indices in book form.

In addition, consider the following sources:

- *The Canadian Encyclopedia* and the annual *Canadian Global Almanac* for details on economic institutions in Canada
- E-STAT for Statistics Canada data on the Canadian economy, society, and population in CD-ROM format, as well as Statistics Canada publications, such as the biennial *Canada Year*

Book, the monthly *Canadian Economic Observer* and its annual historical supplement, the quarterly *Perspectives on Labour and Income*, plus other more detailed publications on particular topics listed in Statistics Canada's catalogue
- Canadian BusinessDisc and Canadian NewsDisc on CD-ROM
- the Bank of Canada's quarterly *Bank of Canada Review* and the Department of Finance's annual *Economic and Fiscal Reference Tables* for recent economic statistics, especially on monetary and financial matters
- the World Bank's annual *World Development Report* and the monthly *OECD Main Economic Indicators* for international statistics
- federal and provincial government bookstores for annual budget papers

Presentation

Based on your research, you should be able to present the results in an essay, an oral presentation, or a debate. Once again, evaluate your work against the basics of critical thinking. Whatever the form of your presentation, you should be able to state the thesis or main argument, give support, and address your points in a logical and orderly way. Prepare an outline to ensure that your presentation is well-structured and organized.

Essay

An essay should be written in a concise and easy-to-follow style. Remember that your general purpose is to inform and persuade, rather than to overwhelm your reader with complicated concepts and terminology. Keep in mind your specific task and the expectations of readers. Double-check to see that, in fact, your essay does what it was supposed to—for example, "explain," "support or refute," "compare," or "analyze." State your thesis clearly in your introduction, any background information your readers will need, support for your thesis, and a conclu-sion, which restates your thesis. Repeatedly revise and edit your writing before handing in the final version.

Class Presentation

Though less formal than an essay, a class presentation requires the same steps of research and preparation. Again, you should structure your discussion using an outline, and credit any sources during your presentation.

Debate

Usually when you debate, the thesis is provided for you. In a formal debate, two sides debate a statement or **proposition**. The side arguing for the proposition, called the **affirmative**, and the side arguing against the proposition, called the **negative**, each have a set period of time to make their original arguments, after which each side is allowed time for a **rebuttal** of the other's arguments. Informal debates often include a statement of the argument and support by either side, then discussion and resolution. In both types of debates, research and preparation are key. Consider *all* sides of the argument. It is also important to remember that the purpose of a debate is to persuade, not to create conflict. Effective debating therefore combines logic and tact.

NOTE

[1]This example and diagram, modified for our purposes, appear in David P. Kreutzer, *Systems Thinking and Dynamic Modeling* (Cambridge, MA: Gould-Kreutzer Associates, 1994), p. 9.

SOURCES

M. Neil Brown and Stuart Keeley, *Asking the Right Questions* (Englewood Cliffs, NJ: Prentice-Hall, 1990).

Stanley L. Brue and Donald R. Wentworth, *Economic Scenes*, 5th ed., (Englewood Cliffs, NJ: Prentice-Hall, 1992.)

Robert Case, *Reading Critically* (Toronto: OISE Press, 1981).

Catherine Harris, "A Guide to Using Statistics," in *Canadian Economic Observer* (Ottawa: Statistics Canada, February 1990), pp. 19–33.

Darrel Hugg, *How to Lie with Statistics* (New York: W.W. Norton, 1954).

David P. Kreutzer, *Systems Thinking and Dynamic Modeling* (Cambridge, MA: Gould-Kreutzer Associates, 1994).

W. Edgar Moore, H. McCann, and J. McCann, *Creative and Critical Thinking*, 2nd ed. (Boston: Houghton Mifflin, 1985).

PART 1

Working With Economics

The Age of Chivalry is gone—that of sophisters, economists, and calculators has succeeded.
— EDMUND BURKE, BRITISH POLITICAL WRITER

Understanding economic principles is important for everyone who votes or participates in the marketplace. How do we go about choosing the products we buy? Do private markets always benefit consumers? What are the best ways to minimize the pollution caused by businesses and households? Can we devise more successful programs to eradicate poverty? Should we expect governments to be doing more to fight unemployment? The next three chapters explore economic principles that can help us find some answers.

CHAPTER 1

The Economic Problem

Economy is the art of making the most out of life.
—GEORGE BERNARD SHAW,
IRISH PLAYWRIGHT

Just as variety adds spice to life, so choice enlivens our everyday existence. Some choices are minor—which pair of shoes to buy, or whether to have a pizza or a hamburger for lunch. Others are more important—where to live, and what career to pursue. Because our resources are limited, every one of our choices has a price. This is a basic fact of human existence that applies equally to individuals and societies. Individuals must decide how to use their limited time and budgets. Societies, meanwhile, must decide how to employ a fixed supply of resources. Thus, both individuals and societies can use economics to analyze their choices and make the best possible decisions.

CHAPTER FOCUS

This chapter focuses on the following:
- the economic problem—the problem of having needs and unlimited wants, but limited resources—that underlies the definition of economics
- the types of reasoning and investigative methods that economists use
- the production choices an entire economy faces, as demonstrated by the production possibilities model
- the three basic economic questions and how various economic systems answer them
- the main economic goals of the Canadian economy and the ways in which they are related

SKILLS FOCUS

After studying this chapter, you will be able to:
- identify independent variables and dependent variables, and note their relationships
- assess economic statements as positive or normative
- explain and apply the concept of opportunity cost
- create a production possibilities curve
- analyze economic systems
- assess and rank economic goals
- note complementary and conflicting economic goals, study the tradeoffs between them and attempts to reconcile conflicting goals, and suggest alternatives

What Economists Do

The Economic Problem

needs: the essentials of life, such as food and shelter

wants: desires for non-essential items

economic problem: the problem of having needs and unlimited wants, but limited resources with which to satisfy them

Every day, we make choices to meet our needs and wants. **Needs** represent the essentials we require in order to live, such as food and shelter. Our needs are limited, but if they are fully satisfied, they are replaced by an inexhaustible range of **wants**, or desires for nonessential items. Wants vary widely from person to person; we may have a special preference for ice-cream sundaes or chocolate cakes, rock concerts or classical recitals, video games or comic books. Because we face so many choices, the sum total of our needs and wants is virtually unlimited. Our resources, however, are not. Thus we have the **economic problem**.

Thinking About Economics

The famous Indian statesman, M.K. (Mahatma) Gandhi, once said, "There is enough for the needy, but not for the greedy." What are the implications of this belief for the economic problem?

Gandhi's statement reveals a way the economic problem can be solved without the help of economics—by curbing our selfish wants. Is such a scenario feasible? For idealistic individuals or small groups, it can be. However, attempts to control the wants of large groups of people have tended to be spectacular failures.

scarcity: the limited nature of resources, which underlies the basic economic problem

economic resources: basic items that are used in all types of production, including natural, capital, and human resources

natural resources: the resources from nature that are used in production, including land, raw materials, and natural processes

The limited nature of resources—or **scarcity**—requires that we make choices based on both noneconomic factors, such as the need for security or a desire for love and respect, *and* economic factors. For many individuals, time and money are most scarce. For societies as a whole, it is the basic items used in all types of production, known as **economic resources**, that are scarce. These resources come not only from nature, but also from human effort and ingenuity. Economic resources are often categorized as natural resources, capital resources, and human resources.

Natural Resources

Natural resources represent nature's contribution to production. These resources include not only land—used for farms, roads, and buildings—but also raw materials such as minerals and forests. As well, natural resources include useful natural processes such as sunlight and water power.

Capital Resources

In economics, **capital resources**, or capital, refers to the real assets of an economy—the processed materials, equipment, and buildings that are used in production. An example is a newspaper printing plant and its printing presses, as well as the processed inputs—paper and ink—used to make newspapers. As economic resources, capital resources do *not* include financial capital such as stocks and bonds. A person's shares in Canadian Pacific, for example, do not add to the economy's stock of real capital. Similarly, the bonds issued by a company such as Bell Canada are viewed as financial capital by their holders, but not as real capital by economists.

capital resources: the processed materials, equipment, and buildings used in production; also known as capital

Human Resources

Human resources include both labour (the various types of human effort employed directly in production) *and* entrepreneurship (the initiative, risk-taking, and innovation needed, for example, to open and run a business). Thus, these resources include the labour of the computer programmer and store clerk, factory supervisor and brain surgeon, farmer and potter, plus the entrepreneurship of the inventor who brings a new product to the market, the head of a multimillion-dollar corporation, the owner of a small variety store, and the student who starts a summer house-painting business. Entrepreneurship is often difficult to pinpoint, but it is this that brings together the natural resources, capital resources, and labour in order to produce a good or service.

human resources: the efforts of people involved in production, including labour and entrepreneurship

Resource Incomes

These three types of economic resources have corresponding incomes, which reflect their contributions to production. When a natural resource is employed, its owner receives a rent, which is the payment for supplying the resource. Similarly, providers of capital resources receive an income in the form of rent for their contribution to production. In return for their labour and entrepreneurship, people are paid wages, salaries, or profit.

Economics Defined

Arising from wants, needs, and scarce resources, **economics** is the study of how to distribute limited resources among alternative ends. Economics is divided into two branches, which are studied separately: microeconomics and macroeconomics.

economics: the study of how to distribute scarce resources among alternative ends

Microeconomics

Microeconomics focuses on the behaviour of individual participants in various markets. How do people decide on the quantities of a particular resource they will consume? How do businesses decide on the quantities of a particular product they will produce? How are prices set within markets? What determines how incomes are distributed to the various participants in an economy? These are the sorts of questions studied in microeconomics.

microeconomics: the branch of economics that focuses on the behaviour of individual participants in various markets

Macroeconomics

macroeconomics: the branch of economics that takes a wide-ranging view of the economy, studying the behaviour of economic sectors

In contrast, **macroeconomics** takes a more wide-ranging view of the economy. It is concerned with entire economic sectors, which are treated as separate entities. The four most important sectors in the economy are households, businesses, government, and foreign markets. How these sectors interact determines a country's unemployment rate, general level of prices, and total economic output. Explaining these larger economic forces is the central task of macroeconomics.

Economic Models

economic models: generalizations about or simplifications of economic reality; also known as laws, principles, or theories

Economists use models to help them understand economic behaviour. **Economic models**—also known as laws, principles, or theories—are generalizations or simplifications of economic reality. As an example, think about the Canadian economy, in which literally millions of separate transactions—sales and purchases—are made each day. Trying to keep track of every sale and purchase for the purpose of understanding economic activity would be impossible. Instead, economists build useful abstractions of reality that allow them to see the *basic* workings of the economy. In other words, a good economic model allows economists to see the forest instead of the trees.

Without even realizing it, we regularly use models. When driving in unfamiliar territory, for example, we often depend on maps. Although an aerial photograph (as shown on the left in Figure 1.1) would be the most

Figure 1.1: Applying an Economic Model

 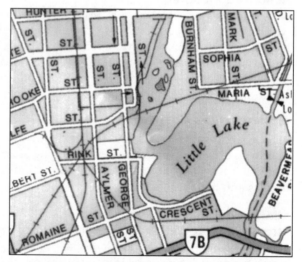

Accurate reproductions of economic reality are as complicated and difficult to decipher as the aerial photograph on the left. Like the road map on the right, a well-designed economic model provides a simplified but reliable guide for those attempting to understand some part of the economy.

SOURCE: © The Queen's Printer For Ontario, 1994. Reproduced with permission.

realistic representation, it is virtually useless as a driving guide. A road map (on the right), however, gives exactly the detail needed to find the way. Similarly, a good economic model can help us understand some facet of economic behaviour without overwhelming us with details.

The Scientific Method

How, then, do economists go about building models to explain economic trends and behaviour? They use the same basic method scientists use in their investigations. First, economists offer a tentative observation or insight about the way the world operates and turn it into a formal statement known as a **hypothesis**. Then they study the relevant facts to see whether the hypothesis is valid.

Cause and Effect

A hypothesis usually includes two or more **variables**, or factors that have measurable values. For example, the price of an item and the quantity that is purchased of that item are two variables. In a hypothesis, variables are connected by a causal relationship, meaning that one variable is assumed to affect another. Suppose you have a hypothesis that states that a rise in the price of cellular phones reduces the number of cellular phones purchased. In this case, the variable that is causing the other to change—known as the **independent variable**—is the price of cellular phones. The variable that is being affected—called the **dependent variable**—is the number of cellular phones purchased.

Inverse and Direct Relationships

The hypothesis proposes what effect one variable will have on another. If the value of one variable is expected to increase as the value of another variable decreases, the variables have an **inverse relationship**. The hypothesis that an increase in cellular phone prices reduces the number of phones sold is an example of an inverse relationship. Two variables can have a **direct relationship**, meaning that, when the independent variable rises or falls, the dependent variable moves in the same direction. A rise in the hourly wage of bank tellers that causes a corresponding rise in the number of people who wish to work in this occupation is an example of a direct relationship.

The Need for Assumptions

In order to focus on the relationship between two variables, economists must make assumptions to temporarily simplify the real world. Let's return to the hypothesis that the quantity of cellular phones purchased is inversely related to their price. Economists must assume that another factor—such as consumer incomes—is not affecting purchases of cellular phones. Assuming that all other factors affecting a dependent variable

hypothesis: a formal statement of a tentative observation or insight, to be tested for its validity

variables: factors that have measurable values

independent variable: the variable in a causal relationship that causes change in another variable

dependent variable: the variable in a causal relationship that is affected by another variable

inverse relationship: a relationship in which a change in the independent variable causes a change in the opposite direction of the dependent variable

direct relationship: a relationship in which a change in the independent variable causes a change in the same direction of the dependent variable

ceteris paribus: the
assumption that all other
things remain the same

remain constant is common in economics. This assumption is known as ***ceteris paribus*** (*pronounced kay'-teh-rees pah'-ri-bus*), which is the Latin expression for "all other things remaining the same." The *ceteris paribus* assumption, as well as any other assumptions that are made, should be outlined explicitly when stating a hypothesis.

Applying the Scientific Method

Figure 1.2 shows the four basic steps of the scientific method: (1) stating the hypothesis, (2) gathering and examining data, (3) testing the hypothesis, and (4) accepting or rejecting the hypothesis. To see how the scientific method is applied to economics, we will look at a simple example and return to it later.

Figure 1.2:   Applying the Scientific Method

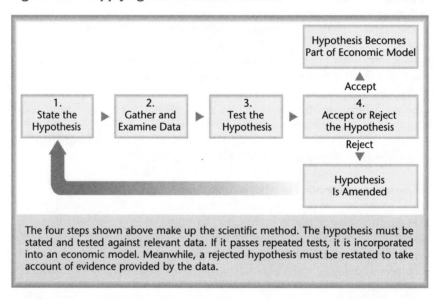

The four steps shown above make up the scientific method. The hypothesis must be stated and tested against relevant data. If it passes repeated tests, it is incorporated into an economic model. Meanwhile, a rejected hypothesis must be restated to take account of evidence provided by the data.

State the Hypothesis

Suppose an economist guesses that a worker's output rises when the worker's job becomes more specialized. This guess could result from a casual observation or simply a hunch. To determine whether it is true, a formal hypothesis must be stated involving two measurable variables. The economist may choose to concentrate on the production of a simple item, such as pins. Thus, the hypothesis is that when specialization, or **division of labour**, is increased in a pinmaking company, the quantity of pins produced per worker increases as well. Meanwhile, all other variables that can affect the quantity of pins produced per worker are assumed to remain the same.

division of labour: the
extent to which jobs of
different workers are specialized into separate tasks

Gather and Examine Data

The economist must gather and examine data that are relevant to the hypothesis. One pinmaking company, Company A, is found to employ 5 workers, each making pins from start to finish, and the company's total output per day is 1000 pins. A second pinmaking company, Company B, employs 10 workers, each performing a specialized task, and their combined output is 50 000 pins a day.

Test the Hypothesis

The collected data must be put in a form that will test the original hypothesis. Because Company A's total output is 1000 pins, the average output of each of the 5 workers is 200 pins (1000 ÷ 5). In contrast, Company B's total output is 50 000 pins, so the average output of each of the 10 workers is 5000 pins (50 000 ÷ 10). Hence, the economist's original hypothesis that greater job specialization leads to higher output per worker is supported by the existing data.

Accept or Reject the Hypothesis

Ideally, hypotheses should be tested repeatedly. To illustrate, the hypothesis relating job specialization to worker output should be tested for more than one industry. If the hypothesis passes such scrutiny, it is accepted as valid and can be used as part of an economic model. If the hypothesis is rejected, however, it can be modified according to the available evidence. For example, the hypothesis that job specialization always adds to worker output might apply to small pinmaking companies, but not necessarily to very large companies.

Deduction and Induction

In applying the scientific method, two approaches or types of reasoning can be used. One approach, known as **deduction**, involves developing a hypothesis *before* examining the facts, and then following the four steps of the scientific method as they appear in Figure 1.2. Therefore, in the pinmaking case, the economist would make the hypothesis about job specialization before gathering and examining the data on pinmaking production.

The second approach, known as **induction**, involves developing a hypothesis only *after* systematically gathering and examining data. Thus, the first two steps of the scientific method are reversed: an economist using the inductive approach (1) collects and studies the data, and then (2) states the hypothesis, (3) tests the hypothesis, and (4) either accepts or rejects the hypothesis. So, for example, researchers who have studied cellular phone prices and the number of cellular phones purchased might then formulate and test a hypothesis about the relationship between prices and quantities purchased.

Depending on the circumstances, one approach will be more useful than the other. In the case of non-numerical relationships, the hypothesis might

deduction: a type of reasoning in which one states a hypothesis before examining the facts

induction: a type of reasoning in which one states a hypothesis after examining the facts

develop from casual observation, before any systematic examination of data takes place. However, in the case of complex numerical relationships, some data will likely need to be gathered before a hypothesis can be stated.

Positive and Normative Economics

While a useful tool, the scientific method cannot be applied to all areas of economics. Economics is, after all, a social science. To understand where the scientific method can be used, we need to distinguish between two types of economic enquiry: positive and normative economics.

positive economics: the study of economic facts and how the economy operates as it does

Positive economics (sometimes called *descriptive economics*) is the study of economic reality and why the economy operates as it does. It is based purely on economic facts rather than on opinions. This type of economics is made up of positive statements, which can be accepted or rejected through applying the scientific method. "Canadians bought 5 million CDs last year" is a positive statement—a simple declaration of fact. A positive statement can also take the form of a condition that asserts that if one thing happens, then so will another: "If rent controls are eliminated, then the number of available rental units will increase." Both declarations of fact and conditional statements can be verified or disproved using economic data.

normative economics: the study of how the economy ought to operate

In contrast, **normative economics** (also called *policy economics*) deals with how the world *ought* to be. In this type of economics, opinions or value judgements—known as normative statements—are common. "We should reduce taxes" is an example of a normative statement. So is "A 1 percent rise in unemployment is worse than a 1 percent rise in inflation." Even people who agree on the facts can have different opinions regarding a normative statement, since the statement relates to questions of ethical values.

BRIEF REVIEW

1. The basic economic problem faced by both individuals and societies is that while human wants are virtually unlimited, the resources to fulfil them are limited, or scarce.

2. Economic resources can be categorized as natural resources, capital resources, and human resources. Each resource has a corresponding income.

3. Whereas microeconomics concentrates on the ways consumers and businesses interact in various markets, macroeconomics takes a broader look at the economy as a whole, and highlights such variables as unemployment, inflation, and total output.

4. Economic models are simplifications of economic reality. They are developed by using the scientific method, which involves formulating and testing hypotheses against real-world evidence. The scientific method can also be applied to positive economics, but not to normative economics.

Economics as an Art

The Craft of Economic Thinking

The Role of Assumptions

One of the most common criticisms of economics is summarized by a well-known joke:

> Three hungry castaways—a physicist, a geologist, and an economist—are stranded on a desert island with a single can of beans to eat, and no can opener.
>
> "I've got the answer," announces the physicist, after thinking about how to extract the beans. "We'll focus sunlight through my eyeglasses to burn a hole in the can."
>
> "Are you crazy?" replies the geologist. "You'll burst it and spill out the beans. Let's punch a hole with a sharp rock."
>
> The economist smiles and shakes his head at their thick-headedness. "No, it's much easier than either of you think. Let's just *assume* we have a can opener."

As the joke implies, economists depend extensively on assumptions, some of them rather creative. Scientists such as physicists and chemists also make assumptions, but theirs are more often assumptions that can be tested in controlled laboratory experiments. They can duplicate circumstances and isolate the variables they are studying from external factors. Economists rarely have this luxury. When people's economic behaviour is studied in artificial laboratory settings, it does not necessarily match real life. To isolate a relationship between two or more variables requires abstracting from the complexity of the real world, then verifying these economic models by studying transactions in actual markets.

Economics as an Art

Many economists prefer to think of their subject simply as a discipline, rather than as a science like physics or chemistry. Some econo-mists argue that they must not only be experts in using the scientific method, but also in creating models of economic reality. Creating such models requires the talent of being able to represent reality in the most "economical" way possible. A good economic model is therefore a little like a sketch by an expert artist such as Leonardo da Vinci; just a few well-chosen lines capture the appearance of the subject, as does da Vinci's sketch below.[1]

The art of model-building in economics is complicated by the fact that economics is a

A good economic model is like an artist's sketch. (Portrait of a Young Woman by Leonardo da Vinci.)

SOURCE: The Royal Collection © 1994. Her Majesty The Queen.

social science, a science that analyzes human behaviour. The way we behave depends partly on our social surroundings: the political, cultural, and economic aspects of the society we live in. Changes in these social surroundings can affect human behaviour; when this happens, economic models may have to be altered as well. This leads to a complex interaction between the science of economics and the reality it tries to explain:

> Economics is an ever-changing discipline. Partly a product of the great ideological debates about the way human society ought to be organized, it also influences the outcome of those debates. Partly based on a theoretical search for abstract truths, it is also rooted in the realities of public policy and the climate of opinion. Partly an explanation of how and why an economic system functions, it is affected by the ways in which economic systems change.[2]

Just as a piece of art is a product of the time and place in which the artist lived, so an economic model reflects the society in which it was developed.

Interestingly, the twentieth century's most illustrious economist, John Maynard Keynes, viewed his subject as science and art. According to Keynes, an economist "must be purposeful and disinterested in a simultaneous mood; as aloof and incorruptible as an artist, yet sometimes as near the earth as a politician."[3] Given such tough

requirements, a first-rate economist is a rare creature indeed. As we'll see in later chapters, Keynes himself was someone who possessed the talents necessary to build a simple yet powerful model of the economy. In fact, his theories form the basis of macroeconomics as we know it today.

SOURCE: De Angelis, Cartoonists and Writers Syndicate.

NOTES

[1]This comparison is made by Maurice Levi in *Economics Deciphered: A Layman's Survival Guide* (New York: Basic Books, 1981), p. 10.
[2]From *The Age of the Economist*, 6th edition, by Daniel R. Fusfeld, copyright © 1990 Scott, Foresman and Company. Reprinted by permission of HarperCollins College Publishers.
[3]John Maynard Keynes, in Robert L. Heilbroner, *The Worldly Philosophers*, 6th ed. (New York: Simon and Schuster, 1986), pp. 286–87.

 **Economic Choice**

How do people make economic choices? They do so by using effectively the scarce resources they have. Two main factors are involved in this decision-making process: utility and cost.

Utility Maximization

Economists assume that, whenever you make an economic choice, you are trying to maximize your own utility. **Utility** can be defined as the satisfaction or pleasure you derive from any action. Let's examine utility maximization with the illustration of you and your lunch. Economists assume first the **self-interest motive**, that is, that you are primarily concerned with your own welfare. So, when deciding among lunch options that cost the same amount of money, you pick the one that gives the most utility. For example, suppose you have $2 to spend at a fast-food restaurant. Two options are available: a pizza slice or a hamburger, each costing $2. How do you make your choice? According to economists, you decide by comparing the utility gained from either product. If the satisfaction from a pizza slice outweighs the pleasures of a hamburger, you'll buy the pizza. If the opposite applies, the hamburger will win out.

utility: the satisfaction gained from any action

self-interest motive: the assumption that people act to maximize their own welfare

Opportunity Cost

Maximizing utility is only one part of making economic decisions. Acquiring anything prevents someone from pursuing an alternative. For example, purchasing a T-shirt for $10 leaves $10 less to spend on other items. So, instead of measuring cost in terms of money, economists use a concept that accounts for the tradeoffs resulting from any economic choice: **opportunity cost.** The opportunity cost of any action is the utility that could have been gained by choosing the best possible alternative.

For example, those of you who would spend $2 to buy a pizza slice at the fast-food restaurant face an opportunity cost equal to the utility that could have been gained by eating a hamburger instead. For those of you who would choose the hamburger, the opportunity cost is the sacrificed pleasure of eating a pizza slice.

Not everything is scarce. A few items, known as **free goods**, exist in such great abundance that they can be acquired without cost. Air is considered one example. However, most of the products that we consume exist in limited quantities. Their scarcity means that they have an opportunity cost, and are said to possess an **economic value**. In order to obtain products with economic value, something—usually money—must be handed over in return.

The concepts of scarcity and opportunity cost also relate to how we spend time, since time passed in one activity means less devoted to another. Suppose a student is deciding whether to spend a free hour watching a TV program or reading a paperback mystery. The opportunity cost of watching the TV program is the pleasure that could have been gained from reading the mystery. Likewise, the opportunity cost of reading the mystery is the benefit sacrificed by not watching the program.

opportunity cost: the utility that could have been gained by choosing an action's best alternative

free goods: items that are so plentiful that they do not have any cost

economic value: the opportunity cost of a product

The Production Possibilities Model

The production possibilities model illustrates the tradeoffs that society faces in using its scarce resources. Like all models, it is an abstraction of the real world based on various simplifications. In this case, the following assumptions are made: only two items are produced, resources and technology are fixed, and all economic resources are employed to their full potential.

Two Products

An immense range of goods and services are produced in the Canadian economy. The production possibilities model, however, narrows the list to only two; for example, bread and saws. A loaf of bread is an example of a **consumer product**, which is an item that gratifies people's needs and wants. A saw, in contrast, is a **capital good**, which is an item that is used to produce other products.

Fixed Resources and Technology

For the model, it is assumed that there is a set amount of available economic resources and that technology remains constant. However, resources can be moved from the production of one good to the other. Workers who assemble saws, for example, can be shifted to the bakery trade.

Full Production

In the production possibilities model, all economic resources are employed; that is, there is no excess. Also, resources are used to their greatest capacity no matter which product they are producing—in this case, bread and saws.

The Production Possibilities Curve

In order to maximize the welfare of its citizens, a society must make economic choices. How many consumer products and capital goods should be produced in a certain year given the resources at the society's disposal? A choice is necessary because producing more of one item means making do with less of the other. This choice is illustrated in Figure 1.3. On the left is the economy's **production possibilities schedule**—a table outlining, in this case, the possible combinations of bread and saws. Expressing the schedule in a graph gives us the economy's **production possibilities curve**. Because there is an inverse relationship between the quantities of bread and saws produced, the curve has a negative slope—from left to right, the curve falls.

As Figure 1.3 demonstrates, it might be possible for the economy to bake 700 loaves of bread and assemble 1 saw in a given year (point *b*). If the output of bread is reduced to 400 loaves, it might also be feasible for the economy to produce 2 saws (point *c*). The extreme cases serve as useful reference points: when all of the economy's resources are devoted to the baking of bread, a total of 800 loaves can be produced annually (point

consumer product: an item that gratifies people's needs and wants

capital good: an item that is used to produce other products

production possibilities schedule: a table that shows the possible output combinations for an economy

production possibilities curve: a graph that illustrates the possible output combinations for an economy

Figure 1.3:   The Production Possibilities Model

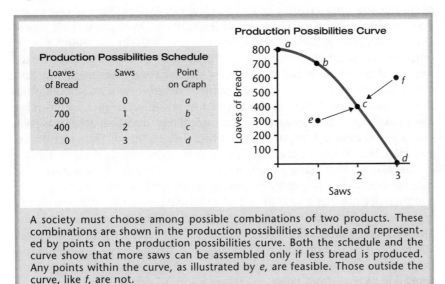

Production Possibilities Curve

Production Possibilities Schedule		
Loaves of Bread	Saws	Point on Graph
800	0	a
700	1	b
400	2	c
0	3	d

A society must choose among possible combinations of two products. These combinations are shown in the production possibilities schedule and represented by points on the production possibilities curve. Both the schedule and the curve show that more saws can be assembled only if less bread is produced. Any points within the curve, as illustrated by *e*, are feasible. Those outside the curve, like *f*, are not.

a), but when the economy devotes all of its resources to making only saws, 3 can be made (point *d*).

The Role of Scarcity

As well as depicting the economic choices a society faces, the production possibilities curve highlights the scarcity of economic resources. The curve is a boundary between all those output combinations that are within reach of an economy, and all those combinations that are unattainable. Anywhere inside the curve, such as point *e* in Figure 1.3, represents a feasible combination of the two products. At point *e*, for example, 300 loaves of bread and 1 saw can be produced. The production of both bread and saws could be increased by moving toward point *c* on the curve. At any point such as *e*, some of an economy's resources are not being fully employed. Hence, all points inside the curve represent a situation of unemployment.

In contrast, point *f* in Figure 1.3 is outside the curve. In this case, the economy would be producing 600 loaves of bread and 3 saws annually. As long as the economy's resources remain constant, this point cannot be reached. More of *both* bread and saws could be made if point *f* were attainable, but the economy's resources are already being fully utilized at point *c*.

The Law of Increasing Opportunity Costs

The notion of opportunity cost is best seen when moving from one point to another on the production possibilities curve. Notice that the curve in

**law of increasing
opportunity costs:**

the concept that as more
of one product is pro-
duced by an economy,
the opportunity cost of
additional units of that
product rises

Figure 1.3 bows out to the right. This shape reflects what is called the **law of increasing opportunity costs**, which states that, as more of one product is produced, its opportunity cost in terms of the other product increases. This law arises from the fact that economic resources do not shift perfectly from one use to another. For example, because of training and experience, some workers are better bakers than they are saw assemblers. When the first saw is assembled, it is made using resources suited to saw assembly rather than to baking bread. Hence, the number of bread loaves sacrificed is relatively small. But if further saws are assembled, resources that are not as well suited to this new task must be shifted from baking bread. Therefore, more and more bread loaves have to be given up in order to gain each new saw.

The law of increasing opportunity costs is illustrated in Figure 1.4. Assume that society begins by producing only bread (point *a* on the curve), and then decides that 1 saw should be assembled (point *b*). The opportunity cost of this first saw is the number of loaves of bread that must be given up. Since bread production falls from 800 to 700 loaves, the new saw costs 100 loaves. This is shown on the schedule and, on the curve, appears as the height of the triangle connecting points *a* and *b*. The same reasoning can be applied in moving from points *b* to *c*—as a second saw is added, bread production drops from 700 to 400 loaves. The opportunity cost of this extra saw is therefore 300 loaves. Finally, in moving from points *c* to *d*, bread production drops another 400 loaves to zero, meaning that the opportunity cost of the third saw is 400 loaves. The opportunity cost of each new saw, in terms of bread, therefore rises from 100, to 300, and then to 400 loaves.

Figure 1.4:   The Law of Increasing Opportunity Costs

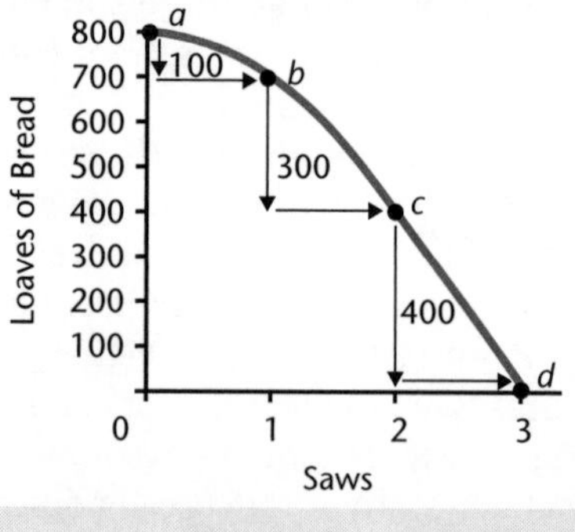

As the production of saws rises from 0 to 1 unit (from points *a* to *b*), the opportunity cost of the first saw is 100 loaves of bread. Further expansion in the output of saws comes at higher opportunity costs: 300 loaves for the second saw (from points *b* to *c*), and 400 loaves for the third saw (from points *c* to *d*).

Thinking About Economics

What happens to the production possibilities curve when the economy's stock of resources increases? Also, what happens if technology improves, allowing the same resources to produce more of both bread and saws?

In each of these cases, the production possibilities curve shifts to the right, meaning that the area of feasible output combinations expands. As a result, the society can choose output combinations that were previously unattainable—more of both items can now be produced. The economy therefore experiences a growth in total output.

BRIEF REVIEW

1. Economists assume that individuals make economic choices among scarce items by maximizing their own utility while minimizing opportunity cost.

2. The production possibilities curve shows the range of choices faced by an economy. It assumes only two products, fixed resources and technology, and full production.

3. Points inside the production possibilities curve are feasible but indicate that not all resources are being used effectively. Conversely, points outside the curve cannot be reached unless resources increase or technology improves.

4. The fact that economic resources are specialized leads to the law of increasing costs. As the economy's production of any item is expanded, that item's opportunity cost rises.

Economic Systems

Basic Economic Questions

Because of the basic economic problem of scarcity, every country, no matter how it chooses to conduct its economic affairs, must answer three basic economic questions: what to produce, how to produce, and for whom to produce.

What to Produce

Countries face economic choices when trying to decide what items to produce, as depicted by the production possibilities curve. For example, baking more bread means assembling fewer saws. Somehow, a country must decide how much of each possible good and service is to be supplied.

Should these decisions be based on past practice, the individual choices of consumers, or government decisions?

How to Produce

Once the question of what to produce has been answered, a country must decide how these items should be produced. Which resources should be employed and in what combinations? For example, should farmers use horse-drawn ploughs and large amounts of labour to produce wheat? Or should they use sophisticated farm machinery and very little labour? And how should these decisions be made? Should the farmers follow tradition, each choose among their many options, or have their production methods specified by government planners?

For Whom to Produce

Each country must also determine how its total output of goods and services will be distributed. How output is divided might be based on custom. Alternatively, each person's ownership of economic resources may be the key factor. Or, the government might distribute output in some other fashion.

economic system: the organization of an economy, which represents a country's distinct set of social customs, political institutions, and economic practices

To answer these three basic economic questions, a country organizes its economy. The result is an **economic system**, which represents the country's distinct set of social customs, political institutions, and economic practices. In the following sections, we will look at three main economic systems: traditional economy, market economy, and command economy. Each of these is a pure or theoretical system, so few economies come close to them. Most economies today are mixed; that is, they combine aspects of the main economic systems. These systems are all founded on different views of what a society's primary aims should be.

Traditional Economy

traditional economy: an economic system in which economic decisions are made on the basis of custom

A **traditional economy** is one in which economic decisions depend on custom. The mix of outputs, the organization of production, and the way in which outputs are distributed tend to be passed on relatively unchanged from generation to generation. Religion and culture tend to be considered at least as important as material welfare. As recently as a century ago, most people lived in traditional economies, but these economies exist today only in isolated pockets. For example, many farmers in the remote country of Nepal still use traditional methods that have existed for generations. Since they are based on tight social constraints, traditional economies are often resistant to change. Still, the long-term outlook for these economies seems clear: increasingly, they are being broken down by expanding consumer wants and the inability of traditional production methods to meet these wants.

Supporters of traditional economies suggest that they offer the advantage of stability. These economies can also be viewed as beneficial because they emphasize the spiritual and cultural aspects of life. However, critics argue that traditional economies' widespread poverty and social restrictions restrain human potential; people must follow the dictates of custom rather than having the freedom to make their own economic choices.

Market Economy

In a **market economy,** individuals are free to pursue their own self-interest. This type of economy is based on the private ownership of economic resources and the use of markets in making economic decisions. In this system—often referred to as capitalism—households use incomes earned from their economic resources by saving some and spending the rest on consumer products. Businesses, conversely, buy resources from households and employ these resources to provide the consumer products demanded by households. Government performs only the political functions of upholding the legal system and maintaining public security. So the government's economic role corresponds to the principle of *laissez faire*, or "let things be."

The transactions between households and businesses in a market economy are illustrated by the circular flow diagram in Figure 1.5. This diagram includes not only households and businesses, but also two markets. A **market** is a set of arrangements between buyers and sellers that allows them to trade items for set prices. **Product markets** are those in which consumer, or final, products are traded. **Resource markets** are those in which economic resources— natural resources, capital resources, and human resources—are traded.

Households and businesses face each other in both sets of markets. In product markets, households are the buyers of consumer products while

market economy: an economic system based on private ownership and the use of markets in economic decision-making

laissez faire: the principle that governments benefit society the most by not interfering in economic activity

market: a set of arrangements between buyers and sellers of a certain item

product markets: markets in which consumer, or final, products are traded

resource markets: markets in which economic resources are traded

Figure 1.5:   The Circular Flow Diagram

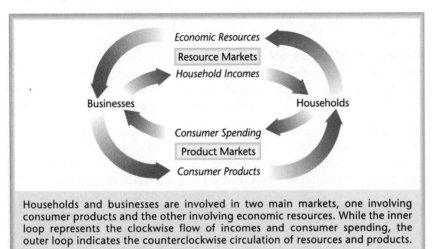

Households and businesses are involved in two main markets, one involving consumer products and the other involving economic resources. While the inner loop represents the clockwise flow of incomes and consumer spending, the outer loop indicates the counterclockwise circulation of resources and products.

circular flows: the circulation of money and the circulation of consumer products and economic resources in the economy

businesses are the sellers. In resource markets, the roles are reversed: households sell resources that businesses purchase so they can produce goods and services. Households and businesses are connected by two **circular flows.** The inner loop in the diagram shows the circulation of money—both household incomes and consumer spending. The outer loop shows the circulation of consumer products and economic resources in the opposite direction.

Benefits of a Market Economy

Placing markets at the centre of economic activity can have benefits. The main benefits are associated with consumer sovereignty, prices, competition, and innovation.

consumer sovereignty: the effect of consumer needs and wants on production decisions

Consumer Sovereignty   Market economies are characterized by **consumer sovereignty**, meaning that the decision of what to produce is ultimately guided by the needs and wants of households in their role as consumers. In other words, consumers use their dollars to "vote" on what types of goods and services should be produced. For example, if households wish to switch some of their consumption dollars from the purchase of stereos to TVs, a chain reaction will occur in the product and resource markets. In product markets, the extra demand for TVs pushes up TV prices, while the lower demand for stereos pushes down stereo prices.

Prices   Prices act as an important signalling device in a market economy. They do this by co-ordinating the activities of buyers and sellers to stop either too much or too little of an item from being produced. In the case of our earlier example, higher TV prices provide businesses, lured by the chance to make higher profits, with an incentive to supply more TVs. Meanwhile, the price drop for stereos causes businesses to cut their stereo production. These shifts in production also result in changes in the employment of economic resources, with more resources being used to make TVs and fewer being used to make stereos.

invisible hand: the tendency for competitive markets to turn self-interested behaviour into socially beneficial activity

Competition   As long as the "**invisible hand**" of competition (as the economist Adam Smith labelled it) is able to operate, a market economy benefits consumers by providing products at the lowest possible prices and by using economic resources in a way that best satisfies consumer needs and wants.

Innovation   The incentive of making a profit in a market economy encourages innovation and entrepreneurship, which help to foster advances in technology. Consumers benefit through improvements to existing products and the introduction of completely new products.

Drawbacks of a Market Economy

The main drawbacks of a market economy are associated with income distribution, possible market problems, and potential instability of total output.

Income Distribution   Without intervention by governments, the distribution of income in a market economy can create significant inequities. If households' incomes are based solely on the ability to supply economic resources, then some individuals in the economy might not earn enough even to provide for their basic needs.

Market Problems   Other deficiencies of market economies arise when private markets do not always operate in a way that benefits society as a whole. Negative external effects of economic activity—for example, pollution—may require intervention by governments to prevent harm to the society. Negative internal effects may also cause governments to step in; for example, when one or a few companies control a certain product market, thus depriving consumers of the advantages of competition.

Instability   Finally, experience has shown that market economies can display considerable instability in the total output produced from year to year. Such fluctuations can harm the economy's participants through substantial variations in prices or employment levels. The recession of 1990–1991, for example, caused tremendous dislocation, with great human cost.

As a result of these deficiencies, there are very few real-world examples of pure capitalism. The closest approximations have occurred in the past; in particular, during the first half of the nineteenth century in Great Britain, when the *laissez-faire* theory of Adam Smith and his followers had its most profound impact.

Command Economy

Opposite to a market economy is a **command economy**, in which all productive property—natural resources and capital—is in the hands of government, and markets are largely replaced by central planning. Rather than being based on consumer sovereignty and individual decision-making, command economies rely on planners to decide what should be produced, how production should be carried out, and how the output should be distributed. For example, in a market economy, decisions made by households about how much to consume and how much to save determine the split between consumer and capital products. In a command economy, however, central planners determine the split based on their judgement of the future needs of the entire economy.

command economy: an economic system based on public ownership and central planning

Benefits of a Command Economy

The reliance on planning rather than markets gives command economies some possible benefits related to income distribution and economic growth.

Income Distribution   A country that adopts a command system can choose to distribute income among its citizens based on considerations other than purely economic ones. In these economies, an attempt is usually made to distribute income more equally than would be the case with market economies.

Economic Growth   Central planners can focus on promoting the rate of economic growth by devoting more resources to capital goods than would be the case in a market economy. This strategy can be particularly effective when an economy is first building a manufacturing sector. During this stage of development, economic growth is closely tied to the quantity of capital goods, such as machines and factories, that an economy possesses.

Drawbacks of a Command Economy

Command economies also have serious drawbacks related to planning, efficiency, and individual freedom. Because of these deficiencies, pure command economies are almost as rare as pure market economies; the closest approximation in contemporary times is North Korea.

Planning Difficulties   Trying to plan an entire economy is a difficult task requiring a tremendous amount of information that is unlikely to be at the planners' disposal. Incorrect estimates of future conditions are all too easy to make, leading to overproduction of some items and underproduction of others.

Inefficiencies   Government ownership of productive property can lead to waste and inefficiency, since command economies cannot depend on the lure of profit to promote the efficient use of resources. Without markets to control individual self-interest, corruption of government officials is also a frequent problem. As well, because planners emphasize *quantity* by setting production quotas, the *quality* of goods and services can suffer.

Lack of Freedom   Opponents of command economies also suggest that putting so much power into the hands of government stifles individual freedom. Because central planners are responsible for so many economic decisions, people living in command economies have limited economic choices. All too often, critics contend, command economies are associated with a lack of political freedom as well.

Mixed Economy

Most countries fall between the extremes of traditional, market, and command economies. A **modern mixed economy** is one that combines both the use of markets and a significant government presence in economic decision-making. Modern mixed economies have proven very popular and take a variety of forms, depending on the relative importance given to

modern mixed economy: an economic system that combines aspects of a market economy and a command economy; production decisions are made both in private markets and by government

private markets and to the economic functions of government. In some countries, such as Canada and the United States, markets play the dominant economic role. In other countries, such as Sweden, the government's economic role is more important. All three examples are illustrated in Figure 1.6, which depicts the range of possible modern mixed economies (along the top edge of the triangle) that exist between the two poles of pure market and command economies.

Figure 1.6:   The Range of Economic Systems

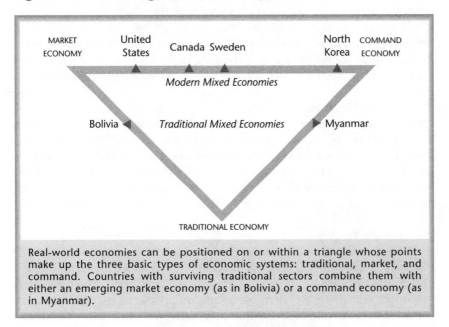

Real-world economies can be positioned on or within a triangle whose points make up the three basic types of economic systems: traditional, market, and command. Countries with surviving traditional sectors combine them with either an emerging market economy (as in Bolivia) or a command economy (as in Myanmar).

While modern mixed economies vary widely, they have some common attributes. Each one includes a **private sector**, in which economic activity is dominated by markets and there is private ownership of productive resources. Each of these economies also includes a **public sector**, in which governments conduct economic activity—often without the use of markets—and own productive resources.

In most modern mixed economies, the distinction between the private and public sectors is not clear-cut. Governments can intervene in the private sector by levying taxes or providing subsidies to some industries. In Canada, for example, the federal government plays a part in the private sector through personal and corporate taxes and the subsidies it provides to business. Government also intervenes in the private sector by imposing regulations, such as environmental laws, on businesses. Also, the government owns some companies, such as Canada Post.

private sector: the part of an economy in which private markets dominate

public sector: the part of an economy in which governments dominate

Countries with entirely traditional economies are rare. However, some countries still possess a significant **traditional sector**, in which economic activity is based on custom and traditional production methods. Economies that possess a traditional sector alongside more modern sectors are known as **traditional mixed economies**. An example is Bolivia, where market-driven industries such as mining co-exist with a traditional sector of peasant farmers. These economies can also involve traditional and command economies, as in the case of Myanmar (formerly Burma). Both of these examples appear in Figure 1.6, in which traditional mixed economies appear on the two sides of the triangle.

Of course, mixed economies, like any other economies, have their advantages and disadvantages. Mixed economies can combine not only the benefits of all sectors from which they are formed, but also the drawbacks. In addition, conflicts can arise between different economic philosophies.

Combined Benefits

The main advantage of mixed economies is that they can display the best features of their component sectors. A private sector can offer consumer sovereignty, the use of prices as a signalling device, the benefits of competition, and the chance for innovation. A public sector can ensure a more equal distribution of income and an emphasis on national goals such as economic growth. A traditional sector can provide continuity and cultural stability.

Combined Drawbacks

Each sector can also bring its weaknesses to a mixed economy. The private sector can bring in market economy deficiencies: inequities in the distribution of income, market problems, and instability. The public sector might contribute deficiencies—planning problems, inefficiencies, and constraints on freedom. The traditional sector can be a source of poverty and social constraints.

Conflicts

Mixed economies must deal with the inevitable conflicts among their component sectors. Each sector emphasizes a distinct view of society's underlying aims—the focus on self-interest in a private sector, wider national objectives in a public sector, and continuity in a traditional sector. As the sectors interact, differences in these views are sure to cause friction.

As an example, consider one of Canada's few remaining traditional industries—the Atlantic inshore fishery. Canadians view government subsidies to those working in this industry in different ways. Some Canadians resent their taxes being used to prop up an uncompetitive industry. Others see these subsidies as a necessary form of regional aid. Still others view the issue not as an economic one, but as a cultural one, since fishing has traditionally been an important part of Atlantic Canada's economy.

The Founder of Modern Economics

Adam Smith and the Invisible Hand

Smith and His Influence

Adam Smith (1723–1790) is known as the father of present-day economics. While he deserves his reputation as a trailblazer, his greatest talent was in combining innovative ideas—many conceived by others—into a theory that had a profound influence on economic thinking, not only in his own time but ever since.

The son of a middle-class Scottish family, he was an avid student, attending universities in both England and Scotland. At the University of Glasgow, he gained a reputation as the classic absent-minded professor who, when distracted by some difficult theoretical problem, would walk for hours, oblivious to his surroundings.

Smith first made a name for himself through his writings in philosophy. He then turned his attention to economic issues. In 1776, after years of research, he published his classic work, *An Inquiry Into the Nature and Causes of the Wealth of Nations,* which brought him both fame and a modest fortune. For generations the book was a standard in economics, and it can still be read profitably today.

ADVANCING ECONOMIC THOUGHT

Adam Smith
SOURCE: The Bettman Archive.

The Industrial Revolution

Smith lived at the beginning of the Industrial Revolution. In the latter half of the 1700s and early 1800s, agriculture lost its central role in the British economy. Through a host of technological innovations, a powerful new manufacturing sector based on labour-saving machinery and steam power took its place. By transforming the lives of common people, this revolution had a profound social and economic impact in many countries, but first in Britain:

> The Industrial Revolution marks the most fundamental transformation of human life in the history of the world recorded in written documents. For a brief period it coincided with the history of a single country, Great Britain. An entire world economy was thus built on, or rather around, Britain, and this country therefore temporarily rose to a position of global influence and power unparalleled by any state of its relative size before or since, and unlikely to be paralleled by any state in the foreseeable future.[1]

The Division of Labour

When Adam Smith was writing *The Wealth of Nations*, these great changes in the British economy were just beginning. As the title of his book suggests, he wished to explain why some countries become more wealthy than others. Smith viewed the division of labour—the degree to which the job of each worker is a specialized task—as the most significant single cause of economic progress. To support this claim, he provided his famous illustration from the trade of pinmaking:

The greatest improvement in the productive powers of labour, and the greater part of the skill, dexterity, and judgement with which it is anywhere directed, or applied, seem to have been the effects of the division of labour....

To take an example,...the trade of the pin-maker; a workman not educated to this business,...nor acquainted with the use of the machinery employed in it,...could scarce, perhaps, with his utmost industry, make one pin in a day, and certainly could not make twenty. But in the way in which this business is now carried on, not only the whole work is a peculiar [i.e., particular] trade, but it is divided into a number of branches, of which the greater part are likewise peculiar trades. One man draws out the wire, another straight[en]s it, a third cuts it, a fourth points it, a fifth grinds it at the top for receiving the head; to make the head requires three distinct operations; to put it on is a peculiar business, to whiten the pins is another; it is even a trade by itself to put them into the paper; and the important business of making a pin is, in this manner, divided into about eighteen distinct operations, which, in some manufactories, are all performed by distinct hands, though in others the same man will sometimes perform two or three of them.[2]

Smith mentioned that he visited a small factory where, through the division of labour, 10 employees produced a total of 48 000 pins a day—4800 times the estimated product of 1 pin per worker when the division of labour was not used!

The Invisible Hand
The benefits associated with the division of labour are not the only reason why some nations are better off than others, according to Smith. Economic progress is also spurred by the self-interest motive, or the desire individuals have to increase their own happiness. "It is not from the benevolence of the butcher, the brewer, or the baker that we expect our dinner," Smith stated, "but from their regard to their own interest. We address ourselves, not to their humanity but to their self-love, and never talk to them of our own necessities but of their advantages."[3] In other words, if people are free to pursue their own private interests, they act in a way that aids the economy as a whole. What causes this is competition. As long as there are many businesses selling a product, the product's price will be driven down to a point where it covers only the businesses' costs, including a reasonable profit for the owners. If the price of the product were any higher, others would enter the industry in order to gain excess profits. Because consumers can buy the product at the lowest possible price, they reap the ultimate rewards of competition.

In more general terms, the forces of individual self-interest and competition ensure that resources are used in ways that promote economic growth and national prosperity. To explain his theory, Smith used a descriptive image that has become part of everyday language. He said that the forces of market competition act like an "invisible hand," so that self-interested behaviour can work to the benefit of all society.

The Principle of *Laissez Faire*

Although Adam Smith pointed out the potential benefits of people's selfish actions, he was not merely acting as a mouthpiece for the business class. As he was quick to point out, individual self-interest ceases to benefit society when competition is lacking. In the case of a monopoly, where a single producer controls an entire market, the business class's selfish motives cause price to be driven to the highest value that the market will bear, meaning that consumers suffer.

Often it is governments that cause monopolies to flourish, said Smith, by offering privileges to a chosen firm. In fact, governments themselves can be considered a type of monopoly. All too frequently, Smith argued, public officials engage in political favouritism or misuse their power for private ends. In doing so, they illustrate how selfish behaviour, when unimpeded by private competition, harms rather than helps society.

Given his sceptical view of government actions, Smith asserted the principle of *laissez faire*, the French term for "let things be"—meaning that, in general, governments should interfere as little as possible in the day-to-day operations of private markets.

Relevance for Today

While modern economists, as a rule, express admiration for Smith's achievements, some of them question the suitability of his theories in contemporary times. They suggest that Smith's "invisible hand" only operates when an economy is made up of many small businesses. However, most modern markets do not meet these requirements. A contemporary American economist named Robert Heilbroner upholds this view:

> Today's market mechanism is characterized by the huge size of its participants: giant corporations and equally giant labor unions obviously do not behave as if they were individual proprietors and workers. Their very bulk enables them to stand out against the pressures of competition, to disregard price signals, and to consider what their self-interest shall be in the long run rather than in the immediate press of each day's buying and selling.[4]

Other economists claim that Smith's conclusions are just as relevant today as they were 200 years ago. Although huge corporations are an important factor in contemporary economies, so are small businesses. And, as various nations become integrated into a single global economy, international competition among companies—both large and small—is playing a greater role than ever before.

Supporters of Smith's relevance also point to the recent growth of private markets in formerly communist and socialist states. They argue that now, even more than before, private competition is preferred over government intervention.

NOTES
[1] From *Industry and Empire: From 1750 to the Present Day* by E.J. Hobsbawm (Penguin Books, 1969), p. 13, copyright © E.J. Hobsbawm, 1968, 1969. Reprinted by permission of Simon & Schuster, Inc.
[2] Adam Smith, *The Wealth of Nations* (Harmondsworth: Penguin, 1983), pp. 109–10.
[3] *Ibid*, p. 119.
[4] *The Worldly Philosophers*, 6th ed. (New York: Simon and Schuster, 1986), p. 59. Copyright © 1953, 1961, 1967, 1972, 1980, 1986, 1992 by Robert L. Heilbroner. Copyright renewed © 1981, 1989 by Robert L. Heilbroner. Reprinted by permission of Simon & Schuster, Inc.

1. Explain how each of the following individuals, in pursuing his or her own self-interest, contributes to the well-being of the economy as a whole.
   a) A medical student pursues her studies to become a neurosurgeon.
   b) An entrepreneur develops a new technology that effectively recycles used glass.
   c) A high school student starts a summer house-painting business to pay for university.
   d) A high school teacher devotes three summers to obtaining a Master's degree, which requires him to research the special needs of some students.

2. How might Adam Smith argue that the "invisible hand" of competition encourages the most efficient use of resources?

3. Suggest the results of each of the following situations in a *laissez-faire* economy, and explain how the "invisible hand" might function in each to benefit the economy. Make specific references to economic variables such as wages, prices, production levels, and levels of unemployment.
   a) Too many businesses are producing Product X.
   b) The quality of goods produced by Company A begins to deteriorate below the level of the quality of goods produced by Company B and Company C.
   c) A series of hospital closures causes a surplus of nurses.
   d) A need develops for a new service that is not yet provided.

4. Research the production process of a current manufacturing industry—for example, the automotive industry in Canada or in Japan—to see how the division of labour applies. Report your findings, and comment on the relevance of Smith's theory to this industry now, new trends in this industry, and so on.

 ## Economic Goals

Choosing economic goals is an issue of normative economics. In other words, it requires making value judgements. The economic goals that various countries strive for are often similar. In 1964, the Economic Council of Canada—which, until recently disbanded, was a federal "think tank" on economic issues—listed what it considered to be the five main goals of the Canadian economy: economic growth, full employment, price stability, income equity, and a viable balance of payments. Many Canadians would add to the list economic efficiency and environmental sustainability.

These seven goals are the focus of later parts of this text. Part 2 of the text centres on how an economy can best achieve the goals of economic efficiency and income equity. Part 3 concentrates on how to attain both price stability and full employment. Finally, Part 4 focuses on issues related to ensuring a viable balance of payments and economic growth. The goal of environmental sustainability is addressed throughout the text. For now, the significance of each of these goals will be briefly summarized.

Economic Efficiency

In general, **economic efficiency** means getting the highest benefit from an economy's scarce resources. In other words, efficiency requires that scarce economic resources be employed in a way that maximizes utility. Attaining this goal depends on two conditions, minimum-cost pricing and marginal-cost pricing, which we'll explore in later chapters.

economic efficiency: employing scarce resources in such a way as to derive the highest benefit

Income Equity

Income equity is achieved when a country's total output is distributed fairly. This begs the question, "What is fair?" Is it fair that the salary of a bank executive is many times higher than the year's wages of a part-time gardener? Or should income be taken from the executive through taxation and then provided to the gardener? In Canada, the question of income equity is further complicated by regional differences. Average incomes for residents of Newfoundland, for example, are significantly lower than for residents of British Columbia. Should the imbalance remain? Some Canadians believe that incomes should be shared in a relatively equal fashion. For others, fairness means that households should receive the bulk of income from any resources they supply. Because value judgements come into play, defining and satisfying the goal of income equity is controversial.

Price Stability

To achieve price stability, Canadian governments try to minimize the country's rate of inflation. **Inflation** is a general rise in prices. As the average price level in the economy increases, households must pay more to buy the same items as before. In other words, the purchasing power of a single dollar falls. Meanwhile, people's money incomes do not necessarily increase along with these higher prices. Those households whose incomes stay the same or grow only slightly are hurt by inflation because they can buy fewer goods and services than they could before.

Problems with inflation were most serious in Canada during the period between the late 1960s and the mid-1980s, when the annual rate of

inflation: a general rise in prices

inflation in Canada was usually in the 5 to 10 percent range and sometimes above 10 percent. By 1986, the purchasing power of a Canadian dollar was about *one quarter* what it had been two decades earlier in 1966. Many households during this period depended on money incomes that lagged behind the climb in prices, which caused considerable hardship. Since then, Canadian governments have gone to great lengths to reach and maintain a relatively stable price level.

Full Employment

unemployment rate: the percentage of a labour force that is involuntarily unemployed

The Canadian government endeavours to have all of the labour force employed. The labour force can be defined as those people who are working, plus those who are involuntarily unemployed and actively seeking employment. The **unemployment rate** is the percentage of the country's labour force that is involuntarily unemployed. Pensioners and full-time students who choose not to have a job are not considered to be involuntarily unemployed; homemakers are also not included in labour force calculations.

The costs of involuntary unemployment are significant both to jobless people and to the entire economy. Being without work represents a waste of personal potential and can bring economic hardship to the unemployed and their families. For the Canadian economy, a high unemployment rate means a lower total output than could otherwise be produced. In terms of the country's production possibilities curve, economic activity takes place *within* the curve, where resources are not used to their full potential.

The problem of involuntary unemployment was most pronounced in Canada during the Great Depression of the 1930s when, in some years, the unemployment rate hovered near 20 percent, thus causing a catastrophe in both human and economic terms. More recently, the costs of unemployment have been highest during the economic downturns that occurred during the early 1980s and early 1990s. While not as high as during the Great Depression, Canada's unemployment rate topped 10 percent for several years in a row during each of these periods. In both cases, the human and economic costs were substantial.

Viable Balance of Payments

balance-of-payments accounts: a summary of all transactions between Canadians and foreigners that involve exchanging Canadian dollars for other currencies

Canadians, like people of other nations, engage in a constant flow of imports, exports, and financial dealings with other countries. These international flows—including importing, exporting, borrowing, and lending—are of great significance to the Canadian economy, since the annual value of trade per person in Canada is higher than that for citizens of any other country in the world. The **balance-of-payments accounts** summarize all transactions between Canadians and foreigners that involve exchanging Canadian dollars for other currencies, such as American dollars or British pounds. Because of Canada's dependence on foreign markets, it is important that Canadian imports and exports should roughly balance one another. Similarly, financial flows in and out of the country need to be more or less evenly matched. As long as these conditions are met, then Canada exhibits a *viable* balance of payments.

Economic Growth

Economic growth, or an increase in the total output of goods and services, shifts the production possibilities curve outward. A rise in the amount of available resources or an improvement in technology can cause this outward shift. Economic growth is an important national goal because it helps to raise the average standard of living for Canadians. Thus, over recent decades the entire Canadian economy has expanded considerably *and* individual Canadians are better off than they were in previous decades. For example, an average Canadian worker in the early 1990s could buy over three and a half times as much with his or her income than could an average worker in the early 1920s. Maintaining the past rates of growth in the Canadian economy will ensure that future generations will achieve even higher living standards.

economic growth: an increase in an economy's total output of goods and services

Environmental Sustainability

Economic activity must be carried out so that the quality of our physical environment can be sustained without significant harm. Already, the world's air, water, and land resources have seriously deteriorated, so much so that there are signs that irreversible damage has occurred. Depletion of the earth's protective ozone layer continues as chlorofluorocarbons (CFCs), a family of chemicals used as refrigerants and in the manufacture of many consumer products, are released. In addition, the greenhouse effect, a potentially devastating global warming trend, seems to be worsening with deforestation and the burning of fossil fuels such as oil and coal. The number of the world's species is also being rapidly reduced, especially in the tropical rainforests, with the accelerating exploitation of the globe's natural resources. To eliminate, or at least minimize, these problems in the future requires adjustments in the way economic activity is now conducted, especially in industrialized countries such as Canada.

Complementary Goals

In some cases, success in reaching one economic goal makes another goal easier to achieve. Goals that are related in this way simplify the task of those in charge of government economic policy, and are said to be complementary. Full employment and economic growth, for example, are considered complementary goals, since government policies that help to push up employment levels in an economy also lead to expanded national output.

Conflicting Goals

Some economic goals, however, are bound to conflict, so that attaining one goal makes another goal more difficult to achieve. For example, price stability and full employment frequently clash, because government measures that bring down the rate of inflation often restrain the level of production in an economy, thus raising the unemployment rate. Similarly, income equity and economic efficiency often clash, since efforts to make the distribution of income more fair can reduce incentives for households to supply their resources. This can mean that an economy's resources are used less efficiently than before. Conflicts like these mean that government policy-makers must set priorities, and this can mean that one goal is achieved at the cost of another.

BRIEF REVIEW

1. Three basic economic questions must be answered by every country: what to produce, how to produce, and for whom to produce.

2. Traditional economies stress the role of custom and tradition. Market economies rely on private property and the operation of markets. Command economies depend on publicly owned property and central planning.

3. Modern mixed economies combine features of both market and command economies in different degrees. Traditional mixed economies include both traditional and modern sectors.

4. The main goals of the Canadian economy are economic efficiency, income equity, price stability, full employment, a viable balance of payments, economic growth, and environmental sustainability. Some of these goals are complementary while others are conflicting.

Key Concepts

needs
wants
economic problem
scarcity
economic resources
natural resources
capital resources
human resources
economics
microeconomics
macroeconomics
economic models
hypothesis
variables
independent variable
dependent variable
inverse relationship
direct relationship
ceteris paribus

division of labour
deduction
induction
positive economics
normative economics
utility
self-interest motive
opportunity cost
free goods
economic value
consumer product
capital good
production possibilities schedule
production possibilities curve
law of increasing opportunity
   costs
economic system
traditional economy
market economy

laissez faire
market
product markets
resource markets
circular flows
consumer sovereignty
invisible hand
command economy
modern mixed economy
private sector
public sector
traditional sector
traditional mixed economies
economic efficiency
inflation
unemployment rate
balance-of-payments accounts
economic growth

Developing Application and Analysis Skills

1. The business lunch has been a tradition among executives in North America for decades. Explain how an economist would interpret the saying: "There's no such thing as a free lunch." Give an example of this in your daily life.

2. How is the concept of opportunity cost basic to the meaning of economics?

3. For each of the situations listed, identify the independent variable and the dependent variable. Then, state whether the relationship between the variables is direct or inverse. Finally, suggest one factor that would have to be assumed constant for the relationship to be examined effectively. Explain your answers.

   a) An increase in time spent studying results in higher grades on economics tests.

   b) A rise in interest rates triggers a decline in the price of government of Canada bonds.

   c) A decline in the value of the Canadian dollar stimulates Canada's export industries.

   d) The inflation rate rises, and wages in several sectors increase.

   e) A flurry of buying on the Toronto Stock Exchange causes the price of popular stocks to rise.

4. Find three to five examples of positive economic statements and normative economic statements in the mass media (for example, in newspapers and magazines or on TV). Clip or note your examples, identify them as either positive or normative, and explain your answers.

5. Interview someone who regularly goes to the movies about his or her age and average

movie consumption per month. Assuming that movie ticket prices will remain constant over the person's lifetime, and assuming that the person lives to be 75 years old, calculate the following:

a) the lifetime cost of movie-going
b) the lifetime opportunity cost of movie-going as compared to depositing the same amount of money in a savings account that pays 4 percent interest annually
c) the lifetime opportunity cost of movie-going as compared to taking an annual vacation (at a standard cost you estimate) during the person's working life (to age 65)

6. a) Construct a production possibilities curve for the following production possibilities schedule.

Production Possibilities Schedule		
Production Scenario	Pairs of Skates	Dozens of Hockey Sticks
A	0	5
B	6	4
C	9	3
D	11	2
E	12	1

b) On your production possibilities curve, locate a point that represents unattainable production of skates and hockey sticks. Under what circumstances would this production level be attainable? Explain.
c) On the curve, locate a point that represents a situation of underemployment of the economy's resources.
d) Identify the opportunity cost for the sixth pair of skates, the ninth pair of skates, the eleventh pair of skates, and the twelfth pair of skates.
e) Explain the significance of the shape of the curve.

7. Form four groups to informally debate economic systems. Each of three groups should analyze one pure economic system—traditional, market, or command—and prepare to defend that system's effectiveness. The fourth group should prepare to facilitate the debate, and then evaluate the arguments presented by the other groups.

8. Rank the seven goals of the Canadian economy according to the importance you feel they have today.

a) Briefly explain your ranking.
b) For each goal, identify the possible tradeoffs.
c) Note which goals are complementary and which are conflicting.

9. a) After reading the editorial on page 37, identify the characteristics of the California smog control program. Based on the article and your experiences, suggest what a more "traditional" approach would have been. What are the advantages and disadvantages of the RECLAIM program? What might be the advantages and disadvantages of a more traditional program?
b) The RECLAIM program is criticized by some as offering big business the opportunity to pay to pollute. Evaluate this criticism, and then propose alternative programs or amendments to this program that you feel would help achieve the goal of environmental sustainability. Support your proposals.
c) Research either the current status of the RECLAIM program and its effectiveness, or a local program that attempts to reconcile two conflicting goals.

10. Write an essay that supports or refutes the following assertion: "The market system—which is driven by the forces of competition and the profit motive—is, because of its economic efficiency, the most effective economic system today."

Laissez-Faire Smog Control

Los Angeles, the smog capital of North America, just may have a sunnier future thanks to the opening on Jan. 1, 1994 of the world's first smog market. Turning smog into a marketable commodity (like pork bellies or cotton) is a business-friendly and cheaper way of reducing pollution. It's an experiment that Canada should follow if it proves successful.

California's South Coast Air Quality Management District set up RECLAIM (Regional Clean Air Incentives Market) as a new way of seriously reducing the industrial pollution in the area. The market includes 390 companies—half are already on line, the remaining companies come on line in July.

Under RECLAIM each company is allocated an annual pollution limit for nitrogen oxides and sulphur dioxides—the two most serious culprits. The company then faces some interesting choices.

It can stay just within the limit.

It can even decide to go *below* the limit, in which case, it can sell its excess credits at whatever price the market will bear. This, in essence, creates an economic incentive to cut emissions while still imposing an acceptable overall ceiling on emission levels.

On the other hand, if the company finds it too costly to immediately install expensive anti-smog controls, it may find it cheaper to buy up pollution credits on the market that would allow it to go over its limit. Thus the company buys itself some time, but only if others are cutting below acceptable standards. This flexibility is extremely important given how badly California was battered by the recession, losing at least 400,000 manufacturing jobs in the last five years.

Initially, trading will be slow as some companies may find it relatively easy to meet the first set of limits. However, the action will pick up as the limits are reduced annually by 5%–8% for the next decade. At that point executives will either attend auctions or whip out their laptops, dial a 900 number and hook up to an electronic bulletin board to buy, sell or swap "pounds of pollution."

Environmentalists may also get in the game and boost the price of polluting by buying up credits on the market and retiring them.

Of course, the big unknown is what a pound of pollution will go for—but only the market has that answer.

Meantime, the smog will be slowly clearing. Los Angeles officials predict industrial sources of nitrogen oxide will be cut by a dramatic 75% and sulphur dioxide by 60% within the 10-year period.

The most important benefit for business, not to mention the local economy, is that reductions will be achieved at half the cost they would have racked up under traditional rules. It's predicted the 390 businesses should realize annual savings of approximately $58 million. This is especially remarkable since prior to RECLAIM businesses were choking on over-regulation with hundreds of individual regulations relating to each piece of polluting equipment. It was becoming unbearable.

While there have been other cases of trading pollution (the Chicago Board of Trade has a secondary market in sulphur-dioxide allowances for power companies) RECLAIM is the most ambitious example of a market remedy for an environmental illness. This is clearly the right path to take if we're ever to achieve sustainable development.

Cleaning the air while cutting the cost to business—what better solution is there?

SOURCE: *The Financial Post* (editorial), 8–10 January 1994, p. S1.

CHAPTER 2

Demand and Supply

Teach a parrot to say demand and supply, and you've created an economist.
— AN OLD JOKE

Each day, we buy an assortment of goods and services—a meal, a snack, maybe a magazine. What determines the price of the french fries we buy at lunchtime? The selection of chocolate bars we find at our local variety store? The types of articles we find in the magazines we read? The answer to all of these questions is demand and supply. In this chapter, we will study the impact of these two forces on our daily lives by analyzing how they operate in individual markets.

CHAPTER FOCUS

This chapter focuses on the following:
- the interaction between demand and supply within product markets
- the nature of demand, changes in quantity demanded, changes in demand, and the factors that affect demand
- the nature of supply, changes in quantity supplied, changes in supply, and the factors that affect supply
- price elasticity of demand and price elasticity of supply

SKILLS FOCUS

After studying this chapter, you will be able to:
- explain the laws of demand and supply, and apply them
- graph demand curves and supply curves
- analyze, graph, and explain the effects of changes in quantity demanded, changes in demand, changes in quantity supplied, and changes in supply
- apply the concepts of price elasticity of demand and price elasticity of supply
- make predictions and recommendations based on demand, elasticity, and total revenue

Markets and Circular Flows

A market exists wherever buyers and sellers trade products—either face-to-face, or indirectly by mail, telephone, or computer. Some markets, such as the market for crude oil, are global in scope. Others, such as the market for hot dogs at a local baseball game, are tiny by comparison.

The Circular Flow Diagram

In the last chapter, we saw how households and businesses interact in two types of markets. Once again, we illustrate these markets and the flow of resources and products in Figure 2.1. In the upper portion of the diagram—the resource markets—households sell economic resources to businesses and receive income resources in return. With these economic resources, businesses produce goods and services, which households purchase in product markets—the lower portion of the diagram. Hence, in the resource markets, there is a flow of economic resources from households to businesses (the outer loop) and a matching flow of resource incomes from businesses to households (the inner loop); in the product markets, there is a flow of consumer products from businesses to households (the outer loop) and a matching flow of consumer spending from households to businesses (the inner loop).

In this chapter, we focus on the flows found in product markets. Because households are the buyers in these markets, their behaviour can be analyzed using the concept of demand. Since businesses are the sellers, their behaviour can be analyzed using the concept of supply.

Figure 2.1: The Circular Flow Diagram

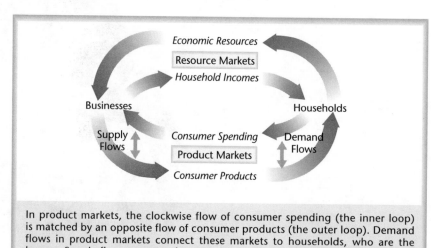

In product markets, the clockwise flow of consumer spending (the inner loop) is matched by an opposite flow of consumer products (the outer loop). Demand flows in product markets connect these markets to households, who are the buyers. Supply flows connect these markets to businesses, who are the sellers.

The Role of Demand

What Is Demand?

Demand is the relationship between the various possible prices of a product and the quantities consumers will purchase at each price. In this relationship, price is the independent variable. **Quantity demanded**— the amount of the product that consumers are willing to purchase at each price—is the dependent variable. To isolate the relationship between these two variables, all other factors affecting price and quantity demanded are assumed to remain constant. Recall that this is the assumption of *ceteris paribus* —"all other things remaining the same."

The Law of Demand

Is the relationship between price and quantity demanded direct or inverse? To answer this question, consider the example of chocolate bars you eat during a week. As shown in the table in Figure 2.2, you might buy two bars per week when each bar is priced at $1.00. If the price rises to $1.25 per bar, you will likely purchase fewer chocolate bars, perhaps one per week at this new price. Conversely, if the price falls to 75 cents, you might buy more bars per week. At this lower price, chocolate bars become a better deal in terms of the satisfaction you get from each dollar spent. Thus you may decide to increase your purchases to three bars per week. This inverse relationship between price and quantity demanded, when all other factors are kept constant, is known as the **law of demand.**

demand: the relationship between the various possible prices of a product and the quantities of that product consumers are willing to purchase

quantity demanded: the amount of a product consumers are willing to purchase at each price

law of demand: states that there is an inverse relationship between a product's quantity demanded and its price

Figure 2.2: **An Individual's Demand Schedule and Curve**

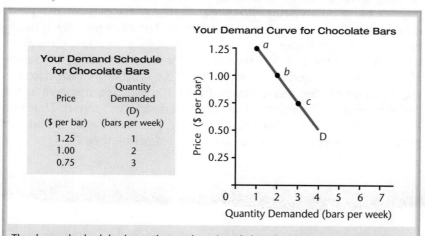

The demand schedule shows that as the price of chocolate bars falls, you are willing to purchase more bars. The demand curve D depicts this same inverse relationship between price and quantity demanded. For example, a fall in price from $1 to 75 cents causes quantity demanded to rise from 2 bars (point *b*) to 3 bars (point *c*).

The Demand Curve

demand schedule: a table that shows possible combinations of prices and quantities demanded of a product

demand curve: a graph that expresses possible combinations of prices and quantities demanded of a product

change in quantity demanded: the effect of a price change on quantity demanded

The quantities demanded of a product at various prices can be expressed in a **demand schedule** like the one in Figure 2.2. Expressing the schedule in a graph, as shown on the right in Figure 2.2, gives us the consumer's **demand curve**, D, for chocolate bars. The demand curve is drawn by placing the price of chocolate bars on the vertical axis and the quantity demanded on the horizontal axis. Note that the independent variable (price) is on the vertical axis, while the dependent variable (quantity demanded) is on the horizontal axis. This is a choice economists have made that differs from the convention in mathematics, in which the independent variable (x) is on the horizontal axis and the dependent variable (y) is on the vertical axis.

The demand curve's negative (downward) slope reflects the law of demand: an increase in the product's price decreases the quantity demanded, and vice versa. Changes such as these are examples of a **change in quantity demanded**, and produce a movement *along* the demand curve. For example, an increase in the price of chocolate bars from 75 cents to $1 decreases the quantity demanded of chocolate bars from three bars (point *c* on the demand curve) to two bars (point *b*).

Thinking About Economics

Is the law of demand ever broken?

While extremely rare, the relationship between a product's price and quantity demanded can be direct, in which case the demand curve for the product has a positive (upward) slope. This may happen when a product's high price is seen as a status symbol. For example, the quantity demanded of a designer shirt may rise when its price rises. Consumers who can afford the shirt are attracted to the item because its high price makes it more fashionable than before. This situation, which can also apply to such products as luxury perfumes and watches, is known as the "Veblen effect." It is named after a famous American economist, Thorstein Veblen (1857–1929), who criticized such purchases and coined the memorable term *conspicuous consumption* to describe them.

Market Demand

Market demand, which can again be shown as a schedule or a curve, is the sum of all consumers' purchases, or quantity demanded, at each price. This is illustrated in Figure 2.3 in the unlikely case that there are just two consumers in the chocolate-bar market—you and a friend—with individual demand curves D_0 (yours) and D_1 (your friend's). While you purchase two bars at a $1 price, your chocolate-loving friend purchases three bars at this same price. The total quantity demanded in the market is therefore five bars. Repeating this procedure at every possible price gives the market demand curve, D_m, on the lower right in Figure 2.3.

market demand: the sum of all consumers' quantity demanded for a product at each price

Figure 2.3:   The Market Demand Schedule and Curve

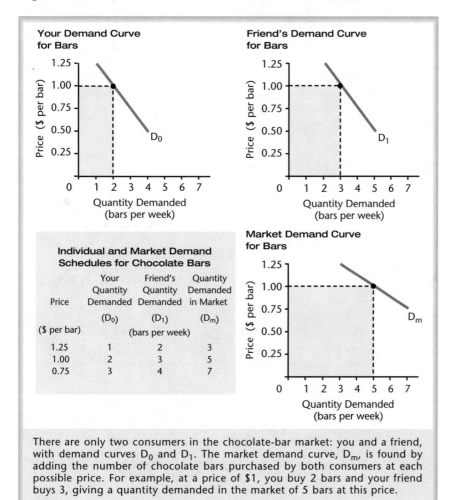

Individual and Market Demand Schedules for Chocolate Bars

Price	Your Quantity Demanded	Friend's Quantity Demanded	Quantity Demanded in Market
	(D_0)	(D_1)	(D_m)
($ per bar)		(bars per week)	
1.25	1	2	3
1.00	2	3	5
0.75	3	4	7

There are only two consumers in the chocolate-bar market: you and a friend, with demand curves D_0 and D_1. The market demand curve, D_m, is found by adding the number of chocolate bars purchased by both consumers at each possible price. For example, at a price of $1, you buy 2 bars and your friend buys 3, giving a quantity demanded in the market of 5 bars at this price.

Changes in Demand

Earlier, we stated that to study the relationship between price and quantity demanded, all other factors that affect these variables must be assumed constant. Now, let us examine these other factors, which are known as **demand determinants**. Demand determinants are factors that can cause the entire market demand curve to shift. The five main demand determinants are the number of buyers in a market, their average income, the prices of other products, consumer preferences, and consumer expectations about future prices and incomes. With each determinant, it must be assumed that all other factors remain constant.

demand determinants: factors that can cause an increase or a decrease in a product's demand

Number of Buyers

When the number of buyers for a certain product increases, more purchases are made. Thus the product's quantity demanded increases, whatever its price. The result is called an **increase in demand**. In a graph, an increase in demand is shown as a shift of the *entire* demand curve to the right. When the number of buyers in a market decreases, quantity demanded also decreases at every price, thus causing the entire demand curve to shift to the left. This result is called a **decrease in demand.**

increase in demand: an increase in the quantity demanded of a product at all prices

decrease in demand: a decrease in the quantity demanded of a product at all prices

Figure 2.4:   Changes in Demand

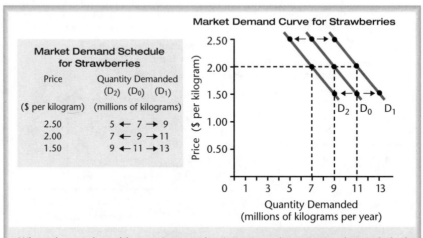

When the number of buyers in a market increases, the quantity demanded of strawberries increases at every possible price. Each point on the demand curve therefore shifts to the right from D_0 to D_1, as from 9 to 11 million kilograms at a price of $2 per kilogram. Similarly, a decrease in the number of buyers pushes down the quantity demanded at every price, shifting the demand curve to the left from D_0 to D_2, as from 9 to 7 million kilograms at a $2 price.

Both cases are illustrated in Figure 2.4 using a hypothetical market for strawberries. The initial quantities demanded in the market are shown in the demand schedule, under D_0. When demand increases, quantity demanded increases at every possible price. For example, at a price of $2, quantity demanded increases from 9 to 11 million kilograms. Thus, on the graph, the original demand curve (D_0) shifts to the right, giving a new demand curve (D_1). When demand decreases, quantity demanded decreases at every price. For example, at a price of $2, quantity demanded decreases from 9 to 7 million kilograms. Thus, the demand curve shifts to the left, from D_0 to D_2.

Income

When consumers' incomes increase, they purchase more luxury products such as expensive jewellery and caviar. Purchases of more basic items, such as milk and shoes, also rise, but by a smaller proportion. Whether for luxury products or for necessities, demand increases, thus shifting the entire demand curve to the right. Products whose demand changes directly with income are known as **normal goods**. There are a few products, known as **inferior goods**, for which incomes have the opposite effect. Turnips and second-hand suits are examples. As incomes rise, consumption of these products falls as buyers switch from turnips to more expensive vegetables, and from second-hand to new suits. The result is a decrease in demand for these products, reflected in a shift to the left of the entire demand curve.

Prices of Other Products

Substitute goods are products that can be consumed in place of one another. When the price of a product rises, consumers choose to purchase more of any reasonable substitute available, thus shifting the substitute product's demand curve to the right. For example, a higher price for butter causes some consumers to switch to margarine, increasing the demand for margarine. If the price of butter falls, however, there will be a decrease in the demand for margarine.

Complementary goods are products that are consumed together, such as cars and gasoline, or compact discs and compact disc players. In the case of complementary goods, an increase in the price of one product causes a decrease in demand for its complement. For example, if the price of cars rises, the demand for gasoline falls. The reverse is also true: a fall in the price of compact discs leads to a rise in demand for compact disc players.

Consumer Preferences

People's preferences also affect buying patterns. A significant shift in consumer concerns over nutrition, for example, causes an increase in

normal goods: products whose demand changes directly with income

inferior goods: products whose demand changes inversely with income

substitute goods: products that can be consumed in place of one another

complementary goods: products that are consumed together

the demand for healthy foods. Consumer preferences are also influenced by current fashion or advertising, as in the case of clothing. This is illustrated by a sudden fad for fringed denim shirts, which increases their demand and shifts the fringed denim shirt demand curve to the right.

Consumer Expectations

The expectations that consumers have about future changes in prices and their own incomes affect their current purchases. For example, if a majority of consumers expect the price of laptop computers to fall, the current demand for laptops decreases. This is because consumers will delay their purchases of laptops until the expected drop in price occurs. Alternatively, if consumers expect their incomes to grow and the prices of products they buy to remain constant—in other words, if they expect their standard of living to rise—their current demand for normal goods will increase and their current demand for inferior goods will decrease.

Change in Quantity Demanded Versus Change in Demand

It is important to note the difference between a *change in quantity demanded* and a *change in demand.* Both types of change are shown in Figure 2.5. As we have seen, a change in quantity demanded results from a change in

Figure 2.5:   Change in Quantity Demanded and Change in Demand

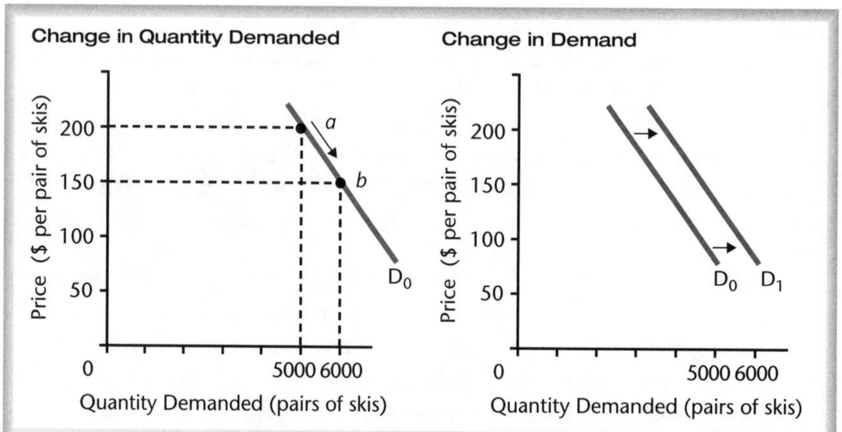

A change in quantity demanded is shown in the left graph as a movement along a single demand curve, D_0, that results from a change in the product's own price. There is a rise in quantity demanded from 5000 to 6000 pairs of skis when the price of skis drops from \$200 to \$150 a pair, causing a movement from point *a* to point *b*. A change in demand is shown in the right graph as a shift in the entire demand curve to the right, from D_0 to D_1. This shift results from a change in a demand determinant, such as consumer incomes.

the product's own price. For example, the number of skis purchased will increase when the price of skis decreases, as shown in the graph on the left in Figure 2.5. Here a movement (from point *a* to point *b*) occurs *along* demand curve D_0, since varying the product's own price does not alter the position of the curve. An increase or decrease in demand, however, results from a change in a demand determinant. The graph on the right shows how an increase in incomes increases the demand for skis, which are a normal good, causing a shift of the entire demand curve for skis from D_0 to D_1.

BRIEF REVIEW

1. In product markets, demand represents the decisions of households purchasing consumer items. Supply in product markets represents the actions of businesses selling these items.

2. The demand curve for a particular product shows the relationship between its price and the quantity demanded, either by an individual consumer or by the market as a whole. According to the law of demand, price and quantity demanded are inversely related.

3. A change in quantity demanded is shown by a movement along a product's demand curve and is caused by a change in the product's own price.

4. A change in demand is shown by a shift of the entire demand curve and is caused by a change in a demand determinant: the number of buyers, their average income, the prices of other products, consumer preferences, or consumer expectations about future prices and incomes.

Spoilt for Choice

William Stanley Jevons and Utility Maximization

Jevons and His Influence

Demand can be related to human psychology if you think of people making purchases to maximize their utility based on their limited budgets. Remember that utility is the satisfaction each individual gains from consuming a variety of goods and services.

William Stanley Jevons (1835–1882), a nineteenth-century English economist, is best known for applying the concept of utility to economics and developing a model of consumption. Jevons found his life turned upside down when, in his teens, his rich family went bankrupt. He was forced to break off his studies to find a job. After working for five years in Australia—during which Jevons taught himself economics—he had

ADVANCING ECONOMIC THOUGHT

William Stanley Jevons

earned enough to return to England and complete his formal education. He went on to become a university professor, a shy man who established his reputation primarily through his writings.

The Law of Diminishing Marginal Utility

Jevons based his model of consumption on the assumption that utility can be measured in units, which he called "utils." According to Jevons, a consumer's total utility—or overall satisfaction gained from consuming a particular product—depends on the number of units he or she purchases. Consider the example of a student drinking cups of cappuccino at a sidewalk café on a summer afternoon. As shown in Figure A, the student's total utility increases with every additional cup he drinks, but each new cup gives him less *extra* pleasure than the one before. This is illustrated in the top graph by the increases in total utility between *ab* and *bc*, and then *cd* and *de:* the shaded areas get steadily smaller. These shrinking areas are highlighted on the marginal utility

Figure A: Total and Marginal Utility

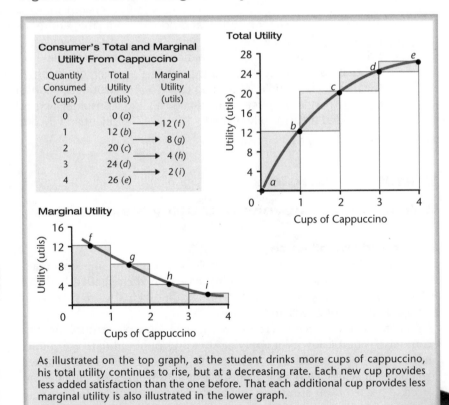

As illustrated on the top graph, as the student drinks more cups of cappuccino, his total utility continues to rise, but at a decreasing rate. Each new cup provides less added satisfaction than the one before. That each additional cup provides less marginal utility is also illustrated in the lower graph.

graph. For each extra cup he drinks, the student's marginal—or extra—satisfaction is less.

The fall in marginal utility at higher consumption levels led Jevons to state what has become a general rule in economics. The *law of diminishing marginal utility* states that, as a consumer purchases more units of a particular product in a given time period, that consumer's extra satisfaction from each additional unit falls. According to Jevons, common sense suggests that this law applies to the consumption of virtually all products. Other economists developed their own versions of the law of diminishing marginal utility, but Jevons' version has remained the most influential.

Choosing One Product Over Another

One of the most important uses of the law of diminishing marginal utility is in helping to understand how much consumers choose to spend on various products. Consider again the student visiting a sidewalk café one afternoon. He arrives with $4 in his pocket, and plans to spend it all on $1 cappuccinos and $2 Danish pastries. To get the most out of his $4, the student should use it in a way that gives him the greatest added satisfaction from each new dollar. In other words, he should make each purchase based on which item gives him the highest marginal utility per dollar. These figures can be found by dividing the student's marginal utilities for cappuccinos and pastries by their prices.

When making his first purchase, the student can choose either 12 utils in extra satisfaction from a cappuccino or 16 utils from a pastry, as shown in columns 2 and 5 of the schedule in Figure B. His marginal utilities per dollar are shown in columns 3 and 6, and on the graphs. Because the 12 utils (12 ÷ $1) per dollar spent on cappuccinos exceeds the 8 utils (16 ÷ $2) per dollar spent on pastries, the student buys a cappuccino. For his second purchase, the student compares the 8 utils (8 ÷ $1) per dollar he could spend on the second cappuccino with the 8 utils per dollar he could spend on his first pastry. Since these marginal utilities per dollar are equal, he buys both items, exhausting his $4.

The Utility-Maximizing Rule

According to the utility-maximizing rule, the student keeps buying both products until the marginal utility per dollar from both cappuccinos and pastries is the same (MU ÷ P_1 = MU ÷ P_2). This economic law, which Jevons developed, applies no matter how many items are being bought. By following the rule, consumers maximize their overall satisfaction, or total utility, from a whole range of products.

Relevance for Today

Jevons' model rests on the assumption that utility is measurable in set units. While his critics suggested that this assumption is unrealistic, others

Figure B: The Utility Maximizing Rule

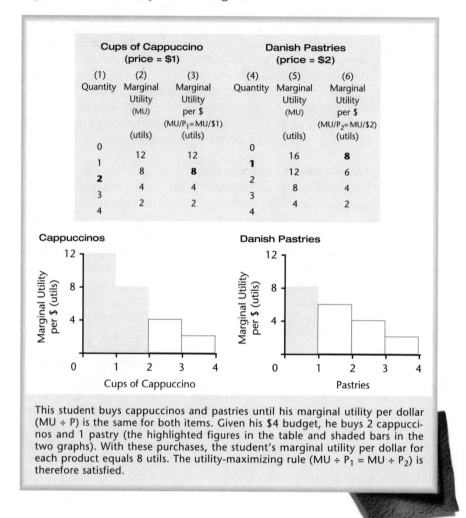

Cups of Cappuccino (price = $1)			Danish Pastries (price = $2)		
(1) Quantity	(2) Marginal Utility (MU) (utils)	(3) Marginal Utility per $ ($MU/P_1 = MU/\$1$) (utils)	(4) Quantity	(5) Marginal Utility (MU) (utils)	(6) Marginal Utility per $ ($MU/P_2 = MU/\$2$) (utils)
0	12	12	0	16	**8**
1	8	**8**	**1**	12	6
2	4	4	2	8	4
3	2	2	3	4	2
4			4		

This student buys cappuccinos and pastries until his marginal utility per dollar (MU ÷ P) is the same for both items. Given his $4 budget, he buys 2 cappuccinos and 1 pastry (the highlighted figures in the table and shaded bars in the two graphs). With these purchases, the student's marginal utility per dollar for each product equals 8 utils. The utility-maximizing rule (MU ÷ P_1 = MU ÷ P_2) is therefore satisfied.

argued that it is a legitimate way to simplify reality. By assuming that utility could be measured, Jevons made a verifiable conclusion concerning the relationship between two observable variables—the quantity of a product individuals wish to consume and the price they pay—and the result is unaffected by how this satisfaction is measured. Recently, economists have used utility theory without assuming measurable units of satisfaction. As long as consumers can say they prefer one set of products to another (without having to state exactly how much more they prefer it), conclusions like those drawn from the law of diminishing marginal utility and the utility-maximizing rule can still be reached.

1. What assumptions about consumers and their behaviour did Jevons make?

2. What aspects of consumer behaviour does the law of diminishing marginal utility help to explain? What aspects of consumer behaviour does the utility-maximizing rule help to explain?

3. What are the possible implications of the law of diminishing marginal utility for suppliers of goods and services? How might suppliers encourage consumers to keep spending? Give an example in your answer.

4. In your opinion, is it valid to say that the satisfaction a person receives from a product cannot be measured? Explain your answer, and give examples.

Price Elasticity of Demand

If the price of a video game falls, then the number of games purchased rises. But by how much? If price is reduced by half, will quantity demanded double or triple, or will it rise by a smaller proportion, such as 10 percent or 20 percent? To answer these questions, we need to understand the **price elasticity of demand** (also called demand elasticity). Price elasticity of demand is the extent to which consumers (and the quantity they demand) respond to a change in price.

price elasticity of demand: the responsiveness of a product's quantity demanded to a change in its price

Figure 2.6: **Elastic and Inelastic Demand Curves**

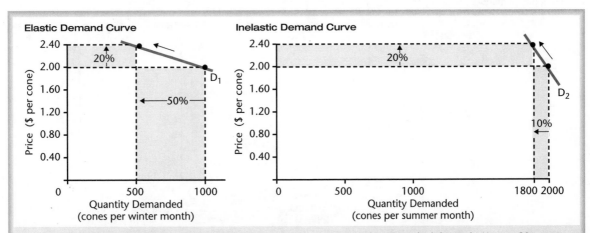

A sidewalk vendor faces an elastic demand curve for ice-cream cones, D_1, shown on the left graph. Here, a 20 percent increase in price from $2.00 to $2.40 leads to a greater 50 percent decrease in quantity demanded, from 1000 to 500 cones. The graph on the right shows an inelastic demand curve, D_2, for the vendor's cones. The same 20 percent increase in price now leads to a smaller 10 percent decrease in quantity demanded, from 2000 to 1800 cones.

Elastic and Inelastic Demand

Consumers can be very responsive or very unresponsive to price changes. Consider Figure 2.6, which shows the demand curves for a sidewalk vendor selling ice-cream cones in two seasons. During the winter, the vendor raises her price by 20 percent, from $2.00 to $2.40. The result is that monthly quantity demanded decreases by 50 percent, from 1000 to 500 cones. If a given percentage change in price causes a *larger* percentage change in a product's quantity demanded, the product has **elastic demand**. Thus, the vendor faces elastic demand in the winter, as shown in the graph on the left. When the vendor increases her price in the summer by 20 percent, from $2.00 to $2.40, monthly quantity demanded decreases only from 2000 to 1800 cones, or 10 percent. If a given percentage change in price causes a *smaller* percentage change in quantity demanded, the product has **inelastic demand**. Inelastic demand for ice-cream cones is shown in the graph on the right.

Perfectly Elastic and Perfectly Inelastic Demand

There are two extreme cases of demand elasticity. When a product has **perfectly elastic demand**, its price remains constant whatever quantities are demanded. Because price never varies, the demand curve is horizontal, as shown in Figure 2.7, on the left. Consider the example of an individual producer, a soybean farmer, who is a *price-taker*—meaning that the farmer has no influence over the market price of soybeans. This farmer would face demand as illustrated by the demand curve D_3. Because the same $100 price

elastic demand: demand for which a percentage change in a product's price causes a larger percentage change in quantity demanded

inelastic demand: demand for which a percentage change in a product's price causes a smaller percentage change in quantity demanded

perfectly elastic demand: demand for which a product's price remains constant regardless of quantity demanded

Figure 2.7: Perfectly Elastic and Perfectly Inelastic Demand

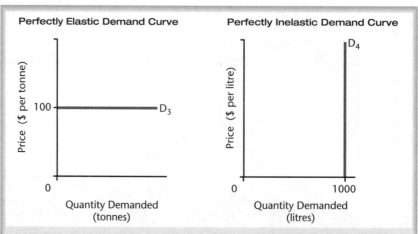

A single farmer of soybeans might face a perfectly elastic demand curve, as shown on the left graph, with a constant price of $100 per tonne. In contrast, a producer of insulin might face a vertical or perfectly inelastic demand curve, as shown on the right graph, with the quantity demanded constant at 1000 L.

per tonne of soybeans applies at all possible amounts demanded, the farmer faces a perfectly elastic demand curve. In contrast, when a product has **perfectly inelastic demand**, quantity demanded is completely unaffected by price. This situation creates a vertical demand curve, as shown in Figure 2.7, on the right. An example is the demand for insulin: since this product is essential to people who have diabetes, they are willing to pay any price for a certain quantity of insulin. This means that the market demand curve for insulin, D_4, is vertical at a given quantity demanded, such as 1000 L.

perfectly inelastic demand: demand for which a product's quantity demanded remains constant regardless of price

Thinking About Economics

Is the slope of the demand curve related to the price elasticity of demand?

Except in cases of perfectly elastic and perfectly inelastic demand, there is no automatic connection between the slope of the demand curve and a product's price elasticity of demand. This is because the slope of the demand curve reflects the change in price divided by the change in quantity demanded, while elasticity is expressed in terms of *percentage* changes in price and quantity demanded. There is a loose connection between the two concepts, however, as shown in Figure 2.6. When two demand curves—one fairly flat and one more steep—are drawn on the same set of axes, the flatter curve (D_1) is more elastic than the steeper curve (D_2) over a given price range. This is because the flatter curve (D_1) is associated with a greater adjustment in quantity demanded, and hence a more elastic demand.

Price Elasticity of Demand and Total Revenue

Demand elasticity plays a role in determining what effect a price change has on **total revenue** (TR). Total revenue is defined, either for an individual business or for all businesses producing the same product, as the price of a product multiplied by its quantity demanded:

$$TR = P \times Q_d$$

total revenue: the total income earned from a product, calculated by multiplying the product's price by its quantity demanded

For example, if the price of a certain product is $4 and 1000 units are purchased, then the total revenue generated is $4000 ($4 × 1000).

Consider how a rise in a product's price affects total revenue for businesses selling the product. The higher price, by itself, increases the revenue pocketed by the sellers, but the accompanying decrease in quantity demanded has the opposite effect. It is the price elasticity of demand that determines which of these two effects—the increase in price or the decrease in quantity demanded—has the greater influence on sellers' total revenue.

Elastic Demand

If demand for a product is elastic, price changes cause large variations in quantity demanded. Since a price increase of a certain percentage causes an even bigger percentage decrease in quantity demanded, sellers' total revenue is reduced. Likewise, a price decrease of a certain percentage causes an even bigger percentage increase in quantity demanded, thus raising total revenue for sellers. So, when demand is elastic, total revenue and the change in price have an inverse relationship—total revenue shifts in the opposite direction to the change in price.

Let's take a look at an example. All-U-Want Videos faces an elastic demand for video rentals, as shown in Figure 2.8. At a price of $5 per video, 500 videos are rented each day. The store's total revenue at this point on the demand curve is $2500 ($5 × 500 videos). This total revenue is represented by the area of the shaded rectangle AB. At a price of $3 per video, 1500 videos are rented each day, pushing up total revenue to $4500 ($3 × 1500 videos), which is represented by the shaded area BC. Therefore, a decrease in price raises the store's total revenue, because the effect of the price decrease is outweighed by the effect of the increased quantity demanded.

Figure 2.8:   Revenue Changes With Elastic Demand

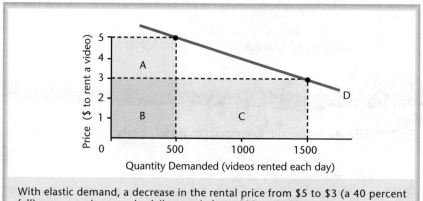

With elastic demand, a decrease in the rental price from $5 to $3 (a 40 percent fall) causes an increase in daily rentals from 500 to 1500 (a 200 percent rise). Total revenue for the business increases from the area AB ($2500 = $5 x 500) to the area of BC ($4500 = $3 x 1500). Thus, the changes in price and total revenue are in opposite directions.

Inelastic Demand

When the demand for a product is inelastic, changes in price have little effect on quantity demanded. Since an increase in price leads to a smaller percentage decrease in quantity demanded, the sellers' total revenue increases. Similarly, a decrease in price causes a smaller percentage increase in quantity demanded, thus causing total revenue to fall. Therefore, when

Figure 2.9:   Revenue Changes With Inelastic Demand

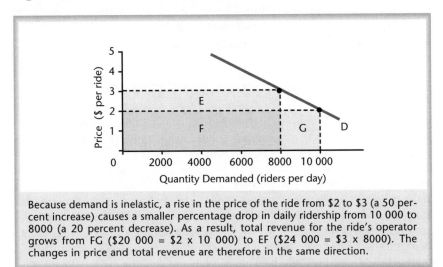

Because demand is inelastic, a rise in the price of the ride from $2 to $3 (a 50 per-cent increase) causes a smaller percentage drop in daily ridership from 10 000 to 8000 (a 20 percent decrease). As a result, total revenue for the ride's operator grows from FG ($20 000 = $2 x 10 000) to EF ($24 000 = $3 x 8000). The changes in price and total revenue are therefore in the same direction.

demand is inelastic, price and total revenue have a direct relationship—total revenue shifts in the same direction as the change in price. Take, for example, a ride at an amusement park that has inelastic demand, as shown in Figure 2.9. With a price of $2, there are 10 000 riders a day. Total rev-enue for the ride's operator is therefore $20 000, as shown by the shaded area FG. If price increases to $3, there are 8000 riders a day and a total rev-enue of $24 000, as shown by the shaded area EF. Therefore, an increase in price adds to the total revenue, because the price increase more than com-pensates for the reduced quantity demanded.

Unit-Elastic Demand

In the case of **unit-elastic demand**, a percentage change in price causes an *equal* percentage change in quantity demanded. Thus, when demand

unit-elastic demand: demand for which a per-centage change in price causes an equal percent-age change in quantity demanded

Figure 2.10:   Demand Elasticity and Changes in Total Revenue

	Price Change	Change in Total Revenue
Elastic Demand	up down	down up
Inelastic Demand	up down	up down
Unit-Elastic Demand	up down	unchanged unchanged

is unit-elastic, a price change leaves total revenue unchanged. This is because the revenue gain caused by a price increase is precisely offset by the lost revenue due to the decrease in quantity demanded. The effect of a price change on total revenue in this case is summarized, along with all other possible cases, in Figure 2.10.

Factors That Affect Price Elasticity of Demand

Four factors affect a product's price elasticity of demand: the portion of consumer incomes devoted to buying the product, consumer access to substitutes, whether the product is a necessity or a luxury, and the time consumers have to adjust to price changes.

Portion of Consumer Incomes

If the price of a product represents a hefty portion of consumer incomes, consumers will be more responsive to price changes. For those consumers who are deciding whether or not to buy a stereo, for example, a price change can determine whether they make the purchase. If stereo prices are cut in half, quantity demanded will rise by a considerably higher percentage. In contrast, consumers who are deciding how much sugar to buy pay little attention to price; a 50 percent drop in the price will cause a much smaller percentage increase in the amount of sugar purchased. The demand for big purchases, therefore, tends to be more elastic than the demand for smaller purchases.

Access to Substitutes

If there are many close substitutes for a product, consumers will be more responsive to changes in the product's price, because they have more options and can easily change their buying patterns. The demand for a particular brand of athletic shoes, for example, will be more elastic than the demand for athletic shoes in general. If only one brand becomes more expensive, its quantity demanded will plummet as consumers substitute cheaper brands. A rise in the price of all athletic shoes, however, will not radically affect quantities purchased. As this example illustrates, the more narrowly a product is defined, the more elastic its demand will be.

Necessities Versus Luxuries

Recall that necessities are essential items—such as bread and milk—that satisfy basic needs rather than wants. Consumers tend to buy similar amounts of necessities regardless of their price; thus necessities tend to have inelastic demand. In contrast, products such as tourist travel, expensive sports cars, and yachts are luxuries that buyers can easily live without. Because these items are expendable, their demand tends to be elastic.

Time

Demand tends to become elastic over time. In the short run, consumers don't generally respond greatly to price. For example, immediately after a price increase, eaters of nachos will not modify their buying habits significantly, and users of furnace oil will continue to purchase furnace oil, regardless of price. Over time, however, consumers change their habits and needs: nacho-eaters might reduce their consumption, and home-owners might change their furnaces so as to use less fuel.

BRIEF REVIEW

1. Price elasticity of demand is the responsiveness of a product's quantity demanded to changes in the product's price.

2. When demand is elastic, a given percentage change in price causes a larger percentage change in quantity demanded. When demand is inelastic, a given percentage change in price causes a smaller percentage change in quantity demanded.

3. Demand is perfectly elastic when the price of a product is constant at all quantities demanded. Demand is perfectly inelastic when the quantity demanded of a product is constant at all prices. Demand is unit-elastic when a percent-

age change in price causes an equal percentage change in quantity demanded.

4. Price and total revenue have an inverse relationship when demand is elastic, but a direct relationship when demand is inelastic. When demand is unit-elastic, total revenue is constant regardless of price.

5. Four factors affect the price elasticity of demand of a product: the portion of consumer incomes the product accounts for, access to substitute products, whether the product is a luxury or a necessity, and the amount of time that elapses after a price change.

The Role of Supply

What Is Supply?

The role of supply is most easily analyzed in competitive markets where the "invisible hand" of competition, identified by Adam Smith, operates. Because the actions of sellers are independent from those of buyers in these markets, the role of supply can be studied separately. In any competitive market, **supply** is the relationship between the various possible prices of a product and the quantities of the product that businesses are willing to put on the market. While the independent variable is again price, the dependent variable is now **quantity supplied**—the amount of the product that businesses are willing to supply at each price. Once again, we can consider both individuals (in this case, individual businesses) and groups (in this case, all businesses producing the same product). **Market supply** is the sum of all producers' quantities supplied at each price. As before, all other factors that affect supply are assumed to be constant.

supply: the relationship between the various possible prices of a product and the quantities of the product that businesses are willing to supply

quantity supplied: the amount of a product businesses are willing to supply at each price

market supply: the sum of all producers' quantities supplied at each price

The Law of Supply

When price changes, quantity supplied changes in the same direction. If the price of strawberries rises, for example, farmers find it desirable to increase the quantity of strawberries they supply, thus increasing total revenue. This direct relationship between price and quantity supplied, when all other factors are kept constant, is called the **law of supply**.

law of supply: states that there is a direct relationship between a product's quantity supplied and its price

The Supply Curve

The law of supply can be illustrated in a **supply schedule**, such as that for the strawberry market in Figure 2.11. Expressing the schedule in a graph gives us the **supply curve** for the strawberry market. As with the demand curve, a change in a product's price causes a movement *along* the supply curve, thus a **change in quantity supplied**. This is illustrated in Figure 2.11 by the movement from point *f* to point *e* on the supply curve. Because of a drop in the price of strawberries from $2.50 to $2.00 per kilogram, the quantity supplied by farmers drops from 13 to 9 million kilograms. The positive (upward) slope of the supply curve illustrates the direct relationship between price and quantity supplied.

supply schedule: a table that shows possible combinations of prices and quantities supplied of a product

supply curve: a graph that expresses possible combinations of prices and quantities supplied of a product

Changes in Supply

While price changes will cause changes in quantity supplied, other factors cause supply to change. These factors, which cause the entire supply

change in quantity supplied: the effect of a price change on quantity supplied

Figure 2.11:   The Market Supply Schedule and Curve

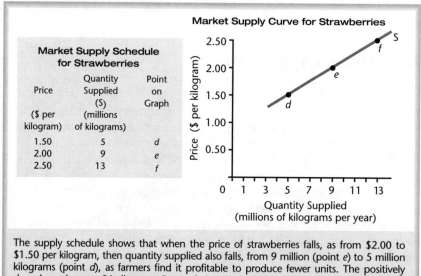

Market Supply Schedule for Strawberries		
Price ($ per kilogram)	Quantity Supplied (S) (millions of kilograms)	Point on Graph
1.50	5	d
2.00	9	e
2.50	13	f

The supply schedule shows that when the price of strawberries falls, as from $2.00 to $1.50 per kilogram, then quantity supplied also falls, from 9 million (point *e*) to 5 million kilograms (point *d*), as farmers find it profitable to produce fewer units. The positively sloped supply curve S indicates a direct relationship between price and quantity supplied.

curve to shift, are known as **supply determinants.** The five main supply determinants are the number of producers, resource prices, the state of technology, changes in nature, and the prices of related products. Once again, with each determinant, we must assume that all other factors remain constant.

Number of Producers

An increase in the number of businesses in an industry causes an **increase in supply**, thus giving a higher quantity supplied at each price, and shifting the supply curve to the right. In contrast, a decrease in the number of businesses in the industry creates a **decrease in supply**, and a corresponding shift of the supply curve to the left. Both cases are illustrated in Figure 2.12 for the strawberry market. The column marked S_0 in the supply schedule gives the quantity supplied by the original number of producers. When the number of producers increases, so does the quantity supplied (indicated by column S_1) at every possible price—for example, from 9 to 11 million kilograms at a price of $2. Thus the supply curve shifts to the right, from S_0 to S_1. Conversely, a decrease in the supply of the product causes the quantities supplied (indicated by column S_2) to decrease at each possible price, from 9 to 7 million kilograms at a price of $2. The supply curve therefore shifts to the left, from S_0 to S_2.

supply determinants: factors that can cause an increase or a decrease in a product's supply

increase in supply: an increase in the quantity supplied of a product at all prices

decrease in supply: a decrease in the quantity supplied of a product at all prices

Figure 2.12: Changes in Supply

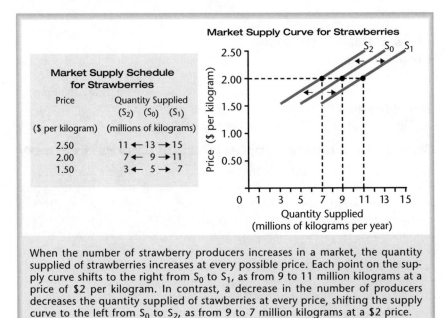

When the number of strawberry producers increases in a market, the quantity supplied of strawberries increases at every possible price. Each point on the supply curve shifts to the right from S_0 to S_1, as from 9 to 11 million kilograms at a price of $2 per kilogram. In contrast, a decrease in the number of producers decreases the quantity supplied of stawberries at every price, shifting the supply curve to the left from S_0 to S_2, as from 9 to 7 million kilograms at a $2 price.

Resource Prices

As discussed in the previous chapter, businesses buy various resources, such as capital resources and natural resources, to produce goods. If there is a price increase for a resource used in a particular industry, costs for businesses in that industry increase. As a result, fewer units of the product can be produced for the same expenditure. Thus businesses will tend to cut back on production, causing the supply curve to shift to the left. For example, an increase in the wages of workers in the apple industry causes a decrease in the supply of apples.

State of Technology

Technological progress affects the supply curve by allowing businesses to use more efficient production methods. With increased efficiency, more units can be produced at every price, so supply will increase. Use of a better grain fertilizer, for instance, causes the supply of barley to increase, shifting the supply curve to the right.

Changes in Nature

Changes in nature—for example, an early frost, record high temperatures, a flood, or an earthquake—can affect the supply of many products, especially agricultural products. A cold, rainy summer in Canada's prairies, for example, will decrease the supply of grains such as wheat. The market supply curve for wheat will therefore shift to the left.

Prices of Related Products

A product's supply can be influenced by changes in the prices of other products. For example, declines in the price of tobacco during the early 1990s caused some Ontario farmers to switch to ginseng, a medicinal root that is popular in East Asia. As a result, the supply for ginseng increased, resulting in a shift to the right of the supply curve.

Change in Quantity Supplied Versus Change in Supply

As in the case of demand, it is important to distinguish between a *change in quantity supplied* and a *change in supply*, both of which are shown in Figure 2.13. An increase or decrease in quantity supplied is the effect of a change in a product's price, and is illustrated by a movement *along* the supply curve. As shown in the graph on the left, a rise in the price of ginseng, which raises the quantity of ginseng produced, is a change in quantity supplied. In contrast, a change in supply is caused by a change in a supply determinant. A change in supply shifts the *entire* supply curve. As shown in the graph on the right, a decrease in the price of tobacco increases the supply of ginseng, causing a shift in the entire supply curve to the right.

Figure 2.13:   Change in Quantity Supplied and Change in Supply

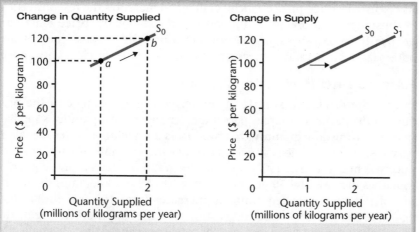

A change in quantity supplied is shown in the left graph as a movement along a single supply curve, S_0, that results from a change in the product's own price. There is a rise in quantity supplied from 1 to 2 million kilograms of ginseng when the price of ginseng rises from $100 to $120 a kilogram, causing a movement from point a to point b. A change in supply is shown in the right graph as a shift in the entire supply curve to the right, from S_0 to S_1. This shift results from a change in a supply determinant—for example, a drop in the price of a related product such as tobacco.

BRIEF REVIEW

1. Supply is the relationship between the various possible prices of a product and the quantities of the product that businesses are willing to put on the market.

2. The law of supply states that there is a direct relationship between the two variables of price and quantity supplied.

3. A change in quantity supplied is caused by a change in price, and is shown as a movement *along* the supply curve.

4. A change in supply is caused by a change in a supply determinant, and is shown as a shift of the *entire* supply curve. The five supply determinants are the number of producers in a market, resource prices, the state of technology, changes in nature, and the prices of related products.

Supply Elasticity

**price elasticity of sup-
ply:** the responsiveness of
a product's quantity sup-
plied to a change in price

As discussed earlier, price elasticity of demand measures the responsiveness of consumers to a change in a product's price. Similarly, **price elasticity of supply** (also called supply elasticity) measures the responsiveness of producers (and the quantity they supply) to changes in the product's own price.

Elastic and Inelastic Supply

elastic supply: supply for
which a percentage change
in a product's price causes
a larger percentage change
in quantity supplied

In the case of **elastic supply**, a certain percentage change in the product's price leads to a larger percentage change in its quantity supplied. In other words, the quantity that producers are willing to offer for sale is very responsive to price changes. Consider the example of a tomato producer, as in Figure 2.14. As shown in the graph on the left, if the price of tomatoes increases by 50 percent, from $2 to $3 per kilogram, the quantity of tomatoes supplied annually increases from 100 000 to 200 000 kg—a 100 percent increase. If, as shown in the graph on the right, the identical 50 percent price increase for tomatoes causes a much smaller 20 percent increase in quantity supplied—from 100 000 to 120 000 kg—then we have **inelastic supply**. In other words, if a product has inelastic supply, a given percentage change in price results in a smaller percentage change in quantity supplied.

inelastic supply: supply
for which the percentage
change in a product's
price causes a smaller percentage change in quanti-
ty supplied

As in the case of demand elasticity, the price elasticity of supply is not the same as the slope of the supply curve. However, when two supply

Figure 2.14:   Elastic and Inelastic Supply

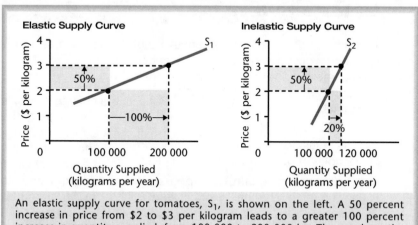

An elastic supply curve for tomatoes, S_1, is shown on the left. A 50 percent increase in price from $2 to $3 per kilogram leads to a greater 100 percent increase in quantity supplied, from 100 000 to 200 000 kg. The graph on the right shows an inelastic demand curve, S_2, for tomatoes. The same 50 percent increase in price now leads to a smaller 20 percent increase in quantity supplied, from 100 000 to 120 000 kg.

curves are drawn on the same set of axes, as in Figure 2.14, then—over a certain price range—the flatter curve (S_1) is more likely to be elastic than the steeper curve (S_2).

Factors That Affect Supply Elasticity

The main factor that affects the price elasticity of supply is the passage of time. In competitive markets, three production periods can be distinguished: the immediate run, the short run, and the long run. The price elasticity of supply differs in each period. In Figure 2.15, we illustrate elasticity for each of the three production periods in the market for strawberries.

The Immediate Run

The **immediate run** is the period during which businesses in a certain industry can make no changes in the quantities of resources they use. In the case of strawberry farming, the immediate run may be for a month. For example, if the price of strawberries suddenly jumps as a result of an increase in demand, then, during the immediate run, farmers are unable to increase their production. Because quantity supplied is constant, the supply curve (S_1), shown on the left, is vertical at a quantity such as 750 000 kg. Thus, for the immediate run, the supply is said to be **perfectly inelastic**.

immediate run: the production period during which none of the resources required to make a product can be varied

perfectly inelastic supply: supply for which a product's quantity supplied remains constant regardless of price

Figure 2.15: Time and Price Elasticity of Supply

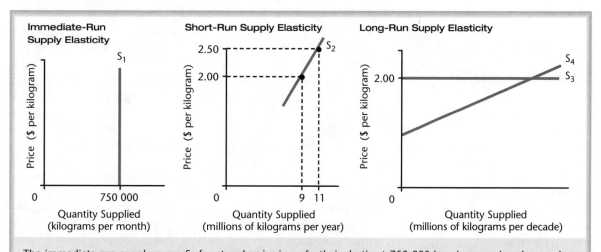

The immediate-run supply curve S_1 for strawberries is perfectly inelastic at 750 000 kg, since a price change does not affect quantity supplied. The short-run supply curve S_2 is either elastic or inelastic, with quantity supplied varying in the same direction as price. The long-run supply curve S_3 shows the case of a constant-cost industry, where supply is perfectly elastic since price is constant at $2 per kilogram for every possible quantity supplied. The long-run supply curve S_4 shows the case of an increasing-cost industry, where price rises as quantity supplied rises.

The Short Run

The **short run** is the period during which the quantity of at least one of the resources used by businesses in an industry cannot be varied. In the case of strawberry farming, the short run is less than a year. If there is a rise in the price of strawberries from $2.00 to $2.50, then during the short run, farmers can increase their production by, for example, using more labour and maximizing the crop with mulch or fertilizers, but they cannot bring more land into production until the next growing season. In this case, illustrated in the middle graph, the price rise causes an increase in quantity supplied from 9 to 11 million kilograms. The supply curve (S_2) for the short run may be either elastic or inelastic. This depends on whether a given percentage change in price causes a bigger or smaller percentage variation in quantity supplied.

The Long Run

In the **long run**, the quantities of all resources used in an industry can be varied. Also, businesses may enter or leave the industry. In the case of strawberry farming, the long run is a period longer than a single growing season—perhaps as long as a decade. Over this period, a rise in the price of strawberries will cause a temporary increase in total revenues beyond what they have been in the past. The lure of these larger revenues leads to more resources being devoted to strawberry production. Not only will existing farmers expand their operations, but new farmers will enter the market. Both of these changes increase the quantity supplied of strawberries. Two results are then possible, depending on whether the industry exhibits constant costs or increasing costs at the new, higher production levels.

If strawberry farming is a **constant-cost industry**, the increase in quantity supplied following a short-run rise in the price of strawberries has no effect on resource prices, since strawberry farmers are not major users of any single resource. The lure of extra revenues keeps production expanding in the long run until the price of strawberries is driven back to its original level. Thus, the price of strawberries does not vary in the long run, regardless of quantity supplied. This means that a constant-cost industry, as shown on the right in Figure 2.15, exhibits a horizontal long-run supply curve (S_3). For the long run, then, supply is said to be **perfectly elastic**.

If strawberry farming is an **increasing-cost industry**, an increase in quantity supplied leads to an increase in the price of a single resource, such as land or farm machinery. This increase results because the industry is a major user of this resource. Again, a short-run rise in the price of strawberries causes production to grow as farmers take advantage of extra revenues. At higher levels of quantity supplied, however, price is again driven down in the long run to its lowest pos-

short run: the production period during which at least one of the resources required to make a product cannot be varied

long run: the production period during which all resources required to make a product can be varied, and businesses may either enter or leave the industry

constant-cost industry: an industry that is not a major user of any single resource

perfectly elastic supply: supply for which a product's price remains constant regardless of quantity supplied

increasing-cost industry: an industry that is a major user of at least one resource

sible price, but price is now above its initial level, since farmers face higher per-unit costs. Hence, the long-run supply curve (S_4) has a positive (upward) slope but is very elastic, showing how quantities supplied are highly sensitive to price changes.

Thinking About Economics

Are the time spans for the three production periods—immediate run, short run, and long run—similar in all industries?

The time spans are not similar in all industries, because production periods depend on the duration, complexity, and inputs for each product's production. In agriculture, the growing season and the life cycle of a specific crop determine the three production periods. In craft industries—such as carpentry or pottery made by hand—where resource quantities can be changed relatively quickly, all three production periods can be much shorter than in agriculture. In contrast, for a complicated manufacturing process, such as airplane production, resource quantities can only be adjusted slowly, thus making the three production periods longer even than in agriculture.

BRIEF REVIEW

1. Price elasticity of supply is the responsiveness of a product's quantity supplied to changes in the product's price.

2. When supply is elastic, a given percentage change in price causes a larger percentage change in quantity supplied. When supply is inelastic, a given percentage change in price causes a smaller percentage change in quantity supplied.

3. Price elasticity of supply is dependent mainly on the production period. In the immediate run, supply is perfectly inelastic, meaning that a change in price has no effect on quantity supplied. In the short run, supply may be elastic or inelastic.

4. In the long run, price elasticity of supply depends on the industry's use of resources. In a constant-cost industry (not a major user of any one resource), supply in the long run is perfectly elastic, with a constant price at all possible quantities supplied. In an increasing-cost industry (a major user of at least one resource), the long-run supply is very elastic, with price rising gradually at higher quantities supplied.

SIDELINE

A Calculating Question

How to Calculate Elasticities

Price Elasticity of Demand

Businesses that can adjust the prices they charge frequently attempt to estimate the effect any price change would have on total revenue. By calculating the impact of their product's price elasticity to see whether or not a change in price would be to their advantage, businesses quantify elasticity— that is, they give it a numerical value.

As we will find in the following example, the larger this numerical value, the greater the price sensitivity—or price elasticity—of the product's demand. If the value is greater than 1, then quantity demanded is sensitive to price changes, and demand is elastic. If the value is less than 1, the quantity demanded is unresponsive to price changes, and demand is inelastic. If the value is 1, then the product is unit-elastic.

Recall the case of All-U-Want Videos (Figure 2.8), which rents 500 videos a day at a price of $5 each, and 1500 videos when the price drops to $3. All-U-Want Videos can use the following formula to calculate the price elasticity of demand. In the formula, Q_d stands for quantity demanded, and Δ stands for change. (The symbol Δ is the Greek capital letter "delta," which signifies a change in some variable.)

$$\text{Price elasticity of demand} = \frac{\Delta Q_d \div \text{average } Q_d}{\Delta \text{ price} \div \text{average price}}$$

$$= \frac{(1500 - 500) \div [(1500 + 500) \div 2]}{(\$3 - \$5) \div [(\$3 + \$5) \div 2]}$$

$$= \frac{1000 \div 1000}{-\$2 \div \$4}$$

$$= \frac{1}{-\frac{1}{2}}$$

$$= (-)2$$

In the numerator and denominator of this formula, the changes in quantity demanded and price, respectively, are divided by each variable's average value. The average quantity demanded is found by adding together the new and old quantities demanded, and then dividing by 2. The same method is used to derive the average price, which is the sum of the new and the old prices divided by 2. Therefore, in the example of All-U-Want Videos, the price elasticity is 2, which means that a certain percentage change in price (calculated using average price) causes twice that percentage change in quantity demanded (calculated using average quantity demanded). Note that the answer is a pure number with no units attached. Its negative sign is also ignored, so that the number is always considered to be positive. A step-by-step approach to calculating the price elasticity of demand is outlined in Figure A.

Figure A: Calculating the Price Elasticity of Demand

The value of the price elasticity of demand can be calculated by completing the following steps, which are illustrated using the demand faced by All-U-Want Videos.

1. Find the new and old quantities demanded (1500 and 500 videos) and the new and old prices ($3 and $5).
2. Calculate the changes in quantity demanded (1500 − 500 = 1000) and price ($3 − $5 = −$2).
3. Calculate the average quantity demanded [(1500 + 500) ÷ 2 = 1000] and the average price [($3 + $5) ÷ 2 = $4].
4. Insert the values found in steps 2 and 3 into the elasticity formula:
   (1000 ÷ 1000) ÷ (−$2 ÷ $4) = (−)2.

Price Elasticity of Supply

Supply elasticity is calculated in a similar way to demand elasticity. When the price elasticity of supply has a value greater than 1, quantity supplied is sensitive to price changes, and supply is elastic. If the value is less than 1, quantity supplied is unresponsive to price changes, and supply is inelastic.

Consider the case of the tomato industry with an elastic supply curve (Figure 2.14). When the price of tomatoes rises from $2 to $3 a kilogram, the quantity supplied by farmers increases from 100 000 to 200 000 kg. The value of the price elasticity of supply for this industry can be found using the following formula, in which Q_s stands for quantity supplied.

$$\text{Price elasticity of supply} = \frac{\Delta Q_s \div \text{average } Q_s}{\Delta \text{price} \div \text{average price}}$$

$$= \frac{(200\ 000 - 100\ 000) \div [(200\ 000 + 100\ 000) \div 2]}{(\$3 - \$2) \div [(\$3 + \$2) \div 2]}$$

$$= \frac{100\ 000 \div 150\ 000}{\$1 \div \$2.50}$$

$$= \frac{0.667}{0.4}$$

$$= 1.67$$

Therefore, the tomato suppliers face a price elasticity of supply of 1.67, which means that a certain percentage change in price causes a percentage change in quantity supplied that is 1.67 times as large (when both percentage changes are calculated using average values). Because there is a direct relationship between price and quantity supplied, the changes in these two variables are always in the same direction. Thus, the numerator and the denominator of the supply elasticity formula are either both positive or both negative, giving a final answer that is always positive. Like the numerical value of demand elasticity, this is a pure number with no units attached. A step-by-step approach to calculating the price elasticity of supply is outlined in Figure B.

Figure B: Calculating the Price Elasticity of Supply

The value of the price elasticity of supply can be calculated in a similar series of steps. Here, the market supply of tomatoes is used as an example.

1. Find the new and old quantities supplied (200 000 and 100 000 kg) and the new and old prices ($3 and $2).
2. Calculate the changes in quantity supplied (200 000 − 100 000 = 100 000) and price ($3 − $2 = $1).
3. Calculate the average quantity supplied [(200 000 + 100 000) ÷ 2 = 150 000] and the average price [($3 + $2) ÷ 2 = $2.50].
4. Insert the values found in steps 2 and 3 into the elasticity formula: (100 000 ÷ 150 000) ÷ ($1.00 ÷ $2.50) = 1.67.

Key Concepts

demand
quantity demanded
law of demand
demand schedule
demand curve
change in quantity demanded
market demand
demand determinants
increase in demand
decrease in demand
normal goods
inferior goods
substitute goods
complementary goods
price elasticity of demand
elastic demand
inelastic demand
perfectly elastic demand
perfectly inelastic demand
total revenue
unit-elastic demand

supply
quantity supplied
market supply
law of supply
supply schedule
supply curve
change in quantity supplied
supply determinants
increase in supply
decrease in supply
price elasticity of supply
elastic supply
inelastic supply
immediate run
perfectly inelastic supply
short run
long run
constant-cost industry
perfectly elastic supply
increasing-cost industry

Developing Application and Analysis Skills

1. a) Explain the law of demand, giving one example from your daily life. For your example, give possible causes for changes in quantity demanded, and possible causes for a change in demand.
   b) Give one example of an exception to the law of demand.

2. A distributor of autographed baseball bats has conducted a study that indicates there is a relationship between the price of bats and the number of bats sold. The study shows that 2000 bats are sold at a price of $50 per bat, 3000 at a price of $40, 4000 at a price of $30, 6000 at a price of $20, and 9000 at a price of $10.

   a) Create a demand schedule and curve showing the demand for autographed bats.
   b) On your graph, show the probable impact on demand if another supplier offered autographed baseballs at half the price of the bats.

3. For each of the following situations, state whether demand for the product(s) will increase, decrease, or stay constant. If demand will change, state which demand determinant is the cause of the change.

a) A rise in pork prices affects beef producers.
b) A downturn in the economy has an impact on the steel industry.
c) A drought in Manitoba raises concerns that wheat prices will rise in the near future.
d) A fall in the price per carton of milk affects the dairy industry.

4. Predict the effect on demand for the products in the following situations. Sketch a graph for each to illustrate your prediction.

a) Cola Company X raises the price for its soft drink, while its competitor, Cola Company Y, does not.
b) Researchers determine that consuming high-fibre foods, such as broccoli, reduces the risk of developing certain cancers.
c) The price of a slice of pizza in the cafeteria rises from $1.50 to $2.00.
d) An aggressive TV advertising campaign for shaving cream starts during the hockey playoff season.
e) Patrons of downtown hot-dog vendors learn that several people have become seriously ill after eating hot dogs sold by their favourite vendor.
f) A shortage of available housing is predicted for the next six months.
g) Grocery stores announce that they expect a price increase for coffee.
h) The price of hamburgers increases in the staff cafeteria.
i) Sixty-five students come to Veblen Secondary School for a conference and swell the lines in the school cafeteria.

5. A worker receives a large pay increase. For each of the following products, predict the effect on the worker's demand for that product, sketch a graph to show the effect, and give an explanation.

a) luxury clothing
b) canned meat
c) public transit
d) evening entertainment
e) steaks

6. For each of the following products, state whether demand would likely be elastic or inelastic, and explain your answers.

a) bread
b) TV
c) Company X's top-of-the-line car speakers
d) cafeteria lunches
e) cough and cold treatments

7. For each of the following products, state whether demand would be elastic or inelastic, and explain your answers. Next, sketch a demand curve for the product. Then, predict the effect of the change described on the product's quantity demanded. Finally, indicate the effect on quantity demanded on your graph.

a) Producers of razor blades announce a 15 percent increase in price.
b) Milk prices are reduced by 30 percent.
c) Gas stations have a price war, and the vendor of Brand Z drops his price by 10 cents a litre.
d) The price of compact discs is reduced by 10 percent.
e) Toronto's largest newspaper announces a 10-cent price increase.

8. Explain why increasing the price of a product with elastic demand reduces the supplier's total revenue. List at least three products to which this would apply.

9. A business that has been selling 3000 cellular phones at a price of $150 each increases its price to $200 per phone and finds that 1800 phones are demanded.
   a) What is the effect on the business's total revenue from cellular phone sales?
   b) Is the demand for cellular phones in this example elastic or inelastic?

10. A new local country band, Neon Moon, is giving a concert this weekend. The demand for tickets is shown in the schedule that follows.
    a) Calculate the total revenue at each price.
    b) At what price does the increase in price no longer offset the decrease in quantity?
    c) What price would you advise the band to set if its total costs for the event are $250? Explain your answer.

Demand Schedule for Neon Moon

Price ($ per ticket)	Quantity (tickets sold)	Total Revenue ($)
3.00	0	_____
2.50	500	_____
2.00	1000	_____
1.50	1500	_____
1.00	2000	_____
0.50	2500	_____

11. In the role of a business owner in your community, explain how you would adjust quantity supplied of your product to a given change in price. (You might use an example from the newspaper.) What might cause a change in supply for your product? Explain your answer.

12. An economist studies the effects of price changes on the number of handmade sweaters offered for sale by a local merchant. She finds out the following: at $80 per sweater, the merchant will offer eight sweaters for sale; at $70, seven sweaters; at $60, six sweaters; at $50, five sweaters; at $40, four sweaters; at $30, three sweaters; at $20, two sweaters; at $10, one sweater.
    a) Create a supply schedule and curve to reflect the economist's findings.
    b) On your graph, predict and show the likely result of the merchant switching to a knitting machine to produce sweaters of equal quality.

13. For each of the following news headlines, state whether supply for the product would increase or decrease, and which determinant is the cause of the change.
    a) Free Trade Brings Competition in Turkey Production
    b) Saskatchewan Farmer Grows Frost-Resistant Strain of Oats
    c) Feds to Raise Tax on Alcohol
    d) Dam Construction Lowers B.C. Cranberry Growers' Irrigation Costs

14. Predict the effect on supply for the products in the following situations. Sketch graphs to illustrate your predictions.

a) A severe frost strikes Florida's orange trees, but leaves the grapefruit crop untouched.

b) Robots increase the production efficiency of a light bulb factory.

c) A tire manufacturer hears that prices for unprocessed rubber are about to drop.

d) An increase in the popularity of computer colour monitors encourages new producers.

e) A labour dispute at a fish processing plant results in a large wage increase for employees.

f) The government introduces tax incentives for producers of bicycle helmets.

15. Predict the impact of the following changes on the supply of the products in the short run and in the long run. Explain your predictions.

a) The price of beef rises by an average of 50 cents a kilogram due to demand in the summer season.

b) High prices for gold affect the number of small companies in the gold-mining industry.

c) Concern over cholesterol causes a generation of Canadians to eat more poultry.

CHAPTER 3

Competitive Dynamics

Everything is worth what its purchaser will pay for it.
— PUBLILIUS SYRUS, ANCIENT ROMAN WRITER

Most markets work so well that we take them for granted. Usually, when we wish to acquire goods and services—a fresh loaf of bread, a pair of shoes in the right size and style, a last-minute holiday package to a Caribbean island—they can be bought quickly and conveniently. If you take a minute to think about it, you will realize what a significant achievement this is. In competitive markets, which contain many independent buyers and sellers, it is the forces of demand and supply that coordinate the plans of buyers and sellers. In this chapter, we will examine how the "invisible hand" of competition accomplishes this important task through the interaction of demand and supply.

CHAPTER FOCUS

This chapter focuses on the following:
- how markets reach equilibrium—the point at which demand and supply meet
- the effects of changes in demand and supply on market equilibrium
- price controls that governments use to override the "invisible hand" of competition, and their effects

SKILLS FOCUS

After studying this chapter, you will be able to:
- show the ways in which competitive markets reach equilibrium
- demonstrate using graphs how changes in demand and supply affect equilibrium in competitive markets
- analyze and evaluate the impact of government price controls on competitive markets

How Competitive Markets Operate

Market Equilibrium

market equilibrium: the stable point at which demand and supply curves intersect

In competitive markets, demand and supply play a key role in co-ordinating the decisions of consumers and producers. Changes in price drive demand and supply to a point of stability, known as **market equilibrium**, where the demand and supply curves intersect. Whenever the market is out of equilibrium—supply can't keep up with demand, for example—the market tries to right itself and achieve equilibrium. To see how equilibrium is achieved, consider the example of the strawberry market that appears in Figure 3.1.

Figure 3.1:   Movement of Price Toward Equilibrium

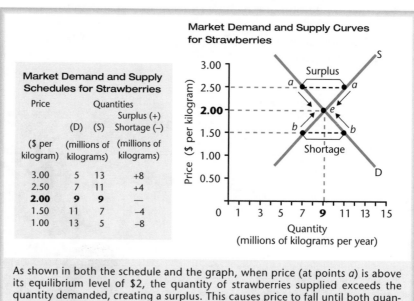

As shown in both the schedule and the graph, when price (at points *a*) is above its equilibrium level of $2, the quantity of strawberries supplied exceeds the quantity demanded, creating a surplus. This causes price to fall until both quantities demanded and supplied equal 9 million kilograms at the equilibrium point (point *e*). If price (at points *b*) is below equilibrium, a shortage results. Price is forced higher until its $2 equilibrium level (point *e*) is again reached.

Effects of a Surplus

surplus: an excess of quantity supplied over quantity demanded

At a price of $2.50 per kilogram, the quantities demanded and supplied of strawberries are 7 and 11 million kilograms, respectively. The quantity supplied exceeds the quantity demanded, so there are 4 million more kilograms of strawberries for sale than consumers wish to purchase. This excess is called a **surplus**. As a result of this surplus, producers are holding unwanted inventories.

The pressures produced by a surplus in a competitive market cause the price to fall. As the price falls, two adjustments take place. First, consumers buy more at the lower price, so that the quantity demanded rises. This increase in quantity demanded is shown as a move down the demand curve in Figure 3.1. Second, producers offer less for sale, so that the quantity supplied drops. This decrease in quantity supplied is shown as a move down the supply curve in Figure 3.1. Both responses reduce the surplus until price comes to rest where quantity supplied matches quantity demanded. Once this happens, the market has reached a stable equilibrium point—at a price of $2 in the case of the strawberry market. At this point, the amount of the product exchanged (9 million kilograms) is simply called "quantity," and can refer to either quantity demanded or quantity supplied.

Effects of a Shortage

When price is below equilibrium, the quantity of strawberries that consumers wish to purchase exceeds the quantity supplied. This excess of quantity demanded over quantity supplied is called a **shortage.** Because of this shortage, some consumers are unable to purchase strawberries. For example, at a price of $1.50, the quantities demanded and supplied in the strawberry market are 11 and 7 million kilograms, respectively, giving a shortage of 4 million kilograms.

shortage: an excess of quantity demanded over quantity supplied

A shortage in a competitive market pushes price higher. Both consumers and producers respond to the price increase. Consumers purchase less, decreasing quantity demanded. At the same time, producers provide more for sale, raising quantity supplied. As a result of these movements up the demand and supply curves in Figure 3.1, the shortage shrinks until the quantities demanded and supplied are again equal at the equilibrium point.

The Role of Price

Notice that, if there is either a shortage or a surplus, the price in a competitive market changes until equilibrium is attained. Only at this point is the pressure for further adjustments eliminated. The market then remains at equilibrium until changes in some demand or supply determinant cause demand or supply to change. Whenever this happens, the shortage or surplus that results will force the market to a new equilibrium point.

Changes in Demand

Consider the case in which the demand for strawberries increases because of a price increase for a substitute product, such as cherries. As a result, as shown in Figure 3.2, the demand curve shifts to the right, from D_0 to D_1. From an equilibrium price of $2.00 and a quantity of 9 million kilograms, quantity demanded shifts to 13 million kilograms. Quantity supplied lags

Figure 3.2:   Effects of Changes in Demand on Equilibrium

Market Demand and Supply Curves for Strawberries

Market Demand and Supply Schedules for Strawberries

Price	Quantity Demanded (D_0) (D_1)		Quantity Supplied (S)
($ per kilogram)	(millions of kilograms)		
3.00	5 → 9		13
2.50	**7 → 11**		**11**
2.00	**9 → 13**		**9**
1.50	11 → 15		7
1.00	13 → 17		5

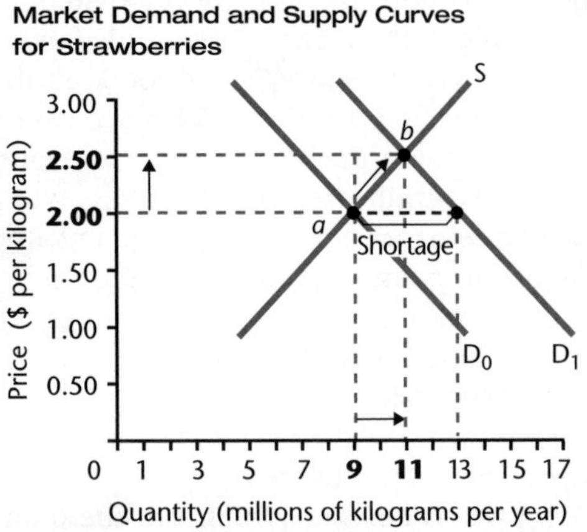

When the demand curve shifts to the right, from D_0 to D_1, there is a shortage of 4 million kilograms at the original equilibrium price of $2.00 (point *a*). As a result, price rises until a new equilibrium point of demand and supply is reached, at point *b*, with a price of $2.50 and a quantity of 11 million kilograms. Both equilibrium price and equilibrium quantity rise from their original values of $2.00 and 9 million kilograms.

behind, at 9 million kilograms, thus creating a shortage of 4 million kilograms in the market (13 million – 9 million). For the market to right itself, price *and* quantity supplied both push up to a new equilibrium price of $2.50 and quantity of 11 million kilograms. So, with an increase in demand, the equilibrium values of both price and quantity rise. A decrease in demand would have the opposite effect, causing the equilibrium values of both price and quantity to fall.

Changes in Supply

The effects of a change in supply can be outlined in a similar fashion. For example, the supply of strawberries may increase because new producers enter the industry. As a result, as shown in Figure 3.3, the supply curve shifts to the right, from S_0 to S_1. From an equilibrium price of $2.00 and quantity of 9 million kilograms, quantity supplied shifts to 13 million kilograms. Quantity demanded lags behind at 9 million kilograms, thus causing a surplus of 4 million kilograms in the market (13 million – 9 million). For the market to right itself, price is driven down until it reaches a new equilibrium value of $1.50, and quantity demanded is driven up to a new equilibrium value of 11 million kilograms. So, with an increase in supply, the equilibrium values of price and quantity move in opposite directions, with price falling and quantity rising. A decrease in supply would have the opposite effects: price would rise and quantity would fall to reach a new equilibrium point.

Figure 3.3:   Effects of Changes in Supply on Equilibrium

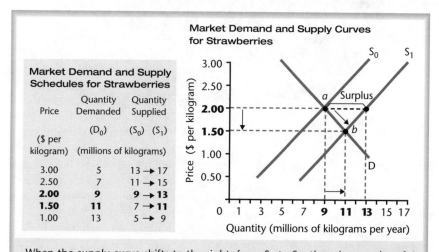

Price	Quantity Demanded	Quantity Supplied	
	(D_0)	(S_0)	(S_1)
($ per kilogram)	(millions of kilograms)		
3.00	5	13 → 17	
2.50	7	11 → 15	
2.00	**9**	**9 → 13**	
1.50	**11**	**7 → 11**	
1.00	13	5 → 9	

When the supply curve shifts to the right, from S_0 to S_1, there is a surplus of 4 million kilograms at the original equilibrium price of $2.00 (point *a*). As a result, price falls until a new equilibrium point of demand and supply is reached at point *b*, with a price of $1.50 and a quantity of 11 million kilograms. In this case, the equilibrium values for price and quantity move in opposite directions, with price falling from $2.00 to $1.50, and quantity rising from 9 million to 11 million kilograms.

Thinking About Economics

Does a change in demand affect quantity supplied, or does a change in supply affect quantity demanded?

Both situations apply. A shift in the demand curve has a significant impact on quantity supplied. Notice in Figure 3.2, for example, that an increase in demand causes a movement upward along the supply curve, meaning that quantity supplied rises as well. Thus, a change in demand pushes quantity supplied in the same direction. With an increase in supply, as depicted in Figure 3.3, there is a movement downward along the demand curve, which causes an increase in quantity demanded. A change in supply therefore drives quantity demanded in the same direction.

SIDELINE

Second-Hand Stories
Supply Shift in the Used-Car Market

Although we may not know it, we often use the concept of equilibrium in forecasting how changes in the demand or supply of a certain product will affect its price and the quantity exchanged. The following article illustrates the power of demand and supply and the concept of equilibrium with the example of used cars.

Auto manufacturers have been watching new-vehicle sales erode like a winter salt-ravaged fender since 1989. So, while Canadians may have purchased more vehicles than ever before—most of them just happened to be used, not new.

The used-vehicle industry estimates between 2.8 million and three million used vehicles are sold in Canada each year, a figure that has been rising since the recession began. Add to this another million vehicles sold within the retail industry through wholesale auctions, and the million-plus new cars and trucks sold each year, and the number of vehicles that changes hands annually—something in the neighbourhood of five million—is staggering.

"We believe, although there's no real hard proof, that the total car market grew, perhaps by quite a bit during this period," says Dennis DesRosiers, president of DesRosiers Automotive Research Inc. in Toronto. He says he doesn't buy into the commonly held belief that the recession has been solely responsible for moving buyers from the new to the used market.

DesRosiers says consumers bought a record number of new cars in between 1986 and 1989. "This left us swimming in supply of three-, four-, and five-year-old used cars," he says. Those are a car's prime resale years.

DesRosiers says this knocked the bottom out of used-car prices. "One of the prime reasons Canadians have bought fewer new cars, particularly in the past two years, is the abundance of high-quality, lower-priced used cars."

He says there are an increasing number— perhaps as high as 50%—of car buyers moti- vated by a need for transportation rather than lust for the latest in automotive trendi- ness. "These people flip between buying new and used vehicles," he says. "And they'll buy whatever the best deal is. They've moved en masse into the used-car market."

A recent Canadian Automobile Association (CAA) survey agrees that price sensitivity is at a record high. The CAA survey shows price is most important for 57% of buyers, compared with 45.5% for reliability, 26% for handling and performance, 18% each for warranty and fuel consumption, and 17% for safety.

Supply Shift

A shift in supply, however, appears immi- nent. Because Canadians have purchased sig- nificantly fewer new cars in the past five years, there is a growing shortage of some three- to five-year-old vehicles, and used-car residual values are beginning to climb signifi- cantly. "There are hardly any used cars to be had," says Mik Panavas, owner of Ontario Auto Auctions Toronto Inc. "There will be a dramatic shortage of used cars for the next two to three years."

Used-car prices will climb as a result. Pricing for new cars, meanwhile, is becoming more aggressive, and buyers have never had more choice because of the intense competition. CAA President Michael McNeil says many consumers are now asking why they should spend money on a used vehicle, when for a few thousand more they can buy new.

SOURCE: Abridged from Robert English, "Second-Hand Market Draws Bargain Hunters," in *The Financial Post*, February 26, 1994 p. 515.

BRIEF REVIEW

1. In a competitive market, the appearance of either surpluses or shortages forces price and quantity toward the intersection of the demand and supply curves. This point represents market equilibrium.

2. An increase in demand—with the demand curve shifting to the right—causes the equilibrium values for both price and quantity to rise. A decrease in demand—with the demand curve shift-ing to the left—causes the equilibrium values for both price and quantity to fall.

3. An increase in supply—with the supply curve shifting to the right—causes the equilibrium price to decrease and the equilibrium quantity to increase. A decrease in supply—with the supply curve shifting to the left—causes the equilibrium price to increase and the equilibrium quantity to decrease.

Price Controls

Sometimes governments see fit to control prices, thus overriding the forces of demand and supply and the "invisible hand" of competition. There are two types of price controls. A **price floor** is a minimum price set *above* the level that would exist in equilibrium. An example is agricultural price supports. A **price ceiling** is a maximum price set *below* the equilibrium level. An example is rent controls. Demand and supply can be used to analyze the effects of government programs to control prices. Because analyzing price controls also involves weighing one goal against another, the analysis depends in part on value judgements and so is part of normative economics.

price floor: a minimum price set above equilibrium

price ceiling: a maximum price set below equilibrium

Agricultural Price Supports

Agricultural markets, with their many independent buyers and sellers, are among the most competitive in the Canadian economy. These markets therefore provide a useful example of the potential difficulties encountered by competitive producers.

Given the nature of demand and supply for most agricultural products, farmers face product prices that can fluctuate widely. Products such as milk and wheat are viewed as necessities by consumers, so demand curves for these items are inelastic, especially in the short run. Similarly, the short-run supply curves for most agricultural products are inelastic, because farmers find it difficult to vary quantity supplied over brief time periods.

Inelastic demand and supply in agricultural markets mean that changes in either demand or supply lead to relatively large price changes. This is illustrated in Figure 3.4, using a hypothetical market for wheat. A decrease in the supply of wheat, due to unfavourable weather, leads to a fairly small decrease in the equilibrium quantity, but a considerable rise in price.

Figure 3.4:   Price Fluctuations in Agriculture

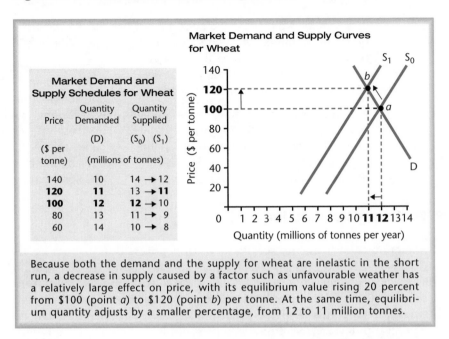

Market Demand and Supply Curves for Wheat

Market Demand and Supply Schedules for Wheat

Price	Quantity Demanded	Quantity Supplied	
	(D)	(S_0)	(S_1)
($ per tonne)	(millions of tonnes)		
140	10	14 →	12
120	**11**	**13** →	**11**
100	**12**	**12** →	**10**
80	13	11 →	9
60	14	10 →	8

Because both the demand and the supply for wheat are inelastic in the short run, a decrease in supply caused by a factor such as unfavourable weather has a relatively large effect on price, with its equilibrium value rising 20 percent from $100 (point *a*) to $120 (point *b*) per tonne. At the same time, equilibrium quantity adjusts by a smaller percentage, from 12 to 11 million tonnes.

Unstable prices, therefore, can cause large fluctuations in farmers' incomes. In years when prices are high, farmers can make substantial profits, but low prices cause widespread losses. Over the long term, farmers also face pressures from the introduction of more sophisticated and expensive production techniques, which make small producers less able to compete with large agribusinesses. Consequently, many Canadian farmers have decided that the returns from agriculture are no longer worth the effort. Canada's farm population is undergoing a gradual but persistent decline, as shown in Figure 3.5.

To counter these difficulties, farmers often request that governments intervene in markets to stabilize prices at favourable levels. In the past, federal and provincial governments have usually responded positively to these demands, not only out of a desire to stabilize prices and farm incomes, but also because the family farm represents a traditional institution that many Canadians wish to see maintained through government intervention.

One type of government program is price supports, illustrated by a hypothetical market for milk in Figure 3.6. Without government intervention, this market would reach an equilibrium price of $1.10 per litre and an associated quantity of 60 million litres sold per year. A government agency pays a minimum or floor price such as $1.30, which is above the equilibrium level. The floor price has two effects: quantity demanded decreases from 60

Figure 3.5: Canadian Farm Population (thousands)

	Canada	Nfld	PEI	NS	NB	Que	Ont	Man	Sask	Alta	BC
1931	3289.2	n.a.	55.5	177.7	180.2	777.0	801.0	256.3	564.0	375.1	102.4
1941	3152.5	n.a.	51.1	143.7	163.7	838.9	704.4	249.6	514.7	384.0	102.4
1951	2912.0	20.0	46.9	115.4	149.9	792.8	702.8	219.2	399.5	345.2	120.3
1956	2746.8	13.1	43.3	98.9	129.0	765.5	683.1	206.7	362.2	332.2	112.7
1961	2128.4	11.1	34.8	58.0	63.3	585.5	524.5	172.9	305.7	287.8	84.7
1966	1960.4	9.2	31.0	46.3	52.0	507.9	498.0	161.7	281.1	286.1	91.4
1971	1489.6	5.2	21.3	27.0	27.5	334.6	391.7	131.2	233.8	237.9	79.4
1976	1056.6	1.5	12.3	12.5	12.2	198.2	286.4	101.9	193.1	190.8	47.8
1981	1039.9	1.9	12.0	17.7	15.0	186.4	279.8	96.4	180.3	190.8	59.7
1986	890.5	1.7	10.3	14.2	12.1	143.4	232.8	84.7	161.5	178.1	51.8
1991	867.3	2.0	8.7	12.8	11.0	128.4	226.8	79.6	159.7	177.2	61.1

Canada's total farm population (which includes all those, including dependents, who depend on farming as their primary source of income) has fallen consistently since 1931. This trend is also reflected in each of the provinces, although there have been several periods during which farm population in some provinces has stayed constant or even increased.

SOURCES: *The Canadian Global Almanac* 1992, p. 642; (Toronto: Global Press, 1992) adapted from Statistics Canada, *Trends and Highlights of Canadian Agriculture and Its People* (December 1992), cat. no. 96-303E, p. 29. Reproduced by authority of the Minister of Industry, 1994.

Figure 3.6: Effects of Price Supports

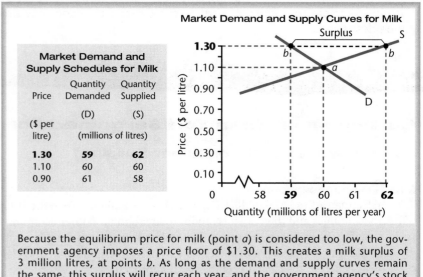

Because the equilibrium price for milk (point *a*) is considered too low, the government agency imposes a price floor of $1.30. This creates a milk surplus of 3 million litres, at points *b*. As long as the demand and supply curves remain the same, this surplus will recur each year, and the government agency's stock of milk will increase.

to 59 million litres, and quantity supplied increases from 60 to 62 million litres. Both effects lead to a surplus of the commodity of 3 million litres per year (62 million – 59 million), which the government agency purchases.

Winners and Losers

Farmers are the obvious winners from price supports. The program causes both price and quantity supplied to increase and also raises farmers' profits. Consumers lose because of the higher prices they pay, while taxpayers lose because they must foot the bill for the government agency's purchases of surplus products. Finally, by causing economic resources to be devoted to the production of unneeded agricultural surpluses, this program also works to the disadvantage of society as a whole. Are the benefits to farmers worth the costs to consumers, taxpayers, and the rest of society? The answer to this question depends on how important you consider the stability and health of the farming sector to be in relation to the costs of supporting the agricultural sector.

Thinking About Economics

How do government agencies dispose of the food stocks they buy because of programs such as price supports?

Government-owned food stocks cannot be sold in Canadian retail markets because this would increase supply and drive down prices. Food is sometimes offloaded in international markets—especially for foreign aid purposes—or sold to industrial users. In some cases, the food may simply be destroyed.

Getting More Than You Bargained For

Alfred Marshall and Consumer Surplus

ADVANCING ECONOMIC THOUGHT

Marshall and His Influence

The Englishman Alfred Marshall (1842–1924) contributed more to the study of microeconomics and the way it is taught today than any other economist. He was the first to establish the use of demand and supply graphs, for example, and the way we conceive of such tricky notions as equilibrium and elasticity owes much to his clear-headed, logical approach.

Marshall was a student at Cambridge University, and went on to spend most of his life there as a professor. Trained as a mathematician, he then switched to economics. Marshall became a model for twentieth-century economists and taught some of the most famous ones.

Consumer Surplus

One of Marshall's most useful contributions related to the interpretation of demand curves. He realized that an individual's demand for a certain item can be seen in two ways. Figure A shows the demand for pizza by an individual pizza lover. Recall that an individual's demand curve tells us how much a person is willing to spend on each unit of the product—in other words, what her quantity demanded is at each price. The curve shows that this consumer will buy one pizza at a price of $12, two pizzas at a price of $9, and three pizzas at a price of $6. According to Marshall, the demand curve can also be viewed in the opposite way. The height of the demand curve at each quantity is the maximum price the consumer is willing to pay for that unit. Therefore, in this example, the consumer is willing to pay up to $12 for her first pizza of the week, $9 for her second, and $6 for her third.

Marginal Benefit

The maximum price a consumer will pay for a certain unit of a product indicates the extra satisfaction, expressed in dollar terms, that he or she receives from consuming that unit. This marginal benefit is closely associated with marginal utility—Jevons' notion of extra satisfaction gained—but is measured in

Alfred Marshall
SOURCE: By Permission of the Master and Fellows of St. John's College, Cambridge.

Figure A: Consumer Surplus for an Individual

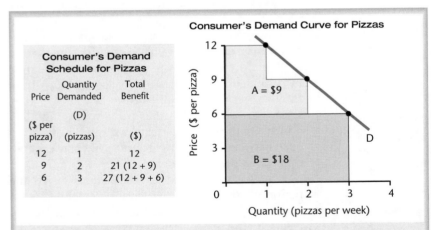

Consumer's Demand Schedule for Pizzas

Price ($ per pizza)	Quantity Demanded (D) (pizzas)	Total Benefit ($)
12	1	12
9	2	21 (12 + 9)
6	3	27 (12 + 9 + 6)

The consumer pays $6 for each of the 3 pizzas, but gets more marginal benefit from the first 2 pizzas. At 2 pizzas, for example, the $9 marginal benefit can be split into the $6 market price and the $3 surplus for that pizza. The consumer's total benefit from eating pizzas is area AB ($12 + $9 + $6 = $27) and the total expenditure is area B ($3 x 6 = $18). So consumer surplus is area A ($27 − $18 = $9).

dollars instead of imaginary "utils." While our pizza consumer gains $12 worth of marginal benefit from her first pizza of the week, the second pizza gives her $9 in marginal benefit, and the third only $6.

Total Benefit

Since any total value is simply the sum of all possible marginal values, it is possible to use marginal benefits to find the consumer's total benefit—in this case, the total amount of satisfaction derived from eating pizzas during the entire week. Our consumer receives marginal benefits of $12, $9, and $6 for the first three pizzas she eats each week. The sum of these three numbers—$27—gives the total benefit gained weekly from pizza consumption. This total benefit is shown as area AB under the demand curve, between zero and three pizzas.

Consumer Expenditure

A consumer's expenditure on a product is simply the market price multiplied by the number of units purchased. With a price of $6 and her consumption of three pizzas per week, our consumer faces a weekly bill of $18. This dollar amount, which represents revenue to the seller, is shown as area B on the graph.

Consumer Surplus

Marshall realized that individuals usually receive more satisfaction from consuming a product than they actually pay for it. This consumer surplus is defined as the net benefit to the consumer from buying a product at its market price, and is found by subtracting the consumer's expenditure from the total received benefit. In the case of our pizza lover, her consumer surplus from pizzas is $9 ($27 – $18). On the graph, consumer surplus is the difference between total benefit (area AB) and expenditure (area B), giving area A.

With the help of the market demand curve, the notion of consumer surplus can be extended to an entire market, as illustrated for the pizza market in Figure B. The market demand curve shows that, at a price of $6, consumers buy 100 000 pizzas per week. By adding together the marginal benefits for each consumer, total benefit appears as the entire area AB beneath the demand curve, up to a quantity demanded of 100 000 pizzas. In contrast, the total expenditure

Figure B: Consumer Surplus for a Market

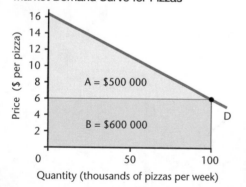

Market Demand Schedule for Pizzas

Price	Quantity Demanded (D)
($ per pizza)	(thousands of pizzas)
16	0
11	50
6	100

Market Demand Curve for Pizzas

A = $500 000

B = $600 000

When consumers in the pizza market are charged a price of $6, they consume 100 000 pizzas. Adding up consumers' marginal benefits for all 100 000 pizzas gives a total benefit in the market equal to area AB. At the same time, consumers' total expenditure on pizzas is area B ($600 000). The total consumer surplus in the market is found by subtracting area B from area A, so it is equal to area A ($500 000).

equals the rectangular area B. Because 100 000 pizzas are purchased at $6, this area equals $600 000 ($6 × 100 000). The consumer surplus for the entire market is the difference between total benefit (area AB) and total expenditure (area B), or the triangular area A. Because this triangle has a height of $10 ($16 − $6) and a width of 100 000, its area equals $500 000 [($10 × 100 000) ÷ 2].

Relevance for Today

Marshall's concept of consumer surplus for an entire market has a wide range of applications. In evaluating a government policy such as rent controls or price supports, economists often try to calculate the policy's effect on consumer surplus in the affected market. If the consumer surplus is larger with the policy than without it, then the policy is worthwhile, since it increases the net benefit to consumers. Using the notion of consumer surplus in this way assumes that people's utilities can be added together in dollar terms, a simplification that is not always appropriate. However, as a rough guide to how different policies affect consumer welfare, the concept is extremely useful.

1. Early economists noticed a puzzling fact about prices. Some of the most useful items, such as water, are very inexpensive, while others that have little real value, such as diamonds, are very expensive. This contradiction is known as the "paradox of value." Give examples of other inexpensive and expensive products to which this concept applies.

2. Using your examples, explain how the concept of consumer surplus can explain this apparent contradiction.

Rent Controls

Another way that governments override the "invisible hand" of competition is with price ceilings, which are upper limits to a price such as rent. A rent-control program was imposed on rental housing in Ontario in the 1970s due to pressure from tenant lobby groups. The effect of rent controls in a hypothetical large community with a competitive rental market is shown in Figure 3.7, assuming that all rental units in this market are identical. Without a rent-control program, equilibrium in the market would occur at a monthly rent per unit of $500 and a total of 2000 units rented per month. Controls push rents below the equilibrium level, to a value of $300. Consequently, quantity demanded increases from 2000 to 2300 units as more consumers enter the market. At the same time, quantity supplied falls from 2000 to 1500 units as landlords find it profitable to provide fewer units than before. The result of this artificially low rent is a shortage of 800 (2300 − 1500) rental units. This shortage makes itself felt through a low vacancy rate for units, meaning that an unusually small percentage of units are available for rent at any given time.

Figure 3.7: Effects of Rent Controls

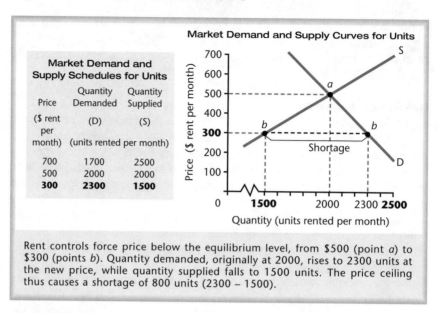

Market Demand and Supply Schedules for Units		
Price	Quantity Demanded	Quantity Supplied
($ rent per month)	(D)	(S)
	(units rented per month)	
700	1700	2500
500	2000	2000
300	**2300**	**1500**

Rent controls force price below the equilibrium level, from $500 (point *a*) to $300 (points *b*). Quantity demanded, originally at 2000, rises to 2300 units at the new price, while quantity supplied falls to 1500 units. The price ceiling thus causes a shortage of 800 units (2300 – 1500).

Quantity supplied is reduced in two ways: new rental construction is cut back, and some existing buildings are demolished or converted to other uses. In the 1980s, for example, many residential buildings in Ontario were turned into co-operatively-owned condominiums.

As a rule, shortages foster underground markets. In the case of rental housing, some landlords and tenants who are subletting their apartments to other tenants charge a fee to choose among people on waiting lists. These fees, or bribes, are known as "key money" and are illegal. To get around the law, key money often takes imaginative forms, such as forced purchases of furnishings at exorbitant prices.

Winners and Losers

According to many critics, rent controls harm society as a whole by driving economic resources away from an important housing market and creating a shortage. Because of the restraints placed on landlords in setting their own price, they are particularly hurt by such controls. Some tenants gain from controls, especially middle-class tenants who have the connections and credentials to acquire the most desirable units. However, the shortage caused by controls pushes many poorer tenants into unregulated units, such as basement flats and rooming houses, with rents that are often higher than for units in the controlled market. Therefore, not only do rent controls lower the stock of rental housing, but they can affect different income groups unfairly.

DEVELOPING INTERPRETATION SKILLS

Home Remedies

The Debate Over Housing Programs

Behind rent controls is the goal that all Canadians will have a decent home. This editorial asks, "What is the best way to ensure that this goal is met?" and gives a number of answers, none of them rent controls.

What is the best way to ensure that lower-income Canadians have a decent roof over their heads? Funny you should ask. In attempting to provide housing for the poor, most Canadian governments have chosen to act like Gosplan, the central planning agency of the defunct Soviet Union. The approach may be wrong, but concern over this multi-billion dollar misguided course of action never seems to have filtered up into public consciousness. That is surprising, because the methods Canadian governments use to house the poor are exactly the opposite of those by which problems of poverty and want are normally dealt with.

Take another example of poverty: the problem of food being too expensive for the poor. There are three possible ways government can deal with this problem. It can order food producers to lower their prices. It can set up its own non-profit farms, and distribute their produce to the poor. Or governments can simply give needy individuals more money, allowing them to afford to buy food on the open market. The right choice is obvious; even governments can see it. No one would seriously propose that the problem of poverty be addressed by laws suppressing prices, or by setting up a bureaucracy of state-owned farms and food stores.

The idea is completely wrong-headed in theory, and the experience of those places where it has been tried—back to the Gosplan example—is even worse. It is far, far cheaper and easier for all concerned to simply give the money directly to those in need, and let them make their own spending decisions.

In the housing game, however, governments have stood this logic on its head. Most provinces, at one time or another, have dabbled with rent controls, which, when applied tightly enough to have any effect, mean forcing landlords to charge below-market prices. Many provinces eventually left the game, with Nova Scotia among them. Others have moved in the opposite direction. Ontario, most significantly, has consistently expanded and tightened rent controls since legislating them in 1975.

"CAN WE AFFORD IT?"

SOURCE: By permission of Keith J. Taylor.

Simultaneously, governments have generally chosen to remedy housing problems among lower-income people not through income transfer programs, but through construction of social housing. Once again, the most committed player has been Ontario, which has more than 220,000 social housing spaces, and has embarked on an ambitious plan to spend billions of dollars building more.

Probably the most comprehensive study of housing policy ever done in Canada—two volumes long, backed by 30 research papers—was Ontario's Commission of Inquiry into Residential Tenancies, headed by Stuart Thom. It found, as everyone knew it would, that the current system of rent control and government-financed social housing doesn't work.

The Thom Inquiry found that rent controls prevent the private market from building new rental housing. In markets with rising demand, rent control puts a cap on supply. It also found, as economists have repeatedly noted, that as an income redistribution scheme for the poor, rent control is a terrible failure. The beneficiaries are those who already have apartments—most of whom are middle- or upper-income. They are the real constituency for rent control.

If tough rent controls are in place, the private sector has little economic interest in building new rental units—leaving the state with no choice but to step in and construct the low-income housing that rent control's distortions prevented the private market from building in the first place.

Governments should be acting as they do in every other sector of the economy: simply transferring sufficient monies to those with insufficient incomes, allowing them to rent or purchase adequate accommodation. This is known as a shelter allowance or housing allowance, and several provinces make limited use of it. British Columbia, New Brunswick and Quebec offer housing allowances to the elderly, and Manitoba's allowance covers families as well. (All still operate social housing, however.)

The Thom Commission lists the many problems with social housing: the number of households which can be assisted is limited by the number of units available; even if there are enough units, they will never be of the right size or in the right location for those requiring housing assistance, and those on waiting lists for social housing (60,000 in Ontario) receive no benefits while they wait.

In sum, Mr. Thom wrote, "the costs associated with socially assisted housing are high and no level of government has the funds to meet fully the demands for assisted housing...*it is clear that assisting low-income households primarily through publicly-financed housing would be a massive undertaking.*"

The Thom Report continues: "The foregoing disadvantages [of social housing] are avoided by housing allowance programs. All households requiring assistance would be given immediate help to pay the rent. There is no need to wait for one of a limited number of subsidized units to come available or for new units to be built, as is the case with socially subsidized housing. Nor is there a need to move in order to receive assistance."

Studies done for the Commission also found that government-built social housing is more expensive than a system of shelter allowances. Here's what one of those studies, *The Costs of Rent Review in Ontario*, concluded about the three options for making housing affordable for low-income people: "A comparison of the costs of rent review [controls], housing allowances and public housing suggests that the greater transfers [costs] are incurred by public housing, followed by rent review and then housing allowance." Yet governments have chosen to pursue the two most expensive options. The price: according to Ontario's Provincial Auditor, new social housing requires an annual subsidy of approximately $12,500 per unit—and $15,000 a year in Metro Toronto.

Delivering money directly to Canadians in need would be far cheaper, it would distort an efficient market economy far less and—most importantly—it would offer greater benefits to low-income Canadians. It would mean the end of a huge bureaucracy that plans, funds, approves and administers social housing. It would get the government out of the business of playing land-lord. It would allow people who have fallen on hard times to stay in their dwellings, instead of forcing them to fight for a space in government housing. It would leave decisions about where to live in the hands of people, not bureaucrats. It's time somebody dusted off the Thom Report.

SOURCE: Adapted from "Cheap housing, Cadillac price tag" (editorial) in *The Globe and Mail*, September 20, 1993, p. A12.

1. Identify the approaches the Ontario govern-ment takes to housing. Suggest possible rea-sons the government might have for each.

2. Assess the recommendation given at the end of the editorial. To what extent do you feel this approach would make good eco-nomic sense?

3. Identify the groups that are affected by housing policy. Outline the possible eco-nomic consequences for each group of a policy giving tax concessions to landlords who provide low-cost accommodation to Canadians in need.

BRIEF REVIEW

1. For various reasons, governments some-times choose to intervene in markets to override the "invisible hand" of compe-tition. Price controls are one form of intervention, and take the form of price floors and price ceilings.

2. Setting a price floor, or a minimum allowable price, in a competitive mar-ket tends to cause surpluses.

3. Setting a price ceiling, or a maximum allowable price, in a competitive mar-ket tends to cause shortages.

Key Concepts

market equilibrium
surplus
shortage
price floor
price ceiling

Developing Application and Analysis Skills

1. a) For the schedules on page 90, draw a graph showing market demand and supply curves for blueberry pies.
   b) On your graph, indicate the equilibrium price for blueberry pies.

   c) On your graph, locate the prices of $6 per pie and $2 per pie. Identify at each price the surplus or shortage that is cre-ated at that price level.

Demand and Supply Schedules for Blueberry Pies

Price ($ per pie)	Quantity Demanded (no. of pies)	Quantity Supplied (no. of pies)
6	10	26
5	14	22
4	18	18
3	22	14
2	26	10

2. Sketch a graph with supply and demand curves for blueberry pies. On your graph, indicate the following and explain the effect on both equilibrium price and equilibrium quantity:

   a) increase in demand
   b) decrease in demand
   c) increase in supply
   d) decrease in supply

3. a) Copy the following schedules for pizzas into your notebook, and then indicate for each price the surplus or shortage that exists, if any.
   b) Indicate at each price level the effect of any surplus or shortage on price.
   c) Indicate the equilibrium price for pizzas.

4. a) For the table below, draw a graph showing the market demand curves (D_0 and D_1) and the market supply curve for blueberry pies.
   b) On your graph, indicate the initial equilibrium price for blueberry pies on curve D_0.
   c) On your graph, indicate the effect of the change in demand to D_1. What is the new equilibrium point?
   d) Suggest two factors that could have caused demand to change as shown.

Demand and Supply Schedules for Blueberry Pies

Price ($ per pie)	Quantity Demanded (no. of pies)		Quantity Supplied (no. of pies)
	D_0	D_1	
6	10 → 18		26
5	14 → 22		22
4	18 → 26		18
3	22 → 30		14
2	26 → 34		10

5. a) For the table on page 91, draw a graph showing the market demand curve and

Demand and Supply Schedules for Pizzas

Price ($ per pizza)	Quantity Demanded (no. of pizzas)	Quantity Supplied (no. of pizzas)	Surplus (+, −)	Impact on Price (up, down)
12	20	80	_____	_____
10	35	65	_____	_____
8	50	50	_____	_____
6	65	35	_____	_____
4	80	20	_____	_____

the market supply curves (S_0 and S_1) for blueberry pies.

b) On your graph, indicate the initial equilibrium price for blueberry pies on curve S_0.

c) On your graph, indicate the effect of the change in supply to S_1. What is the new equilibrium point?

d) Suggest two factors that could have caused supply to change as shown.

Demand and Supply Schedules for Blueberry Pies

Price ($ per pie)	Quantity Demanded (no. of pies)	Quantity Supplied (no. of pies)	
		S_0	S_1
6	10	26 →	34
5	14	22 →	30
4	18	18 →	26
3	22	14 →	22
2	26	10 →	18

6. The schedules opposite show demand and supply for corn in the immediate run and the short run.

a) Draw a graph showing the initial market demand curve (D_0) and the initial market supply curve (S_0) for corn.

b) Explain why the supply of corn is perfectly inelastic in the immediate run. Mark the equilibrium price and quantity on your graph (E_0).

c) Add to your graph a demand curve (D_1) reflecting a change in demand. Describe the effect on equilibrium price and quantity on your graph, and mark the new equilibrium point (E_1).

d) Add to your graph a supply curve (S_1) reflecting the change in supply from the immediate run to the short run. Describe the effect of the supply change on equilibrium price and quantity on your graph. Mark the new equilibrium point on your graph (E_2).

e) What do you conclude about the effect on price and quantity when supply is perfectly inelastic and demand increases? What would be the effect if demand decreased?

Demand and Supply Schedules for Corn

Price ($ per tonne)	Quantity Demanded (no. of tonnes)		Quantity Supplied (no. of tonnes)	
	(D_0)	(D_1)	(S_0)	(S_1)
52.50	90 →	130	130 →	170
45.00	110 →	150	130 →	150
37.50	130 →	170	130 →	130
30.00	150 →	190	130 →	110
22.50	170 →	210	130 →	90
15.00	190 →	230	130 →	70

7. What is the effect on price when supply is elastic and demand increases? What is the effect if demand decreases? Explain your answers.

PART 2

Efficiency and Equity

That action is best which procures the greatest happiness for the greatest numbers.

—Francis Hutcheson, British philosopher

To answer the three basic economic questions—what to produce, how to produce, and for whom to produce—any society must decide on the relative significance of efficiency and equity. These two goals, which lie at the heart of microeconomics, are often in conflict. While most of us would agree that society should try to achieve the greatest happiness for the greatest number of people, differences of opinion are common when weighing the importance of gaining the most benefits from the economy's scarce resources (efficiency) against the importance of distributing the country's total output fairly (equity).

In modern mixed economies such as Canada's, the private sector has traditionally stressed the goal of efficiency, while the public sector—especially in the decades since World War II—has tended to focus on the goal of income equity. In the chapters that follow, we will examine the impact of each goal and how they are related. We will also examine the impact of an important third goal—environmental sustainability.

CHAPTER 4

Costs of Production

Knowledge is the only instrument
of production that is not subject to
diminishing returns.
—J.M. CLARK, AMERICAN ECONOMIST

There is an old saying: "There's no such thing as a free lunch." In other
words, everything has a cost. This chapter highlights one of the most
important types of cost—how production creates expenses for businesses.
In the future, if not already, most of us will have a close connection with
a business as an employee or owner. All of us have a connection to businesses by virtue of being consumers. For now, we will ignore the selling
side of business to look at how businesses are organized, how they make
decisions about production processes, and how they deal with production
costs. In later chapters, we will look again at sales revenues to see the crucial role production costs play in determining the profits companies earn.

CHAPTER FOCUS

This chapter focuses on the following:
- major organizational forms of business—sole proprietorships, partnerships, and corporations
- economic costs (explicit and implicit) of production, and economic profit
- short-run (total, average, and marginal) products and costs, and the law of diminishing returns
- long-run results of production (economies of scale, constant returns to scale, and diseconomies of scale), and long-run costs

SKILLS FOCUS

After studying this chapter, you will be able to:
- understand how businesses are organized and how their performance is measured
- identify fixed and variable costs in industries
- graph total, average, and marginal product curves, and identify the ranges of increasing returns, diminishing returns, and negative diminishing returns
- calculate and graph total, marginal, average, fixed, and variable costs, and explain the relationships among these costs
- describe the main cost concepts that are relevant in the long run
- outline the three types of returns to scale and their importance

Business Organization

business: an enterprise that brings individuals, financial resources, and economic resources together to produce a good or service for economic gain

A **business** is an enterprise that brings individuals, financial resources, and economic resources together to produce a good or service for economic gain. There are about one million businesses in Canada. Of that number, many are small; more than three-quarters of Canadian businesses have annual sales revenues of less than $5 million. However, 5000 businesses together account for almost half the total revenue received by Canadian business as a whole.

The vast majority of businesses take one of the following forms: sole proprietorship, partnership, or corporation. A co-operative, which is a business owned and run jointly by its members, is significant in certain sectors and regions but is overall a less popular option.

Sole Proprietorships and Partnerships

sole proprietorship: an unincorporated business that is owned by a single person

A business that is owned by a single person is a **sole proprietorship**. A business that is owned by two or more people is a **partnership**. There are few legal restrictions on establishing these forms of business, and their simple structure gives them the flexibility to adapt to new market situations. However, they are a viable option only for small enterprises. This is because of the principle of *unlimited liability*, which means that owners of sole proprietorships and partnerships are responsible for their company's obligations. In other words, the personal belongings and private savings of the owners may be seized to pay off lenders and suppliers if a business cannot pay its outstanding debts.

partnership: an unincorporated business that is owned by two or more people

Corporations

corporation: a company that has a legal status independent of its owners

A **corporation** is a company that has a legal status independent of its owners. In the eyes of the law, a corporation is a legal entity, like a person, and

Figure 4.1: Types of Businesses in Canadian Manufacturing (1990)

	Percentage of Total Businesses	Percentage of Total Sales Revenue
Sole Proprietorships	2%	< 1%
Partnerships	< 1%	< 1%
Corporations	97%	98%
Co-operatives	< 1%	1%
	100%	100%

In 1990, about 97 percent of all Canadian manufacturers were corporations. When viewed as a percentage of total sales revenue for businesses in manufacturing, the domination of corporations in manufacturing is even greater, accounting for 98 percent of total sales revenue in 1990.

SOURCE: Adapted from Statistics Canada, *Manufacturing Industries of Canada, 1990* (March 1994), cat. no. 31-203, pp. 282–83. Reproduced by authority of the Minister of Industry, 1994.

has the obligations of any person doing business. Ownership in a corporation is gained by buying shares. The shares of many corporations are bought or sold among a wide range of individuals, making the connection between the corporation and its owners looser than for sole proprietorships or partnerships. Many shareholders have nothing to do with the day-to-day operations of the business, but the money they invest allows the corporation to be formed and to expand.

The process of establishing a corporation, which involves government fees and lawyers' bills, is sometimes too expensive for small businesses. But most large businesses find the convenience of operating as a corporation worth the expense. Corporate shareholders enjoy the advantage of *limited liability*, meaning they can lose only what they put into the business. Given this protection to owners, a large corporation can raise funds by selling shares to many interested buyers. In manufacturing, corporations are the prevalent form of business organization. Figure 4.1 shows the significance of corporations in Canadian manufacturing, both in terms of the percentage of all enterprises and their share of sales.

Production, Costs, and Profit

Production is the process of transforming a set of resources into a good or service that has economic value. The resources used in production are known as **inputs**. Recall that natural resources, capital resources, and human resources are the three economic resources used in production. Inputs for most businesses include all three of these *factors of production*. **Output** is the result of this production, the quantity of a good or service that is produced.

Businesses and the industries in which they operate fall into one of three sectors depending on the type of production: primary, secondary, or service (also known as "tertiary"). The primary sector includes industries that extract or cultivate natural resources, such as mining, forestry, fishing, and agriculture. The secondary sector involves fabricating or processing goods and includes, among other industries, manufacturing and construction. Finally, the service sector includes trade industries (both retail and wholesale) such as banking and insurance, and the new information industries. Despite the differences among these three sectors, they all follow the same production principles.

Productive Efficiency

In producing a certain good or service, businesses can typically choose from several processes, each using a different combination of inputs. A **labour-intensive process** is one that employs more labour and less capital to produce a certain quantity of output. Conversely, a **capital-intensive process** uses more capital and less labour to produce the same quantity of output.

production: the process of transforming a set of resources into a good or service that has economic value

inputs: the resources used in production

output: the quantity of a good or service that results from production

labour-intensive process: a production process that employs more labour and less capital

capital-intensive process: a production process that employs more capital and less labour

Suppose you have started a small clothing company, Pure 'n' Simple T-Shirts. You rent a building to use as a factory, and buy a supply of materials. Before hiring workers or buying sewing machines, you discover that you can make 250 T-shirts a day by using one of two possible production processes, each involving a different combination of workers and machines. The combinations of labour and capital employed in each process are shown in Figure 4.2. Process A is labour-intensive, since it requires more workers and fewer machines to produce 250 T-shirts per day. Process B is capital-intensive, since it requires more machines and fewer workers.

Figure 4.2:   Choosing a Production Process

	Workers (labour)	Sewing Machines (capital)
Process A	4	2
Process B	3	3

Pure 'n' Simple T-Shirts can produce a daily output of 250 T-shirts with one of two possible combinations of workers and sewing machines. Process A is a more labour-intensive process, while Process B is a more capital-intensive process.

productive efficiency:

making a given quantity of output at the lowest cost

How does a business decide which production process to use? Owners who want to earn as much profit as possible should try to maximize the business's **productive efficiency**, which means making a given quantity of output with the least costly mix of inputs. Selecting the most efficient process therefore depends both on the quantity of each input used and on the prices of these inputs. Let's look again at the example of Pure 'n' Simple T-Shirts. As the owner, you can maximize your business's productive efficiency by using the lowest-priced combination of workers and sewing machines needed to turn out the daily output of 250 T-shirts. You find that the daily cost of a worker (an hourly wage, plus employee benefits) is $100, while the daily cost of a sewing machine (including wear and tear on the machine, use of electricity, and maintenance) is $25. All other costs for the business (for example, rent of the building) remain constant no matter which process is used, so they can be ignored in making this decision. With Process A, the daily costs of employing four workers and two machines come to $450 [($100 × 4 workers) + ($25 × 2 machines)]. In contrast, the daily costs of employing three workers and three machines with Process B are $375 [($100 × 3 workers) + ($25 × 3 machines)]. In this case, productive efficiency is maximized by using the capital-intensive Process B.

Economic Costs

Businesses face two types of costs: explicit costs and implicit costs. **Explicit costs** are payments made by a business to businesses or people outside of it. Explicit costs are also referred to as "accounting costs" because they include all the costs that appear in the business accounting records. These costs include such items as payments made for workers, buildings, machinery, and materials. For Pure 'n' Simple T-Shirts, for example, the explicit costs of producing 250 T-shirts a day using Process B include $375 for labour and machinery. In addition, the business may face a whole range of other accounting costs that add up to $675 per day. The daily explicit costs for the business are therefore $1050 ($375 + $675).

In contrast, **implicit costs** are estimates of what owners give up by being involved with a business—the opportunity cost, in other words, of pursuing this course of action over another. Implicit costs relate to the resources provided by the owners. One implicit cost is **normal profit**, or the minimum return that owners must receive to keep their funds tied up in their business. To calculate normal profit, owners must determine the highest possible return they could have received by using their funds and entrepreneurship skills in another way. Consider again the T-shirt company. You might estimate that, if you closed down the business and used the proceeds to purchase a partnership in your friend's catering business, you could earn a return of $50 a day. Another implicit cost is the wages that owners sacrifice by providing labour to the business. If, for example, you devote labour by working as the manager of Pure 'n' Simple T-Shirts, you might estimate the value of your work as $150 a day, which is what you could earn by working for someone else. The sum of these two costs means that the implicit costs for Pure 'n' Simple T-Shirts are $200 ($50 + $150) per day.

Recall that economists define "cost" as opportunity cost, which includes any sacrificed opportunity that results from some course of action, even if no outright monetary payment is made. Thus, the **economic costs** encountered by a business are all the opportunity costs involved in production, and include both explicit and implicit costs. So, for Pure 'n' Simple T-Shirts, the explicit costs of producing 250 T-shirts per day are $1050, and the implicit costs are $200. The total economic costs faced by the business are therefore $1250:

$$\text{Economic costs} = \text{explicit costs} + \text{implicit costs}$$
$$\$1250 = \$1050 + \$200$$

Economic Profit

When economic costs are subtracted from total revenue, the excess is known as **economic profit**. If this gives a negative figure, the business faces a negative economic profit, or a loss. The daily economic profit of

explicit costs: payments made by a business to businesses or people outside of it

implicit costs: the owner's opportunity costs of being involved with a business

normal profit: the minimum return necessary for owners to keep funds in their business

economic costs: a business's total explicit and implicit costs

economic profit: the excess of a business's total revenue over its economic costs

The Profit Game

Measuring Business Performance

Economists and accountants differ in how they look at costs and profits. Although economists consider the broader picture of opportunity costs, they must still understand the concepts accountants use to measure a business's performance. Business performance is measured using two basic accounting records: *balance sheets* and *income statements*.

The Balance Sheet

A balance sheet shows a business's financial position at a particular point in time; thus, it gives a "snapshot" of the business's financial status at that time.

One side of the balance sheet lists the business *assets*, or items of value that the business owns. The other side of the balance sheet lists the claims against the business assets. These claims are either *liabilities*, which are the company's obligations to make payments to others, or *owner's equity*, which represents the owner's stake in the business (there may also be more than one owner). Owner's equity is found by adding the value of all assets, and then subtracting the value of all liabilities.

A balance sheet can be used for several purposes, one of which is to help determine a business's *solvency*, or its ability to meet its debts. To measure solvency, accountants calculate the business's debt/equity ratio, which is the total value of the liabilities divided by the owner's equity. A low value for this ratio is a sign of financial health, since the company can likely pay off any upcoming obligations it has to lenders.

Take, for example, Jumbo-Dogs, a sidewalk cart owned by your friend, who used some savings and a loan from his parents to start the business after graduating. As shown in Figure A, the business has three assets: a bank deposit, food inventory, and a hot-dog cart. The business has one liability, its outstanding $2000 loan, along with owner's equity of $5000. The debt/equity ratio for the business is therefore 0.4, which is found by dividing the value of liabilities by the value of owner's equity:

$$\text{Debt/equity ratio} = \frac{\text{total liabilities}}{\text{owner's equity}}$$

$$0.4 = \frac{\$2000}{\$5000}$$

Compared to most businesses, Jumbo-Dogs has a low debt/equity ratio, meaning that there is little chance that it will soon become insolvent. At present, the business's cash holdings of $1900 are almost equal to its outstanding debt of $2000. Even if the entire loan came due in the very near future, the $100 inventory could soon be turned into cash as well. Assets that can be quickly transformed into money are known as *liquid assets*.

The Income Statement

An *income statement* measures a business's activities over a given period of time. The income statement lists both the business's total sales (or revenue earned) and total expenses (the explicit costs incurred over the period of time). The difference between sales and expenses is the business's profit. The income statement for Jumbo-Dogs is shown in Figure B.

Figure A: Balance Sheet for Jumbo-Dogs

Balance Sheet
December 31, 1995

Assets		Liabilities	
Cash	$1900	Loan from parents	$2000
Food inventory	100		
Hot-dog cart	5000	**Owner's equity**	5000
	$7000		$7000

The assets of the business include cash of $1900, unsold food inventory of $100, and the hot-dog cart, which has an estimated value of $5000. The claims on company assets include the $2000 remaining on the loan from the owner's parents as well as $5000 in owner's equity.

Figure B: Income Statement for Jumbo-Dogs

Income Statement
For the year 1995

Total Sales		$50 000
Expenses		
Food	$15 000	
Fuel	3 500	
Depreciation	1 000	
Interest on loan	500	
Total expenses		$20 000
Total profit		$30 000

The business's accounting profit of $30 000 is found by deducting total explicit costs of $20 000 from its total revenue of $50 000. The explicit costs include payments for food and fuel (for a propane tank), $500 interest on the business's loan, and wear and tear on the hot-dog cart—depreciation—estimated at $1000.

Depreciation

One explicit cost that deserves special note is *depreciation*, or the reduction in the value of a company's long-lived tangible, or durable, assets.

(Land is a special durable asset that does not depreciate because it lasts indefinitely). Depreciation is the result of age and wear and tear on an asset. As an asset depreciates, its value on the business's balance sheet falls, with a depreciation charge being subtracted from the income statement each year.

Let's consider Jumbo-Dogs again. At the beginning of the year, the owner bought a hot-dog cart for $6000. Because the cart has an expected life span of six years, the value is depreciated over the six-year life, giving a yearly depreciation of $1000 ($6000 ÷ 6 years). Therefore, at the end of the first year, the hot-dog cart has a value of $5000, and the income statement in Figure B shows a depreciation charge of $1000.

Durable assets have different life spans, so they depreciate at different rates. For example, because a building is a longer-lasting asset than most machinery, the annual depreciation charge for a building is usually proportionately less than that for machinery. Of all the explicit costs, depreciation is the only item that does not entail an outright payment of cash by the business. In the example of Jumbo-Dogs, the $1000 depreciation charge is not withdrawn from the deposits of the company. Therefore, to reflect the cash position of the company for the year, the depreciation charge would be added to the accounting profit.

Accounting Versus Economic Profit

The main purpose of an income statement is to show the business's accounting profit, which appears at the bottom of the statement, and is found by deducting total expenses from total sales. So, Jumbo-Dogs has an accounting profit, or "bottom line," of $30 000, as shown in Figure B and below.

Accounting profit = total revenue − explicit costs
$30 000 = $50 000 − $20 000

Because accountants consider only a business's explicit costs in their measure of profit—

whereas economists consider both explicit *and* implicit costs — accounting profit always exceeds economic profit by the amount of implicit costs. Therefore, calculating the economic profit of Jumbo-Dogs would involve measuring not only total sales and total expenses, but also the business's implicit costs, as shown in Figure C. Imagine the owner estimates that, by working for the company, he sacrifices $25 000 a year in wages. In addition, he estimates that he could have earned $3000 a year by devoting his funds and entrepreneurial skills to another business. This $3000 is called a normal profit. Implicit costs therefore equal $28 000. As a result, Jumbo-Dogs' implicit costs of $28 000—as well as its explicit costs of $20 000—are subtracted from the $50 000 in total revenue to give an annual economic profit for the company of $2000 [$50 000 – ($28 000 + $20 000)].

Figure C: Calculation of Economic Profit for Jumbo-Dogs

Total Revenue		$50 000
Explicit Costs		
Food	$ 15 000	
Fuel	3 500	
Depreciation	1 000	
Interest on loan	500	
Total explicit costs		$20 000
Implicit Costs		
Owner's wage	$25 000	
Normal profit	3 000	
Total implicit costs		$ 28 000
Economic profit		$ 2 000

Jumbo-Dogs' economic profit is calculated by subtracting both explicit and implicit costs—$20 000 and $28 000, respectively—from total revenue. The $2000 economic profit is lower than the $30 000 accounting profit, shown in Figure B, by the $28 000 in implicit costs.

1. Just as a company's balance sheet shows a company's financial position at a given point in time, an individual's statement of net worth shows that individual's financial position at a given point in time. Calculate the net worth of the person described in the following hypothetical situation:

   Mary Ann McCalister is a university student who works part-time. She has $765 in the bank and two $1000 Canada Savings Bonds. Her compact car has a value of $7000, and the furniture in her apartment is worth approximately $2500. She owns a limited-edition print worth approximately $300, and her gold earrings, chain, and bracelet are valued at $1200. The outstanding balance on her car loan is $4254, and Mary Ann owes her parents $1875 for a tuition loan.

2. The owner of a bicycle store is going to see his accountant for a "financial check-up." Based on the following information, determine the extent to which the health of his business has improved or deteriorated over the past year.

   The business owns the store building, which has a market value of $125 000, but has a mortgage on it with $35 000 principal outstanding. Inventories in the store are valued at $18 500, and the equipment and tools used by the assembly and repair staff are valued at $3500. There is $2375 cash in the bank. The business has a line of credit at the bank (in effect, a pre-arranged loan option), of which it has used $17 800. Last year at this time, the business had a debt/equity ratio of 2.87.

Pure 'n' Simple T-Shirts can be found by calculating total revenue and subtracting economic costs. If 250 T-shirts are sold at a price of $6 each, then the total revenue gained by producing 250 T-shirts is $1500 ($6 × 250 shirts). When the economic costs of $1250 are deducted, we get an economic profit of $250 ($1500 − $1250):

$$\text{Economic profit} = \text{total revenue} - \text{economic costs}$$
$$\$250 = \$1500 - \$1250$$

BRIEF REVIEW

1. The major forms of business organization are sole proprietorship, partnership, and corporation. Sole proprietorships and partnerships are common choices for small businesses, while larger businesses tend to be corporations.

2. Production processes may be labour-intensive or capital-intensive. To achieve productive efficiency, a business must choose the production process that is the cheapest way to produce a certain quantity of output.

3. Economic costs, as opposed to accounting costs, include both explicit costs (payments to those outside the business) and implicit costs (opportunity costs owners sustain by running the business).

4. Economists measure profitability using economic profit, which is found by deducting both explicit and implicit costs from a business's sales revenue.

 ## Production in the Short Run

Recall from Chapter 2 that the short run is the period during which quantities of one or more of a business's inputs cannot be varied. In manufacturing, companies usually cannot adjust the quantity of machinery they use or the size of their factories on short notice. In agriculture, there is typically an additional quantity that cannot be varied—the land available for cultivation. Inputs that cannot be adjusted in the short run are known as **fixed inputs**. Inputs that can be adjusted are known as **variable inputs**. Typically, variable inputs in the short run include the labour and materials a business uses in production. For example, as owner of Pure 'n' Simple T-Shirts, you are considering adjusting your current production of 250 shirts a day. You have already bought three sewing machines and cannot acquire more without a considerable delay. Hence, the three machines represent a fixed input for your business in the short run. But you can change the number of workers you employ, so labour represents a variable input in the short run.

fixed inputs: inputs whose quantities cannot be adjusted in the short run

variable inputs: inputs whose quantities can be adjusted in the short run

Total, Average, and Marginal Product

total product: the overall quantity of output produced with a given workforce

To increase production of a certain good or service, a business must employ more of all variable inputs, including workers. The result is a rise in **total product**, which is the overall quantity (q) of output associated with a given workforce. The employment of labour is a convenient measure of a company's scale of production, since labour is a variable input in making virtually all products. But businesses also use other variable inputs, such as natural resources or semi-processed goods.

Once again, let's look at Pure 'n' Simple T-Shirts. Say you conduct a few experiments to see what happens to total product for your business when the number of workers employed is changed but the number of sewing machines—three—remains constant. As shown in columns 1 and 2 of Figure 4.3, an increase in workers from three to four causes an increase in total production from 250 to 270 shirts per day.

Figure 4.3:   Production in the Short Run

(1) Labour (L) (workers per day)	(2) Total Product (q) (T-shirts per day)	(3) Marginal Product ($\Delta q / \Delta L$) (T-shirts per day)	(4) Average Product (q/L) (T-shirts per day)
0	0		—
1	80	80	80
2	200	120	100
3	250	50	83.3
4	270	20	67.5
5	280	10	56
6	270	–10	45

As the number of workers increases, total product increases until the fifth worker is hired. Marginal product peaks when the second worker is hired and becomes negative at the same point that total product begins to drop. Meanwhile, average product peaks at 2 workers.

average product: the quantity of output produced per worker

marginal product: the extra output produced by an additional worker

In addition to total product, two other concepts are important when analyzing production in the short run. **Average product** is the quantity of output produced per worker, and is found by dividing total product (q) by the quantity of labour (L) employed. **Marginal product,** in contrast, is the additional output produced when an additional worker is hired. Marginal product is calculated by dividing the change in total product (Δq) by the change in the amount of labour employed (ΔL). (The symbol Δ is the Greek capital letter "delta," which signifies a change in some variable.)

Columns 3 and 4 of Figure 4.3 list the marginal and average products for Pure 'n' Simple T-Shirts. When employing three workers, the workforce's average product is 83.3 shirts per day (250 shirts ÷ 3 workers). If a fourth worker is added, the marginal product of this worker is 20 shirts, which comes from subtracting the old total product (250 shirts) from the new total product (270 shirts), and dividing the difference by the change in the workforce from three to four:

$$\text{Average product} = \frac{\text{total product (q)}}{\text{number of workers (L)}}$$

$$83.3 \text{ shirts} = \frac{250}{3}$$

$$\text{Marginal product} = \frac{\text{change in total product } (\Delta q)}{\text{change in workforce } (\Delta L)}$$

$$20 \text{ shirts} = \frac{(270 - 250)}{(4 - 3)}$$

Thinking About Economics

Since marginal product is the "extra" product created by a change in an input, it relates to two *levels of inputs. How can this be shown in a schedule?*

In a table, such as Figure 4.3, marginal product is shown halfway between the values for total and average product. This is because marginal product is defined as a *change* from one employment level to another. So, for example, in column 3 the marginal product of 20 shirts for the fourth worker is shown between the rows for 3 and 4 workers. The same principle also applies to expressing the marginal product on a graph; the marginal product of 20 shirts for the fourth worker will be plotted halfway between the horizontal co-ordinates for 3 and 4 workers.

Diminishing Marginal Returns

The marginal product values in Figure 4.3 reflect a law that applies to production in the short run. According to the **law of diminishing marginal returns**, at some point—as more units of a variable input are added to a fixed input—the marginal product will start to decrease. It is possible to prove the law of diminishing returns through a type of argument known by the Latin term *reductio ad absurdum* (pronounced *re-dook´-shio ad ab-surd´-um*). This type of argument verifies a statement by showing that its opposite leads to absurdity. For the law of diminishing marginal returns, consider what would happen if you used a flower pot to grow food. If the law of diminishing marginal returns were false, then, as you used more labour, the total product of food grown in the flower pot

law of diminishing marginal returns: at some point, as more units of a variable input are added to a fixed input, the marginal product will start to decrease

would rise at a faster and faster rate, until the world's entire food supply could be provided from this single pot. Since this conclusion is obviously absurd, the law of diminishing marginal returns must be true.

Increasing Versus Diminishing Returns

Pure 'n' Simple T-Shirts' total product is shown in the top graph of Figure 4.4, and its marginal product and average product are shown in the bottom graph. Both graphs can be divided into three ranges, according to the

Figure 4.4:   Total, Marginal, and Average Product

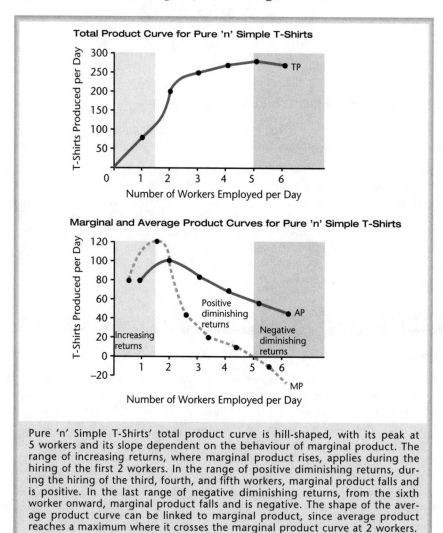

Pure 'n' Simple T-Shirts' total product curve is hill-shaped, with its peak at 5 workers and its slope dependent on the behaviour of marginal product. The range of increasing returns, where marginal product rises, applies during the hiring of the first 2 workers. In the range of positive diminishing returns, during the hiring of the third, fourth, and fifth workers, marginal product falls and is positive. In the last range of negative diminishing returns, from the sixth worker onward, marginal product falls and is negative. The shape of the average product curve can be linked to marginal product, since average product reaches a maximum where it crosses the marginal product curve at 2 workers.

behaviour of marginal product in each range. In the bottom graph's first range, known as increasing returns, marginal product rises as more workers are added. In the top graph's first range, total product rises at a higher and higher rate, giving the curve a positive slope that gets steeper. During the second range, called positive diminishing returns, marginal product begins to fall, but is still positive. Total product in this second range continues to rise but at a lower rate, so that the curve becomes flatter. In the final range, known as negative diminishing returns, marginal product falls below zero and total product decreases. Points in this last range will never be chosen by the business.

Average Versus Marginal Product

The shape of the average product curve reflects an important series of rules governing the relationship between average and marginal values. The average rises if the marginal value is above the average value. The average value stays constant if it equals the corresponding marginal value. Finally, the average value falls if the marginal value is below the average value.

These rules are borne out by the bottom graph in Figure 4.4. At first, marginal product is above average product, so that average product must be rising. At two workers, average product crosses the marginal product curve, so that values for both must be equal. Here average product is constant, meaning it has a zero slope. Beyond this point, marginal product is below average product, causing average product to fall.

The rules that connect marginal and average values can be used in a variety of situations. To help explain these rules, we'll use an illustration

Figure 4.5: A Student's Marginal and Average Marks

	Marginal Mark	Average Mark
Test 1	$\frac{36}{50}$	$\frac{36}{1} = 36$
Test 2 (Case A)	$\frac{34}{50}$	$\frac{(36 + 34)}{2} = 35$
(Case B)	$\frac{36}{50}$	$\frac{(36 + 36)}{2} = 36$
(Case C)	$\frac{38}{50}$	$\frac{(36 + 38)}{2} = 37$

On the first test, the student receives a mark of 36, which represents both her marginal and average marks. In Case A, the marginal mark of 34 on the second test is below the previous average, so the average mark falls to 35. In Case B, the marginal mark on the second test equals the previous average, so the average stays the same at 36. In Case C, the marginal mark of 38 on the second test is above the previous average, so the average mark rises to 37.

every student is familiar with—marks. Suppose there are two tests in a course, each worth 50 marks, with a student's final grade calculated as the sum of the two marks. A student's *marginal mark* is the mark on each test, while her *average mark* is the total earned so far divided by the number of completed tests. For example, say the student has received a marginal mark of 36 out of 50 on the first test. Her initial average is also 36, which comes from dividing 36 by 1, as shown in Figure 4.5. If the student receives a marginal mark of 34 out of 50 on the second test, her average on the two tests falls to 35 [(36 + 34) ÷ 2]. The student's average mark has declined, because her new marginal mark of 34 is below her previous average of 36. On the other hand, she may get another mark of 36 on the second test. Because her new marginal mark is the same as her previous average, this student's average stays the same at 36 [(36 + 36) ÷ 2]. Finally, if the student receives a mark of 38 on the second test, her average rises to 37 [(36 + 38) ÷ 2]. In this case, her average rises because her new marginal mark is greater than her previous average. All three of these cases are shown in Figure 4.5.

Costs in the Short Run

In the short run, just as businesses use fixed and variable inputs, they face corresponding fixed and variable costs. **Fixed costs** (FC) do not change when a business changes its quantity of output, since these costs relate to fixed inputs such as machinery and land. **Variable costs** (VC), in contrast,

fixed costs: economic costs for inputs that remain fixed at all quantities of output

Figure 4.6:   Short-Run Costs for Pure 'n' Simple T-Shirts

(1) Labour (L)	(2) Total Product (q)	(3) Fixed Costs (FC)	(4) Variable Costs (VC)	(5) Total Cost (TC) (FC + VC)	(6) Marginal Cost (MC) (ΔTC/Δq)	(7) Average Fixed Costs (AFC) (FC/q)	(8) Average Variable Costs (AVC) (VC/q)	(9) Average Cost (AC) (AFC + AVC)
0	0	825	0	825				
1	80 →80	825	140	965 →140	1.75	10.31	1.75	12.06
2	200 →120	825	300	1125 →160	1.33	4.13	1.50	5.63
3	250 →50	825	425	1250 →125	2.50	3.30	1.70	5.00
4	270 →20	825	535	1360 →110	5.50	3.06	1.98	5.04
5	280 →10	825	640	1465 →105	10.50	2.95	2.29	5.24

Columns 1 and 2 are from Figure 4.3, while columns 3 and 4 represent possible fixed and variable costs for the business. The remaining columns are based on calculations shown in the table. Total cost in column 5 is the sum of the fixed and variable costs. Marginal cost in column 6 is found by dividing the *changes* in total cost by the *changes* in total product. Columns 7 and 8 are derived by dividing fixed and variable costs by total product. Average cost in column 9 is the sum of the average fixed and average variable costs.

relate to variable inputs, which change when a business adjusts the quantity produced. The most important variable costs are wages and payments for materials used in production. **Total cost** (TC) is the sum of all inputs, both fixed and variable, and is found by adding fixed and variable costs at each quantity of output.

variable costs: economic costs for inputs that vary at each quantity of output

The short-run costs for Pure 'n' Simple T-Shirts are shown in Figure 4.6. The company's fixed costs (column 3) reflect its expenditures on such inputs as factory rent and machinery, and are a constant $825, regardless of how many shirts are produced. In contrast, variable costs (column 4) rise along with output. Therefore, at the level of three workers, total cost (column 5) is $1250 ($825 + $425):

total cost: the sum of all fixed and variable costs at each quantity of output

$$\text{Total cost (TC)} = \text{fixed cost (FC)} + \text{variable cost (VC)}$$
$$\$1250 = \$825 + \$425$$

Marginal Cost

Marginal cost (MC), or the extra cost of producing an additional unit of output, is one of the most important cost concepts in economics. Marginal cost is found by calculating the change in total cost (ΔTC) that results whenever a new worker is hired, and then dividing this change by the change in total product (Δq) that results from employing another worker. So, for example, the marginal costs for Pure 'n' Simple T-Shirts at each output level are shown in column 6 of Figure 4.6. When the fourth worker is hired, total cost in column 5 rises by $110 ($1360 – $1250), and total product, in column 2, increases by 20 shirts (270 – 250). Therefore, the marginal cost of each of these additional 20 shirts is $5.50 ($110.00 ÷ 20 shirts).

marginal cost: the extra cost of producing an additional unit of output

Figure 4.7:   The Marginal Cost Curve

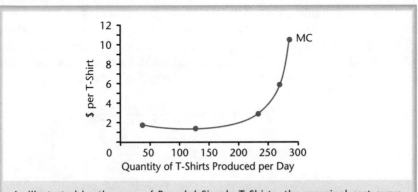

As illustrated by the case of Pure 'n' Simple T-Shirts, the marginal cost curve (MC) is shaped like the letter "J." At low output levels, the extra cost of each unit produced falls. However, the marginal cost of each new unit starts to rise when diminishing returns set in.

$$\text{Marginal cost (MC)} = \frac{\text{change in total cost } (\Delta TC)}{\text{change in total product } (\Delta q)}$$

$$\$5.50 = \frac{\$110.00}{20 \text{ shirts}}$$

Figure 4.7 shows that the marginal cost curve is shaped like the letter "J." Early in the process of adding labour, the addition of each new worker produces an even greater increase in output than the existing labour. So, the marginal cost for each new worker falls as long as marginal product keeps increasing. But when diminishing marginal returns set in, marginal product starts to decline. From this point, each new worker produces fewer extra units of output than the previous worker, and the marginal cost connected with adding a new worker is greater for each extra unit of output. Marginal cost therefore rises as long as marginal product continues to fall.

Per-Unit Costs

While marginal cost is based on changes in a business's total product, per-unit costs are expressed in terms of a single level of output. These costs are related to a business's fixed costs, variable costs, and total costs. Hence, there are three separate types of per-unit costs: average fixed cost, average variable cost, and average cost.

Average Fixed and Average Variable Cost

average fixed cost: the fixed cost per unit of output

average variable cost: the variable cost per unit of output

Average fixed cost (AFC) is the fixed cost per unit of output, and is calculated by dividing the business's fixed costs (FC) by its total product (q). Similarly, **average variable cost** (AVC) is the variable cost per unit of output, and is calculated by dividing the business's variable costs (VC) by total product (q). For example, for Pure 'n' Simple T-Shirts, the average fixed and average variable costs are found in columns 7 and 8 of Figure 4.6. When three workers are employed, the business's fixed costs of $825.00 are divided by the total product of 250 shirts, giving an average fixed cost of $3.30. Similarly, the $425.00 variable costs at this employment level are divided by 250 shirts, resulting in an average variable cost of $1.70.

$$\text{Average fixed cost (AFC)} = \frac{\text{fixed costs (FC)}}{\text{total product (q)}}$$

$$\$3.30 \text{ per shirt} = \frac{\$825.00}{250 \text{ shirts}}$$

$$\text{Average variable cost (AVC)} = \frac{\text{variable costs (VC)}}{\text{total product (q)}}$$

$$\$1.70 \text{ per shirt} = \frac{\$425.00}{250 \text{ shirts}}$$

Figure 4.8 shows in a graph the average fixed cost for Pure 'n' Simple T-Shirts. When no shirts are produced, the denominator of the average fixed cost formula is zero, meaning that average fixed cost is an infinitely high number. Average fixed cost then falls as the business's total product increases, since the denominator in the formula rises. Therefore, the average fixed cost curve has a negative (downward) slope, which becomes flatter as output rises.

Figure 4.8:   The Family of Short-Run Cost Curves

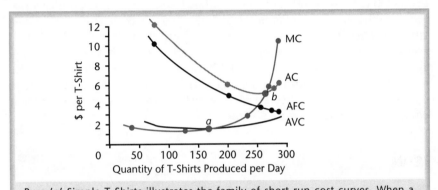

Pure 'n' Simple T-Shirts illustrates the family of short-run cost curves. When a business's output of a certain product rises, the average fixed cost curve (AFC) falls. The average variable cost curve (AVC) declines until it reaches point *a*, where it meets the marginal cost curve (MC), after which the AVC curve rises. The average cost curve (AC) also falls, and then rises. It reaches a minimum at point *b*, where it meets the MC curve.

In contrast, the average variable cost curve shown in Figure 4.8 is saucer-shaped, reflecting its connection with the associated marginal cost curve. At the initial quantities of output, marginal cost is below average variable cost, causing average variable cost to decline. Where the two curves meet (at point *a*)—where the marginal and average values are equal—the average variable cost curve has a zero slope and reaches its minimum. At higher output levels, marginal cost is above average variable cost, causing average variable cost to rise.

Average Cost

Average total cost, or simply **average cost** (AC), is the business's total cost per unit of output. Average cost is the sum of average fixed cost and average variable cost at each quantity of output. So, for example, in column 9 of Figure 4.6, when Pure 'n' Simple T-Shirts produces 250 shirts, average fixed cost is $3.30 and average variable cost is $1.70, giving an average cost of $5.00 ($3.30 + $1.70)

average cost: the sum of average fixed cost and average variable cost at each quantity of output

$$\text{Average cost (AC)} = \text{average fixed cost (AFC)} + \text{average variable cost (AVC)}$$
$$\$5.00 \text{ per shirt} = \$3.30 + \$1.70$$

Like the average variable cost curve, the average cost curve in Figure 4.8 is saucer-shaped. It represents the sum of the values plotted for the average fixed cost curve and the average variable cost curve. At an output level of 250 shirts, for example, the $5.00 average cost is the sum of the heights of the average fixed cost curve ($3.30) and the average variable cost curve ($1.70). At lower output levels, average cost is high because of average fixed cost. Once average cost has passed its lowest point, its rise is due to the impact of expanding average variable cost. The average cost curve reaches its minimum at point *b*, where it intersects the marginal cost curve. This relationship parallels the relationship between the average variable cost and marginal cost. Therefore, marginal cost provides the minimum values for both the average variable cost curve and the average cost curve. In each case, an average value remains constant when it equals its associated marginal value.

BRIEF REVIEW

1. In the short run, production is governed by the law of diminishing returns which states that, as more units of a variable input are added to a fixed input, the marginal product will start to decrease at some point.

2. Because of the law of diminishing marginal returns, the marginal product curve is hill-shaped. The total and average product curves are also hill-shaped, because of their connections with changes in marginal product.

3. Marginal cost, or the extra cost of producing another unit of output, is inversely related to marginal product. The marginal cost curve is shaped like the letter "J."

4. Average fixed cost represents fixed costs per unit of output. Its curve has a negative slope and is flatter at higher output levels. Average variable cost, or variable costs per unit of output, has a saucer-shaped curve that reaches its minimum where it crosses the marginal cost curve.

5. Average cost, or total cost per unit of output, is the sum of average fixed and average variable costs at given output levels. The curve for average cost is saucer-shaped, and reaches a minimum where it intersects the marginal cost curve.

Production in the Long Run

As we discussed in Chapter 2, the long run is the period in which quantities of all resources used in an industry can be adjusted. So, even those inputs that had been fixed in the short run—such as machinery, buildings, and cultivated land—can be adjusted in the long run. Because all inputs can vary in the long run, the law of diminishing marginal returns no longer has the same importance as in the short run. Instead, new questions arise. If a business increases all inputs used to produce a certain product, how will the output of the product change, and what effect will these increases have on costs? There are three possible results: economies of scale, constant returns to scale, and diseconomies of scale.

Economies of Scale

Economies of scale occur when a business increases all inputs for a certain product by a given percentage and the output rises by an even higher percentage. For example, if a car manufacturer doubles all inputs used to make a certain car model (that is, increases all inputs by 100 percent), and total output of the car more than doubles (increasing by, for example, 150 percent), the manufacturer enjoys economies of scale. Virtually all businesses experience economies of scale over the initial range of output. There are three basic causes of economies of scale: division of labour, specialized capital, and specialized management.

economies of scale: a situation in which a percentage increase in all inputs causes a larger percentage increase in output

Division of Labour
As Adam Smith illustrated with the pinmaking factory over two centuries ago, increases in the scale of production and worker specialization can go hand in hand. Performing fewer tasks allows workers to become more efficient at their jobs. As a result, Smith concluded, quantities of output tend to rise more quickly than the number of workers producing them. The impact of the division of labour is just as prevalent today in labour-intensive production. For example, if a very small restaurant where workers do everything expands, then workers can begin to specialize in either food preparation or service, thus making both sets of workers more efficient in the tasks they do.

Specialized Capital
In most manufacturing industries, an increased scale of production is associated with the use of specialized machinery. If a car manufacturer increases the quantity of all its inputs, for example, capital equipment can have more specialized functions, so that it performs fewer tasks more efficiently than before.

constant returns to scale: a situation in which a percentage increase in all inputs results in an equal percentage increase in output

diseconomies of scale: a situation in which a percentage increase in all inputs causes a smaller percentage increase in output

Specialized Management

The same principle that underlies the division of labour applies to management. When the scale of production is small, there are few managers. Each is forced to deal with a wide range of duties, some of which they are better at performing than others. An accounting expert may need to devise a marketing strategy, or a production manager may have to deal with personnel problems. Along with an increased scale of production, more managers are hired, with each assigned to the area in which he or she has the most expertise.

Constant Returns to Scale

In contrast to economies of scale, in the case of **constant returns to scale**, a business that increases inputs a given percentage will see output increase by the same percentage. This may be the case for the artisan making pottery; doubling her input also doubles her output. Constant returns to scale usually result when making more of an item requires repeating exactly the same tasks used to produce previous units of output.

SOURCE: Franklin, *The Financial Post*

Diseconomies of Scale

The last possible case is **diseconomies of scale**, or decreasing returns to scale, in which a business that increases inputs to a product's production by a certain percentage sees output increase by a smaller percentage. For example, a 100 percent increase in all inputs used by a copy shop may lead to its output rising by only 75 percent. There are two major reasons for diseconomies of scale: management difficulties and limited natural resources.

Management Difficulties

Continual expansion in the scale of production will eventually make a business so cumbersome to administer that managers face problems in coordinating operations to ensure efficient production. Virtually all businesses reach an output level above which management difficulties cause diseconomies of scale to become dominant.

Limited Natural Resources

In primary industries, such as fishing or forestry, a business may be able to acquire only a limited supply of easily available natural resources, even in the long run. In this case, an output level is reached above which further increases in all inputs lead to a smaller rise in output, resulting in diseconomies of scale.

Costs in the Long Run

The concept of returns to scale is useful in analyzing the effect on a business's costs when inputs that are fixed in the short run become variable. Figure 4.9 shows the case of a magazine publishing company that expands its printing plant three times, and faces a different short-run average cost curve for each plant size. With each expansion of the plant, the curve shifts to the right, demonstrating the effects of the increased output.

When the plant is first expanded, the short-run average cost curve fall from AC_1 to AC_2. This shift results from economies of scale. Recall that average cost is found by dividing total cost by the quantity of output. With economies of scale, output rises more rapidly than the total cost of inputs, so that average cost falls as the scale of production increases.

With the second plant expansion, the shift of the short-run average cost curve (from AC_2 to AC_3) reflects constant returns to scale. Output and the total costs of inputs rise at the same rate when the plant is expanded this second time, so the average cost curve moves horizontally as the output of magazines rises.

With the final plant expansion, the company's short-run average cost curve not only shifts to the right but also rises (from AC_3 to AC_4). This shift reflects diseconomies of scale. Since the printing plant's output is rising less rapidly than the total cost of input costs, the average cost curve rises as the production of magazines continues to increase.

Long-Run Average Cost

A business's **long-run average cost** in producing a certain product is the minimum short-run average cost at each possible level of output. Figure 4.9 shows that the long-run average cost curve is made up of the lowest possible points from the short-run average cost curves. Given a wide range of possible plant sizes, the long-run AC curve is smooth and saucer-shaped, with only one point represented from each short-run curve. As depicted in Figure 4.9, long-run average cost falls in the initial output Range A because of economies of scale, remains the same in Range B due to constant returns to scale, and rises in Range C because of diseconomies of scale.

long-run average cost: the minimum short-run average cost at each possible level of output

Figure 4.9:   Long-Run Average Costs

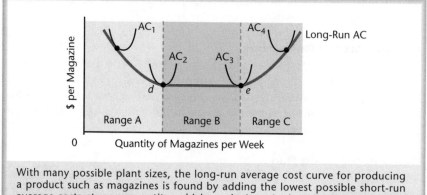

With many possible plant sizes, the long-run average cost curve for producing a product such as magazines is found by adding the lowest possible short-run average costs at every quantity, which results in a single point being included from each short-run curve. The long-run AC curve has three ranges. Range A has a negative slope, reflecting economies of scale between the average cost curves AC_1 and AC_2. Range B is horizontal, indicating the constant returns to scale between AC_2 and AC_3. Range C has a positive slope, showing diseconomies of scale beyond the AC_3 curve.

Industry Differences

While virtually all businesses face a saucer-shaped long-run average cost curve, these curves are not necessarily symmetrical for all industries. Often in an industry, one range (or portion of the curve) will dominate the long-run average cost. Figure 4.10 illustrates long-run average cost curves characteristic of manufacturing industries, craft industries, and primary industries.

Manufacturing Industries

Manufacturing industries tend to exhibit an extended range of economies of scale due to the degree to which specialization is possible in the use of both labour and capital. This is particularly true of companies in which assembly-line techniques are used. It is not until output is very large that the conditions leading to constant returns to scale and diseconomies of scale become relevant. The long-run average cost curve faced by businesses in most manufacturing industries is shown in Figure 4.10, on the left. In this case, the curve falls over a wide range of input levels before briefly levelling out, and then rising.

Craft Industries

In contrast, craft industries are dominated by constant returns to scale. Because raising output levels of crafts tends to depend on repeating exactly the method of production, an increase in input usually results in an equal increase in output. Hence, except at very low or very high levels of output, the long-run average cost curves for producers of items such as handmade pottery are horizontal, as in the middle graph of Figure 4.10.

Primary Industries

Diseconomies of scale, meanwhile, are most prevalent for businesses in primary industries, as in some types of fishing, where the limits of resource supplies are particularly acute. In this case, the slope of the long-run average cost curve becomes positive at a relatively low level of output, as shown in Figure 4.10, on the right.

Figure 4.10:   Possible Long-Run Average Cost Curves

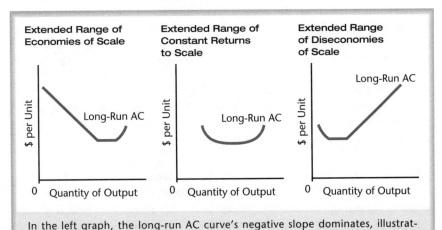

In the left graph, the long-run AC curve's negative slope dominates, illustrating a wide range of economies of scale, as usually occurs in assembly-line manufacturing. The middle graph shows the long-run AC curve when the horizontal range of constant returns to scale dominates, which is characteristic of craft industries. In the right graph, the positive slope dominates, illustrating the range of diseconomies of scale, as is common in primary industries.

Thinking About Economics

How do returns to scale influence the size of businesses in a certain industry?

The predominance of economies of scale in an industry increases the chances that businesses in the industry are large. Because of their lower long-run average costs, big companies have a competitive advantage over smaller rivals. It is economies of scale, for example, that explain the gigantic size of most companies in the automobile industry. In contrast, smaller companies tend to prevail in industries characterized by constant returns to scale or diseconomies of scale, because there is no cost disadvantage associated with low output levels.

ADVANCING

ECONOMIC

THOUGHT

John Kenneth Galbraith

SOURCE: UPI/Bettmann

Critic of the Modern Corporation

John Kenneth Galbraith and the Role of Management

Galbraith and His Influence

John Kenneth Galbraith has been one of Canada's most notable intellectual exports. Born in 1908 near Port Talbot, Ontario, he studied agricultural economics at what is now the University of Guelph. He then emigrated to the United States, where, as a professor at Harvard University, he became one of the most widely known economists of the past few decades.

A prolific writer, Galbraith caused considerable debate in the 1960s and 1970s about the role of the modern corporation. He popularized the view that corporate managers possess the real decision-making power in modern capitalist economies. These managers, according to Galbraith, are more interested in their own prestige and income than they are in making profit.

Financing Corporate Activity

To follow Galbraith's argument, we must first consider how corporations finance their operations. Unlike other types of businesses, corporations can acquire funds by issuing stocks and bonds.

Stocks   Corporations sell stocks (also known as shares) through the stock market to buyers, who are known as shareholders. Stockbrokers act as go-betweens in this market, buying and selling stocks on behalf of their customers. People who purchase stocks of a certain corporation do so because they expect to receive dividends, which are periodic payments by the corporation to its shareholders. Shareholders may also expect the price, or resale value, of a company's stock to increase as its profit outlook improves. However, there are no guarantees to shareholders—the company may not perform as expected and dividends may not be declared (corporations are not required to pay dividends). Also, changing conditions in the stock market can cause price fluctuations for a wide range of stocks.

Bonds   Corporations can also raise funds by selling bonds. A bond is a type of loan that is governed by a formal contract, which sets out when the borrower will provide interest payments, and also when the original amount of the loan (known as the principal) will be paid back to the bondholder. Corporate bonds differ from other loan contracts in that they can be bought and sold. If the bondholder wishes to convert a bond into cash, he or she does not return the bond to the borrower, but sells it to an interested buyer. Unlike shareholders, bondholders are considered to be lenders to the corporation, rather than its owners. Unless a corporation becomes insolvent, bondholders have no say in the company's operations.

Separation of Ownership and Control

According to Galbraith, the ways that corporations raise funds can cause a separation of ownership and control. Most large corporations have no single shareholder owning a significant portion of the shares, but are owned and managed by different groups. On the one hand, the owners are the corporation's shareholders, who receive income through dividends and higher stock prices. On the other hand, the corporation's managers are, strictly-speaking, employees. The interests of these two groups, according to Galbraith, do not coincide. A corporation's managers may be more interested in maximizing the company's sales revenue rather than its profit, since, as the corporation expands, so will the managers' salaries and power in the organization. Managers may also siphon off profit by providing themselves with generous perks and rewards. While such actions go against shareholder interests, managers do not have to fear reprisals as long as the stake of each shareholder in the company is small enough to rule out a costly examination of management actions.

Relevance for Today

Galbraith's outlook has been influential with the general public and with some economists, although others downplay its relevance. His critics suggest that recent developments in stock markets have tended to increase the power of shareholders over management. During the 1980s, much attention was focused on the frequency of corporate takeovers, in which one company buys a sufficiently large portion of another company's shares to control its operations. Corporate takeovers can either be friendly or hostile, depending on how those taking over a company view its current managers. When a takeover is hostile, managers are often turfed out, especially if they have been looking after their own interests rather than maximizing the company's profit. According to Galbraith's critics, the ever-present threat of a hostile takeover helps to ensure that managers act in the shareholders' interests. Critics also cite the growing clout of investment funds, whose administrators often own significant portions of even a large corporation's shares, giving them control over the behaviour of the corporation's managers.

1. According to Galbraith, why do the interests of corporate managers and shareholders conflict? How do Galbraith's critics respond to this argument?

2. Find at least three examples in the mass media (for example, in newspapers, in magazines, on TV) of corporate activities mentioned in the essay (for example, declaration of dividends, takeovers, change of management). Clip or note your examples. For each, identify the activity and, if applicable, explain whether it supports or refutes Galbraith's argument.

BRIEF REVIEW

1. When, in the long run, all inputs can be varied, there are three possible results for a business: economies of scale, constant returns to scale, and diseconomies of scale.

2. Economies of scale exist when a given percentage change in inputs causes an even greater percentage change in output. Division of labour, specialized capital, and specialized management are the major causes.

3. Constant returns to scale exist when a given percentage change in inputs causes an equal percentage change in output. When production of any additional product depends on repeating exactly the tasks used to produce the previous product, constant returns prevail.

4. Diseconomies of scale exist when a given percentage change in inputs causes a lower percentage change in output. Management difficulties and limited natural resources are the major causes.

5. The long-run average cost curve is saucer-shaped, reflecting ranges first of economies of scale, then constant returns to scale, and finally diseconomies of scale.

6. In general, economies of scale dominate in manufacturing industries, constant returns to scale dominate in craft industries, and diseconomies of scale dominate in primary industries.

Key Concepts

business
sole proprietorship
partnership
corporation
production
inputs
output
labour-intensive process
capital-intensive process
productive efficiency
explicit costs
implicit costs
normal profit
economic costs
economic profit
fixed inputs

variable inputs
total product
average product
marginal product
law of diminishing marginal returns
fixed costs
variable costs
total cost
marginal cost
average fixed cost
average variable cost
average cost
economies of scale
constant returns to scale
diseconomies of scale
long-run average cost

Developing Application and Analysis Skills

1. Create a table to compare sole proprietorships, partnerships, and corporations in terms of their ownership, organization, advantages, and disadvantages.

2. You have decided to open a driveway-sealing business this summer to pay tuition for courses you plan to take next year. Before you start your business, however, you need to do some planning and organizing. You will also need to borrow money to purchase the necessary supplies and equipment to get started. Your plan, if well-written, will help you convince the loans manager at your bank that you are a good risk. Write a plan that addresses the following considerations:

   a) the name of your company, the type of business organization you have chosen, and your reasons for choosing that type of business organization
   b) the nature of the production process and what inputs are necessary
   c) whether the business will be labour-intensive or capital-intensive, and what (if any) capital items you will use in the production process
   d) your expected level of output in the first summer
   e) how you will maximize your company's efficiency, the obstacles to efficiency you foresee, and how you plan to overcome these obstacles
   f) the explicit costs of the business, and when and how often they will be incurred
   g) your expectation of normal profit, how you'd calculate this, and any other implicit costs

   h) how you will determine the company's success

3. An investment counselling company has a total revenue of $159 000. Accountants have determined that the explicit costs of the business are $75 000. The owner, who has invested $40 000 in the business, knows that she could be earning 10 percent on the funds if they were used in another way, and she could be earning at least $90 000 as a stockbroker with the company she worked for before opening her business.

   Calculate the following:

   a) accounting profit (if any) for the business
   b) economic costs of the business
   c) economic profit (if any) for the business

4. Which measure of profit—economic profit or accounting profit—do you feel is the most meaningful indicator of the financial status of a business? Explain your answer.

5. For each of the following businesses, suggest one fixed cost and one variable cost:

   a) market gardening
   b) word-processing
   c) car rental agency
   d) clothing wholesaler
   e) cellular phone manufacturer

6. A business that is capable of producing a total product of 60 units per day by employing 10 workers finds that it can produce a total product of 105 units per day by employing 11 workers. Calculate the

average product in both situations. What is the marginal product?

7. The table below shows the production of hockey sticks by a Canadian business. Using the figures, draw a graph that shows the following:

a) total product curve
b) average product curve
c) marginal product curve
d) the ranges of increasing returns, positive diminishing returns, and negative diminishing returns

		Production in the Short Run		
(1) Labour (L) (workers)	(2) Total Product (q) (hockey sticks per day)	(3) Marginal Product (MP) (hockey sticks per day)	(4) Average Product (AP) (hockey sticks per day)
0	0		—
		160	
1	160		160
		240	
2	400		200
		100	
3	500		166.6
		40	
4	540		135
		−40	
5	500		100

8. Using the short-run costs given in Figure 4.6, do the following:

a) Create a graph showing the fixed cost, variable cost, and total cost curves.
b) Explain the relationship between total cost and variable cost as output increases.
c) Show how total cost and variable cost illustrate the law of diminishing returns.
d) Create another graph showing the average fixed cost, average variable cost, average cost, and marginal cost curves. Explain the relationship of marginal cost to both average variable cost and average cost.

9. a) Copy and complete the table on page 123 of short-run costs for The Leather Works, which manufactures leather vests.
b) Create a graph showing fixed cost, variable cost, and total cost.
c) Create another graph showing average fixed cost, average variable cost, average cost, and marginal cost.
d) Explain, using your graphs, the law of diminishing returns.

10. For each of the following industries, identify whether they would tend to have economies of scale, constant returns to scale, or diseconomies of scale. Then explain each term. Finally, sketch a long-run average cost curve for each industry.

a) logging industry in New Brunswick
b) solar panel manufacturing
c) software development industry
d) handcrafted sweater industry

Short-Run Costs for The Leather Works								
(1) **Labour** **(L)** **(workers)**	**(2)** **Product** **(q)** **(vests** **per day)**	**(3)** **Fixed** **Costs** **(FC)**	**(4)** **Variable** **Costs** **(VC)**	**(5)** **Total** **Cost** **(TC)**	**(6)** **Marginal** **Cost** **(MC)**	**(7)** **Average** **Fixed Cost** **(AFC)**	**(8)** **Average** **Variable** **Cost** **(AVC)**	**(9)** **Average** **Cost** **(AC)**
0	0	20	0	—				
					—			
1	3	20	20	—		—	—	—
					—			
2	7	20	40	—		—	—	—
					—			
3	10	20	60	—		—	—	—
					—			
4	12	20	80	—		—	—	—
					—			
5	13	20	100	—		—	—	—

CHAPTER 5

The Nature of Markets

Modern business is a complex, fast-moving thing. The fit and educated survive. The remainder go into politics.

—HERBERT SURPLIS, CANADIAN JOURNALIST

How do the operations of a giant company like Bell Canada differ from those of a small-town restaurant or a single broccoli farmer? From an economist's perspective, the main distinction is the type of market in which each producer does business. In this chapter, we'll examine the four market structures and how much businesses within each can influence the prices and demand for the products they sell. We'll also consider how a company's ability to influence its market position affects the interests of consumers.

CHAPTER FOCUS

This chapter focuses on the following:
- the four market structures—perfect competition, monopolistic competition, oligopoly, and monopoly—and the characteristics of each
- the demand conditions for businesses in each market structure
- nonprice competition through product differentiation and advertising
- industrial concentration—how it is measured, and the arguments for and against it

SKILLS FOCUS

After studying this chapter, you will be able to:
- classify businesses according to the markets within which they operate
- analyze the economic behaviour of businesses in their markets
- differentiate between price-takers and price-makers
- sketch the demand curves for individual businesses and markets
- draw conclusions about the importance of nonprice competition
- analyze the costs and benefits of industrial concentration

Market Structures

While product markets come in all shapes and sizes, each has one of four structures: perfect competition, monopolistic competition, oligopoly, or monopoly. The number of businesses involved in the market, whether or not a standard product is being sold, and the ease with which businesses can enter and exit the industry all determine the market structure.

Perfect Competition

The ideal form of competition allows for the unobstructed operation of demand and supply forces, as outlined in previous chapters. This market structure, known as **perfect competition**, has three main characteristics: many buyers and sellers, a standard product, and easy entry to and exit from the industry. In a perfectly competitive market, businesses consider the price of the product they sell to be determined by the forces of demand and supply. While common in agriculture, perfectly competitive markets are not common in other sectors of the economy.

perfect competition: a market structure characterized by many buyers and sellers of a standard product and easy entry to and exit from the industry

Many Buyers and Sellers

The most important feature of perfectly competitive industries is that there are large numbers of buyers and sellers. For example, in the Canadian broccoli market there are many consumers and many farmers. As a result, no single participant is large enough to affect the outcome in the industry.

Standard Product

In a perfectly competitive market, each business supplies a product that is indistinguishable from that of other businesses. One farmer's crop of broccoli, for example, is not noticeably different from that same variety of broccoli produced by other farmers.

Easy Entry and Exit

Finally, for a market to be perfectly competitive, businesses must be free to enter or exit the industry. Compared with most other industries, for example, it is relatively easy for farmers to transfer resources from the production of other crops to the growing of broccoli. Similarly, farmers can leave the broccoli market with little difficulty by devoting resources to alternative agricultural uses.

Monopolistic Competition

monopolistic competition: a market structure characterized by many buyers and sellers of slightly different products and easy entry to, and exit from, the industry

Monopolistic competition is the structure most prevalent in the service sector, and applies, for example, to the restaurant industry. This market structure is characterized by a large number of businesses (though not as many as in a perfectly competitive industry), perceptible differences among the products of competitors, and easy entry and exit of businesses. Product differences can be related to location, quality, or the image consumers have of each product.

Oligopoly

An **oligopoly** is a market in which there are only a few businesses, and entry to the industry is restricted. Oligopolies are extremely common in the Canadian economy, as illustrated by the steel, automobile, and insurance industries. The products sold in oligopolies may or may not vary, depending on the particular market. For example, in the steel industry, a standard product is produced, whereas the automobile and insurance industries offer some variety among their products.

oligopoly: a market structure characterized by only a few businesses offering standard or similar products and restricted entry to the industry

Monopoly

A **monopoly** is an industry in which a single business supplies a product with no close substitutes. This market structure is the exact opposite of perfect competition. Monopolies are relatively common in the Canadian economy. Bell Canada, for example, has a monopoly over local telephone services in Ontario and Quebec. Other notable Canadian monopolies include Canada Post and Via Rail. Monopoly companies are not always large; small companies, such as a caterer with exclusive rights to sell food at a certain sports stadium, can be monopolies as well.

monopoly: a market structure characterized by only one business supplying a product with no close substitutes and restricted entry to the industry

Entry Barriers

Markets that are oligopolies and monopolies require entry barriers to continue as such. **Entry barriers** are economic or institutional obstacles that stop potential competitors from setting up in an industry where economic profits are being made. There are six main entry barriers: economies of scale, market experience, restricted ownership of resources, legal obstacles, market abuses, and advertising.

entry barriers: economic or institutional obstacles to businesses entering an industry

Economies of Scale

In industries where established companies benefit from economies of scale, and therefore decreasing average costs in the long run, small companies just entering the market will be unable to charge as low a price. In the extreme case, known as a **natural monopoly**, economies of scale mean that it makes sense to have only one supplier of a product. This applies to public utilities, which provide such products as water and electricity, and services such as public transit. Having more than one company would require a large-scale duplication of inputs, thus leading to high per-unit costs and product prices.

natural monopoly: a market in which only one business is economically viable because of economies of scale

Market Experience

Even in cases where economies of scale are not predominant, well-established businesses may have a cost advantage over potential rivals simply because of their experience. A business can learn from experience how to supply a product more efficiently, thus decreasing its per-unit costs at all possible output levels.

Restricted Ownership of Resources

When one or a few businesses control supplies of a resource to make a product, they effectively bar other businesses from entering the industry. One example of such control is the South African company De Beers, which owns or controls over 80 percent of the world's supply of diamonds.

Legal Obstacles

Legislation regarding, for example, patents or licences can act as barriers to entry. A patent gives the exclusive right to produce, use, or sell an invention for a given period (now 20 years in Canada). This exclusive right allows individuals and companies to reap some rewards of their innovations. Some companies can become monopolies with patented products, as did the patent-holder for the artificial sweetener aspartame, known as Nutrasweet. Government licensing, too, can create closed or regulated markets. For instance, only Canada Post has the legal right to provide regular mail service, making it a monopoly in this industry. Similarly, only a certain number of Canadian television or radio stations have broadcast rights within different regions of the country, thus making these broadcasting industries oligopolies.

Market Abuses

Established businesses in an industry may use unfair practices to maintain their dominant positions. A business might, for example, temporarily drop the price of its product below average cost to drive a new competitor out of business. This illegal strategy is known as **predatory pricing**. At one time, predatory pricing was used in the international airline industry; some large companies would cut fares only to increase them once upstart competitors had gone into bankruptcy.

predatory pricing: an unfair business practice of temporarily lowering prices to drive out competitors in an industry

Advertising

The use of advertising as an entry barrier is most common in oligopolies, such as the beer and soft-drink industries. Because consumer preference for these products is so dependent on promotion, established companies with large advertising budgets can often stop small competitors from gaining a significant toehold in these markets. For example, Canada's two largest beer companies, Molson Breweries and John Labatt Ltd., use advertising to help them maintain their sales, which represent over 90 percent of total quantity demanded in the Canadian beer market.

Market Power

Businesses in perfectly competitive markets—or perfect competitors, as they may be called—are price-takers because they are forced to take the price for their product that is set by the market forces of demand and supply. In contrast, businesses in the remaining three types of markets have some influence over a product's price, so they are price-makers. In other words, these businesses have some measure of **market power**, or the ability to affect the price they charge. A business's market power depends on the number of competitors in the industry, the business's size, and the elasticity of its product's demand curve.

market power: a business's ability to affect the price of the product it sells

Number of Competitors

The fewer the number of rivals in an industry, the more leeway a business has to vary its price without having to worry about the responses of competitors. A small-town newspaper with no competitors, for example, has more market power than a big-city newspaper with several competitors.

Size

A business's market power is also greater when it is large in relation to its industry. A major computer software producer such as Microsoft, for example, has more freedom to vary the prices of its products than do its smaller rivals.

Price Elasticity of Demand

Finally, an inelastic demand curve for a product enhances the business's market power because a variation in price will have only a minor effect on the quantity the business sells. Thus, for example, a business producing a patented life-saving drug has greater market power than does a clothes manufacturer with an elastic demand curve for its product.

Thinking About Economics

How much market power do businesses in each type of market possess?

As a rule, a business in a monopoly (a monopolist) has the most market power. It deals with no competitors and has the largest possible size in relation to the industry. Because the monopolist sells a product with no close substitutes, the product's demand curve tends to be less elastic than for other products. A company in an oligopoly (an oligopolist) commonly has substantial market power because of the small number of competitors and the company's large size relative to the industry. A business in a monopolistically competitive market (a monopolistic competitor) has less market power because it faces many competitors and is small in relation to its market. Moreover, because it sells a product with close substitutes, its demand curve is relatively elastic. Finally, a perfect competitor has no market power because of its role as a price-taker.

Figure 5.1: Attributes of Market Structures

	Perfect Competition	Monopolistic Competition	Oligopoly	Monopoly
Number of Businesses	very many	many	few	one
Standard Product	always	never	sometimes	not applicable
Entry and Exit of New Businesses	very easy	fairly easy	difficult	very difficult
Market Power	none	some	some	great
Example	farming	restaurants	automobile manufacturing	public utilities

BRIEF REVIEW

1. Product markets have one of four structures: perfect competition, monopolistic competition, oligopoly, or monopoly.

2. The market structure, or degree of competition in a market, is determined by the number of buyers and sellers in the market, whether or not a standard product is being sold, and the ease with which businesses can enter or exit the market.

3. In monopolies and oligopolies, potential competitors face the entry barriers of economies of scale, market experience, restricted ownership of resources, legal obstacles, market abuses, and advertising.

4. A business's market power, or ability to be a price-maker, is affected by the number of rivals in the industry, its size in relation to its industry, and the elasticity of its product's demand curve.

 ## Demand Differences

Producers face many of the same sorts of costs. However, because of the different market structures in which they operate, producers face significantly different demand conditions.

Perfect Competition

Because a perfect competitor is a price-taker, it must accept the price dictated by the market forces of demand and supply. Thus, the individual

business's demand curve is different from the market demand curve. Recall that the market demand curve (D_m) has a negative slope, because price and quantity demanded are inversely related. Because a perfect competitor is one of many businesses in a market, the quantity it chooses to supply has no effect on equilibrium price and quantity in the market. See the graph for the T-shirt market in Figure 5.2, on the left. The intersection of the market demand and supply curves, D_m and S_m, gives the equilibrium price of $6 per T-shirt. No matter how many shirts Pure 'n' Simple T-Shirts supplies, it will sell all it produces at a price of $6 per shirt. Thus, the individual business's demand curve, D_b, is horizontal, or perfectly elastic, at a price of $6 as shown in Figure 5.2, on the right.

"I don't know if I agree with your method of bringing customers into the store!"

SOURCE: Courtesy of Arnie of Arnietoons.

Figure 5.2:   Demand Faced by a Perfect Competitor

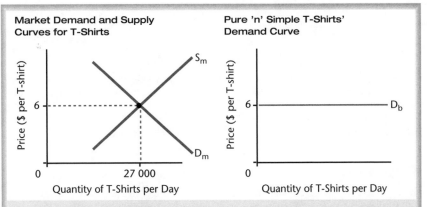

Market Demand and Supply Curves for T-Shirts

Pure 'n' Simple T-Shirts' Demand Curve

Equilibrium in the T-shirt market occurs where the market demand and supply curves, D_m and S_m, meet as shown in the graph on the left. The equilibrium price ($6) sets the position of the business's demand curve, D_b, in the graph on the right.

business's demand curve: the demand curve faced by an individual business, as opposed to an entire market

Monopolistic Competition

Because it has some ability to influence the price it charges, a monopolistic competitor faces a different type of demand curve. Consider the example of the Jaded Palate, a restaurant that serves highly spiced Cajun food. Customers of this restaurant view its food as distinct from that of nearby restaurants, none of which specialize in this cuisine. If the Jaded Palate raises the average price of its meals from $10 to $11, as shown in Figure 5.3, it will lose some, but not all, of its customers. Quantity demanded will fall from 200 to 100 meals a day. If the restaurant lowers the average price of meals from $10 to $9, there will be an increase in quantity demanded, from 200 to 300. Hence, the restaurant faces the demand curve D_b. Since customers see other restaurants as possible substitutes, a percentage change in the price of a meal causes an even greater change in quantity demanded. In other words, the monopolistic competitor's demand curve is elastic.

Figure 5.3:   Demand Faced by a Monopolistic Competitor

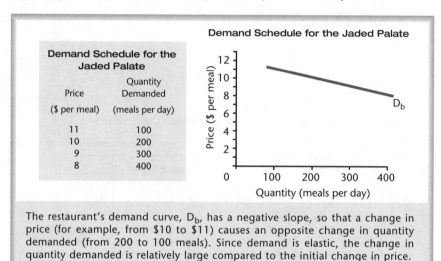

Demand Schedule for the Jaded Palate

Price ($ per meal)	Quantity Demanded (meals per day)
11	100
10	200
9	300
8	400

The restaurant's demand curve, D_b, has a negative slope, so that a change in price (for example, from $10 to $11) causes an opposite change in quantity demanded (from 200 to 100 meals). Since demand is elastic, the change in quantity demanded is relatively large compared to the initial change in price.

Oligopoly

mutual interdependence: the relationship among oligopolists, in which the actions of each business affect the other businesses

In the case of an oligopoly, the fact that each business makes up a considerable part of the market leads to **mutual interdependence**. This is a situation where businesses in the industry cannot afford to ignore their competitors' actions that might indirectly affect sales. Because of mutual interdependence, businesses in an oligopoly can operate in either of two ways: as rivals, or as fellow players who co-operate to increase combined profits.

Rivalry Among Businesses

market share: a business's proportion of total market sales

Businesses in an oligopoly where rivalry prevails are concerned with maintaining their **market share**, or the proportion of total market sales they control. Because their actions influence rivals, these businesses must take into account the reactions of competitors whenever they consider a price change. They must then predict how the responses of other businesses will influence their own market share.

Let's consider the hypothetical situation of Universal Motors and its luxury car, the Centaur. If Universal Motors increases its price for the Centaur, competitors will likely keep the prices of their luxury cars constant in order to increase their sales. Thus, Universal Motors will lose some of its market share to its competitors. If, in contrast, Universal Motors lowers its price for the Centaur, its competitors will reduce their prices as well, so as not to lose market share. Thus, Universal Motors' market share will remain constant. These actions and reactions among rival companies in an oligopoly are summarized in Figure 5.4.

Figure 5.4:   Actions and Reactions Among Rivals in an Oligopoly

Action of Company A	Effect on Probable Response of Competitors	Effect on Company A's Market Share	Company A's Quantity Demanded
raise price	keep prices constant	product now high-priced, so market share falls	large decrease as market share lost to competitors
lower price	match price drop	since all companies selling at lower price, Company A's market share stays constant	small increase as lower prices for all companies attract new buyers

Now, let's continue the example of Universal Motors in Figure 5.5. If the original price of the Centaur is $30 000, a price increase to $35 000 will cause competitors to keep their prices constant, and the market share for Centaurs will drop from 20 000 to 10 000 cars. The change in quantity demanded (from point *b* to point *a*) causes the demand curve for this price range to be fairly flat. If Universal Motors lowers the price of the Centaur from $30 000 to $20 000, competitors will lower the prices of their cars. Sales of Centaurs will increase—from 20 000 to 25 000—but not in equal proportion to the price drop. Thus, the demand curve for this price range (from point *b* to point *c*) is steep. As shown on the graph in Figure 5.5, the result is a **kinked demand curve**—a demand curve with two segments, one fairly flat and one steep, with the kink or bend at the original price of $30 000 (point *b*). This kinked demand curve is typical of oligopolies in which businesses jostle one another for profit and market dominance.

kinked demand curve: a demand curve with two segments, one fairly flat and one steep, that is typical of rival oligopolists

Figure 5.5: Demand Faced Among Rivals in an Oligopoly

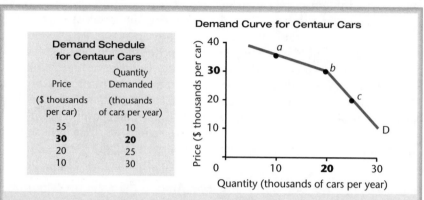

Demand Schedule for Centaur Cars

Price ($ thousands per car)	Quantity Demanded (thousands of cars per year)
35	10
30	**20**
20	25
10	30

The demand curve for Centaur cars is shown as two differently sloped segments. When Universal Motors raises the price above $30 000, competitors keep their prices constant to raise their sales. The results are a substantial drop in the quantity demanded of Centaurs, and a flat demand curve (from point *b* to point *a*). If price moves below $30 000, competitors are forced to drop their prices as well. Thus, quantity demanded for Centaurs increases by only a minor amount, producing a steep demand curve (from point *b* to point *c*).

price leadership: an understanding among oligopolists that one business will initiate all price changes in the market and the others will follow by adjusting their prices and output accordingly

collusion: oligopolists acting together as if they are a monopoly

cartel: a union of oligopolists who have a formal market-sharing agreement

Co-operation Among Businesses

Oligopolists can also co-operate in ways that are against the interests of consumers. In an oligopoly, for example, there may be an unspoken understanding that one company—usually the largest—acts as the price leader. In a case of **price leadership**, other companies will follow any price change initiated by the price leader, and adjust their output accordingly. In the past, price leadership has occurred in the automobile and farm-machinery industries. Oligopolies may take their co-operation even further. When oligopolists band together—either secretly or openly—as if they were a monopoly, they are practising **collusion**. In this case, they act jointly to maximize total profits. To do so, the businesses must first estimate the most profitable output level, and then agree to restrict production in order to keep the total market output down and price high. When this sort of agreement among producers is a formal one, the businesses together are known as a **cartel**. The best-known example of a cartel is OPEC, the Organization of Petroleum Exporting Countries.

Monopoly

As sole supplier of a product, a monopolist faces the same demand curve as that for the entire market—a curve with a negative slope. Therefore, the monopolist has considerable ability to influence price. Figure 5.6 gives the example of Megacomp, the only seller of large supercomputers.

Figure 5.6:   Demand Faced by a Monopolist

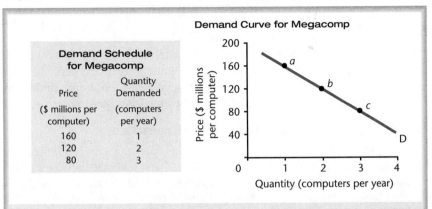

The demand curve for the individual business is identical to the market demand curve, D. As D shows, if Megacomp increases the price from $120 million to $160 million, quantity demanded decreases from 2 to 1 computer.

Nonprice Competition

Because of the similarities they share, monopolistic competition and oligopoly are often lumped together in a general category known as *imperfect competition*. In addition to changing product prices, imperfectly competitive firms can compete in another way. **Nonprice competition** refers to the efforts of imperfectly competitive producers to increase demand for their products by swaying consumer preferences. The two strategies used are product differentiation and advertising.

nonprice competition: efforts to increase demand through product differentiation, advertising, or both

Product Differentiation

Product differentiation is a company's attempt to distinguish its product from that of competitors. Designer labels on a clothing manufacturer's jeans, or an "exclusive" set of toppings on a pizza restaurant's product are examples of product differentiation. The changes made to a product may be cosmetic—slick packaging, for example—or they may be substantial. Product differentiation has two goals: to increase demand (thus raising the quantity demanded at every price), and to decrease demand elasticity (so that prices can be increased without losing customers to competitors). Meeting both goals increases a business's profit and market power.

product differentiation: efforts to make a product distinct from that of competitors

Advertising

Advertising can play two roles in imperfectly competitive markets. It can provide the consumer with information, as with newspaper classified ads, and it can promote consumer preferences for a product, as is commonly the case for radio and television ads. Advertising has the same two goals as product differentiation: to increase demand for the product, and to make the demand more inelastic. For example, a producer of athletic shoes, such as Nike, advertises in order to raise the quantity demanded of its shoes at every possible price. The producer also aims to make consumers less likely to switch brands if Nike shoes go up in price. Again, the company's profit and market power are increased if its advertising strategy meets the two goals.

Nonprice Competition and Business

For a single imperfectly competitive business, product differentiation and advertising increase both revenues and costs. Total revenue increases when the demand for the business's product increases and the demand becomes more inelastic. However, the business's total costs increase because of the extra costs of undertaking nonprice competition. If the gain in total revenues outweighs the extra costs of product differentiation and advertising, profits are increased. Whether or not this extra profit can be made depends on how easy it is to influence consumer preferences. Businesses in oligopolies typically find advertising a profitable strategy, especially when large advertising budgets serve as an entry barrier. Not surprisingly, businesses in such markets are Canada's top advertisers, as shown in Figure 5.7.

Figure 5.7:   Canada's Top Advertisers (1992)

	$ Millions
1. Government of Canada	113.2
2. General Motors	109.0
3. Proctor & Gamble	99.6
4. The Thomson Group	81.6
5. Sears Canada	59.0
6. The Molson Companies	57.4
7. Eaton's of Canada	46.3
8. BCE	44.8
9. John Labatt Ltd.	40.9
10. Imasco	38.9
11. Unilever	38.5
12. Kraft General Foods Group	37.9

SOURCE: Nielsen Marketing Research

Nonprice Competition and the Consumer

For the consumer, product differentiation leads to higher prices by raising per-unit costs and enhancing an individual business's market power. However, consumers will likely have more choices because of businesses' efforts to differentiate their products. So, for example, the fact that TVs produced by competing companies are distinctive raises the average price of TVs, but gives consumers a wider selection of possible features than they would otherwise have had.

The impact of advertising on the consumer is also mixed. In some cases, advertising is anti-competitive, leading to more market power for established firms. However, advertising can also increase competition. By giving new companies the chance to familiarize buyers with their products, advertising can offer consumers more choice. In this case, advertising lessens the market power of established businesses and leads to more industry flexibility. An example that portrays both possible effects is the Canadian soft-drink industry. This market is an oligopoly that for decades was dominated by two giant businesses, Coca-Cola and PepsiCo, whose market power was enhanced by their high levels of advertising. However, partly through the effects of advertising, smaller private-label producers (usually connected with supermarket chains) have recently become major players, with a combined market share of almost 30 percent in 1993.

BRIEF REVIEW

1. A perfectly competitive business is a price-taker, and thus faces a horizontal demand curve, with the price being set by the market.

2. A monopolistic competitor faces an elastic demand curve with a negative slope.

3. Oligopolies are characterized by mutual interdependence. Rivalry among oligopolists creates a kinked demand curve because of competitors' responses to price changes. Co-operation among oligopolists may lead to price leadership or collusion. If collusion is formal and explicit, the companies make up a cartel.

4. Monopolists face the demand curve of the entire market—a curve with a negative slope.

5. Product differentiation and advertising are forms of nonprice competition common in imperfectly competitive markets. Their effect on the consumer is mixed.

Industrial Concentration

It is usually fairly obvious that an industry is either perfectly competitive or monopolistic. Most industries, however, fall between the two extremes, and therefore represent some form of imperfect competition. It is not always easy to establish whether an imperfectly competitive industry is monopolistically competitive or an oligopoly. The most common

concentration ratio:

the percentage of total sales revenue in a market earned by the largest businesses

indicator is a **concentration ratio**, which is the percentage of total sales revenue in a market earned by the largest business firms.

Concentration ratios are commonly measured for the four largest business firms in any market, in which case they are known as four-firm ratios. An industry might be considered to be a monopolistic competition if its four-firm ratio is below 50 percent. If the four-firm ratio is above 50 percent, the industry is considered to be an oligopoly. So, for example, if a certain market has total annual sales revenues of $100 million, with the four largest companies having sales of $42 million, $27 million, $14 million, and $8 million, the four-firm ratio is 91 percent $\left(\frac{42 + 27 + 14 + 8}{100} \times 100\%\right)$ In this case, the industry is considered an oligopoly. Concentration ratios for selected Canadian industries are shown in Figure 5.8.

Figure 5.8:   Concentration Ratios in Selected Canadian Industries (1988)

	Share of Industry Sales by Four Largest Businesses
Tobacco products	98.9
Petroleum and coal products	74.5
Transportation equipment	68.4
Beverages	59.2
Metal mining	58.9
Paper and allied industries	38.9
Electrical products	32.1
Printing, publishing, and allied industries	25.7
Food	19.6
Finance	16.4
Machinery	11.3
Retail trade	9.7
Clothing industries	6.6
Construction	2.2

Sales in industries such as tobacco products, beverages, and transportation equipment are dominated by the four top businesses in each industry, indicating high levels of concentration. Meanwhile, in industries such as retail trade, clothing, and construction, the four top businesses in each industry have a much smaller proportion of industry sales, indicating low levels of concentration.

SOURCE: Statistics Canada, *Annual Report of the Minister of Industry, Science and Technology under the Corporations and Labour Unions Return Act, Part 1 — Corporations 1988* (October 1991), cat. no. 61-210, p. 94. Reproduced by authority of the Minister of Industry, 1994.

About half of Canada's manufacturing industries have four-firm ratios of over 50 percent, and can therefore be classified as oligopolies. Many Canadian service industries are concentrated as well. Compared to the United States, Canada has relatively small markets, each of which are more likely to be dominated by just one or a few businesses. It has been estimated that, overall, about three-fifths of Canadian economic activity takes place in concentrated markets that are either monopolies or oligopolies. In the U.S. economy, the corresponding estimate is just over one-fifth.

Concentration ratios are not foolproof indicators of market structure, however. Statistics Canada includes only domestic businesses in its calculations and defines each market as for all of Canada. In markets where there is significant international trade, official concentration ratios underestimate competition by ignoring the role of imports. So, for example, Canada's motor vehicle industry would appear less concentrated if foreign imports were taken into account. In markets that are highly localized, meaning that one or two businesses dominate certain regions, national concentration ratios overestimate the level of competition. For example, while the many radio broadcasters in Canada would result in low official concentration ratios, the fact that most broadcasters operate in highly concentrated regional markets would not be reflected.

The Debate Over Industrial Concentration

The effect of market power on the economy can be studied in the context of **industrial concentration**, which refers to the domination of a market by one or a few large companies. Because of their small numbers and great size, these companies possess significant market power. Figure 5.9 gives some indication of how large some individual Canadian companies are in relation to Canadian business as a whole.

industrial concentration: market domination by one or a few large businesses

Figure 5.9: Concentration in the Canadian Economy (1992)

In Nonfinancial Industries, Share of Assets and Share of Revenues for 25 Leading Enterprises

	Assets	Revenues
Foreign	4.9	7.3
Canadian		
Private enterprises	13.2	7.6
Government enterprises	15.6	4.5
	33.7%	19.4%

Canada's leading 25 enterprises (ranked by assets) control about a third of total assets in nonfinancial industries. Of this, the bulk was controlled by Canadian enterprises—both private and government-owned. In terms of sales revenue in nonfinancial industries, the leading 25 enterprises (ranked by revenues) have a less significant share.

SOURCE: Statistics Canada, *Parliamentary Report of the Minister of Industry, Science and Technology under the Corporations and Labour Unions Return Act, Part 1 — Corporations* (December 1993), cat. no. 61-220, pp. 49, 52. Reproduced by authority of the Minister of Industry, 1994.

Can industrial concentration work to the advantage of consumers? To answer this question, we must weigh the costs and the benefits of huge companies dominating a given market.

Economies of Scale Versus Market Power

Defenders of industrial concentration emphasize the role of economies of scale. They say this is especially important in a time when businesses are more likely than ever to compete in huge global markets. In many industries, only large businesses with a substantial market share can produce the quantity of output necessary to take advantage of economies of scale. As a result, these big businesses have lower per-unit costs than would perfectly competitive businesses in the same market. These cost savings may then be passed on to consumers in the form of lower prices. Critics of industrial concentration say that the benefits of economies of scale must be weighed against the market power held by large monopolists and oligopolists. This market power allows big companies to charge a higher price than would occur with more competition in the market.

Technical Innovation

Some people have argued that "big business" is needed to promote innovation and technological advances. However, recent evidence points to the opposite conclusion. Companies in highly concentrated industries—either monopolies or oligopolies—tend not to innovate as rapidly as those in more competitive markets, where the continual jockeying for profit encourages improvements in products and production processes.

BRIEF REVIEW

1. Concentration ratios are measures of the percentage of total sales revenue in a market as earned by the biggest companies within the industry. These ratios suggest the degree of competition in an industry, although they do have some deficiencies.

2. Industrial concentration has its supporters and its critics. The arguments for and against concentration centre around economies of scale, excess market power, and technical innovation.

Stoking the Fires of Competition

Anti-Combines Legislation in Canada

Laws aimed at preventing industrial concentration and abuses of market power are known as *anti-combines legislation*. Canada's anti-combines laws date back to 1889, but until recently were largely unsuccessful.

That violations were considered criminal offences was one reason for the lack of success. Criminal cases require that guilt be established beyond a reasonable doubt. This requirement does not easily make use of economic analysis—analysis that is so vital to considering anti-competitive behaviour. A second reason is that Canadian governments have traditionally been less opposed to industrial concentration than those in other countries, the United States in particular. Many Canadians have argued that domestic businesses need to be large in order to be internationally competitive, especially in sectors with significant economies of scale. Canada's lawmakers, therefore, have typically given the goal of international competitiveness and efficiency greater weight than domestic competition.

The Competition Act of 1986 was a major reform of Canada's anti-combines legislation. It offered a combination of criminal and civil provisions, strengthened penalties, and built on the almost century-long experience of anti-combines legislation and prosecution. The Act covers business practices that prevent or lessen competition, including the practices described in the following sections. Of these, the first three are still criminal offences, with penalties ranging from fines to possible imprisonment of company executives, while the last two are considered civil matters, which are reviewed by a government-administered panel known as the Competition Tribunal.

Conspiracy

Businesses that conspire or agree to fix prices, allocate markets, or restrict entry to markets can be charged under the Competition Act. In order for a business to be found guilty, its actions must be proven to unduly restrain competition. Violators can face fines of up to $10 million or prison terms of up to five years. One case of conspiracy involved nine real estate boards in five provinces. After complaints from customers and some industry members about commissions, services, and other practices, an investigation began. The Canadian Real Estate Association came forward to settle the matter, which was resolved out of court.

Bid-Rigging

Companies that bid on contracts may arrange among themselves who will win each contract and at what price. By taking turns at winning bids and by inflating prices, all conspirators are winners. Unlike the more general conspiracy charge, bid-rigging is considered an automatic offence; undue restraint does not have to be proven. In a recent case, three heating equipment suppliers were convicted on six counts of sharing out the market, in part by rigging bids; each company was fined $1000 on each count. Penalties are at the courts' discretion, but reflect the seriousness with which the courts view the crime, and so can include, for example, $1 million fines and five-year prison terms.

Predatory Pricing

The policy and practice of temporarily dropping a price for a product below its average cost to drive a new competitor out of business is a criminal offence. In one case, a company provided free supplies of a drug to hospitals. Because the company's goal was to generate long-term sales after eliminating competition, the company was fined $50 000.

Abuse of Dominant Position

Companies that control most of the sales in a market are not allowed to use their dominant position to engage in anti-competitive behaviour. One recent case of abuse involved the Canadian maker of (and former patent-holder for) the artificial sweetener aspartame, known as NutraSweet.[1] According to the findings of the Competition Tribunal, the company had used its power to have several major purchasers of aspartame sign long-term contracts to buy NutraSweet exclusively, rather than the products of the competition. The company was not allowed to enforce these old contracts or to negotiate new ones of the same sort. Typically, the Tribunal requires that the guilty company cease its anti-competitive behaviour. The Tribunal can also use stronger measures to restore competition in the market; for example, by requiring partial break-up of a business into smaller units.

Mergers

A merger is the combining of two companies into one. The Competition Tribunal has the power to prohibit a merger in Canada—no matter what the size or nationality of the companies involved—if the merger could prevent or substantially reduce competition. Exceptions are often made if a merger will increase efficiency and pass on savings to consumers. In practice, it is uncommon for the Tribunal to disallow a merger. Mergers can be of three sorts, depending on the connection between the companies involved.

Horizontal Merger　A horizontal merger combines former competitors. One example of a horizontal merger is the 1989 purchase of Wardair by its rival, Canadian Airlines International. Horizontal mergers allow businesses to take advantage of the economies of scale that arise from combining production. Horizontal mergers can also reduce the level of competition in the market, thereby giving the new, combined company more market power and potential profit.

Vertical Merger　A vertical merger combines a business and its supplier. A steelmaker that purchases an iron ore mine is one example, as is a fashion design company merging with a clothing wholesaler. Vertical mergers can guarantee a supply of needed inputs or can ensure distribution of the product. For example, McDonald's has taken over many of its food suppliers, and PepsiCo's acquisition of Pizza Hut ensured that PepsiCo soft drinks are sold in these restaurants.

Conglomerate Merger　A conglomerate merger combines businesses in unrelated industries. The main reason for such mergers is to help companies smooth out fluctuations in profit that occur during booms and recessions. A company whose profit plummets during a downturn in the economy—a manufacturer of luxury yachts, for example—might decide to purchase a chain of discount hardware stores, which are not affected in the same way.

SOURCES:
Consumer and Corporate Affairs Canada, *Competition Policy in Canada: The First Hundred Years;* Robert S. Nozick and Charlotte Neff, *The Annotated Competition Act* (Toronto: Carswell, 1987), pp. 78, 79, 83.
[1]Fagan and Drew, "Nutrasweet case to set precedent," in *The Globe and Mail,* 10 January 1990, pp. B1, B5.

Prophet of Capitalism's Doom

The Economic Theories of Karl Marx

Marx and His Influence

Karl Marx (1818–1883) is best known as the founder of the international socialist and communist movements. He was born in the German state of Prussia, studied philosophy, and worked as a journalist before beginning his career as a political activist. Exiled from both Germany and France, he moved to England where, with his close friend Friedrich Engels (1820–1895), he applied his revolutionary views to the fields of philosophy, history, and economics.

Of these three subjects, it was what he called "the confounded ramifications of Political Economy," that gave him the most headaches. In his mammoth three-volume work, *Das Kapital*, Marx developed his theory of economics. He concluded that capitalism, by its very nature, is unjust.

Marx's View of Capitalism

Marx's years in England allowed him to witness first-hand the effects of the British Industrial Revolution. By the mid-1800s, manufacturing was the mainstay of Britain's economy, and a large portion of the population had moved from rural areas to the burgeoning new cities in hopes of finding jobs in manufacturing. In the long run, the industrial transformation experienced in Britain enhanced the economic well-being of the majority of citizens of industrialized countries. But in Marx's day, the benefits of the Industrial Revolution seemed to be limited to the wealthier members of society. Living conditions were horrendous for the labouring classes living and working in the rapidly expanding urban areas:

> And what cities! It was not merely that smoke hung over them and filth impregnated them, that the elementary public services—water-supply, sanitation, street-cleaning, open spaces, and so on—could not keep pace with the mass migration of men into cities, thus producing, especially after 1830, epidemics of cholera, typhoid and an appalling constant toll [from] air pollution and water pollution.... The new city populations...[were] pressed into overcrowded and bleak slums, whose very sight froze the heart of the observer.[1]

Marx's Theory of Capitalism

The Labour Theory of Value   Marx blamed these conditions on capitalism itself. His attack was based on his "labour theory of value," in which prices of products depend on how much labour goes into producing them. According to

Karl Marx

A scene reflecting Marx's view of capitalist exploitation contrasts the toil of workers with the idleness of their employer on horseback.

ADVANCING ECONOMIC THOUGHT

this theory, only company owners (whom Marx called capitalists) have the financial resources to hire workers and sell the resulting output. By paying wages that are less than the value workers contribute to production, company owners are able to skim off a portion of value for themselves. By doing this, they engage in capitalist exploitation of their workforce.

The Theory of Exploitation   An example will help explain Marx's theory. It may take a worker four hours to make a shirt and eight hours to make a suit. According to Marx, the price of the shirt should then be half that of the suit; say the prices of the two products are $40 and $80, respectively. If so, workers producing either two shirts or one suit in an eight-hour day create $80 of value. Let's assume that daily wages in the textile trade are $50, and that the cost of materials plus daily wear and tear on the machines each worker uses is $10. The portion of value kept by the capitalist, or each worker's "surplus value," is therefore $20 [$80 − ($50 + $10)] as shown in the table below.

Marx's Theory of Exploitation

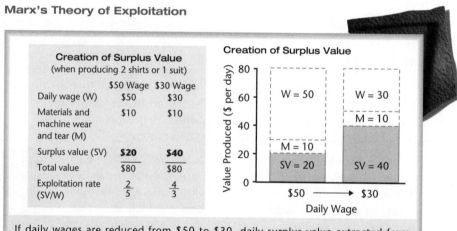

If daily wages are reduced from $50 to $30, daily surplus value extracted from each worker is increased (the shaded portions in the bar graphs). As a result, surplus value as a proportion of daily wages also increases.

SOURCE: Adapted from Stanley L. Brue, *The Evolution of Economic Thought*, 5th ed. (Fort Worth: The Dryden Press, 1994), p.195.

Dynamics of Capitalism

With time, Marx argued, the rate of exploitation by capitalists would worsen, meaning that surplus value would increase as a proportion of the daily wage. This could happen either through further decreases in wages or a lengthening of the workday.

Decreased Wages   Capitalists try to slash wages as much as possible. The daily wage in our example could drop from $50 to $30, while the cost of materials, plus the wear and tear on machines, remains constant at $10. As a result, surplus value would rise to $40 [$80 − ($30 + $10)]. Surplus value as a proportion of the daily wage would then increase from $20/$50 to $40/$30.

Lengthening of the Workday   Capitalists also have an incentive to raise the number of hours workers put in each day. This expands the daily value created by each worker. As long as the daily wage remains the same, surplus value as a proportion of this wage would again rise.

Communist Revolution

Marx believed that capitalist exploitation would worsen the living standards of workers until, finally, workers would revolt violently, first in the nations of Western Europe, which were most industrialized at the time Marx was writing, and later in other parts of the world. The overthrow of capitalism would usher in a socialist age based on common ownership of property. Once socialist ownership had been consolidated, true communism would arrive. Governments would disappear and people would be able to live in complete liberty. Society's guiding principle would then be "from each according to his abilities, and to each according to his needs."[2]

Relevance for Today

Marx's theories have been the source of continuing controversy. His detractors challenge the usefulness of the labour theory of value and the notion of surplus value. They argue that other economic resources, such as capital and entrepreneurship, make their own contributions to production, and that owners of these resources must receive a payment so that they will keep supplying their resources to businesses.

   At the same time, Marx has had a significant impact on the world. Socialists—who advocate that the community as a whole own and control the means of production, distribution, and exchange—have held power in many countries. Among socialists, communists have accepted the bulk of Marx's theories and applied them in countries subject to communist rule. In most countries, however, Marx's influence has been less direct. Labour movements, for example, owe much to Marx's theories of capitalist exploitation. Through gradual reform, rather than revolution, socialists in countries such as Canada have played a major part in social reform and in creating modern mixed economies in which governments are much more important than they were a century ago.

NOTES

[1]Adapted from *Industry and Empire: From 1750 to the Present Day* by E.J. Hobsbawm, (Penguin Books, 1969). Copyright © E.J. Hobsbawm, 1968, 1969. Reprinted by permission.
[2]Karl Marx, *Critique of the Gotha Program*, 1875.

1. For the textile industry example given previously, imagine that each worker's wages are reduced to $20 per day, but the other costs remain the same. Create a bar graph to show the resulting change in surplus value. How does surplus value change as a proportion of the daily wage?

2. Imagine that the daily wage of a textile worker remains at $50, but the workday is lengthened to 16 hours, causing each worker to double production to $160 per day and increasing the other costs (materials and wear on machines) to increase to $20 per worker.
   a) Create a bar graph to show the new surplus value per worker.
   b) Explain how the surplus value changes as a proportion of the daily wage.
   c) Explain whether the company owners are worse off or better off as a result of the lengthened workday.

3. What factors present in modern economics have been responsible for preventing Marx's predictions from being realized? Explain your answer.

4. Research one aspect of Marx's work. What, if any, are some positive effects of this work? Present your findings in a report.

Key Concepts

perfect competition
monopolistic competition
oligopoly
monopoly
entry barriers
natural monopoly
predatory pricing

market power
business's demand curve
mutual interdependence
market share
kinked demand curve
price leadership
collusion

cartel
nonprice competition
product differentiation
concentration ratio
industrial concentration

Developing Application and Analysis Skills

1. For each of the four market structures—perfect competition, monopolistic competition, oligopoly, and monopoly—identify one real company that typifies a business in this market. (You might find examples in your community, in the newspaper, on TV, and so on.) In supporting your choices, identify the attributes of each market structure.

2. Classify each of the following businesses according to its market structure, and give reasons for your classification. Then, sketch a demand curve for the business, and explain how the demand curve compares with the demand curve for the relevant market.
   a) a vendor of tomatoes at a farmers' market
   b) the company that runs the cafeteria at your school

c) a chain of movie theatres

d) an internationally known chain of donut shops

e) a major steel manufacturer

f) a major Canadian chartered bank

g) a cable television company in Toronto

3. For each of the following hypothetical newspaper headlines, explain in which market structure the business operates. Then, explain the extent to which the business is a price-taker or price-maker. Finally, describe the economic behaviour of each business using the terms you have learned in this chapter (for example, "predatory pricing").

   a) Universal Motors Leads the Way—Standard Anti-Lock Brakes for All Models!

   b) ABC Airlines and XYZ Airlines to Increase Transatlantic Fares

   c) Three Top Construction Companies Arranged "Sweet Deal" for Bridge

   d) Lola Cola Introduces Line of Caffeine-Free Soft Drinks

   e) Neighbourhood Brewing Co. Bows Out After Bitter Price War

   f) Coffee Growers Cutting Back After Record Harvest

   g) Happy Hour Draws Dance Crowd to Queen Street

4. The fast-food hamburger industry in North America is a classic example of how businesses use nonprice discrimination. Research and write an essay about the uses, costs, and benefits of nonprice discrimination. Give examples from the burger business to support your conclusions.

5. For each of the situations that follow, identify the market structure in which the business operates. Then, sketch the demand curve each business would face before making the change described. Finally, describe the impact of the change on the demand curve, and give reasons for your answer.

   a) ZEUS, a manufacturer of non-aspirin medication, changes the name of its medication to ZEUS-Flu at the height of the influenza season.

   b) The sole television cable company in a rural area raises the monthly price of its service by 50 percent.

   c) The manufacturer of cigarette Brand Z raises the price of its product.

   d) A cod vendor at a local fish market raises the price of his catch.

   e) A producer of jet airliners announces a price increase for its most competitive model.

   f) The producer of a well-known shampoo announces that a scientific study proves that the shampoo prevents baldness in male users.

6. What advantages and disadvantages do product differentiation and advertising present to the producer and the consumer? Give examples in your answer.

7. If total sales for Canadian businesses that produce in-line skates are $176 million and the four largest producers have sales of $70 million, $45 million, $15 million, and $10 million, can this industry be classified as an oligopoly? Explain your answer.

8. Identify and research an example of industrial concentration in North America in the past or present. In a research paper, examine the market structure in which the concentration takes place, the economic behaviour of the business(es) involved, and the economic and social costs and benefits.

CHAPTER 6

The Role of Profit

> It is not from the benevolence of the butcher, the brewer, or the baker that we expect our dinner but from their regard to their own interest.
>
> —ADAM SMITH, SCOTTISH ECONOMIST

Ask most businesspeople why they are in business and they'll give one answer—to make a profit. In fact, profits are expected, so economists consider "normal profit" an implicit cost of doing business. As the driving force behind business activity, profit is the key to understanding how businesses behave. In this chapter, we'll examine how the quest for profit is carried out by businesses in the four market structures. We'll also look at how profit-making activity leads to significantly different results depending on the extent of competition in a market.

CHAPTER FOCUS

This chapter focuses on the following:
- the profit-maximizing rule
- how businesses in each market structure maximize profits
- the effects of profit-maximizing behaviour on consumers in each market structure
- the short-run and long-run outcomes of profit-maximizing behaviour
- natural monopolies and how governments regulate them

SKILLS FOCUS

After studying this chapter, you will be able to:
- compare the ways in which businesses in each market structure maximize profits, and how their actions affect consumers in the short and the long run
- use graphs and tables to determine profit-maximizing output levels for perfect competitors, monopolistic competitors, oligopolists, and monopolists
- demonstrate a business's profit using revenue, cost, and profit rectangles
- analyze a business's costs and revenues for breakeven and shut-down points
- evaluate methods that governments use to regulate monopolies

 **Perfect Competition**

How do businesses make operating decisions? They do so by comparing a range of potential revenues and costs. All businesses—whether they are perfect competitors, monopolistic competitors, oligopolists, or monopolists, and whatever their product—use the same general methods in pursuing maximum profit. However, each business must apply the methods differently, according to the market structure in which it operates. To examine profit-maximizing decisions and actions, we'll look first at perfect competitors—the "price-takers." As price-takers, perfectly competitive businesses accept one price, and can maximize their profits only by finding the optimum quantity of output.

Revenue Conditions

Given the horizontal demand curve the business faces, the perfect competitor's total revenue (TR), or the overall earnings from selling a product, is calculated by multiplying the product's price by each potential quantity of output (q). For example, if Pure 'n' Simple T-Shirts sells 250 shirts at a price of $6, then its total revenue is $1500 ($6 × 250). In addition to total revenue, the perfect competitor can examine two other revenue concepts to help make operating decisions: average revenue and marginal revenue.

Average Revenue

average revenue: a business's total revenue per unit of output

Average revenue (AR) is the business's total revenue per unit of output (q). When Pure 'n' Simple T-Shirts sells 250 shirts and its total revenue is $1500, its average revenue equals $6 per unit of the product:

$$\text{Average revenue (AR)} = \frac{\text{total revenue (TR)}}{\text{quantity of output (q)}}$$

$$\$6 \text{ per shirt} = \frac{\$1500}{250 \text{ shirts}}$$

Note that average revenue for Pure 'n' Simple T-Shirts equals each shirt's $6 price. For all businesses, regardless of the market structure in which they operate, price will equal average revenue. This is because price can be defined in the same way as average revenue—as the business's total revenue per unit of output. The only exception to this rule occurs when a business practises price discrimination, or charging different prices to different customers for exactly the same product.

Marginal Revenue

marginal revenue: the extra total revenue earned from an additional unit of output

Marginal revenue is the extra total revenue (ΔTR) earned when the business sells another unit of output (Δq). For example, if Pure 'n' Simple

T-Shirts has an increase in total revenues from \$1500 to \$1620 when it increases its output from 250 to 270 shirts, then the marginal revenue of each of these last 20 shirts is \$6:

$$\text{Marginal revenue (MR)} = \frac{\Delta TR}{\Delta q}$$

$$\$6 \text{ per shirt} = \frac{\$120}{20 \text{ shirts}}$$

Relationship Between Revenue Conditions and Demand

As the case of Pure 'n' Simple T-Shirts illustrates, average and marginal revenues are always equal for a perfectly competitive business. This follows from the fact that average revenue (or price) is constant at all possible quantities of output. Recall that when an average value such as average revenue is constant, it equals its related marginal value—which in this case is marginal revenue.

Figure 6.1 illustrates the relationships among price, average revenue, and marginal revenue for our example of Pure 'n' Simple T-Shirts. In the table, the values for price (column 1), marginal revenue (column 4), and average revenue (column 5) are identical. The demand curve this perfect competitor faces also represents the business's average revenue and marginal revenue curves. Because the business is a price-taker, this combined curve shows a constant value at all quantities of output. Thus, for a perfectly competitive business:

$$\text{Price (P)} = \text{Average revenue (AR)} = \text{Marginal revenue (MR)}$$

The Short Run

Because the forces that affect perfectly competitive markets in the short run are different from those in the long run, the actions of individual businesses depend on the relevant time period. We'll begin by analyzing how perfect competitors operate in the short run.

Profit Maximization

Regardless of the market it operates in, any business can maximize its profit by following a single **profit-maximizing rule**: produce the quantity of output (q) at which marginal revenue and marginal cost intersect.

> Profit-maximizing rule: Marginal revenue (MR) = Marginal cost (MC)

Of course, this may result in an awkward quantity, such as 5.73 units, in which case the producer would choose the closest whole number, such as 6 units.

What happens if the condition MR = MC is not met? If each new unit of output is still providing more extra revenue to the business than it adds

profit-maximizing rule: produce at the level of output where marginal revenue and marginal cost intersect

Figure 6.1: Revenues for a Perfect Competitor

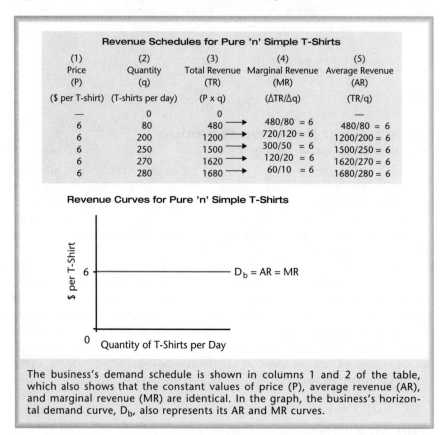

Revenue Schedules for Pure 'n' Simple T-Shirts

(1) Price (P) ($ per T-shirt)	(2) Quantity (q) (T-shirts per day)	(3) Total Revenue (TR) (P x q)	(4) Marginal Revenue (MR) (ΔTR/Δq)	(5) Average Revenue (AR) (TR/q)
—	0	0		—
6	80	480	480/80 = 6	480/80 = 6
6	200	1200	720/120 = 6	1200/200 = 6
6	250	1500	300/50 = 6	1500/250 = 6
6	270	1620	120/20 = 6	1620/270 = 6
6	280	1680	60/10 = 6	1680/280 = 6

Revenue Curves for Pure 'n' Simple T-Shirts

D_b = AR = MR

$ per T-Shirt

6

0

Quantity of T-Shirts per Day

The business's demand schedule is shown in columns 1 and 2 of the table, which also shows that the constant values of price (P), average revenue (AR), and marginal revenue (MR) are identical. In the graph, the business's horizontal demand curve, D_b, also represents its AR and MR curves.

in cost, output should be increased in order to maximize profit. So, for example, if a business has a marginal revenue of $3 at its current output level, but the marginal cost of producing this unit is $2, the business is wise to increase its output. Recall that profit is the difference between total revenue and total cost. In this case, each additional unit of output is adding more revenue ($3) than it is costing ($2), so the profit added by this unit is $1. Profit-adding units such as these should be produced no matter how small the contribution to profit. Once output is raised to the level at which marginal revenue and marginal cost are equal, any further increase in output would cause the business's profit to fall. So, for example, if a business produces beyond the output level at which marginal revenue and marginal cost are both $3, the business will soon find the marginal revenue of $3 surpassed by a marginal cost of $4. Hence, each additional unit is subtracting from profit, and output should be returned to the point at which marginal revenue and marginal cost are equal.

Thinking About Economics

Does the profit-maximizing rule also apply when a business is making a loss at all possible quantities of output?

Yes. In this case, the profit-maximizing rule is used to determine the quantity at which the business makes the minimum possible loss. Since a loss is simply a negative profit, this means finding the output level with a negative profit that is closest to zero. For example, if a loss-making business is choosing between two output levels that provide negative profits of –$100 and –$300, it can minimize its loss by selecting the first of these output levels.

So, perfect competitors, like all other businesses, must determine their profit-maximizing output by looking at the business's cost and revenue figures. Pure 'n' Simple T-Shirts, for example, would examine the data in Figure 6.2 and ask: "At what output level does marginal revenue intersect with marginal cost?" If the marginal revenue and marginal cost figures are graphed, as shown, we can see that the profit-maximizing point occurs at point *a*. As the closest associated whole number is 270, Pure 'n' Simple T-Shirts should choose a quantity of 270 T-shirts.

This point can be checked against the table in Figure 6.2. The figures for marginal revenue (column 3) and marginal cost (column 4) would pass through the same values nearest the output of 270 T-shirts (column 1). To verify this result, a business's owners might calculate the total profit they would make at every possible quantity of output. The highest positive (or lowest negative) profit figure in this column corresponds to the profit-maximizing quantity. In the case of Pure 'n' Simple T-Shirts, the owner would subtract total cost (column 8) from total revenue (column 7), to give total profit (column 9). So, scanning column 9, it is clear that the best choice is again at 270 shirts, where total profit reaches its highest value of $260 ($1620 – 1360).

While the profit-maximizing point can be verified with the table, using a graph to find this point has a bonus: the graph immediately shows whether or not the business is earning an economic profit. When price (P) exceeds average cost (AC) at the profit-maximizing output, the business enjoys a short-run economic profit. If price is less than average cost, the business suffers a loss, or negative profit. In the special case where price and average cost are equal, the business is making no economic profit, and is said to be at its **breakeven point**. Note, however, that at this point the business is still making a normal profit.

Business's breakeven point: P = AC

Using a graph to show the profit-maximizing point has another bonus: with a graph, we can see immediately the relationship of a business's

breakeven point: the level of output where price (or average revenue) equals average cost

Figure 6.2:   Profit Maximization for a Perfect Competitor

Profit Maximization Table for Pure 'n' Simple T-Shirts

(1) Total Product (q)	(2) Price (P) (=AR)	(3) Marginal Revenue (MR)	(4) Marginal Cost (MC) ($\Delta TR/\Delta q$)	(5) Average Variable Cost (AVC) (VC/q)	(6) Average Cost (AC) (TC/q)	(7) Total Revenue (TR)	(8) Total Cost (TC)	(9) Total Profit (TR – TC)
0	6					0	825	–825
		6	1.75					
80	6			1.75	12.06	480	965	–485
		6	1.33					
200	6			1.50	5.63	1200	1125	75
		6	2.50					
250	6			1.70	5.00	1500	1250	250
		6	5.50					
270	**6**			**1.98**	**5.04**	**1620**	**1360**	**260**
		6	10.50					
280	6			2.29	5.24	1680	1465	215

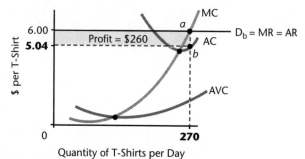

Profit Maximization Graph for Pure 'n' Simple T-Shirts

The quantity of output at which the business maximizes its short-run profit—or minimizes its short-run loss—is found using either a graph or a table. On the graph, the profit-maximizing output is found where the MR and MC curves intersect at point *a*. Total profit is the area of the shaded rectangle, the width of which is the profit-maximizing output (q) and the height of which is the average revenue (AR) minus average cost (AC) at points *a* and *b*. In the table, this profit-maximizing output occurs where marginal cost (MC) in column 4 passes through the same values as the constant marginal revenue (MR) in column 3. The answer can be verified by calculating total profit at every output level, as in column 9, and then finding the output level at which the highest positive (or lowest negative) profit is possible.

profit to its revenue and costs. The "revenue rectangle" has a height that is equal to price and a width that is equal to the quantity of output. The "cost rectangle" has a height that is equal to average cost and a width that is again equal to the quantity of output. The "profit rectangle" is the area of the revenue rectangle less the area of the cost rectangle. So, for example, in Figure 6.2 the marginal cost curve and marginal revenue curve for Pure 'n' Simple T-Shirts intersect at the profit-maximizing point. As we know from the table also, this point is closest to an output level of 270 shirts and a price of $6 per shirt. Thus, the company's revenue rectangle has an area of $1620 ($6 price × 270 quantity). The cost rectangle has an area of $1360 ($5.04 average cost × 270 quantity). The profit rectangle, then, is the shaded area of $260 profit ($1620 − $1360).

When Should a Business Close?

Would Pure 'n' Simple T-Shirts remain in business if it were making a loss? In the short run, the business would likely continue to operate as long as it earned sufficient revenue to pay its variable costs. The remaining fixed costs would have to be paid in the short run whether or not the company stayed in business. As long as a business's total revenue more than covers its variable costs, it is better off remaining in business rather than shutting down and still having to pay its fixed costs. If total revenue were to fall below variable costs, however, the business would not be able to even fund its day-to-day operations, and it would have no choice but to close down.

Recall that total revenue for a business is found by multiplying price by the quantity of output (TR = P × q). Recall also that variable costs are found by subtracting fixed costs from total cost at any given output level (VC = TC − FC), and average variable cost is variable costs divided by quantity (AVC = VC ÷ q). So that we may consider the question of whether or not a business should continue to operate, let's take a look at average variable cost in another way: variable costs equal average variable cost multiplied by quantity (VC = AVC × q). Now, we can establish a relationship between price and average cost by looking at the formula for total revenue (TR = P × q), and the formula for variable costs (VC = AVC × q). Recall that as long as variable costs do not exceed total revenue, the company should stay in business; if the variable costs begin to exceed total revenue, the company should shut down. Cancelling the quantity of output (q)—because it is a common element in both these expressions—means that total revenue exceeds variable costs as long as price is greater than average variable cost. Variable costs exceed total revenue when average variable cost exceeds price. At the point that total revenue and variable costs (or average variable cost and price) are equal, the business reaches its **shutdown point**:

$$\begin{aligned} VC &= TR \\ (AVC \times q) &= (P \times q) \\ AVC &= P \end{aligned}$$

Business's shutdown point:

shutdown point: the level of output where price (or average revenue) equals average variable cost

Let's consider our example of Pure 'n' Simple T-Shirts in Figure 6.3. When receiving a price of $6.00 per T-shirt (at point *a*), the company is maintaining a positive economic profit. If, for some reason, the price drops to $5.00, the business reaches its breakeven point (point *b*). At the lowest point on the average variable cost curve, at $1.50 (point *c*), average variable cost equals price, thus variable costs equal total revenue. Point *c* is Pure 'n' Simple T-Shirts' shutdown point. If the price falls further, to a price such as $1.40 (point *d*), the company closes down its operations, since total revenue no longer covers variable costs.

Figure 6.3:   Supply Curve for a Perfect Competitor

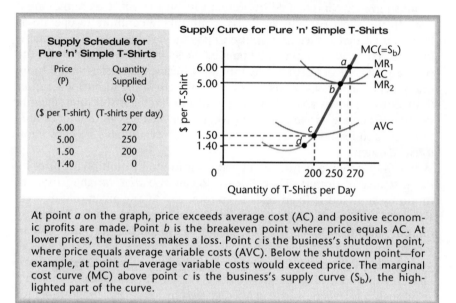

Supply Schedule for Pure 'n' Simple T-Shirts

Price (P)	Quantity Supplied (q)
($ per T-shirt)	(T-shirts per day)
6.00	270
5.00	250
1.50	200
1.40	0

At point *a* on the graph, price exceeds average cost (AC) and positive economic profits are made. Point *b* is the breakeven point where price equals AC. At lower prices, the business makes a loss. Point *c* is the business's shutdown point, where price equals average variable costs (AVC). Below the shutdown point—for example, at point *d*—average variable costs would exceed price. The marginal cost curve (MC) above point *c* is the business's supply curve (S_b), the highlighted part of the curve.

Business's Supply Curve

Figure 6.3 also sheds light on how a change in price influences the operations of a perfectly competitive business. For example, if price falls from $6 to $5, the profit-maximizing output for Pure 'n' Simple T-Shirts changes from 270 to 250 shirts. At the same time, the business's economic profit falls to zero, since point *b* is the breakeven point. Notice that the effect of this price change on the business's quantity supplied is shown as a movement along the marginal cost curve (MC). Because the various profit-maximizing points for the business are all on the marginal cost curve, at least a portion of it represents the **business's supply curve**, S_b. The business's supply curve shows the quantity of output supplied by the business at every possible price. If price moves below the shutdown point (point *c*), Pure 'n' Simple T-Shirts will no longer be in business and its output will fall to zero. Hence, only that part of the marginal cost curve above this point is the business's supply curve (the highlighted part of the MC curve).

business's supply curve: a curve that shows the quantity of output supplied by a business at every possible price

Market Supply Curve

The market supply curve, S_m, for a perfectly competitive industry is created using the supply curves for all businesses in the market. So, for the T-shirt market in which Pure 'n' Simple T-Shirts operates, we have the supply curve S_m as illustrated in Figure 6.4. If there are 100 businesses all identical to Pure 'n' Simple T-Shirts in the industry, then the market supply curve for T-shirts is found by adding the profit-maximizing outputs produced by all 100 businesses at each possible price. Thus, at a price of $6, the quantity supplied in the market would be 27 000 shirts (270 shirts × 100 businesses), given that each business's output is 270 shirts.

Figure 6.4:   Supply Curves for a Perfectly Competitive Business and Market

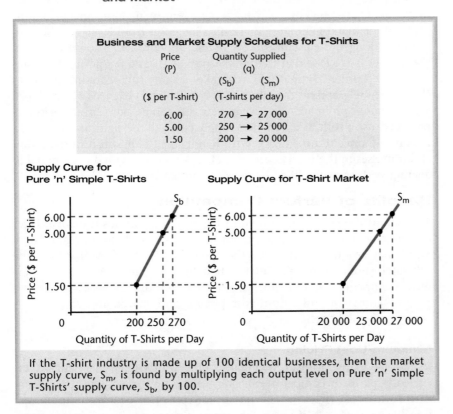

Business and Market Supply Schedules for T-Shirts		
Price (P)	Quantity Supplied (q)	
	(S_b)	(S_m)
($ per T-shirt)	(T-shirts per day)	
6.00	270 →	27 000
5.00	250 →	25 000
1.50	200 →	20 000

If the T-shirt industry is made up of 100 identical businesses, then the market supply curve, S_m, is found by multiplying each output level on Pure 'n' Simple T-Shirts' supply curve, S_b, by 100.

The Long Run

In the long run, ease of entry into and exit from an industry in a perfectly competitive market becomes a crucial factor. Short-run profits and losses cause perfectly competitive markets to move toward a point of long-run equilibrium. Entrepreneurs enter industries where an economic profit can be made, and leave those industries where there are losses. Movement to and from the industry continues until all the businesses in the market reach long-run equilibrium, at which they are just breaking even, with price equalling average cost and a normal profit being made.

The operation of these long-run competitive forces is illustrated in Figure 6.5 for the T-shirt market. We will assume that this is a constant-cost industry in which input prices are fixed regardless of the quantity of T-shirts produced. As a representative business in this industry, Pure 'n' Simple T-Shirts is originally in long-run equilibrium at a price of $5 (point *a* on the left), which is determined by the intersection of the market demand and supply curves, D_0 and S_0, at point *c* on the graph on the right. At this price, Pure 'n' Simple T-Shirts produces 250 shirts per day. Since price equals average cost, it is breaking even, or making zero economic profit. If the market demand for T-shirts increases from D_0 to D_1, the conditions of long-run equilibrium are temporarily broken. The new price in the market is $6, found at the intersection of D_1 and S_0 (point *d*). At this new price, Pure 'n' Simple T-Shirts makes a short-run economic profit, as shown on the graph on the left, since price (point *b*) exceeds average cost. This economic profit acts as a lure to new companies, who enter the industry and cause a shift in the market supply curve to the right, from S_0 to S_1. As a result, price returns to $5. With long-run equilibrium restored (point *e*), businesses in the market are again breaking even with a price equal to average cost, as exemplified by Pure 'n' Simple T-Shirts.

Benefits of Perfect Competition

The long-run equilibrium shown in Figure 6.5 illustrates the advantages of perfectly competitive markets for buyers. It also helps explain Adam Smith's assertion that, through the "invisible hand" of competition, the self-interest of producers ultimately benefits consumers. As long as a perfectly competitive market in long-run equilibrium meets two requirements—known as minimum-cost pricing and marginal-cost pricing—consumers will benefit.

Minimum-Cost Pricing

In addition to operating at the break-even point (where price equals average cost), perfectly competitive businesses in long-run equilibrium practise **minimum-cost pricing**. The minimum-cost price equals the minimum possible average cost. If businesses weren't charging the minimum possible average cost as their price, they would change the scale of production and reduce average costs even further in order to maximize profit. By charging the minimum-cost price of $5 when it is in long-run equilibrium, Pure 'n' Simple T-Shirts, for example, is choosing the least costly combi-

minimum-cost pricing: the practice of setting price where it equals minimum average cost

**Figure 6.5: Long-Run Equilibrium for a Perfectly
Competitive Business**

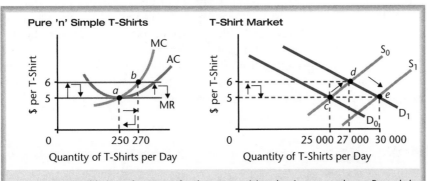

Long-run equilibrium for a perfectly competitive business, such as Pure 'n'
Simple T-Shirts, is shown on the left at point a, where price equals both marginal cost and minimum average cost. Associated with this point is the equilibrium point c for the entire market on the graph on the right. An increase in market demand for T-shirts from D_0 to D_1 shifts equilibrium in the T-shirt market to
point d, at both a higher price and a higher quantity. At the new profit-maximizing point for the business (point b on the left graph), a positive profit is
being made, since price now exceeds average cost. The lure of economic profit
causes new businesses to enter the market. Assuming that this is a constant-cost
industry, the market supply curve shifts to the right, from S_0 to S_1, until price is
driven back down to its original level at point e. On the left graph, Pure 'n'
Simple T-Shirts returns to its long-run equilibrium point a because of these
competitive forces.

nation of inputs. Moreover, it is making zero economic profit, so that all
these cost savings are passed on to T-shirt buyers. The purchasing power
of consumers' incomes when acquiring T-shirts is therefore maximized.

Marginal-Cost Pricing
In long-run equilibrium, perfectly competitive businesses also practise
marginal-cost pricing, meaning they produce at an output level where
price equals marginal cost. The fact that they do so follows from the
equality of marginal revenue and price for perfectly competitive firms.
The profit-maximizing rule means that perfect competitors choose the
quantity of output at which marginal revenue and marginal cost intersect. Since marginal revenue and price are identical for individual businesses, the profit-maximizing rule can be expressed, also, as the condition that price equals marginal cost.

If each business's marginal cost incorporates all possible costs to society,
then a perfectly competitive market in long-run equilibrium operates at a
price that fully reflects the product's opportunity cost. Furthermore, if all
markets in an economy are close to being perfectly competitive, society's

marginal-cost pricing:
the practice of setting
price where it equals
marginal cost

scarce resources are distributed among industries in a way that maximizes the overall satisfaction of consumers. This is because the prices of various products accurately reflect the extra costs of producing them. Considering again the example of T-shirts, if they are priced at $6 while the marginal cost of an additional T-shirt is $3, then more of society's resources should be devoted to T-shirt production. Otherwise, consumers who derive less than $6 worth of satisfaction from this product are not purchasing it, even though many of them would be willing to pay more than the product's marginal cost. Production in this market should therefore be increased.

BRIEF REVIEW

1. All businesses—whatever market structures they operate in—can maximize profits by finding the output level at which marginal revenue intersects marginal cost.

2. A business's economic profit is positive if price is greater than average cost. When price and average cost are equal, the business is at its breakeven point, with economic profit at zero. If price is lower than average cost, then the business is operating at a loss, or negative economic profit.

3. Beyond the breakeven point, where price falls below average cost, a perfect competitor will continue business until the shutdown point, where price equals minimum average variable cost. A perfectly competitive business's supply curve is only the portion of its marginal cost curve that is above the shutdown point.

4. In long-run equilibrium, perfectly competitive businesses break even. They also operate at the minimum-cost and marginal-cost prices, thereby benefiting consumers.

 ## Monopolistic Competition

Because they are price-makers, monopolistic competitors must choose both a level of output and a price when attempting to maximize profits. Thus they apply the profit-maximizing rule in a different way than do perfectly competitive businesses.

Revenue Conditions

Figure 6.6 shows the relationships among price, marginal revenue, and average revenue for a monopolisitic competitor, the Jaded Palate restaurant. In the table, price (column 1) and average revenue (column 5) are equal, just as they are for perfect competitors. However, marginal revenue and average revenue are no longer necessarily the same. Recall that if an average value such as average revenue declines, then its corresponding marginal value (marginal revenue) is below it. For example, when the Jaded Palate sells its first 100 meals, the restaurant's average and marginal revenues both equal $11. But once the next 100 meals are added, average revenue falls to $10. For this to happen, the last 100 meals must each have a lower marginal revenue of $9. Therefore, in the accompanying graph, the demand (D) and average revenue (AR) curves for the Jaded Palate are identical, but demand and marginal revenue (MR) are equal only at their initial points of zero quantity. As the quantity of output for the restaurant rises, marginal revenue drops below price. This follows from the connection between average and marginal values.

Figure 6.6:   Revenues for a Monopolistic Competitor

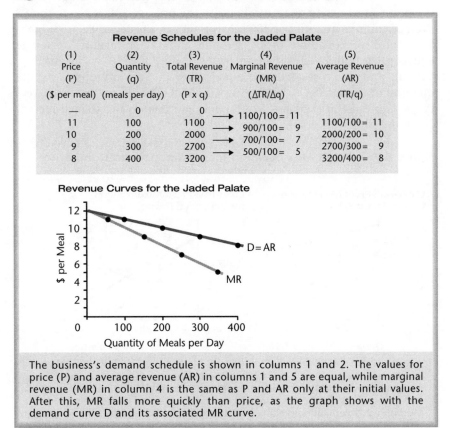

Revenue Schedules for the Jaded Palate

(1) Price (P) ($ per meal)	(2) Quantity (q) (meals per day)	(3) Total Revenue (TR) (P x q)	(4) Marginal Revenue (MR) ($\Delta TR/\Delta q$)	(5) Average Revenue (AR) (TR/q)
—	0	0		
11	100	1100	1100/100 = 11	1100/100 = 11
10	200	2000	900/100 = 9	2000/200 = 10
9	300	2700	700/100 = 7	2700/300 = 9
8	400	3200	500/100 = 5	3200/400 = 8

Revenue Curves for the Jaded Palate

The business's demand schedule is shown in columns 1 and 2. The values for price (P) and average revenue (AR) in columns 1 and 5 are equal, while marginal revenue (MR) in column 4 is the same as P and AR only at their initial values. After this, MR falls more quickly than price, as the graph shows with the demand curve D and its associated MR curve.

The Short Run

Given its ability to choose price, the monopolistic competitor maximizes its short-run profit by first finding the appropriate quantity of output, and then using this quantity level to determine the highest possible price it can charge. These typical profit-making activities are illustrated on the left in Figure 6.7. In addition to the business's demand and marginal revenue curves, the graph shows the relevant curves for marginal cost and average cost. Once again, in order to maximize profit, the business must find the point at which marginal revenue and marginal cost intersect. This is point *a*, which is at the profit-maximizing quantity of 200 meals. Price is then set at $10 by drawing a vertical line up to the business's demand curve at point *b*, and then across to the price axis.

The Jaded Palate could be making an economic profit or loss in the short run, or it could be breaking even. As in the case of perfect competitors, the answer can be found by comparing price and average cost at the profit-maximizing quantity. Because the price of $10 is above the $8 average cost at a quantity of 200 meals (point *c*), the Jaded Palate is making a positive economic profit. On the graph, the revenue rectangle equals price multiplied by the quantity of output ($10 × 200 meals = $2000), and the cost rectangle equals average cost multiplied by the quantity of output ($8 × 200 meals = $1600). Therefore, the profit rectangle equals $400 ($2000 – $1600) and is shown as the shaded rectangle in the short-run graph.

Figure 6.7:   Profit Maximization for a Monopolistic Competitor

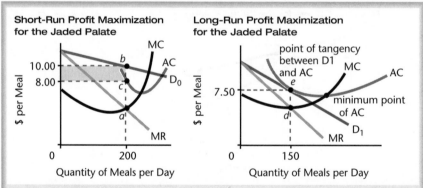

On the left, the business's short-run profit is maximized at point *a*, where the marginal revenue (MR) and marginal cost (MC) curves intersect at a quantity of 200 meals. The $10.00 price is found by drawing a vertical line up to point *b* on the business's demand curve, D₀, and then across to the price axis. The business's total profit is shown by the shaded rectangle, which has a height equalling the difference between price at point *b* and average cost (AC) at point *c*. The width of the rectangle equals the profit-maximizing output (200 meals). On the right, the long-run profit-maximizing output of 150 meals occurs at the point where MR and MC are equal (point *d*). The price of $7.50—which equals long-run AC—is point *e* on the business's long-run demand curve (D₁).

The Long Run

It is in the long run that the competitive elements of monopolistic competition become evident. Because short-run economic profits are being made in the restaurant industry, new businesses enter the market in the long run. The graph on the right in Figure 6.7 shows how the increase in both competition and supply shifts demand (from D_0 to the new D_1 curve) for established restaurants such as the Jaded Palate. Once again, the market adjusts: profits go down and, eventually, long-run equilibrium is reached at point e. Besides showing the Jaded Palate's demand and marginal revenue curves, the graph on the right shows the marginal cost and average cost curves in the long run. The profit-maximizing point where marginal revenue equals marginal cost now occurs at a quantity of 150 meals (point d). The new price is $7.50, which is found at point e on the long-run demand curve, D_1.

Note that monopolistic competitors reach neither the minimum-cost nor the marginal-cost pricing conditions in long-run equilibrium. Since average cost and price are equal at point e on Figure 6.7, the business is breaking even in the long run. However, this price does *not* equal the minimum point on the average cost curve. This minimum-cost price could only be achieved at a higher output for each business. Figure 6.7 also illustrates that in the long run, for monopolistic competitors, price (point e) is greater than marginal cost. This means that too few units of output are produced for price to reflect the product's full opportunity cost.

Oligopoly

We have already seen in Chapter 5 how an oligopoly that is characterized by rivalry among competitors faces a kinked demand curve. Recall that the kinked demand curve is based on the different responses of competitors when the business either raises or reduces its price. In Figure 6.8, when Universal Motors increases the price of its Centaur car, rivals do not increase their prices. Thus, the quantity demanded of Centaurs decreases sharply, giving the flatter segment of the demand curve. Were Universal Motors to decrease its price on the Centaur, rivals would follow suit, so the change in quantity demanded would be small, giving the steeper segment of the demand curve.

Revenue Conditions

The marginal revenue for Centaur cars is shown in the table and on the graph in Figure 6.8. Just as with the demand curve, the marginal revenue curve has two distinct segments. In this case, however, the flatter segment and the steeper segment do not meet, but must be joined by a vertical line at the quantity of 20 000 cars, the quantity associated with the $30 000 price.

Figure 6.8:   Profit Maximization for an Oligopolist

Profit Maximization Table for Centaur Cars

(1) Price (P) (=AR) ($ thousands per car)	(2) Quantity (q) (thousands of cars per year)	(3) Total Revenue (TR) (P x q) ($ millions)	(4) Marginal Revenue (MR) (ΔTR/Δq) ($ thousands per car)	(5) Marginal Cost (MC) ($ thousands per car)	(6) Average Cost (AC) ($ thousands per car)
—	0	0			
$35	10	350	35	15	30
30	**20**	**600**	25	10	**20**
20	25	500	−20	15	19
10	30	300	−40	25	20

Profit Maximization Graph for Centaur Cars

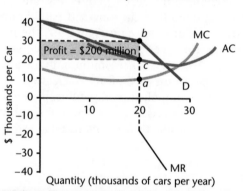

In an oligopoly characterized by rivalry, a business faces a kinked demand curve, D, with two segments. The marginal revenue curve also has two segments; however, the segments are separate, so they must be joined with a vertical line. On the graph, the marginal revenue (MR) and marginal cost (MC) curves meet at point *a*, giving a profit-maximizing output level of 20 000 cars. To determine price for these 20 000 cars, we must look to the demand curve; at a quantity demanded of 20 000, the price should be $30 000 (point *b*). According to the table also, the values of marginal revenue (column 4) and marginal cost (column 5) pass through the same values around an output level of 20 000.

Profit Maximization

To maximize profit, the oligopolist, like all businesses, must follow the profit-maximizing rule. Therefore, Universal Motors should produce at the output level where the marginal revenue and marginal cost curves intersect, at point *a* in Figure 6.8, or 20 000 cars. According to the demand curve, this quantity of cars should be sold at a price of $30 000 (found by extending a vertical line from a quantity of 20 000 to the demand curve,

THE ROLE OF PROFIT

at point *b*, which aligns on the price axis with a $30 000 price). Looking at the table in Figure 6.8, we can see that marginal cost and marginal revenue pass through the same values closest to an output of 20 000 cars.

At the profit-maximizing point, an oligopolist may make a positive, negative, or zero economic profit in the short run. When average cost is below price at the business's profit-maximizing output, the business makes a positive economic profit. When average cost is above price at the profit-maximizing output, the business makes an economic loss. When average cost and price are equal at the profit-maximizing output, the business breaks even. In the case of Universal Motors, at the output level of 20 000 cars and the price of $30 000 (point *b* in Figure 6.8), the average cost is $20 000 (point *c*). Therefore, the company makes an economic profit on Centaur cars equal to quantity multiplied by the difference between price and average cost, or $200 million [20 000 × ($30 000 – $20 000)]

The kinked demand curve—which applies equally in both the short run and the long run—explains why rival oligopolists tend to keep prices constant even as costs change. In the case of the Centaur illustrated in Figure 6.8, as long as the marginal cost and marginal revenue curves intersect at a quantity of 20 000, Universal Motors will not change its price. Only if marginal cost changed so dramatically that its curve and the marginal revenue curve no longer intersected at 20 000 (the vertical connection between the two segments) would Universal Motors change its price.

As in the case of monopolistic competitors, oligopolists achieve neither the minimum-cost nor the marginal-cost pricing conditions. Because of limited competition created by barriers to entry, an oligopolist that faces rivals can remain indefinitely at one price, such as $30 000 in Figure 6.8. At this price, the business is making a positive economic profit and fails to reach the output level where average cost is at its lowest value. So, the minimum-cost pricing condition is broken. The condition of marginal-cost pricing is also broken; as Figure 6.8 shows, the price of $30 000 is greater than marginal cost. The same conclusions apply for colluding oligopolists, as the prices they charge are even higher.

Thinking About Economics

Why are there no supply curves for businesses in imperfectly competitive markets?

A supply curve is relevant only when a business plans how much output to produce at various prices. Perfect competitors do this, but not sellers in other types of markets. Given its demand curve, a monopolistic competitor or oligopolist chooses *one* output level and then charges the highest possible price the demand allows at that quantity. It is therefore impossible for an imperfectly competitive business to devise a supply curve that is independent of the demand conditions it faces.

BRIEF REVIEW

1. A monopolistic competitor faces a marginal revenue curve that equals its corresponding demand curve only at their initial (zero) values. From that point, the marginal revenue curve falls faster than does the demand curve.

2. In the short run, a monopolistic competitor can make an economic profit or loss. In the long run, however, competitive forces drive monopolistic competitors to a breakeven point.

3. An oligopolist in a market that is characterized by rivalry faces a marginal revenue curve of two disconnected segments, one steeper than the other. These segments are associated with the two portions of the kinked demand curve.

4. Because of limited competition, oligopolists can make an economic profit even in the long run.

5. Imperfectly competitive businesses satisfy neither the minimum-cost nor the marginal-cost pricing conditions met by perfectly competitive businesses in the long run.

 **Monopoly**

Unlike businesses in other market structures, the monopolist does not have to worry about competitors when it chooses its profit-maximizing point. In contrast to the horizontal demand curve the perfect competitor faces, the monopolist faces a negatively sloped demand curve for the entire market.

Revenue Conditions

Figure 6.9 shows the demand and revenue conditions for Megacomp, the sole seller of supercomputers. As for monopolistic competitors and oligopolists, only the initial values for Megacomp's price and marginal revenue (columns 1 and 4 of the table) are equal. As the graph also demonstrates, marginal revenues drop below price when output increases. Notice that the curves look similar to those for the Jaded Palate (Figure 6.7). The difference is that Megacomp's demand curve is less elastic. This is because the monopolist is selling a product with no close substitutes.

Profit Maximization

With its ability to set price, Megacomp applies the profit-maximizing rule in the same way as imperfectly competitive sellers. Both in the short run and the long run, the profit-maximizing output is found where marginal revenue intersects marginal cost. As shown in Figure 6.9, the marginal rev-

Figure 6.9:   Profit Maximization for a Monopolist

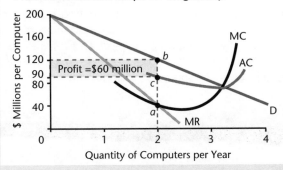

Profit Maximization Table for Megacomp

(1) Price (P) (AR)	(2) Quantity (q)	(3) Total Revenue (TR) (P x q)	(4) Marginal Revenue (MR) (ΔTR/Δq)	(5) Marginal Cost (MC)	(6) Average Cost (AC)
($ millions per computer)	(computers per year)	($ millions)	($ millions per computer)	($ millions per computer)	($ millions per computer)
	0	0			
			160	60	
160	1	160			140
			80	40	
120	**2**	**240**			**90**
			0	70	
80	3	240			83
			−80	150	
40	4	160			100

Profit Maximization Graph for Megacomp

On the graph, the profit-maximizing output is found at the intersection of the marginal revenue (MR) and marginal cost (MC) curves (at point *a*.) At this output of 2 computers, the demand curve gives a price (at point *b*) of $120 million (determined by drawing a vertical line from the quantity of 2 to the demand curve, then across to the price axis). The table also shows that marginal revenue and marginal cost pass through the same values around an output of 2 computers and a price of $120 million. On the graph, Megacomp's profit ($60 million) is the area of the shaded rectangle, with a height equalling the difference between price (point *b*) and average cost (point *c*), and with a width equalling the quantity of 2.

enue and marginal cost curves for Megacomp intersect at point *a*, at a quantity of 2 computers. Once again, the price for this output level is determined by the demand curve. At the quantity of 2, the demand curve gives a price (at point *b*) of $120 million. The table shows the same results: marginal revenue (column 4) and marginal cost (column 5) pass through the same values nearest the quantity of 2 computers and price of $120 million.

Like other companies, the monopolist may be making an economic profit or a loss, or it may be breaking even, depending on whether the business's average cost is above, below, or equal to price. Because in our example Megacomp has an average cost of $90 million (at point *c*) that is below the $120 million price (point *b*), it is making a positive economic profit. The business's profit rectangle has a height equal to the distance between points *b* and *c* ($30 million = $120 million – $90 million) and a width of 2 computers, giving a total economic profit of $60 million.

Thinking About Economics

How easy is it for a monopolist, such as Megacomp, to estimate the profit-maximizing values for price and quantity?

The task requires estimating both demand and costs. Whereas the perfect competitor has an easy time of estimating demand conditions (because market price is the only factor to be determined), monopolists (as well as imperfectly competitive businesses) have a harder task of estimating how much consumers will buy at each possible price. As far as cost estimates are concerned, all businesses must estimate how much explicit and implicit costs would be at each possible output level. When a business sells more than one item, it must also distribute its costs among these various products.

Notice that, like both monopolistic competitors and oligopolists, a monopolist satisfies neither of the conditions for consumer benefit: minimum-cost pricing and marginal-cost pricing. Because the monopolist has no competitors due to barriers to entry, it can keep its price constant in the long run. In the case of Megacomp, this price would be $120 million, as shown in Figure 6.9. Since price does not equal the lowest possible average cost, the minimum-cost pricing condition is not met. Similarly, this price is not equal to the business's marginal cost, meaning that the marginal-cost pricing condition is not met either.

Monopoly Versus Perfect Competition

To see the impact on price and quantity of a monopoly, let's compare them with price and quantity in a perfectly competitive market. To do this, we'll consider what would happen if a perfectly competitive market in long-run equilibrium were transformed into a monopoly.

The market demand and supply curves for the T-shirt industry are shown in Figure 6.10. Equilibrium for a competitive market occurs at the intersection of these curves (point *a*), with a price of $4 and a quantity of 22 000 shirts. If the industry becomes one large company, the market demand curve remains the same no matter what the industry structure. With the change to a monopoly, the demand curve for the entire market becomes the business's demand curve. There is a significant change, however. Now that the business is a monopolist, the relationship between price (given by the demand curve) and marginal revenue is no longer equal; as was the case for Megacomp, the marginal revenue curve falls below the demand curve.

Figure 6.10:   Monopoly Versus Perfect Competition

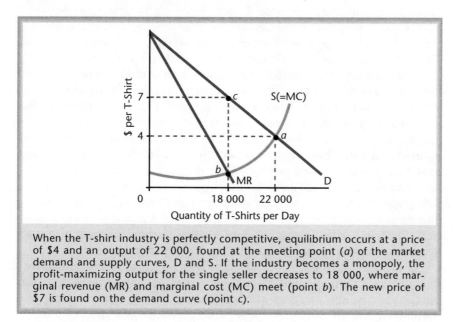

When the T-shirt industry is perfectly competitive, equilibrium occurs at a price of $4 and an output of 22 000, found at the meeting point (*a*) of the market demand and supply curves, D and S. If the industry becomes a monopoly, the profit-maximizing output for the single seller decreases to 18 000, where marginal revenue (MR) and marginal cost (MC) meet (point *b*). The new price of $7 is found on the demand curve (point *c*).

Next let's consider supply. Recall that a perfect competitor's supply curve shows the quantity of output supplied by the business at each possible price, and is represented by a portion of the marginal cost curve. In turn, the market supply curve is the sum of all supply curves of businesses in the market. After the change to a monopoly, production facilities remain the same as before, with inputs originally owned by the perfectly competitive producers now in the hands of one business. When the monopolist combines the cost figures for these various facilities, it finds a marginal cost curve that is merely an extension of the perfectly competitive supply curve, shown in Figure 6.10.

Effects on Price and Quantity

The T-shirt monopoly's profit-maximizing output is 18 000, where the new marginal revenue and marginal cost curves intersect (point *b*). At this output level, the price is $7 (point *c*), as found on the demand curve.

Thus, with the transformation from perfect competition to monopoly, T-shirts become more expensive and fewer of them are produced.

Regulation of Natural Monopolies

When an industry is a natural monopoly, economies of scale mean that the single business can produce a product at a significantly lower per-unit cost than could several companies. To ensure that these cost savings are passed on to the consumer, governments usually intervene in natural monopolies. Either they provide the service through a government-owned corporation (as in the case of Canada Post), or they regulate the single private company in the market (just as the Canadian Radio-television and Telecommunications Commission regulates cable television businesses).

Public agencies that regulate monopolies have a difficult task. Not only must regulators estimate each business's costs, they must also try to choose the "best" possible price for the monopolist to charge. Consider the case of a company that is the sole provider of cable television in a particular province. Because it is a natural monopoly, economies of scale dominate its long run. Thus, the lowest point (point *d*) of the long-run average cost curve tends to have a position above demand at the relevant quantity, as shown on the left in Figure 6.11. With no regulation, as shown on the left graph, the business will base its output and price on the profit-maximizing point—point *a*, where marginal revenue and marginal cost intersect. Price and output are at $45 and 1 million subscribers (point *b*), and the business makes economic profits equal to the shaded rectangle.

At first glance, the task for the regulatory agency seems straightforward: force the monopolist to operate at a point that satisfies both the minimum-cost and marginal-cost pricing conditions. Unfortunately, it's more complex. Operating at a level where average cost reaches a minimum (point *d* on the left graph) is not a viable option for the business because at this output level of 2.5 million subscribers the price that the company can charge (at point *e*) is lower than average cost.

Marginal-Cost Price

As an alternative, the monopoly could be forced to select the marginal-cost price, where the marginal cost curve crosses the demand curve. This scenario is shown on the middle graph in Figure 6.11. Thus, the business would choose an output of 2 million subscribers at a price of $15 (point *f*). At this point, price reflects the opportunity cost of scarce resources used in the industry but, because price is below the business's average cost at this output level (point *g*), the business is again making an economic loss. Since no business will continue with long-term losses, the government might give the monopolist a subsidy equalling the loss *if* the government considers the product desirable. The business can then break even when it charges the marginal-cost price. Some government-run monopolies

Figure 6.11: Regulating a Natural Monopoly

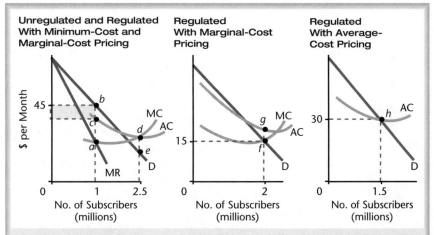

On the left, the unregulated company chooses price and quantity at $45 and 1 million cable TV subscribers using points *a* and *b*, and makes a profit equal to the shaded profit rectangle. Regulating price for minimum-cost and marginal-cost pricing (at point *e*) would result in the company making a loss, since the average cost is higher (at point *d*). Regulating with marginal-cost pricing, shown on the middle graph, would give a price of $15 and quantity of 2 million subscribers (at point *f*). Given that average cost is higher (at point *g*), the business again makes a loss. Regulating with average-cost pricing, shown on the right, would give a price of $30 and quantity of 1.5 million subscribers (at point *h*), allowing the business to break even.

receive such subsidies. Urban transit companies, for example, depend on subsidies from provincial or municipal governments so that prices can be kept below average costs.

Average-Cost Price
Public subsidies are usually not feasible for private companies. Taxpayers tend to disapprove of their money going to big business, even if it enables these companies to charge a socially beneficial price. Therefore, another approach must be used. Often the regulator will use **average-cost pricing**, so that the monopolist can break even without public funds. This option is shown on the graph on the right in Figure 6.11—the average cost and demand curves meet at $30 and 1.5 million subscribers (point *h*).

As a practical matter, regulators applying the average-cost price do not undertake the cumbersome task of estimating the cost and demand curves of the regulated business. Instead, they control profits directly. A business's **accounting-profit rate**, or rate of return, is its accounting profit divided by owner's equity and expressed as a percentage:

average-cost pricing: the practice of setting price where it equals average cost

accounting-profit rate: a measure of a business's profitability, calculated as its accounting profit divided by owner's equity

fair rate of return: the maximum accounting-profit rate allowed for a regulated monopoly

$$\text{Accounting-profit rate} = \frac{\text{accounting profit}}{\text{owner's equity}} \times 100\%$$

The regulating agency imposes a ceiling, such as 8 percent or 9 percent, on the profit rate the business can earn. This **fair rate of return** is arrived at by estimating how much the business needs to cover both explicit costs (such as wages and outlays on materials) and implicit costs (in particular, the business's normal profits).

While it is often the only viable method of regulation, setting a fair rate of return leads to inefficiencies. Because of profit controls, there is little incentive for the company's managers to control costs. Indeed, the easiest way for the business to raise its price is by inflating costs. Generous perks, bloated payrolls, and plush offices are then paid for by consumers in the form of higher prices. Regulators try to overcome such problems by imposing performance standards on the business, but these standards are difficult to implement.

"Gentlemen you've asked me about this company's performance...I'd have to say... about the same."

SOURCE: Courtesy of Arnie of Arnietoons.

BRIEF REVIEW

1. The monopolist faces a demand curve that is equal to marginal revenue only at its initial value. Marginal revenue drops more quickly than price as output rises.

2. A monopolist can make a positive economic profit in both the short run and the long run, and meets neither of the minimum-cost and marginal-cost pricing conditions.

3. A monopolist necessarily charges a higher price and produces a lower quantity than would a perfectly competitive industry in the same market.

4. Regulators force natural monopolies to charge either a marginal-cost price, in which case public subsidies must be provided, or an average-cost price, where the businesses are just breaking even.

Key Concepts

average revenue
marginal revenue
profit-maximizing rule
breakeven point

shutdown point
business's supply curve
minimum-cost pricing
marginal-cost pricing

average-cost pricing
accounting-profit rate
fair rate of return

Can Capitalism Survive?

Joseph Schumpeter and the Prospects for Capitalism

Joseph Schumpeter (1883–1950) is one of the most famous economists of the twentieth century, and the originality of his ideas and breadth of his learning have been matched by few others. Born to a middle-class business family, he enjoyed an aristocratic upbringing after his father died and his mother married a high-ranking military commander in the Austrian army. Schumpeter studied law and economics at the prestigious University of Vienna. After working as a lawyer, he took up a career as a professor of economics. For a brief period after World War I, he served as the Minister of Finance in the Austrian government. In the 1930s, the political turmoil surrounding the rise of the Nazis in Germany caused him to move to the United States, where he taught for many years at Harvard University.

Schumpeter and His Influence

Schumpeter's work is fascinating because of his ability to combine seemingly contradictory ideas. While a strong supporter of capitalism and private markets, he devised a theory of capitalist development that has interesting parallels with the work of Karl Marx. Like Marx, Schumpeter used not only the tools of economics but also the other social sciences. He was therefore able to highlight the role played by politics and culture in affecting economic conditions.

The crucial player in Schumpeter's theory of capitalism is the entrepreneur. For Schumpeter, entrepreneurs are much more than risk-takers—they are innovators who, through imagination and creativity, supply new products or adopt new types of technology. While not necessarily inventors, they are able to bring fresh ideas to the marketplace. As Schumpeter noted:

> To carry any improvement into effect is a task entirely different from the inventing of it, and a task, moreover, requiring entirely different kinds of aptitudes. Although entrepreneurs of course *may* be inventors just as they may be capitalists, they are inventors not by nature of their function but by coincidence and vice versa.[1]

Joseph Schumpeter
SOURCE: The Bettmann Archive

Schumpeter saw entrepreneurs as the driving forces of economic progress. He believed that a capitalist system would ensure the fastest possible pace of technological change, because capitalism allows entrepreneurs to keep the profits resulting from their innovations.

According to Schumpeter, the importance of perfectly competitive markets is overrated in economic theory. In real capitalist economies, he said, competition usually takes place between a few rivals in oligopolistic markets. In pursuit of profit and market power, the rivals introduce new products and production methods, which in turn lead to economic growth and revitalize the capitalist system. Schumpeter called this process "creative destruction," since it destroys parts of the economy at the same time as it creates new ones.

Predictions for the Future

Given Schumpeter's opposition to socialism and his strong support for capitalism, we might expect that he would predict the downfall of socialism and final victory of capitalism throughout the world. On the contrary, he believed that in the long run capitalism was doomed, not because of its internal economic contradictions, but because of cultural and political trends flowing from its success. Hence, in answer to the question, "Can capitalism survive?" he gave the straightforward answer, "No. I do not think it can."[2]

According to Schumpeter, because of the advantages they possess, giant companies will gradually take over most industries. In the process, the innovative spirit that once guided them will be crushed, as the imaginative entrepreneur is replaced by the cautious professional manager at the helm of business. Without the entrepreneur, there will no longer be a force in society to support the institution of private property.

At the same time, the growing class of intellectuals—professors, writers, and journalists—that live well off the prosperity provided by the capitalist system, will use their persuasive powers to turn others against capitalism. Therefore, a majority of people will also become opposed to property rights. Why are so many intellectuals hostile to capitalism? Because, stated Schumpeter, most of them are outsiders who are much more competent at criticizing the system than they are at working within it.

Schumpeter predicted that the elimination of the entrepreneur and the new popular hostility toward capitalism would lead to more government involvement in the economy. Attempts would be made by government bureaucrats to smooth out economic fluctuations as well as reduce inequalities in the distribution of incomes. Gradually, the role of private property would shrink, and capitalist societies would turn toward socialism—of either the democratic or the authoritarian variety.

Relevance for Today

It is important to note that Schumpeter developed his theories before and during World War II, *before* the massive expansion in government activity that took place in developed capitalist countries such as Canada. In the 1960s and 1970s, as criticism of capitalist institutions became common in Canada and other countries, many commentators suggested that Schumpeter's forecasts contained a good deal of truth. Are his predictions still as applicable in the 1980s and 1990s as they were in previous decades? Some would argue that there has been a resurgence in entrepreneurship and popular support for capitalism that now makes Schumpeter's theories less relevant than they once were.

> During the late 1960s...Schumpeter's predictions seemed to be coming true. Third world nations, newly liberated from Europe, turned to socialism. By the early 1970s, Ph.D.'s were driving taxicabs and blasting the establishment. But what did the 1980s bring us? Yuppies, short hair, striped shirts, and a parade of underdeveloped nations trading *Das Kapital* in for *Dress for Success*. Even the [former] Soviet Union strives to revise its...economy. Nobody urges centralized planning anymore.... Even if a return to market mechanisms does not magically turn poverty into wealth, at least governments have jettisoned rigid, ideological abhorrence of market economic systems.[3]

But, right or wrong, Schumpeter's work provides a classic example of how economic theorizing can be made to include not only economic factors but also political and social trends.

NOTES

[1] Joseph A. Schumpeter, *The Theory of Economic Development* (New York: Oxford University Press, 1961), pp. 88–89.

[2] Joseph A. Schumpeter, *Capitalism, Socialism and Democracy* (New York: Harper & Row, 1976), p. 61, as quoted in *New Ideas From Dead Economists* by Todd G. Buchholz. Copyright © 1989 by Todd G. Buchholz. Used by permission of Dutton Signet, a division of Penguin Books USA Inc.

[3] From *New Ideas From Dead Economists* by Todd G. Buchholz. Copyright © 1989 by Todd G. Buchholz. Used by permission of Dutton Signet, a division of Penguin Books USA Inc.

1. Give and explain three specific examples of "creative destruction" in the local, national, or global economy today.

2. Schumpeter believed the innovation of the entrepreneur to be the key to capitalism. With this in mind, assess the state of capitalism in Canada today, and then predict its future in a short essay.

3. The Industrial Revolution in the late 1700s and early 1800s was a period of technological innovation that transformed Britain's economy and ushered in a period of unprecedented economic growth from which the capitalist system took root. Research this period of economic history, then prepare a report examining the extent to which this period supports Schumpeter's theory.

Ted's Excellent Adventure:

The Debate Over a Growing Multimedia Empire

If Joseph Schumpeter were alive today, he would no doubt point to the Canadian media magnate Ted Rogers as exemplifying the entrepreneur. The following article and editorial give two perspectives on the owner of Rogers Communications, just as he was poised to take over Maclean Hunter Ltd.

The trouble with spotting hot trends and riding them to commercial success is that real trends take time. Yet there is also a paradox. The most successful businesspeople are like Wayne Gretzky: they get there before the puck does.

And make a profit doing it.

Ted Rogers has long been such a player.

In the 1950s, the telephone companies could have gone into cable TV but chose against it. Instead, a few Canadian entrepreneurs did—among them the aforementioned Rogers—and Canada is now the most cabled country in the world. Fully 72% of Canadians subscribe to cable; the system is available to 95% of all homes.

In the 1960s, when only 5% of Canadians could even tune in to a new-fangled thing called FM radio, Ted Rogers bought CHFI, an FM radio station. Today, everyone seems to own more FM radios than they have ears to listen with. Coming soon: portable in-car FM radios coupled with digital, recordable CD players.

Fifteen years ago, Rogers risked his reputation, once again, on cellular telephones—well before most people even held the notion that one day they'd want to be summoned wherever they sat by someone they'd rather avoid. Today, Rogers Cantel Communications offer more than big-city gadgets for high-pressure insurance agents—cellular phones are available to 85% of Canadians.

Through it all, Cantel Chief Executive Officer George Fierheller was saying this week, Ted Rogers's business philosophy has always been simple: "Find a need and fill it."

But Rogers is an even rarer bird. He's a visionary, and there's more to what he does all day than finding needs and filling them.

While others banter about whether the "Information Superhighway" is a pipeline or a pipedream, Ted Rogers is getting on with building that very thing by offering to take over Maclean Hunter Ltd., Canada's largest publisher.

By combining Rogers and Maclean Hunter with its trade publications, directories, newspapers, and consumer magazines, Rogers adds instant content to the electronic delivery mechanisms he already possesses. That synergy is critical, because it is content, not technology, that will drive future infotech success.

But there's something else happening here that's well worth celebrating: the renaissance of the entrepreneur-owners.

In the new economy, large old-line companies will only be successful if there's an individual at the top with an overarching vision. And the guts to take a risk.

Rogers Communications, in fact, is today a large corporation. But it's a large corporation run by a visionary Canadian.

Ted Rogers knows he isn't just fishing for an entity called Maclean Hunter; he's out there chasing tomorrow.

SOURCE: Adapted from Rod McQueen, "MH Can Fill Up Rogers' Pipeline," in *The Financial Post*, 3 February 1994, p. 5.

Canadians communicate with each other by telephone, computers, fax machines and through the media of radio, television, newspapers, magazines and books.

With his successful $3 billion takeover of Maclean Hunter Ltd., Ted Rogers has become Canada's undisputed multimedia mogul, controlling a corporate octopus with tentacles that reach into nearly every communications field.

As Rogers sees it, he's defending Canada from foreign media giants: "If we're to maintain a distinctive Canadian voice, it's essential we build companies of comparable scale and sophistication. It's vital to have strong Canadian companies at the forefront of the electronic highway."

But with such a concentration of power, there's a grave risk that the "distinctive voice" of Canada could become the voice of Ted Rogers alone. As Ian Morrison of the Friends of Canadian Broadcasting put it, "What you're getting is something that approaches mind control."

In cable TV alone, the deal could give Rogers and his allies control over the bulk of the market in a string of major cities, including Vancouver, Calgary and Victoria; in the greater Metro Toronto area, his monopoly would extend into 70 per cent of homes.

Since cable technology is changing from a one-way delivery network for broadcasters to an interactive medium for providing a vast array of consumer services, Rogers' monopoly would give him awesome new powers.

Take electronic home shopping, for example. Whether it's ordering pizza by television, checking out real estate from an armchair, or doing your banking with a channel-changer in your hand, Ted Rogers could decide whom you're going to do business with.

Newspapers are exploring the possibility of delivering classified ads through your TV set. If Rogers decides that he's going to supply this kind of service, would he give equal access to all newspapers which wanted to compete?

Or would he price some potential competitors out of the market, grant his own Toronto Sun Channel 1 for classified ads, and relegate others to Channel 396?

Rogers has dismissed all these concerns: "In the multimedia environment of the future," he said, "we must broaden these policies to ensure that there is fair, open and equal access for all voices, from *Chatelaine* to *The Toronto Star*, from CBC Newsworld to MuchMusic...You have my word that with Rogers, there will be total access to everyone on equal terms."

No matter how sincere Rogers is, public policy cannot be based on personal expressions of good will alone.

With the takeover of Maclean Hunter, he is driving Canada on to the on-ramp of the information superhighway. But Canadians have no idea where it may take them.

SOURCE: Abridged from "Who Will Have Access to the King's Highway?" (editorial) from *The Toronto Star*, 13 March 1994, p. C2.

Developing Application and Analysis Skills

1. Explain the relevance to modern business of the chapter's opening quotation. Based on the chapter, what can you add to the quotation?

2. The owner of Tom Thumb Tomatoes sells 600 kg of tomatoes at a price of $2 per kilogram, and finds that she can increase her revenue to $1296 when she sells another 48 kg.

   a) Calculate total revenue, average revenue, and marginal revenue for this product at each output level.
   b) Is the business an example of a perfect competitor? Explain.
   c) Identify and explain the relationship among the business's price, marginal revenue, and average revenue. What factors are responsible for this relationship?

3. A craftsperson sells 42 handmade purses for a total revenue of $3780, and finds that he can increase his revenue by $90 when he produces another purse. The total cost of production rises by $87 when this additional purse is produced.

   a) Determine whether or not the craftsperson should produce the additional purse.
   b) Calculate and explain what would happen to profit if one more purse, which adds $80 to total revenue and $91 to total cost, is produced.

4. a) Using the table for Paula's Perfectly Competitive Pottery Products, create a graph showing the total revenue and total cost curves for the business. Indicate on the graph the areas of possible profit or loss.
   b) Copy and complete the table for Paula's Perfectly Competitive Pottery Products.
   c) Create a second graph for the business showing the marginal revenue, marginal cost, and average cost curves. Indicate the profit-maximizing point, as well as areas of possible profit or loss.

5. a) Copy and complete the table for Harry's Handmade Tiffany Lamps.
   b) Create a graph showing the business's marginal cost, marginal revenue, average cost, and average variable cost curves.
   c) Indicate on your graph the profit-maximizing point.
   d) Outline and label the revenue, cost, and profit rectangles.
   e) Indicate on your graph the breakeven point. Explain why the business breaks even at this point.
   f) Indicate on your graph the shutdown point. Explain why the business shuts down at this point.

6. What are the three most important decisions that a perfect competitor faces? Explain.

7. Sketch the demand curve for a perfect competitor and the demand curve for a monopolistic competitor. Account for the difference between the two curves.

8. a) Copy and complete the table for Differentiated Portraits (page 180) a monopolistically competitive business that sells family portrait packages.
   b) Create a graph showing the demand (average revenue) and marginal revenue curves. Explain the relationship between the curves.
   c) Plot and draw the marginal cost and average cost curves, and then indicate the cost, revenue, and profit rectangles. Finally, indicate the profit-maximizing level of output.
   d) Confirm the profit-maximizing level of output using the table.

Profit Maximization Table for Paula's Perfectly Competitive Pottery Products

Price	Quantity	Marginal Revenue	Marginal Cost	Total Revenue	Total Cost	Average Cost	Profit
	0			0	30		
—	1	—	—	30	58	—	—
—	2	—	—	60	78	—	—
—	3	—	—	90	94	—	—
—	4	—	—	120	108	—	—
—	5	—	—	150	124	—	—
—	6	—	—	180	144	—	—
—	7	—	—	210	176	—	—
—	8	—	—	240	226	—	—
—	9	—	—	270	306	—	—
—	10	—	—	300	426	—	—

Profit Maximization Table for Harry's Handmade Tiffany Lamps

Price (P) ($ per lamp)	Quantity (q) (lamps)	Fixed Cost (FC)	Variable Cost (VC)	Total Cost (TC)	Average Fixed Cost (AFC)	Average Variable Cost (AVC)	Average Cost (AC)	Marginal Cost (MC)	Marginal Revenue (MR)
120	0	120	0	—					
120	1	120	30	—	—	—	—	—	—
120	2	120	42	—	—	—	—	—	—
120	3	120	60	—	—	—	—	—	—
120	4	120	100	—	—	—	—	—	—
120	5	120	195	—	—	—	—	—	—
120	6	120	388	—	—	—	—	—	—
120	7	120	752	—	—	—	—	—	—

Price (P) ($ per package)	Quantity (q) (packages)	Total Revenue (TR)	Marginal Revenue (MR)	Average Revenue (AR)	Total Cost (TC)	Marginal Cost (MC)	Average Cost (AC)	Total Profit (TR – TC)
90	1	—		—	70		—	—
85	2	—	—	—	100		—	—
80	3	—	—	—	120	—	—	—
75	4	—	—	—	140	—	—	—
70	5	—	—	—	175	—	—	—
65	6	—	—	—	230	—	—	—
60	7	—	—	—	345	—	—	—
55	8	—	—	—	540	—	—	—

Profit Maximization Table for Differentiated Portraits

e) Describe the possible effects of advertising on the demand curve for the business. Outline and explain other possible effects.

9. a) Copy and complete the table for Fly-by-Night Airlines, an oligopolist.
   b) Create a graph showing the demand (average revenue) and marginal revenue curves. Explain the nature of the demand curve.
   c) Add the marginal cost and average cost curves to your graph.
   d) Locate and label the profit-maximizing level of output, and then indicate the cost, revenue, and profit rectangles.
   e) Confirm the profit-maximizing level of output using the table.
   f) Describe the possible effects of advertising and of product differentiation on the demand curve for the business.

10. a) Using the table for Neutron, create a graph showing the demand (average revenue) and marginal revenue curves for this business, a maker of the only nuclear-powered vehicle in Canada.
   b) Plot marginal and average costs, and draw curves for each.
   c) On your graph, locate and mark the profit-maximizing point.
   d) Indicate the cost, revenue, and profit rectangles.

11. Identify the methods that governments use to regulate prices charged by natural monopolies. In your opinion, how effective is each of these methods? Rank the methods according to effectiveness, and explain your ranking.

12. With a group, research one natural monopoly—for example, a public utility—and develop a case study with the information you discover. Include the following in your case study:

   a) extent of services provided
   b) rate structures and pricing
   c) regulatory process
   d) economies of scale
   e) an evaluation of the overall efficiency of this natural monopoly

Profit Maximization Table for Fly-by-Night Airlines

Price (P) ($ per fare)	Quantity (q) (fares)	Total Revenue (TR)	Marginal Revenue (MR)	Marginal Cost (MC)	Average Cost (AC)
0	0	0			
			70	30	
70	10	—			60
			50	20	
60	20	—			40
			−40	20	
40	25	—			36
			−80	60	
20	30	—			40

Profit Maximization Table for Neutron

Price (P) ($ thousands per car)	Quantity (q) (cars)	Total Revenue (TR) ($ thousands)	Marginal Revenue (MR) ($ thousands)	Marginal Cost (MC) ($ thousands)	Average Cost (AC) ($ thousands)
	0	0			—
			320	120	
320	10	3200			280
			160	80	
240	20	4800			180
			0	138	
160	30	4800			166
			−160	302	
80	40	3200			200

Resource Markets

We have one asset, and that's people.

—Sylvia Ostry, Canadian economist

Two activities unite all businesses: they sell products and they hire resources. So far, we have concentrated on the selling. Now, we'll start to explore how businesses use economic resources. How many workers should a particular company hire? Is it worthwhile for the business to purchase and use another machine? Should a farmer use more land to grow a crop? In this chapter, we'll focus on how businesses make choices about the economic resources they use; later, we'll turn our attention to the roles households and governments play in these decisions.

CHAPTER FOCUS

This chapter focuses on the following:
- how businesses maximize profits by choosing how much of each economic resource to use
- the demand for resources by businesses that are price-takers and price-makers in the markets in which they sell their products
- the supply of labour, how wage rates are determined, and labour market equilibrium
- factors that change resource demand
- price elasticity of resource demand and the factors that determine it

SKILLS FOCUS

After studying this chapter, you will be able to:
- calculate and graph the marginal revenue product and marginal cost for a business
- locate and explain the profit-maximizing employment level for businesses that are price-takers and price-makers in their product markets
- graph labour supply and demand curves and locate equilibrium
- predict and explain the effects on a resource market of changes in the price of a resource, in product demand, and in technology, and the use of substitute and complementary resources
- outline the factors that affect the demand elasticity of a resource

How Resource Markets Operate

In past chapters, we have concentrated on product markets—the markets in which consumer goods and services are traded. Now, we'll take a look at the other half of the picture—resource markets, in which economic resources are traded. Recall that in resource markets, shown as the upper portion of the circular flow diagram in Figure 7.1, households sell economic resources to businesses (the outer loop), and households receive income resources in return (the inner loop). So, for their contribution of natural resources (including land), capital resources, and human resources (including labour and entrepreneurship), households receive income resources in the form of rent, wages, interest, and profit.

Figure 7.1:   The Circular Flow Diagram

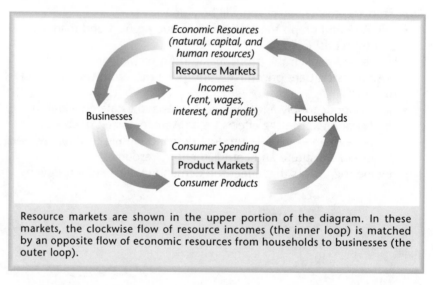

Resource markets are shown in the upper portion of the diagram. In these markets, the clockwise flow of resource incomes (the inner loop) is matched by an opposite flow of economic resources from households to businesses (the outer loop).

When analyzing resource markets, economists are especially interested in the way that resource prices are set, since these prices play a crucial role in determining people's incomes. For example, the relevant price in a labour market is the **wage** (sometimes known as the salary), which is the amount earned by a worker for providing labour for a certain period—an hour, a day, a month, or a year. It is important to remember that resource markets are affected by a wide array of factors. While social customs, governments, and labour unions each play a part in determining resource prices, the interaction of demand and supply remains the central feature in these markets. Indeed, demand and supply conditions often influence resource markets *despite* outside intervention. In this chapter, we focus on the forces of demand and supply.

wage: the amount earned by a worker for providing labour for a certain period of time; sometimes known as salary

The Demand for Resources

Unlike the demand for consumer items, the demand for resources is determined indirectly. Since resources are used to produce final goods and services, it is the demand for these products that ultimately determines how much of the resources are demanded. For example, the number of printing presses demanded by a newspaper publishing company depends on the demand for the company's product. If the newspaper attracts more readers, the company will respond by increasing production, and therefore buying more printing presses. Similarly, the number of workers hired by a car manufacturer depends on demand in the car market. A drop in the demand for cars will lower the demand for workers, resulting in hiring freezes and, perhaps, even layoffs.

To calculate resource demand, economists use the **marginal productivity theory**, which states that businesses use resources based on how much extra profit these resources provide. Therefore, when deciding whether or not it is profitable to buy one more unit of a resource, businesses consider two factors: the resource's marginal product, and the marginal revenue provided by each new unit of output produced. To illustrate the resource choices a business makes, we'll look at businesses with varying power in product markets.

marginal productivity theory: the theory that businesses use resources based on how much extra profit these resources provide

Product and Resource Price-Taker

Let's first consider the example of a strawberry farm. We'll assume that the strawberry market is perfectly competitive, that the farmer hires labour in a perfectly competitive resource market, and that factors other than output and labour remain constant. So, the farmer hires workers in a market with many buyers and sellers, each of them having no effect on the prevailing price of the resource—namely, the hourly wage for farm workers. Therefore, the strawberry farm is a price-taker in both its product and resource markets.

Marginal Revenue Product

According to marginal productivity theory, a business decides how much of a resource to use based on the resource's marginal product and marginal revenue.

Marginal Product

The strawberry farmer must first estimate how much output will be added by hiring a new worker while all other factors remain constant. In other words, the farmer must determine one worker's marginal product. Columns 1, 2, and 3 of the table in Figure 7.2 show the results. For the sake of simplicity, we assume that diminishing returns for labour set in with the very first worker. At harvest time, the farmer hires more labour and the total quantity of strawberries picked per hour increases, as shown in column 2. Because of diminishing returns, however, the marginal product of labour, shown in column 3, declines. For example, when the second worker is hired, the total product of strawberries rises from 10 to 18 kg, giving a marginal product for the second worker of 8 kg (18 − 10). With the third worker, the total product rises from 18 to 24 kg, giving a marginal product for the third worker of only 6 kg (24 − 18).

Figure 7.2: Labour Demand and Supply for a Product and Resource Price-Taker

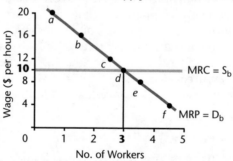

Labour Demand and Supply Schedules for a Strawberry Farm

(1) Labour (L) (no. of workers)	(2) Total Product (TP) (kilograms)	(3) Marginal Product (MP) ($\Delta TP/\Delta L$) (kilograms)	(4) Output Price (P) ($ per kilogram)	(5) Total Revenue (TR) (P x TP)	(6) Marginal Revenue Product (MRP = ΔTR)	(7) Marginal Resource Cost (MRC = W) ($ per hour)
0	0		2	0		
1	10	10	2	20	20 (a)	10
2	18	8	2	36	16 (b)	10
3	**24**	6	**2**	**48**	12 (c)	10
4	28	4	2	56	8 (e)	**10** (d)
5	30	2	2	60	4 (f)	10

Labour Demand and Supply Curves for a Strawberry Farm

The price-taking business's demand for labour, D_b, is found by calculating the marginal revenue product (MRP), or the change in the business's total revenue from hiring each new worker. The business's supply curve, S_b, is the marginal resource cost (MRC) of each new worker. Since the business can hire workers at a constant wage of $10 per hour, S_b is a horizontal line, and the business's profit-maximizing employment level of labour is 3 workers at point *d*.

Marginal Revenue

Once the marginal product of each worker is determined, the farmer must calculate the marginal revenue gained by selling the additional strawberries. Because the farmer is a price-taker in the perfectly competitive strawberry market, the price of strawberries is constant, and the price and marginal revenue for strawberries are equal. Hence, the farmer only needs to know the price of strawberries to find marginal revenue. Figure 7.2 shows the price of strawberries in column 4 as $2 per kilogram.

The effects of marginal product and marginal revenue on the business's demand for labour are summarized by the concept of **marginal revenue product** (MRP), which is the change in total revenue associated with employing each new unit of a resource—in this case, each new worker. Because it represents the *extra* revenue provided by the *extra* units of output produced by each new worker, marginal revenue product incorporates both marginal revenue and marginal product. The table in Figure 7.2 shows total revenue in column 5 (found by multiplying each total product value by price), and the marginal revenue product (the change in total revenue) in column 6. Expressing the marginal revenue product on the graph gives us the marginal revenue product curve. So, in the strawberry farm example, total revenue is $20 (10 × $2) when employing one worker, and $36 (18 × $2) when employing two workers. Therefore, the marginal revenue product of the second worker is the difference between the two amounts, or $16 ($36 − $20), shown on the graph at point *b*.

Labour Demand and Supply

Given this information, it is a straightforward task for the strawberry farmer to find the profit-maximizing employment of labour. The extra cost of each additional unit of a resource for the business is referred to as **marginal resource cost** (MRC). In the case of the strawberry farmer who is a price-taker in the labour market, and therefore a "wage-taker," marginal resource cost is simply the prevailing wage paid to farm workers. In our example, the wage is $10 per hour. According to the marginal productivity theory, the employer will use additional resources as long as marginal resource cost does not exceed marginal revenue product. Therefore, our strawberry farmer will hire three workers, because each of the first three workers adds revenue ($20, $16, and $12, respectively) greater than the $10 cost per worker. Beyond this point, it is not profitable to hire more workers, since the extra revenue that each worker will provide the business will be less than the extra cost of that worker.

Expressed on the graph in Figure 7.2, the marginal revenue product curve represents the **business's labour demand curve**, D_b. The business's labour demand curve shows how many workers are demanded by a business at each possible wage. The demand curve has a negative (downward) slope because businesses find it profitable to employ more workers at lower wages. The marginal resource cost curve represents the **business's labour supply curve**, or S_b. This curve shows how many

marginal revenue product: the change in total revenue associated with employing each new unit of a resource

marginal resource cost: the extra cost of each additional unit of a resource

business's labour demand curve: a graph showing the possible combinations of workers demanded by a business at each possible wage

business's labour supply curve: a graph showing the possible combinations of workers supplied to a business at each possible wage

workers are supplied to a business at each possible wage. Because the business is a price-taker in the resource market, this curve is horizontal. No matter what action the strawberry farmer takes, the wage is fixed at the equilibrium wage determined by the entire market.

Profit-Maximizing Employment Rule

The profit-maximizing point for the business occurs at the intersection of its demand and supply curves for labour, D_b and S_b. In other words, the business will hire workers up to the point where marginal revenue product and marginal resource cost are the same. This result provides a general **profit-maximizing employment rule** for resources. No matter what market a business operates in, it should use a resource up to the point where the resource's marginal revenue product equals its marginal resource cost.

profit-maximizing employment rule: states that a business should use a resource up to the point where the resource's marginal revenue product equals its marginal resource cost

$$\text{Profit-maximizing employment: rule} \quad \text{Marginal revenue product (MRP)} = \text{Marginal resource cost (MRC)}$$

Thinking About Economics

Is marginal productivity theory equally applicable to economic resources other than labour?

In theory, a business should make choices about all economic resources based on each resource's marginal revenue product and marginal resource cost. In practice, however, marginal revenue product tends to be calculated for labour and for natural resources, but not for the other economic resources. This is because both labour and natural resources can be measured in standardized units—for example, an hour of a certain type of labour, or a hectare of a certain grade of land.

In contrast, it's usually harder to calculate marginal revenue product for capital goods. While it is possible to calculate the marginal revenue product of a particular material or type of machine used by a business, this cannot be done for an entire investment project—when a business contemplates building a factory, for example. One investment project differs so much from another that it is impossible to count them in standardized units. Because they are physically indivisible, they must be counted in monetary terms—the number of dollars a business needs to undertake a certain investment project. Entrepreneurship is also difficult to measure because it is intangible. Therefore, it is not possible to calculate the marginal revenue product of a given "unit" of entrepreneurship, and its demand and supply must be treated in qualitative, not quantitative, terms.

Notice that the profit-maximizing employment rule parallels the profit-maximizing rule (outlined in the previous chapter), which is used by businesses to decide levels of output. Recall that the profit-maximizing rule states that, in order to maximize profits, a business should produce the quantity of output at which marginal revenue and marginal cost intersect, since up to this point every unit of output has a marginal revenue that exceeds its marginal cost. Similarly, a business can maximize its profits by using a resource up to the point at which marginal revenue product equals marginal resource cost. By doing so, the business employs all units that give more extra revenue than they add to the business's costs.

Market Demand and Supply

Now, if we assume that all 1000 employers of farm workers in the region have marginal revenue product curves identical to the one shown in Figure 7.2, we can derive the **labour market demand curve**, D_m. The labour market demand curve shows how many workers are demanded in a competitive labour market at each possible wage. By adding the labour demand curves of all businesses in this market, we have the labour market demand schedule and curve shown in Figure 7.3. For example, at an hourly wage of $14, each of the 1000 farmers demands two workers, which gives a total labour demanded of 2000. If the wage were to drop to $10, each farmer would demand three workers, raising total labour demanded in the market to 3000.

Corresponding to this market demand for farm workers is a **labour market supply curve**, S_m, which shows the total supply of workers offering

labour market demand curve: a graph showing the possible combinations of workers demanded in a certain labour market at each possible wage

labour market supply curve: a graph showing the possible combinations of workers supplying their labour in a certain labour market at each possible wage

Figure 7.3:   Demand and Supply in a Competitive Labour Market

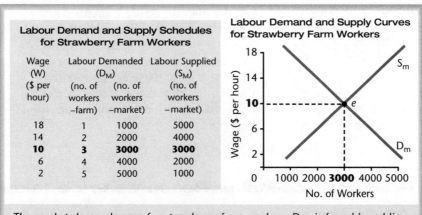

Labour Demand and Supply Schedules for Strawberry Farm Workers

Wage (W) ($ per hour)	Labour Demanded (D_M) (no. of workers –farm)	(no. of workers –market)	Labour Supplied (S_M) (no. of workers –market)
18	1	1000	5000
14	2	2000	4000
10	**3**	**3000**	**3000**
6	4	4000	2000
2	5	5000	1000

Labour Demand and Supply Curves for Strawberry Farm Workers

The market demand curve for strawberry farm workers, D_m, is found by adding together the workers demanded by each farm at various wages. In a competitive labour market, this demand curve and the market supply curve, S_m, intersect at equilibrium point e, where the wage is $10 for 3000 workers employed.

their services in a certain labour market at each wage. This curve has a positive (upward) slope because, in general, higher wages in a given market encourage more workers to offer their labour in that market. Suppose for our strawberry market that wages increase from $10 per hour to $14 per hour. Figure 7.3 shows that this wage increase would increase the quantity of farm workers supplied from 3000 to 4000. Figure 7.3 also demonstrates another feature of resource markets that is similar to that in product markets: equilibrium occurs at the intersection of the labour market supply and demand curves.

BRIEF REVIEW

1. Resource markets, like product markets, are governed by the forces of demand and supply. However, the demand for resources is determined indirectly.

2. Based on marginal productivity theory, businesses decide how much of a resource to use based on the resource's marginal revenue product, or MRP (the change in total revenue associated with each new unit of resource), and marginal resource cost, or MRC (the extra cost to the business of employing each additional unit of resource).

3. The profit-maximizing employment rule states that businesses should use a resource up to the point where its marginal revenue product equals its marginal resource cost.

4. In practice, marginal productivity theory is best applied to labour and natural resources because they can be measured in standardized units.

5. The marginal revenue product curve represents the business's resource demand curve. The marginal resource cost curve represents the business's resource supply curve.

6. In a perfectly competitive resource market, the business is a price-taker; therefore, the resource supply curve is a horizontal line. In this market, the profit-maximizing employment level occurs where the business's resource demand and supply curves intersect.

7. In a perfectly competitive resource market, the market's resource demand is the sum of the individual businesses' resource demand. The market's resource supply is the sum of all the individual resource owners' resource supply. Equilibrium is the point at which the market demand and market supply curves for the resource intersect.

 **Product Price-Maker/Resource Price-Taker**

What happens to resource demand and supply if the business is an imperfect competitor or a monopolist in its product market? In these cases, the business has some control over the price of its product, or is a product price-maker. To see how the business's resource demand curve is determined, let's assume that the labour market is perfectly competitive, making the business a resource price-taker.

To illustrate, let's consider Nirvana Cushions, a small manufacturer that sells its product in a monopolistically competitive product market and hires unskilled workers in a competitive labour market. To decide how many workers to hire, Nirvana Cushions uses the concept of marginal revenue product. However, unlike a price-taker in output markets, Nirvana faces a product demand curve with a negative (downward) slope. As the business increases its output of cushions, the price it can charge for each cushion falls.

Marginal Revenue Product

As with the strawberry farmer, Nirvana Cushions must first find the marginal product of each new worker. Again, we'll assume that diminishing returns set in at the very first worker. Figure 7.4 shows the results in table columns 1 to 3. So, while the marginal product of the first worker is 4 (4 − 0), the marginal product of the second worker is 3 (7 − 4).

Next, the business must find the marginal revenue of each new worker. Because the business is an imperfect competitor, the price is not constant at all quantities of output. So, for example, Nirvana Cushions finds that there is sufficient demand to produce four cushions per hour if they sell at a price of $8 each, but demand dictates that, if seven cushions are produced per hour, they would have to sell at a price of $6 each. The possible prices for each output level are shown in column 4 in Figure 7.4. Column 5 shows the resulting total revenues (total product multiplied by price). The change in total revenue from one production level to the next, the marginal revenue product, is shown in column 6. Expressed on a graph, the marginal revenue product figures give the marginal revenue product curve. So, the business has a total revenue of $32 (4 × $8) when employing one worker, and $42 (7 × $6) when employing two workers. The marginal revenue of the second worker, therefore, is $10 ($42 − $32), shown on the graph as point *h*.

The distinguishing feature of the marginal revenue product curve of a business that has some power to set product prices is that it is less elastic than that for a perfect competitor, which is a price-taker. At Nirvana Cushions' higher employment levels, for example, the marginal revenue product falls for two reasons. Not only does the marginal product decrease because of diminishing returns, but also because the price that the business can charge for its product decreases as production increases.

Labour Demand and Supply

Recall that the profit-maximizing employment rule applies to all businesses regardless of their power in the product and resource markets. This means that once Nirvana Cushions knows its marginal revenue product, it can determine its profit-maximizing employment level. According to the rule, the business should employ a resource up to the

**Figure 7.4: Labour Demand and Supply for a Product
Price-Maker/Resource Price-Taker**

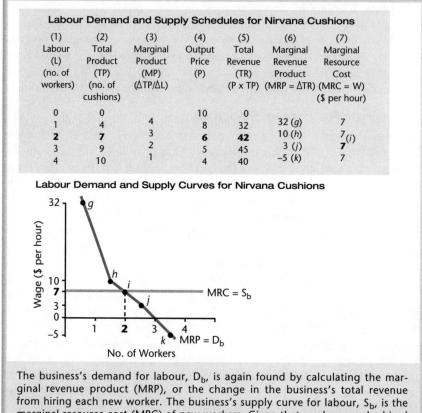

Labour Demand and Supply Schedules for Nirvana Cushions

(1) Labour (L) (no. of workers)	(2) Total Product (TP) (no. of cushions)	(3) Marginal Product (MP) (ΔTP/ΔL)	(4) Output Price (P)	(5) Total Revenue (TR) (P x TP)	(6) Marginal Revenue Product (MRP = ΔTR)	(7) Marginal Resource Cost (MRC = W) ($ per hour)
0	0		10	0		
1	4	4	8	32	32 (g)	7
2	**7**	3	**6**	**42**	10 (h)	7 (i)
3	9	2	5	45	3 (j)	**7**
4	10	1	4	40	–5 (k)	7

The business's demand for labour, D_b, is again found by calculating the marginal revenue product (MRP), or the change in the business's total revenue from hiring each new worker. The business's supply curve for labour, S_b, is the marginal resource cost (MRC) of new workers. Given that workers can be hired at a constant wage of $7 per hour, S_b is a horizontal line, and the business's profit-maximizing employment level of labour is 2 workers at point *i*.

point where the marginal revenue product of the resource equals its marginal resource cost. Recall that Nirvana Cushions is assumed to be a wage-taker in a competitive labour market where individual employers have no influence. Suppose the prevailing wage for unskilled workers is $7 per hour. Given this wage, Nirvana Cushions will hire two workers, since each provides a higher marginal revenue product than their $7 marginal resource cost. As before, the marginal revenue product curve is the business's labour demand curve, D_b, and the horizontal marginal resource cost curve is the business's labour supply curve, S_b. The profit-maximizing employment level occurs at point *i*, where the two curves intersect in Figure 7.4.

Market Demand and Supply

If the resource market is competitive, the degree of competition in the product market doesn't affect how the market demand for a resource is determined. Therefore, Nirvana Cushions' demand for unskilled workers is combined with all other businesses' demand for unskilled workers to find the market demand. As with the market for farm workers, the supply of unskilled workers will have a positive (upward) slope. Once again, the intersection of the demand curve and the supply curve gives the equilibrium point for the labour market.

Changes in Resource Demand

Resource demand can change for a variety of reasons. There are three main resource demand determinants: changes in product demand, changes in other resource prices, and technological innovation. Each demand determinant affects the business's marginal revenue product, which in turn causes a change in resource demand.

Product Demand

Recall that the demand for resources depends on the demand for the consumer products these resources help to produce. Therefore, when the demand for a certain product changes, the demand for resources used to produce the product changes in the same direction. As more people use computers in their leisure time, for example, the demand for computer programmers will increase. Meanwhile, if skiing becomes less popular as a pastime, the demand for ski-lift operators will decline.

Changes in product demand affect the demand for resources through changes in product prices. For example, if the demand for strawberries increases, their price increases, and each strawberry farm worker's marginal revenue product increases as well. Each strawberry farmer's marginal revenue product curve shifts to the right, as does the business's demand curve for labour. Therefore, the entire market demand curve for farm workers shifts to the right. In the same way, a decrease in the demand for cushions decreases the price Nirvana Cushions can charge, which, in turn, decreases each worker's marginal revenue product and reduces the business's demand for labour.

Other Resource Prices

Resources used in a particular production process can be related in two ways. **Complementary resources** are used together, as in the case of steam shovels and steam-shovel operators. When two resources are complementary, the price for one resource and the demand for the other resource have an inverse relationship. So, for example, if steam shovels drop in price, the number of these machines will increase, and the demand

complementary resources: resources that are used together

labour productivity:
the quantity of output produced per worker in a given period of time; the average product of labour

substitute resources:
resources that can be used in place of one another without affecting output

for the labour of steam-shovel operators will increase as well. In this case, there is also an increase in **labour productivity**, which is the quantity of output produced per worker in a given period of time—in other words, the average product of labour—for either a business or an industry.

Substitute resources, in contrast, are resources that can be used in place of one another without affecting the business's or industry's output. The price for one resource and the demand for the substitute resource have a direct relationship. So, for example, if steam shovels drop in price, use of these machines will increase, and demand for manual labour will decrease.

Technological Innovation

A third resource demand determinant is technological innovation. Suppose a new cushion-producing machine is introduced at Nirvana Cushions. If labour and the new machinery are complementary resources, the workers' productivity will increase and Nirvana Cushions' demand for labour will increase. However, if Nirvana Cushions' workers and the new machinery are substitute resources, the use of this new machine will reduce the marginal product of each worker, and Nirvana's demand for labour in this industry will decrease.

DEVELOPING
INTERPRETATION SKILLS

SOURCE: © 1993 Paul Duginski

1. What comment on technological progress does the cartoon make? Do you agree or disagree with the cartoonist's viewpoint? Explain your answer.

2. Give one specific example of technological innovation. Then, list possible benefits and possible drawbacks of this innovation.

Thinking About Economics

How does the increased use of capital resources in the Canadian economy affect Canadian workers?

Recall that businesses producing a certain product can usually choose from among production processes that combine different proportions of inputs. For a given quantity of output, a labour-intensive process employs more labour and less capital resources, while a capital-intensive process employs less labour and more capital resources. The use of more capital-intensive methods of production by Canadian businesses affects parts of Canada's workforce in different ways. As a rule, highly skilled labour benefits when more capital-intensive forms of production are used. Since this labour is usually a complementary resource to new forms of machinery, the employment of more capital by Canadian businesses raises the productivity as well as the demand for skilled labour, therefore boosting wages and employment for these workers.

The effects of capital-intensive production processes on semiskilled and unskilled labour are more indefinite. In the past, automated production processes in manufacturing industries often called for workers to perform simplified and highly repetitive tasks. In these cases, labour was a complementary resource to machinery: continued automation increased labour demand and raised both wages and employment levels. However, in the last few decades, new types of capital resources have increasingly substituted for semiskilled and unskilled labour. As the use of capital resources increases, the demand for semiskilled or unskilled labour decreases, thereby decreasing the equilibrium wage and workers employed.

In general, the use of more capital-intensive techniques in Canadian industry has raised Canadian workers' living standards and gradually led to improved working conditions. However, because of the differential effects of automation on skilled and on semiskilled and unskilled labour, Canadian workers are being forced to become continually more skilled and productive.

Nuala Beck

SOURCE: Nuala Beck.

Shifting Gears

Nuala Beck and the New Economy

What is happening in the economy? And what are the signs of change? These are the questions that Canadian economist Nuala Beck asked herself when she saw the Canadian and world economies changing in ways that didn't fit the old models and measures. In the following excerpt from her book Shifting Gears: Thriving in the New Economy, *Beck outlines how the current transformation of the Canadian economy is part of a long-term evolutionary process.*

We really only need to turn the clock back about 150 years to see how we got where we are today.

By identifying three circles, each representing an economic movement that shaped the period from 1850 to the present, I had stumbled on a key to understanding the forward movement of our economy today. I've called these models the *commodity-processing,* or C Circle; the *mass-manufacturing,* or M Circle; and the *technology,* or T Circle. Each circle contains certain key, common elements; each makes sense of vast economic changes that otherwise don't fit into a sensible pattern; each is the natural extension of the one preceding. Specific industries, even the economies of entire nations, can be defined by their place inside these circles. And once that's determined, their future—and yours—can be foretold with a remarkable degree of precision.

After running my original musings through the gauntlet of hard economic analysis, it became clear that the key to each circle is a single, crucial ingredient whose abundant supply, at steadily falling prices, acts as a springboard, or catalyst, to levels of growth never before witnessed. In the commodity-processing era (the C Circle), it was cheap steel. In the succeeding mass-manufacturing era (M Circle), it was energy, specifically oil, whose discovery in vast quantities around the turn of the century fuelled the consumer-driven manufacturing boom that shifted the center of economic power to the United States from Britain.

Today, in the T (technology) Circle, the world is being driven by huge supplies of another product that was unknown outside the closely guarded doors of Texas Instruments and one or two other research laboratories thirty years ago—semiconductors, or microchips, so cheap and plentiful they can be stuck in watches to tell you when it's time to wake up. The technological leader in this circle is Japan, but America isn't nearly so far back as its internal and external critics like to think.

Besides those single, vital building blocks, each circle has other identifying traits.

• Every era has its *engines*—a handful of strategic industries that drive the entire economy and typically have risen rapidly out of humble origins. The roaring engines of the C Circle were steel, railways, textiles and coal.

These were superseded in the mass-manufacturing era by autos, housing, machine tools and retailing. The T Circle, as you might guess, has been turbo-driven by computers and semiconductors, as well as telecommunications, instrumentation and the health and medical industry.

- Every era has its *virtuosos*—the innovative entrepreneurs, scientists and engineers who use existing technology merely as a stepping stone to new methods, processes and products, rather than endlessly reinventing the wheel.

- Every era can be defined by the *technology* these innovators develop. They spend their working lives looking for that better mousetrap, whether it's Henry Ford and his sturdy Model-T car or Jack Kilby and his microchips. (Ironically, Kilby, the Texas Instruments scientist who invented the first integrated circuit the size of a matchhead, never stopped using the slide rule that his pocket calculator made obsolete in 1971.) When they find it, the stage is set for the next explosive round of growth.

- Every era has its *technological pacesetters*, from Britain in the commodity-processing circle, to the United States and Germany in the manufacturing era, to Japan and the U.S. today. The key is the financial might needed to develop the better mousetraps.

- Every era has its own *management practices*. The C Circle, for example, saw the appearance of the first truly giant firms, cartels and trusts that weren't dependent on the whims of royalty or the vagaries of the trade winds. It was here that the foundation was laid for the first great industrial fortunes—a departure from the land- or merchant-based wealth of old.

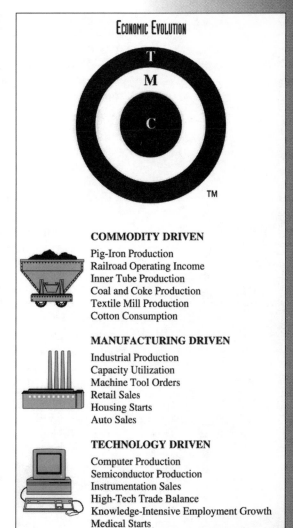

ECONOMIC EVOLUTION

COMMODITY DRIVEN

Pig-Iron Production
Railroad Operating Income
Inner Tube Production
Coal and Coke Production
Textile Mill Production
Cotton Consumption

MANUFACTURING DRIVEN

Industrial Production
Capacity Utilization
Machine Tool Orders
Retail Sales
Housing Starts
Auto Sales

TECHNOLOGY DRIVEN

Computer Production
Semiconductor Production
Instrumentation Sales
High-Tech Trade Balance
Knowledge-Intensive Employment Growth
Medical Starts

- Every era has its *philosophers*, the gurus who spend most of their time formulating theories about an economy that no longer exists and may never have—except in their ideal universe.

- Every era has its *fast track*—the jobs that lead somewhere and provide the best chance of hitching dreams to reality in the workplace. In the M Circle, blue-collar workers achieved a level of prosperity beyond the wildest imaginings of previous generations. For the first time, factory laborers had the American dream within their grasp. Many acquired homes of their own, annual vacations, private transportation and other advantages that had long been the sole preserve of the rich.

Today, it's the workers in the new economy who have the best hope for a secure future. Individual computer or communication companies may come and go, but the worker with T Circle skills will still be better off than those being kicked off the assembly lines of the incredible shrinking auto industry and other outdated sectors. Seniority doesn't matter much when the company has sunk to the bottom of the lake. Everybody drowns, no matter what position they had in the boat!

- Every era has its *losers*—industries that were once a major economic force but are now more or less in permanent decline. Just ask the rail manufacturers or pig-iron producers.
- Every era has its *emerging industries*—fledgling sectors destined to carry the world into the next great period of growth, but still seeking a firm foothold. Once it was automobile manufacturing. Today, it's genetic engineering and artificial intelligence.
- Every era has its *roadblocks*, easily identifiable barriers that have to be overcome before the transition can be completed.

A natural limitation on the growth of the commodity-processing circle was the lack of standards—in everything from education and electricity to railroad tracks. In the manufacturing era, assembly-line technology overcame the severe restrictions on capacity caused by the old batch, or piecemeal, system of production, while rapid transportation removed the major roadblock to market access, and integration of design, production and marketing shunted aside idea-strangling bureaucracies. The current technology-driven circle has developed through the application of electronics and miniaturization to largely remove the limitations of existing energy and materials. Without the magic of integrated circuits, computers would be way too unwieldy and far too expensive for ordinary mortals like you and me to ever make use of them.

- Every era *organizes work* in a particular way, linked to the needs and goals of society at the time, which is why change is doubly painful. Not only does the nature of the work change, so does the social structure that underpins it. The aboliton of child labor and other worker reforms in the C Circle (when some industries were known as "slaughterhouses" for the high death rate of employees, some barely out of diapers) was, in its own time, as revolutionary a move as the organization of work along assembly lines in the M Circle and the later rise of middle management and the development of a professional class.

What doesn't (and can never) work is the grafting of old approaches and structures onto the new economy. That's why companies that have failed to make the successful leap from one circle to the next seem so unbelievably incompetent. Giants like General Motors once represented all the strengths and glories of the mass-manufacturing era. Yet today they are described in unflattering terms—"bloated," "groping," "slow" and "sloppy"—prisoners caged in their own past.

The startling fact of life in Canada is that 70 percent of Canadians are already employed in the new economy, which shows just how well we have adjusted.

It pays to be a supplier of the right materials, and although many Canadians don't realize it, their country is emerging as the principal provider of many of the commodities needed by the technology-driven economy. We are so wrapped up in our wintry view of our future that we don't realize how incredibly lucky—and smart—we've been over the years. It's no secret, for example, that nickel is *the* metal of the new economy, while copper is the dark horse, and Canada happens to be one of the world's principal sources of both.

As supreme hewers of wood, miners of metals and drawers of water, Canadians have been uniquely well placed to serve both the commodity-processing centers of mother Britain and the manufacturing dynamos of the neighboring giant to the south. In return, Canada has had one of the world's fastest-growing economies for decades. The bumpy ride that we're experiencing right now is caused simply by the shifting of gears as we move from supplying the stuff to the declining old economy. For people who aren't used to driving at high speeds, that's always a challenge.

SOURCE: Abridged from *Shifting Gears: Thriving in the New Economy* by Nuala Beck. Copyright 1992 by Nuala Beck. Published by HarperCollins Publishers Ltd., pp. 19–24, 43–44.
PHOTO SOURCE: Nuala Beck is author of *Shifting Gears: Thriving in the New Economy* (HarperCollins 1992) and is President of Nuala Beck & Associates Inc., Management Consultants for the New Economy. The New Economy™ is the trademark of Nuala Beck & Associates Inc.

1. Summarize the traits of the present (technology) era and one other era. Use both information from the excerpt and from your own research to provide examples (of engines, virtuosos, technology, and so on) for each trait.

2. Research employment levels in Canadian industries now, 10 years ago, and 20 years ago. Place each industry within a circle—the commodity-processing circle, the mass-manufacturing circle, or the technology circle. In proportion to the whole, how has employment in each of the circles changed over the last 20 years?

3. Write a research essay focusing on one decade in Canada's economic history as a supplier of natural resources.

4. Find evidence of the technology era in the media. You could clip articles from newspapers and magazines or make notes on a TV business program, for instance. Based on your findings, make and explain predictions for the future for each type of economic resource, for the organization of work, and for management practices.

 **Price Elasticity of Resource Demand**

Just as with demand in product markets, demand in resource markets can be elastic or inelastic. The price elasticity of resource demand indicates the responsiveness of businesses using a resource to variations in its price. In general, there are four factors that affect price elasticity of resource demand: the rate of decline in the marginal product of a resource, the price elasticity of product demand, the resource's proportion of the business's total costs, and the availability of substitute resources.

Rate of Decline in Marginal Product

The more rapid the decline in the marginal product of a resource, the steeper the business's marginal revenue product curve. Since the marginal revenue product curve equals the business's demand curve for the product, the steeper the decline in a resource's marginal product, the less elastic the resource demand becomes. For example, if introducing new robotic machinery in a car manufacturing plant causes the marginal product of auto workers to fall more rapidly than before, the marginal revenue product of auto workers becomes steeper, and the demand for auto workers becomes less elastic.

Price Elasticity of Product Demand

Because the demand for resources is a derived demand, the price elasticity of a product influences the producer's decisions about the resources needed to make that product. When the demand for a product is inelastic, the company producing the product will find that at higher output levels it will charge significantly less. Therefore, the business's marginal revenue product and the associated resource demand curve will be less elastic also. So, for example, the owners of Nirvana Cushions have less elastic demand for labour than does the strawberry farmer, who faces elastic demand.

Proportion of Total Costs

When the cost of a certain resource makes up a large proportion of a business's overall costs, the demand for the resource tends to be more elastic. For example, the quantity of labour demanded by wheat farmers will not vary much when there is an adjustment in wages, since wage costs are a small percentage of total costs. In contrast, the demand for capital equipment such as combine harvesters is much more elastic because these costs represent a large percentage of wheat farmers' costs.

Substitute Resources

A resource with many substitutes has a more elastic demand curve than a resource that is indispensable to the production process. For example, the demand for labour in the auto industry tends to be more elastic than in the hotel and restaurant industry, since the opportunity to substitute capital for labour is much greater in manufacturing.

When Resource Markets Are Uncompetitive

The Case of Monopsony

Price-Takers Versus Price-Makers in Resource Markets

In this chapter, we've looked at cases in which the resource market is competitive, with many individual buyers and sellers. Because each competitive participant is small in comparison to the market, no single business has an effect on the price of a

resource, and businesses are price-takers. In some resource markets, however, competition does not prevail. In the extreme, called *monopsony*, there is only one buyer (known as a monopsonist) in a resource market.

To see how the monopsonist contrasts with the resource price-taker, let's look again at the strawberry farm example. Suppose that one

Profit-Maximizing Employment for a Monopsonist

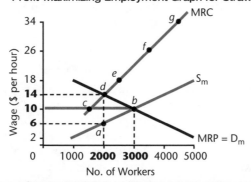

Profit-Maximizing Employment Table for Strawberry Farms Inc.

(1) Labour Supplied (L_S)	(2) Wage (W)	(3) Total Labour Cost (L_S x W)	(4) Marginal Resource Cost (MRC) ($\Delta(W \times L_S)/\Delta L_S$)	(5) Labour Demanded (L_D)	(6) Marginal Revenue Product (MRP)
1000	2	2000	10 (c)	1000	16
2000	**6** (a)	**12 000**	**18** (e)	**2000**	12 >**14** (d)
3000	**10** (b)	**30 000**	26 (f)	**3000**	8 >**10** (b)
4000	14	56 000	34 (g)	4000	4
5000	18	90 000		5000	

Profit-Maximizing Employment Graph for Strawberry Farms Inc.

When the market for strawberry farm workers is competitive, it reaches equilibrium at the intersection of the market demand and supply curves, D_m and S_m, at point *b*, with a wage of $10 and an employment level of 3000 workers. The new monopsonist buyer faces an MRP curve equal to D_m, but its MRC curve is above S_m because increases in the wage paid to additional workers affect the cost of all workers. According to the market supply curve, the monopsonist may pay a lower wage of $6 and hire 2000 workers, as shown at point *a*.

giant company, Strawberry Farms Inc., buys all 1000 strawberry farms in a given region. Before, when the labour market for strawberry farm workers was competitive, the $10 hourly wage was determined by the intersection of the market demand (D_m) and market supply (S_m) curves, as shown again in the figure. Now that Strawberry Farms Inc. is the sole buyer in the market, however, it can act as a wage-maker.

Marginal Revenue Product As always, the business's purchases of labour resources are governed by the profit-maximizing employment rule, which states that the business should utilize a resource up to the point where the marginal revenue product of the resource equals its marginal resource cost. The marginal revenue product curve for the new giant business's workforce is the same as the market demand curve, D_m, which was derived from the individual marginal revenue product curves for the old competitive producers. So, for example, when moving from 2000 to 3000 workers, the marginal revenue product for Strawberry Farms Inc. is $12 as shown in columns 5 and 6 of the table.

Marginal Resource Cost The marginal resource cost, however, is different for the monopsonist. Previously, each of the competitive producers accepted the prevailing wage rate of $10 so they had a constant marginal resource cost, which is shown by a horizontal line on the graph. In contrast, this new giant company may set the wage, since it faces the labour supply curve (S_m) of the entire market. So, for Strawberry Farms Inc., employing 2000 workers means paying an hourly wage of $6 (point a), and increasing employment to 3000 workers means providing a higher wage of $10 (point b) in order to attract new workers to the market.

When it employs more workers, the monopsonist must pay the higher wage to *all* workers—both old and new. As a result, the marginal resource cost for the business rises more quickly than does the market supply curve, S_m. In the table, columns 1 to 4 provide the basis of the marginal resource cost curve. Columns 1 and 2 show the quantity of labour supplied at each possible wage. Multiplying the quantity of labour by the wage gives the total labour cost for the company, as shown in column 3. The marginal resource cost, in column 4, is the extra total labour cost for each additional worker. So, for example, when the company employs 2000 workers at a $6 wage, its total labour cost is $12 000 ($6 × 2000). Increasing employment to 3000 workers at a $10 wage increases the total labour cost to $30 000 ($10 × 3000). The new 1000 workers therefore cost an extra $18 000 ($30 000 − $12 000), which translates into a marginal resource cost of $18 for each new worker ($18 000 ÷ 1000) at point e on the graph.

Profit-Maximizing Employment With the marginal resource costs known, Strawberry Farms Inc. can apply the profit-maximizing employment rule. Using the rule, the company will hire 2000 workers, the employment level at which marginal revenue product and marginal resource cost are equal (point d). According to the labour market supply curve (S_m), the wage for 2000 workers is $6, which is lower than the $10 wage paid to workers when the industry was competitive.

Thus, as a general rule, a monopsonist in a resource market pays a lower price for a resource than would businesses in a competitive resource market. Because of its price-making power in the resource market, the monopsonist cuts its costs and thereby raises its profit.

BRIEF REVIEW

1. The profit-maximizing employment rule also applies to businesses that are price-makers in their product markets. A business should use a resource up to the point where its marginal revenue product and marginal resource cost curves intersect. As long as the resource market is competitive, this point occurs where the business's resource demand and supply curves intersect.

2. The marginal revenue product is less elastic for a business that is a price-maker in its product market than for a business that is a price-taker. The decline in a resource's marginal revenue product is more rapid not only because of the diminishing marginal product but also because of price variations.

3. Resource demand can be affected by changes in product demand, changes in other resource prices, and technological innovation.

4. The price elasticity of resource demand is determined by the rate of decline in the marginal product of a resource, the price elasticity of demand for the product, the proportion of a business's total costs that the resource accounts for, and the availability of substitute resources.

Key Concepts

wage
marginal productivity theory
marginal revenue product
marginal resource cost
business's labour demand curve
business's labour supply curve

profit-maximizing employment rule
labour market demand curve
labour market supply curve
complementary resources
labour productivity
substitute resources

Developing Application and Analysis Skills

1. a) Copy and complete the production schedule for blueberries.
  b) Create a graph showing the total product and marginal product curves.
  c) Explain the relationship described by the curves.
  d) Explain the significance of the relationship for the blueberry farmer.

2. a) Copy and complete the table for Bountiful Blueberry Farm, assuming that the market for blueberry farm workers is competitive.
  b) Create a graph showing the labour demand and labour supply curves the blueberry farmer faces.
  c) On your graph, indicate the profit-maximizing employment level.
  d) Suppose the farmer proposes hiring six workers. What would you advise him or her to do?

Production Schedule for Blueberries

Employment Level	Labour (no. of workers)	Total Product (kilograms of blueberries)	Average Product (kilograms of blueberries)	Marginal Product (kilograms of blueberries)
A	0	0	—	
B	1	20	____	____
C	2	36	____	____
D	3	48	____	____
E	4	56	____	____
F	5	60	____	____
G	6	60	____	____
H	7	56	____	____
I	8	48	____	____

Labour Demand and Supply Schedules for Bountiful Blueberry Farm

Labour (no. of workers)	Total Product (kilograms of blueberries)	Marginal Product (kilograms of blueberries)	Output Price ($ per kilogram)	Total Revenue ($)	Marginal Revenue Product ($ per kilogram)	Marginal Resource Cost ($ per hour)
0	0		2	____		
1	15	____	2	____	____	10
2	27	____	2	____	____	____
3	36	____	2	____	____	____
4	42	____	2	____	____	____
5	45	____	2	____	____	____

e) Suppose the prevailing wage for blueberry farm workers were changed to $14 per hour. Outline the effect on the farmer's labour demand and labour supply.

3. Suppose that the price for a perfect competitor's product rises. Illustrate the effects of the price increase by reordering the following statements in a logical sequence:

a) The product's price rises.
b) More labour is demanded by the business.
c) Marginal revenue product increases.
d) Marginal revenue increases.
e) The demand curve for labour shifts.

4. Suppose a copper-mine business, Catalina Copper Mines, owns a large copper-producing facility in a remote part of Canada. The following table shows the market labour demand and supply for copper-mine workers in the region. Because it was facing stiff competition from foreign producers, Catalina Copper Mines updated its equipment and established a profit-sharing program with employees, which the business hoped would increase efficiency and profits. In addition to a negotiated wage, the workers would share in any profits the company earned. After six months, Catalina Copper Mines regained its competitive edge over the foreign producers. However, a year later, the business was jeopardized when a replacement for copper wire was found that was less expensive and a better electrical conductor. To protect the regional economy from a major economic collapse, the federal and provincial governments announced subsidies to the national copper-mining industry.

Market Labour Demand and Supply Schedules for Copper-Mine Workers		
Wage ($ per hour)	Labour Demanded (no. of workers)	Labour Supplied (no. of workers)
36	2 000	10 000
28	4 000	8 000
20	6 000	6 000
12	8 000	4 000
4	10 000	2 000

a) Using the schedules, show the labour demand and supply curves for the copper-mining industry.
b) Identify the equilibrium price and quantity of labour for copper-mine workers.
c) Sketch on your graph the impact of each of the changes experienced at Catalina Copper Mines:
   i) Copper-mine workers increase their efficiency.
   ii) A replacement for copper wire is found.
   iii) Governments announce a subsidy program for the copper-mining industry.

5. Sketch a graph showing labour market demand and supply curves for knitting-machine operators. Then, show on your graph the impact of each of the following changes. Explain each result.

   a) Demand for sweaters increases.
   b) The price of knitting machines falls.
   c) The price of robotic substitutes for knitting-machine operators falls.

6. Consider the effect of each of the following scenarios on elasticity of demand for one resource Savoy Manufacturing uses in production. Sketch a graph to explain these effects.

   a) Demand for Savoy Manufacturing's product becomes less elastic.
   b) The marginal product of each new unit of resource declines rapidly.
   c) More substitute resources become available.
   d) Resource costs make up a smaller proportion of total costs than they previously did.

CHAPTER 8

Wages, Rent, Profit, and Interest

Nothing like a splendid new resource to start the battles.
—JEAN HOWARTH, CANADIAN SHORT STORY WRITER

Who gets what in an economy? In the Canadian economy, this question is decided primarily in resource markets. For most Canadians, the size of their pay cheques is the biggest determinant of income, but pay cheques vary greatly among Canadian workers. In this chapter, we'll explore the factors that affect incomes from labour. We'll also look at other resource incomes, rent and profit, and a resource-related financial income, interest. Lastly, we will look at how important each income is to the total incomes of Canadians.

CHAPTER FOCUS

This chapter focuses on the following:
- the factors that affect wages, including productivity, education, experience, job conditions, regional disparities, market power, and discrimination
- the types, structure, collective bargaining practices, and impact of labour unions in Canada
- rent, the market for land, the equilibrium value of land rent, and changes in demand for land
- profit, and the functions it serves
- interest, how it's determined, the market for loanable funds, how the forces of demand and supply affect loanable funds, and the factors that determine the interest rate for an individual loan
- the share of total incomes of Canadians accounted for by each type of income

SKILLS FOCUS

After studying this chapter, you will be able to:
- research and compare occupations to analyze the factors responsible for wage differences
- assess various means of determining income from labour
- graph and explain the impact of unions on labour markets
- research and debate possible tradeoffs in labour disputes
- describe and explain changes in corporate profit, and assess their relationship to other incomes
- demonstrate various effects on the market for loanable funds by using graphs
- apply what you've learned about wages, human capital, interest rates, and the market for loanable funds to education and career choices

 **Wages**

In the last chapter, we looked specifically at how the forces of demand and supply determine the wage in a given labour market. Recall that we're using the term "wage" generally to include salaries and other forms of payment for labour. In each labour market, the workforce constitutes a small, noncompeting group with limited opportunities to move from one labour market to another. Steelworkers, for example, can compete among themselves for many jobs in the manufacturing sector, but not likely for jobs as accountants in the financial services sector; in the same way, accountants might compete for jobs as business managers, but not for jobs as heart surgeons. Now, let's look at the big picture of many markets and of various jobs, and the factors that determine wages for Canadian workers.

Wage Determinants

Looking at the wider, national labour market highlights the tremendous differences among Canadians' incomes gained from labour. Figure 8.1 shows the distribution of earnings (defined as wages and self-employed income) in the Canadian economy. In 1991, four out of ten Canadian earners made less than $15 000 annually. At the other end of the scale, less than one in five Canadian earners made $40 000 or more. (These figures are earnings before taxes.)

Figure 8.1:   Distribution of Earnings (1991)

Earnings	Percentage of All Earners
Under $5000	17.2
$5000–$9999	12.7
$10 000–$14 999	10.4
$15 000–$19 999	9.2
$20 000–$24 999	9.3
$25 000–$29 999	9.0
$30 000–$34 999	7.7
$35 000–$39 999	5.9
$40 000–$44 999	4.8
$45 000–$49 999	3.6
$50 000–$59 999	4.8
$60 000 and over	5.4
	100.0

Earnings of Canadians varied widely, with about 4 out of 10 Canadian earners making less than $15 000 annually. In contrast, just under 1 in 5 Canadian earners made $40 000 or more annually.

SOURCE: Statistics Canada, *Earnings of Men and Women, 1991* (January 1993), cat. no. 13-217, p. 40. Reproduced by authority of the Minister of Industry, 1994.

There are seven main determinants of wage levels in labour markets: labour productivity, education, experience, job conditions, regional disparities, market power, and discrimination.

Labour Productivity

As seen in the previous chapter, in a given job market the level of labour productivity, or the output per worker in a given time, determines the wage of that worker. Among the determinants of labour income, productivity is the most important. The output of each worker varies because of such factors as the worker's ability to do the job, the use of complementary resources, and the state of technology. With more capable workers, additional complementary resources, or a technological innovation, the marginal revenue product of each worker rises, pushing up the demand for labour as well as the prevailing wage.

Education

In general, the more education a worker needs to perform a job, the higher the pay. As Figure 8.2 shows, families headed by someone with a university degree earn about twice as much annual income as families headed by someone with only up to eight years of school. (Statistics Canada defines "family head" as the husband in families with a husband and a wife, the parent in single-parent families, or the eldest person in other families.) The most significant differences in average annual incomes are between families headed by those with some high school education and those with high school diplomas only ($43 737 compared to $52 968, or a 21 percent increase for the graduate), and for families headed by those with postsecondary diplomas and those with university degrees ($54 967 compared to $79 347, or a 44 percent increase for the university graduate). Work that requires job-related training tends to have a higher

Figure 8.2:   Education and Average Family Income (1992)

Education	Average Family Income
University degree	$79 347
Postsecondary diploma	54 967
Some postsecondary	53 421
High school graduate	52 968
Some high school	43 737
0 to 8 years of school	38 248

Annual family incomes rise with the educational level achieved by the family head. Average earnings for families whose heads have a university degree are double those for families whose heads have completed the eighth grade or less of schooling.

SOURCE: Adapted from Statistics Canada, *Income Distributions by Size in Canada, 1992* (December 1993), cat. no. 13-207, p. 71. Reproduced by authority of the Minister of Industry, 1994.

marginal revenue product than does work that requires very little job-related training, so education is linked to labour productivity. Therefore, education has an impact on labour demand.

Education also has an impact on labour supply. As every student knows, education is costly and time-consuming. For example, students who undertake a full-time postsecondary program have not only out-of-pocket costs such as tuition and books, but also an important opportunity cost: the income that could have been earned by entering the workforce immediately. Of course, students who attend public postsecondary institutions do not bear the entire cost of their education (taxpayers, through government programs, pick up the remainder). Education provides benefits; acquiring skills and knowledge may itself be a reward for the work and effort involved. Just the same, a worker entering the labour force with a higher education tends to expect a return on his or her education investment.

Economists view work-related education as an investment in **human capital**, which is the income-earning potential of a person's skills and knowledge. According to this perspective and ignoring the consumption component of education (the skills and knowledge a student acquires), an educational program is only worthwhile if the expected rise in the individual's lifetime income outweighs the sum of that education's direct and indirect costs.

human capital: the income-earning potential of a person's skills and knowledge

Thinking About Economics

Suppose three friends graduating from high school choose different career paths: the first enters the workforce directly as a clerical worker, the second enrolls in a university arts program for a major in English literature with a focus on medieval literature, and the third pursues a degree in computer science. What do these decisions suggest about the friends' economic choices?

According to the economic view of human capital, by not making a further investment in education, the first friend sacrifices possible income gains later in life for immediate earnings. In other words, receiving a dollar in purchasing power now is worth much more to this individual than receiving greater purchasing power in the future. The English major is willing to give up immediate income for future benefit, and will likely have a future income greater than the first friend's, but perhaps not as much as he would if he pursued another type of postsecondary education. From this economic viewpoint, this friend sees the knowledge he will gain from his postsecondary education primarily as a consumption item. The third friend is also willing to give up immediate income for future increases in welfare. She views education as an investment in her human capital to increase future earning power and, hopefully, as a source of pleasure as well.

Experience

Experience is another determining factor of income levels. On-the-job experience increases a worker's productivity, pushing up the demand for the worker's labour and the wage rate. In many industries, workers gain certain privileges the longer they work for a single employer. Because of these **seniority rights**, older workers are often paid higher wages and can apply first for promotions and overtime work, allowing them to earn higher incomes than their younger colleagues.

The positive effect of workplace experience on earnings is one of the main reasons why average incomes rise with age during the first part of a person's working life. Figure 8.3 shows the relationship between age and family income. As the age of the head of the family rises to the 45 to 54 age range for men and to the 55 to 59 range for women, average family income increases; thereafter, incomes tend to decrease as more workers retire.

seniority rights: the workplace privileges provided to workers who have the longest experience with their employer

Figure 8.3:   Age and Average Family Income (1992)

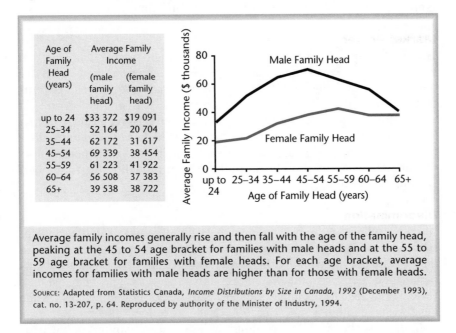

Age of Family Head (years)	Average Family Income (male family head)	(female family head)
up to 24	$33 372	$19 091
25–34	52 164	20 704
35–44	62 172	31 617
45–54	69 339	38 454
55–59	61 223	41 922
60–64	56 508	37 383
65+	39 538	38 722

Average family incomes generally rise and then fall with the age of the family head, peaking at the 45 to 54 age bracket for families with male heads and at the 55 to 59 age bracket for families with female heads. For each age bracket, average incomes for families with male heads are higher than for those with female heads.

SOURCE: Adapted from Statistics Canada, *Income Distributions by Size in Canada, 1992* (December 1993), cat. no. 13-207, p. 64. Reproduced by authority of the Minister of Industry, 1994.

Job Conditions

Often two occupations provide very different earnings even when productivity and education levels in each occupation are the same. One reason for this discrepancy is that working conditions in the two occupations can make one less appealing than the other. In order to attract workers to less appealing occupations, employers must offer higher wages. For example, garbage collectors receive higher wages than most other unskilled workers, in part because of their unattractive working conditions.

Regional Disparities

Wage differences often have a geographic dimension. In Canada, workers in the same occupation often earn different incomes depending on the region they live in. For example, a fishplant worker in British Columbia may earn more than a worker doing the identical job in Newfoundland. In a perfectly functioning labour market, workers in a single occupation would move from one part of the country to another until wage disparities in this occupation were eliminated. However, labour tends to be immobile. Even when workers find moving economically feasible, they and their families may be reluctant to adjust to new jobs, schools, and surroundings. Labour immobility is especially pronounced for multiple-income families because of the added difficulty of two or more people changing jobs. Immobility is also common among older workers, who tend to be more settled in their jobs and communities.

Market Power

labour unions: workers' organizations that negotiate with employers about wages, working conditions, and job benefits

The market power workers have also affects their wages. One way that workers can increase their market power is by using their collective power through labour unions and professional associations. **Labour unions** are workers' organizations that negotiate with employers on such issues as wages, working conditions, and job benefits. As a rule, earnings in labour markets that are unionized tend to be higher than in nonunionized markets. Professional organizations for such groups as medical doctors and lawyers can also play a similar role in providing their members with market power.

Discrimination

job discrimination: hiring, wage, and promotion decisions based on criteria other than a worker's credentials or performance

Discrimination, too, can play a role in determining wages. **Job discrimination** occurs when decisions regarding hiring, wages, or promotion are based on some trait of the worker other than credentials or performance. Job discrimination stems from the prejudices of employers and may be based on a variety of factors; for example, gender, race, age, or physical ability. While job discrimination in a variety of forms is illegal, it does still exist.

job segregation: the discriminatory division of occupations

In its most obvious form, job discrimination means workers doing identical work in a company receive different pay. A less obvious form is **job segregation**, which is the discriminatory division of occupations. In Canada, job segregation on the basis of gender has been widely studied, and has resulted in remedial legislation based on the notion of equal pay for work of equal value. Under such legislation, job segregation—for example, where a male-dominated labour market is paid more than a comparable female-dominated labour market—can be addressed.

Figure 8.4:   The Impact of Job Segregation

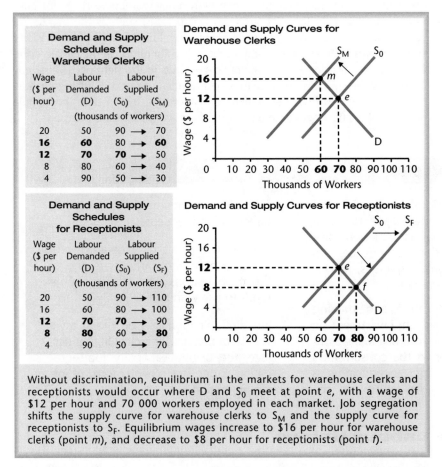

Wage ($ per hour)	Labour Demanded (D)	Labour Supplied (S₀)		(S_M)
		(thousands of workers)		
20	50	90	→	70
16	**60**	80	→	**60**
12	**70**	**70**	→	50
8	80	60	→	40
4	90	50	→	30

Demand and Supply Schedules for Warehouse Clerks

Demand and Supply Curves for Warehouse Clerks

Wage ($ per hour)	Labour Demanded (D)	Labour Supplied (S₀)		(S_F)
		(thousands of workers)		
20	50	90	→	110
16	60	80	→	100
12	**70**	**70**	→	90
8	**80**	60	→	**80**
4	90	50	→	70

Demand and Supply Schedules for Receptionists

Demand and Supply Curves for Receptionists

Without discrimination, equilibrium in the markets for warehouse clerks and receptionists would occur where D and S_0 meet at point *e*, with a wage of $12 per hour and 70 000 workers employed in each market. Job segregation shifts the supply curve for warehouse clerks to S_M and the supply curve for receptionists to S_F. Equilibrium wages increase to $16 per hour for warehouse clerks (point *m*), and decrease to $8 per hour for receptionists (point *f*).

Figure 8.4 shows the hypothetical example of competitive labour markets for warehouse clerks and receptionists. For convenience, we will assume that the wage rate in each occupation would be $12 per hour, at the intersection of the labour demand and labour supply curves, if the markets weren't discriminatory. Suppose employers decide to hire men exclusively to be warehouse clerks and women exclusively to be receptionists. In the male-dominated warehouse clerk market, the supply curve shifts to the left (to S_M), thereby increasing the equilibrium wage to $16 per hour. This new supply curve reflects discrimination not only in hiring warehouse clerks, but in many other occupations as well. Because male workers face a wide range of opportunities for attractive, high-paying employment, they will only enter the market for warehouse clerks at relatively high wages.

Women who would prefer to be employed in traditionally male-dominated occupations must instead apply, along with other women workers, for positions in traditionally female-dominated occupations, such as the market for receptionists. Because women are crowded into a limited range of job markets, supply curves in these markets shift to the right. Therefore, in the female-dominated receptionist market, the supply curve shifts to the right (to S_F), thereby decreasing the equilibrium wage to $8 per hour. As a result of job segregation, therefore, wages in male-dominated occupations are higher than they would otherwise be, and wages in female-dominated occupations are lower.

BRIEF REVIEW

1. Wages vary significantly in the Canadian labour market. Factors that determine wage levels are labour productivity, education, experience, job conditions, regional disparities, market power, and discrimination.

2. Work-related education and training can be viewed as an investment in human capital, or an individual's earning power. Ignoring the consumption aspect of knowledge, an education is worthwhile when its returns, in the form of future income gains, exceed its direct and indirect costs.

3. The positive effect of experience and seniority rights on earnings is one of the main reasons why family income tends to rise with age.

4. Job discrimination can be based on a variety of factors: for example, gender, race, age, or physical ability. Job segregation is one less obvious form of job discrimination.

 ## Labour Unions

The impact of Canadian labour unions is considerable. Their influence extends not only to wage rates, but also to working hours, workplace standards, and employment levels in various labour markets. Before exploring their impact, we'll first consider the types, structure, and procedures of unions.

Types of Unions

There are two main types of labour unions—industrial unions and craft unions—each of which influences labour markets in different ways.

industrial union: a labour union of workers in a certain industry, no matter what their occupations

Industrial Unions

An **industrial union** includes workers in a certain industry, no matter what their occupations. Hence, these unions are also referred to as inclusive unions, and are most common in sectors that primarily use unskilled and semiskilled labour. The automobile, steel, and forestry industries are examples. Figure 8.5 takes a look at the effect of an industrial union on the steelmaking industry. This example is based on two simplifying assumptions: all workers in the industry are assumed to perform identical tasks so that they earn the same wage, and the market for steelworkers is a competitive one. Without a union, the market for steelworkers would reach equilibrium at an hourly wage of $18, with 140 000 workers employed. By bargaining with employers, an industrial union is able to raise the wage to $22 an hour. Each member's earnings are increased, but at a cost—employment in the labour market is reduced to 120 000, creating an excess supply of 40 000 workers.

Figure 8.5:   The Impact of Industrial Unions

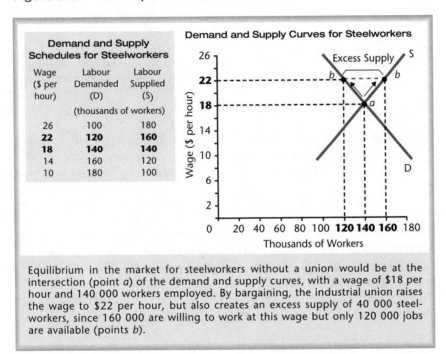

Wage ($ per hour)	Labour Demanded (D)	Labour Supplied (S)
	(thousands of workers)	
26	100	180
22	**120**	**160**
18	**140**	**140**
14	160	120
10	180	100

Demand and Supply Schedules for Steelworkers

Equilibrium in the market for steelworkers without a union would be at the intersection (point *a*) of the demand and supply curves, with a wage of $18 per hour and 140 000 workers employed. By bargaining, the industrial union raises the wage to $22 per hour, but also creates an excess supply of 40 000 steelworkers, since 160 000 are willing to work at this wage but only 120 000 jobs are available (points *b*).

Craft Unions

A **craft union** includes workers in a particular occupation. Craft unions restrict whom they allow to be members, so they are also referred to as exclusive unions. They are common in skilled trades such as printing as well as in some parts of the construction industry, such as carpentry and bricklaying. In any labour market dominated by a craft union, acquiring a *union card* is an essential first step in being allowed to work. To become a member of such a union, a worker often must complete an apprenticeship pro-

craft union: a labour union of workers in a particular occupation

Figure 8.6:   The Impact of Craft Unions

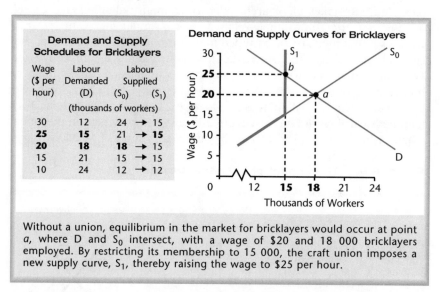

Demand and Supply Schedules for Bricklayers		
Wage ($ per hour)	Labour Demanded (D)	Labour Supplied (S₀) (S₁)
	(thousands of workers)	
30	12	24 → 15
25	**15**	**21 → 15**
20	**18**	**18 → 15**
15	21	15 → 15
10	24	12 → 12

Without a union, equilibrium in the market for bricklayers would occur at point *a*, where D and S_0 intersect, with a wage of $20 and 18 000 bricklayers employed. By restricting its membership to 15 000, the craft union imposes a new supply curve, S_1, thereby raising the wage to $25 per hour.

gram and write a licensing examination. While craft unions' requirements attempt to ensure craft standards, they also allow unions to determine the supply of workers in the market and to negotiate higher wages for their members.

Figure 8.6 shows the results of a craft union's membership restrictions on an otherwise competitive market for bricklayers. Without a union, equilibrium in the market would occur at the intersection of D and S_0, with 18 000 bricklayers employed at an hourly wage of $20. The introduction of a craft union means the number of workers in the trade is limited to 15 000 or less. The result is a kinked supply curve, S_1, which becomes vertical at the membership limit. Market equilibrium moves to a lower employment level of 15 000 workers and a higher wage of $25 per hour.

The Structure of Labour Unions

Most Canadian labour unions are composed of local bargaining units, known as union locals, which are part of national or international unions, which are themselves part of larger central organizations called federations or congresses. While some individual unions, called *local unions*, are local in organization and exist in isolation, most unions gain support from being connected to a larger network of unions.

Union Locals

Unionized workers in a certain factory, company, or geographical area are represented by a union local. Members of the local elect their own executive, a committee that negotiates with employers and signs a labour agreement. Union locals are part of larger unions that aid locals in collective bargaining and other tasks, such as recruiting new members.

A union local's clout depends on the proportion of eligible workers who are members. A **closed shop** is a specific job market (one workplace, for instance) in which all workers covered by a collective agreement must be union members. Related to a closed shop is a **union shop,** in which all workers must become union members after a certain period of employment. Both closed shops and union shops give a union local more power than does an **open shop**, in which union membership is not compulsory for workers.

National and International Unions

Many Canadian labour unions are either national or international in scope. National unions have their headquarters as well as all of their locals in Canada. An example is the Canadian Union of Public Employees (CUPE), Canada's largest union, with a total membership of 412 242 in 1993. Other union locals may be part of international unions, which represent about a quarter of Canadian unionized workers. International unions usually have their headquarters, as well as most of their locals, in the United States. The United Food and Commercial Workers International Union, for example, had a Canadian membership of 170 000 in 1992.

The role of international unions in Canada has dwindled over the past decade, as some Canadian branches of international unions have separated to form their own national unions. The most notable case was the split in 1985 of the Canadian branch of the International Union of United Automobile, Aerospace and Agriculture Workers of America (UAW). The result of the split was Canada's sixth-largest union, known as the Canadian Automobile Workers (CAW, or known officially as the National Automobile, Aerospace, and Agricultural Implement Workers Union of Canada), with a 1993 membership of 170 000.

Federations and Congresses

The majority of unions are affiliated with one or more federations or congresses. These central organizations do not directly govern member unions. Instead, they provide a collective voice for unionized labour. Federations and congresses may lobby government to reflect labour interests in legislation and can settle disputes between unions.

As shown in Figure 8.7, about 80 percent of Canada's union membership is affiliated with at least one central organization. Almost 60 percent of unionized workers in Canada are allied with the Canadian Labour Congress (CLC). Other unions belong to the smaller Canadian Federation of Labour (CFL) or several Quebec-based federations, most notably the

closed shop: a specific labour market in which all workers covered by a collective agreement must be union members

union shop: a specific labour market in which all workers covered by a collective agreement must become union members after a certain period of employment

open shop: a specific labour market in which union membership is not compulsory

Figure 8.7: Union Affiliation in Canada (1992)

Congress Affiliation		Percentage of Total Union Membership
Canadian Labour Congress (CLC)		57.8
CLC only	36.6	
Also affiliated with AFL-CIO	21.2	
Confederation of National Trade Unions (CNTU)		6.2
Canadian Federation of Labour (CFL)		5.2
CFL only	0.2	
Also affiliated with AFL-CIO	5.0	
AFL-CIO only		4.1
Other central organizations		4.5
Unaffiliated unions		19.0
Independent local organizations		3.2
		100.0

The bulk of unions—about 80 percent—belong to one or more central organizations. The Canadian Labour Congress (CLC) is the largest Canadian central federation, including almost 60 percent of Canadian union members. Smaller Canadian central organizations include the Quebec-based Confederation of National Trade Unions (CNTU) and the Canadian Federation of Labour (CFL).

SOURCE: Labour Canada, *Directory of Labour Organizations in Canada, 1992–93*, cat. no. L2-2-1992, p. xiii. Reproduced with permission of the Ministry of Supply & Services Canada, 1994.

Confederation of National Trade Unions (CNTU). The American-based AFL-CIO also has ties with Canadian unions, while about a fifth of unionized workers in Canada are represented by unaffiliated unions or by independent local organizations.

Collective Bargaining

collective bargaining: the process of union representatives negotiating with employers over workers' wages, hours, and working conditions

Unions represent the interests of their members primarily through collective bargaining. **Collective bargaining** is the process of union representatives negotiating with employers over such issues as workers' wages, hours, and working conditions. As a result of collective bargaining, unions and employers make collective agreements to which both parties are bound for a set period of time. Unions also become involved in disputes over, for example, worker suspensions. Generally, unions and employers come to a settlement through face-to-face bargaining. Failing that, unions and employers go to mediation or arbitration. If no settlement is reached, work may be disrupted through work-to-rule campaigns, strikes, lockouts, or the hiring of replacement workers.

Mediation and Arbitration

mediation: the process of having an outside party determine and propose a settlement to employers and unions

When unions and employers cannot come to an agreement, they may seek help through a process known as **mediation.** An outside party known as a mediator is appointed, usually with the help of government officials. After studying the positions and proposals of union and management, the mediator makes a series of recommendations that each side is free to accept or reject.

Disputes are sometimes settled through a similar procedure called **arbitration**. Like a mediator, an arbitrator is an outside party, typically appointed with government help. However, the decision of an arbitrator is binding on both parties; they must accept the settlement.

Working to Rule

If no settlement is reached, a union may elect to use a tactic called **working to rule**, whereby union members work strictly within the bounds of their job descriptions. In a work-to-rule campaign, workers slow down normal operations, but continue to receive their pay. However, they refuse to work overtime or do anything else that is not strictly required by their jobs. A successful work-to-rule campaign pressures both sides to return to the bargaining table.

Strikes

Unions may also elect to stage a **strike** against the employer by effectively ceasing work. Usually, a strike forces a business to shut down, thereby pressuring management to return to the bargaining table. Unions, too, are under pressure as their members have no income except for payments from any strike funds amassed through their members' union dues, or membership payments. Sometimes unions will hold rotating strikes, with groups of workers striking for set periods of time in order to slow down work. During strikes, union members typically picket the workplace. **Picketing** means that the striking workers take strategic positions around the outside of the workplace, usually with signs to publicize their cause, and may try to turn back customers, employees who are still working, and delivery people transporting goods to or from the business.

Lockouts and Replacement Workers

Employers may elect to use a lockout to speed a settlement. A **lockout** literally locks union employees out of the workplace and temporarily stops work. As in the case of strikes, both sides are affected by this action: the business usually ceases operations and employees lose their incomes. In some cases, businesses that lock out employees or who have striking employees may hire replacement workers (sometimes called "scabs" by unions) to carry out the duties of permanent employees. While they can serve as powerful weapons, lockouts and scab labour poison relations between the company and its regular employees, as well as create antagonism between the regular and the replacement workers.

arbitration: the process of having an outside party determine and dictate a settlement to employers and unions

working to rule: the union tactic of members slowing down work by adhering strictly to their job descriptions

strike: the union tactic of members ceasing to work

picketing: the practice of striking workers taking positions around the outside of the workplace, usually with signs, to publicize their cause to others

lockout: the employer tactic of barring workers from the workplace

Unions and the Canadian Economy

Since the 1930s, when only one out of five Canadian workers was union-ized, labour unions have grown in membership. Unions now represent just under four out of ten of Canada's paid nonagricultural workers. As shown in Figure 8.8, union membership rose substantially as a percentage of these workers during the 1940s and early 1950s. Growth fell off in the

Figure 8.8:   Union Membership in Canada

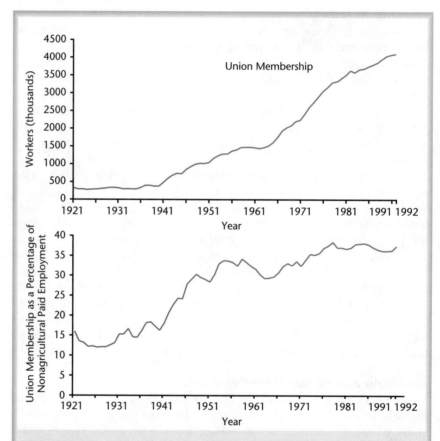

In general, the number of workers in Canada who are union members has grown steadily, as shown on the top graph. The proportion of Canadian workers — other than agricultural workers — who are union members has also risen, as shown on the bottom graph. From a low point of 12 percent in 1926, the proportion rose to its highest point of 38.8 percent in 1984.

SOURCES: Adapted from F.H. Leacy, ed., *Historical Statistics of Canada, 2nd ed.* (Ottawa: Statistics Canada, 1983), pp. 175–77; Labour Canada, *Directory of Labour Organizations in Canada, 1992–93*, cat. no. L2-2-1992, p. xii. Reproduced by authority of the Minister of Industry, 1994.

late 1950s and 1960s as most workers in easily organized manufacturing sectors were already members. Because of the growth in Canada's expanding public sector in the early 1970s, membership rose rapidly. Since then, relative to the total number of workers, membership has decreased slightly.

The recent stagnation in union membership results from the shift of Canada's workforce from the unionized manufacturing sector to less unionized service industries. As shown in Figure 8.9, the role of unions in Canadian service industries varies enormously. Unions are even more prevalent in public administration, communications, public utilities, and transportation than they are in manufacturing. However, there are many service industries—for example, those connected with retailing, finance, and real estate—in which union representation is scanty, and it is in such sectors that significant new employment has been created.

There is also a notable difference in union representation based on the gender and age of workers, as illustrated in Figure 8.9. Male workers dominate many manufacturing jobs, while women are better represented in expanding service industries. Hence, it is no surprise that the percentage of men who are union members is higher than that for women. The same argument applies when comparing workers on the basis of age. Workers aged 45 and up are heavily represented in the manufacturing

Figure 8.9: Union Membership by Industry, Gender, and Age (1990)

Industry	Percentage of Paid Workers Who Are Union Members	Gender and Age	Percentage of Paid Workers Who Are Union Members
Public administration	61.3	**Men**	36.1
Communications and public utilities	60.1	**Women**	29.7
Transportation	47.9		
Manufacturing	39.3	**Both Genders**	
Mining	37.5	16–24	15.4
Construction	32.7	25–34	32.4
Retail and wholesale trade	24.8	35–44	39.8
Finance, insurance, and real estate	9.0	45–54	44.0
Agriculture	5.9	55–64	40.7

Union membership is most prevalent in public administration, while agriculture has the lowest percentage of union members. Males are more likely to be union members than females, and the prevalence of union membership tends to increase with age, peaking in the 45 to 54 age bracket. Reproduced by authority of the Minister of Industry, 1994.

SOURCE: Morley Gunderson and W. Craig Riddell, *Labour Market Economics*, 3rd ed. (Toronto: McGraw-Hill Ryerson, 1993), p. 329. Based on unpublished data from Statistics Canada, The Labour Market Activity Survey 1990. Reproduced by authority of the Minister of Industry, 1994.

sector, so are more likely to be unionized than workers who are younger than 45.

Studies suggest that wages in unionized occupations tend to exceed those in nonunionized occupations by about 10 to 25 percent. Unions do increase wages in unionized labour markets. However, workers who cannot find employment in unionized occupations crowd into nonunionized trades in much the same way as job segregation causes some workers to be pushed into a small range of occupations. Because the supply of labour increases in these labour markets and because workers lack the market power that unions would otherwise give them, employers are able to pay lower wages. Therefore, unions influence wages in both unionized and nonunionized occupations, and *average* wages in the entire economy are not greatly affected by union activity.

BRIEF REVIEW

1. In unionized labour markets, unions have a significant influence on wages, working hours, workplace standards, and employment levels.

2. Industrial unions represent all workers in a certain industry, so they negotiate wages across an industry; craft unions represent workers in a particular occupation; and, they can both affect the supply of labour in the market and negotiate wages.

3. Unions tend to be national or international in scope and have branches, which are called locals. Most unions are affiliated with federations or congresses.

4. While unions and employers usually reach a settlement through face-to-face bargaining, they can also use mediation or arbitration to settle disputes. Sometimes settlements are reached only after work is disrupted through work-to-rule campaigns, strikes, lockouts, or the hiring of replacement workers.

5. While wages in unionized labour markets tend to be higher than those in nonunionized labour markets, labour unions do not greatly affect average wages in the Canadian economy overall.

Rejecting McUnion

Unions have a long history in certain sectors, but only a foothold in others. This article reports the outcome of an attempt to unionize one such workplace by a student who worked there.

Workers at a McDonald's Restaurant of Canada Ltd. outlet in Orangeville, Ont. rejected a proposal to become the first unionized McDonald's franchise in the world. The workers—many of them teenagers—sported "Just say no" buttons before voting 77 to 19 February 24, 1994 against joining the Service Employees International Union.

The vote was held after 17-year-old Sarah Inglis—a three-year veteran of McDonald's—spearheaded a union drive at the fast-food restaurant. She claimed that staff members were being treated poorly and that they need to win "dignity and respect." In all, 67 of the 102 Orangeville workers signed union membership cards by the end of September 1993. That strong majority entitled the union to automatic certification, but a lawyer representing other workers raised objections before the Ontario Labor Relations Board. Many of the workers who signed cards subsequently changed their minds.

Opinions varied about how the vote should be interpreted. Roy Ellis, vice-president of human resources for McDonald's Restaurants of Canada, said the vote showed how much the teens—and others—enjoyed working for the company. But academics and labor leaders said that McDonald's teamwork corporate

SOURCE: The Toronto Star/P. Power

philosophy helped overturn the union drive. Said Pradeep Kumar, a professor of industrial relations at Queen's University in Kingston, Ont.: "There's a brainwashing that goes on in fast-food companies like McDonald's where you're told you're not part of the team if you unionize." Despite the defeat of the yearlong attempt to organize her co-workers, Inglis declared a victory, pointing out that the debate over the union has already a positive effect on working conditions at the restaurant.

SOURCE: Adapted from *Maclean's* "Rejecting McUnion," 7 March 1994, p. 43.

Rent

rent: the payment for use of a productive resource that is available only in a fixed amount

So far, we have concentrated on the income from labour. Now, let's turn to a second resource income: rent. **Rent** is defined very precisely in economics as the payment for use of a productive resource that is available in only a fixed amount. Note that it is distinct from the term "rent" in more general use. For example, the total monthly payment to a landowner by a tenant often includes not only economic rent (payment for a resource in fixed supply), but also payment for utilities, maintenance, and administration, plus a normal profit for the owners. Land is the most significant resource that provides rent. With few exceptions (for example, when landfilling or drainage systems create more land), land is available in only a fixed supply. For example, Ontario has a fixed land supply of 891 190 km².

The Market for Land

To see how the rent for land is determined, we must make a number of assumptions. We'll assume that we can separate economic rent from payments for any buildings or improvements made on the land; we'll assume that the market for land is competitive, with many buyers and sellers; and we'll assume that each unit of land is of the same quality.

The Equilibrium Value of Rent

Figure 8.10 shows demand and supply for land in a particular region. Because there is a fixed supply of land, the supply curve is perfectly inelastic, or vertical at its fixed amount. Demand, however, is variable; quantity demanded decreases at higher rents and increases at lower rents. Therefore, the demand curve for land has a negative (downward) slope. Market equilibrium occurs at a rent of $1000, where the two curves intersect. Since we've assumed that we can separate economic rent from other payments, this $1000 is entirely payment for the land.

Changes in Demand

Because the supply of land cannot change, only a change in demand can change the equilibrium value of rent. Recall from Chapter 7 that the demand for resources is determined indirectly, because it is derived from demand for other products. Therefore, the main factor that can change demand for land is a change in the price for the products the land is used to produce. Suppose that the land in the region we're considering is devoted entirely to cattle ranching and that all cattle ranchers are renting land from landowners. In Figure 8.11, the demand is shown as D_0 and point *a* is the equilibrium. If the price of beef rises, cattle ranchers will find they can increase their revenue for each unit of land. As a result, cattle ranchers will demand more land at every possible price, thus shifting the demand curve to the right, to D_1. The change in the demand will cause the equilibrium value of rent to rise to $1200 (point *b*.)

Figure 8.10:   Equilibrium in the Market for Land

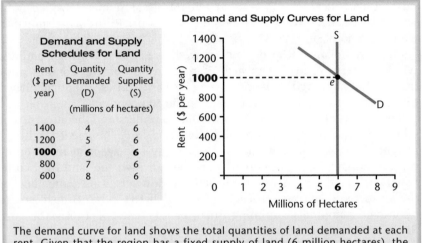

The demand curve for land shows the total quantities of land demanded at each rent. Given that the region has a fixed supply of land (6 million hectares), the supply curve for land is a vertical line. Equilibrium occurs at point *e*, giving a rent of $1000 for each hectare of land.

Figure 8.11:   Changes in the Demand for Land

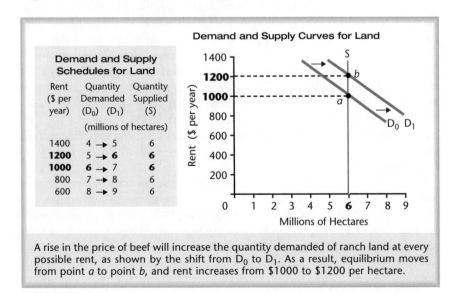

A rise in the price of beef will increase the quantity demanded of ranch land at every possible rent, as shown by the shift from D_0 to D_1. As a result, equilibrium moves from point *a* to point *b*, and rent increases from $1000 to $1200 per hectare.

David Ricardo
SOURCE: The Bettmann Archive

Reaping the Rewards
David Ricardo and the Theory of Rent

Ricardo and His Influence

In the generation after Adam Smith, several influential thinkers worked to extend his theories. Of this group, now known as the classical economists, David Ricardo (1772–1823) left the greatest mark. Unlike most who have made a study of economic questions, Ricardo had practical experience in business.

Born in Holland, Ricardo later moved to England with his parents, where he went on to amass such a great fortune on the London stock market that he retired to the country in his early forties. There, he turned his attention to the subject known as "political economy."

Like others of his time, Ricardo wanted to understand the questions of who gets what in an economy, and why. To do this, he needed a theory of rent. The issue of land rent was especially important in nineteenth-century Britain, because most farmers did not own the land they cultivated but leased it from a small group of landowners, mostly members of the aristocracy. By coincidence, in February of 1815, four British writers published pamphlets outlining theories of rent; of those theories, Ricardo's became the standard.

Ricardo's Theory of Rent

According to Ricardo's theory, the rent to a landowner for a certain piece of farmland equals the excess revenue that remains after paying all other costs, including the farmer's normal profit. Why do landowners receive all this surplus revenue? They do so because the quantity of the land is fixed. Farmers bid against one another to rent each parcel of land; this bidding process raises the rent for each parcel to its maximum possible value.

Suppose, for example, that wheat farmers lease four different grades of land. The table and graph on the next page show the output of wheat per hectare on each grade of land. While grade A land provides an annual crop of 50 kg per hectare, the other grades each produce, respectively, 40, 20, and 10 kg. For all grades of land, farmers have a cost of $100 per hectare for all other inputs. This figure includes not only explicit production costs, such as wages, but also implicit costs, such as the farmer's normal profit.

So, with the output and costs now established, we can determine rent according to Ricardo's theory. For each hectare of land, rent equals the farmer's revenue less the production costs of $100. If the price of wheat is $5, the 50 kg output from a hectare of grade A land gives the farmer a total revenue of $250 per hectare. Therefore, rent for this particular grade of land is the total revenue less the production costs, or $150 ($250 − $100). Because lower-quality land produces a lower output, and therefore lower

Ricardo's Theory of Rent

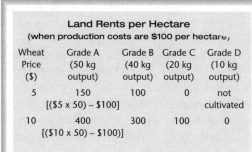

Wheat Price ($)	Land Rents per Hectare (when production costs are $100 per hectare)			
	Grade A (50 kg output)	Grade B (40 kg output)	Grade C (20 kg output)	Grade D (10 kg output)
5	150 [($5 x 50) – $100]	100	0	not cultivated
10	400 [($10 x 50) – $100)]	300	100	0

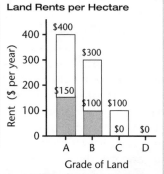

The production costs are constant at $100 per hectare with different grades of land, but the output of wheat per hectare varies from 10 to 50 kg. The table and bar graph show the resulting land rents given two wheat prices: $5 and $10 per kilogram. If the price of wheat is $5 per kilogram, the rents for the three highest grades of land would be $150, $100, and $0, respectively. On the bar graph, the shaded areas indicate the rent at the $5 price. If the price of wheat increased to $10 per kilogram, the rents on the highest grades of land would rise and the fourth grade (D) would enter production, as indicated by the unshaded areas on the bar graph.

SOURCE: Adapted from Stanley L. Brue, *The Evolution of Economic Thought*, 5th ed. (Fort Worth: The Dryden Press, 1994), p.116.

revenue, the lower grades of land have lower rents. For example, a hectare of grade C land produces an output of 20 kg of wheat, giving the farmer a revenue of $100 (20 kg × $5 per kg); after the costs of $100 are paid from the revenue, the rent stands at zero ($100 – $100). The lowest grade of land, grade D, would not be cultivated since the production costs ($100) exceed its revenues (10 kg × $5 per kg = $50).

In Ricardo's theory, the rent of a hectare of agricultural land depends on the price of the product it produces. So, in our example, an increase in the price of wheat to $10 would increase the rents on each grade of land. For example, the rent of a hectare of grade A land would rise to $400, or the difference between the farmer's new revenue ($10 × 50 kg = $500) and the constant production costs ($100). Similarly, the rents for grades B and C land rise to $300 and $100 per hectare, respectively, and grade D land would be brought into production with a rent of zero, since its revenue now matches production costs. Grade D land therefore represents the new margin of cultivation.

Rent and Population Growth   Ricardo's explanation of rent played an important part in his predictions for the future, which he outlined in

Principles of Political Economy and Taxation, first published in 1817. As population increased, said Ricardo, the less productive land would have to be brought into production as premium-quality land became fully utilized. Wheat output per worker would therefore decline, meaning the price of wheat would gradually rise. Because bread was such an important staple in the diets of workers and their families, higher wheat prices would push up the wages that employers would have to pay. And these higher wages, said Ricardo, would lower businesses' profits.

Who would benefit from these trends? It would not be employers, whose profits would shrink, nor workers, whose higher wages would only keep up with costs. It would be well-off landowners who would reap the rewards as higher food prices forced up rents. Unlike other classes in society, said Ricardo, these landowners provided no productive service themselves, but were simply fortunate enough—probably through inheritance—to have gained ownership of an essential economic resource.

The Corn Laws   Already renowned for his theories, Ricardo became famous for applying them when he served as a representative in Britain's parliament. One of the most contentious issues facing the British government in which Ricardo served was whether or not to abolish the country's Corn Laws. These laws restricted the purchase of foreign wheat (or "corn" as it was then called) through a system of tariffs, or taxes on imports. The tariffs, which were meant to aid British farmers, raised average wheat prices. Therefore, Ricardo argued, the tariffs helped no one but the wealthy landowners who benefited from increased rents. While the Corn Laws were not repealed until after Ricardo's death, his theories and political involvement were both important in the struggle against these laws.

Henry George and the Single Tax Movement
While Ricardo did not draw any radical conclusions from his theory of rent, others did. In later decades of the nineteenth century, the privileged position of landowners, both in Europe and North America, increasingly came under attack. One of the most zealous critics of landowners was the American journalist and economist Henry George (1839–1897).

Should those lucky enough to own land be able to make often lavish unearned incomes from this ownership at the expense of productive capitalist employers and workers? Like many reformers, George thought not, and in his well-known book, *Progress and Poverty* (1879), he set out his solution: all taxes should be replaced by a 100 percent tax on land rent.

According to George and his many supporters, this tax would have far-reaching benefits. Because the amount of land is fixed by nature, imposing a land rent tax would not reduce the supply of land. Moreover, the revenues from this tax would be so great that all other taxes could be repealed. Repealing all other taxes would stimulate greater production.

George's proposal was so popular that, at the end of the nineteenth century, his name was almost a household word in Britain and North America. However, no government ever adopted the single tax. Most economists criticized it, stating that such a tax would harm many poor people (for example, elderly widows) and might cause huge social upheavals as all landowners found the return on their investments completely wiped out. Critics also pointed out that much of what is classified as land rent in fact represents the landowner's payment for other items, such as interest payments and the depreciation of buildings on the land. Recent critics point to the increase in government spending, which would mean that 100 percent land rent taxes could no longer provide sufficient revenues to replace all other taxes.

1. Evaluate Ricardo's predictions about the dynamics of population increases, the rising price of wheat, and increasing rents. Consider in your evaluation factors such as technology, interest rates, and labour markets.

2. Sketch a graph to show the demand and supply curves with the Corn Laws in effect, and after their repeal. Explain, with reference to your graph, why Ricardo was opposed to the Corn Laws.

Thinking About Economics

Does the economic analysis for land apply to other types of productive resources?

It does only if the other resources have a fixed supply. Consider a natural resource such as minerals or water. If the known supply is limited (and therefore fixed), payments over and above the costs for extracting, processing, and distributing the resource can be called economic rents.

There is another interesting application of the economic theory of rent. A few lucky individuals, such as star athletes or entertainers, owe their success to the talents they possess. We might consider their talents as having a fixed supply. Therefore, much of the income earned by these people is really an economic rent that pays them for making their talents available in the market. Consider, for example, the hockey superstar Wayne Gretzky. We could consider a portion of his multimillion-dollar yearly salary to be a wage, but most of it is a rent to the team owners who want to reap the rewards of having "The Great One" on their team.

BRIEF REVIEW

1. In economics, rent is the payment for use of a productive resource that is available in only a fixed quantity.

2. Land is an example of an economic resource that provides a rent income. Since the supply of land is fixed, the supply curve is perfectly inelastic. Only changes in the demand for land can affect the equilibrium value of its rent.

3. Because resource demands are derived demands, the major factor that can change the demand for land is a change in the price of the products that the land is used to produce.

 Profit

Profit is another resource income. Recall that economic profit is a business's total revenue less total implicit and explicit costs. In other words, a positive economic profit is the income paid to owners of a business after all other resource payments have been made. Critics of the capitalist system attribute profit to the power of business owners rather than to their contribution to the economy. While it is true than profits can be excessive, profit can also serve some positive functions in private markets by acting as a return on risk-taking, a measure of a business's effectiveness, and a source of funds for future investment.

Return on Risk-Taking

Profit provides a return to entrepreneurs for their risk-taking. Businesses initiate change but are themselves affected by external changes. Owners attempt to predict the future—for example, consumer spending, resource costs, and the demand for their product—but their speculations are always uncertain. No one will assume such risks in a private-market economy unless they can expect at least a normal profit in return. Profit therefore provides an incentive for people to take these risks.

Measure of Effectiveness

Profits give some indication of how well a business is run, thereby giving those inside and outside the business a tool to judge the business's success. If a business makes a high economic profit while others in the same industry suffer losses or merely break even, this suggests good management of the successful business. So, profits can help investors decide what businesses to invest in. Profit levels can also indicate the health of an industry as a whole, and its future. Therefore, profits can help entrepreneurs decide whether or not to enter a particular market. If businesses in a competitive market make positive economic profits, other businesses will enter the market and try to capture some of this profit for themselves. If businesses in the market are negative, some businesses will leave over time.

Source of Funds

Profits can also be used by a business to purchase assets such as buildings, plant, and equipment. Instead of borrowing money or finding new owners who are willing to invest their money, businesses can either replace or increase their assets by using past earnings.

Interest

Another form of income that contributes to the overall incomes of Canadians is interest. While related to the supply of capital resources, interest is best seen as a financial income. When money is lent to a consumer or business, the lender requires that not only the **principal** (the loan amount) be paid back, but also that **interest** (a payment for use of the money) be paid. Interest, in effect, is payment to the lender for the opportunity cost of the money being used in one way over another. In other words, interest is the price of borrowing money.

Interest is determined as a percentage of the principal, which is known as the **interest rate.** The interest rate, or rate of return on loanable funds, is one of the key prices in the economy.

Consider the example of a travel agency, Mariposa Vacations, which decides to borrow $2000 from the bank. The bank agrees to lend the money for a year, and sets the interest rate at 5 percent *per annum*. Interest rates are typically given as *per annum*, or per year. Therefore, at the end of the year, Mariposa Vacations will pay back the principal ($2000), plus interest at a rate of 5 percent (0.05 × $2000 = $100), for a total of $2100 ($2000 + $100).

The Loanable Funds Market

What determines the interest rate for an entire economy? According to the loanable funds theory, the interest rate is simply the price of **loanable funds.** These funds are all the monies made available by lenders to borrowers. Exchanges in the loanable funds market may take place through an intermediary or directly. In the example of Mariposa Vacations, the bank serves as the go-between in the lending process. Chartered banks, as well as other deposit-taking institutions such as trust companies and credit unions, gather funds from depositors to make loans to borrowers. Among friends and family or with a large company, lending is often done directly.

While you and a friend might have a verbal agreement, General Motors, for example, might issue a **bond** for the amount of money it

principal: the amount of a loan, excluding interest

interest: the payment to a lender for use of money loaned

interest rate: the percentage rate with which interest on loans is determined

loanable funds: all the monies made available to lenders by borrowers

bond: a contract between a borrower and the holder of the contract that entitles the holder to interest plus repayment at the maturity date

wants to borrow. Bonds are formal contracts that set out the amount borrowed, the borrower, the period of time until maturity, the interest rate, and when interest is to be paid. When a bond "matures," the bond issuer pays the principal back to the bond holder. Bonds can be bought and sold among lenders.

Demand for Loanable Funds

The demand for loanable funds comes from all participants in the economy. Governments borrow so that they can finance expenditures without immediately increasing taxes. Consumers often borrow to purchase big-ticket items such as houses or cars, so that they can spread out payments over a period of time. Businesses, however, are the main borrowers in the Canadian economy.

Businesses borrow funds to invest in projects that they believe will make a profit. When analyzing business investment, it is important to make a distinction between a business's real and financial assets. A business's **real capital** is made up of assets such as buildings and equipment used to produce goods and services. These assets depreciate; that is, their value decreases over time, so that a business must recognize the fall in value, or **depreciation**, each year in its accounts. Investing in profit-making projects usually means adding to that store of real capital. However, to buy this real capital means using **financial capital**, or cash, bonds, and shares. Note that a **share** (or stock) gives partial ownership of a corporation to the shareholder, who expects to receive periodic payments in the form of dividends, and hopes to sell the share at a profit later.

Suppose that the hypothetical corporation Far North Corp. begins the year with real capital assets valued at $100 000. These assets depreciate 20 percent annually, meaning that they lose $20 000 in value in the first year. If the business puts $30 000 into investment projects, the year-end value of its real capital will rise to $110 000 [($100 000 – $20 000) + $30 000)]. To get the $30 000 for investment projects, the business could use past earnings, issue shares to investors, or borrow money. If Far North Corp. chooses borrowing over its other options, the company must demand $30 000 from the market for loanable funds.

In the market for loanable funds, as in all markets, those who demand funds are concerned with the price they must pay. This applies to all borrowers: consumers, governments, and businesses. As the interest rate on loans goes up, the cost of the loan (the interest payments) can exceed the loan's benefits. Therefore, the demand for loanable funds and the interest rate are inversely related. Figure 8.12 shows the resulting demand curve with a negative (downward) slope. When, for example, the interest rate rises from 6 percent to 8 percent, the demand by borrowers for loanable funds decreases from $160 billion to $140 billion.

real capital: assets such as buildings, equipment, and materials used by businesses to produce goods and services

depreciation: the decrease in value of durable real assets over time

financial capital: assets in the form of cash, bonds, and shares

share: partial ownership of a corporation, which entitles the shareholder to dividends and, hopefully, a profit once the share is sold; also called a stock

Figure 8.12:   Equilibrium in the Loanable Funds Market

Demand and Supply Schedules for Loanable Funds		
Interest Rate	Funds Demanded	Funds Supplied
(% per year)	(D)	(S)
	($ billions)	
10	120	200
8	140	180
6	**160**	**160**
4	180	140
2	200	120

Demand and Supply Curves for Loanable Funds

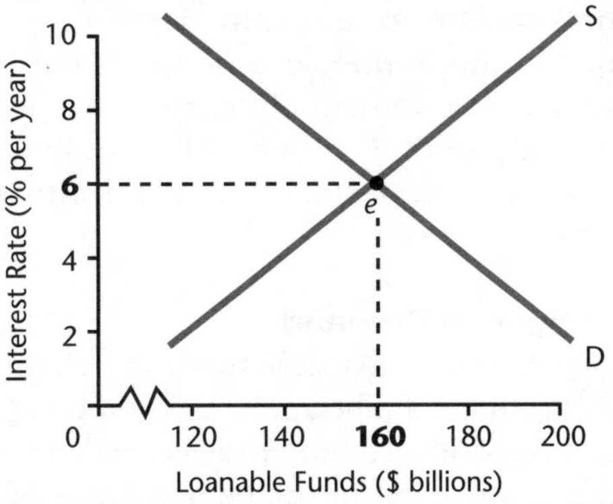

While the demand for loanable funds by borrowers is inversely related to the interest rate, the supply of funds by lenders is directly related. In this case, quantities demanded and supplied are equal at an equilibrium interest rate of 6 percent, at point *e*.

Supply of Loanable Funds

While businesses and governments sometimes have temporary savings, which contribute to the supply of loanable funds, the supply comes primarily from household savings. In the circular flow of markets, consumers not only purchase products and supply labour, but also save and provide funds to the loanable funds market by, for example, banking their savings. Whenever a household engages in saving, it postpones consumption and the benefits that consumption would have had. Households (as we'll call them in their role not as consumers, but as savers) provide their savings to the loanable funds market in order to make interest income.

Just as businesses may have a profit after paying all costs from their total revenues, a household may have an excess after paying all basic costs (for example, food, shelter, and clothing) from its incomes (for example, wages). The household can decide how to spend or save any excess. When deciding how much to save, the household must weigh the psychological costs of delaying consumption against the benefits of earning interest income and greater security for the future. If the interest rate rises, the income earned from each dollar of saving rises as well. Since saving provides greater benefits, it is likely that households will choose to save more, leading to a greater supply of loanable funds. Therefore, the supply of loanable funds is directly related to the interest rate, as shown in Figure 8.12. For example, a rise in the interest rate from 6 percent to 8 percent would cause the supply of loanable funds to increase from $160 to $180 billion.

The Equilibrium Interest Rate

Equilibrium in the loanable funds market occurs at the intersection of the demand and supply curves. In Figure 8.12, equilibrium is at the interest rate of 6 percent. This equilibrium value can change depending on outside factors that affect either the demand for or supply of loanable funds.

Changes in Demand

The demand for loanable funds can change for a variety of reasons, thereby affecting equilibrium in the market. Anything that increases the profitability of investment projects will increase the demand for loanable funds. A rise in consumer purchases of big-ticket items also raises the demand for loanable funds. Governments, too, can increase demand. In all three cases, expanding demand causes both equilibrium values for the interest rate and the quantity of loanable funds exchanged to rise, as shown in Figure 8.13.

Figure 8.13:   Changes in the Demand for Loanable Funds

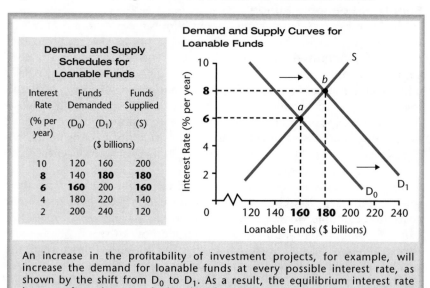

Demand and Supply Schedules for Loanable Funds

Interest Rate (% per year)	Funds Demanded (D_0)	Funds Demanded (D_1)	Funds Supplied (S)
		($ billions)	
10	120	160	200
8	140	**180**	**180**
6	**160**	200	**160**
4	180	220	140
2	200	240	120

An increase in the profitability of investment projects, for example, will increase the demand for loanable funds at every possible interest rate, as shown by the shift from D_0 to D_1. As a result, the equilibrium interest rate increases from 6 percent (point a) to 8 percent (point b).

Changes in Supply

The main factor determining the supply of loanable funds is the saving habits of households. If, for example, households decide to reduce the amount they save, they decrease the supply of loanable funds, and the interest rate rises.

Range of Interest Rates

Equilibrium in the loanable funds market does not mean that all loans have the same interest rate. At any one time, interest rates in the market will range above and below the equilibrium rate. The interest rate charged on a particular loan depends on four factors: the borrower's credit risk, the loan period, whether or not collateral is provided, and the size of the loan.

Credit Risk

When deciding whether to lend funds to a borrower, a lender tries to establish the borrower's **credit risk**, which is the assessed likelihood of the borrower not repaying the loan. In the case of a business, if the business has healthy profits, a solid history and a strong future in the industry, a small existing debt, and a record of repaying loans on time, the credit risk is low. So, for example, Bell Canada would likely pay a lower interest rate than would a new goldmining business with no track record.

credit risk: the assessed likelihood of a borrower not repaying a loan

Loan Period

In general, the shorter the time before the loan must be repaid, the lower the interest rate; the longer the time, the higher the interest rate. In effect, the borrower pays for the added time the lender won't have that money available and for the added risk of an extended loan period. For example, a lender might be willing to lend funds for a single year at an annual interest rate of 8 percent, but the same borrower would be charged an annual rate of 10 percent for a two-year period.

Collateral

Lenders often have the security of **collateral**, which are assets pledged by a borrower as security. If a loan is not repaid, the lender acquires these assets. Collateral can take a variety of forms. For example, a mortgage is a loan whose collateral is in the form of land and buildings. As a rule, lenders demand a higher interest rate on loans that are not secured with collateral than on those that are secured with collateral.

collateral: assets pledged by a borrower as security against a loan; these assets can be seized by the lender if the loan is not repaid

Size of the Loan

The larger the loan, the lower its interest rate. Because lending involves certain administration charges—for example, for paperwork and collections—that do not change substantially with the size of the loan, it is cheaper for the lender to make one loan for $1 million rather than 50 loans for $20 000 each.

BRIEF REVIEW

1. Profit is the income paid to owners of a business after all other resource payments have been made. Profit acts as a return on risk-taking, as a measure of a business's effectiveness, and as a source of investment funds.

2. Interest is the income earned on money that is lent. According to the loanable funds theory, the demand for and supply of loanable funds determines the interest rate.

3. Demand for loanable funds is determined mainly by business investment projects and by government borrowing. Supply is determined mainly by household savings.

4. The interest rate an individual borrower pays depends on the borrower's credit risk, the loan period, whether or not collateral is provided, and the size of the loan.

Shares of Total Income

How important is each income in the total incomes of Canadians? What share does each income have, and how have these shares changed in recent years? Unfortunately, there are practical obstacles to finding accurate

Figure 8.14:   Shares of Net Domestic Income

Year	Net Domestic Income ($ millions)	Wages and Salaries (%)	Corporate Profits (%)	Interest Income (%)	Proprietors' Income and Rent (%)
1926	4 294	55.3	12.4	3.2	29.1
1933	2 559	70.1	8.9	4.3	16.7
1943	8 907	64.2	13.9	2.9	18.9
1953	20 582	63.5	14.5	2.7	19.3
1963	36 277	67.1	13.7	4.3	15.0
1973	98 419	70.6	13.5	5.7	10.2
1983	316 275	70.1	10.9	11.5	7.5
1993	534 472	75.3	6.6	10.0	8.0

Since 1926, the share of wages and salaries in Canada's net domestic income has gradually risen from about 55 percent to about 75 percent. Meanwhile, the share of corporate profits has fluctuated with the level of economic activity. After staying relatively constant for several decades, interest income has risen from about 3 percent to 10 percent since 1963. Finally, proprietors' incomes and rent have fallen from about 29 percent in 1926 to 8 percent in 1993.

SOURCES: Adapted from Statistics Canada, *Canadian Economic Observer, Historical Statistical Supplement 1992/93* (July 1933), cat. no. 11-210, vol. 7, table 1.1; *Canadian Economic Observer, Statistical Summary* (April 1994), cat. no. 11-010, p. 3. Reproduced by authority of the Minister of Industry, 1994.

answers to these questions. Economists must use the four main classifications of income used by government statisticians to measure economic activity in the entire Canadian economy.

The total income earned by households in Canada is known as **net domestic income**, which can be divided into four main categories: wages and salaries, corporate profits, interest income, and proprietors' incomes (including rent). In 1993, for example, Canada's net domestic income was $534.5 billion, of which $402.5 billion was in the form of wages and salaries, $35.4 billion in corporate profits, $53.6 billion in interest income, and $43.0 billion in proprietors' incomes and rent. As shown in Figure 8.14, wages and salaries formed 75.3 percent, corporate profits 6.6 percent, interest income 10.0 percent, and proprietors' incomes 8.0 percent of Canada's 1993 net domestic income.

net domestic income: the total income earned by Canada's households

Wages and Salaries

Not surprisingly, the bulk of net domestic income goes to labour in the form of wages and salaries (measured before any tax payments), including fringe benefits paid on behalf of workers by employers, such as contributions to unemployment insurance and workers' compensation. Over the past decades, the share of wages and salaries in Canada's net domestic income has gradually increased from just above 50 percent in 1926 to 67 percent by 1963. Since then, the figure has remained above 70 percent. As Figure 8.14 makes clear, the rise in the share of wages and salaries is related to a corresponding fall in the share of proprietors' incomes and rent. This trend is due to a gradual movement of Canadians away from agriculture, an industry in which employment earnings often take the form of proprietors' income.

Corporate Profits

Corporate profits include all corporate earnings before taxes are paid, representing the total amount made by incorporated businesses as a result of their production. Also added into corporate profits is a special accounting item known as the inventory valuation adjustment, which includes any increases in the value of business inventory due to a general rise in prices throughout the economy. The share of corporate profits in Canada's net domestic income tends to vary with the overall state of the economy. During boom periods, corporate profits are relatively high as a proportion of net domestic income. This is illustrated in Figure 8.14 by the 1953 figure of 14.5 percent. Economic downturns cause a drop in the share of corporate profits, as shown by the 1993 value of just 6.6 percent.

Interest Income

Interest income represents the payments made by businesses on their outstanding bonds and loans as well as a minor account representing miscellaneous investment income, such as royalties received by individuals. Figure 8.14 shows that, after remaining in the 2 to 5 percent range from 1926 to 1963, interest income as a share of Canada's net domestic income rose, and equalled 10 percent in 1993. This increase reflects the recent preference of businesses for bonds over shares as a way to raise funds.

Proprietors' Incomes and Rent

Proprietors' incomes include the earnings of all unincorporated businesses—sole proprietorships and partnerships, including self-employed professionals and farmers. The nature of many small businesses is such that their earnings are made up of various types of resource payments. Given the difficulty of separating rent from other forms of small business income, all rent payments are added to this category as well. Since the 1920s, proprietors' incomes and rent have fallen from 29.1 percent to a 1993 figure of 8.0 percent. As already noted, this reflects the gradual decrease in the prevalence of self-employed farmers in the Canadian economy.

BRIEF REVIEW

1. The total income earned by Canadian households is measured by government statisticians using the concept of net domestic income, which categorizes income as wages and salaries, corporate profits, interest income, and proprietors' incomes and rent.

2. Since the 1920s, the shares of net domestic income going to wages and salaries as well as to interest income have tended to increase. While the share going to corporate earnings has fluctuated widely, the share going to proprietors' incomes and rent has decreased.

Key Concepts

human capital	collective bargaining	interest rate
seniority rights	mediation	loanable funds
labour unions	arbitration	bond
job discrimination	working to rule	real capital
job segregation	strike	depreciation
industrial union	picketing	financial capital
craft union	lockout	share
closed shop	rent	credit risk
union shop	principal	collateral
open shop	interest	net domestic income

Developing Application and Analysis Skills

1. a) Choose one occupation to research with other students. (For example, mail carrier, nurse, automobile assembler, bricklayer, bank teller, teacher, plumber, medical technician, software developer). Research the chosen occupation as a group. Based on your research, write a job description and identify the wage rate, education and experience required, working conditions, market power, and any regional dispari- ties or discrimination for that occupation.

   b) Report your findings to the class, and compare the results of your study with other students.

2. A massive computer software and hardware company is going through a period of change, and proposes that the basis for determining workers' pay should also change. Consider each of the following methods for determining workers' pay. For each method, suggest the possible advan- tages and disadvantages both to the work- ers and to the company, as well as jobs for which the method would be particularly appropriate and particularly inappropriate.

   a) seniority
   b) piece-work—a set pay rate per "piece" produced by a worker
   c) managers' discretion
   d) commission—a percentage of sales
   e) contribution to company profit or loss

3. Sketch a graph showing demand and sup- ply curves for workers in a depressed region's perfectly competitive labour mar- ket. Illustrate on your graph the effect on wages if regional disparities were eliminat- ed, and explain the results.

4. The following schedules reflect the demand and supply for data-entry workers in a per- fectly competitive labour market prior to an industrial union being formed.

Demand and Supply Schedules for Data-Entry Workers		
Wage ($ per hour)	Labour Demanded (D) (workers)	Labour Supplied (S) (workers)
15	50	90
13	60	80
11	70	70
9	80	60
7	90	50

   a) Create a graph showing the demand and supply curves for data-entry workers.
   b) Identify the equilibrium wage.
   c) Suppose a union forms and collectively bargains with employers. Demonstrate on your graph the possible impact of the union's agreement.
   d) What costs and benefits did formation of the union have for workers? Explain your answer.
   e) How might the union increase both wages and the number of workers demanded? Demonstrate the change on your graph.

5. Study the following graphs, and then do the following:

   a) Explain the relationships that exist among changes in average hourly earnings, changes in wage settlements, and changes in inflation or "cost of living" (as indicated by CPI, which we'll discuss in Chapter 11).
   b) Explain the relationships that exist between changes in wage settlements and work stoppages.
   c) Suggest what greater economic trends the changes reflect.

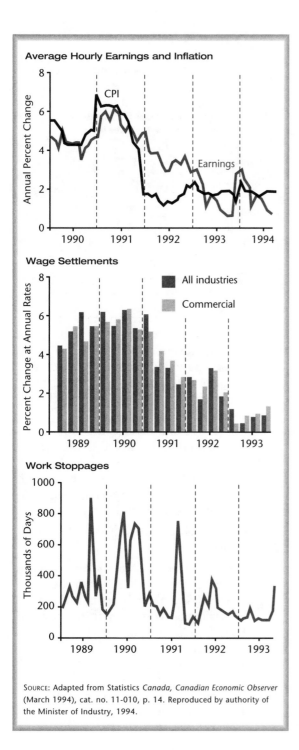

Average Hourly Earnings and Inflation

Wage Settlements

Work Stoppages

SOURCE: Adapted from Statistics *Canada, Canadian Economic Observer* (March 1994), cat. no. 11-010, p. 14. Reproduced by authority of the Minister of Industry, 1994.

6. a) Research and prepare a report detailing the structures and processes the provincial government has in place to deal with wage disputes involving police officers, doctors, and teachers. In your report, be sure to consider legislation regarding mediation, arbitration, working to rule, lockouts, and replacement workers.

b) Prepare to debate, and then debate the following statement: "In order to better serve the interests of society, workers who provide essential services should not be allowed to strike."

7. a) Copy the following graph, which gives the supply and demand curves for professional athletes.

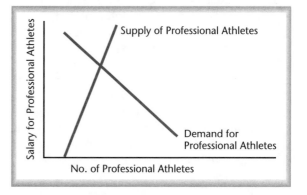

b) Indicate on your graph the equilibrium salary and quantity of professional athletes.

c) Explain whether the supply of professional athletes is elastic or inelastic.

d) Explain whether the demand for professional athletes is elastic or inelastic.

e) What factors might cause the supply of professional athletes to increase or decrease? Explain your answer, and sketch the results on your graph.

f) What factors might cause the demand for professional athletes to increase or decrease? Explain your answer, and sketch the results on your graph.

g) What factors could cause the elasticity of supply and demand for professional athletes to change? Sketch the results on your graph.

h) Give an example of a highly paid sports star. In your opinion, what part of this athlete's pay might be viewed as rent? Why?

8. a) Study the following graph, and then describe what happened to total corporate profit margins between 1989 and the first part of 1992. Suggest what economic factors might have been responsible for this trend.

b) Suggest, based on the changes shown in total corporate profits, what changes might have taken place in net domestic income over the same period of time.

Corporate Profit Margins

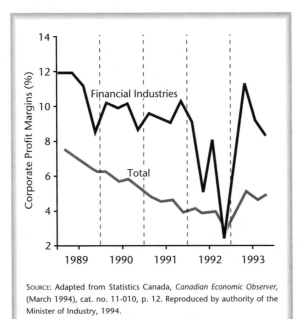

SOURCE: Adapted from Statistics Canada, *Canadian Economic Observer*, (March 1994), cat. no. 11-010, p. 12. Reproduced by authority of the Minister of Industry, 1994.

9. In the early 1990s, many questions were raised about the pay received by sports stars, entertainers, and corporate executives. For example, 1993 earnings were reported as the following for selected high-earners: Toronto Blue Jay player Joe Carter, $7 million; singer Bryan Adams, an estimated $35 million; talk-show host Oprah Winfrey, $66 million; president and CEO of Canadian Tire Corporation Ltd. Stephen E. Bachand, $3.2 million. Are they worth it? Whether or not they are, is the pay justifiable in the context of what other workers make, of peoples' needs, and of the economy as a whole? Let's focus on corporate executives. Some argue that executives who create value should be rewarded, and the rewards should relate to the company profits. Others argue that, regardless of the company profits, there should be a limit. For example, the philosopher Plato believed that no one should earn more than five times the pay of the lowest-paid worker in the community, and Ben & Jerry's Ice Cream sets its corporate limit at seven times. Write an essay on this issue. In your essay, state and explain your beliefs about how pay for corporate executives should be determined.

10. What effect on the loanable funds market might each of the following situations have? Sketch a graph for each situation, showing the market forces before and after.

a) An increase in automobile sales is reported by auto manufacturers.

b) When a recession is forecasted, consumer spending drops.

c) Banks begin to offer more flexible repayment terms to borrowers.

d) A housing boom results in an increase in mortgage applications.

e) Growth in the computer industries encourages new project development.

CHAPTER 9

The Role of Government

Government is an art, not a science, and an adventure, not a planned itinerary....
—DONALD CREIGHTON, CANADIAN HISTORIAN

Imagine that one person enjoys all the luxuries of a consumer culture, while another can barely scrape by. Alternatively, imagine that a business's profit-making activity pollutes a resource that is shared with neighbours. What is fair? What is reasonable? What could or should be done, and how? In mixed market economies such as Canada's, governments deal not only with competition in the market, as we have seen in previous chapters, but also with the distribution of income and with spillover effects. In this chapter, we examine: the distribution of income among Canadian households; the tools the Canadian government uses to promote income equity, especially transfer payments and taxation; the extent of poverty in Canada; and, spillover effects.

CHAPTER FOCUS

This chapter focuses on the following:
- the distribution of income among Canadian households, how this distribution is measured, and the factors underlying the distribution
- how government intervenes with transfer payments and taxes, and the effectiveness of this intervention
- the causes of poverty and the way poverty is measured
- the Canadian welfare society and its impact on Canadians
- spillover costs and benefits, and how the government addresses these issues

SKILLS FOCUS

After studying this chapter, you will be able to:
- calculate changes in average incomes resulting from transfer payments and taxation
- graph and analyze Lorenz curves
- consider the effect of a wealth tax and the reasons for its absence
- assess the possible uses of poverty measures
- apply the concept of a poverty line to your community
- relate the causes of poverty to barriers to escaping it, and then propose a remedy
- examine one issue related to income equity that is currently in the mass media
- differentiate among progressive, regressive, and proportional taxes, and explain the effects of various components of personal income tax
- identify spillover costs and benefits, and how a government might intervene to correct these issues

The Distribution of Income

In the last chapter, we examined the incomes from resources, the factors that affect these incomes, and the importance of each type of income in the Canadian economy. Now we'll look at who gets what, and why.

Income Shares

To get an overview of who gets what in an economy, economists typically rank Canadian households by income and then categorize households into five groups based on their income levels. Each group therefore represents 20 percent, or one-fifth, of the total number of Canadian households. Figure 9.1 shows the pre-taxation income levels of the five groups for various years. In 1992, the fifth of Canadian households with the lowest incomes received a small proportion—a mere 4.6 percent—of all households' total pre-tax income, while the fifth of Canadian households with the highest incomes received 43.6 percent. The groups in-between the extremes received 10.3 percent, 16.7 percent, and 24.8 percent, respectively.

Looking at the figures for selected years, one can see that there has been surprisingly little change in income distribution since the 1950s. For example, in 1951, the fifth of Canadian households with the lowest incomes received 4.4 percent of all households' total pre-tax income, whereas the fifth with the highest incomes received 42.8 percent.

Figure 9.1: **Income Distribution in Selected Years**

	Percentage of Total Pre-tax Income Received by Each Fifth of Households					Average Income (1992)
	1951	1961	1971	1981	1992	
Lowest 20%	4.4	4.2	3.6	4.5	4.6	$10 169
Second 20%	11.2	11.9	10.6	10.9	10.3	22 673
Third 20%	18.3	18.3	17.6	17.6	16.7	36 786
Fourth 20%	23.3	24.5	24.9	25.2	24.8	54 607
Highest 20%	42.8	41.1	43.3	41.8	43.6	95 984
Average of total						$44 044

Selected incomes from five decades show the income distribution to Canadian households. Proportionally, the shares have not changed considerably since 1951. Consistently, the group of households with the highest income received over 40 percent of the total income, while the group of households with the lowest income received less than 5 percent.

SOURCES: Statistics Canada, *Incomes of Non-Farm Families and Individuals in Canada, Selected Years 1951–65* (June 1969), cat. no. 1100-506, p. 78; Statistics Canada, *Income Distributions by Size in Canada, 1983* (March 1985), cat. no. 13-207, p. 93; Statistics Canada, *Income Distributions by Size in Canada, 1992* (December 1993), cat. no. 13-207, p. 147; Statistics Canada, *Income After Tax, Distributions by Size in Canada, 1992* (March 1994), cat. no. 13-210, p. 28. Reproduced by authority of the Minister of Industry, 1994.

The Lorenz Curve

Comparing distributions of income for different years can be a cumbersome task given the amount of information included in Figure 9.1. Therefore, economists simplify matters by summarizing the results on a graph. However, rather than simply presenting the shares of each one-fifth of households, economists present the *cumulative* distribution of income. The **Lorenz curve**, as this graph is known, conveniently summarizes how equally or unequally income is distributed.

To see how the Lorenz curve does this, take another look at the income distribution for 1992 given in Figure 9.1. Seen as separate shares of total pre-tax income, the figures—4.6 percent, 10.3 percent, 16.7 percent, 24.8 percent, and 43.6 percent—don't seem to say a lot. However, we can look at the first and second groups together; then the first, second, and third groups together; and so on. The results are shown in Figure 9.2. For example, whereas the 20 percent of Canadian households with the lowest incomes receive 4.6 percent of the total income, the 40 percent of households with the lowest incomes receive 14.9 percent, and the 60 percent of households with the lowest incomes receive 31.6 percent. Plotted on a graph—with the variables being the percentage of families and the percentage of income—these figures give the Lorenz curve. The points *a, b, c, d,* and *e* represent the *cumulative* income shares.

Lorenz curve: a graph showing the cumulative distribution of income among a country's households

Figure 9.2:   The Lorenz Curve

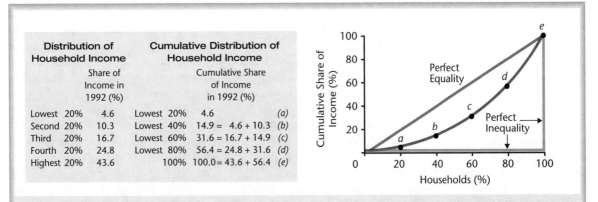

Distribution of Household Income		Cumulative Distribution of Household Income		
	Share of Income in 1992 (%)		Cumulative Share of Income in 1992 (%)	
Lowest 20%	4.6	Lowest 20%	4.6	(a)
Second 20%	10.3	Lowest 40%	14.9 = 4.6 + 10.3	(b)
Third 20%	16.7	Lowest 60%	31.6 = 16.7 + 14.9	(c)
Fourth 20%	24.8	Lowest 80%	56.4 = 24.8 + 31.6	(d)
Highest 20%	43.6	100%	100.0 = 43.6 + 56.4	(e)

Point *a* on the graph shows that the group with the lowest income received 4.6 percent of the total pre-tax income in 1992. Point *b* shows that the groups receiving the lowest 40 percent of pre-tax income in 1992 received 14.9 percent (4.6 + 10.3). Each subsequent point shows the cumulative income distribution; therefore point *e* shows that 100 percent of households earned 100 percent of total incomes. Connecting all the points gives the Lorenz curve. To contrast, the extremes of perfect equality and perfect inequality are shown. The closer the Lorenz curve is to the curve representing perfect equality (and the farther from the curve of perfect inequality), the more equally incomes are distributed.

Interpreting the Lorenz Curve

To see what this curve tells us about the distribution of income among Canadian households, it can be compared to Lorenz curves for two hypothetical economies with income distributions at the extremes: perfectly equal, and perfectly unequal.

Perfect Equality

The first hypothetical Lorenz curve represents the case of *perfect equality*, where each household earns an identical amount. Therefore, 20 percent of households receive 20 percent of the total income, 40 percent receive 40 percent, 60 percent receive 60 percent, and so on. The result is the 45-degree line shown in Figure 9.2 The closer the actual Lorenz curve is to this hypothetical case—in other words, the less bow-shaped it is—the more equal the distribution of incomes in the economy.

Perfect Inequality

At the other extreme of income distribution is *perfect inequality*, with only one household receiving all of the economy's income, while all other households receive nothing. The hypothetical Lorenz curve in this circumstance would follow the horizontal and vertical axes of the graph, as shown by the two thick lines in Figure 9.2 forming a right angle at the bottom right-hand corner. The closer the Lorenz curve is to this hypothetical case—meaning the more bow-shaped it is—the more unequal the distribution of income.

Governments and Income Distribution

As stated in Chapter 1, among their numerous goals Canadian governments have the goal of income equity. Recall that income equity is achieved when a country's total output is distributed fairly among its citizens. Before dealing with the question, "What is fair?" let's first examine how Canadian governments can affect the distribution of income among Canadian households—through the payments they make to households, and through the way they levy personal income taxes.

The Effect of Transfer Payments

transfer payments:
government payments to households or other levels of government

Transfer payments are government payments to either households or other levels of government. In both cases, transfer payments are not payments for goods and services, but legally granted payments. Examples are Old Age Security, Unemployment Insurance, and federal transfer payments to the provinces and territories, known as the Canada Assistance Plan, that help to pay for provincial and local welfare programs.

Figure 9.3 shows the impact of government transfer payments on the distribution of income in 1992. Column 1 shows the shares of income that went to each one-fifth of Canadian households *before* any adjustments by government. Column 2, which repeats the 1992 data from Figure 9.1, shows the distribution of income among the same income groups *after* government transfer payments were received by households. Note that the shares of income going to the three-fifths of households with the lowest incomes—especially the lowest one-fifth—increased as a result of these transfer payments. Meanwhile, the shares of income going to the other two groups—particularly the highest income group—decreased.

Figure 9.3: Distribution of Household Income (1992)

	Income Before Transfer Payments and Taxes (1)		Pre-tax Income (2)		Income After Transfer Payments and Taxes (3)	
	Income Share	Average Income	Income Share	Average Income	Income Share	Average Income
Lowest 20%	0.7%	$ 1 242	4.6%	$10 169	5.5%	$ 9 843
Second 20%	7.5	14 177	10.3	22 673	11.5	20 533
Third 20%	16.4	30 973	16.7	36 786	17.5	31 180
Fourth 20%	26.5	50 163	24.8	54 607	24.7	44 151
Highest 20%	49.0	92 823	43.6	95 984	40.8	72 790
	100.0%	$37 876	100.0%	$44 044	100.0%	$35 699

Both government transfer payments to households and personal income taxes raise the share of income going to the three-fifths of households with the lowest incomes, especially the fifth with the lowest income. In contrast, the shares of income going to the two-fifths of households with the highest incomes decrease with the effects of transfer payments and taxation.

SOURCE: Statistics Canada, *Income After Tax, Distributions by Size in Canada, 1992* (March 1994), cat. no. 13-210, p. 28. Reproduced by authority of the Minister of Industry, 1994.

The Effect of Taxes

Governments collect taxes in many forms—for example, personal income taxes, sales and excise taxes, and corporate taxes—many of which we will deal with later in this chapter. While each of these taxes affects households, personal income taxes have the most direct impact on household income. Column 3 in Figure 9.3 shows the distribution of income to households after *both* personal income taxes are paid and transfer payments are received. Comparing columns 2 and 3 shows that the income shares going to the two-fifths of households with the highest incomes are further reduced by the effect of taxation; however, not as much as by the effect of transfer payments. In comparison, the effect of taxation increases the shares of income going to the three-fifths of households with the lowest incomes.

Combined Effect of Transfer Payments and Taxes

Overall, government intervention in the form of transfer payments and taxation have the greatest effect on income shares for those households at the extremes. As Figure 9.3 shows, the income share for the fifth of Canadian households with the lowest income rises from 0.7 percent before any transfer payments or taxes to 5.5 percent with the effects of both transfer payments and taxes. This translates into a change in average income from $1242 to $9843. Meanwhile, the income share for the fifth of Canadian households with the highest income is cut from 49.0 percent to 40.8 percent, for a change in average income from $92 823 to $72 790.

Reasons for Income Inequality

The differences in incomes of individual households can be attributed to a variety of causes. Recall from Chapter 8 that wages and salaries make up over 70 percent of Canada's net domestic income. Hence, the factors that determine wages outlined in Chapter 8—labour productivity, education, experience, job conditions, regional disparities, market power, and discrimination—play an important role in income inequality. However, not all income inequalities are related to wages; profit, rent, and interest, for example, also play a part. In addition to the factors that determine wages, three other factors contribute to income inequality: risk-taking, ability, and wealth.

Risk-Taking

Risk-taking in an economy can take a variety of forms. For example, the risks that entrepreneurs take mean that their profit earnings fluctuate widely. While unsuccessful risk-takers often face the threat of hardship and bankruptcy, successful risk-takers reap significant rewards.

Ability

Because of different abilities, some individuals may pursue careers in high-paying areas while others make no earnings at all. Those individuals who find their talents in short supply—star athletes or gifted computer programmers, for instance—can sometimes earn extravagantly high incomes due to their special abilities.

Wealth

wealth: ownership of financial assets, such as stocks and bonds, or real assets, such as buildings and land

Most rent and interest incomes flow from the ownership of **wealth**. Wealth takes the form of financial assets, such as stocks and bonds, or real assets, such as buildings and land. There are two main ways to acquire wealth: through one's own saving, or by inheriting wealth from others.

Interestingly, wealth tends to be much more unequally distributed than income. Figure 9.4 shows the share of wealth held by the top 1 percent, 5 percent, and 20 percent of households in various years for four countries: Sweden, Canada, France, and the United States. In Canada, the

Figure 9.4:   Distribution of Wealth in Selected Countries

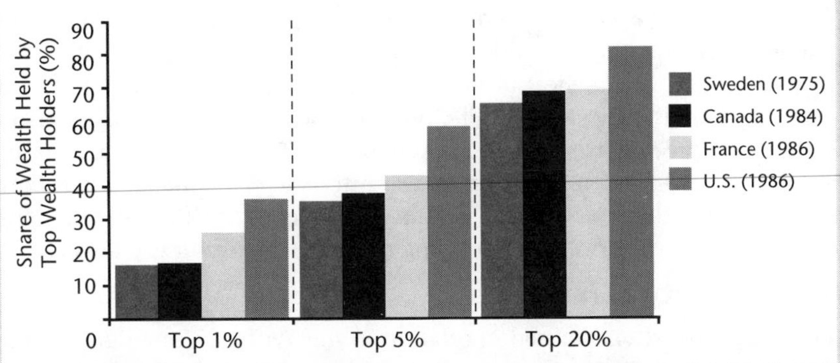

In 1984, the top 1 percent of Canadian households held 16.8 percent of Canada's wealth, the top 5 percent held 37.5 percent, and the top 20 percent held 68.8 percent. In Canada, the distribution of wealth among households is more equal than it is in France or the United States, but less so than in Sweden.

SOURCE: Reprinted with the permission of University of Toronto Press, Inc.

top 1 percent owned 16.8 percent of the country's total wealth, while the top 5 percent owned 37.5 percent, and the top 20 percent owned 68.8 percent. This last figure is significantly higher than the 40.8 percent share for the top one-fifth income group after transfer payments and taxes. While less equally distributed than in Sweden, wealth in Canada is distributed more evenly among households than it is in either France or the United States.

Thinking About Economics

Is income inequality necessarily a bad thing?

While gross inequalities in income are undesirable, a perfect equality of incomes is not necessarily desirable because of the tradeoff between equity and efficiency. Without differences in incomes, the incentive to undertake further education, to take unpleasant jobs for greater pay, to save one's earnings, and to take risks would be severely hampered. Without some degree of income inequality, an economy's total output would be below its highest possible level. The goal of income equity is, therefore, usually interpreted as *reducing*, rather than *eliminating*, the inequalities that would exist in a pure market economy.

 **Poverty**

poverty: a situation in which a person's income is not adequate to provide the necessities of life

One of the main reasons behind the economic goal of income equity is the desire to minimize poverty. **Poverty** is a situation in which a person's income is inadequate to provide the necessities of life, such as food, clothing, and shelter. In practical terms, defining poverty is difficult. All would agree that food is a necessity of life, but what sort of food should a person be able to afford? Also, should such products as TVs and radios be considered necessities in a rich industrialized country such as Canada, when they are luxuries in other countries? These are examples of the kinds of questions governments must address when trying to define and minimize poverty.

The Poverty Line

poverty line: an income level below which a household is classified as poor

In Canada, poverty is defined in relation to the average Canadian income and expenditures. The average Canadian family spends 34.7 percent of its household pre-tax income on food, clothing, and shelter. Statistics Canada defines as poor any household that spends an additional 20 percent, or a total of 54.7 percent, on these items. For simplicity, Statistics Canada uses this relationship to identify a **poverty line**, or income level below which a household is classified as poor.

In dollar terms, the poverty line depends on the number of household members and the size of the community they live in, since people in rural areas or small towns can live more cheaply than those in urban centres. Figure 9.5 shows the poverty lines as determined for 1992. For example,

Figure 9.5: The Poverty Line for Various Households (1992)

Size of Household Unit	Urban Areas (categorized by size)				Rural Areas
	500 000 and over	100 000 to 499 999	30 000 to 99 999	Less than 30 000	
	($ 1992)				
1 person	16 186	13 883	13 787	12 829	11 186
2 persons	20 233	17 354	17 234	16 036	13 982
3 persons	25 163	21 583	21 433	19 943	17 390
4 persons	30 460	26 126	25 945	24 142	21 050
5 persons	34 049	29 205	29 002	26 986	23 531
6 persons	37 638	32 284	32 059	29 830	26 012
7 or more persons	41 227	35 363	35 116	32 674	28 493

The poverty line varies among household sizes and the households' community size. Within a given household category, a household would be considered poor if its income were below the income listed.

SOURCE: Statistics Canada, *Income Distributions by Size in Canada, 1992* (December 1993), cat. no. 13-207, text table VII. Reproduced by authority of the Minister of Industry, 1994.

the poverty line would be a yearly income of $30 460 for a household of four persons living in a large city, or a yearly income of $11 186 for an unattached individual living in a rural area.

Causes of Poverty

The reasons for income inequality necessarily play a role in one of its extremes—poverty. A declining industry in one region, for example, might lay off workers, thereby causing them hardship as they develop new skills and look for new opportunities. For the working poor, the market value of their skills may simply be too low to provide a livelihood. Alternatively, job segregation might play a role. Inequalities of income distribution compounded by inequalities of wealth distribution can heighten the differences between the "haves" and the "have-nots." The results are apparent in the incidence of poverty.

Incidence of Poverty

How common is poverty among different groups in Canadian society? Using Statistics Canada's definition, an estimated 4 508 000 Canadians lived in poverty in 1992, of which 1 265 000 were children under the age of 18. As a proportion of Canada's total population, the number of poor Canadians has been falling in the last few decades. While 27.9 percent of families and 49.2 percent of unattached individuals were classified as poor in 1961, 13.3 percent of families and 39.7 percent of unattached individuals were classified as poor in 1992.

Note that Statistics Canada's definition of poverty using a low-income cut-off (LICO) has been criticized for depending on an arbitrary measure— the average proportion of income spent by Canadians on food, clothing, and shelter. As a result of the criticism, Statistics Canada has introduced a measure intended to complement LICO. Known as the low-income measure (LIM), this measure is a fixed percentage (50 percent) of *median* family income, adjusted for family size. Using LIM, Statistics Canada calculates the "incidence of low income." Although LIM, like LICO, simplifies and uses an arbitrary percentage, it provides another perspective on low income. In 1992, for example, 14.5 percent of Canadians were classified as having low incomes using LIM, as opposed to 16.8 percent using LICO.

Figure 9.6 shows how the incidence of poverty among households (defined by LICO) is classified by certain characteristics: the sex of the household head, and his or her age, employment status, and education, as well as the region in which the household lives.

Gender and Household Type

In general, poverty rates are considerably higher among unattached individuals of either sex than among families, with 39.7 percent of all unattached individuals being poor as opposed to 13.3 percent of all families. Unattached females are more likely to be poor than unattached males, while single-parent families tend to be poorer than two-parent families.

Figure 9.6:   The Incidence of Poverty (1992)

	Percentages of Households Below the Poverty Line in 1992	
	Families	**Unattached Individuals**
	13.3	39.7
Gender and Household Type		
Married couples with children	9.6	
Single-parent families (female head)	47.8	
Single-parent families (male head)	16.4	
Unattached males		33.8
Unattached females		45.1
Age of Household Head		
24 and under	41.5	58.8
25–34	18.6	27.2
35–44	12.9	27.3
45–54	8.6	33.7
55–64	11.4	45.8
65 and over	8.5	48.4
Weeks Worked by Household Head in 1992		
None	27.1	59.6
1–9 weeks	34.0	80.6
10–19 weeks	26.0	67.2
20–29 weeks	20.2	47.0
30–39 weeks	18.7	45.4
40–48 weeks	13.2	32.0
49–52 weeks	5.6	14.8
Education of Household Head		
0–8 years of schooling	17.7	61.9
Some secondary education	18.1	48.6
Graduated from high school	13.7	35.0
Some postsecondary	13.5	48.2
Postsecondary certificate or diploma	10.5	28.9
University degree	7.0	20.8
Region		
Atlantic provinces	13.8	44.6
Quebec	14.8	48.9
Ontario	11.1	33.6
Prairie provinces	15.2	41.4
British Columbia	13.5	34.1

The greatest incidence of poverty is among unattached individuals, women, single-parent families, families with a household head under 25 or over 64 in age, the unemployed, and those with minimal education. Differences in poverty rates also exist among regions.

SOURCE: Statistics Canada, *Income Distributions by Size in Canada, 1992* (December 1993), cat. no. 13-207, pp. 164, 166–69. Reproduced by authority of the Minister of Industry, 1994.

Age

Households headed by the youngest group (24 and under) and the oldest group (65 and over, unattached individuals) are more heavily represented among the ranks of the poor than are other households.

Employment

While poverty is more common among the unemployed, as expected, a notably high proportion of the employed are poor as well. Indeed, of families classified as poor, over half of the heads—50.6 percent in 1992—were employed for at least part of the year. This group, known as the "working poor," is often found in primary industries such as fishing, where wages are low and seasonal employment is common.

Education

Those households headed by a person with less education (no high school diploma) have the highest poverty rates. As we saw in Chapter 8, education affects wage levels. As a result, education level attained is a factor of poverty for the working poor.

Region

Poverty also varies from region to region. Historically, poor households tend to be concentrated in certain regions, particularly the Atlantic provinces and parts of Quebec. However, poverty exists throughout Canada. For example, a third of Canada's poor live in Ontario.

BRIEF REVIEW

1. The pre-tax income share of each fifth of households in Canada has not changed significantly in the last 40 years.

2. The Lorenz Curve, which expresses cumulative income distribution, demonstrates the extent to which there is perfect equality or perfect inequality in income distribution.

3. Governments affect income distribution through both transfer payments to households and taxes, especially personal income taxes. Transfer payments and taxation most affect the income shares of the highest and lowest income groups.

4. Factors that determine wages, as well as risk-taking, ability, and wealth, play a part in income inequality.

5. In Canada, poverty is defined in relation to the average Canadian income and expenditures on necessities. The poverty line, which depends on household type, is the income level below which a household is classified as poor.

6. Poverty is most prevalent among unattached individuals (especially women), single-parent families (especially those headed by women), the unemployed, and those under 25 and over 64 years old. Certain regions in Canada also have higher poverty rates.

 **The Canadian Welfare Society**

welfare society: a society in which the government plays a major role in attempting to ensure the economic well-being of its citizens

A mixed economy such as Canada's can be described as a **welfare society**, in which the government plays a major role in attempting to ensure the well-being of its citizens. Although the welfare society has become an integral part of life in industrialized countries such as Canada, it is a relatively recent creation. Before the 1930s, Canadian government maintained the legal system, provided education up to the secondary school level, and encouraged markets to develop. Health care and universities were left largely in the hands of the private sector, and unemployment insurance was not available. In comparison to the present, a *laissez-faire* attitude characterized the relationship between government and business.

Change began with the Great Depression of the 1930s. Faced with widespread unemployment and deprivation, Canadians demanded that government attend to the economic welfare of its citizens. From the 1930s to the 1970s, the role of Canadian governments—especially at the federal level—continued to expand. The question "What is fair?" has become perhaps the most important question that Canadian governments face, and their welfare programs are part of the answer. Now the welfare society in Canada includes a host of government programs: payments to adults with children, retirement funds for the elderly, insurance

Figure 9.7: Government Expenditures (1993–94)

Federal (1993–94)		Provincial (1993)		Local (1993)	
		($ billions)			
Transfers to persons					
Old age security	19.9	Goods and services	49.2	Goods and services	46.9
Unemployment insurance benefits	18.4	Transfers to		Transfers to	
Veterans' allowances and pensions	1.9	Persons	34.8	Persons	3.5
Transfers to other levels of government	27.1	Businesses	6.7	Businesses	1.0
Subsidies	13.3	Municipalities	28.2	Provinces	0.1
Foreign aid	2.7	Hospitals	22.7	Debt charges	4.2
Payments to Crown corporations	4.9	Debt charges	24.1		55.7
Defence	11.3		165.7		
Government operations	22.2				
Debt charges	38.5				
	160.2				

Federal government spending for the budgetary year of 1993–94 was dominated by transfer payments to persons and debt charges, which together make up almost half of federal spending. The main components of provincial spending are expenditures on goods and services, and transfers to persons, municipalities, and hospitals. Expenditures on goods and services dominate local government spending.

SOURCES: Department of Finance, *The Budget Plan* (February 1994), p. 56; Statistics Canada, *Canadian Economic Observer, Statistical Summary* (May 1994), cat. no. 11-010, pp. 7–8. Reproduced by authority of the Minister of Industry, 1994.

for unemployed workers, welfare payments for those who cannot work, subsidies for higher education, free health care, free schooling, and subsidized public housing for low-income families.

While all of these programs promote the general goal of ensuring Canadians' economic welfare, it is the transfer payments made to supplement incomes that most significantly address the specific goal of income equity. In Canada, transfer payments are made by all three levels of government; however, the federal government takes the leading role. Note that transfer payments are made not only by government to citizens, but also from one level of government to another. For example, the federal government makes transfer payments to the provinces and territories for education and health care. Figure 9.7 shows the expenditures of three levels of government. For the federal government, transfer payments to persons are the most important category of expenditure, followed by debt charges, which are interest payments on the government's own debt. The expenditures of provincial and local governments are more heavily weighted toward purchases of goods and services, although transfers to persons are also an important component of total provincial spending.

Universality Versus Means Testing

Some transfer payments to households are based on the principle of **universality.** The principle of universality means that benefits apply to all individuals, no matter what their incomes. An example is Old Age Security, which is received by all Canadians aged 65 and over. Universal programs have the advantage of treating everyone in the same way. As a result, there is no social stigma attached to receiving benefits, and no Canadians left out of a program who might resent the expenditures; therefore, there is strong support for continuing the program. However, universal programs also have drawbacks. Their main weakness is their expense: in order to provide substantial help to those who need it most, a large sum of money must be paid to *all* recipients.

In recent years, there has been a move toward **means testing**, whereby transfer payments vary according to a recipient's income. Examples of means-tested programs are the Guaranteed Income Supplement for the elderly and the Child Tax Credit received by parents. The main advantage of these programs is that benefits can be directed to those who need them most, so poor households receive the highest payments. However, governments may use means testing to limit spending by narrowing qualifications.

Transfer Payments to Households

There are six main types of transfer payments to households: Old Age Security, the Guaranteed Income Supplement, the Child Tax Credit, the Canada Assistance Plan, Unemployment Insurance, and the Quebec and Canada Pension Plans. The first four of these programs require no payments

universality: the principle applied to transfer payments whereby benefits are provided to all, regardless of income

means testing: a procedure whereby transfer payments vary according to a recipient's income

whatsoever from recipients. The last two programs require some contribution from workers and employers.

Old Age Security

Old Age Security (OAS) is a universal federal program that provides benefits to all Canadian residents once they reach age 65. Under the program, each unattached individual aged 65 and over receives a set dollar amount monthly ($381.60 as of April 1993), with married couples receiving exactly twice as much. Because the payments are considered part of the recipient's taxable income, well-off households pay much of their benefits back in the form of personal income taxes. For example, 1993 recipients with taxable incomes over $53 215 had all of their benefits "clawed back" through taxes.

Guaranteed Income Supplement

The Guaranteed Income Supplement (GIS) is a means-tested federal program that boosts the incomes of elderly Canadians whose only other primary source of income is Old Age Security. There is a maximum dollar supplement that can be received annually ($453.49 for a single pensioner as of April 1993). The recipient then loses $1 in benefits for every $2 of income from any source other than Old Age Security.

Child Tax Credit

The Child Tax Credit is a federal program that provides payments to parents of children under 18 years old. It is means tested, with low-income households receiving more than well-off households, many of whom receive no credit whatsoever.

Canada Assistance Plan

The Canada Assistance Plan (CAP) is a cost-sharing program that helps fund the welfare services provided by provincial, territorial, and municipal governments to individuals or households unable to support themselves through their own earnings. For example, single-parent families with low incomes, individuals who are unable to work due to disability, and families in crisis can benefit. Under this program, the federal government pays about half (less for residents of Ontario, B.C., and Alberta) of the costs of the program.

Unemployment Insurance

Unemployment Insurance (UI) is a federally run insurance program to aid people unemployed because of job loss, temporary sickness, or the birth or adoption of a child. The program is funded by compulsory contributions from employees and their employers, with any shortfall being made up through federal tax revenues. Employees pay a certain percentage of their earnings (3 percent in 1993), while their employers pay 1.4 times this amount. Benefits vary slightly among regions. In general, individuals with a minimum of 10 to 20 weeks of employment are eligible to receive benefits at 57.5 percent of their previous earnings for 17 to 50 weeks. During this period, recipients must file claims stating that they are actively looking for work.

Because the Unemployment Insurance program applies in the same way to all workers, there is little connection between benefits to and contributions from individual recipients. Workers in occupations with a high risk of unemployment, such as in the construction and resource industries, are subject to the same rules as those in comparatively low-risk occupations, such as in the public service.

Quebec and Canada Pension Plans

The Quebec and Canada Pension Plans (QPP and CPP) are parallel programs that provide workers in Quebec and the rest of Canada with payments after retirement. Like private pension plans, the QPP and CPP require that contributions be made to receive future benefits, so in one sense they are self-financing. Employees and their employers pay an equal percentage (2.5 percent for each for a total of 5.0 percent in 1993) of the worker's annual income, with self-employed workers paying the full percentage (5.0 percent).

Criticisms of the Welfare Society

While providing much-needed assistance to many households, Canada's welfare society has been the subject of widespread debate. As Figure 9.3 highlighted, government intervention in the form of transfer payments and taxation quite dramatically affects the incomes of households in the lowest income group. However, critics have pointed to three main problems with transfer payments to households: they discourage employment, they lead to inequities, and they are ineffective.

Disincentives to Work

According to critics, three programs in particular discourage employment: welfare, Unemployment Insurance, and government-run pension plans. Welfare plans vary across Canada, but most of them set up financial hurdles to employment, with some recipients receiving more income from welfare than they would upon initially entering the workforce.

Canada's Unemployment Insurance program has been criticized for worsening the very problem it is meant to counteract. By allowing repeated claims for benefits with no penalty, the program encourages workers to stay in occupations and regions of the country in which the risk of unemployment is considerable. Moreover, the high contributions paid by employers discourage them from creating new jobs.

The QPP and CPP have been criticized largely for their funding. Both are financed on a "pay-as-you-go" basis: the benefits paid out in any given year are funded by the benefits paid in. With the aging of the "baby-boom generation" and other demographic changes, it is estimated that workers' and employers' payments will have to rise to 9.1 percent (or about 4.6 percent each for employers and employees) by the year 2011 to cover the costs. This projected increase, critics argue, would discourage employment and job creation.

More generally, critics claim, Canada's welfare society indirectly discourages work by increasing taxes for individuals and businesses. With high tax rates, people have less incentive to seek employment and businesses have less incentive to hire them.

Inequities and Abuses

Some people argue against the principle of universality, which ensures that Old Age Security is paid to all households, not just those in need. The same criticism is directed at Unemployment Insurance; it is paid to both well-off individuals and those in need. Critics also note abuses of programs. Unemployment Insurance, for example, might be claimed by individuals who have little intention of acquiring a permanent job, but who may work for brief periods each year in order to claim extended benefits.

Ineffectiveness

Lastly, critics argue that welfare programs are hampered by overlapping bureaucracies, high administrative costs, and a lack of focus. They contend that due to this lack of focus and despite the large amounts spent on maintaining Canada's welfare society, the programs do not sufficiently alleviate poverty. In particular, the welfare society is not well-suited to helping the large group of working poor.

BRIEF REVIEW

1. Canada's welfare society has developed since the 1930s. As well as instituting free health care, schooling, and so on, governments have established programs requiring transfer payments to households, the main purpose of which is to promote income equity.

2. Some transfer payments to households are based on the principle of universality, with all Canadians receiving the same payment. Other programs are means tested; that is, benefits are determined by the recipient's income.

3. The main transfer payment programs to households are Old Age Security, the Guaranteed Income Supplement, the Child Tax Credit, the Canada Assistance Plan, Unemployment Insurance, and the Quebec and Canada Pension Plans.

4. Government transfer payment programs are criticized for discouraging employment, fostering inequities and abuses, and not sufficiently alleviating poverty.

Thinking About Economics

Can the problems associated with Canada's welfare society be solved while maintaining the benefits that flow from this system?

Many economists believe that Canada's welfare society can be made more effective. The solution they propose is known as a *guaranteed annual income*, which could replace virtually all current transfer payments to households. Under this proposed program, Canadians would be guaranteed a certain income. Those who earn no income themselves would receive the entire amount from the government. Those who earn some private income would have their government payment decreased by a certain amount for every dollar of private income. Say, for example, the guaranteed minimum were set at $20 000 per year and the deduction for each dollar of private earnings set at 50 cents. A household with no private earnings would receive $20 000. If it started to have private earnings of $2000, its payment would be reduced by $1000 ($2000 × 0.50), for a new government payment of $19 000. Therefore, with a total income of $21 000 ($19 000 + $2000) the household would still be better off than if it did not have any private income. As private earnings rose further, the government payment would gradually drop, finally disappearing altogether.

What advantages would such a system bring? Supporters of a guaranteed annual income plan claim it would correct each of the major problems associated with the current patchwork of transfer payment programs. By ensuring that households are made better off when they earn private income, such a plan provides a strong incentive to work. The plan would also do away with many of the inequities associated with present programs by ensuring that government funds are paid to those who are most in need. Finally, by streamlining Canada's welfare system, the plan would save on administrative costs and help ensure that government funds are used in the most effective manner to minimize the incidence of poverty in Canada. However, it must be pointed out that this proposal focuses on paid work and income earning to the exclusion of some other considerations—for example, the worth of homemaking, the needs of families with young children, and different requirements of individuals who are unable to work. Any streamlined program would have to address these other considerations as well.

 **Taxation**

tax: a payment required by government from individuals or businesses, with no direct good or service being provided in return

A **tax** is a payment required by government from individuals or businesses, with no direct good or service being provided in return. The main purpose of taxation is to finance state activity, but taxes may also be designed to promote income equity or improve outcomes in private markets. As shown in Figure 9.8, taxes by all three levels of government in Canada have increased considerably over past decades in relation to the size of the entire economy. The federal government, which plays the biggest role in operating Canada's welfare programs, takes the largest share of taxes.

Figure 9.8:   Taxes in the Canadian Economy

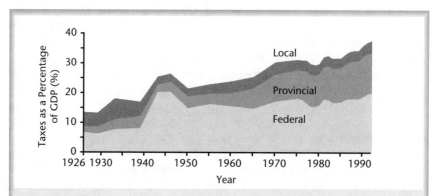

Since the 1920s, the increasing importance of the public sector in the Canadian economy has led to increased taxes (including contributions for such programs as UIC and CPP/QPP) in relation to the size of the economy. While taxes represented just over 10 percent of Gross Domestic Product (GDP) in 1926, they represented just under 40 percent by 1992.

SOURCES: Adapted from Statistics Canada, *National Income and Expenditure Accounts, Annual Estimates, 1926 to 1989*, cat. no. 13–531, and CANSIM matrices 2711 to 2713 and 6713 to 6714 (March 1993), reprinted in Canadian Tax Foundation, *The National Finances, 1993* (Toronto, 1993), p. 3:12. Reproduced by authority of the Minister of Industry, 1994.

Principles of Taxation

How should the burden of taxes be shared among taxpayers? Two principles can be applied in deciding whether or not the burden of a tax is distributed in a manner that is fair to all taxpayers: the principle of benefits received, and the principle of ability to pay.

benefits received: the principle applied to taxation whereby taxes are geared to the benefits each taxpayer gains from government activity

Benefits Received

The principle of **benefits received** suggests that taxes should be geared to the benefits each taxpayer gains from government activity. In this case, government services are paid for in the same ways that products are bought and sold in the private sector. The benefits-received principle is the guiding philosophy behind some taxes. The proceeds from a tax on gasoline, for example, are often earmarked for road construction and maintenance, thereby allowing governments to have drivers who use the most gasoline—and use the roads the most—pay the most for road upkeep.

Ability to Pay

A more common tax philosophy is based on the principle of **ability to pay**. According to this principle, taxes should vary in proportion to a taxpayer's financial resources—in particular, income. As sensible as the principle may be, it is difficult to measure ability to pay. For example, do all individuals earning $40 000 have the same ability to pay taxes, or does their taxpaying capacity also depend on other factors, such as the number of dependent children they support? Suppose a person's income rises by 50 percent, from $40 000 to $60 000. Should his or her tax bill also rise by 50 percent, or by some larger or smaller percentage?

ability to pay: the principle applied to taxation whereby taxes vary in proportion to a taxpayer's financial resources

Taxes and Income

Taxes are related to income in three possible ways, with a certain type of tax being either progressive, regressive, or proportional.

Progressive Taxes

A **progressive tax** is one that increases as a proportion of income as the income increases. In other words, well-off taxpayers are taxed more in both dollar terms *and* percentage terms. For example, someone making an annual income of $10 000 might pay 10 percent of total income, or $1000, for a certain tax, but a person making $20 000 a year might pay 15 percent of total income, or $3000, for that same tax.

progressive tax: a tax that increases as a proportion of income as income increases

Regressive Taxes

In contrast, a **regressive tax** is one that decreases as a proportion of income as income increases. In other words, taxpayers with low incomes pay proportionately more of their incomes for the tax than do well-off taxpayers, even though the well-off taxpayer may pay more as a dollar amount. For example, one taxpayer making $10 000 a year might pay 8 percent in tax, or $800, while another taxpayer with an annual income of $20 000 might pay 6 percent, or $1200, for the same tax.

regressive tax: a tax that decreases as a proportion of income as income increases

Proportional Taxes

Finally, a **proportional tax** is one that remains constant as a proportion of income for all incomes. Therefore, while taxpayers with vastly different incomes pay proportionately the same tax, the well-off taxpayer pays a higher dollar amount. For example, with a 6 percent tax rate, one taxpayer with an annual income of $10 000 would pay $600 in tax, while another taxpayer with an annual income of $20 000 would pay $1200.

proportional tax: a tax that remains constant as a proportion of income for all incomes

Types of Taxation

Canadian governments at the federal, provincial, and local levels use five main types of taxation to raise funds: personal income taxes, sales and excise taxes, property taxes, and corporate income taxes.

Personal Income Taxes

capital gains: earnings from selling an asset, such as land, at a higher price than it was purchased for

marginal tax rates: tax rates that are calculated as percentages of each *extra* dollar of taxable income

Personal income taxes are collected by the federal government, the proceeds being shared with the provinces and territories (except in Quebec, where federal and provincial income taxes are collected separately). Households pay taxes not only on their income from supplying resources, but also on any transfer payments they receive. Households also pay income tax on **capital gains**, which are earnings from selling an asset such as a bond or a piece of land at a higher price than it was purchased for.

Figure 9.9 shows the federal income tax rates. Note how the tax rates go up as income increases. These rates are called **marginal tax rates**, meaning that they are calculated as percentages of each *extra* dollar of taxable income. So, for example, households in the lowest income bracket, with 1993 taxable incomes of up to $29 590, were taxed at 17 percent. Therefore, a household making the maximum would pay $5030 in taxes ($29 590 × 0.17). In contrast, a household in the next tax bracket—with taxable income between $29 591 and $59 180—would pay 17 percent on its first $29 590 of taxable income, but 26 percent on income above that amount. Thus, a household that earns the maximum for the second tax bracket, or $59 180, would pay $5030 on the first $29 590 (using the 17 percent rate), plus $7693 on the remaining $29 590 (using the 26 percent rate), for a total tax bill of $12 723. Households in the highest possible tax bracket are taxed on each new dollar of income at a marginal tax rate of 29 percent.

Households may be allowed a variety of deductions that reduce their taxable income. For example, contributions to registered retirement savings plans can reduce the dollar amount on which a household is taxed.

Figure 9.9:   Federal Personal Income Tax Rates (1993)

Levels of Taxable Income	Marginal Tax Rate
$0 to $29 590	17%
$29 591 to $59 180	26%
$59 181 or more	29%

In 1993, households with taxable income in the first tax bracket—between $0 and $29 590—paid 17 cents on each dollar of income. Those in the second tax bracket—between $29 591 and $59 180—paid 26 cents on every dollar earned above $29 590. Those in the third income bracket paid 29 cents on every dollar earned above $59 180.

SOURCE: Condensed from *Tax Facts and Figures 1993* published by Coopers & Lybrand, Chartered Accountants.

In addition to these deductions, households may also claim a variety of tax credits, which directly reduce their tax bill.

Outside Quebec, provincial personal income taxes are simply a percentage of the federal tax bill added onto the taxpayer's bill. These percentages vary among the provinces and territories, as shown in Figure 9.10. Newfoundland taxes at the highest rate, with the province adding an extra 69 percent to households' tax bills in 1993. In contrast, residents of the Northwest Territories enjoy the lowest rate—45 percent in 1993.

Figure 9.10:   Provincial and Territorial Personal Income Tax Rates (1993)

Province	Percent of Federal Tax
Newfoundland	69.0
Prince Edward Island	59.5
Nova Scotia	59.5
New Brunswick	62.0
Ontario	58.5
Manitoba	52.0
Saskatchewan	50.0
Alberta	45.5
British Columbia	52.5
Northwest Territories	45.0
Yukon	48.0
Nonresidents	52.0

Personal income taxes going to provinces and territories are determined as a percentage of the taxpayer's federal tax bill. So, for example, a taxpayer in Nova Scotia pays his or her federal tax bill, and then 59.5 percent of that amount again to the province.

SOURCE: Condensed from *Tax Facts and Figures 1993,* published by Coopers & Lybrand, Chartered Accountants.

Figure 9.11:   Tax Revenues for All Levels of Government (1990–91)

	$ Billions	Percent of Total
Personal income taxes	100.4	48.5
Sales and excise taxes	55.8	27.0
Property taxes	23.1	11.2
Corporate income taxes	18.3	8.8
Miscellaneous taxes	9.3	4.5
	206.9	100.0

Personal income taxes are the most important source of revenue for the state, followed by sales and excise taxes, property taxes, and corporate taxes.

SOURCE: Statistics Canada, *Public Finance Historical Data 1965/66–1991/92,* cat. no. 68-512, reprinted in Canadian Tax Foundation, *The National Finances, 1993* (Toronto, 1993) p. 4:2. Reproduced by authority of the Minister of Industry, 1994.

As shown in Figure 9.11, personal income taxes made up 48.5 percent of total tax revenues for all levels of government in 1990–91.

Sales and Excise Taxes

Sales and excise taxes, which made up 27 percent of total tax revenues in 1990–91, are levied by both federal and provincial governments on goods and services. **Sales taxes** are usually charged on a wide range of goods and services, and are calculated as a percentage of the prices of these products. For example, a general 7 percent sales tax means that 7 cents is paid on each $1 spent on goods and services. In contrast, **excise taxes** are charged on particular products such as gasoline, liquor, and tobacco, and are often expressed as a dollar amount per unit of quantity, rather than in terms of percentages of product price.

Customs duties, also known as tariffs, are a special type of excise tax. They are levied on imported goods by the federal government. While customs duties provide the government with revenue, their main purpose is to push up the prices of foreign goods, thereby encouraging consumers to purchase Canadian-made products.

Property Taxes

Property taxes are charged by local governments on buildings and land. For taxation purposes, these assets are assigned a value—often *not* their potential price in the real estate market, but some arbitrary dollar amount set in the past. Then, each year, the local government establishes a tax rate in terms of mills (or thousands) of property value. For example, a mill rate of 80 means that property owners are charged $80 for each $1000 in property value. As shown in Figure 9.11, property taxes made up 11.2 percent of Canadian governments' total tax revenues in 1990–91.

Corporate Income Taxes

Corporate income taxes are paid by corporations to governments as a percentage of their annual profits. As with personal income taxes, corporations are allowed to make deductions from their total income in calculating taxable profit. The resulting dollar amount is then taxed at a constant marginal rate of 28.0 percent by the federal government, with most provincial governments "piggybacking" on this rate as in the case of personal income taxes. In the budget year 1990–91, corporate income taxes represented 8.8 percent of total tax revenues for all levels of government, as shown in Figure 9.11.

sales taxes: taxes that are charged on a wide range of products, and calculated as a percentage of their prices

excise taxes: taxes that are charged on particular products, and often expressed as a dollar amount per unit of quantity

Thinking About Economics

Are Canadian taxes progressive, regressive, or proportional?

Because of the range of marginal rates for different income brackets, Canada's personal income tax system is progressive, with the rich paying a larger proportion of their incomes than do the poor. This is so despite tax shelters that the rich can use to reduce their taxable incomes. In contrast, sales and excise taxes tend to be regressive, since the poor spend a higher proportion of their incomes on consumption items than do the rich, who are more likely to save part of their incomes. Property taxes (at least those on buildings rather than those on land) are also often regressive, largely because the poor devote a higher proportion of their incomes to housing than do the rich. Corporate income taxes are more difficult to classify as either progressive or regressive. To the extent that these taxes reduce the income of shareholders—a rich group in Canadian society—they are progressive. However, corporations that have considerable market power may succeed in passing on the burden of the tax to consumers in the form of higher prices for their products. In this case, the corporate tax is regressive in a similar way to a sales tax.

BRIEF REVIEW

1. Taxes are payments required by government from individuals and businesses. Over past decades, taxation has increased as a proportion of the overall Canadian economy, with federal taxes representing the largest share.

2. Taxes may be based on the benefits received by a taxpayer from government activity, or on the taxpayer's ability to pay.

3. Taxes that are progressive increase as a proportion of income as income increases. Taxes that are regressive decrease as a proportion of income as income increases. Taxes that are proportional remain constant as a proportion of all incomes.

4. Canadian governments use five main types of taxation: personal income taxes, sales and excise taxes, property taxes, and corporate income taxes.

SIDELINE

Taxation Blues

The Debate Over the Goods and Services Tax

In 1991, the federal government made a controversial change in Canada's tax system: it introduced the Goods and Services Tax (GST). Rarely has a tax been so disliked by Canadian taxpayers, so much so that many taxpayers demanded its replacement. To examine why, let's first look at why the GST was introduced.

Drawbacks of the Federal Sales Tax

Prior to the GST, the federal government had a Federal Sales Tax (FST), also known as the manufacturer's sales tax. Under the FST, a 13.5 percent tax was levied on the sales value of all Canadian manufactured goods. The tax was "hidden" to consumers in that it was built into final retail prices, rather than added on top. Therefore, most consumers were unaware of its existence.

As it stood, the FST had some major drawbacks: its narrow base, the possibility of tax avoidance, its effect on exports, and its effect on the poor.

Narrow Base   Only one-third of all products bought by Canadians were taxed under the FST. Forty percent of FST revenues, for example, came from consumer spending on just five types of products: tobacco, alcohol, automobiles, auto parts, and fuels. If the government had chosen to raise the FST rate, the tax would have put an extra burden on buyers and sellers of this narrow range of products.

Tax Avoidance   Businesses could avoid paying the FST because of the method used to calculate the tax, and because of an increasing number of exemptions. The FST was calculated on the basis of business costs; however, certain types of businesses had gained exemptions. So, for example, if a company created a special subsidiary to perform the marketing function for its products, this marketing subsidiary, because of exemptions, would pay no FST. In comparison, a compa-

SOURCE: John Larter/The Calgary Sun

ny that had not created a subsidiary would pay more tax while producing the same product. As a result, the total dollar amount of taxation was reduced, and unfairly so. Also, by battling the federal government in court, businesses were gradually able to carve out a wider range of possible cost exemptions.

Effect on Exports   The FST was applied on both products sold to Canadians and products sold in foreign markets. By raising the prices of Canadian manufactured goods in foreign markets, the tax reduced sales of Canada's exports, thereby hurting employment in the related industries.

Effect on the Poor   Like all sales taxes, the FST was regressive. Because Canadians with low incomes spend a higher proportion of their incomes on consumption items, they were more affected by the FST than were Canadians with high incomes.

How the GST Operates

The GST differs from the FST in two key ways: it applies to virtually all goods and services, and it is a "value-added" tax. As a result of its broad base—which includes almost everything but food (as of 1994)—the tax rate could be kept to 7 percent. Because it is a "value-added" tax, the GST is charged on the value added by businesses to a good or service at each stage of production.

The following example illustrates how a value-added tax works. In this example, logging, paper-making, and retailing are the stages in producing and selling a pad of paper.

Transaction 1   Wood with a value of $1 is sold by the logging company to the paper-maker. Because the logging company adds the full $1 in value, the tax that is paid on this transaction is 7 cents (7 percent of $1). This tax is collected by the logging company and passed on to the federal government.

Transaction 2   The paper-maker manufactures the pad of paper, which is sold to the retailer for $4. A tax of 28 cents (7 percent of $4) is charged on this transaction. The paper-maker collects the tax, but before handing it over to the government is able to claim an "input tax credit" for the 7 cents tax paid to the logging company in transaction 1. Hence, the company pays a net tax of only 21 cents (28 cents – 7 cents) to the government. This represents 7 percent of the $3 value that the paper-maker adds to production—the $4 it gains from selling the paper minus the $1 it was charged for the necessary input.

Transaction 3   When a consumer buys the pad of paper at a retail price of $6, he or

Calculating the GST				
Transaction	Value of Sale	Tax on Sale (0.07 x value of sale)	Input Tax Credit (tax paid at previous stage)	Net Tax on Value Added (tax on sale less input tax credit)
1. Wood sold by logging company	$1.00	$0.07	—	$0.07
2. Paper sold by paper-maker	$4.00	$0.28	$0.07	$0.21
3. Paper sold to consumer	$6.00	$0.42	$0.28	$0.14
				$0.42

When the wood is sold to the paper-maker for $1, a tax of 7 cents is charged. When the paper-maker sells the resulting pad of paper to the retailer for $4, a tax of 28 cents is charged; however, the paper-maker claims a 7-cent input tax credit for tax already paid, and therefore pays a net tax of 21 cents. When the pad is finally sold to the consumer at a price of $6, the retailer collects 42 cents in tax, but claims a 28-cent input tax credit for tax already paid; therefore, the retailer pays 14 cents. The net taxes paid at each stage add up to the full 42 cents in tax paid by the consumer.

she pays a tax of 42 cents (7 percent of $6). Before transferring this amount to the government, the retailer claims an input tax credit for the 28 cents in tax paid to buy the paper. Thus, the retailer's net tax is the remaining 14 cents (42 cents – 28 cents). This is 7 percent of the $2 value added by the retailer in buying the pad of paper for $4 and selling it for $6.

Impact of the GST

The response of Canadians to the GST stems from its three main attributes: multi-stage coverage, broad base, and visibility.

Multi-Stage Coverage Because the GST is levied at all stages of production, and because legal tax avoidance is not possible, the GST is more fair than the FST. The input tax credits received by businesses make it possible for the government to exempt goods and services sold outside the country, thereby keeping down the prices of exports and helping export industries. Export businesses can claim input tax credits on any taxes they pay to suppliers.

Broad Base The GST's broad base of goods and services has both positive and negative effects. On the positive side, it allows the federal government to raise more tax revenue. A portion of these revenues is channelled into a "GST credit" to taxpayers with low incomes, thereby helping to over-come the tax's regressive aspects. Another advantage of the GST's broad base—at least for government policy-makers—is that it allows for increases in the tax rate without placing an undue burden on consumers and producers of a narrow range of products.

The disadvantages of the broad base have attracted the most attention. Not only does the GST apply to more products than did the FST, it also covers many more businesses. All companies whose taxable sales exceed $30 000 have to collect the tax. For these businesses—especially the numerous small businesses in the service sector—this task adds to the cost of doing business. Many commentators suggest that the GST has led to more "under-the-table" transactions in parts of the service sector, so that unscrupulous businesses and consumers can evade the tax.

Visibility Ironically, one of the most contentious aspects of the GST is incidental to its operation. Unlike the FST, the GST is visible to consumers when they pay for their purchases. Supporters of this feature say that Canadians should be aware of the taxes they pay. Others point out that the tax seems more intrusive in Canadians' daily lives. Making the GST—or any replacement—more palatable to Canadian consumers seems to mean making the tax less noticeable.

SOURCE: This material is drawn from the discussion in Evelyn Jacks' book, *Jacks on GST* (Toronto: McGraw-Hill Ryerson, 1991).

Spillover Effects

spillover effects: external effects of economic activity, which have an impact on outsiders who are not producing or consuming a product

Government spending and taxation are not only geared to promoting income equity and competition. Governments also play a part in dealing with the external effects of economic activity. These **spillover effects** arise whenever outsiders are affected by the production or consumption of a particular product. Spillover effects occur in even the ideal case of a perfectly competitive market, simply because no market exists in isolation. Governments often step in to see that all costs and benefits—private and public—are accounted for. Sometimes government intervention takes the form of direct spending. Figure 9.12 shows how government spending is categorized.

Figure 9.12:   Government Spending (1990–91)

Function	$ Billions	Percentage
General services	18.7	6.0
Protection of persons and property	23.6	7.6
Transportation and communications	15.1	4.9
Health	41.6	13.4
Social services	67.1	21.7
Education	36.8	11.9
Resource conservation and industrial development	12.8	4.1
Debt charges	62.7	20.3
Other	31.1	10.1
Total	309.5	100.0

The above figures represent the consolidated spending in the budget year 1990–91 for Canada's federal, provincial, territorial, and local governments. Note the extent of social services, health, and education expenditures.

Source: Statistics Canada, *Public Finance Historical Data 1965/66–1991/92*, cat. no. 68-512, p. ix. Reproduced by authority of the Minister of Industry, 1994.

Spillover Costs and Benefits

Spillover effects may take the form of either costs or benefits.

Spillover Costs

Spillover costs are the negative effects of producing or consuming a product that fall on outsiders, not market participants. Environmental pollution is the most common example. Recall that some resources called *free goods,* such as air, can be used free of charge. Still other resources, such as water, have prices that do not reflect the resource's value. Any damage caused to these resources through market activity creates substantial costs for society as a whole.

Producers making products that have negative external effects focus only on their private costs as they make supply decisions. Consequently, the prices for these products are insufficient to cover both private and spillover costs. Figure 9.13 illustrates spillover effects with the example of gasoline used by motor vehicles. Assuming that the market for gasoline is perfectly competitive and free of government intervention, equilibrium occurs at point *b*, the intersection of the demand and supply curves D and S$_0$, with a price per litre of $1.50 and a quantity of 6 million litres.

spillover costs: negative external effects of producing or consuming a product

Figure 9.13: The Impact of Spillover Costs

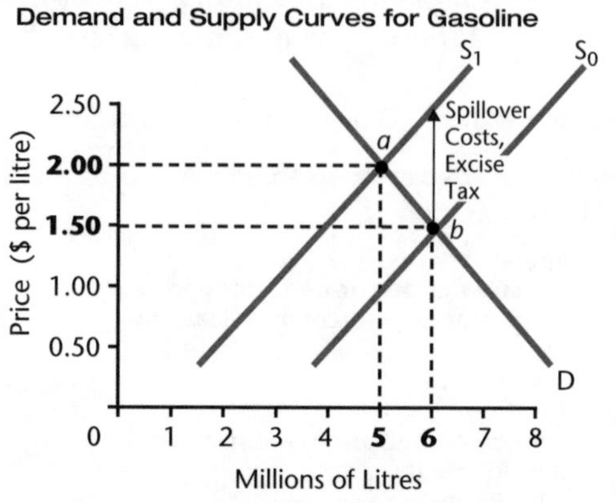

Demand and Supply Curves for Gasoline

Demand and Supply Schedules for Gasoline

Price	Quantity Demanded	Quantity Supplied	
($ per litre)	(D)	(S_0)	(S_1)
	(millions of litres)		
2.50	4	8 → 6	
2.00	5	7 → 5	
1.50	6	6 → 4	
1.00	7	5 → 3	
0.50	8	4 → 2	

Without government intervention, equilibrium occurs at point *b*, at a price of $1.50 per litre and a quantity of 6 million litres of gasoline. To account for spillover costs, the government may impose an excise tax of $1.00 per litre. As a result, the supply curve shifts from S_0 to S_1, moving equilibrium to point *a*, at a price of $2.00 per litre and a quantity of 5 million litres.

Because of the pollution created by both the production and the consumption of gasoline, spillover costs are associated with this product. If these spillover costs are an extra $1 for each litre of gas, a new supply curve, S_1, can be drawn that incorporates the additional cost per litre. Whereas the old supply curve, S_0, reflects the *private* costs of producing one more litre of gasoline, the new supply curve, S_1, reflects the *private* and *public* costs of this production.

Where should the market operate? Applying the rule of marginal cost pricing, price in this market should equal the height of the supply curve (which reflects marginal cost), once both private and spillover costs are accounted for. In other words, equilibrium should occur at point *a*, the intersection of D and S_1, at a price of $2 and a quantity of 5 million litres. Without government intervention, 1 million too many litres of gasoline are produced and consumed. To achieve the preferred outcome, the government can levy an excise tax on gasoline equalling $1 per litre. This succeeds in shifting the supply curve from S_0 to S_1, and ensures that the oversupply of gasoline is corrected.

Spillover Benefits

spillover benefits: positive external effects of producing or consuming a product

Spillover benefits are positive external effects of producing or consuming a product. Education is an important example, since society as a whole gains from this service. From an economic perspective alone, education is considered beneficial because of the increased work and income-earning opportunities it affords each individual, and because it enriches the nation's human resources. More generally, education is seen as a social good because it helps Canadians to lead more informed, fulfilled, and productive lives.

Suppose that students are considering an education in engineering. Figure 9.14 gives a hypothetical example. As in any education and career choice, the students would weigh the costs and benefits of obtaining an engineering degree. With the private market for an engineering education being perfectly competitive, the demand and supply curves D_0 and S have equilibrium point a, with a yearly tuition per student of $4000 and an enrollment of 10 000 students.

Figure 9.14:   The Impact of Spillover Benefits

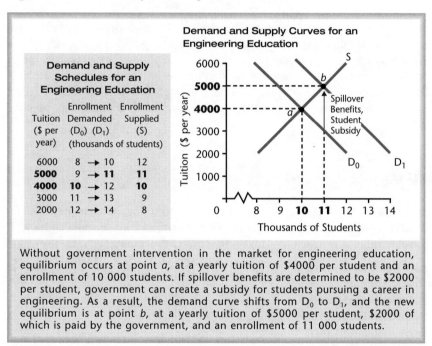

Demand and Supply Schedules for an Engineering Education			
	Enrollment	Enrollment	
Tuition	Demanded		Supplied
($ per year)	(D_0)	(D_1)	(S)
	(thousands of students)		
6000	8 → 10		12
5000	9 → **11**		**11**
4000	**10** → 12		**10**
3000	11 → 13		9
2000	12 → 14		8

Without government intervention in the market for engineering education, equilibrium occurs at point a, at a yearly tuition of $4000 per student and an enrollment of 10 000 students. If spillover benefits are determined to be $2000 per student, government can create a subsidy for students pursuing a career in engineering. As a result, the demand curve shifts from D_0 to D_1, and the new equilibrium is at point b, at a yearly tuition of $5000 per student, $2000 of which is paid by the government, and an enrollment of 11 000 students.

Because society as a whole benefits from having trained engineers, there are spillover benefits. To see how much engineering education should be undertaken from society's perspective, we must estimate the spillover benefits of this education. Suppose the result is $2000 per student per year. As a result, a new demand curve, D_1, can be drawn that incorporates the private and public benefits.

Again applying the rule of marginal cost pricing, price in this market should equal the height of the supply curve (which reflects marginal cost), once both private and spillover benefits are accounted for. In other words, equilibrium should occur at point *b*, at the intersection of S and D_1, with an annual tuition of $5000 and an enrollment of 11 000 students. However, if private benefits alone were accounted for, only 10 000 students (point *a*) would be enrolled, thereby creating a shortfall of 1000 students. To increase enrollment to the desired level, the government could subsidize engineering education by giving prospective students vouchers to be turned in to the engineering school. The school would then turn in these vouchers to the government for $2000 per voucher. As a result, the demand curve for engineering education would shift to the right, thereby ensuring that society produces more engineers than would a fully private and competitive market.

Public Goods

public good: a product whose benefits cannot be restricted to certain individuals

At the extreme, there are some products for which private benefits and spillover benefits cannot be separated. A **public good** is a product whose benefits cannot be restricted to certain individuals. In other words, while many consumers may pay for the product, others may get a "free ride." Lighthouses are an example, as is national defence. In this situation, the only option is to dispense with markets and have government provide these products.

BRIEF REVIEW

1. Spillover effects are the external effects of economic activity that arise because no market exists in isolation.

2. Spillover effects can be negative or positive. Spillover costs, such as pollution, are the harmful effects of producing or consuming a product. Spillover benefits, such as those associated with education, are the positive effects of producing or consuming a product.

3. Governments often step in to see that public, as well as private, costs and ben-

efits are accounted for. Governments might, for example, intervene with taxes to correct an oversupply in the case of spillover costs, or with subsidies to correct a shortfall in the case of spillover benefits.

4. Public goods are products whose benefits cannot be restricted to certain individuals. Governments often step in to provide these goods rather than leave them to private markets.

The Doomsday Prophet

Thomas Malthus and Population Growth

ADVANCING ECONOMIC THOUGHT

Malthus and His Influence

Known as the "doomsday prophet" for his gloomy predictions of the economic and social future, Thomas Malthus (1766–1834) was an influential economist in his time, as well as a clergyman. Malthus' theories and predictions sprang from an unlikely source: a reform-minded writer named William Godwin (1756–1836), who believed that future society would be transformed by science and human reason. Wars, disease, and crime would finally come to an end, Godwin thought, and the need for government would vanish. Malthus' *Essay on Population* (1798), in which he published his arguments against Godwin's vision, was destined to be one of the most influential economic works of the nineteenth century.

Malthus' basic point was that utopian visions of the future ignore the negative effects of population growth. According to Malthus, food production and population levels expand at different rates. At best, he said, food increases in what mathematicians call an algebraic progression (1, 2, 3, 4...) as more variable inputs are devoted to a certain amount of usable land. In contrast, population increases in a geometric progression (1, 2, 4, 8...), with levels doubling again and again in a set period. Malthus estimated this period to be 25 years.

Given these assumptions, it was easy for Malthus to predict a discrepancy between food production and the needs of the population. The following time chart shows numbers taken from Malthus' *Essay*. For convenience, population and food stocks in Year 1 are set equal to 1 unit. Food production expands by 1 unit every 25 years as population doubles in the same period. After 225 years, population will have outstripped food by a factor of just over 50 (512 ÷ 10) to 1.

Thomas Malthus

Source: By courtesy of the National Portrait Gallery.

A Malthusian Time Chart

Year	1	25	50	75	100	125	150	175	200	225
Food	1	2	3	4	5	6	7	8	9	10
Population	1	2	4	8	16	32	64	128	256	512

If food grows by 1 unit every 25 years but population doubles over the same period, then after 225 years food production will be 10 times higher but population will be 512 times higher.

Source: Henry William Spiegel, *The Growth of Economic Thought* (Durham, NC: Duke University Press, 1971), p.272.

Malthus warned of desperate circumstances if his predictions came true, and outlined how population growth could be slowed by either a decrease in the birth rate or an increase in the mortality rate. He had little faith that the number of births would decrease; however, he did feel that at some point, if birth rates did not fall, a limited food supply would bring on misery, famine, plagues, or war, thereby decreasing the population.

Implications and Influence of Malthus' Theory

Based on his assumptions, Malthus believed that aid to those in need would be self-defeating, as it would encourage people to survive and thrive. In the long run, he said, this population growth would result in starvation. During the nineteenth century, Malthus' views had a powerful effect on government policies. In England, for example, aid to people who were physically able to work was restricted to those willing to give up their possessions and move into a workhouse, where prolonged labour brought them virtually no pay—only room and board.

Social reformers attacked this "Malthusian" policy, calling it misguided and cruel. The appalling conditions in English workhouses were exposed in many books and pamphlets, Charles Dickens' fictional account *Oliver Twist* being the most famous. Not surprisingly, it was because of Malthus' work that economics was dubbed "the dismal science" by its critics.

Relevance for Today

Fortunately, Malthus' dire predictions have proven to be wrong, at least in those countries with which he was directly concerned. While he later refined the logic of his arguments, their foundations were shaky. Malthus implied that the state of technology would remain fixed; however, the dramatic changes in technology since his day have increased food production in most countries. Malthus also overlooked the extent to which large families were the result of economic necessity. In his own day, high infant mortality rates and the lack of old age pensions meant that large families provided parents with security in old age. Also, during his time, child labour provided extra income to a family. Today, with social welfare programs, child labour laws, and the means to limit population growth, population growth rates in industrialized countries have been far below what Malthus imagined. Indeed, in some of these nations, the rate is close to zero.

While population growth continues to be a *global* concern (which we'll address in Chapter 18), the history of Malthus' theory has a valuable lesson: care must be taken in applying economic models to the real world and to government policy.

1. Summarize Malthus' population theory as outlined in this essay.

2. Research one specific era (a decade, for example) to identify one of the prevailing economic theories of that time. In a research essay, outline the theory, its assumptions, its social and economic context, and its influence. Finally, explain whether you agree or disagree with the theory, and why.

Key Concepts

Lorenz curve
transfer payments
wealth
poverty
poverty line
welfare society
universality
means testing
tax
benefits received
ability to pay

progressive tax
regressive tax
proportional tax
capital gains
marginal tax rates
sales taxes
excise taxes
spillover effects
spillover costs
spillover benefits
public good

Developing Application and Analysis Skills

1. Using the data in Figure 9.3, do the following:

a) For each of the five income groups, calculate the changes in average income from income before transfers and taxes, to pre-tax income, to income after transfer payments and taxes.

b) Comment on the results, noting and explaining the most significant changes.

2. a) Figure 9.2 gives the Lorenz curve based on incomes prior to taxation but after transfer payments. Using the data from Figure 9.3, create a graph giving two

Lorenz curves: one using income shares prior to taxes and transfer payments, and another after both taxes and transfer payments.

b) Compare the results. Given the goal of taxation and transfer payments—income equity—how effective do you think government intervention is?

3. The following table shows the share of post-tax income received by each 20 percent of income earners, from lowest to highest, in selected countries for various years. On one

Income Shares in Selected Countries					
Country	Share of income received by each 20 percent of income earners				
	1 (lowest)	2	3	4	5 (highest)
France	4.2	9.7	16.2	22.8	47.1
Japan	5.1	12.4	16.8	21.7	41.9
Sweden	7.3	14.1	19.0	24.7	35.0
United Kingdom	6.1	12.2	18.4	24.0	39.3
United States	4.9	10.9	17.5	24.6	42.1
Canada	5.2	12.0	18.0	24.2	40.5
Average	5.5	11.9	17.7	23.7	41.0

SOURCE: L. Osberg, *Economic Inequality in Canada* (Toronto: Butterworths 1981), p. 24.

large graph, draw and label a Lorenz curve for each country. Then, rank the countries from most equal to least equal income distribution.

4. Although capital gains taxes are levied when a taxpayer dies, there are no longer any Canadian taxes on the transfer of wealth from one generation to the next. In this respect, Canada differs from most other industrialized countries, which levy "wealth taxes" on gifts and inheritances.

   a) What effect does the lack of a wealth tax have on Canada's distribution of wealth and income?
   b) Outline the possible advantages and disadvantages of a tax on Canadian wealth. Suggest why Canadian governments do not levy such a tax.
   c) In your opinion, should Canadian governments levy a wealth tax? Explain your answer in detail.

5. Research the current poverty lines applicable to your community. Based on community wages, costs, and other economic factors, create a realistic composite sketch of what living below the poverty line entails for one hypothetical household of a size you choose. For example, if your assumption is that the household spends 54.7 percent of its income on necessities, identify in real terms what this dollar amount might be able to buy.

6. a) Two main barriers to escaping poverty are an inability to find work, and low wages in jobs where employment is possible. How are the causes of poverty and these barriers related? Give specific examples in your answer.
   b) Propose and explain a government policy that would help individuals overcome these barriers.

7. Collect from newspapers and magazines at least 10 articles concerning income inequality,

taxation, specific transfer payment programs, and/or the welfare society in general. Research one of the current issues addressed in the articles—current government procedures, arguments for or against any proposals, and so on. Present your results in a research essay.

8. Based on what you've learned from this chapter and any research for previous activities, write an opinion paper in response to the following statement: "Canada's system of transfer payments and taxation has evolved into a wasteful, inefficient, and ineffective response to Canada's realities. Rather than solving the problems this system was meant to address, it creates more problems, and should be replaced by a guaranteed annual income program."

9. Consider the effects of each of the following taxes. Identify each tax as progressive, regressive, or proportional, and explain your answer.

   a) a federal personal income tax at a rate that increases with every extra dollar of income
   b) a federal personal income tax at a constant rate
   c) a property tax at a constant rate
   d) taxes paid on gasoline
   e) a 7 percent tax on gains realized through real estate sales

10. Research the following factors that determine personal income taxes. Explain how each affects the distribution of income or wealth:

   a) personal deductions
   b) child tax credit
   c) retirement savings plan contributions
   d) pension contributions
   e) investment losses
   f) university tuition
   g) medical expenses
   h) charitable donations

11. a) Analyze the following bar graph and identify the trend it illustrates.

b) Suggest the impact of this trend on income distribution in general, on Canada's welfare society, and on taxation.

c) Considering the implications for Canada as a whole, state whether you believe this to be a positive or a negative trend. Support your answer.

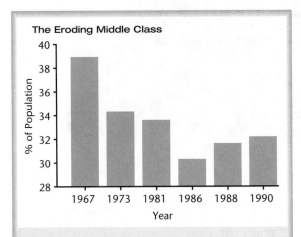

The Eroding Middle Class

NOTE: Government specialists define the middle class as those earning between 75 percent and 150 percent of the average wage.

SOURCE: Adapted from Statistics Canada, *Survey of Consumer Finances* Special Tabulations, Analytical Studies Branch (9 September 1992). Reproduced by authority of the Minister of Industry, 1994.

12. Using the examples cited in this chapter, what are the opportunity costs of Canadian governments taxing spillover costs and subsidizing spillover benefits?

13. Suggest for each of the following activities the spillover costs or benefits, and the forms of intervention the government is taking or might take:

a) the production of automobile tires
b) the production of nuclear-generated power
c) recycling industries
d) public libraries
e) wilderness conservation areas

P A R T   3

Economic Stability

In the long run we are all dead. Economists set themselves too easy, too useless a task if in tempestuous seasons they can only tell us that when the storm is long past the ocean is flat again.

—JOHN MAYNARD KEYNES, ENGLISH ECONOMIST

So far, we have concentrated on the microeconomic issues associated with efficiency, income equity, and the environment. In this section, we turn our attention to macroeconomics, with its emphasis on ensuring economic stability. All of us feel the impact of fluctuations in the Canadian economy. Particularly for those Canadians who lose their jobs or see the purchasing power of their incomes drop, economic instability is more than just an abstraction. The next six chapters investigate the measurements of economic health, the nature and causes of fluctuations in the Canadian economy, and the ways in which these fluctuations can be reduced through government policy.

CHAPTER 10

Measures of Economic Activity

All progress is precarious, and the solution of one problem brings us face to face with another problem.
—Martin Luther King Jr., American civil rights and religious leader

How healthy is the Canadian economy? How productive is Canada? Are the incomes of Canadians rising or falling? How do living standards in Canada compare with those in other countries? Just as you use a thermometer to check your temperature, nations must diagnose and understand their economic health before they can respond to questions such as these ones. This chapter examines various indicators of Canadian economic health, especially the most prominent measure—Gross Domestic Product (GDP). In later chapters, we will consider GDP further and examine additional measures, what they indicate, and the economic realities of stability and instability.

CHAPTER FOCUS

This chapter focuses on the following:
- Gross Domestic Product (GDP), and the two approaches to calculating it
- the components of GDP
- per capita GDP, and how it may be used to compare GDPs of different years or different countries
- some limitations of GDP as an economic indicator
- other economic measures developed from the national income accounts

SKILLS FOCUS

After studying this chapter, you will be able to:
- explain the GDP identity
- illustrate the components of GDP using the two approaches for calculating it
- outline the causes of statistical discrepancy, and the difference between GDP and GNP
- differentiate between intermediate and final products, and suggest value-adding processes
- categorize transactions as included in or excluded from GDP, and explain them
- interpret tables and graphs containing data that relate to GDP
- demonstrate flows of resources and money in an economy
- evaluate and explain the extent to which GDP indicates living standards in an economy
- propose measures that would indicate the economic health and living standards in your community

Gross Domestic Product

National Income Accounts

national income accounts: accounts showing the levels of total income and spending in the Canadian economy

Keeping track of the Canadian economy is the task of Statistics Canada, a federal agency. This agency prepares the country's **national income accounts**, which give various measures of total income and spending in the Canadian economy. Recall that businesses track revenues and expenditures in their accounts and show any resulting profit on an income statement, thereby allowing managers and owners to pinpoint ways of improving a business's performance. National income accounts play a similar role for the economy as a whole. They allow us to evaluate the performance of the Canadian economy and to compare it with other nations' economies. National income accounts also help government policymakers find ways to improve the economy.

Measuring Gross Domestic Product

Gross Domestic Product: the total dollar value at current prices of all final goods and services produced in Canada over a given period

A variety of measures of economic activity can be developed from the national income accounts. Of these, the most common measure in Canada is **Gross Domestic Product**, or GDP. GDP is the total dollar value of all final goods and services produced in the economy over a given period. The dollar value is calculated at current prices, and the period is typically a year. As Figure 10.1 shows, GDP uses *dollar* value because it effectively simplifies the picture; dollar value is a way to quantify and combine a wide range of goods and services.

Two Views of GDP

Canada's GDP is calculated using two approaches, one measuring income and the other measuring spending. Figure 10.2, which illustrates the circular flow for a simple economy where only consumer products are sold, shows both approaches. The diagram shows two economic sectors: households and businesses. Recall that whereas the inner (clockwise)

Figure 10.1:   Calculating Gross Domestic Product

Product	Current Price (P)	Annual Output (Q)	Total Dollar Value (P × Q)
Surgical lasers	$1000	3	$3000
Milkshakes	2	1000	2000
			GDP = $5000

It is impossible to add together the economy's annual output of surgical lasers and milkshakes without taking into account dollar values. If 3 surgical lasers and 1000 milkshakes are produced, then GDP is the sum of both outputs valued at their current prices.

loop represents the flow of money, the outer (counterclockwise) loop represents the flow of products and resources. The upper portion of the diagram shows the economy's resource markets, in which human, capital, and natural resources are sold by households for incomes. The **income approach** to GDP involves adding together all the incomes in the economy to give GDP. The lower portion of the diagram shows the economy's product markets, in which final goods and services are sold by businesses to households. The **expenditure approach** to GDP involves adding together all consumer spending in the economy to give GDP.

income approach: a method of calculating Gross Domestic Product by adding together all incomes in the economy

expenditure approach: a method of calculating Gross Domestic Product by adding together all spending in the economy

Figure 10.2:   Circular Flows in a Simple Economy

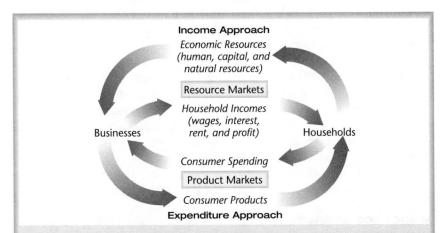

Households and businesses meet in both resource and product markets. The inner (clockwise) loop represents the flow of money. The outer (counterclockwise) loop represents the flow of products and resources. As shown in the upper portion of the diagram, in the resource markets, human, capital, and natural resources are sold by households for incomes. As shown in the lower portion of the diagram, in the product markets, final goods and services are sold by businesses to households. The income approach to GDP measures the flow of incomes in the upper portion; the expenditure approach measures the flow of spending in the lower portion.

The GDP Identity

In the simple economy shown in Figure 10.2, because all spending on final consumer products ends up as some form of household income, annual income equals annual spending. As a result, GDP found using the income approach and GDP found using the expenditure approach are the same. This relationship between the two approaches is known as the **GDP identity**:

GDP expressed as total income $\equiv$ GDP expressed as total spending

The triple-lined identity sign in this formula—a stronger version of the equals sign (=)—indicates that the expressions on either side are identical.

GDP identity: Gross Domestic Product calculated as total income is identical to Gross Domestic Product calculated as total spending

The GDP identity applies not only to the simplified economy shown in Figure 10.2, but also to the entire Canadian economy. So, Statistics Canada uses both approaches—the income approach and the expenditure approach—to calculate GDP. However, Statistics Canada does not restrict itself to consumer products; instead, it considers incomes from and expenditures on all goods and services in Canada.

 ## The Income Approach

Income Components of GDP

As discussed in Chapter 8, wages, rent, profit, and interest make up Canadian incomes. Human, capital, and natural resources give Canadians wages, rent, and profit. Although not strictly a resource income, interest forms part of Canadian incomes. These four payments form the basis of GDP calculated using the income approach. As we mentioned in Chapter 8, because of practical difficulties in distinguishing resource earnings, Statistics Canada applies its own classification system: wages and salaries, corporate profits, interest income, and proprietors' incomes (including rent).

To these four classes of income, Statistics Canada adds three other classifications: indirect taxes, depreciation, and a statistical discrepancy account. These three categories help to balance GDP that is calculated using the income approach with GDP that is calculated using the expenditure approach. Using the income approach, GDP is the sum of all seven categories.

Wages and Salaries
Wages and salaries are the largest income category, representing close to 60 percent of GDP. This category includes direct payments to workers in both business and government, as well as employee benefits such as contributions to employee pension funds.

Corporate Profits
This category includes all corporate profits declared to the government, including the profits paid as corporate income tax, the profits paid out to corporate shareholders as dividends, and the profits put back into the business. The final subcategory of profits put back into the business, or **retained earnings,** represents the funds that corporations keep for new investment.

retained earnings: profits kept by businesses for new investment

Interest Income
Interest income includes interest paid on business loans and bonds and, to a lesser extent, income such as royalty payments. This category also includes adjustments to the value of businesses' unsold products. This category does not, however, include interest payments made by consumers and government, since consumer loans and government debt are viewed simply as transfers of purchasing power.

Proprietors' Incomes and Rents

Proprietors' incomes include the earnings of sole proprietorships and partnerships, including self-employed professionals and farmers. These incomes are received by owners for supplying various types of resources to their businesses. The income to landlords from renting property is also included in this category.

Indirect Taxes

Indirect taxes, such as provincial sales taxes, are charged on products rather than levied against households or businesses. Because of this, they would not be included as part of GDP using the income approach, but would be using the expenditure approach. To balance the results from the two approaches, taxes (minus any subsidies businesses receive) are added to income-based GDP.

Depreciation

Recall that durable assets—such as buildings, equipment, and tools—wear out and need to be replaced. This is considered a cost of doing business, and shows up in the expenditure approach to GDP. To balance the two approaches to calculating GDP, the income approach must also include depreciation.

Statistical Discrepancy

Because businesses' and individuals' records might be faulty or missing, GDP figures for the two approaches do differ. Therefore, the GDP figures are actually estimates, and any discrepancy between them is known as a

Figure 10.3: Canada's Gross Domestic Product (1993)

Income Approach ($ billions)		Expenditure Approach ($ billions)	
Wages and salaries	402.5	Personal consumption (C)	432.9
Corporate profits	38.2	Gross investment (I)	130.2
Interest income	50.7	Government purchases (G)	150.8
Proprietors' incomes and rents	43.0	Net exports (X – M)	–0.8
Indirect taxes	89.4	Statistical discrepancy	–2.4
Depreciation	84.5		
Statistical discrepancy	2.4		
Gross Domestic Product	710.7	**Gross Domestic Product**	710.7

With the income approach, GDP is the sum of incomes and balancing items, as shown on the left. With the expenditure approach, GDP is the sum of expenditures, as shown on the right. Both totals are reconciled with an equal amount for statistical discrepancy.

SOURCE: Adapted from Statistics Canada, *National Income and Expenditure Accounts, Quarterly Estimates, Fourth Quarter 1993* (March 1994), cat. no. 13-001, vol. 41, no. 4, pp. 3, 5. Reproduced by authority of the Minister of Industry, 1994.

statistical discrepancy. To balance the two figures, Statistics Canada divides the difference between the two approaches. As shown in Figure 10.3, the discrepancy was $4.8 billion in 1993. Half the amount ($2.4 billion) is added to the lower figure, the income-based estimate of GDP, and half ($2.4 billion) is deducted from the higher figure, the expenditure-based GDP estimate.

The Expenditure Approach

GDP found using the expenditure approach is the sum of purchases in product markets. In order to explore this in greater detail, we must first distinguish between categories of products. Later, we will examine the categories of expenditures.

Categories of Products

final products: products that will not be processed further and will not be resold

Final products are those that will not be processed further and will not be resold. How much the ultimate user pays for the product determines the value of a final product. An example might be a pad of paper bought at the corner store. In contrast, **intermediate products** are those that will be processed further or will be resold. Advertising services bought by a soft-drink manufacturer or clothing bought by a wholesaler are examples. How a product is used determines whether it is a final product or an intermediate product. For example, flour that is bought by a household for home baking is a final product; however, flour that is bought by a bakery to make bread to be sold is an intermediate product.

intermediate products: products that will be processed further or will be resold

To understand why the distinction matters, consider that some products will be sold many times in product markets—first as intermediate products, and then as final products. The products to make a pad of paper, for example, may be sold once by the logging company to the paper producer, a second time by the paper producer to the retailer, and a third time by the retailer to you. Since the cost of the wood may be $1 out of the retail price of $4, the value of the final product covers the value of the wood used to make it.

double counting: the problem of adding to GDP the same item at different stages in its production

value added: the extra worth of a product at each stage in its production; a concept used to avoid double counting in calculating GDP

If the values of all products—final and intermediate—were included in the GDP calculations, we might have the problem of **double counting**. Double counting would cause estimates of GDP to be too high and not reflect the real activity in the economy. To avoid this problem, the concept of **value added** is applied to GDP. This concept helps quantify the extra worth of the product at each stage in its production. Figure 10.4 uses the example of the pad of paper to show the results of double counting and how the concept of value added deals with it. Statistics Canada subtracts the value of all purchases of intermediate goods and services by businesses from the value for which intermediate and final products are sold.

Figure 10.4:   Value Added in Making Paper

Production Stage	Total Value Paid/Received	Value Added	Business That Adds Value
1. Wood is cut and transported to paper mill	$1.00	$1.00	logging company
2. Paper is processed and sold to retailer	2.75	1.75 (2.75 – 1.00)	paper company retailer
3. Paper is sold by retailer to consumer	4.00	1.25 (4.00 – 2.75)	
	$7.75	$4.00	

A pad of paper is produced from wood that is (1) cut and transported, and (2) processed into paper, which is sold to a retailer. Then (3) the paper is sold by the retailer to the consumer. The value added by each business at each production stage is the value of the business's output, less its cost of materials. The sum of the values added at all stages of production represents the price of the pad of paper when it is finally sold.

Categories of Purchases

Expenditure-based GDP is calculated on the basis of almost all purchases in the Canadian economy. Few products are excluded, and those that are included fall into four categories. Note, once again, that figures for GDP calculated using this approach are adjusted for any statistical discrepancy.

Excluded Purchases

Before we examine the categories of purchases included in GDP, let's examine those that are excluded because they are not related to current production. There are two types: financial exchanges and second-hand purchases.

Financial Exchanges   A gift of money—between family members, for example—is not a transaction included in GDP for the simple reason that the transaction just shifts purchasing power from one party to another. Similarly, bank deposits and purchases of stocks are not included; however, payments for any financial service—bank service charges or a commission to a stockbroker—are included.

Second-Hand Purchases   Purchases of second-hand, or used, goods are also excluded from GDP because these products have already been counted at their first sale to a consumer. In other words, including second-hand purchases in GDP would double count, or overestimate, the value of products sold.

Included Purchases

Purchases included in GDP calculations fall into four categories: personal consumption (C), gross investment (I), government purchases (G), and net

expenditure equation:
the equation that states
that GDP is the sum of
personal consumption (C),
gross investment (I), government purchases (G),
and net exports (X – M)

personal consumption:
household spending on
goods and services

nondurable goods:
goods that are consumed
just once

durable goods: goods
that are consumed repeat-
edly over time

gross investment:
purchases of assets that
are intended to produce
revenue

inventories: stocks of
unsold goods and materials

capital stock: the total
value of productive assets
that provide a flow of
revenue

net investment: gross
investment minus
depreciation

exports (X – M). Each of these categories contributes to the circular flow of money in the Canadian economy. The following **expenditure equation** shows that GDP is simply the sum of these four types of spending.

$$GDP = C + I + G + (X - M)$$

Personal Consumption   **Personal consumption** (C) is household spending on goods and services. These purchases make up the largest component, about 60 percent, of GDP. Of the goods and services consumed, **nondurable** goods, such as food, are consumed just once. **Durable goods**—such as bikes and compact discs—are consumed repeatedly over time.

Gross Investment   The second component of expenditure in GDP is **gross investment** (I). This category includes purchases of assets that are intended to produce revenue. Gross investment varies—usually from between 15 and 25 percent of GDP—from year to year. The most important spending in this category is on equipment and machines used by businesses—for example, a carpenter's purchase of a lathe or a newspaper publisher's purchase of a printing press. Expenditures by government agencies on equipment and machines also fall into this category.

Gross investment also includes changes in the dollar value of unsold goods and materials, known as **inventories**. So that businesses can meet unexpected demand for particular products without stopping production to wait for deliveries of inputs, they often keep inventories of inputs on hand. Because these inventories are income-producing assets, an increase in an economy's inventories over a given year is seen as positive investment spending. In contrast, a decrease in inventories is seen as negative investment spending.

The construction of all buildings, including houses and apartments, is considered another part of gross investment. Owner-occupied housing is added here, rather than as part of personal consumption, because owner-occupied dwellings *could* be rented out by the owner to make an income. From an economic perspective, homeowners make an investment when they purchase their properties, and then rent to themselves.

Gross investment is related to the economy's **capital stock**, which is the total value of productive assets that provide a flow of revenue. Recall that capital assets, such as machinery and equipment, depreciate in value over time. Subtracting annual depreciation of an entire economy's capital assets from new gross investment gives **net investment**. Net investment therefore represents the yearly change in the economy's stock of capital.

Consider the example in Figure 10.5. An economy has $200 billion of capital stock at the beginning of a year and depreciation of $40 billion during the year. If gross investment over the same period is $100 billion, then net investment equals $60 billion ($100 billion – $40 billion). This $60 billion represents the amount by which the capital stock expands during the year. So, by year's end, the value of the economy's capital stock is $260 billion ($200 billion + $60 billion).

Figure 10.5:   Net Investment and Capital Stock

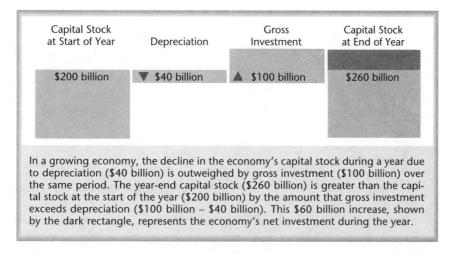

Capital Stock at Start of Year	Depreciation	Gross Investment	Capital Stock at End of Year
$200 billion	▼ $40 billion	▲ $100 billion	$260 billion

In a growing economy, the decline in the economy's capital stock during a year due to depreciation ($40 billion) is outweighed by gross investment ($100 billion) over the same period. The year-end capital stock ($260 billion) is greater than the capital stock at the start of the year ($200 billion) by the amount that gross investment exceeds depreciation ($100 billion – $40 billion). This $60 billion increase, shown by the dark rectangle, represents the economy's net investment during the year.

Thinking About Economics

Does gross investment include spending on education and training?

As discussed in Chapter 8, education can be considered an investment in human capital, with knowledge and skills representing a vital part of an economy's productive assets. Some economists argue that Statistics Canada should include at least some spending on education as part of gross investment *and* add human capital to its estimate of Canada's total capital stock. Statistics Canada does not do this because of the difficulty in separating out the investment component of education. Instead, education appears either as part of personal consumption or government purchases.

While they cannot be included in GDP, it is interesting to highlight the sources of funds for investment. Recall from Chapter 8 that the money used for capital investment comes not only from businesses' retained earnings but also from households' **personal saving** (S). By depositing funds in banks and by investing in stocks and bonds, households provide a flow of personal savings to businesses. Figure 10.6

personal saving: funds saved by households

Figure 10.6:   The Circular Flow of Funds in Financial Markets

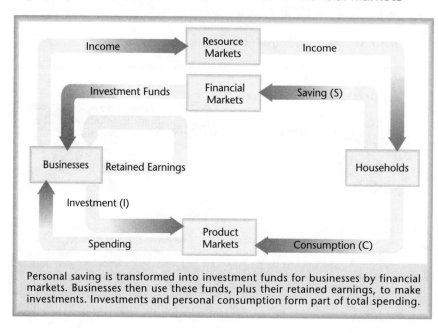

Personal saving is transformed into investment funds for businesses by financial markets. Businesses then use these funds, plus their retained earnings, to make investments. Investments and personal consumption form part of total spending.

shows this flow of funds for investment, as well as the flow of incomes from businesses to households.

government purchases:

current government spending on goods and services

Government Purchases   **Government purchases** (G) include current spending by all levels of government on goods and services, and typically make up about 20 percent of GDP. The federal government buying a battleship for the armed forces and a municipality hiring a paving company to do road repairs are two examples of government spending.

Some types of government spending are not included in this category. Government transfer payments to households, such as those detailed in Chapter 9, are excluded from government purchases since they are simply a redistribution of purchasing power. For the same reason, government subsidies to businesses are also excluded. Both transfer payments and government subsidies are viewed instead as negative taxes, meaning they are tax payments in reverse. Expenditures by government-owned agencies on income-producing assets—for instance, hydro-electric dams built by Ontario Hydro, or post offices built by Canada Post—are also excluded from government purchases, because these amounts are considered part of gross investment.

As outlined in Chapter 9, government spending is partly financed through taxes from both households and businesses. Governments also finance their spending through borrowing, which takes place in financial markets. Figure 10.7 shows the role of government in the economy's circular flow of money.

Figure 10.7:   Government and the Circular Flow

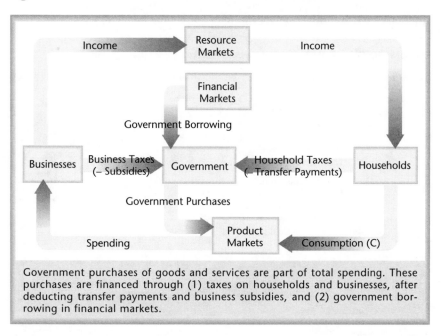

Government purchases of goods and services are part of total spending. These purchases are financed through (1) taxes on households and businesses, after deducting transfer payments and business subsidies, and (2) government borrowing in financial markets.

Net Exports   This final category of purchase includes purchases of Canadian goods and services by foreigners, or **exports** (X). Suppose, for example, that a British consumer buys a Canadian cellular phone, or an American tourist spends a night in a Canadian hotel. Because payments for these transactions remain in the Canadian circular flow of money, export spending contributes to GDP. This expenditure category also accounts for **imports** (M), or Canadian purchases of foreign goods and services. Such spending includes, for example, a Canadian cheese-lover buying French cheese, a Canadian steelmaker buying a Japanese-made casting machine, or a Canadian police force buying an American radar device. Because payments for these transactions leave the Canadian circular flow of money, import spending is subtracted from GDP.

To reconcile spending inside and outside the Canadian economy in calculating GDP, Statistics Canada uses the category of net exports (X – M), or exports minus imports. When represented as **net exports,** these purchases represent a small fraction of GDP; however, the values of exports and imports viewed separately each account for over 25 percent of GDP.

Figure 10.8 shows the roles of exports and imports in the circular flow of the Canadian economy. Note that foreigners also play a part in the Canadian economy by lending to and borrowing from financial markets. Foreign loans to the Canadian economy (flows into the economy) tend to

exports: foreign purchases of Canadian goods and services

imports: Canadian purchases of foreign goods and services

net exports: exports minus imports

exceed Canadian loans to foreigners (flows out of the economy). As a result, foreign involvement in financial markets tends to create a net increase in the Canadian economy.

Figure 10.8:   Foreign Markets and the Circular Flow

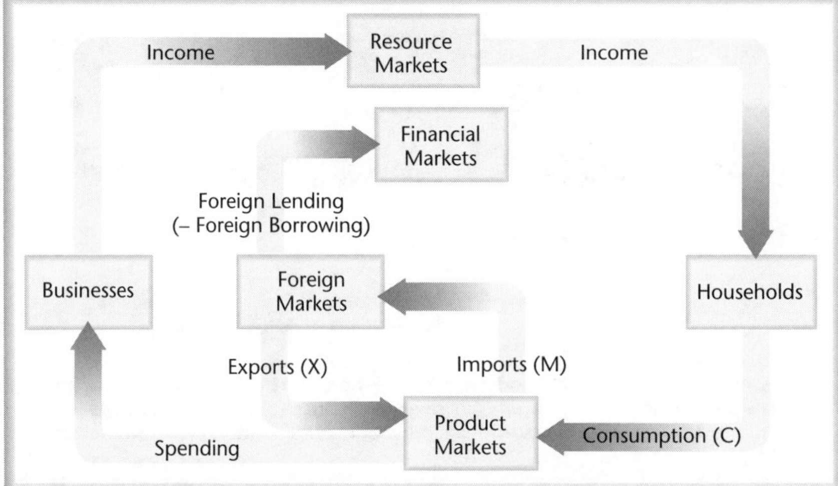

Whereas exports are part of total spending in product markets, imports are deductions from total spending. Foreign lending, after subtracting foreign borrowing, creates a net increase in flows to Canadian financial markets.

BRIEF REVIEW

1. Statistics Canada prepares the national income accounts to measure the economic health of Canada.

2. The most prominent measure of economic activity is Gross Domestic Product (GDP), which is the total dollar value of all final goods and services produced in the economy over a given period.

3. GDP can be calculated by adding all incomes in resource markets or all expenditures in product markets. After including several balancing items and a statistical discrepancy, the two approaches give the same figure.

4. Using the income approach, GDP is the sum of four main income items—wages and salaries, corporate profits, interest income, and proprietors' incomes (including rent)—plus indirect taxes and depreciation.

5. The expenditure approach depends on the concept of added value to avoid double counting of purchases.

6. Using the expenditure approach, GDP is the sum of personal consumption, gross investment, government purchases, and net exports, but neither financial exchanges nor second-hand purchases.

GDP and Living Standards

What does GDP say about life in Canada? How do living standards in Canada today compare with past living standards? And how does Canadian economic performance compare with that of other countries? To answer these questions, **per capita GDP**, or GDP per person, is frequently used as a measure.

A country's GDP divided by its population is its per capita GDP. So, for example, in 1993, Canada's GDP was $710 723 million and its population was 28.753 million. Hence, per capita GDP was $24 718 per person:

$$\text{Per capita GDP} = \frac{\text{GDP}}{\text{population}}$$

$$\$24\ 718 = \frac{\$710\ 723\ 000\ 000}{28\ 753\ 000}$$

per capita GDP: GDP per person, calculated as GDP divided by population

Adjustments to Per Capita GDP

Depending on how per capita GDP is to be used, either of two adjustments can be made to it: inflation adjustments or exchange-rate adjustments.

Inflation Adjustments

Because prices change over the years, per capita GDP must be adjusted when comparing economic well-being in the same country in different years. This is done by using **real GDP**, which is GDP expressed in constant dollars from a given year (currently, 1986 is the base year). When a country's real GDP is divided by its population, the result is **per capita real GDP**, or real GDP per person. This adjustment allows comparisons to be made between per capita GDP despite changes in price. For example, Canada's 1993 real GDP, expressed in 1986 dollars, was $573 433 million. Given Canada's 1993 population of 28.753 million, per capita real GDP in 1993 was $19 943. In contrast, the per capita real GDP for 1986 was $19 297 ($505 666 million ÷ 26.2038 million).

real GDP: GDP expressed in constant dollars from a given year

per capita real GDP: GDP per person, expressed in constant dollars from a given year

$$\text{Per capita real GDP} = \frac{\text{real GDP}}{\text{population}}$$

$$\$19\ 943 = \frac{\$573\ 433\ 000\ 000}{28\ 753\ 000}$$

Exchange-Rate Adjustments

To compare various countries' per capita GDP for a given year, we must adjust for the different currencies. This is done by expressing all countries' GDPs in one currency, the standard being the American dollar. For example, per capita GDP for 1992 in the United States was $23 215 in U.S. dollars, while Canada's per capita GDP for 1992 in U.S. dollars was

$20 541. When expressed in a common currency, Canada's GDP is slightly lower than that of the United States.

Limitations of GDP

As with any economic indicator, it is important to distinguish what specifically is being measured by GDP and what that measure indicates. Recall that GDP is a measure of the total dollar value of all final goods and services produced in an economy over a given period. GDP does indicate economic activity and, to some extent, living standards. However, like all indicators, it has quantitative and qualitative limitations.

Excluded Activities

Because GDP represents the market value of goods and services produced in an economy, it does not include some types of productive activities. Excluding these activities means that GDP can understate economic activity and living standards.

nonmarket activities:
productive activities that take place outside the marketplace

Nonmarket activities—such as housework, unpaid child care, and the work of "do-it-yourselfers"—take place outside the marketplace, so they are excluded from GDP. However, these productive activities have a vital impact on the living standards of Canadians.

underground economy:
all the productive transactions that go unreported

The **underground economy** includes all the productive transactions that are unreported and, therefore, also left out of GDP. One example of a transaction in the underground economy is smuggling, which is an illegal activity. In contrast, other "under-the-table" transactions may be for legal purchases—for example, gardening services that are paid for by cash or barter so that taxes on these transactions can be avoided.

Thinking About Economics

How large is Canada's underground economy?

Estimates of the size of Canada's underground economy vary widely. Some economists have tried to measure the underground economy by studying how much cash is held by the public, since underground transactions are commonly paid for with cash to escape detection. Using this method, it has been estimated that Canada's underground economy is equal to anywhere from 10 to 25 percent of GDP, meaning that it has an annual value of $70 billion or more. Statistics Canada's own studies suggest that Canada's underground economy is much smaller—between 1 and 5 percent of GDP. Because of the difficulty in gathering data, these are only "guesstimates."

Product Quality

Today's GDP includes purchases of products not available a few decades ago—personal computers, fax machines, and VCRs, to name only a few. As well, many other products, such as cars and photocopiers, have increased substantially in quality with little or no rise in price. GDP, which can only add up selling prices, cannot fully capture these quality improvements.

Composition of Output

Another limitation related to the dollar-value basis of GDP is that it tells us nothing about what is produced and purchased. Suppose one country dedicates most of its GDP to military uses, but another country dedicates the same GDP to health care and education for its citizens. While the GDPs may be the same, the countries' living standards would differ considerably.

Income Distribution

As outlined in Chapter 9, incomes may be distributed in a range of ways, with profound effects on the living standards of individuals. GDP does not reflect how output is distributed among a country's citizens. So, for example, citizens in two countries with the same per capita GDP may have very different living standards if one country's income is equally distributed, while most of the other country's income is in the hands of a few.

Leisure

Although we might be able to work every waking hour, most of us consider leisure a requirement for a satisfactory standard of living. However, leisure is not bought and sold in the market, so it can't be accounted for by GDP. Thus, although the average Canadian work week has gradually become shorter—to almost half of what it was a century ago—GDP has no way of representing this change. Because of this, GDP understates economic well-being.

The Environment

Since GDP quantifies economic activity in terms of its dollar value, it does not adequately represent another factor: the environment. GDP does not differentiate between economic activities that are harmful to the environment and those that are not, and it may not effectively represent spillover costs and benefits. So, for example, while the clean-up following an oil spill would be added to GDP, the creation of a new nature preserve would likely not be added.

SIDELINE

Canadians Live Best

Indicators of well-being are numerous. One that draws on a wide range of statistics is the human development index used by the United Nations.

Canada has again been judged the best place in the world to live.

A United Nations report, which ranks countries in terms of "human development," placed Canada ahead of Switzerland and Japan for 1992, the last year for which relevant statistics are available.

Top Scorers

Canada leads the world in the "human development index," based on income, life expectancy, and educational attainment.

Rank	Country
1	Canada
2	Switzerland
3	Japan
4	Sweden
5	Norway
6	France
7	Australia
8	United States
9	Netherlands
10	United Kingdom

SOURCE: *The Human Development Report*, published for UNDP by Oxford University Press.

It's the second time in the five years the index has been compiled that Canada has topped the list of 173 countries—the previous occasion being 1990.

The ranking does not mean Canadians enjoyed the highest standard of living in the world, however.

As the report, compiled by the U.N. Development Program, indicates, the rankings are based on a combination of three factors: average income, life expectancy and educational attainment.

A more detailed analysis of what the report calls the "human development index (HDI)" shows that Canada ranks ahead of all industrialized countries in only one category, over-all enrolment in schools. But it is in the top 10 in most categories.

Canada ranks fifth in real per capita gross domestic product, a widely accepted measure of wealth, behind the United States, Switzerland, Germany and Japan.

In terms of longevity, Canada ranks sixth, with an average life expectancy of 77.2 years.

Although they did not count in the human development index, Canada rated highly in several other factors. It was near the top in percentage of wealth that went to education and health-care spending, and in ownership of such commodities as automobiles and television sets.

It scored seventh in income distribution, the percentage of income earned by the top 20 and bottom 20 per cent of the population, and eighth in the income disparity between men and women in the country.

The report acknowledges the index is not the last word in measuring human development, but argues that the three broad categories—wealth, knowledge and longevity—offer a sound measurement for the "relative socio-economic progress of nations."

SOURCE: Southam News, "Canadians Live Best, U.N. Study Finds Again," *The Toronto Star*, 28 May 1994, p. A3.

 ## Other Economic Measures

Statistics Canada uses the national income accounts to calculate other measures, which are employed in various ways to indicate economic activity. While the following relate closely to GDP and to income, upcoming chapters will explore additional measures that indicate economic health and living standards.

Gross National Product

Gross National Product (GNP) is the total income acquired by Canadians both within Canada and elsewhere. Note that, while GDP focuses on incomes made in *Canada*, GNP focuses on the earnings of *Canadians*.

To calculate GNP, two adjustments to GDP must be made. Income earned from Canadian investments by foreigners—interest payments on a Canadian government bond held in Japan, for example—is deducted from GDP. Although included in GDP, such earnings are not part of the earnings of Canadians. Also, income earned from foreign investments by Canadians—a stock dividend from an American company paid to a Canadian shareholder, for example—is added to GDP. While not included in GDP, this income is part of Canadians' earnings.

These two adjustments can be made in an investment income account. Because, traditionally, foreign investment in Canada has been higher than Canadian investment in foreign markets, the account gives *net* investment income to foreigners, and is subtracted from GDP to give GNP. As Figure 10.9 shows, Canadian GNP is less than Canadian GDP.

Gross National Product: the total income acquired by Canadians both within Canada and elsewhere

Figure 10.9: Deriving Gross National Product (1993)

($ billions)	
Gross Domestic Product (GDP)	710.7
Deduct: Net investment income to foreigners	(–)24.7
Gross National Product (GNP)	686.0

GNP is less than GDP because foreign investment in Canada exceeds Canadian investment in foreign markets.

SOURCE: Statistics Canada, *National Income and Expenditure Accounts, Quarterly Estimates, Fourth Quarter 1993* (March 1994), cat. no. 13-001, vol. 41, no. 4, p. 89. Reproduced by authority of the Minister of Industry, 1994.

Net Domestic Income

In Chapter 8, we saw how net domestic income (NDI) represents what is earned by households supplying resources in Canada. As shown in Figure 10.10, NDI is GDP minus those amounts that are not earnings from current

Figure 10.10: Deriving Other Income Measures (1993)

($ billions)

Gross Domestic Product (GDP)	710.7
Deduct: Indirect taxes	(–)89.4
Depreciation	(–)84.5
Statistical discrepancy	(–)2.4
Net Domestic Income (NDI)	534.4
Add: Government transfer payments	112.8
Other payments to persons	72.7
Deduct: Earnings not paid out to persons	(–)59.8
Net investment income to foreigners	(–)24.7
Personal Income (PI)	635.4
Deduct: Personal taxes and other personal transfers to government	(–)145.6
Disposable Income (DI)	489.8

Net domestic income is less than GDP because some payments included in GDP do not represent resource earnings. Personal income is greater than net domestic income because amounts received by households exceed amounts earned. Finally, disposable income is less than personal income because of the effect of personal taxes.

SOURCE: Adapted from Statistics Canada, *National Income and Expenditure Accounts, Quarterly Estimates, Fourth Quarter 1993* (March 1994). cat. no. 13-001, vol. 41, no. 4, pp. 9, 11, 13, 19, 31. Reproduced by authority of the Minister of industry 1994.

production—namely, indirect taxes, depreciation allowances, and the statistical discrepancy.

Personal Income

personal income: the income actually received by households

Personal income (PI) is the income actually *received* by households. To calculate it, adjustments are made to net domestic income, as shown in Figure 10.10.

Transfer Payments
One adjustment to personal income is the addition of government transfer payments to net domestic income. Even though transfer payments are unrelated to earned income, they are received by households. Thus, they are excluded from net domestic income but are part of households' personal income.

Other Payments to Persons
Other payments to persons are primarily from governments to households, the most important being interest payments paid by governments on the debt they owe. Like transfer payments, these are not part of resource earnings

but are nonetheless received by households. Hence, they must be included in personal income.

Earnings Not Paid Out to Persons
Earnings not paid out to persons include taxes on corporate profits and retained earnings. These items must be subtracted from net domestic income to find personal income, since they are earned, but not received, by households.

Net Investment Income to Foreigners
Just as net income from Canadian investments going to foreigners must be subtracted from GDP to give GNP, this net investment income must be subtracted to give personal income. These income payments are part of both GDP and net domestic income, but are not received by Canadian households.

Disposable and Discretionary Income
Household income after personal taxes and other personal transfers to government have been subtracted from personal income is called **disposable income,** or DI, as shown in Figure 10.10. Households use some of their disposable income to buy necessities such as food, housing, and clothing. Any amount left over is referred to as **discretionary income**, which may either be saved or spent on nonessential items.

disposable income: household income minus personal taxes and other personal transfers to government

discretionary income: disposable income minus purchases of necessities

BRIEF REVIEW

1. To make comparisons among years and countries, GDP is expressed per capita, or per person. To compare GDP for different years, it is adjusted for inflation to derive real GDP, and then expressed per capita. To compare GDP among countries, a common currency must be used, usually American dollars.

2. GDP has its limitations as an indicator of living standards: it excludes nonmarket activities and the underground economy; it does not reflect changes in product quality or what specific products a country is producing; it cannot account for income distribution or leisure; and, it cannot adequately account for environmental spillover costs and benefits.

3. Other measures of economic activity and income include Gross National Product, net domestic income, personal income, disposable income, and discretionary income.

Thinking Globally

Hazel Henderson and GNP

After moving to New York City with her family, Hazel Henderson saw firsthand one outcome of economic growth: pollution. Her daughter's sooty face and persistent morning cough from the pollution started Henderson's career as an economist.

Hazel Henderson

In 1964, Henderson founded one of the first grassroots environmental organizations in the U.S.—Citizens for Clean Air. Back then, pollution stood for progress. Henderson, 57, hasn't stopped fighting for a saner, greener, healthier world. She, however, treads an unbeaten path as an economic guerrilla.

The unsoapable soot on her daughter's face, she realized, stemmed from the industrial economic system—a system that has a voracious appetite for resources, then pretends it has nothing to do with environmental and health consequences.

Economics, she realized, is politics in disguise and the environmental movement doesn't touch on the bigger problem of a bulimic economic system.

Railing at the line that she had become a "sincere lady who just doesn't understand that cleaning up the air was uneconomic," she read everything she could on economics and went into combat with condescending industrial potentates.

By 1967, the Harvard Business Review published her article called "Should Business Tackle Society's Problems?"

In 1978, she published *Creating Alternative Futures: The End of Economics.* In 1981, she published *The Politics of the Solar Age: Alternatives to Economics,* both as big as booster seats.

"I knew there must be something terribly wrong with economics if keeping it healthy meant people had to get sick," she said during a visit to Vancouver.

Consider this. The Exxon Valdez oil spill creates millions of dollars' worth of economic activity around the blighted Alaskan coast. Cleanup, public relations and an inquiry are *good* for the gross national product. Environmental, health and social problems *add* to GNP rather than subtract from it.

For a real look at progress and success, the debit side has to be factored in, not ignored, she says. But the present economic system plays the denial game very well. It's a system that cannibalizes itself, a parasite that kills its host.

Henderson wants to include environmental and social costs of development in the economic accounting system. Right now, she says, the end-all, be-all, of economic success is growing GNP. It will, in the end, mean a lower standard of living and lower profit margins—but then whoever said businesses had to keep growing and growing, making bigger and bigger profits? Whoever said the privileged few have to gourmandize at the expense of the lower classes and of future generations?

Current economics rewards resource depletion rather than taxing it and values cheap land, cheap labor, low taxes and weak environmental laws, says Henderson. It rewards over-developed nations and impoverishes developing ones. It panders to greed and profits and expansion and has the pretence of science, while ignoring the simple law of thermo-dynamics.

Henderson says that a new economics, for example, would make the polluter, not the taxpayer, pay for pollution cleanup. Polluting products would include the cost of disposal and recycling. Prices would, in effect, reflect *total* costs.

"We need to encourage more green technologies and tax the hell out of waste and destruction," says Henderson.

She would redeploy and retrain workers for environmentally benign industries. She would provide guaranteed incomes for people stranded in environmental sunset industries, a cheaper alternative to corporate bailouts and continued environmental and social damage.

She would decentralize, localize and seek global cooperation in development.

"Think globally, act locally," is her favorite motto.

As recently as 10 years ago, corporations such as B.C. Hydro dismissed Henderson's ideas. They're now inviting her to speak at conferences. "The social, environmental costs of industrial development are coming in. You can't sweep them under the rug any more," said Henderson before she spoke at a B.C. Hydro conservation conference in May 1990.

The next day, she was back at her energy efficient cottage in St. Augustine, Fla., before heading to Budapest for a conference on the future. The cottage roof, painted white, eliminates the need for air conditioning in her tropical environment.

Henderson, a consultant to organizations in more than 30 countries, makes about 200 speeches a year to grassroots organizations, enlightened corporations, colleges, agencies and planning groups, mostly outside the U.S. She talks to Soviet officials and meets with Chinese think-tank members regularly on how to make the shift to green technologies.

She operates on the Robin Hood principle—charge the rich and give to the poor. She fetches $3,000 for a corporate appearance but pays her own way to speak in China.

During the pit stops at home, she transports herself on an "unstealable" 20-year-old rusty five-speed Schwinn bicycle, grows flowers, writes poetry and cosies up in her 2,000-book library. Two phones and a fax machine connect her to the outside world.

She says that economics, like ecology, comes from the Greek word *oikos*, meaning house and home. It's supposed to be about providing goods and services efficiently. But it's now about artificial needs and wants, created through corporate advertising.

Henderson's metaphor for economics is a cake. The top layer is the official market economy of money transactions. But two other layers—social/familial/community activities and Mother Nature—are missing from today's "science" of looking after house and home.

"Karl Marx and Adam Smith both discount nature in exactly the same way and discount unpaid work," she says.

Economists, Henderson feels, are hired guns, like lawyers. The only difference is, economists are passed off as scientists. "An absolutely wonderful way of psyching out the ordinary citizen," she says. "Part of my message has always been: never let an economist get away with saying they are experts on efficiency. Ask 'For whom?' and 'In what time frame?' Generally you'll find it's efficiency for the client in the short term."

"Economists confuse money with real wealth and GNP scorecard distorts the kind of debate needed about what's valuable," Henderson says. "If we paid less attention to money and more attention to *real* wealth—like creative people, healthy ecosystems, healthy people, education, nutrition—it will put us on track to a sustainable future," she says.

"Power flows from the economic system; power is defined by money, the control of capital and the ability to control political processes. We allow money changers to take control in this hypnosis about money," she says. "It's a form of control that's so subtle—people are buying into disempowerment."

"The most glaring problem is, it doesn't show the poverty gap and whether it's widening or narrowing or how much energy is being used to produce a unit of GNP. We can watch money, income, GNP and stock markets go up while everything else may be going to pot."

She wants nations to set up data banks codifying their value systems—"a cultural DNA code"—to incorporate into economics.

Solar cars, renewable energy systems, mass transit, organic agriculture, preventive health care, recyclable products, education, reforestation, information industries, desert greening, pollution control, day care and elder care—this is the stuff of developing sustainably.

In Florida, says Henderson, conservationists offered an alternative to a coal-fired power plant meant to boost air conditioning energy. Planting shade trees would have reduced the ambient air by eight degrees Fahrenheit, just what the plant was intended to do. But the plant went ahead anyway, she says.

Despite being ignored for decades, Henderson sees the world catching up. "Mass media have discovered the environment and 20-year-old issues. For many of us in the field, things are unfolding predictably.

"Things are happening in many, many chinks and niches. Every institution is changing just a little bit and people in many institutions are rethinking and orchestrating millions of different decisions. It will eventually reach critical mass," she says. "It's time to give Karl Marx and Adam Smith a decent burial."

SOURCE: Abridged from Mia Stainsby, "Back when clean air was a dirty term," in *The Vancouver Sun*, 3 November 1990, pp. D3, D4.

1. What criticisms of current economics and economists does Henderson make? What suggestions does she have for improving both? To what extent do you agree or disagree with her views?

2. a) What is the economic ideal that Henderson envisions? Evaluate this ideal in terms of its costs and benefits.
   b) Compare this ideal with those envisioned by Adam Smith and Karl Marx.

Key Concepts

national income accounts
Gross Domestic Product
income approach
expenditure approach
GDP identity
retained earnings
final products
intermediate products
double counting
value added
expenditure equation
personal consumption
nondurable goods
durable goods
gross investment
inventories

capital stock
net investment
personal saving
government purchases
exports
imports
net exports
per capita GDP
real GDP
per capita real GDP
nonmarket activities
underground economy
Gross National Product
personal income
disposable income
discretionary income

Developing Application and Analysis Skills

1. Examine Figure 10.3. Using specific examples, explain what is meant by the "GDP identity."

2. In writing or diagrams, outline the following:
   a) the various components of GDP calculated using the income approach
   b) the various components of GDP calculated using the expenditure approach
   c) possible causes of the statistical discrepancy between the two approaches
   d) how GNP compares with GDP, and why

3. For each of the following industries, suggest examples of intermediate products and final products. Also, suggest a process by which each industry could add value to its products.
   a) steelmaking industry
   b) winemaking industry
   c) music industry
   d) travel industry

4. For each of the following, explain why the transaction would or would not be included in GDP.
   a) inline skates are bought at a garage sale
   b) a real estate agent sells a house
   c) a provincial government subsidizes a new company
   d) a builder contracts to build a house
   e) a vendor sells hot dogs
   f) a federal ministry purchases 10 new photocopiers
   g) a Dutch-based multinational corporation pays dividends to a Canadian investor
   h) interest is paid to the foreign holder of a Government of Canada bond
   i) a Canadian family buys a new car manufactured in Mexico
   j) a Canadian family buys a new car manufactured by a foreign company in an Ontario plant

5. a) Study the figure that follows.
   b) Describe the changes in the components of GDP.
   c) Suggest and explain what economic circumstances the figure indicates.

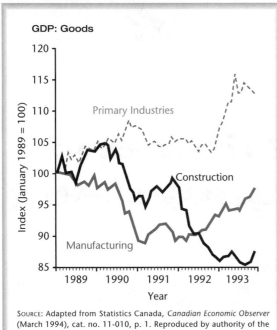

GDP: Goods

Index (January 1989 = 100)

Primary Industries

Construction

Manufacturing

1989 1990 1991 1992 1993

Year

SOURCE: Adapted from Statistics Canada, *Canadian Economic Observer* (March 1994), cat. no. 11-010, p. 1. Reproduced by authority of the Minister of Industry, 1994.

6. Using a circular flow diagram, illustrate the effects of a declining economy on the flow of money and resources within the economy.

7. In the role of a newspaper columnist, and using what you've learned from this chapter, write a column to explain to your readers the apparent contradiction in the following headline: "Living Standards Slide Despite Ever-Increasing GDP."

8. Propose at least three measures that would indicate the economic health or living standards of your community. In a report, identify and explain what each would measure, what the measure would indicate, and the measure's particular strengths or weaknesses.

CHAPTER 11

Inflation and Unemployment

Unemployment and inflation still pre-occupy and perplex economists...and everyone else.

—JAMES TOBIN, AMERICAN ECONOMIST

Ask working Canadians what economic prospect concerns them the most, and the answer will likely be unemployment. Ask a pensioner the same question and, chances are, the answer will be inflation. Our anxiety over these two economic evils is not misplaced; in fact, price stability and full employment are among Canada's most important economic goals. This chapter explores the effects of a trend of rising prices, how the trend is measured, and how it tends to hurt most those who can afford it least. In this chapter, we'll also examine unemployment: how it is measured, its causes, and its costs, not only for individuals but for the entire economy.

CHAPTER FOCUS

This chapter focuses on the following:
- inflation, its two measures—the consumer price index and the GDP deflator—and their limitations
- nominal and real incomes, both for individuals and the entire economy
- the effects of inflation
- how the labour force and unemployment are defined
- limitations of the official unemployment rate
- frictional, structural, cyclical, and seasonal unemployment
- full employment, the reasons for recent changes in unemployment, and the costs of unemployment

SKILLS FOCUS

After studying this chapter, you will be able to:
- graph consumer price index changes, and calculate inflation rates
- examine and demonstrate how inflation influences the economic well-being of individuals and the entire economy
- propose and create a student consumer price index
- calculate the size of the labour force, and calculate participation rates and unemployment rates
- calculate the GDP gap
- differentiate between the various types of unemployment and assess their economic costs
- examine a contemporary situation of extreme inflation or unemployment

 **Inflation**

Inflation, as introduced in Chapter 1, is a general increase in the prices of goods and services in an entire economy over time. Suppose, for example, that Canada has an annual inflation rate of 3 percent this year. Some prices are rising, others are remaining constant, while still others may be falling; however, the *overall* rise in prices is 3 percent. In exceptional cases—most notably during the 1930s—prices may remain constant, in which case the inflation rate is zero, or there may be a general decrease in prices. A general decrease in the level of prices is called **deflation**. To explain why Canadian governments stress the goal of price stability, let's first examine inflation in detail, how it is measured, and its implications for the economy.

deflation: a general decrease in the level of prices

The Consumer Price Index

The tool most commonly used to measure overall changes in prices is the **consumer price index** (CPI). This index monitors price changes in a representative "shopping basket" of consumer products. To determine what typical Canadian households buy, Statistics Canada surveys their buying habits every few years.

consumer price index: a measure of price changes for a typical basket of consumer products

A simple illustration, as given by Figure 11.1, allows us to see how the consumer price index indicates price changes. Suppose the shopping basket includes only two items—hamburgers and milkshakes. An investigator conducting a survey in 1994 finds that each month an average consumer buys 10 hamburgers at $2 each and 30 milkshakes at $1 each. In

Figure 11.1: Simple Consumer Price Index

	Results of 1994 Survey			
	Prices	**Quantity Consumed per Month**	**Expenditure per Month**	**Weights**
Hamburgers	$2.00	10	$20	$20 ÷ $50 = 0.4
Milkshakes	$1.00	30	$30	$30 ÷ $50 = 0.6
			$50	

	Prices in 1995	
	Prices	**1995 Price × 1994 Quantity**
Hamburgers	$2.20	$2.20 × 10 = $22.00
Milkshakes	$1.05	$1.05 × 30 = $31.50
		$53.50

In this simplified economy, 10 hamburgers and 30 milkshakes fill the monthly shopping basket of an average consumer. If the value of this basket rises from $50.00 to $53.50 during the course of a year, the annual inflation rate is 7 percent, with the consumer price index moving from 1.00 to 1.07.

other words, the typical consumer spends $20 on hamburgers and $30 on milkshakes, for a total of $50 per month. Therefore, two-fifths (0.4) of the consumer's total budget is spent on hamburgers and three-fifths (0.6) on milkshakes. These fractions represent the **item weights**, or proportions of each good in the total cost of the shopping basket.

To give a point of comparison for prices in subsequent years, the year in which the survey is conducted acts as the **base year.** The combined price of the representative products in the base year is considered the reference point, and the index in the base year is set at 1. Suppose, in our example, that the prices of hamburgers and milkshakes rise to $2.20 and $1.05 in 1995. Based on the quantities determined by the 1994 survey, the amount spent each month on hamburgers and milkshakes can be calculated. In other words, the same quantity of hamburgers at the new hamburger price (10 × $2.20) and the same quantity of milkshakes at the new milkshake price (30 × $1.05) give a total cost of $53.50 ($22.00 + $31.50). Compared with the 1994 total cost ($50.00) of the same products, prices have risen $3.50 ($53.50 − $50.00) or 7 percent from the base year [($3.50 ÷ $50.00) × 100]. Hence, the 1995 consumer price index is 1.07.

While it includes many more items, the actual CPI is calculated by Statistics Canada in the same way. Figure 11.2 shows the item weights for the major components of the CPI. Every month, the prices of products included in the CPI shopping basket are researched in a variety of Canadian cities. The index is calculated from the results. In the typical

item weights: the proportions of each good in the total cost of the basket of consumer goods used to calculate CPI

base year: the survey year used as a point of comparison in subsequent years

Figure 11.2:   **Consumer Price Index Weights (1986)**

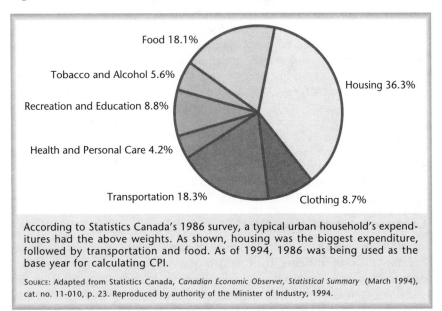

According to Statistics Canada's 1986 survey, a typical urban household's expenditures had the above weights. As shown, housing was the biggest expenditure, followed by transportation and food. As of 1994, 1986 was being used as the base year for calculating CPI.

SOURCE: Adapted from Statistics Canada, *Canadian Economic Observer, Statistical Summary* (March 1994), cat. no. 11-010, p. 23. Reproduced by authority of the Minister of Industry, 1994.

case of rising prices, the percentage increase in the consumer price index represents the inflation rate. For example, if the CPI has a value of 1.00 at the end of one year and a value of 1.10 at the end of the next year, the inflation rate over the year has been 10 percent. In other words, the change in the index (1.10 − 1.00), expressed as a percentage [(0.10 ÷ 1) × 100], is the inflation rate (10 percent).

Nominal Versus Real Income

cost of living: the amount consumers must spend on the entire range of goods and services they buy

The consumer price index is useful in helping consumers determine the **cost of living**, or the amount they must spend on the entire range of goods and services they buy. In particular, the CPI allows consumers to judge how much better or worse off they are as a result of inflation. Suppose, for example, a consumer's monthly income increases from $1000 to $1050 during a year when the CPI rises from 1.00 to 1.10. If the consumer's own monthly purchases roughly correspond to those in the representative "shopping basket," he can evaluate the personal impact of inflation. To see how this consumer's purchasing power is affected by inflation, we can express his **nominal income,** or income valued in current dollars, as a **real income**, or income expressed in constant base-year dollars. To determine real income, the consumer's nominal income ($1050.00) is divided by the value of the consumer price index (1.10):

nominal income: income expressed in current dollars

real income: income expressed in constant base-year dollars

$$\text{Real income} = \frac{\text{nominal income}}{\text{CPI}}$$

$$\$954.55 = \frac{\$1050.00}{1.10}$$

In other words, the consumer's monthly income of $1050.00 has a purchasing power of $954.55 when valued in constant base-year dollars. His income has not increased proportionally with the cost of living. For the consumer's purchasing power to keep up with inflation, his income would have to increase by the same percentage as the increase in prices—that is, by 10 percent, or $100 ($1000 × 0.10), to $1100 ($1000 + $100).

As our example shows, the purchasing power of a current dollar is inversely related to the consumer price index: the lower the CPI, the higher the purchasing power of nominal income; and, the higher the CPI, the lower the purchasing power of nominal income. Therefore, those whose incomes increase at a higher rate than the rise in prices have a higher standard of living. On the other hand, those whose incomes increase at a lower rate than the rise in prices are worse off than before.

Limitations of the CPI

As with any economic indicator, the consumer price index has a number of limitations. In this case, they consist of the following: consumer differences, changes in spending patterns, and product quality. In some circumstances, these limitations can severely reduce the index's usefulness.

Consumer Differences

Individual consumption patterns do not always match those of the typical urban household. Hence, the consumer price index may not apply to many consumers' individual cost of living. Consider, for example, a fashion-conscious reader. This person tends to spend a larger proportion of her budget on clothing and books than the typical consumer and, consequently, might travel less than the average consumer. For this individual consumer, the official index understates the impact of price changes in clothing and books, but overstates the impact of price changes in travel fares.

Changes in Spending Patterns

While Statistics Canada regularly surveys households to update both the contents and the item weights of the "shopping basket," changes in consumption patterns are ongoing and gradual. For example, more cellular phones and CD players were steadily purchased in the early 1990s. Also, consumers tend to buy less of items whose prices rise the most. Over time, these products have too high a weight in the CPI basket, meaning that the index overstates the rate of inflation.

Product Quality

The index cannot reflect changes in quality that are unmatched by changes in price. For example, items in the CPI shopping basket such as medicines and stereos may improve tremendously in quality, yet their prices may not increase proportionally with quality, and may even fall. So, while the standard of living may increase because of the increased quality, this will not be reflected in the CPI.

The GDP Deflator

Another indicator of price changes is the **GDP deflator.** Unlike the CPI, which focuses on a small number of consumer items, the GDP deflator measures price changes for all goods and services produced in the economy, and weights them in terms of the economy's total output. The item weights in this index are altered yearly, depending on how goods and services are represented in current GDP. While this frequent updating increases the accuracy of the GDP deflator, it means that values for this index are not as quickly available as values for the consumer price index. Because of this drawback, the GDP deflator receives less publicity than the CPI. Given the difference in the way they are calculated, the two indicators give similar but not identical estimates of inflation.

Figure 11.3 shows how the GDP deflator is calculated in a simplified economy that produces only computer microchips. In 1994, which is the base year, the GDP deflator is equal to 1. In order to calculate the value of the GDP deflator in each subsequent year, the output of each year is multiplied by the current price per microchip and divided by the same output in base-year

GDP deflator: an indicator of price changes for all goods and services produced in the economy

prices. For example, the 1995 output of microchips is 2000 and the price is 30 cents. This $600 value of output (2000 × $0.30) is divided by the same output in 1994 prices (2000 × $0.20), or $400, to give a GDP deflator of 1.5 ($600 ÷ $400). The result shows that the general price level has risen by one-half between 1994 and 1995. In other words, the inflation rate was 50 percent.

Figure 11.3:   Simple GDP Deflator

(1) Year	(2) Output of Microchips	(3) Current Price	(4) Output at Current Price (2) × (3)	(5) Output at 1994 Price (2) × $0.20	(6) GDP Deflator (4) ÷ (5)
1994	1000	$0.20	$ 200	$200	1.0
1995	2000	0.30	600	400	1.5
1996	2500	0.40	1000	500	2.0

The GDP deflator in any year is calculated by taking the economy's annual output at current prices (column 4) and dividing by this same output valued in base-year dollars (column 5). While the GDP deflator has a value of 1 in 1994, which is the base year, it rises in proportion with the prices of the economy's output.

Nominal Versus Real GDP

Just as nominal incomes for an individual household can be adjusted to take account of price changes, so the value of the economy's entire output can be adjusted for inflation. Recall that real GDP (or real output) is GDP expressed in constant dollars from a chosen base year. In contrast, **nominal GDP** (or nominal output) is GDP expressed in current dollars. Recall that real income for the individual household measures the purchasing power of that household over time. In the same way, real GDP gives an indication of the purchasing power of an entire economy. To find the real GDP, economists and statisticians divide nominal GDP by the GDP deflator:

nominal GDP: Gross Domestic Product expressed in current dollars

$$\text{Real GDP} = \frac{\text{nominal GDP}}{\text{GDP deflator}}$$

This formula can be applied to Canada's GDP in Figure 11.4 to give GDP in constant base-year (1986) dollars. Canada's nominal GDP was $710.7 billion in 1993. This amount divided by the GDP deflator, which was 1.2394, gives a real GDP of $573.4 billion ($710.7 billion ÷ 1.2394). The same approach can be used for years prior to the base year. For example, Canada's 1968 nominal GDP was $75.4 billion. This amount divided by the GDP deflator, which is 0.3, gives a real GDP for 1968, expressed in 1986 dollars, of $251.3 billion ($75.4 billion ÷ 0.3). Notice that when the adjusting number is more than 1, as in 1993, nominal

GDP is reduced or *deflated* to find real GDP. In the opposite case, where the index falls short of 1, as in 1968, nominal GDP is expanded or *inflated* when this adjustment is made.

Figure 11.4:   Finding Real Gross Domestic Product

(1) Year	(2) Nominal GDP (current $ billions)	(3) GDP Deflator (1986 = 1.00)	(4) Real GDP (1986 $ billions) (2) ÷ (3)
1968	$ 75.4	0.3000	$251.3
1986	505.7	1.0000	505.7
1993	710.7	1.2394	573.4

Canada's real GDP in any year is found by dividing the economy's nominal GDP, which is expressed in current dollars, by the value of the GDP deflator. While Canada's nominal output rose from $75.4 to $710.7 billion between 1968 and 1993, the nation's real output in 1986 dollars increased by a much smaller amount, from $251.3 to $573.4 billion.

SOURCES: Statistics Canada, *Canadian Economic Observer, Historical Statistical Supplement, 1992/93* (July 1993), cat. no. 11-210, vol. 7, pp. 5, 27; Statistics Canada, *National Income and Expenditure Accounts, Quarterly Estimates, Fourth Quarter 1993* (March 1994), cat. no. 13-001, vol. 41, no. 4, pp. 7, 43. Reproduced by authority of the Minister of Industry, 1994.

Inflation's Effects

Figure 11.5 shows Canada's inflation record since 1926. After a period of deflation during the Great Depression of the 1930s, significant inflation occurred during and immediately after World War II. Relatively low rates of inflation during the 1950s and 1960s were then followed by gradually rising rates during the 1960s and 1970s. Since the mid-1980s, inflation rates have again gradually fallen to low levels.

Why are high inflation rates, such as those experienced by Canadians during the 1970s and early 1980s, such a serious problem? Inflation redistributes purchasing power among different groups in ways that can be both economically harmful and unjust; in other words, purchasing power keeps pace with inflation for some individuals but not for others. To see the effects of inflation, we will look at its effects on household incomes and on borrowing and lending.

Incomes

If a household's income increases steadily every year but inflation rises at a higher rate, the household loses purchasing power. So, for example, this year's dollars buy fewer groceries than did last year's dollars, even with the expanding income. If, in contrast, the same household has an income that increases at roughly the same rate as inflation, the household

Figure 11.5:   The Inflation Rate

The graph shows annual inflation rates as measured by changes in the GDP price deflator. While deflation occurred during the early 1930s, inflation has been the dominant trend ever since. Inflation was most pronounced after World War II, during the 1970s, and in the early 1980s. In the late 1980s and early 1990s, the inflation rate dropped tremendously.

SOURCES: Adapted from Statistics Canada, *Canadian Economic Observer, Historical Statistical Supplement, 1992/93* (July 1993), cat. no. 11-210, vol. 7, p. 27; Statistics Canada, *Canadian Economic Observer, Statistical Summary* (March 1994), cat. no. 11-010, p. 22. Reproduced by authority of the Minister of Industry, 1994.

maintains its purchasing power. In other words, each year's dollars buy about the same amount of groceries. Therefore, whereas some households may feel the full impact of inflation on their living standards, others may have the impact cushioned by income adjustments.

Many labour unions negotiate income adjustments for their members. As a result, workers' wages are adjusted using the consumer price index, or cost of living, as it is popularly known. In the collective agreement, provisions for these adjustments are called **cost-of-living-adjustment (COLA) clauses.** When workers' incomes automatically increase by the rate of inflation, they are called **fully indexed incomes.** In this case, nominal income rises at the same rate as prices, so real income stays the same. For example, if the inflation rate between 1994 and 1995 is 10 percent, a worker originally earning a monthly income of $1000 receives a new monthly income of $1100, thereby maintaining purchasing power. The worker's real income in 1994, using 1994 as the base year, is $1000 ($1000 ÷ 1.00). In 1995, the same worker's real income, expressed in 1994 dollars, is again $1000 ($1100 ÷ 1.10).

Other people may receive incomes that are only partially indexed or are fixed. These are the people—including, for example, pensioners, unskilled and nonunionized workers, and recipients of government

cost-of-living-adjustment clauses: provisions for income adjustments to accommodate changes in price levels, which are included in wage contracts

fully indexed incomes: nominal incomes that automatically increase by the rate of inflation

transfer payments—who lose the most from inflation. **Partially indexed incomes** rise more slowly than the inflation rate, causing real incomes to fall. Suppose, for example, that a single parent has only welfare payments of $1000 per month as income. If the inflation rate is 10 percent between 1994 and 1995, the household needs a 10 percent rise, or an extra $100, in nominal income to maintain its purchasing power. If the payments increase by only 7 percent, they rise by $70, for a total of $1070 per month. Using 1994 as the base year, the household's real income falls from $1000.00 in 1994 to $972.73 ($1070.00 ÷ 1.10) in 1995.

In contrast to indexed and partially indexed incomes, **fixed incomes** are nominal incomes that stay at the same nominal dollar amount. In other words, these incomes do not change at all in response to inflation. Suppose, for example, that a pensioner receives a set monthly payment of $1000. Any increase in prices will cause purchasing power to decrease and, thereby, the pensioner's real income will be reduced. So, with the same hypothetical 10 percent inflation rate between 1994 and 1995, the pensioner's real income, expressed in 1994 dollars, drops from $1000.00 in 1994 to $909.09 ($1000.00 ÷ 1.10) in 1995.

Borrowing and Lending

As discussed in Chapter 8, the forces of demand and supply in the loanable funds market, the duration of the loan, the loan size, the individual's credit risk, and whether collateral is provided determine the interest rate at which money is lent. Whatever interest rate is established, if the lender loans funds at an interest rate that is not adjusted for inflation, the lender may lose out.

To illustrate, we have to distinguish between two types of interest rates. The **nominal interest rate** is the interest rate expressed in money terms. This is the interest rate expressed per annum, as discussed in Chapter 8. For example, Mariposa Vacations borrows $2000 at 5 percent per annum. At the end of the year, Mariposa Vacations will pay back the principal ($2000), plus interest (0.05 × $2000 = 100), for a total of $2100 ($2000 + $100).

In contrast, the **real interest rate** is the nominal interest rate minus the rate of inflation.

Real interest rate = nominal interest rate – inflation rate

If the inflation rate is 3 percent in the year that Mariposa Vacations takes out the loan, then the loan's real interest rate is 2 percent—the 5 percent nominal interest rate minus the 3 percent rate of inflation. The real interest rate reflects the fact that, because of inflation, the funds lent (the principal) have less purchasing power at the end of the one-year term than they did at the time the loan was made. Thus, the bank lending to Mariposa Vacations receives $100 (5 percent) in nominal interest at the end of the year, but only $40 (2 percent) in real interest.

partially indexed incomes: nominal incomes that increase by less than the rate of inflation

fixed incomes: nominal incomes that remain fixed at some dollar amount regardless of the rate of inflation

nominal interest rate: the interest rate expressed in money terms

real interest rate: the nominal interest rate minus the rate of inflation

inflation premium: a percentage built into a nominal interest rate to anticipate the rate of inflation for the loan period

Once the nominal interest rate has been agreed upon, it is fixed. So, lenders try to anticipate the rate of inflation for the loan period and build it into the nominal interest rate. This rate built into the nominal interest rate is known as the **inflation premium**. Lenders, therefore, determine what real interest rate they desire and add an inflation premium to determine the nominal interest rate:

Nominal interest rate = desired real interest rate + inflation premium

For example, the manager at Mariposa Vacations' bank may have anticipated a 2 percent inflation rate and wanted a real interest rate of 3 percent. So, on the $2000 one-year loan, she expected the bank would receive real interest of $60 ($2000 × 0.03) and an inflation premium of $40 ($2000 × 0.02) to compensate for the reduced purchasing power of the original $2000 principal.

What happens if the inflation rate turns out to be higher than lenders anticipated? Suppose, in our example, the inflation rate is actually 4 percent instead of 2 percent. As a result, the bank actually receives only 1 percent real interest—that is, the 5 percent nominal rate minus the 4 percent inflation rate. This is substantially less than the 3 percent real interest rate the bank manager anticipated. Because the inflation rate is higher than anticipated, the real interest rate is lower than the desired real interest rate, and creditors are worse off.

BRIEF REVIEW

1. Inflation is a general increase in the prices of goods and services in the entire economy. A general fall in prices is known as deflation.

2. The consumer price index (CPI) is one indicator of inflation, or changes in the cost of living. The CPI measures price changes in a typical "shopping basket" of consumer products.

3. Whereas nominal income is expressed in current dollars, real income is expressed in constant base-year dollars. Real income equals nominal income divided by the current value of the CPI.

4. The GDP deflator measures price changes for all goods and services

produced in the economy, and weights them in terms of the economy's total output. Nominal GDP divided by the current value of the GDP deflator gives the economy's real GDP, or real output.

5. The extent to which inflation affects individuals' purchasing power varies. Those people whose incomes are fully indexed to inflation rates maintain purchasing power. However, those with partially indexed or fixed incomes lose purchasing power.

6. Lenders also lose from inflation if inflation is higher than they anticipated with the inflation premium.

Unemployment

Recall from Chapter 1 that another economic goal of Canada is full employment. Of all economic statistics, the unemployment rate is the one most often highlighted in the media, discussed by politicians, and noticed by Canadians. For most people, the prospect of involuntary unemployment provokes considerable anxiety. To see why, we must understand unemployment, how it is measured, and its implications for individuals and for the economy as a whole.

The Labour Force Survey

Statistics Canada keeps track of the Canadian workforce through a monthly survey of about 59 000 households. These households are a random sample of the **labour force population**, which includes all residents of Canada over 15 years of age except those living in the Northwest Territories and Yukon, on Native reserves, and in institutions (for example, jails and psychiatric hospitals), and full-time members of the armed forces. The **labour force** is made up of those people in the labour force population who either have jobs or are actively seeking employment. By its definition, the labour force leaves out such groups as pensioners who do not have jobs and are not looking for work. It also excludes those who have given up looking for a job, as well as full-time homemakers who, while they work, do not do so in the formal job market.

The **participation rate** is the percentage of the entire labour force population that makes up the labour force. For example, in 1993 Canada's labour force was 13.946 million and the labour force population was 21.392 million, so the participation rate was about 65 percent. In other words, of the defined labour force population, about 65 percent is participating in the labour market:

$$\text{Participation rate} = \frac{\text{labour force}}{\text{labour force population}} \times 100$$

$$65.2\% = \frac{13\ 946\ 000}{21\ 392\ 000}$$

Statistics Canada also examines the participation rates of specific groups of people. Figure 11.6 shows recent trends in labour force participation for women and men in two age groups. As shown, the participation rates for all women have increased steadily over recent decades. In contrast, the participation rates for men between the ages of 15 and 24 have fluctuated, and those for men aged 25 years and over have decreased slightly. This decline is largely due to the growing popularity of early retirement. Overall, the participation of young people in the labour force is higher than it was in the past.

labour force population: the population, with specific exclusions, from which Statistics Canada takes a random sample for the labour force survey

labour force: all people who either have a job or are actively seeking employment

participation rate: the percentage of the entire labour force population that makes up the labour force

Figure 11.6: **Participation Rates**

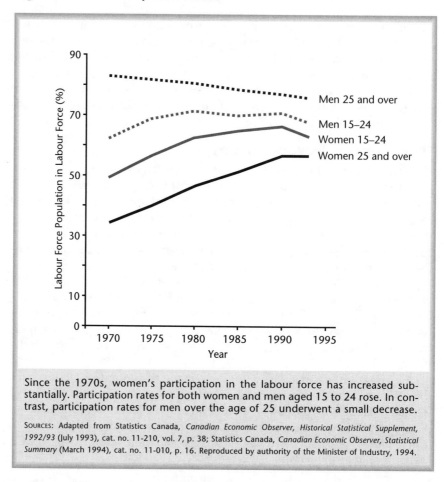

Since the 1970s, women's participation in the labour force has increased substantially. Participation rates for both women and men aged 15 to 24 rose. In contrast, participation rates for men over the age of 25 underwent a small decrease.

SOURCES: Adapted from Statistics Canada, *Canadian Economic Observer, Historical Statistical Supplement, 1992/93* (July 1993), cat. no. 11-210, vol. 7, p. 38; Statistics Canada, *Canadian Economic Observer, Statistical Summary* (March 1994), cat. no. 11-010, p. 16. Reproduced by authority of the Minister of Industry, 1994.

The Official Unemployment Rate

Once the labour force has been defined, its members can be divided into those who are employed and those who are unemployed. The official unemployment rate is the number of unemployed people in the labour force as a percentage of the entire labour force. For example, Canada's 1993 labour force of 13.946 million people was composed of 12.383 million people who were employed and 1.562 million who were not. Therefore, the unemployment rate was 11.2 percent:

$$\text{Unemployment rate} = \frac{\text{unemployed in labour force}}{\text{labour force}} \times 100$$

$$11.2\% = \frac{1\ 562\ 000}{13\ 946\ 000}$$

Figure 11.7 summarizes the relationships among Canada's population, labour force, labour force population, and unemployed labour force.

Drawbacks of the Official Unemployment Rate

Because of the way the official unemployment rate is calculated, it may either understate or overstate the true level of unemployment in the Canadian economy. Critics of this official rate point to the following factors: underemployment, discouraged workers, and dishonesty.

Figure 11.7:   The Canadian Labour Force (1993)

$$\text{Participation rate} = \frac{\text{labour force}}{\text{labour force population}} \times 100 = \frac{13\,946\,000}{21\,392\,000} \times 100 = 65.2\%$$

$$\text{Unemployment rate (\%)} = \frac{\text{unemployed in labour force}}{\text{labour force}} \times 100 = \frac{1\,562\,000}{13\,946\,000} \times 100 = 11.2\%$$

In 1993, Canada's total population was 28.753 million. Of this number, 21.392 million were considered part of the labour force population. The labour force constituted 65.2 percent of the labour force population, or 13.946 million. Of this labour force, 88.8 percent, or 12.383 million, were employed. The remaining 1.562 million in the labour force were unemployed, giving an unemployment rate of 11.2 percent.

SOURCE: Statistics Canada, *Labour Force Annual Averages 1993* (February 1994), cat. no. 71-220, p. 8-2. Reproduced by authority of the Minister of Industry, 1994.

Underemployment

The official unemployment rate makes no distinction between part-time and full-time employment, nor does it reflect the appropriateness of the work. While some part-time workers prefer part-time work, others would want full-time work if it were available. Also, in hard times, some workers may have to work at jobs that do not fully utilize their skills and education. Thus, we have the problem of **underemployment**. It is sometimes argued that the official rate understates unemployment by ignoring underemployed workers.

Discouraged Workers

Unemployment statistics also do not take into account people who, after searching for a job without luck, give up looking. Because they are not actively seeking employment, these **discouraged workers** are not considered part of the labour force. Again, it is sometimes argued that this causes the official rate to understate unemployment.

The number of underemployed and discouraged workers rises during an economic downturn, since job prospects—especially for full-time work—are at their bleakest. During the recession of the early 1990s, for example, estimates suggested that the numbers of underemployed and

underemployment: the problem of workers being underutilized, either as part-time workers or by working at jobs not appropriate to their skills or education

discouraged workers: unemployed workers who have given up looking for work

discouraged workers would have added up to 10 percent to the official unemployment rate.

Dishonesty

People responding to Statistics Canada's labour market survey may state that they are actively looking for work when, in fact, they are not. While the extent to which such dishonesty affects the unemployment rate is difficult to measure, it does make it possible for the official rate to overstate unemployment.

Types of Unemployment

When examining unemployment, we should distinguish among four types: frictional, structural, cyclical, and seasonal unemployment.

Frictional Unemployment

Workers who are temporarily between jobs or have begun looking for their first jobs are experiencing **frictional unemployment**. A dental assistant who has left one job voluntarily to look for another and a recent college graduate looking for career-related work are examples. Frictional unemployment is a permanent feature of labour markets, and represents about 3 percent of the labour force at any given time.

Structural Unemployment

Another type of unemployment arises largely from structural changes in the economy. **Structural unemployment** is due to a mismatch between people and jobs—unemployed workers cannot fill the sorts of jobs that are available. This type of unemployment occurs primarily because of gradual changes in the economy. Long-term adjustments in what items are produced (for example, the current shift from goods to services), how they are produced (largely due to technological change), and where they are produced cause such unemployment.

Because of these changes, workers lose out; they're displaced. Consider a worker who loses her job in manufacturing because of automation. She might not yet have the skills for the expanding service sector. In the same way, an unemployed fisherman living in a remote village cannot easily take advantage of employment opportunities elsewhere. Because gaining new skills, moving to obtain work elsewhere, and developing new industries in a region all take time, structural unemployment can persist for long periods.

Cyclical Unemployment

Economies and businesses must cope with ups and downs (which we'll discuss in Chapter 12), causing unemployment to rise and fall. This type of unemployment is called **cyclical unemployment**. An auto worker, for example, may work overtime in periods of strong consumer demand for cars, but be laid off in leaner times.

frictional unemployment: unemployment due to being temporarily between jobs or looking for a first job

structural unemployment: unemployment due to a mismatch between people and jobs

cyclical unemployment: unemployment due to the ups and downs of economies and businesses

DEVELOPING

INTERPRETATION SKILLS

The Age of the Part-Timer

The Shift From Full-Time Work

Increasingly over the last few decades, part-time jobs have replaced full-time jobs. What has caused the trend toward part-time work? Is this trend likely to be reversed? In which sectors is part-time work becoming most pervasive? The following article offers some answers to these questions.

Darin Doberstein, 24, has been working as a grocery store cashier for most of the past six years since he graduated from high school, putting in 18 to 20 hours a week doing something he likes—dealing with people.

Until his hours were cut back recently, he could count on about 24 hours of work a week. He'd prefer to work full-time, but knows that business is just too slow. "They just don't need it now."

The young Toronto man has plenty of company. In June 1993, according to Statistics Canada, there were 848,000 people—double the number from three years earlier—in the same position: part-timers who want full-time work.

Part-timers—70 per cent of whom are women—make less money than full-timers.

Mr. Doberstein, for example, not only works fewer hours than a full-timer at his store, but his $13.83-an-hour wage is about $3 less than his full-time counterparts make.

Statistics Canada doesn't track the incomes of full-time and part-time workers as such, but the Economic Council of Canada has estimated that in 1987 the hourly earnings of part-timers were roughly three-quarters those of full-time workers.

What may surprise many people is the fact that in each of Canada's latest two recessions, part-time work continued to grow while employers shucked off hundreds of thousands of full-time jobs.

In the past three years, the number of part-time jobs grew by 266,000. The unemployment rate is still at 11.4 per cent, because full-time employment fell by almost 500,000.

But the job shift is more than just a consequence of the recession. Part-time employment has been growing steadily since the 1950s, and not just in Canada. Every industrialized country in the world has been shifting from making goods to producing services and as the Economic Council pointed out in a 1991 report, "Part-time employment is overwhelmingly a service-sector phenomenon." In 1991, 89 per cent of all part-time jobs were in the service sector.

The shift, driven by a combination of new technologies and globalized production, amounts to what former ECC chairwoman Judith Maxwell calls a revolution in the workplace.

"Employers have fewer permanent positions," she said in a recent speech. "Those that are permanent tend to be mainly high-paid jobs with good benefits packages. They tend to hire people for short-term, temporary or part-time work."

Part-time work is most common in industries such as retail trade, accommodation, food and beverage service, personal and household services, and amusement and recreation. In each of those, part-timers now make up more than 30 per cent of the work force.

Full-time jobs are still the rule in the goods-producing sector that takes in manufacturing and construction and in services such as transportation and communications, financial services and the public service.

That pattern also helps explain why part-time work has grown and full-time work fallen in the past few years. The recession in the early 1990s was particularly hard on goods-producing industries as factories closed their doors, construction projects dried up and battered airlines and railways laid off thousands of people, most of them full-time employees.

Mr. Doberstein, for one, hasn't given up his hopes for full-time work. He likes the grocery business and he's planning to take community college courses in the fall in the hope of working his way into a management job some day.

SOURCE: Abridged from Bruce Little, "Full-time work on the decline," in *The Globe and Mail*, 19 July 1993, pp. A1, A2.

Evaluate the trend toward more part-time jobs. In your opinion, is this a positive economic trend in the short term and long term, or a negative trend? Support your answer.

Where Part-Timers Work

	Industry Share of Total Jobs (%)	Part-Timers' Share of Industry Jobs (%)
Total economy	100	16
Goods sector	28	6
Services sector	72	20
Services Sector breakdown		
Accommodation, food, beverage	6	36
Personal, household	2	35
Recreation	1	33
Retail trade	13	31
Other services	3	24
Health, social	10	24
Education	7	19
Finance, insurance, real estate	6	13
Business services	6	12
Transportation, communications	6	8
Wholesale trade	5	7
Public administration	7	6

SOURCE: Statistics Canada.

Seasonal Unemployment

seasonal unemployment: unemployment due to the seasonal nature of some occupations and industries

In some Canadian industries—agriculture, construction, and tourism, for example—work is seasonal, with lower employment in the winter months. As a result, some workers experience **seasonal unemployment**. Compared with many other countries, seasonal unemployment is particularly significant in Canada, given its climate and the importance of its primary resource industries. So that month-to-month comparisons can be made without the influence of seasonal unemployment, Statistics Canada calculates seasonal changes and adjusts the official unemployment rate accordingly.

Full Employment

Defining **full employment** is a tricky task. In effect, full employment is the highest reasonable expectation of employment for the economy as a whole, and is defined in terms of a **natural unemployment rate**. This rate includes frictional unemployment, but traditionally excludes cyclical unemployment. This rate also excludes seasonal unemployment, which is already omitted from the official unemployment rate using the seasonal adjustment.

full employment: the highest reasonable expectation of employment for the economy as a whole

natural unemployment rate: the unemployment rate that defines full employment

In the 1950s and 1960s, full employment in the Canadian economy was defined by the Economic Council of Canada as a natural unemployment rate of 3 percent. In other words, full employment was 100 percent labour force employment minus 3 percent frictional unemployment. As Figure 11.8 shows, the unemployment rate, which reached almost 20 percent during the Great Depression of the 1930s, decreased considerably over the following decades. However, full employment—as it was defined—was only occasionally achieved.

Figure 11.8: The Unemployment Rate

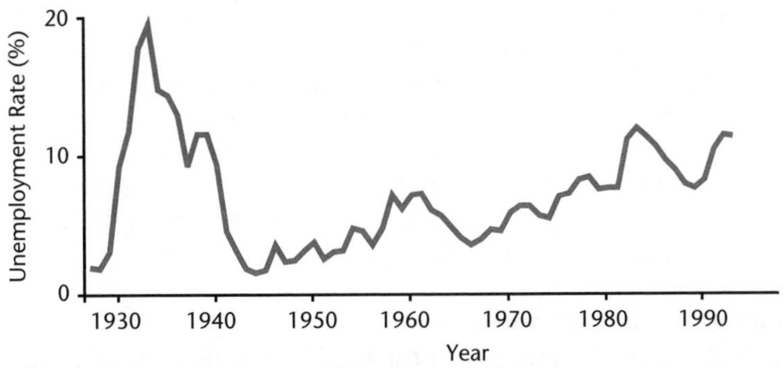

After rising significantly in the 1930s, the unemployment rate fell to 2 to 4 percent for much of the 1940s and 1950s. Since the late 1950s, the rate has gradually risen. Much of this increase can be attributed to a rise in natural unemployment.

SOURCES: Adapted from (for 1966–1993) Statistics Canada, *Canadian Economic Observer, Historical Statistical Supplement, 1992/93* (July 1993), cat. no. 11-210, vol. 7, p. 38; adapted from (for 1926–1965) *National Income and Expenditure Accounts, Annual Estimates 1926–1986* (June 1988), cat. no. 13-531, pp. 214–15. Reproduced by authority of the Minister of Industry, 1994.

Since the 1970s, the unemployment rate has been well over 3 percent. In light of recent economic trends and thinking, many economists argue that in addition to frictional unemployment—which will always exist—the definition of full employment should also accommodate at least some structural unemployment. This, they say, is because structural unemployment *can* be reduced, but only very gradually. While definitions of full employment in the 1990s vary, most include a natural unemployment rate of between 6 percent and 8 percent.

Increases over the past few decades in both the actual and the natural unemployment rates represent worrisome trends. Several factors are often highlighted in explaining these trends.

Structural Change

Recall that structural adjustments in an economy occur whenever there are changes regarding what products are produced, as well as in how and where they are produced. Over the past few decades, the pace of structural change in the Canadian economy has accelerated. The OPEC oil crisis, the growth of the service sector and shrinking of the traditional manufacturing sector, and the removal of many international trade barriers have each led to the displacement of workers and therefore caused increases in long-term structural unemployment.

Unemployment Insurance

Most unemployed workers today have a significant advantage over those in previous generations. The financial cushion provided by unemployment insurance allows job seekers to devote more time and effort to searching for employment than in the past, which increases frictional unemployment. Reforms to unemployment insurance in the early 1970s also made it easier for those experiencing seasonal and structural unemployment to claim benefits. Thus, unemployment insurance can be a factor in increasing the unemployment rate. Overall, it is estimated that this factor has added between 0.5 percent and 2.0 percent to the unemployment rate since the 1970s.

Changing Participation Rates

Recall from Figure 11.6 that, over the last few decades, young people have added to the labour force. Not only do they add to the supply of unskilled labour when they first enter the labour force but, as they acquire skills and work experience, they also suffer greater frictional unemployment than more experienced workers. As a result, the increased participation rates among young Canadians have swelled the ranks of the unemployed.

Minimum Wage

Minimum wage levels set by the provinces have increased a great deal in the past few decades. For young people in particular—who are more likely than others to be affected by minimum wage laws—this has meant an increase in the number of people looking for work. For example, a 1980 Canadian study suggested that a 10.0 percent increase in the minimum wage reduces employment by 1.0 percent for male teenagers and 2.7 percent for female teenagers.

Thinking About Economics

How do minimum wages cause unemployment?

A minimum wage has the same effect on the market for unskilled labour as industrial unions do in other labour markets. By creating a wage floor *above* equilibrium, the minimum wage creates a surplus, with a greater supply of workers than there are available jobs at that wage. In evaluating the effectiveness of minimum wages, the higher wages received by employed workers must be weighed against the unemployment caused for others.

The Costs of Unemployment

High unemployment rates hurt both individuals and the Canadian economy as a whole. As Figure 11.9 shows, the rates vary from province to province and among groups of people. To jobless workers and their families, unemployment, especially for extended periods, can create stress and discouragement, disrupt family life, lower self-esteem, and cause financial hardship. The economy as a whole loses the output the worker could have produced.

The cost of unemployment for the entire economy is indicated by the **GDP gap**, which is the dollar value by which **potential output**, or the real output associated with full employment, exceeds actual real output.

GDP gap: the difference between potential and actual real output, or Gross Domestic Product, of an economy

potential output: the real output, or Gross Domestic Product, associated with full employment

Figure 11.9: Unemployment Rates by Province, Gender, and Age (1993)

Province		Gender and Age	
Newfoundland	20.2	Women	
Prince Edward Island	17.7	15–24	15.0
Nova Scotia	14.6	25 and over	9.6
New Brunswick	12.6		
Quebec	13.1	Men	
Ontario	10.6	15–24	20.2
Manitoba	9.2	25 and over	10.1
Saskatchewan	8.0		
Alberta	9.6		
British Columbia	9.7		

Unemployment rates vary from province to province. 1993 rates were highest among the Atlantic provinces and Quebec, and lowest in Saskatchewan. Rates for women are slightly lower than for men, and young people were more likely to be unemployed than those over the age of 25.

SOURCE: Statistics Canada, *Canadian Economic Observer, Statistical Summary* (May 1994), cat. no. 11-010, pp. 16, 59. Reproduced by authority of the Minister of Industry, 1994.

According to Okun's Law—named after the American economist Arthur Okun—for every percentage point that the unemployment rate exceeds the natural unemployment rate, the GDP gap is 2.5 percent.

In 1993, for example, the real GDP in 1986 (constant) dollars was $573.4 billion, while the unemployment rate was 11.2 percent, or 3.7 percent above an assumed natural unemployment rate of 7.5 percent. According to Okun's Law, real output could have been 9.25 percent (3.7 × 2.5) higher than if unemployment equalled the natural rate. In other words, in 1986 dollars, the 1993 real GDP could have been $53.0 billion ($573.4 billion × 0.0925) higher.

While the concept of the GDP gap is difficult to apply because of disagreements over the natural unemployment rate, it gives a good indication of the substantial cost of unemployment, not just to those workers who are directly affected, but to the economy as a whole.

BRIEF REVIEW

1. The labour force population is Canada's population over age 15, with some exclusions.

2. The participation rate is the percentage of those in the labour force population who make up the labour force, which includes all those people who are employed or who are actively seeking work within the formal economy. Participation rates for women and young people have risen considerably in the last few decades.

3. The official unemployment rate is the percentage of the labour force that is unemployed.

4. The official unemployment rate, which has risen significantly in the last few decades, does not take into account underemployment, discouraged workers, or dishonest answers given in labour market surveys.

5. Unemployment can be categorized as frictional, structural, cyclical, and seasonal.

6. Full employment is the highest reasonable expectation of employment for the economy as a whole, and is defined in terms of a natural unemployment rate. Traditionally, the natural unemployment rate only accommodated frictional unemployment; now, however, many economists believe it should include at least some structural unemployment.

7. The costs of unemployment are profound and numerous for unemployed workers and their families. Unemployment costs to the economy as a whole equal the sum of each unemployed worker's potential output, which can be understood with the concept of the GDP gap.

The Economics of Age Distribution

David Foot and the Future

What economic indicators can we apply to our personal lives? One Canadian economist and demographer suggests that, because large groups of peers make a difference in the economy, our ages can give us insights into our economic futures. In the following 1993 interview with journalist Micki Moore, David Foot outlines some effects of Canada's huge "baby-boom generation" (people born between 1947 and 1966), its smaller "baby-bust generation" (people born between 1967 and 1979), and its "baby-boom echo generation" (people born after 1979).

ADVANCING ECONOMIC THOUGHT

David Foot

SOURCE: Footwork Consulting Inc.

Professor David Foot is a University of Toronto economist and Canada's most outspoken demographer. Studying the relationships between economics and population trends and how they apply to private and public policy, Foot has been put centre stage, peering into the future, discussing an array of issues from unemployment to housing to crime. Knowing the year you were born, claims Foot, helps you understand where you're headed and what to expect.

Foot's predictions over the years have challenged conventional wisdom, yet many of them have proved to be true. Here's what he had to say.

Micki Moore: With daily news of company shut-downs, people being laid off and a never-ending recession, what insights can we learn from demographics about our economic future?

David Foot: The baby boomers in Canada started to be born in 1947. The first baby boomers are now 46 years old. If you look at the demographic profile in Canada it looks like a rectangle—lots of people born in 1947 through the 1950s and early 1960s. So we have a blunt front end of people born in the 1940s and early 1950s who are now in their 40s.

Corporate structures look like triangles...so there simply aren't enough jobs at the top of those corporations to fit all the baby boomers. The smart corporate strategy is to flatten the corporate structure—flatten the triangle. So there are six steps to the top instead of 20 steps.

M.M.: Doesn't that still mean letting people go?

D.F.: It depends on whether you're in the downsizing mode. If you flatten the structure, one occupation is not going to serve you anymore in life—you're going to move around a lot and constantly have to retrain and re-educate throughout your whole lifetime. And it's the portable general skills—good written and oral communications, computer skills, good analytical skills, teamwork skills—that are important.

We need "followership" training, not leadership training, because there will be a lot of people working at the same level and you'll be a follower on more teams than you'll be a leader.

In fact, don't look for a job in the narrow occupation you've always been in. Start to generalize your skills. People may have five different occupations in a lifetime.

If you're also in the downsizing mode, why don't corporations put every employee on four days a week at 80% salary? It downsizes by 20%, keeps all your employees and that knowledge base in the work force. I don't understand why we have to adopt this American competitive short-term firing strategy. Where is the sharing and caring Canadian solution?

M.M.: Why aren't people spending? Who has the money?

D.F.: The people who have the money are in the 55 to 64 age group. These were the people who were born in the Depression of the 1930s; they had a tough beginning to life, but fewer people were born and thus there were fewer people to compete with. They were teenagers during World War II. They had a tough start, paid their dues up front. Then they entered the job market in the postwar reconstruction era of the 1950s. They never had to worry about getting a job or being promoted, so they went out and got more of everything over the 1950s and 1960s, including children.

On average, by 1960, there were four children per family. That was a smart investment because over the 1970s and 1980s those kids grew up and started to demand their parents' houses and drove up the value of houses. Then they started to demand stocks and bonds and drove up the value of those assets.

Those born in the 1930s had little competition, never had to worry about finding a job and then their children drove up the value of all their assets.

They're the richest group in Canada, but you're a spender in your 20s and 30s, you're a saver in your 50s and 60s. They've already bought everything they wanted.

M.M.: We constantly hear that our children's college degree will not guarantee job security like their parents', so what's in store for these young adults?

D.F.: None of that has to be true. There is one group in Canada that has been very disadvantaged, the back quarter of the baby boom, born between 1960 and 1966. Now they would be 27 to 32. Often known as Generation X, there's a lot of them out there, so there's a huge competition for jobs in their peer group. And the baby boomers ahead of them drove up the price of housing and took all the good educational opportunities and jobs.

The baby bust generation is currently aged 14 to 25. There's a few of them and, therefore, little competition for jobs—that's why babysitting prices have been going up even though there's a recession. They've done very well getting part-time jobs during school. But now they've entered the job market in a recession when there are no jobs. But there's a potential for them to do even better than their parents if we ever get out of the recession.

M.M.: We've heard, ad nauseam, about the baby boomers, how they have profoundly affected us in every aspect of our lives. When is all of this over?

D.F.: It's not over 'til they die. That's in another 50 years!

M.M.: What is the demographic impact of those boomers in the following areas?

D.F.:

Women

They have more power because there's more of them in the work force and, at the high end of the baby boom, women are gradually reaching senior management positions. In my students, there's roughly equal employment between men and women. But in the corporate boardrooms, you don't see many women (in the private sector). So the real challenge will be whether the women in their late 40s get to the top and break the glass ceiling. There are a lot more women now poised in the right position, at the right age, with the right work experience to move to the top. If they don't make it, that will be clear evidence that sexism is still rampant in the workplace.

Education

The boomers started to have their kids in the '80s so there was an echo generation born. That echo group is probably on its way down in numbers in the '90s because those women are now in their 30s and it's much more difficult to get pregnant in your late 30s.

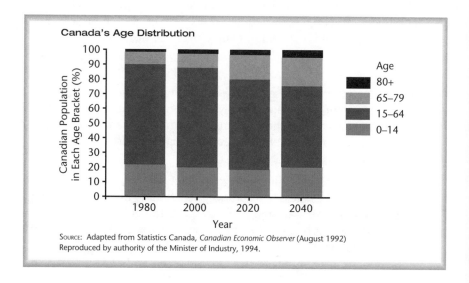

SOURCE: Adapted from Statistics Canada, *Canadian Economic Observer* (August 1992)
Reproduced by authority of the Minister of Industry, 1994.

In the '80s so many more children were born, not because fertility has gone up, but because there's so many more women in their prime child bearing years—late 20s and early 30s. The front end of the echo children are now 13 and they've entered high school this fall, so high school enrollments which have been declining for the past 15 years will gradually start to climb again. That's why there's this push on education and we're building all these schools but many will be empty 10 years from now. It's ridiculous.

Senior Citizens

Otto von Bismarck [the nineteenth-century German Chancellor who pioneered government-financed pensions] chose retirement age as 65 in the 1880s when people only lived until 57, so he didn't expect anyone to reach retirement age. We've kept that constant for 100 years even though life expectancy has risen 20 years. Is it any surprise that our pensions are in trouble? We'll probably have to raise the retirement age to solve the problem. We tend to think of seniors as poor, on a fixed income. But now that we've got inflation under control and interest rates are low, the seniors are complaining because they're not getting their interest income: they have savings, and it's the interest on that savings that gives them the discretionary income to go on holidays. It's an interesting reversal.

The richest group in Canada is going to retire soon. Do you think we should be giving them senior citizens discounts? We do have to worry about the older seniors, who are mostly women born around World War I. They do not have careers or they married men who did not have transferable pensions.

For the first time in postwar history the seniors market is splitting into two distinct markets: a rapidly growing poorer older woman's market and a much slower growing richer young seniors market. So I think senior citizens discounts should be given to people over 75, not over 65.

SOURCE: Abridged from "Close encounters: Stepping into the future with demographer David Foot," *The Sunday Sun*, 26 September 1993, p. 20. Courtesy of *The Toronto Sun*.

1. Foot contends that the larger social and demographic context in which we live and work significantly affects our economic present and future. Find at least three examples from your life or from those of your siblings, parents, or grandparents that support Foot's theory. Discuss your examples in a group.

2. Arrange to have representatives from a variety of industries—for example, the real estate, life insurance, health care, financial planning, and service industries—form a panel to speak to your class about the effects of demographics on their industries and about their predictions for the future. Before the panel discussion, prepare opening questions to ask, and ask your guests to read the preceding interview.

Key Concepts

deflation
consumer price index
item weights
base year
cost of living
nominal income
real income
GDP deflator
nominal GDP
cost-of-living-adjustment clauses
fully indexed incomes
partially indexed incomes
fixed incomes
nominal interest rate
real interest rate

inflation premium
labour force population
labour force
participation rate
underemployment
discouraged workers
frictional unemployment
structural unemployment
cyclical unemployment
seasonal unemployment
full employment
natural unemployment rate
GDP gap
potential output

Developing Application and Analysis Skills

1. Examine the table on page 332, and do the following:

a) On a graph, plot the CPI for the years given in the table.

b) Explain the significance of the year 1986.

c) Based on the CPI, estimate what a car bought in 1986 for $12 000 would cost in nominal dollars in 1992.

d) What is the overall rate of inflation between 1986 and 1992?

e) Suppose that an office manager has a nominal income in 1971 of $10 000 per year. According to the CPI, what nominal income would she have to receive in 1992 to maintain her purchasing power?

f) Consider the other indexes. For each, suggest for whom in the economy the index would be particularly relevant.

2. a) Research the current rate of inflation.

b) Based on this, suggest a likely interest rate for a $1000 five-year student loan, and explain your answer.

c) Calculate the interest to be paid at the end of the first year. Identify what would be nominal interest and what would be real interest.

3. a) Suppose last year has been established as the new base year. Now the CPI is at 1.09. What is the current rate of inflation?

b) Given this rate of inflation, what is the real income of people whose nominal income for this year is $45 000?

4. Propose and create a student consumer price index. To do so, list items typically purchased by you and your peers, determine the quantities you buy, check prices, and monitor prices over an extended period of time. Present your findings in a report.

Price Indexes (1986 = 100)					
	Consumer Price Index		Industrial Product Price Index	Raw Materials Price Index	New Housing Price Index
	All Items	Annual Percentage Change			
1961	23.9	1.0	25.3	n.a.	n.a.
1971	31.9	2.9	30.7	n.a.	n.a.
1981	75.5	12.4	83.6	104.0	95.8
1986	100.0	4.2	100.0	100.0	100.0
1987	104.4	4.4	102.8	107.3	113.8
1988	108.6	4.0	107.2	103.8	125.6
1989	114.0	5.0	109.4	107.2	142.2
1990	119.5	4.8	109.7	111.6	144.3
1991	126.2	5.6	108.6	104.7	134.3
1992	128.1	1.5	109.1	105.7	134.3

n.a. = not available

SOURCE: Minister of Industry, Science and Technology, *Canada Year Book 1994* (Ottawa: 1993), p. 614. Reproduced by authority of the Minister of Industry, 1994.

5. Differentiate between the consumer price index and the GDP deflator. In what circumstances is one a more useful indicator than the other, and vice versa? Explain.

6. Explain the effect of inflation on the following people:
   a) people with fixed incomes
   b) unionized workers
   c) salespeople on commission
   d) lenders and borrowers

7. Determine the real GDP for an economy in which the nominal GDP is $533 billion and the GDP deflator is 1.1.

8. Copy the table on page 333 for a simple economy that produces only two products, bicycles and axes. Complete the table, using 1995 as the base year.

9. Suppose the GDP for a country in its base year of 1995 was $500 billion. Calculate the 1996 GDP in 1996 dollars for this country if the GDP deflator is known to be 1.2 and the growth rate of real GDP is 5 percent. What is the 1996 nominal GDP per capita if the 1996 population is 10 million?

10. Based on what you've learned in the chapter, suggest what advantages and disadvantages of each of the following types of investments might have:
   a) shares in a corporation
   b) interest-bearing investments, such as bonds

11. Suppose a country has a population of 40 million aged 15 and older (none of whom are excluded from the labour force population), an employed population of 21 million, and an unemployed population of 9 million who are seeking work.

   a) Calculate the labour force.
   b) Calculate the participation rate.
   c) Calculate the unemployment rate.
   d) Account for the numbers of people not included in the labour force, and explain.

	Axcycle's GDP (1995–1997)						
Year	Output (no. of bicycles)	Current Price ($ per bicycle)	Output (no. of axes)	Current Price ($ per axe)	Nominal GDP ($)	Real GDP ($)	GDP Deflator
1995	1500	500	3000	25	_____	_____	_____
1996	2000	525	3500	26	_____	_____	_____
1997	2000	530	3500	30	_____	_____	_____

12. Suppose full employment in Canada is defined as including a natural unemployment rate of 7.5 percent; however, the actual unemployment rate is 9.5 percent this year, and real GDP is $700 billion. Apply Okun's Law to calculate the following:

a) the GDP gap
b) the potential output in constant dollars

13. Using terminology from this chapter, describe the employment circumstances of each of the following people. For each, identify the economic costs and, if any, the economic benefits of the circumstances described.

a) a construction worker is out of work for the month of February
b) a graphic artist is laid off for six months during a recession
c) a person with a Ph.D. in microbiology drives a cab for a living
d) a parent decides to stay at home with his infant child
e) a former middle manager returns to school to update her skills
f) after a year of searching for a job, a musician is employed "under the table" doing bookkeeping
g) by chance, the person in f) finds work in the formal economy, teaching others how to use computer programs for bookkeeping.

14. Examine a contemporary situation in which either inflation or unemployment has been extreme. You might focus on a particular community, industry, or region. In a report, identify and explain the possible causes of the inflation or unemployment, its effects, any solutions proposed or implemented, the effectiveness of these solutions, and the current situation.

CHAPTER 12

Economic Fluctuations

> It's a recession when your neighbor loses his job; it's a depression when you lose yours.
>
> —HARRY TRUMAN, AMERICAN PRESIDENT

For decades, real output and average living standards in Canada have gradually increased, but the economy rarely grows steadily. Sometimes, production and incomes increase sharply; at other times, they inch up or even fall. Such fluctuations occur in all free-market economies, with occasionally devastating results. During the Great Depression of the 1930s, for example, real output in Canada dropped by over 25 percent, while unemployment soared. In the late 1960s, the opposite happened: an overheated economy led to accelerating inflation, which significantly reduced some Canadians' living standards. More recently, the recession of the early 1990s led to layoffs and plant closings throughout Canada, leaving a legacy of displaced workers and lost production.

CHAPTER FOCUS

This chapter focuses on the following:
- aggregate demand and aggregate supply
- the effect of the general price level on total expenditures
- aggregate demand factors and aggregate supply factors
- the economy's equilibrium and how it differs from its potential
- injections to and withdrawals from the economy
- the business cycle of expansion and contraction, with its peaks and troughs

SKILLS FOCUS

After studying this chapter, you will be able to:
- construct aggregate demand and supply curves and explain changes in them
- outline the ways in which the economy reaches equilibrium
- outline the factors that determine the level of investment in the economy
- differentiate between equilibrium and potential output
- apply the concept of the business cycle to explain the causes of economic instability
- demonstrate and explain relationships that exist among economic variables at various stages in the business cycle

Aggregate Demand

What determines the connections among inflation, unemployment, and levels of spending and real output in the Canadian economy? As in the case of individual markets, the explanation can be given in terms of demand and supply. First, we'll look at how the concept of demand can be applied to the economy as a whole to see the relationship between the general price level and total spending in the economy, which is known as **aggregate demand** (AD).

Recall that total spending on an economy's goods and services is the sum of four components: consumption, investment, government purchases, and net exports. The primary groups responsible for this spending are households, businesses, governments, and foreigners. Total spending in an economy, adjusted for changes in the general price level, is referred to as **real expenditures**, and is calculated using the GDP price deflator. Suppose, for example, that $1080 billion in nominal dollars are spent in Canada in a year in which the GDP deflator has a value of 1.2. Therefore, real expenditures, or total output purchases, equal $900 billion ($1080 billion ÷ 1.2) in constant dollars.

Economists attempt to identify the factors that influence real expenditures. One of the most important factors is the price level, since changes in prices cause changes in spending. In other words, not only is price level used to *calculate* real expenditures, it also *affects* real expenditures.

The Aggregate Demand Curve

Aggregate demand can be expressed in a table known as the **aggregate demand schedule**, or on a graph known as the **aggregate demand curve** (AD). Figure 12.1 shows an aggregate demand schedule and an aggregate demand curve. Just as with a demand curve for a single product, the price variable is placed on the vertical axis of the graph, and the output variable is placed on the horizontal axis.

Recall that price and quantity demanded of a single product almost always have an inverse relationship: as price rises, quantity demanded decreases, and vice versa. The same can be said for the general price level and real expenditures, although for different reasons. Whereas quantity demanded of a certain product is affected by the law of diminishing marginal utility, the amount spent in the entire economy is affected by two entirely different factors: wealth and foreign trade. Note that the response to a change in the price level is a movement *along* the aggregate demand curve.

Wealth

In Chapter 9, we saw that a household may have wealth in the form of financial assets, as well as real assets. The nominal values of these

aggregate demand: the relationship between the general price level and total spending in the economy

real expenditures: total spending in an economy, adjusted for changes in the general price level

aggregate demand schedule: the relationship between the general price level and total spending in the economy expressed in a table

aggregate demand curve: the relationship between the general price level and total spending in the economy expressed on a graph

Figure 12.1:   Aggregate Demand

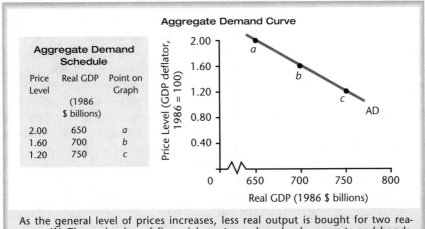

As the general level of prices increases, less real output is bought for two reasons. (1) The real value of financial assets, such as bank accounts and bonds, decreases. As a result, households feel less wealthy, so they reduce their consumption spending. (2) Net export spending is reduced as both foreigners spend less on Canadian exports and Canadian residents spend more on imports.

financial assets—such as bank accounts and retirement savings plans—stay the same no matter what the price level; however, their real values change with any rise or fall in the price level. To find the real value of financial assets, their nominal value must be divided by the price level:

$$\text{Real value of financial assets} \quad = \quad \frac{\text{nominal value of financial assets}}{\text{price level}}$$

When the price level rises, the real value of households' financial assets decreases. Because consumers feel they have less wealth, they spend less on consumption items. As a result of this **wealth effect**, real expenditures drop.

Foreign Trade

Changes in the price level also influence foreign trade. When the price level in Canada rises, Canadian exports become more expensive for foreigners. As a result, sales in foreign markets fall, causing a decrease in export expenditures. At the same time, products imported into Canada become cheaper relative to higher-priced domestic products. Therefore, import expenditures by Canadians rise. The **foreign trade effect**—as this combination of effects is known—involves a decrease in net exports (X – M), and thus a decline in real expenditures.

wealth effect: with changes in the price level, the real value of households' financial assets changes, causing households to adjust their spending

foreign trade effect: with changes in the price level, expenditures on imports change in the same direction, while expenditures on exports change in the opposite direction

Changes in Aggregate Demand

aggregate demand factors: variables that cause changes in total expenditures at all price levels

In addition to the price level, other factors can influence total spending. However, these factors, called **aggregate demand factors**, change total spending at *all* price levels. In other words, they *shift* the aggregate demand curve. Recall that spending has four components—consumption, investment, government purchases, and net exports. When factors other than price level affect any of these components, they in turn affect total real expenditures.

Suppose, for example, that government purchases increase (in constant dollars) by $50 billion. Because government spending is a component of total expenditures, the aggregate demand curve shifts to the right by $50 billion, as shown in Figure 12.2, from AD_0 to AD_1. This change is known as an **increase in aggregate demand**. Similarly, a decrease in another component of real expenditures, such as consumption spending, would cause a decrease in total expenditures. This **decrease in aggregate demand** would be represented by a shift in the aggregate demand curve to the left.

increase in aggregate demand: an increase in total expenditures at all price levels

decrease in aggregate demand: a decrease in total expenditures at all price levels

Figure 12.2:   Changes in Aggregate Demand

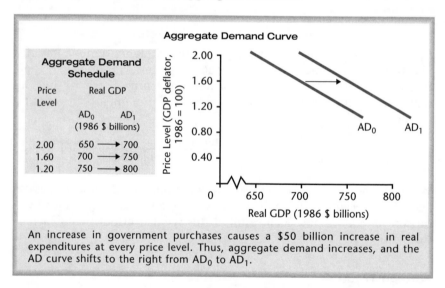

An increase in government purchases causes a $50 billion increase in real expenditures at every price level. Thus, aggregate demand increases, and the AD curve shifts to the right from AD_0 to AD_1.

Aggregate demand factors can be categorized by the spending component they immediately affect. As we consider each in turn, we must assume that all other aggregate demand factors and the price level remain constant.

Consumption

Recall that personal consumption and saving are the two uses of disposable income. Thus consumer spending is decided when households determine how much to spend or save. Changes in disposable income, wealth, consumer expectations, and interest rates can all affect consumer spending. With any change in consumer spending, total expenditure changes also, thereby shifting the aggregate demand curve.

Disposable Income

The most significant determinant of consumer spending is the level of disposable income (DI) in the entire economy. The economy's total disposable income may change as a result of changes in population or changes in disposable income per household. Higher income taxes, for example, decrease household disposable income. Disposable income and consumer spending have a direct relationship. So, when disposable income rises, there is a rise in consumer spending, thereby adding to total expenditures and shifting the aggregate demand curve to the right.

Wealth

In Chapter 9, we learned that wealth and income are quite different. Whereas income consists of earnings received over time, wealth is made up of financial and real assets. Real assets (such as houses and appliances) and financial assets (such as stocks and bonds) are measured at a particular point in time. We've already considered the wealth effect—the effect of the price level on the value of wealth, which then influences consumer spending. Factors other than price level can affect wealth, however, and in turn affect consumer spending. For example, if stock prices jump, households owning stocks enjoy increased wealth; as a result, these households will likely spend more of their disposable income. Aggregate demand will increase and the aggregate demand curve will shift to the right. Conversely, an increase in consumer debt means that households lose wealth. Households reduce their spending as a result, and aggregate demand decreases.

Consumer Expectations

As we saw in Chapter 2, consumer expectations influence the demand for a single product. Similarly, these expectations can affect aggregate demand by changing general consumption patterns. If consumers expect prices to rise—for example, because of a calamity such as war or a flood—they will spend more now and save less. As a result of this higher consumer spending, aggregate demand increases, and the aggregate demand curve shifts to the right. In the same way, if consumers expect their incomes to rise soon, they again spend more and save less, causing an increase in aggregate demand.

Interest Rates

Because households often borrow to purchase durable goods, such as cars and furniture, changes in real interest rates can affect their purchasing decisions. If the real interest rate falls, consumers are more likely to borrow in order to buy big-ticket items. Consumer spending rises, and the aggregate demand curve shifts to the right. Conversely, a jump in the real interest rate has the opposite effect: because consumer spending falls, aggregate demand decreases, and the aggregate demand curve shifts to the left.

Investment

The investment component of aggregate demand is limited to *planned* investment, which excludes unintended changes in inventories. As we saw in Chapter 8, investment represents spending on projects where earning a profit is anticipated.

real rate of return:

constant-dollar extra profit provided by a project each year stated as a percentage of the project's initial cost

How does a business decide whether or not to make an investment? The business first calculates all the expected revenues and costs of the project in constant dollars. Then it calculates the project's **real rate of return**, which is the constant-dollar extra profit provided by the project each year stated as a percentage of the project's initial cost. Let's consider our example from earlier chapters, Pure 'n' Simple T-Shirts. As its owner, you are deciding whether to buy a $100 sewing machine, which is expected to last for one year. After its effects on day-to-day operating costs are taken into account, the machine is expected to add $112 in constant dollars to your business's net revenue. The extra profit gained from purchasing the machine is therefore $12 ($112 − $100). Thus, the machine's real rate of return, as a percentage of its $100 price, is 12 percent [($12 ÷ $100) × 100%].

Because most businesses borrow money to finance their investment projects, they will pursue projects for which the return on the project exceeds, or at least equals, the real interest rates they will be charged. In other words, any project is undertaken if its annual benefit is greater than or at least equal to its annual cost.

We've focused on a single business; now let's turn our attention to the entire economy. Suppose that businesses in the economy are considering four possible investment projects. Projects A, B, C, and D each have a cost of $15 billion. However, their real rates of return differ. Project A has a real rate of return of 10 percent, B a rate of 8 percent, C a rate of 6 percent, and D a rate of 4 percent. Figure 12.3 shows the projects' respective profits as rectangles. While each rectangle has the same width, representing the projects' uniform $15 billion cost, the heights differ to reflect the different rates of return.

To see how interest rates affect investment in the economy, let's place the real interest rate on Figure 12.3, also on the vertical axis. Recall that only investment projects with a real rate of return equal to or greater than the prevailing real interest rate will be undertaken. So, if the real interest rate is 12 percent, businesses in the economy would not invest in any project since none provides a sufficient real rate of return to cover the cost of borrowing. This is shown as point *a* in Figure 12.3. If the real interest rate falls to 8 percent, businesses in the economy will invest in

Figure 12.3:   Investment Demand

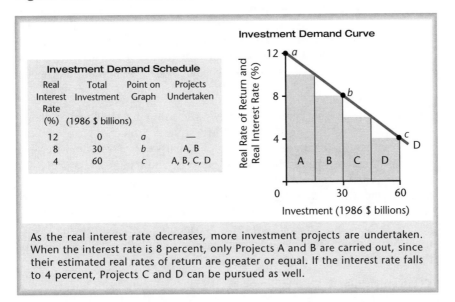

Investment Demand Schedule

Real Interest Rate (%)	Total Investment (1986 $ billions)	Point on Graph	Projects Undertaken
12	0	a	—
8	30	b	A, B
4	60	c	A, B, C, D

Investment Demand Curve

As the real interest rate decreases, more investment projects are undertaken. When the interest rate is 8 percent, only Projects A and B are carried out, since their estimated real rates of return are greater or equal. If the interest rate falls to 4 percent, Projects C and D can be pursued as well.

Projects A and B, as shown by point *b*, because their real rates of return equal or exceed the costs of borrowing. As a result, investment in the economy rises to $30 billion. Finally, if interest rates drop even further, to 4 percent, businesses in the economy will invest in Projects A, B, C, and D, as shown by point *c*, thereby increasing investment in the economy to $60 billion. This relationship between interest rates and investment is known as **investment demand**. Investment demand can be expressed in a table, called the **investment demand schedule**, or on a graph, called the **investment demand curve** (D_I).

Now that we have seen how total investment in the economy is determined, it is easier to recognize the various aggregate demand factors related to investment. A rise in investment causes an increase in aggregate demand, thereby shifting the aggregate demand curve to the right. Conversely, a fall in investment causes a decrease in aggregate demand, thereby shifting the aggregate demand curve to the left. Investment not only changes because of interest rates, as we've seen, but also because of business expectations and production costs.

Interest Rates

As shown by the investment demand curve in Figure 12.3, real interest rates and investment have an inverse relationship. Hence, a rise in real interest rates causes a decrease in aggregate demand, and a fall in real interest rates causes an increase in aggregate demand.

investment demand: the relationship between interest rates and investment

investment demand schedule: the relationship between interest rates and investment expressed in a table

investment demand curve: the relationship between interest rates and investment expressed on a graph

Business Expectations

Business expectations—whether optimistic or pessimistic—can affect investment demand. If businesses anticipate that profits will increase, investment demand rises, thereby causing an increase in aggregate demand. Conversely, if businesses anticipate that profits will drop, investment demand falls, leading to a decrease in aggregate demand.

Production Costs

Changes in businesses' production costs also influence the level of investment by altering the profitability of investment projects. A rise in businesses' costs—for example, due to higher corporate taxes—reduces real rates of return for various investment projects, and makes it less likely that these projects will be pursued. As a result, investment spending decreases and the aggregate demand curve shifts to the left. In contrast, a technological breakthrough that reduces production costs increases the real rates of return in those industries that use the technology, thereby making investment projects more feasible. As a result, investment spending increases, and the aggregate demand curve shifts to the right.

Government Purchases

A rise in government purchases—such as highway construction, for example—causes an increase in aggregate demand, while a fall in government purchases causes a decrease in aggregate demand. Recall that this component of spending does not include government transfer payments, such as those discussed in Chapter 9; Old Age Security payments, for example, are classified as negative taxes, which flow *from* rather than *to* governments.

Net Exports

As seen earlier, net exports can vary due to changes in the price level. For example, a drop in the Canadian price level increases net exports, because Canadian exports are cheaper in foreign markets and imports are made more expensive in Canada. As a result of this foreign trade effect, a change in the price level influences total spending in the economy, which is expressed as a movement along the aggregate demand curve.

Other factors that affect net exports—and that cause a *change* in aggregate demand—include incomes in foreign countries and foreign exchange rates. The effect of changes in these factors is represented by a shift in the aggregate demand curve.

Foreign Incomes

Suppose incomes rise in a foreign country such as France. French citizens will be able to purchase more products as a result. Not only will they purchase French products, but also those of other countries. As a result, Canadian net exports to France will likely rise, thereby increasing Canada's aggregate demand and shifting the aggregate demand curve to the right. Conversely, a fall in foreign incomes will likely reduce Canadian net exports, thereby decreasing Canada's aggregate demand and shifting the aggregate demand curve to the left.

Exchange Rates

An **exchange rate** is the value of one nation's currency in terms of another currency. As we will see in more detail in Chapter 16, the value of the Canadian dollar can be expressed in any other currency, but is usually compared to American dollars. So, the exchange rate can show how many American cents are needed to buy one Canadian dollar. A rise in the value of the Canadian dollar—for example, from 75 to 80 cents— means more U.S. currency is needed to purchase Canadian funds. In this example, Canada's currency becomes more expensive for Americans to purchase. At the same time, U.S. currency becomes cheaper for Canadians to purchase, since we get more of it—80 cents as opposed to 75 cents—in exchange for one Canadian dollar.

If the Canadian dollar goes up in value, exports from Canada become more expensive for Americans. So, a product priced at $1 in Canada costs not 75 cents in American funds but 80 cents. At the same time, American products imported into Canada fall in price when expressed in Canadian currency. One Canadian dollar now buys American products with a U.S. price of 80 cents, whereas before the same dollar could buy American products with a U.S. price of only 75 cents.

Because of the impact of exchange rates on prices, net exports fall when the Canadian dollar goes up in value. Aggregate demand decreases and the aggregate demand curve shifts to the left. A drop in the value of the Canadian dollar has the opposite effect: net exports rise, thereby increasing aggregate demand and shifting the aggregate demand curve to the right. The effects of this and other aggregate demand factors are summarized in Figure 12.4.

exchange rate: the value of one nation's currency in terms of another currency

Thinking About Economics

Which of the components of aggregate demand is most likely to vary?

While consumption, government purchases, and net exports all vary substantially, investment is the most unstable element in aggregate demand. One reason for its volatility is the *accelerator effect*. This occurs when a relatively small proportional change in consumption leads to a larger proportional change in investment. For example, an expected 10 percent rise in consumption spending may cause businesses to invest 100 percent more in capital goods than they would have if consumption were expected to stay constant. Similarly, an expected reduction in consumption can lead to a magnified decrease in investment. Investment that arises from the accelerator effect is known as *induced investment*.

Figure 12.4:   Shifts in the Aggregate Demand Curve

Aggregate demand increases, thereby shifting the AD curve to the right, with the following:	*Aggregate demand decreases, thereby shifting the AD curve to the left, with the following:*

(1) An increase in consumption due to
    (a) a rise in disposable income
    (b) a rise in wealth
    (c) an expected rise in prices or incomes
    (d) a fall in interest rates

(2) An increase in investment due to
    (a) a fall in interest rates
    (b) an expected rise in profits
    (c) a fall in production costs

(3) An increase in government purchases

(4) An increase in net exports due to
    (a) a rise in foreign incomes
    (b) a fall in the value of the Canadian dollar

(1) A decrease in consumption due to
    (a) a fall in disposable income
    (b) a fall in wealth
    (c) an expected fall in prices or incomes
    (d) a rise in interest rates

(2) A decrease in investment due to
    (a) a rise in interest rates
    (b) an expected fall in profits
    (c) a rise in production costs

(3) A decrease in government purchases

(4) A decrease in net exports due to
    (a) a fall in foreign incomes
    (b) a rise in the value of the Canadian dollar

BRIEF REVIEW

1. Aggregate demand is the relationship between the price level and total spending in the economy. This relationship can be expressed in an aggregate demand schedule or on an aggregate demand curve (AD).

2. Total spending in the economy, adjusted for inflation, is known as real expenditures, and includes the spending of households, businesses, governments, and foreigners.

3. The general price level and total spending in the economy have an inverse relationship, thereby giving the aggregate demand curve a negative slope.

4. Both the wealth effect and the foreign trade effect, which arise from price level changes, cause movements *along* the aggregate demand curve.

5. In contrast, aggregate demand factors cause a change in total spending at all price levels, thereby *shifting* the aggregate demand curve. Anything that changes consumption spending, investment, government purchases, or net exports shifts the aggregate demand curve.

 **Aggregate Supply**

aggregate supply: the relationship between the general price level and real output produced in the economy

So far in this chapter, we have focused on the role of spending in the economy. Now, let's turn our attention to the role of production. **Aggregate supply** is the relationship between the general price level and real output produced in the economy. Figure 12.5 shows aggregate supply expressed in a table, called the **aggregate supply schedule**, and on a graph, called the **aggregate supply curve** (AS).

The Aggregate Supply Curve

As Figure 12.5 shows, price level and real output are directly related, giving the aggregate supply curve a positive slope. At higher price levels in the economy, businesses are encouraged to produce more; at lower price levels, businesses may not be able to make a profit or break even in the short run, so they reduce output. Variations in an economy's output caused by changes in the price level result in movements *along* the aggregate supply curve.

aggregate supply schedule: the relationship between the general price level and real output expressed in a table

aggregate supply curve: the relationship between the general price level and real output expressed on a graph

Figure 12.5:   Aggregate Supply

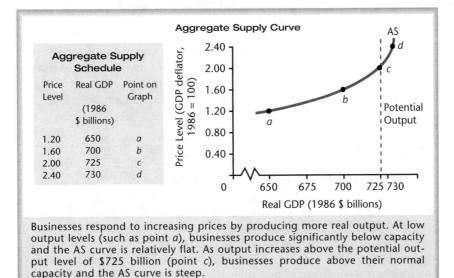

Businesses respond to increasing prices by producing more real output. At low output levels (such as point *a*), businesses produce significantly below capacity and the AS curve is relatively flat. As output increases above the potential output level of $725 billion (point *c*), businesses produce above their normal capacity and the AS curve is steep.

Recall from Chapter 11 that unemployment reduces real output from what it could be. If full employment were achieved—in other words, if only natural unemployment occurred—the economy would reach its potential output. If, as sometimes happens, the unemployment rate temporarily falls below the natural unemployment rate, real output rises temporarily above potential output.

Let's consider the hypothetical example in Figure 12.5. Potential output—the real output associated with full employment—has a value of $725 billion. The real output level, as shown by the aggregate supply curve (AS), is much lower than its potential at point *a*, but greater than the potential output at point *d*. Notice that, above the potential output level, the aggregate supply curve becomes very steep. This shows that businesses are producing above their normal capacity, which is possible in the short run only if businesses employ overtime labour and temporarily rent new machinery. These temporary measures mean that any expansion in real output—for example, from $725 billion (point *c*) to $730 billion (point *d*)—is associated with a large increase in businesses' per-unit costs and, therefore, in the price level. Conversely, at real output levels below the potential output, the production capacity of businesses is underutilized, with some labour and capital equipment either working part-time or sitting idle. A rise in real output, as from $650 billion (point *a*) to $700 billion (point *b*), can be made with a relatively small increase in per-unit costs and thus in the price level.

 ## Changes in Aggregate Supply

aggregate supply factors: variables that change total output at all price levels

Of course, other factors in addition to the price level can influence real output. However, these factors, known as **aggregate supply factors**, change real output at *all* price levels. In other words, they *shift* the aggregate supply curve. Once again, as we examine each in turn, we must assume that all other aggregate supply factors and the price level remain constant.

Input Prices

short-run increase in aggregate supply: an increase in total output at all price levels, with no change in potential output

Aggregate supply assumes steady input prices for the businesses that are producing the output. Changes in input prices—which can occur frequently over brief periods of time—alter production costs. When a rise in the price of an input pushes up production costs, businesses reduce their real output and the aggregate supply curve shifts to the left. Note, however, that nothing happens to change the economy's potential output. Conversely, if the price of an input decreases, production costs fall. Businesses then raise their real output, causing the aggregate supply curve to shift to the right, while the economy's potential output stays the same. These changes apply to the short run, so they are called a **short-run increase in aggregate supply** and a **short-run decrease in aggregate supply**, respectively. Figure 12.6 shows an example.

short-run decrease in aggregate supply: a decrease in total output at all price levels, with no change in potential output

Resource Supplies

long-run increase in aggregate supply: an increase in total and potential output at all price levels

Over the long term, supplies of resources in an economy—especially human and capital resources—tend to grow. With any such increase, businesses produce more real output at every price level. In other words, more inputs over the long run increase aggregate supply, as well as the economy's potential output. Figure 12.7 shows the outcome—a **long-run increase in aggregate supply**. The reverse is also possible. With a long-run reduction in the amounts of any resource, businesses will pro-

Figure 12.6: A Short-Run Change in Aggregate Supply

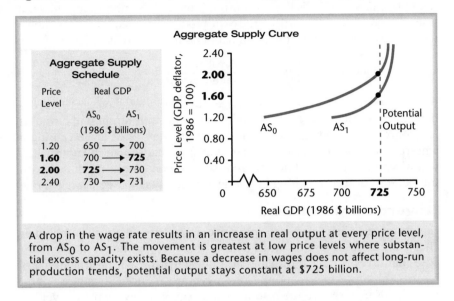

A drop in the wage rate results in an increase in real output at every price level, from AS_0 to AS_1. The movement is greatest at low price levels where substantial excess capacity exists. Because a decrease in wages does not affect long-run production trends, potential output stays constant at $725 billion.

Figure 12.7: A Long-Run Change in Aggregate Supply

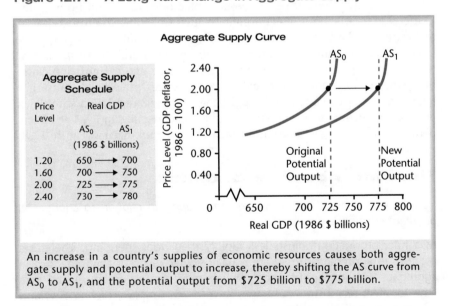

An increase in a country's supplies of economic resources causes both aggregate supply and potential output to increase, thereby shifting the AS curve from AS_0 to AS_1, and the potential output from $725 billion to $775 billion.

duce lower real output at all prices, thereby causing a **long-run decrease in aggregate supply**, which is accompanied by a reduction in the economy's potential output.

long-run decrease in aggregate supply: a decrease in total and potential output at all price levels

Productivity

Recall that productivity is the real output produced per unit of input over a given period of time. In particular, labour productivity is found by dividing a nation's real output by the total number of hours worked by its labour force:

$$\text{Labour productivity} = \frac{\text{real output}}{\text{total hours worked}}$$

Increases in productivity are due largely to technological progress. A technological innovation raises productivity when the same amount of economic resources can produce more real output at every price level, causing a long-run increase in aggregate supply similar to that shown in Figure 12.7. Likewise, a technological decline reduces the real output produced with the same resources, resulting in a long-run decrease in aggregate supply.

Government Policies

Government policies can also influence aggregate supply through their effects on the business environment in an economy. For example, suppose that taxes rise for businesses and households. Because the after-tax returns on supplying economic resources are reduced, businesses and households may reduce the resources they supply at every price level. As a result, real output falls, causing a long-run decrease in aggregate supply. Conversely, lower taxes may encourage businesses and households to increase their supply of economic resources, leading to an increase in real output and a long-run increase in aggregate supply.

Government regulations, such as environmental and safety standards, typically raise per-unit costs for businesses. Hence, more regulation causes businesses to produce less real output at every price level, causing a long-run decrease in aggregate supply. Similarly, less regulation stimulates production, leading to a long-run increase in aggregate supply. The effects of these and other aggregate supply factors are summarized in Figure 12.8.

Thinking About Economics

How important are changes in aggregate supply in relation to changes in aggregate demand?

As a rule, production adjusts less rapidly than does spending. Therefore, changes in aggregate supply are usually slower to occur than changes in aggregate demand. Input prices, which may change quickly, often take time to affect real output. Changes in resource supplies, technology, and government policies tend to occur even more gradually. While aggregate supply is more stable than aggregate demand over the short run, the long-run effect of aggregate supply on the economy can be profound.

Figure 12.8: Shifts in the Aggregate Supply Curve

Aggregate supply increases, thereby shifting the AS curve to the right, and potential output stays the same with the following:

(1) A decrease in input prices due to
  (a) a fall in wages
  (b) a fall in raw material prices ✓

Aggregate supply increases, thereby shifting the AS curve to the right, and potential output increases with the following:

(2) An increase in supplies of economic resources due to
  (a) increased labour supply
  (b) increased capital stock
  (c) increased land and natural resources ✓
  (d) increased entrepreneurship

(3) An increase in productivity due to technological progress

(4) A change in government policies: ✓
  (a) lower taxes
  (b) less government regulation

Aggregate supply decreases, thereby shifting the AS curve to the left, and potential output stays the same with the following:

(1) An increase in input prices due to
  (a) a rise in wages
  (b) a rise in raw material prices

Aggregate supply decreases, thereby shifting the AS curve to the left, and potential output decreases with the following:

(2) A decrease in supplies of economic resources due to
  (a) decreased labour supply
  (b) decreased capital stock
  (c) decreased land and natural resources
  (d) decreased entrepreneurship

(3) A decrease in productivity due to technological decline

(4) A change in government policies:
  (a) higher taxes
  (b) more government regulation

BRIEF REVIEW

1. Aggregate supply is the relationship between the price level and real output produced in the economy. This relationship can be expressed in an aggregate supply schedule or on an aggregate supply curve (AS).

2. Because higher prices encourage increased real output and vice versa, the price level and real output have a direct relationship, thereby giving the aggregate supply curve a positive slope.

3. Since real output may not reflect full use of all resources—for example, labour—an economy may not reach its potential output.

4. While changes in the price level cause movement *along* the aggregate supply curve, aggregate supply factors—changes in input prices, supplies of economic resources, productivity, and government policies—*shift* the curve and so change real output of an economy and aggregate supply.

5. Short-run changes in aggregate supply, caused by varying input prices, do not change an economy's potential output. However, long-run changes in aggregate supply do change an economy's potential output in the same direction.

Equilibrium

Aggregate Demand and Supply

So far, we've been looking at aggregate demand and aggregate supply separately. Now we'll consider them together. What happens if real output at a certain price level exceeds real expenditures? Alternatively, what happens if real output at a certain price level falls short of what an economy would spend? Figure 12.9 presents answers to these questions. As with demand and supply in a competitive market for an individual product, the forces underlying aggregate demand and aggregate supply push the economy to an equilibrium point. An economy's equilibrium price level and real output occur at the intersection of the aggregate demand and aggregate supply curves.

Inventory Changes

Unintended changes in inventories cause price levels and real outputs to reach equilibrium. We'll look at the two possibilities: the results of an inventory increase and of an inventory decrease.

Results of an Inventory Increase

Suppose the general price level is above the equilibrium price level, at 2.00 (points *a*). At this price level, real output exceeds real expenditures,

Figure 12.9: An Economy in Equilibrium

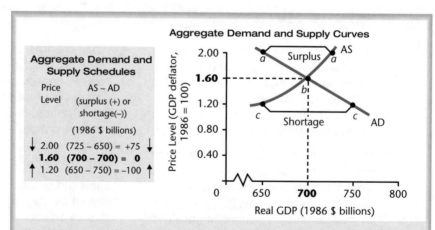

If the price level, at points *a*, is above its equilibrium level of 1.60, real output exceeds expenditures. An unintended rise in inventories causes businesses to lower prices until output and expenditures are the same, at $700 billion (point *b*). When the price level is below its equilibrium value (points *c*), there is an unintended fall in inventories. Businesses increase prices until equilibrium is reached (point *b*).

meaning that more is produced than is purchased in the economy. Businesses have an unintended increase in inventories—in other words, a surplus—which represents **positive unplanned investment**. As a result of this surplus, prices of individual products decrease, pushing down the general price level.

The general decrease in prices influences both households and businesses. Because of the wealth and foreign trade effects, the response of buyers is to increase spending. So, real expenditures in our example increase toward point *b*. Meanwhile, lower prices cause businesses to decrease real output. These trends continue until real output and real expenditures are equal at the equilibrium point (point *b*).

Results of an Inventory Decrease

Suppose, on the other hand, that the price level is below its equilibrium value, at 1.20 (points *c*). Expenditures exceed production, creating a shortage. This leads to an unintended decrease in inventories, known as a **negative unplanned investment**. Because particular products are in short supply, prices rise. The response of buyers is to decrease spending. Meanwhile, the higher price level causes businesses to raise real output. These trends continue until real output and real expenditures are equal at the equilibrium point (point *b*).

The Role of Unplanned Investment

Notice that, in the case of either an inventory increase or decrease, unplanned investment plays a central role in stabilizing the economy. Unplanned investment is positive when the price level is above its equilibrium value and negative when the price level is below its equilibrium value, and in each case unplanned investment is identical to the discrepancy between aggregate demand and aggregate supply.

This is illustrated by the aggregate demand and supply schedules in Figure 12.9. The $75 billion discrepancy between aggregate demand and aggregate supply at a price level of 2.00 means there is an unintended increase in inventories of $75 billion. Hence, there is unplanned investment of $75 billion. Likewise, the shortage of $100 billion that appears at the 1.20 price level translates into an unintended $100 billion drop in inventories. Unplanned investment is therefore –$100 billion.

Injections and Withdrawals

The tendency of an economy to move toward equilibrium can also be outlined by looking at the flows of income payments and consumption purchases that connect resource and product markets. There are three flows, known as **injections**, that add to the main income-spending stream: investment (I), government purchases (G), and exports (X).

positive unplanned investment: an unintended increase in inventories; a surplus

negative unplanned investment: an unintended decrease in inventories; a shortage

injections: additions to an economy's income-spending stream

withdrawals: deductions
from an economy's
income-spending stream

Corresponding to these injections are three outward flows of money, known as **withdrawals**. Withdrawals, which divert funds from the income-spending stream, are saving (S), taxes (T), and imports (M).

There is no need for these individual injections and withdrawals to be equal. Even those injections and withdrawals related to the same sector can have different values. To see why, we'll look at each related pair of injections and withdrawals in turn.

Investment and Saving

Recall that personal savings from households provide the bulk of funds in the loanable funds market. Most funds are borrowed by businesses for investment. However, the amount saved and the amount invested in an economy are not equal for three reasons. First, recall that companies keep a portion of their profits to reinvest. These retained earnings supplement personal savings in financing investment. Second, governments also borrow money. The more governments borrow, the less personal savings end up in the hands of businesses. Third, we must also consider the foreign flows we've already discussed. Because foreign lending usually exceeds foreign borrowing, foreign funds add to Canadian savings available for investment.

Government Purchases and Taxes

Recall that transfer payments and business subsidies are viewed as negative taxes. Government purchases usually exceed taxes. To make up for the discrepancy, governments borrow funds in financial markets. In the odd case that taxes exceed government purchases, governments can use their excess revenues to pay off some of their outstanding debt.

Exports and Imports

From 1989 to 1993, Canada's imports of both goods *and* services were greater than its exports. In other words, Canadians spent more on foreign products than they received in revenues from selling products to foreigners. At the same time, foreign lenders typically provide funds to Canadian financial markets, and foreign borrowers remove funds from these markets. Overall, foreign lending tends to be greater than foreign borrowing. So, the surplus of foreign lending makes up for the shortfall in net exports. We will explore this subject further in Chapter 16.

Total Injections and Withdrawals

While individual injections and withdrawals are not necessarily equal, there is an important connection between them that applies when an economy is at equilibrium. If the circular income-spending stream is thought of as a flow of water—a water-ride at an amusement park, for example—then it is easy to see what will happen if the amount of water flowing into this stream is more or less than the water flowing out. If inward flows exceed outward flows, the amount of water circulating in the stream must be increasing. Conversely, if inward flows are less than outward flows, the amount of water must be decreasing. Only if inward and outward flows are equal will the water-ride function well. Viewed in this way, comparing total injections and withdrawals provides a way of explaining macroeconomic equilibrium that complements the approach using aggregate demand and aggregate supply.

Total injections are the sum of investment, government purchases, and exports $(I + G + X)$. Total withdrawals are the sum of saving, taxes, and imports $(S + T + M)$. Just as only the planned portion of investment is included in real expenditures to find aggregate demand, only planned investment is included in total injections.

Total injections $(I + G + X)$ and total withdrawals $(S + T + M)$ may be equal or unequal, as Figure 12.10 demonstrates. In the case shown in the upper portion of Figure 12.10, where total injections exceed total withdrawals, flows into the income-spending stream are greater than flows out. Hence, the income-spending stream rises and speeds up. In other words, real output and spending in the economy expand.

The middle diagram shows the other extreme. If total withdrawals exceed total injections, flows into the income-spending stream are less than outflows. Hence, the income-spending stream falls and slows down. In other words, real output and spending in the economy contract.

Finally, in the case of equilibrium, as shown in the bottom portion of Figure 12.10, total injections equal total withdrawals. Because inward and outward flows match, the income-spending stream circulates at a steady rate, so that real output and spending in the economy stay constant.

Equilibrium Versus Potential Output

An economy's equilibrium point can occur at its potential output, as illustrated in Figure 12.11. If so, then unemployment at equilibrium equals the natural unemployment rate.

Recessionary Gaps

While the situation shown in Figure 12.11 is possible, an economy's real output rarely equals its potential output. If equilibrium output is below its potential level, unemployment is above the natural unemployment rate. In this case, the difference between equilibrium output and potential output is known as a **recessionary gap**. Figure 12.12 shows on the left an economy with a recessionary gap of $25 billion. This is the amount by which real output would have to increase from its equilibrium value of $700 billion in order to attain its potential level of $725 billion.

recessionary gap: the amount by which equilibrium output falls short of potential output

Figure 12.10: Equilibrium With Injections and Withdrawals

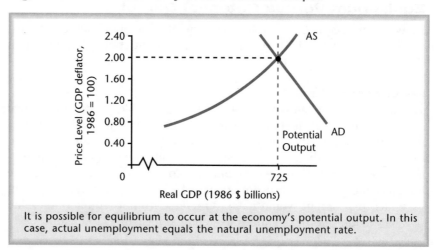

When injections are greater than withdrawals, as in the top diagram, real output and spending increase. When injections are less than withdrawals, as in the middle diagram, real output and spending decrease. When injections and withdrawals are equal, as in the bottom diagram, real output and spending stay the same.

Figure 12.11: An Economy at Its Potential Output

It is possible for equilibrium to occur at the economy's potential output. In this case, actual unemployment equals the natural unemployment rate.

Figure 12.12: Recessionary and Inflationary Gaps

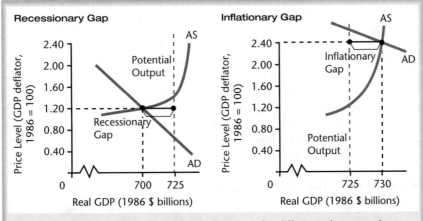

When real output falls short of potential output, the difference between the two is a recessionary gap, as shown on the left. In contrast, when real output temporarily exceeds its potential level, the difference between the two is an inflationary gap, as shown on the right.

Inflationary Gaps

If equilibrium output is above its potential output, unemployment is temporarily below the natural unemployment rate. Inflation will accelerate if this situation persists. When equilibrium output exceeds potential output, therefore, the discrepancy is called an **inflationary gap**. Figure 12.12 shows on the right an economy with an inflationary gap of $5 billion. In this case, the equilibrium output of $730 would have to fall by $5 billion to achieve the potential output of $725 billion.

inflationary gap: the amount by which equilibrium output exceeds potential output

BRIEF REVIEW

1. An economy's equilibrium price level and real output occur at the intersection of the aggregate demand and aggregate supply curves.

2. The economy moves toward equilibrium through the workings of positive and negative unplanned investment—in other words, surpluses and shortages.

3. When an economy is at equilibrium, total injections (I + G + X) equal total withdrawals (S + T + M). If total injections exceed total withdrawals, real output rises and the economy expands. If the reverse is true, real output falls and the economy contracts.

4. If equilibrium output is less than potential output, the difference between the two is a recessionary gap. When equilibrium output exceeds potential output, the discrepancy in the output levels is an inflationary gap.

Business Cycles

Recessionary and inflationary gaps do not happen at random. Instead, they occur in a sequence based on fluctuations in real output and expenditures. As a rule, a sustained rise in real output, known as a period of **expansion** or recovery, is followed by an extended period of falling real output, known as a **contraction**. These rises and falls in real output constitute a pattern known as the **business cycle**.

Figure 12.13 shows the business cycle in simplified form. The long-run trend of potential output to rise is shown by a dashed line. Actual output moves toward and away from this potential output in a cycle of successive contractions and expansions.

expansion: a sustained rise in real output of an economy

contraction: a sustained fall in real output of an economy

business cycle: the cycle of expansions and contractions in the economy

Figure 12.13:   The Business Cycle

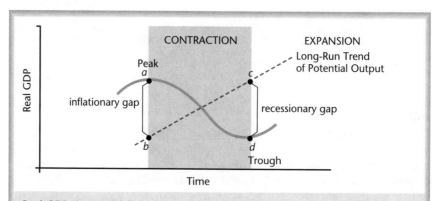

Real GDP rises and falls in a cycle of expansion and contraction. These fluctuations can be compared with a trend line that represents long-run growth potential. The distance between actual output and the trend line represents the size of either the economy's inflationary gap (as in the case of points *a* and *b*) or the economy's recessionary gap (as in the case of points *c* and *d*).

Actual Versus Potential Output

When actual output exceeds potential output, the resulting inflationary gap is the difference between real output (point *a*) and potential output (point *b*). Real output then falls below its potential level shown by the trend line. In this case, the recessionary gap is the amount by which real output falls short of its potential—in other words, the difference between potential output (point *c*) and real output (point *d*).

Contraction

peak: the point in the business cycle at which real output is at its highest

Consider the case of an economy that has reached its **peak**. At this point (point *a*), the economy is said to be experiencing a boom, which occurs when real GDP is at its highest value in the business cycle. The inflationary gap has reached its maximum width, unemployment is at its lowest possible level, and real output can grow no larger in the short run. From this point, the economy must contract.

Causes of a Contraction

Economic contractions originate with events that occur in the previous boom. Peak levels of spending and real output drive up the demand for production inputs, such as labour and raw materials. Higher demand pushes up the prices for these inputs. As a result, production costs for businesses increase. If we concentrate on changes in aggregate demand, higher production costs cause falling real rates of return for investment projects. Investment spending decreases, thereby shifting the aggregate demand curve to the left.

The Role of Expectations

The decrease in aggregate demand can be magnified by the reactions of both households and businesses to initial reductions in spending and output. To understand how this occurs, recall that spending by both households and businesses is influenced by expectations of the future. Households vary consumption expenditures depending on their anticipation of future prices and incomes, while businesses decide how much to invest based on estimates of future profit.

Expectations of the future are often made simply by extending current trends. Sometimes this can create a self-fulfilling prophecy. That is, if the economy is experiencing reductions in real output and spending, then many households and businesses assume that income and spending will drop further. As a result, there will likely be decreases in three types of spending: consumption, investment, and exports. The prospect of lower future incomes causes households to spend less, especially on durable items. Similarly, the decline in spending that businesses expect causes a drop in real rates of return for investment projects, leading to further declines in investment. The effect on exports occurs because periods of contraction usually arrive in various countries simultaneously. Therefore, it is probable that foreign consumers and businesses are reacting in the same way as their domestic counterparts, thus reducing exports. In other words, the expectations of businesses and households create a downward spiral in which declines in real output lead to further declines in spending and in output. Enough pessimism creates the very economic conditions people fear.

SOURCE: Alan King, The Ottawa Citizen

"Well, we tried to come up with a name that would really scare people"

Effects of a Contraction

Figure 12.14 shows the effects of a decrease in aggregate demand from AD_0 to AD_1. Equilibrium output declines from its initial value of $730 billion (point f)to a final value of $700 billion (point e). As a result, unemployment gradually rises above its natural unemployment rate, with the initial inflationary gap of $5 billion turning into a recessionary gap of $25 billion. At the same time, there is downward pressure on prices. If inflation is originally zero, as in Figure 12.14, then the price level falls from 2.40 to 1.60, causing deflation.

Figure 12.14:   Expansion and Contraction

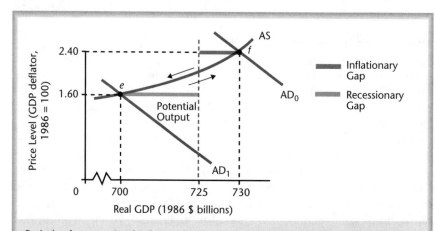

Periods of contraction lead to a decrease in aggregate demand, shifting the curve from AD_0 to AD_1. This leads to a fall in equilibrium output from $730 to $700 billion (points f to e). As a result, the initial inflationary gap of $5 billion turns into a recessionary gap of $25 billion. Periods of expansion reverse the change, causing the curve to shift from AD_1 to AD_0, and increasing equilibrium output (points e to f).

Recessions and Depressions

In general, the longer the period of declining real output, the more serious its effects. A decline in real output that lasts for six months or more is known as a **recession**. A **depression** occurs if the reduction in real output is particularly long and harsh, as happened during the early 1930s.

Expansion

The spiral of worsening expectations and declining real output does not last indefinitely. Sooner or later, the economy reaches a **trough** where real output is at its lowest possible value in the business cycle. In Figure 12.13, this occurs at point d. At this point, not only is the economy's recessionary gap at its widest, but unemployment is at its highest level. After this turning point, the dampening effect of expectations is counteracted by other factors, and the economy enters a phase of expansion.

recession: a decline in real output that lasts for six months or more

depression: a particularly long and harsh period of reduced real output

trough: the point in the business cycle at which real output is at its lowest

Thinking About Economics

Which sectors of the economy are most affected by a downturn?

While a recession or a depression is felt in every sector, those industries that make capital goods or durable consumer goods, such as automobiles and appliances, are hardest hit. This is because purchases of these products can be postponed until after the downturn has ended. In contrast, producers of nondurable consumption items—especially necessities such as food and utilities—are less affected by the downturn. Households can reduce their spending on nondurable products, but they cannot postpone these purchases.

Causes of an Expansion

The seeds of a recovery are planted in the latter stages of the previous period of contraction. The low levels of spending and production associated with a trough reduce the demand for production inputs, in particular the demand for labour and raw materials. As a result, prices for these resources are pushed down. With lower production costs, businesses' real rates of return for investment projects increase, raising investment. The aggregate demand curve therefore shifts to the right.

As in periods of contraction, expectations play a role in maintaining a recovery. Rising real output and spending lead to optimistic forecasts of continuing growth. Therefore, consumption, investment, and exports all increase. Consumers react to the prospect of higher incomes by spending more, especially on durable goods. At the same time, businesses increase their investment because optimism causes further rises in estimated real rates of return. Finally, in the case where other countries are experiencing similar trends, foreign buyers also increase their spending and buy more exports. Increased consumer spending, business investment, and exports lead to continual increases in aggregate demand, until a new peak is reached and the stage is set for another period of contraction.

Effects of an Expansion

Figure 12.14 also shows the effects of an expansion. In this case, the aggregate demand curve shifts to the right, from AD_1 to AD_0. Because of the rise in equilibrium output, the original recessionary gap is turned into an inflationary gap. Corresponding to this movement, the unemployment rate goes from above to below its natural rate, while the accompanying rise in the general price level causes inflation.

BRIEF REVIEW

1. Real output rarely equals potential output. Instead, output and expenditures generally follow a cycle of expansions and contractions, which together make up the business cycle.

2. The highest output occurs at a peak in the business cycle. From this point, the economy must contract, so aggregate demand decreases. Consumer and business expectations magnify the downward trend.

3. The lowest output occurs in a trough in a business cycle. From this point, the economy must expand, so aggregate demand increases. Again, expectations magnify the upward trend.

ADVANCING ECONOMIC THOUGHT

Economist Extraordinaire

John Maynard Keynes and the Transformation of Macroeconomics

Keynes and His Influence

The best blueprint for a model economist comes from the century's most illustrious one—John Maynard Keynes (1883–1946). An Englishman, he was a well-rounded and energetic individual who wrote on mathematics, formulated economic policy as an adviser to the British government and a director of its central bank, and served as a representative at international conferences, such as the Paris Peace Conference that ended World War I. On top of all of this, Keynes found time to be a college administrator, edit a major economics journal, produce theatre, chair an insurance company, and serve as an investment trust manager, while accumulating a considerable personal fortune through his own investments.[1]

Keynes came from a privileged background—his father was an economist and his mother was a city politician. After a time at the exclusive boarding school Eton, Keynes studied mathematics at Cambridge University, where he began a lifelong association with the Bloomsbury Group, an influential circle of English writers and artists with a shared taste for the unconventional and a reputation for snobbery.

In response to the Great Depression plaguing North America and Europe, Keynes published his book *The General Theory of Employment, Interest, and Money*. By 1936, when the book was published, millions of jobless people had given up hope of finding work, and capitalism seemed to many to be on the verge of self-destruction, just as Karl Marx had predicted decades earlier. There was a widespread call for government intervention to combat the Depression. Keynes, however, went one step further: he supported the call for government intervention with a coherent theo-

John Maynard Keynes

ry, which stressed the role played by aggregate demand in determining output in the macroeconomy.

Keynes and his followers were able to convince most politicians and economists that action was needed. The government programs they advocated were later viewed as crucial in hastening the end of the Depression. Keynesian ideas dominated macroeconomics from after World War II to the 1970s, when events brought about a new period of questioning and debate.

Neoclassical Theory

Prior to Keynes' influence, most economists held the opinion that economic slowdowns—even those as severe as the Great Depression—are self-correcting. This view of the economy, referred to as neoclassical theory, is based on two major assumptions: flexible labour markets and Say's Law.

Flexible Labour Markets   According to neoclassical economists, both the demand and supply of labour depend on the real wage rate, or wages expressed in constant base-year dollars, rather than the nominal wage rate, which is valued in current dollars. Neither workers nor employers are fooled by price changes; therefore, they adjust their behaviour only when the purchasing power of wages changes. Employers demand less labour at higher real wage rates, while workers choose to supply more. As Figure A illustrates, the labour market can be shown using the demand and supply curves D_L and S_L.

Neoclassical economists distinguished between two types of unemployment: voluntary and involuntary. Voluntary unemployment exists when-

Figure A: A Flexible Labour Market

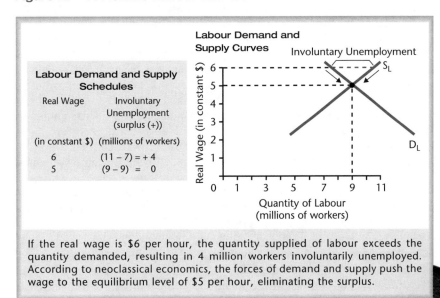

If the real wage is $6 per hour, the quantity supplied of labour exceeds the quantity demanded, resulting in 4 million workers involuntarily unemployed. According to neoclassical economics, the forces of demand and supply push the wage to the equilibrium level of $5 per hour, eliminating the surplus.

ever workers decide that real wages are not high enough to make work worthwhile. In contrast, involuntary unemployment—when someone wants to work at the current real wage rate but cannot find a job—is of much greater concern to policy-makers. According to neoclassical economics, involuntary unemployment occurs when market demand and supply create a surplus—for example, at a $6 real wage rate, as shown in Figure A. As long as labour markets are flexible, the market forces of demand and supply eradicate the surplus—for example, when market forces push wages toward an equilibrium point of $5. Because markets are flexible, involuntary unemployment is no more than a short-run problem.

Say's Law Neoclassical economists also assumed that periods of underspending in the economy are short-lived. Their view was based on a principle known as Say's Law, first outlined by the French economist Jean-Baptiste Say. Using the circular flow of money in the economy, Say argued that supply automatically creates its own demand. That is, we produce goods and services in order to purchase others. A tailor makes clothes, for example, in order to have funds to buy other products. Therefore, the production of goods and services generates enough funds to purchase them.

Keynesian Theory

Keynes challenged both of the assumptions of neoclassical economics. Having done so, he provided a theory that explained how involuntary unemployment and underspending had become chronic problems during the Depression.

Challenge to Flexible Labour Markets Keynes believed, unlike the neoclassical economists, that workers were influenced by *money illusion*. By this, he meant that workers would respond to changes in nominal wages, rather than real wages and purchasing power.

Consider a case in which prices fall, as they did during the Great Depression. If the price level drops by 10 percent, workers should not mind if their nominal wages are cut by 10 percent as well, because real wages and purchasing power are not affected. However workers *do* mind, according to Keynes. Workers see a decrease in nominal income as a drop in living standards, and trade unions tend to reject nominal wage cuts. Therefore, the nominal wage rate does not move despite downward pressure.

Figure B illustrates Keynes' view of labour markets. The quantity demanded and supplied of labour both vary with the nominal wage rate. Because the nominal wage will not decrease despite market pressure, the involuntary unemployment caused by a nominal wage such as $8 can last indefinitely. Only if there is an increase in spending, shifting demand to the right, will this unemployment be reduced.

Challenge to Say's Law Keynes proved that while Say's Law seems to be common sense, it is valid only if all income in an economy is spent. According to Say's Law, reduced spending is only temporary; total expendi-

Figure B: An Inflexible Labour Market

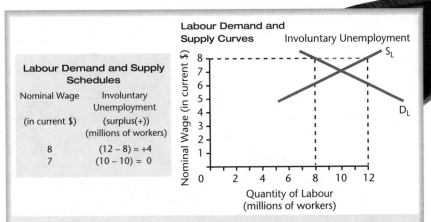

Labour Demand and Supply Schedules	
Nominal Wage	Involuntary Unemployment
(in current $)	(surplus(+)) (millions of workers)
8	(12 – 8) = +4
7	(10 – 10) = 0

At a nominal wage of $8 per hour, 4 million workers are involuntarily unemployed. According to Keynesian economics, because these nominal wages will not respond to downward pressure, the market does not move toward the equilibrium wage of $7 per hour. Instead, involuntary unemployment persists.

tures and production soon balance each other out. Neoclassical economists believed that this occurs since total withdrawals and injections can be equal *at any output*. According to their view, interest rates charged in financial markets will vary until withdrawals leaving the circular flow are matched by injections.

Despite its superficial appeal, this argument is flawed. Output levels—not interest rates—adjust to bring about a balance between total injections and withdrawals. When injections are less than withdrawals, output falls until a new equilibrium level is reached. It is only *at this equilibrium output* that Say's Law is true, with injections and withdrawals the same. Also, this output is quite possibly associated with high unemployment. Hence, Keynes concluded that underspending is not necessarily self-correcting. So governments must step in to create the needed jobs.

NOTE
[1]D.E. Moggridge, *Keynes* (London: Macmillan, 1976), p. 12.

1. Explain the importance of flexible labour markets to the neoclassical interpretation of involuntary unemployment.
2. Describe economic situations in which the neoclassical assumptions would prove to be invalid.
3. Using labour demand and supply curves, demonstrate on a graph how Keynes believed the problem of involuntary unemployment could be solved.
4. Find evidence in current news that supports or refutes Keynes' arguments concerning money illusion and the labour market.

SIDELINE

Crystal Ball Economics

Forecasting the Future

Attempting to predict the future is a popular, though often futile, pastime. Accurate forecasts of economic conditions benefit households, businesses, and governments. A home-buyer who can correctly predict changes in interest rates, for example, can decide on the best time to take out a mortgage. Similarly, if business managers can successfully predict the future spending on the items their companies sell, they are able to make more cost-effective decisions. Finally, government officials can use predictions of the business cycle to plan economic policy.

Statistical Models

One way to predict economic conditions is with statistical models. These models are composed of equations that summarize macroeconomic behaviour in numerical terms. For example, one equation is an estimate of aggregate demand. The slope and position of the aggregate demand curve are approximations based on past economic behaviour. Possible values of the variables in the equation can then be "plugged in" to forecast movements of the curve.

There are several well-known models of the Canadian economy, including one formulated by the Bank of Canada known as RDX2. These models require large amounts of data and use sophisticated statistical techniques. However, the models are not always reliable indicators of the future. The complexity of an economy can only be approximated by a model, especially when the model is based on past economic relationships.

Composite Index   One forecasting tool that is used to predict turning points in the business cycle is the Statistics Canada composite index.[1] This index is calculated monthly, and is a weighted average of 10 *leading indicators*. Whereas leading indicators show movement that precedes changes in the GDP, *lagging indicators* show movement that follows changes in the GDP. The stock market is one example of a leading indicator, since share prices reflect expectations of the future. In contrast, the unemployment rate lags behind the GDP, because there is usually a delay between changes in business revenues and new hiring or layoffs.

Five indicators that are included in the composite index—furniture and appliance sales, retail sales of other durable goods (such as automobiles), new orders for durable goods, a shipment-to-inventory ratio of finished goods, and a house-spending index—highlight consumer demand for durable goods as well as factors that affect investment. Changes in any of these indicators point to corresponding future changes in the GDP.

Future GDP movements are also directly related to current employment trends. This link is captured by two other indicators that are part of the composite index: employment in business and personal services, and the average work week in the manufacturing sector.

Because Canadian exports form part of the GDP and are dependent on the health of foreign economies, one key foreign economy is reflected in the composite index. The most recent value of the American composite index is included in the Canadian composite index.

The final ingredients of the composite index, which represent financial and money markets, are the Toronto Stock Exchange 300 share price index (known as the TSE 300) and a measure of money supply called M1. While movements in share prices reflect expected changes in corporate profits, alterations in the money supply are directly tied to future spending plans. Changes in either measure point to similar future changes in the GDP.

Generally, the composite index must move in the same direction for three consecutive months before it is said to forecast changes in the GDP. In the past, the composite index has often successfully forecasted turning points in the business cycle. However, use of the index is complicated by the length of time it takes to collect values for all of its 10 components. Also, the index can give false predictions. The following example illustrates both successes and failures. The index successfully predicted the start of the recession, since it began falling four months before the sustained drop in GDP in 1990. However, the index failed to give adequate warning of the rise and fall that occurred in 1991.

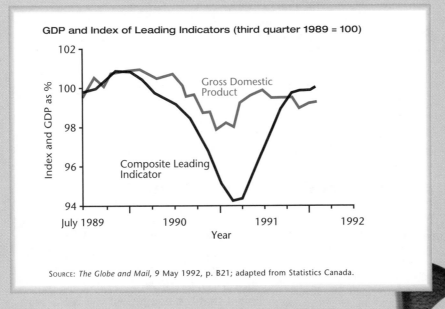

GDP and Index of Leading Indicators (third quarter 1989 = 100)

SOURCE: *The Globe and Mail*, 9 May 1992, p. B21; adapted from Statistics Canada.

NOTE

[1]Bruce Little, "Leading indicators lag sometimes," in *The Globe and Mail*, 9 May 1992, p. B21.

Key Concepts

aggregate demand
real expenditures
aggregate demand schedule
aggregate demand curve
wealth effect
foreign trade effect
aggregate demand factors
increase in aggregate demand
decrease in aggregate demand
real rate of return
investment demand
investment demand schedule
investment demand curve
exchange rate
aggregate supply
aggregate supply schedule
aggregate supply curve
aggregate supply factors

short-run increase in aggregate supply
short-run decrease in aggregate supply
long-run increase in aggregate supply
long-run decrease in aggregate supply
positive unplanned investment
negative unplanned investment
injections
withdrawals
recessionary gap
inflationary gap
expansion
contraction
business cycle
peak
recession
depression
trough

Developing Application and Analysis Skills

1. Explain the effect of each of the following situations on aggregate demand. Sketch aggregate demand curves to illustrate each effect.

a) The government purchases $1 billion worth of computer hardware from a Canadian company.

b) Investors in Canadian mutual funds are wiped out by a stock market crash.

c) A sudden increase in corporate profits is announced by a majority of Canadian corporations.

d) A serious recession results in widespread layoffs and cutbacks for most businesses.

e) A new technology lowers prices for appliances.

f) Prior to an election, the government decreases income tax rates.

g) Interest rates drop 2 percent for consumer and business loans.

2. Atomic Automobile Corporation is exploring the feasibility of spending $5 million to install robots in its assembly plant, which produces the Neutron, the world's first nuclear-powered car. Analysts have determined that the equipment will last at least one year before it needs to be replaced, and that it will add $5.5 million in constant dollars to the business's net revenue.

a) For the economy that Atomic Automobile Corporation is a part of, sketch an aggregate demand curve prior to the company making any investment. Indicate on your graph the change that the investment would make to aggregate demand.

b) If the prevailing interest rate is 9 percent, should the company make this investment? Explain your answer.

3. Explain the impact of each of the following situations on aggregate supply. Sketch aggregate supply curves to illustrate each case, and show the effect on potential output.

   a) Labour productivity rises due to technological innovation in the car industry.
   b) Supplies of natural gas increase when a new gas deposit is discovered.
   c) Wages for unskilled labour rise because of new minimum wage legislation.
   d) Corporate taxes fall.

4. Why do prices tend to rise as an economy's output reaches its potential? Explain in writing and use a graph to demonstrate your answer.

5. Using the aggregate demand and aggregate supply schedules (above right), draw a graph to show the aggregate demand (AD_0) and aggregate supply (AS_0) curves for a hypothetical economy. From your graph, determine the following:

   a) for AD_0 and AS_0, the equilibrium price and output level for the economy
   b) the equilibrium price and output level for the economy if aggregate supply remains constant (at AS_0), but an increase in investment spending changes aggregate demand to AD_1
   c) the equilibrium price and output level for the economy if aggregate demand remains constant (at AD_0), but an increase in the supply of labour resources changes aggregate supply to AS_1

Aggregate Demand and Aggregate Supply Schedules for Hypothetical Land				
Price Level	**Real GDP**			
	AD_0	AD_1	AS_0	AS_1
(real \$)	**(\$ billions)**			
30	5 ⟶ 9		12 ⟶ 16	
25	7 ⟶ 11		11 ⟶ 15	
20	9 ⟶ 13		9 ⟶ 13	
15	11 ⟶ 15		7 ⟶ 11	
10	13 ⟶ 17		3 ⟶ 7	

6. Study the following graph, and then comment on the relationship among the components of spending. Suggest reasons for this relationship.

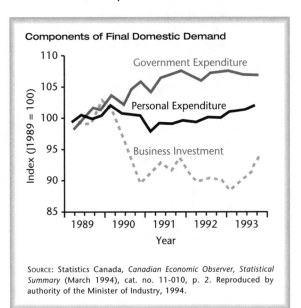

Components of Final Domestic Demand

SOURCE: Statistics Canada, *Canadian Economic Observer, Statistical Summary* (March 1994), cat. no. 11-010, p. 2. Reproduced by authority of the Minister of Industry, 1994.

7. a) Study the table opposite. Identify the following and give support for your answer:

- years in which the economy expanded
- years in which the economy contracted
- peaks
- troughs

b) Comment on the relationship between real investment and real GDP. Suggest possible reasons for this relationship.

8. At what stages in the business cycle can we reasonably expect to see planned investment, positive unplanned investment, and negative unplanned investment? Explain your answers.

9. a) With reference to the factors that affect aggregate demand and aggregate supply, describe the possible ways a recessionary gap can be eliminated.

b) Do the same for an inflationary gap.

c) Demonstrate each change on a graph.

10. For each stage in the business cycle, explain what would happen to the following economic variables:

a) unemployment
b) the CPI
c) consumer confidence
d) labour disputes and strikes
e) government expenditures and revenues
f) interest rates
g) stock prices
h) household savings
i) utilization of factories

Year	Annual Percentage Change in Real Investment ($ 1986)	Annual Percentage Change in Real GDP ($ 1986)
1980	9.9%	1.5%
1981	11.2	3.7
1982	–10.6	–3.2
1983	0.9	3.2
1984	2.2	6.3
1985	9.4	4.8
1986	6.2	3.3
1987	10.8	4.2
1988	10.4	5.0
1989	6.0	2.4
1990	–3.4	–0.2
1991	–2.1	–1.7
1992	–1.3	0.7
1993	0.7	2.4

SOURCES: Adapted from Statistics Canada, *Canadian Economic Observer, Statistical Summary* (April 1994), cat. no. 11-010, p. 4; *Canadian Economic Observer, Historical Statistical Supplement, 1992/93* (July 1993), cat. no. 11-210, vol. 7, p. 7. Reproduced by authority of the Minister of Industry, 1994.

11. Suppose you were about to invest in stocks. In terms of your investment plans, how would you respond to each stage in the business cycle? Explain your answer.

12. According to an argument known as the paradox of thrift, an economy that attempts to save more may sometimes save less because of the links between saving, consumption, aggregate demand, real output, employment, and incomes.

   a) Study the causal loop diagram opposite, and explain the causes and effects.
   b) Identify the stage in the business cycle where the paradox of thrift is a factor.
   c) List and explain the factors that are responsible for the final decrease in saving.
   d) Create a causal loop diagram that demonstrates the factors involved in economic expansion.

13. Research and outline the possible implications of a current economic policy for consumer and business confidence.

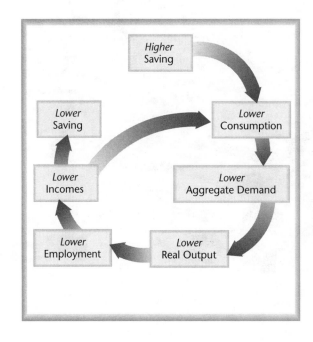

CHAPTER 13

Fiscal Policy

Democracy will defeat the economist
at every turn at its own game.
—HAROLD INNIS, CANADIAN ECONOMIST
AND HISTORIAN

Should governments sit idly through the upheavals caused by the
business cycle? Certainly not, according to John Maynard Keynes,
the founder of modern macroeconomics. Governments can do plenty to
stabilize the economy—not only during downturns when unemployment
is high, but also during inflationary upswings. Governments can use certain policies to achieve economic stability; for example, they can spend
more money or reduce taxes to cause changes in total spending and
aggregate demand. This chapter examines the theory behind such policies
and their outcomes.

CHAPTER FOCUS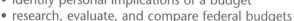

This chapter focuses on the following:
- expansionary and contractionary fiscal policies, which are used by governments seeking economic stability
- the effects of automatic stabilizers
- the multiplier effect of fiscal policy, as determined by the marginal propensities to consume and withdraw
- the benefits and drawbacks of fiscal policy, and principles that may guide such policy
- budget surpluses and deficits, and their impact on public debt and public debt charges

SKILLS FOCUS

After studying this chapter, you will be able to:
- distinguish between expansionary and contractionary fiscal policies, and outline both their possible outcomes and their tradeoffs
- examine the implications of a budget reduction process
- calculate, graph, and explain the multiplier effect in various economic situations
- note the relationships among fiscal policy, public debt, and aggregate demand, and assess the opportunity cost of public debt charges
- identify personal implications of a budget
- research, evaluate, and compare federal budgets

Fiscal Policy

The Goal of Stabilization

stabilization policy:
government policy designed to lessen the effects of the business cycle

In order to lessen the effects of downs and ups in the business cycle—particularly unemployment and inflation—governments use stabilization policies. A **stabilization policy** attempts to influence the amounts spent and produced in an economy. The goal of such a policy is to keep the economy as close as possible to its potential output. At this point, only natural unemployment exists and the price level is constant.

Stabililization policies fall into two categories, depending on the state of the economy and the effect on the economy the policy is meant to have. When total output is below its potential, policy-makers want to eliminate the recessionary gap—in other words, reduce unemployment and stimulate total output. Policies with these goals are called **expansionary policies**.

expansionary policies:
government policies designed to reduce unemployment and stimulate output

In contrast, if the economy is booming, policy-makers want to cut the inflationary gap—in other words, stabilize prices and bring the economy back to its potential output. Policies with these goals are called **contractionary policies**.

contractionary policies:
government policies designed to stabilize prices and reduce output

Stabilizing the Business Cycle

Assuming that it can be applied quickly and effectively, stabilization policy may be used to smooth out the business cycle. Figure 13.1 shows how stabilization policy can reduce the severity of economic troughs and peaks, and the recessionary and inflationary gaps associated with them. The closer the economy stays to the long-run trend of potential output, the lower will be the social costs of unemployment and inflation to the country's citizens.

Figure 13.1:   Stabilization Policy and the Business Cycle

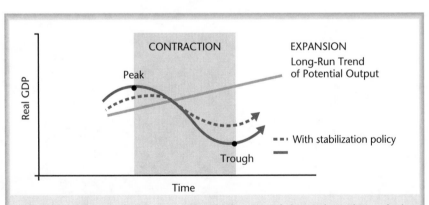

Effective stabilization policy minimizes the severity of the peaks and troughs in the business cycle. Differences between actual output and the long-run trend of potential output are therefore smaller, thus reducing recessionary and inflationary gaps.

In general, governments can affect spending and output levels in an economy through two sets of instruments. First, recall that governments have an extensive impact on the economy through, for example, taxation and government purchases. Because a government's annual budget sets out what the government will tax and spend, the budget becomes an instrument of stabilization policy. Such a policy is called **fiscal policy**, "fiscal" meaning "budgetary." The twelve-month period to which the budget applies is called the **fiscal year**. Governments can also exert their influence on interest rates and the economy's money supply. A policy that uses these tools is called **monetary policy**. We'll focus on fiscal policy in this chapter, and turn our attention to monetary policy in the next chapter.

Use of Fiscal Policy

Governments apply fiscal policy during any part of the business cycle. So, during a recession or depression, government action is geared toward increasing spending and output in the economy. Such **expansionary fiscal policy** involves increasing government purchases, decreasing taxes, or both. In contrast, during an inflationary boom, government policy-makers concentrate on restraining output and spending. Such **contractionary fiscal policy** involves decreasing government spending, increasing taxes, or both.

Injections and Withdrawals

One way to see how fiscal policy works is to look at injections and withdrawals. Recall from Chapter 12 that investment, government purchases, and exports make up injections to the income-spending stream; saving, taxes, and imports are withdrawals from the stream.

With expansionary fiscal policy, governments increase their purchases and so raise injections to the circular flow. As a result, injections increase relative to withdrawals, and the total flow increases. Reducing taxes has the same effect. By withdrawing less from the income-spending stream, withdrawals decrease relative to injections, and the total flow increases. As the total flow increases, equilibrium output is pushed up.

Contractionary fiscal policies have the opposite effect. Governments that reduce their purchases reduce injections to the circular flow. As a result, injections decrease relative to withdrawals, and the total flow decreases. Increasing taxes has the same effect; withdrawals increase relative to injections, and the total flow decreases. As the total flow decreases, equilibrium output is pushed down.

Aggregate Demand

Another way to look at fiscal policy is through its effects on aggregate demand and aggregate supply. In order to increase aggregate demand so that the economy expands to its potential, policy-makers increase government purchases, cut taxes, or both. Increasing government spending

fiscal policy: government stabilization policy that uses taxes and government purchases as its tools; budgetary policy

fiscal year: the twelve-month period to which a budget applies

monetary policy: government stabilization policy that uses interest rates and the money supply as its tools

expansionary fiscal policy: government policy that involves increasing government purchases, decreasing taxes, or both to stimulate spending and output

contractionary fiscal policy: government policy that involves decreasing government purchases, increasing taxes, or both to restrain spending and output

has an immediate effect on aggregate demand since government purchases are a component of real expenditures. As Figure 13.2 demonstrates, the equilibrium price level and output are pushed up as a result.

Figure 13.2:   Expansionary Fiscal Policy

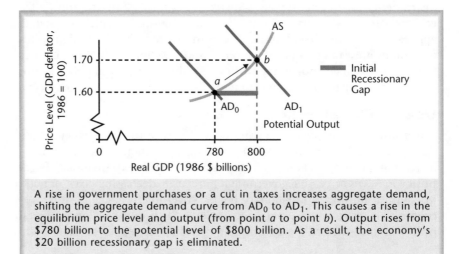

A rise in government purchases or a cut in taxes increases aggregate demand,
shifting the aggregate demand curve from AD_0 to AD_1. This causes a rise in the
equilibrium price level and output (from point *a* to point *b*). Output rises from
$780 billion to the potential level of $800 billion. As a result, the economy's
$20 billion recessionary gap is eliminated.

The effect of tax cuts is less immediate. Cutting taxes enables households and businesses to spend more, so both consumption and investment increase, thereby shifting the aggregate demand curve to the right.
Again, Figure 13.2 illustrates the results.

If a government has a contractionary fiscal policy—in other words, if it
wants to decrease aggregate demand so that the economy contracts to its
potential—policy-makers will decrease government purchases, increase
taxes, or both. As with expansionary fiscal policy, the effect of decreasing
government purchases is immediate, while the effect of increasing taxes
is less so. Figure 13.3 illustrates both cases. Decreased government purchases reduce aggregate demand, thereby shifting the aggregate demand
curve to the left. Increased taxes reduce households' disposable income
and businesses' profits. Consumption and investment both decline, thereby reducing aggregate demand and shifting the aggregate demand curve
to the left.

discretionary policy:

intentional government
intervention in the economy, such as budgeted
changes in spending
or taxation

Automatic Stabilizers

As we've seen, fiscal policy involves adjusting government purchases or
taxes. These actions are intentional; laws must be passed and budgets
brought down. Because it is up to a government's discretion to take these
actions, fiscal policy is known as **discretionary policy**. In contrast, some

Figure 13.3:   Contractionary Fiscal Policy

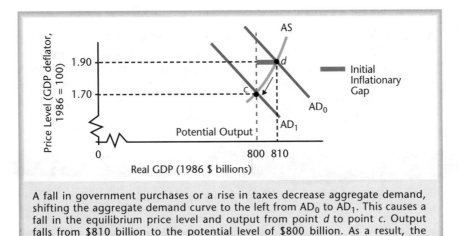

A fall in government purchases or a rise in taxes decrease aggregate demand, shifting the aggregate demand curve to the left from AD_0 to AD_1. This causes a fall in the equilibrium price level and output from point *d* to point *c*. Output falls from $810 billion to the potential level of $800 billion. As a result, the economy's $10 billion inflationary gap is eliminated.

stabilizing forces are automatic—that is, they do not involve the direct involvement of government decision-makers.

Recall from Chapter 9 the taxation and transfer payment programs such as progressive income taxes, Unemployment Insurance, and welfare payments. These established programs act as **automatic stabilizers** in the business cycle. In a period of contraction, **net tax revenues** (taxes minus transfers and subsidies) decrease; during a period of expansion, net tax revenues increase. As a result, spending and aggregate demand are stimulated in a downturn and suppressed in an upswing, thereby helping to smooth out the business cycle.

To see how automatic stabilizers work, let's first consider an economy that is contracting. Because household incomes and business profits fall, the taxes that a government can collect from households and businesses also fall. As jobs are lost and businesses suffer, government transfer payments and subsidies are increased. Both trends cause a decline in net tax revenues. Because incomes are bolstered by one program and taxes are reduced by the other, spending increases over what it would have been, helping to push the economy toward its potential output.

When the economy expands, the opposite happens. Personal incomes and business profits increase. As a result, governments collect more in taxes. Because the nation is more prosperous and employment is high, transfer payments and subsidies are reduced. Both trends cause a rise in net tax revenues. Because taxes are increased, spending and aggregate demand decrease, helping to push the economy back down to its potential output.

automatic stabilizers: built-in measures, such as taxation and transfer payment programs, that lessen the effects of the business cycle

net tax revenues: taxes collected, minus transfers and subsidies

Thinking About Economics

How significant are automatic stabilizers in the Canadian economy?

As discussed in Chapter 9, the expanding role of Canadian governments since World War II has led to a substantial increase in rates of taxation as well as rising expenditures on transfer payments. Higher tax rates and more generous transfer payments have both served as important automatic stabilizers in the Canadian economy during recent decades—a point that is stressed by economists who support greater government involvement in the economy.

BRIEF REVIEW

1. Governments use stabilization policies to minimize ups and downs in the business cycle. Such policies are categorized as expansionary or contractionary policies depending on the state of the economy and the effect of the policy on the economy.

2. Fiscal policy affects spending and output through taxes and government purchases. Monetary policy affects spending and output through interest rates and the economy's money supply.

3. Expansionary fiscal policy involves increasing government purchases,

decreasing taxes, or both. Such a policy increases aggregate demand and pushes up the equilibrium price level and output.

4. Contractionary fiscal policy involves decreasing government purchases, increasing taxes, or both. Such a policy decreases aggregate demand and pushes down the equilibrium price level and output.

5. In contrast to discretionary policies, automatic stabilizers are built-in factors that affect aggregate demand and minimize the impact of inflationary and recessionary gaps.

 ## The Spending Multiplier

Government decision-makers must have some way of estimating, in terms of dollar values, the impact that their policies will have on the economy. In general, a certain dollar change in government purchases or taxation does not cause the same dollar change in total real output. Like a pebble dropped in a pond causes ripples, fiscal policy has a multiplier effect.

The Multiplier Effect

The **multiplier effect** is the magnified impact of any spending change on aggregate demand. It assumes that the price level stays constant. So, the multiplier effect is the change in spending at one price level, multiplied by a certain value to give the resulting change in aggregate demand.

Let's consider an example. Suppose the government institutes an expansionary fiscal policy. As part of this policy the government pays Spender A, a trade consultant, $1000 for her services. The economy's output rises by $1000, and the consultant's revenues rise by $1000. (We'll assume for this example that the consultant incurs only negligible costs.) This consultant spends half of the amount she earns on a Canadian product and uses the rest for saving, imports, and taxes. In other words, she pays $500 to the supplier of a Canadian product, Spender B, thereby increasing Spender B's income (assuming that B also has negligible costs). The economy's total output has been expanded again by $500, with the remaining $500 withdrawn from the income-spending stream by Spender A in the form of saving, imports, and taxes. Spender B, with his $500 in new income, spends $250 on Canadian products and uses the other $250 on saving, imports, and taxes. His $250 purchase also has an impact on the Canadian economy and provides income to someone else. And on it goes. Any given purchase made by the government has an initial effect, a secondary effect, and so on.

As the example illustrates, the inclination to spend and the inclination to save or otherwise withdraw funds from the economy both determine the multiplier effect. These factors are summarized by the concepts of marginal propensity to consume and marginal propensity to withdraw.

Marginal Propensity to Consume

Marginal propensity to consume (MPC) is the effect on domestic consumption of a change in income, and applies to individual households and the economy as a whole. In effect, MPC answers the question: "If income increases this amount, how much extra will be spent on domestic goods and services?" MPC is defined as the change in consumption on domestic products as a proportion of the change in income.

$$\text{MPC} = \frac{\text{change in consumption on domestic items}}{\text{change in income}}$$

Marginal Propensity to Withdraw

As the earlier example illustrated, not all income is spent, and what is may not be spent on domestic products. As a result, some income does not reappear in the circular flow. Recall from Chapter 12 that there are three types of withdrawals: saving, taxes, and imports. Part of income is saved, part is paid out in taxes, and part is used to buy imports. The

multiplier effect: the magnified impact of a spending change on aggregate demand

marginal propensity to consume: the effect on domestic consumption of a change in income

marginal propensity to withdraw: the effect on withdrawals—saving, imports, and taxes—of a change in income

marginal propensity to withdraw (MPW) is the effect on withdrawals of a change in income. It is defined as the change in total withdrawals as a proportion of the change in income.

$$\text{MPW} = \frac{\text{change in total withdrawals}}{\text{change in income}}$$

Let's consider the concepts of MPC and MPW together. Suppose a person's income rises by $1000. Of that, the consumer spends $300 on domestic products but saves the rest. In this case, the marginal propensity to consume is 0.3 ($300 ÷ $1000), while the marginal propensity to withdraw is 0.7 ($700 ÷ $1000). Note the relationship between the values of the marginal propensities to consume and withdraw: their sum equals 1.0. This is always the case because income is either spent on domestic consumption or withdrawn from the circular flow as saving, imports, or taxes.

$$1.0 = \text{MPC} + \text{MPW}$$
$$1.0 = 0.3 + 0.7$$

To see in detail how the multiplier effect works, let's consider our example of the trade consultant again. The marginal propensities to consume and withdraw in each round, or stage, of spending help to determine the multiplier effect. Figure 13.4 illustrates the example.

Figure 13.4:   The Effect of a Rise in Government Purchases

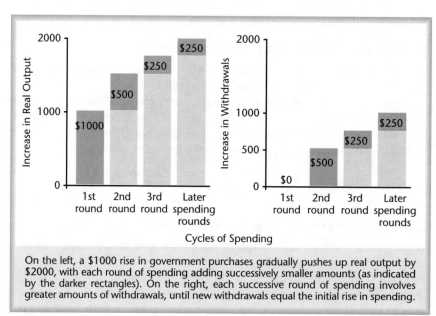

On the left, a $1000 rise in government purchases gradually pushes up real output by $2000, with each round of spending adding successively smaller amounts (as indicated by the darker rectangles). On the right, each successive round of spending involves greater amounts of withdrawals, until new withdrawals equal the initial rise in spending.

First Round

Recall that the government pays Spender A, a trade consultant, $1000. Not only does her income rise, but the economy's output also rises by $1000. The effect is illustrated on the left in Figure 13.4.

Second Round

Spender A starts the second round of spending by using the extra $1000 in income. Because her marginal propensity to consume is 0.5 ($500 ÷ $1000) and her marginal propensity to withdraw is also 0.5 ($500 ÷ $1000), she puts an extra $500 into the circular flow, but withdraws $500 in the form of saving, imports, and taxes. As a result, the economy's real output undergoes a further rise of $500.

Third Round

Recall that Spender B spends $250 of his $500 in income on domestic products, and an equal amount on saving, imports, and taxes. Therefore, Spender B's marginal propensity to consume is 0.5 ($250 ÷ $500), and his marginal propensity to withdraw is also 0.5 ($250 ÷ $500). Figure 13.4 shows that he adds another $250 to the economy's real output.

Later Spending Rounds

The same process of spending providing income, which is then spent domestically or withdrawn, repeats, with expenditures and withdrawals getting smaller in each round. For example, if the spender in the fourth round also has a marginal propensity to consume of 0.5, another $125 ($250 × 0.5) will be added to the economy's real output. This process finally ends when real output has risen by a total of $2000.

Injections and Withdrawals

To see why total output grows by $2000, let's turn our attention to the withdrawals that have occurred with each spending round, shown on the right in Figure 13.4. Notice that with each subsequent round of spending, there are new withdrawals. Eventually, total withdrawals equal $1000. This result can be interpreted in terms of injections and withdrawals, or leakages.

Before the expansionary fiscal policy, the economy was in equilibrium, with injections and withdrawals equal. As a result of the government's discretionary policy—that is, its $1000 planned increase in government purchases—total injections exceed total withdrawals, causing output to increase. In each round of spending, withdrawals increase. This expansion continues until withdrawals equal the initial discretionary injection. At this point, injections and withdrawals are both $1000 higher than they were before government purchases were increased.

spending multiplier:
the value by which an initial spending change is multiplied to give the total change in real output

The Spending Multiplier

Now that we've seen the multiplier effect in action, we'll give it a numerical value. The **spending multiplier** is the value by which the initial spending change is multiplied to give the total change in output—in other words, the shift in the aggregate demand curve.

$$\text{Total change in output} = \text{initial change} \times \text{spending}$$
$$\text{(shift in AD curve)} \qquad \text{in spending} \qquad \text{multiplier}$$

In our example, because initial spending rose by $1000 and total output increased by $2000, the spending multiplier equals 2. This figure can be found by rearranging the above equation to isolate the multiplier:

$$\text{Spending multiplier} = \frac{\text{total change in output (shift in AD curve)}}{\text{initial change in spending}}$$

$$2 = \frac{\$2000}{\$1000}$$

If total output increased instead by $3000 as a result of a $1000 increase in government purchases, then the multiplier would be 3 ($3000 ÷ $1000).

To see what determines the value of the spending multiplier, recall that the economy's total output expands until new withdrawals equal the initial government purchase—the new injection. In our original example, the marginal propensity to withdraw was 0.5, meaning that 50 cents were withdrawn for every $1 of new output in the economy. Output therefore had to expand by $2000 to create the needed $1000 in new withdrawals, giving a spending multiplier of 2. If the marginal propensity to withdraw had been 0.33, then 33 cents would have been withdrawn for each dollar of new output. Hence, output would have had to increase by $3000 to create $1000 in extra withdrawals, giving a spending multiplier equal to 3.

These examples point to the inverse relationship between the marginal propensity to withdraw and the spending multiplier. If MPW is 0.5, the multiplier equals 2. If MPW is 0.33, the multiplier is 3. Therefore, the spending multiplier is the reciprocal of the marginal propensity to withdraw.

$$\text{Spending multiplier} = \frac{1.0}{\text{MPW}}$$

$$2.0 = \frac{1.0}{0.5}$$

Effect of a Tax Cut

The multiplier effect can be applied to the other stimulus that governments use: tax cuts. Recall that tax cuts can also be applied to expand the economy. Lower taxes leave households and businesses with more funds to spend and invest. In this case, the initial spending stimulus of the tax cut is multiplied by the spending multiplier, or the reciprocal of MPW.

The result is an increase in total output, shown as a shift in the aggregate demand curve.

In contrast to government purchases, a tax adjustment has a smaller initial effect on spending. Recall our example of a $1000 government purchase from Spender A. Spender A's initial transaction with the government was added directly to real output before taking into account further rounds of spending. If a tax cut reduces Spender A's taxable income by $1000, however, some of this amount would be withdrawn from the circular flow before its first effect on real output. Only that amount used to buy domestic products represents the initial spending increase. For example, if the marginal propensity to consume is 0.5, then the initial change in spending on domestic items is $500 ($1000 × 0.5). This $500 spending increase is then multiplied by the spending multiplier, or 2 (1.0 ÷ 0.5). As a result, the aggregate demand increases by $1000 ($500 × 2), which is less than the $2000 increase caused by an initial $1000 government purchase.

Relevance of the Spending Multiplier

Recall that throughout our discussion of the multiplier effect, we've assumed that the price level is constant. However, what happens to the spending multiplier if price levels vary?

As shown in Figure 13.5, fiscal policy affects the price level as well as output. Recall from Chapter 12, however, that the slope of the aggregate supply curve is steeper as it reaches or surpasses the potential output level. So, as shown in Figure 13.5, when the aggregate demand curve

Figure 13.5: The Multiplier Effect and Price Changes

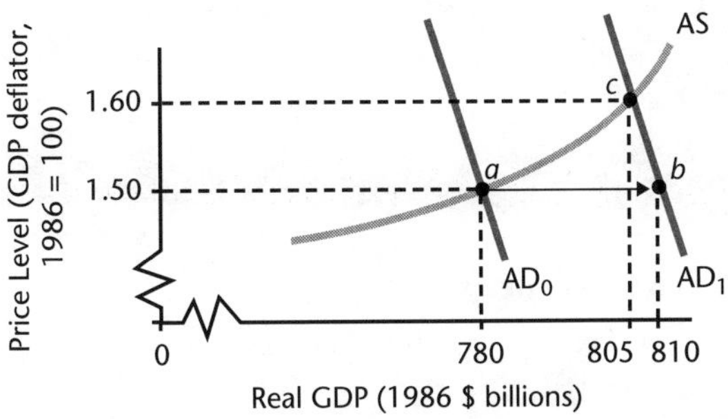

If spending affected output alone, with a spending multiplier of 1.5, a $20 billion rise in government purchases would push the output from $780 billion (point *a*) to $810 billion (point *b*). However, since price level is also affected, the shift from AD_0 to AD_1 causes equilibrium to move to point *c*, with an output of $805 billion and a price level of 1.60. Because of the slope of the AS curve, the closer an economy is to its potential, the greater a change in aggregate demand will have on price level instead of output.

shifts to the right from AD_0 to AD_1, it moves to a steeper portion of the aggregate supply curve. In this case, the change in the equilibrium point, from point *a* to point *c*, means that while both price levels and output rise, the price level rises proportionally more than does output. So, in general, when the economy is close to its potential level, the increase in aggregate demand translates into higher price levels more than into expanded production. In other words, with the stated goal being a stable economy and expanded output, expansionary fiscal policy is less effective the closer the economy is to its potential. Similar reasoning applies to contractionary fiscal policy. When the economy is above its potential, a decrease in aggregate demand means that both price level and total output fall. However, price level falls proportionally more than total output does.

In summary, because of possible changes in the price level, the multiplier effect is less definite than the use of a simple formula would indicate. However, the multiplier calculation is nonetheless useful in indicating the *maximum* change in equilibrium output following a certain fiscal policy.

Thinking About Economics

How large is the spending multiplier in the Canadian economy?

Several estimates of the Canadian spending multiplier have been made. The average value is about 1.5. If this figure is correct, then, as Figure 13.5 illustrates, a $20 billion jump in government purchases shifts the aggregate demand curve to the right by $30 billion. However, given the positive slope of the aggregate supply curve, this change means a rise in the price level as well as in total output. In this case, output would rise by $25 billion.

Benefits of Fiscal Policy

Fiscal policy has two benefits as a stabilization tool: its regional focus, and the direct impact it has on spending.

Regional Focus

Parts of Canada may be more affected than others by the business cycle. Fortunately, discretionary fiscal policy can focus on particular regions. For example, during a recession, new government purchases or tax cuts can be targeted to regions where unemployment rates are highest. In a boom, spending cuts and tax hikes can be concentrated on the regions where inflation is at its worst. Similarly, automatic stabilizers have the greatest effect in regions that need them the most. For example, the greatest Unemployment Insurance payments go to regions with the highest unemployment. This is because net tax revenues drop in hard-hit regions during recessions and rise in those regions where the economy is overheated during booms.

Impact on Spending

As indicated by the previous discussion of the multiplier effect, the influence of a stabilization policy is tied to its initial effect on spending. Monetary policy influences spending through a fairly elaborate chain of events. In contrast, fiscal policy has a more straightforward impact—at least when altering government purchases. The first spending adjustment is then assured, since the government itself initiates the change.

Drawbacks of Fiscal Policy

Offsetting the benefits of fiscal policy are three main drawbacks: policy delays, the political visibility of this policy, and its effects on public debt.

Delays

While automatic stabilizers work promptly to stabilize the economy, discretionary measures are sometimes delayed. Three time lags can slow down fiscal policy-makers: the recognition lag, the decision lag, and the impact lag.

The **recognition lag** is the amount of time it takes policy-makers to realize that a policy is needed. Suppose that economic growth suddenly slows. A few months may pass before statistical evidence of this becomes available. It may then take several more months for policy-makers to decide whether this represents a minor fluctuation or the start of a recession.

The **decision lag** is the period that passes while an appropriate response is formulated and implemented. Suppose policy-makers have decided that, indeed, the economy is entering a recession. They must then decide what to do about it. Should they increase government purchases, reduce taxes, or use some combination of the two measures? Once they've decided, the policy must be passed into law and included in a budget.

Finally, once the policy is implemented, there is an **impact lag**—the time that elapses between implementing the policy and its having an effect on the economy. In the case of government spending to combat a recession, for example, the many rounds of spending must take place before the full multiplier effect is felt in the economy.

As a result of these time lags, a year or more may pass between the cause and the effect of a fiscal policy. Meanwhile, the economy may already have

recognition lag: the amount of time it takes policy-makers to realize that a policy is needed

decision lag: the amount of time needed to formulate and implement an appropriate policy

impact lag: the amount of time between a policy's implementation and its having an effect on the economy

moved to a completely different point in the business cycle. In the extreme case, the use of fiscal policy may *worsen* the business cycle by stimulating output during upswings and suppressing it during downturns.

Political Visibility

Discretionary fiscal policy is a highly visible element of government activity. Not surprisingly, therefore, it is often affected by political as well as economic considerations. Voters are likely to respond more favourably to increases in government purchases and cuts in taxes than they are to spending decreases and tax hikes, regardless of the appropriateness of these policies for the economy. As a result, political parties understandably favour expansionary fiscal policy, especially when an election is coming up.

Public Debt

While there remains a political bias toward expansionary policy, the federal government has used stimulative measures more sparingly in recent recessions. This reluctance to increase government purchases or decrease taxes is related to Canada's **public debt**, which is the total amount owed by the federal government as a result of its past borrowing. Public debt, which is owed by Canadian taxpayers to owners of Canadian government bonds, totalled about $500 billion at the end of 1993.

Each year, the federal government spends large sums related to its debt. **Public debt charges** are the amounts paid out each year by the federal government to cover the interest charges on its public debt. Just as payments of interest on a bank loan do not reduce the principal of the loan, public debt charges do not reduce the overall size of the public debt.

In 1993–94, for example, the federal government's public debt charges were $38.5 billion. This figure represented an average interest rate of about 8 percent [($38.5 billion ÷ $500 billion) × 100%] that the federal government paid to the bondholders who owned its $500 billion debt.

Public debt has been growing rapidly in recent years, so that now public debt charges are by far the largest single expenditure made by the federal government. In 1993–94, for example, a third of every federal tax dollar went to pay interest on Canada's public debt. Because the government has not been able to reduce the public debt, when an individual bondholder cashes in a Canadian government bond the government replaces the funds by selling more bonds. Recently, worries over this trend have constrained the use of expansionary fiscal policy. As a result, such a policy—which has the potential to expand Canada's public debt further—has been used less.

public debt: the total amount owed by the federal government as a result of its past borrowing

public debt charges: the amounts paid out each year by the federal government to cover the interest charges on its public debt

BRIEF REVIEW

1. The multiplier effect—the magnified impact of fiscal policy on aggregate demand—is determined by the marginal propensity to consume and the marginal propensity to withdraw.

2. Assuming a constant price level, the spending multiplier is the value by which an initial spending change is multiplied to give the total change in real output.

3. Because a new injection brings about new withdrawals that equal the initial injection, the spending multiplier is the reciprocal of the marginal propensity to withdraw.

4. In the case of a tax cut, the initial spending adjustment is less than the change in taxes because a portion of the tax cut represents withdrawals from the circular flow of spending and income.

5. While fiscal policy can target certain regions and have a direct impact on spending, it also suffers from delays, problems associated with political visibility, and its impact on public debt.

Impact of Fiscal Policy

Budget Surpluses and Deficits

Government expenditures and revenues are affected both by discretionary fiscal policy and by the workings of automatic stabilizers. In the unlikely case where a government's expenditures and revenues are equal, the government is running a **balanced budget**.

In general, government expenditures and revenues are not equal. When a government's revenues exceed its expenditures, there is a **budget surplus**. For example, in 1969–70 the federal government's total expenditures were $14.4 billion and its total revenues were $14.2 billion. Therefore, the budget surplus was $0.2 billion.

> Budget surplus = government revenues – government expenditures
> $0.2 billion = $14.4 billion – $14.2 billion

In contrast, when a government's expenditures exceed its revenues, there is a **budget deficit**. For example, in 1993–94 the federal government's total expenditures were $160.4 billion and its total revenues were $114.7 billion. Therefore, the budget deficit was $45.7 billion:

> Budget deficit = government expenditures – government revenues
> $45.7 billion = $160.4 billion – $114.7 billion

The size of a government's surplus or deficit in relation to the economy's overall GDP gives an indication of what type of discretionary fiscal policy is in operation, as well as the built-in effects of automatic stabilizers.

balanced budget: the situation where a government's expenditures and revenues are equal

budget surplus: the situation where a government's revenues exceed its expenditures

budget deficit: the situation where a government's expenditures exceed its revenues

Surpluses

In some unusual cases, budget surpluses are related to discretionary fiscal policy. For example, a government might decide to suppress the inflationary effects of an economic boom by cutting defence spending and raising income taxes. However, it is more likely that budget surpluses are the result of built-in factors. During a boom, for example, rising tax revenues that outweigh transfer payments can sometimes cause provincial budgets to show a surplus.

Deficits

Budget deficits sometimes indicate active expansionary policies that increase government expenditures or reduce revenues. During an economic downturn, for example, the federal government may increase its spending on roads and bridges, or it may institute a temporary sales-tax cut to stimulate household spending. Budget deficits more often come about as a result of automatic stabilizers. For instance, fewer jobs and less spending during a recession lead to rising Unemployment Insurance benefits and sagging income tax revenues. Both of these trends push the federal budget into a deficit position.

Impact on Public Debt

Because federal surpluses and deficits have not balanced each other over the long run, they have had a tremendous impact on the size of Canada's public debt. When the federal government has a budget deficit, which is most common, the public debt increases by the same amount. For example, Canada's public debt at the start of the 1993 fiscal year was $465.3 billion. Because the federal government ran a budget deficit of $45.7 billion in 1993–94, its public debt at the start of the 1994–95 fiscal year increased to $511.0 billion ($465.3 billion + $45.7 billion). In the rare case of a federal budget surplus, the public debt can be reduced by the same amount. For example, when the federal government ran a $0.2 billion budget surplus in 1969–70, its public debt was reduced from $18.7 billion at the beginning of the fiscal year to $18.5 billion (18.7 billion – $0.2 billion) at the beginning of the next fiscal year.

Fiscal Policy Guidelines

There are three principles that guide government fiscal policy: annually balanced budgets, cyclically balanced budgets, and functional finance.

Annually Balanced Budgets

annually balanced budget: the principle that government revenues and expenditures should balance each year

Those who criticize government intervention in the economy tend not to support fiscal policy. In general, these critics suggest that any fiscal policy that is used must be guided by the principle of an **annually balanced budget**. In other words, revenues and expenditures should balance every year. So, for example, new spending programs must be matched with higher taxes. In essence, by advocating an annually balanced budget, these critics dismiss active fiscal policy as an option.

Opponents of this principle suggest that it is based on faulty reasoning. While an annually balanced budget might make sense for a particular household, it is not necessarily appropriate for society as a whole. After all, the business cycle does not span one year, but many. During an economic contraction, for example, tax revenues decrease. To balance the budget, a government would have to reduce government purchases, thereby worsening the slump in spending. This problem occurred during the early years of the Great Depression in Canada.

Cyclically Balanced Budgets

A less stringent principle—and one that has more supporters—is that of a **cyclically balanced budget**. In other words, government revenues and expenditures need not be balanced every year, but they should balance over one business cycle. The deficits from periods of contraction should roughly equal the surpluses from periods of expansion.

Functional Finance

The principle of **functional finance** stems from the view that policy-makers should concern themselves primarily with correcting fluctuations caused by the business cycle. Rather than trying to balance budgets either annually or over the business cycle, governments should base a year's fiscal policy on the needs of the economy.

In practice, the choice of fiscal policy guidelines depends on the government's belief in fiscal policy as an effective tool for stabilizing the economy. The defenders of functional finance are those who see fiscal policy as a powerful stabilization tool, while economists who back a cyclically or annually balanced budget tend to be less convinced of fiscal policy's effectiveness.

Recent Fiscal Policy

The predominant view of fiscal policy in Canada has undergone a profound change since the mid-1980s. Similar changes have taken place in other industrialized nations. In the 1970s and early 1980s, functional finance was the guiding principle behind fiscal policy in Canada and many other countries. Since then, there have been attempts—so far largely unsuccessful in Canada's case—to move toward cyclically balanced budgets.

In Canada, this change in view relates primarily to increased budget deficits and their impact on the economy as a whole. Figure 13.6 shows the federal budget deficits and the combined deficits of provincial and territorial governments as proportions of Canada's nominal GDP for the years 1981–82 to 1993–94. For example, in relation to Canada's 1993 nominal GDP of $710.7 billion, the federal government's $45.7 billion budget deficit in 1993–94 was 6.4 percent [($45.7 billion ÷ $710.7 billion) × 100%]. Similarly, provincial and territorial governments, when viewed

cyclically balanced budget: the principle that government revenues and expenditures should balance over the course of one business cycle

functional finance: the principle that government budgets should be geared to the yearly needs of the economy

as a single unit, had a combined budget deficit in 1993–94 of $21.2 billion, which as a share of nominal GDP was 3.0 percent [($21.2 billion ÷ $710.7 billion) × 100%]. Because this period spans two recessions and one prolonged boom, it illustrates the changing view of fiscal policy.

Total government deficits were highest during the periods corresponding to the recessions of the early 1980s and early 1990s. As we'll see, however, there were significant differences in fiscal policy. During and just after the slump of the early 1980s, the overall budget deficits of Canadian governments were about 10 percent of Canada's nominal GDP. The budget deficits of the lower levels of government, which were relatively small, came about largely because of automatic stabilizers as tax revenues fell with slumping output and incomes. The large federal deficits were due not only to automatic stabilizers, but also to the use of discretionary expansionary policy by government policy-makers. In particular, the federal government increased purchases of goods and services to counteract the effects of sagging output and incomes.

Following the recession of the early 1980s, the Canadian economy experienced a prolonged period of economic growth, with first a recovery and then a boom occurring in the later years of the decade. By 1988, when the unemployment rate was under 8 percent, the Canadian economy was at or above its potential output. Despite these boom conditions, budgets did not show an overall surplus. In fact, the combined deficits of federal, provincial, and territorial governments were still about 5 percent of nominal GDP in 1988 and 1989.

During and just after the downturn of the early 1990s, the combined deficits of the lower levels of government were much more significant in comparison to the size of the federal deficit. As a result, the overall budget deficits of all levels of government were again nearly 10 percent of Canada's nominal GDP. However, these deficits were less a result of discretionary policy than of automatic stabilizers. This difference resulted from worry over the increased public debt and reduced confidence in the effectiveness of discretionary fiscal policies to counteract a recession.

Thinking About Economics

Why have budget deficits become common for Canadian governments through all phases of the business cycle?

Many observers believe that Canada has entered a harmful deficit–debt spiral. Past dependence on federal budget deficits has expanded Canada's public debt, which in turn has raised annual interest payments on the public debt. The same trend is also noticeable for provincial governments. Greater debt charges for all levels of government increases their spending, which in turn increases deficits even more. Left unchecked, this trend could lead to even higher government deficits and debt levels in the future.

Figure 13.6: Budget Deficits Relative to GDP

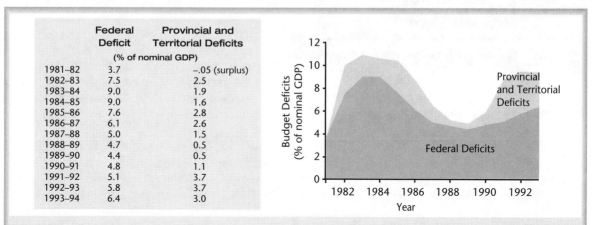

	Federal Deficit	Provincial and Territorial Deficits
	(% of nominal GDP)	
1981–82	3.7	–.05 (surplus)
1982–83	7.5	2.5
1983–84	9.0	1.9
1984–85	9.0	1.6
1985–86	7.6	2.8
1986–87	6.1	2.6
1987–88	5.0	1.5
1988–89	4.7	0.5
1989–90	4.4	0.5
1990–91	4.8	1.1
1991–92	5.1	3.7
1992–93	5.8	3.7
1993–94	6.4	3.0

Federal budget deficits (darker area) and the combined budget deficits for provincial and territorial governments (lighter and darker areas) are shown as percentages of Canada's nominal GDP. Recessions in the early 1980s and early 1990s each caused an increase in budget deficits. While the increase in the early 1980s was mainly due to the federal government, the increase in the early 1990s was split between the federal and the lower levels of government.

SOURCE: Statistics Canada, *Public Sector Assets and Liabilities, Historical Overview* (March 1994), cat. no. 68-508, p. I. Reproduced with permission of the Ministry of Supply and Service Canada, 1995

BRIEF REVIEW

1. When government expenditures equal revenues, the budget is balanced. Budget surpluses—when revenues exceed expenditures—rarely occur. Most frequently, expenditures exceed revenues, resulting in a budget deficit.

2. Repeated budget deficits—in periods of both expansion and contraction—have caused Canada's public debt to balloon.

3. Fiscal policy may be based on three possible guidelines: annually balanced budgets, cyclically balanced budgets, or functional finance. At the federal level, functional finance has been the guiding principle in Canada since the 1970s, although cyclically balanced budgets are increasingly favoured.

Mountain or Mirage?

The Debate Over Public Debt

At first sight, the figures are astounding. From 1982, when public debt was under $5000 per Canadian, the federal government's debt rose by 1994 to over $17 000 per capita. And supplementing this 1994 figure is another $5400 that each Canadian owes because of the debts of provincial and territorial governments—making a total of over $22 000 a head.[1]

Has public debt skyrocketed out of control, are the potential costs of this debt exaggerated by those who want less government involvement in the economy, or does the truth lie somewhere in-between? Because the costs are great whatever the truth—huge debt at one extreme, potentially reduced government programs at the other—this is a question not only for economists and policy-makers, but also for the public as a whole. Let's take a look at opposite perceptions.

Debt Problems Are Overemphasized

People who believe that the negative aspects of public debt have been exaggerated give four main arguments: public debt can increase current output, most of this debt is owed to ourselves, we should take into account the assets created by this debt, and as a percentage of GDP the debt is still lower than it has sometimes been in the past.

Benefits of Public Debt   As discussed in Chapter 12, the amount by which real output falls short of its potential level is known as the GDP gap. This shortfall represents the perma-nent loss of output due to high unemployment. To the extent that expansionary fiscal policy minimizes the GDP gap, it provides a significant benefit—both by supplementing the economy's output and by reducing the human costs of unemployment. According to this argument, any disadvantages caused by the increases in federal debt are minor in comparison to its posi-tive contribution to economic growth.

Debt to Ourselves   The federal government issues bonds to deal with the debt. However, most bonds—about three-quarters of the total value—are actually money Canada owes to Canadian bondholders. Supporters of fiscal policy stress this number's significance. They argue that, when interest is paid on Canadian-owned public debt, funds are simply taken from one group of Canadians in the form of taxes or new borrowing and given to anoth-er group of Canadians. In other words, the total "economic pie" doesn't get bigger or smaller—just the sizes of the slices.

Assets Versus Liabilities   When debt is used to create productive assets, it can be defended in the same way as the debt acquired by businesses for investment purposes. While Canadian govern-ment investment in capital goods—at least as defined in the national accounts—has fallen in recent decades as a percentage of GDP, supporters of fiscal policy suggest that the problem lies in the definitions. They believe that we should define productive assets more widely to include the country's human resources, whose worth is pro-moted through such expenditures as education. Unfortunately, it is difficult to put a value on a country's stock of productive assets when they are broadly defined in this way.

Comparisons With the Past   Because of substantial inflation and economic growth over the years, debt trends expressed in current-year dollars are inadequate. A much better indication of the economy's ability to bear public debt is to express the debt as a percentage of nominal GDP, as shown in the figure below. For example, the $511.0 billion public debt at the end of the 1993–94 year equalled 72 percent of the 1993 nominal GDP of $710.7 billion [($511.0 ÷ $710.7) × 100%]. In contrast, the federal government's debt charges of $38.5 billion equalled 5.4 percent [$38.5 ÷ $710.7) × 100%]. It is interesting to note that, when measured in this way (column 3), public debt has sometimes been at higher levels than in the early 1990s. For example, Canada's public debt in 1936–37, while only $3.1 billion in nominal dollars, was 67 percent of that year's GDP. By 1946–47, after federal borrowing to help finance Canada's involvement in World War II, public debt was over 100 percent of that year's GDP—a figure much higher than the 1993–94 level of 72 percent.

Public Debt Is a Major Problem

People who are concerned about present levels of public debt concentrate on a different set of arguments: the growth of public debt charges in relation to the size of the economy, the recent expansion of provincial and territorial government debt, the apparent limits to future tax increases, and the potential future burdens that government debt may place on Canadians.

Public Debt Charges Although public debt as a proportion of GDP is lower today than during some other periods in Canada's history, public debt charges—or the annual interest payments on this debt—have risen substantially. As shown in column 4 of the figure, public debt charges as a percentage of GDP were much higher in the 1980s and 1990s than in any previous decade since the 1920s, with public debt charges reaching 6 percent of nominal GDP in the late 1980s. This trend was due to high real

Public Debt and GDP
(billions of current dollars)

(1) Year	(2) Public Debt (billions of current-year $)	(3) Public Debt (% of nominal GDP)	(4) Public Debt Charges (% of nominal GDP)
1926–27	2.3	46	2.5
1936–37	3.1	67	3.0
1946–47	12.7	107	3.9
1956–57	11.4	35	1.5
1966–67	17.2	27	1.8
1976–77	39.9	20	2.4
1984–85	206.3	46	5.0
1989–90	357.8	55	6.0
1993–94	511.0	72	5.4

As a percentage of nominal GDP, public debt rose between the 1920s and 1940s, and then fell until the 1980s. However, high interest rates during the 1980s meant that, as a percentage of nominal GDP, public debt charges were higher than ever before.

SOURCE: Department of Finance, *Quarterly Economic Review: Special Report* (March 1992), pp. 33–34, and *The Budget Plan* (February 1994), p. 50. Reproduced by authority of the Minister of Industry, 1994.

interest rates during the 1980s. A subsequent drop in real interest rates in the early 1990s eased the problem somewhat, but public debt charges remain high when compared to the past.

Provincial and Territorial Debt   The comparison of public debt and nominal GDP shown in the figure underestimates the overall expansion of debt for all levels of government in Canada. In former decades, the debts of provincial and territorial governments in Canada tended to be relatively minor. At the end of the 1981–82 fiscal year, for example, the combined net debts of provincial and territorial governments represented only 4 percent of Canada's GDP. By the end of the 1993–94 fiscal year, however, this combined debt stood at $155 billion, or 22 percent of the country's GDP. Adding this debt to the federal debt means that the total debt of all levels of government had reached over 90 percent of GDP.[2]

Tax Limits   As total government debt charges rise, Canadian governments can keep their budget deficits in check either by increasing taxes or by reducing other expenditures, known as program spending. In the past, tax increases have

commonly been used as a way of limiting budget deficits. However, in recent years, Canadians have grown more reluctant to shoulder further tax burdens, making it unlikely that tax rates can rise much beyond present levels. As a result, future increases in government debt charges will likely force governments to engage in unpopular cuts in program spending.

Potential Future Burdens   Many economists argue that public debt will impose future burdens on the entire Canadian economy. According to the *crowding out effect*, higher levels of government borrowing raise demand in the market for loanable funds, which we considered in Chapter 8. This leads to an increase in interest rates, causing businesses to reduce their investment spending. The result is a lower future stock of real capital in the economy and hence a lower rate of economic growth.

Another potential burden of public debt is the portion owed to foreigners. While just under one-quarter of Canada's combined federal and provincial/territorial debt is now foreign-held, this proportion has risen considerably in recent decades.[3] Unlike the case of domestically held debt, interest payments on this debt represent a transfer of purchasing power from Canadians to foreigners. The higher the proportion of public debt owed to foreigners, therefore, the greater this transfer will be in the future.

SOURCE: Vance Rodewalt, *The Calgary Herald*.

NOTES
[1]Statistics Canada, *Public Sector Assets and Liabilities: Historical Overview* (March 1994), pp. xiv, 1, 5.
[2]*Ibid.*, p.1.
[3]OECD, *OECD Economics Surveys 1992–1993* (1993), p. 41.

Research the issues raised in the essay. Then, conduct a class debate on the following resolution: "The current level of Canada's public debt *and* excessive budget deficits not only threaten our economic well-being, but also jeopardize our economic sovereignty."

Rethinking Government

Judith Maxwell and Social Deficits

A leading economist, Judith Maxwell has chaired the now-defunct Economic Council of Canada. In 1994, at the time that she was Associate Director of Policy Studies at Queen's University and head of Queen's–University of Ottawa Economic Projects, Maxwell was also appointed Director of the Bank of Canada. Following an extended recession in Canada, Maxwell offered the following insights.

Fiscal and social deficits go hand in hand. They spring from the same origins and require common solutions. The danger is that, in the process of cutting expenditure to reduce the fiscal deficit, we will destroy the good part of public services, and make the social deficit even worse than it is now.

We all know the extent of the fiscal deficit: the statistics are indeed chilling. The social deficit, however, cannot be measured in cold statistics. Certainly the current unemployment rate of about 11% understates the problem. But the social deficit is even more obvious in the high proportion of children and young people who arrive at school not ready to learn. Some are hungry, some are hurting and others are just "not focussed." It is also evident in the high rates of dependency on unemployment insurance and social assistance by people who have at least some earnings from work.

The social and the fiscal deficits combined explain (but do not excuse) why some people would remove their consent to be governed. They point out vividly just how important the next five years will be for Canada. Will the current trends continue? Or will they be reversed so that Canada can become the civil and caring society we pretend it is? That reversal will only come, it seems to me, if we can restore the credibility of our governing institutions.

In rethinking government, we have to remind ourselves why governments exist, why they are such unique institutions and then how their relationship with citizens has been altered over time.

In the 1860s, the family was self-sufficient. Government did not have a social role but rather provided the legal framework, defended the colonies' borders and played an economic development role (sponsoring canals, railways, land settlement and so on). It was the church that ran the charities for the destitute. By the 1930s, the municipalities had taken responsibility for relief and for public education.

In the 1940s, there was a major evolution in political thinking in response to depression, war and the intellectual contribution of Keynes. The Marsh Report mapped out a role for government in redistribution and then the *White Paper on Reconstruction* set the framework for an extraordinary expansion of both the economic and the social roles of govern-

Judith Maxwell

ment. This led to deliberate decisions to intervene through reallocation of resources and the redistribution of income (family allowances) to prevent a post-war slump. This period also saw the early steps toward fiscal federalism—a system of interregional sharing intended to bind the country together.

The social contract implicit in those documents from the 1940s could be roughly summarized as follows: citizens made a commitment to work and to pay taxes in return for state-funded insurance against temporary unemployment, old age, poor health and certain family responsibilities. The state committed to introduce policies that would ensure high levels of employment.

The Social Safety Net[1]

	1975	1992	Share of GDP 1975	1992
	($ billion)		(%)	
Federal				
Old Age Security and Guaranteed Income Supplement	3.8	18.8	2.2	2.7
Unemployment Insurance	3.1	18.0	1.8	2.6
Canada Pension Plan	0.5	12.9	0.3	1.9
Family allowances	2.0	2.9	1.2	0.4
Total federal	**9.4**	**52.6**	**5.5**	**7.6**
Provincial				
Social assistance[2]	1.8	13.6	1.0	2.0
Worker's Compensation	0.5	4.3	0.3	0.6
Quebec Pension Plan	0.2	3.9	0.1	0.6
Total provincial	**2.5**	**21.8**	**1.5**	**3.2**
TOTAL	**11.9**	**74.4**	**6.9**	**10.8**

	1975	1991	1975	1991
	($ billion)		(%)	
Consolidated government expenditures				
Health	9.0	41.6	5.2	6.2
Education	10.7	38.8	6.2	5.7
Total health and education expenditures	**19.7**	**80.4**	**11.4**	**11.9**

[1] Excludes tax expenditures.
[2] Includes municipal programs and programs for the elderly.

SOURCES: Safety net expenditures based on National Income and Expenditure Accounts. Health and education expenditures based on Public Accounts (FMS basis). Reprinted by authority of the Minister of Industry, 1994.

This contract framed political decisions through the next 25 years; the final element was Medicare, enacted in 1968.

By 1975, a relatively mature safety net was in place. But, by coincidence, the bottom dropped out of revenues in the mid-1970s. In effect, the slump in productivity growth after the oil shock had begun to erode the very foundations of this vision of peace, order and good government. Basically, revenues stopped growing at the pace to which Canadians had become accustomed, yet no adjustments were made to the social contract.

We financed these safety net transfers (excluding health and education) in 1975 with about 7% of GDP. Many programs have actually been tightened up since then—especially through amendments to unemployment insurance and the curtailment of indexing. Yet the share of GDP required to finance these same transfers in 1992 was 11%. This reflects higher rates of dependency on the safety net, and, as I argue below, inefficient *incentives* in the design of these programs. If public spending on health and education expenditures are included as part of the safety net, then they add another 12 percentage points to the share of GDP devoted to the social envelope.

These costs are becoming overwhelming. We are obviously forced to stop and think about whether or not governments really should be providing all these services.

Rationale for Redistribution

I think that the rationale for government's social role is, if anything, stronger than it was in the 1940s. In a sense, the social role of government is to provide the underpinnings necessary to permit a society to adapt to changing circumstances.

In the urban wage economy, people cannot be self-sufficient. They cannot grow their own food, build their own homes and make their own clothes or provide nursing care to the family. They must sell their labour to provide the income needed to buy goods and services. This labour market embodies a lot of risk-taking—risk that there will not be a job, risk of job change, risk the wage earned will not cover all the family's needs.

The social contract originated in an era where the typical family had one breadwinner and that person could earn enough to support another adult and several children or other dependents. In short, there was someone at home to take care of the family. Now, vulnerability has increased for three reasons:

- The labour market has become less stable because the nature of work has changed. Layoffs tend to be permanent, rather than temporary; and there are many jobs that do not provide enough income to support a family. Canada's labour market produces far more instability and turnover than is the case in most other industrial countries—although the US market produces even more.

- Families now depend on two incomes and, generally speaking, there is no one home during the day to do the home making and care giving. (Politicians who campaign door to door have observed that the only people at home during the day are those who are on welfare, unemployed, or working the night shift.) In these circumstances, the family is compelled to contract out many tasks that used to be done at home—child care, elder care. However, as yet, markets for these services are not fully developed. The work goes underpaid or unpaid, and both the quantity and, in many cases, the quality of services fall short of people's needs.

- There is extraordinary pressure on workers to upgrade their skills, but the support structure to permit people to take time out for study is very uneven.

In considering the scope of a new social contract, then, we need to think not only about the pooling of risks in the labour market, but also about the support for families and children and about ways to foster investment in human capital. The key concern becomes the capacity of new generations to be healthy and productive citizens.

What is worrying is that we are currently devoting so much money to the 1945 version of the social contract while there is so much evidence of a growing *social deficit*, accompanied by the risk of creating an underclass. That alone should make the case that it is time to rethink the social contract in order to create a new blueprint for government action. This means rethinking the political values that describe the obligations and the rights of all the players—governments, citizens, employers, unions and interest groups.

How Can Governments Be More Efficient?

Virtually everything that government does requires a contract. Financing education or health implies a contract with a school board or a hospital. Delivering programs directly necessitates a collective agreement with the public servants doing the work. Delivering programs through intermediaries—non-governmental organizations, a private firm or a crown corporation—requires a contract with the management.

The essence of good government is ensuring that these contracts are written in such a way that the supplier—the school board, the hospital, the public servants or the crown corporation—has an incentive to provide the best quality at the lowest possible price. At the same time, the design of the service or program must be such that there is an incentive for the citizen or the user to use that service efficiently—to take only as much as they need, in full recognition of the cost to society.

You can see immediately that this is a huge task, since we are talking about services where the typical product or outcome cannot be measured and where there is seldom an explicit cost or price known to either the producer or the user. The essence of good government is to get as close as possible to the most efficient incentives, despite these obvious barriers.

The mistake that got us off on the wrong track in the 1970s was the assumption that behaviour would not be unduly influenced by the way programs were designed. Let's consider two examples where incentives (or disincentives) play a role: post-secondary education and labour market training policies.

Post-Secondary Education

Universities (and colleges) in Canada are under immense stress. They are being asked to do more for less. Enrolments are breaking records, students are being turned away, tuition fees are controlled, and provincial operating grants are declining. Yet, in a recent paper, I concluded that the governing structure in universities has been so badly eroded that these institutions are incapable of reform from within. When operating grants are reduced, the universities go through a laborious process of across-the-board cuts which cannot help but diminish the standard of education. If we do not break through this barrier soon, we could do long-lasting damage to the capacity of our universities.

The incentives here are wrong in a number of ways. Students have no idea of the value of the programs they are in. If you pay 10% of the cost of a service, you will use it at a different pace than if you are paying 30% or even 50%. Similarly, if universities were in a situation where their revenues depended on the degree to which they could fulfil students' needs, we would see an increase in the value placed on teaching, and a readiness to provide programs that students want.

The way to improve the incentives to the suppliers—the universities—and to the students involves deregulating tuition fees (which, of course, come under provincial jurisdiction) and reforming student loans to make them available to all students. The loans should be repaid through the tax system, contingent upon future earnings. At the same time, we need more means-tested grants for students from low-income backgrounds to ensure that they have adequate access.

Labour Market Training Policies

Somehow, Canada's labour market programs have created or reinforced the wrong expectations among many employers in both the public and the private sectors. They still believe that training is a responsibility of the state, so they wait for the end product to come out of the education and training system, rather than invest in the promotion of human skills themselves. They believe that they can put an ad in the paper and find the trained workers they need. (If they cannot, it is government's or someone else's fault.) Many also believe that layoffs are the route to competitiveness.

My colleague Gordon Betcherman is putting the finishing touches to a report called *The Canadian Workplace in Transition,* which will demonstrate, very clearly, that employers who invest in training, and make a commitment to the existing work force through enlightened policies on workplace cooperation, compensation and family-friendly work arrangements, reap the reward in the form of faster productivity growth.

Clearly, we need to create an incentive structure that is more in tune with the realities of the employer–employee relationship. This does not eliminate the need for public training programs—for the unemployed, the disadvantaged, the self-employed and for young people still in the education system. But recognition of the relationship between employer and employee should affect our attitude toward workplace training.

Conclusions

We need to establish a new social contract between the citizen and the state. That contract will have to take account of the changed circumstances of Canadian families and lower expectations about future revenue growth. It presumably will involve a new set of obligations for both parties. Reform of major programs within the social contract should revolve around getting the incentives right—so that the supplier of the service and the user are both encouraged to be efficient.

How feasible is all of this? On the optimistic side, I can point to two kinds of evidence. First, it appears that Canadians have not given up on government. They continue to look to their elected representatives and officials to solve the nation's problems. Second, there is a recurring cycle in the trust people place in government. The degree of trust intensifies markedly around the time of a national election, as we have seen since October [1993], and then wanes when reality or mistakes become evident. There appears, then, to be a window of opportunity for introducing considered reforms—reforms capable of winning public support.

On the pessimistic side, there is the daunting task of changing expectations about what we mean by social and economic security. Being competitive means securing the best possible chances for employment and income. But being competitive also implies a continuous process of coping with change. As the pressure increases, we need a stronger commitment to collective security and greater attention to preventing a social deficit.

We have to break with the notion that governments can protect citizens from every cold wind. We also have to break with the notion that governments can let the cold winds blow to make Canadians competitive, without putting in place the supporting reforms on the social side.

The real challenge here is to manage both the timing and the expectations. I am not suggesting that the fiscal problem can be corrected simply by reforming the social safety net. Many of the major program areas will take time to reform. And it will take even more time for a new set of incentives to begin to influence the behaviour of suppliers and users.

But reforming the social safety net is part of the solution to the long-term fiscal problem. There are many who would argue that we need a quick reduction in government deficits, and are prepared to slash and burn to make that happen. Certainly if we look at the two provinces that have made the most progress in bringing their books back into balance— New Brunswick and Saskatchewan—it is necessary to make some hard decisions across the whole range of government activities.

What the federal government cannot afford to do is break trust with Canadians. It has to show a capacity for building and healing through sensible and far-reaching reforms to the social infrastructure at the same time as the deficit is being addressed. This obviously cannot be done by the federal government alone. In almost all the key areas, the provinces have the jurisdiction and are also major players in the design of the major social programs. I think that the obvious fiscal distress in all regions of the country forces them to work together.

My ultimate argument is that you cannot restore political legitimacy solely by being fiscally correct. That is a necessary, but not a sufficient condition for restoring the credibility of government. The adjustments in expenditures and revenues have to be framed in the context of a new social contract which responds to the needs and aspirations of Canadians and which is consistent with their ability to pay.

SOURCE: Judith Maxwell, "Rethinking the social role of government," in *Policy Options*, July–August 1994, pp. 54–58. Reproduced by kind permission of Judith Maxwell, Associate Director, School of Policy Studies, Queen's University.

1. What is the main idea conveyed by Maxwell?

2. In your opinion, which problem is more serious—the fiscal deficit or the social deficit? Explain.

3. a) System dynamics experts believe that the structure of a system determines behaviour within the system, and that behaviour within the system determines events that relate to the system. With this in mind, summarize in writing or in a causal loop diagram Maxwell's analysis of postsecondary education.

   b) Evaluate the analysis and the proposal given.

4. a) Work in groups to survey members of your community (relatives, friends, neighbours, teachers) for their definition of "social and economic security."

   b) From your survey results, draft one definition of social and economic security.

   c) Consider your definition in light of current economic realities, and then draft a new social contract.

   d) Present your social contract to the class for discussion.

Key Concepts

stabilization policy
expansionary policies
contractionary policies
fiscal policy
fiscal year
monetary policy
expansionary fiscal policy
contractionary fiscal policy
discretionary policy

automatic stabilizers
net tax revenues
multiplier effect
marginal propensity to consume
marginal propensity to withdraw
spending multiplier
recognition lag
decision lag
impact lag

public debt
public debt charges
balanced budget
budget surplus
budget deficits
annually balanced budget
cyclically balanced budget
functional finance

Developing Application and Analysis Skills

1. Copy and complete the chart below. For each economic situation, sketch a graph demonstrating the situation and the results of any policies.

2. "The more progressive the tax system, the more automatic stabilizers work to diminish the severity of the business cycle." Assess the accuracy of this statement by making specific reference to the content of the chapter.

3. a) Research the saving habits of Canadians and citizens of another country, and suggest reasons for the differences or similarities you discover.
   b) Suggest how the spending multipliers of the two countries might compare, and explain why.
   c) Suggest the implications of your findings for policy-makers in each country.

4. a) Calculate the MPC in an economy where a $6 billion increase in government purchases results in an initial increase of $2 billion in domestic consumption spending.
   b) Calculate the MPW for this example.
   c) Suggest why there would have been this change in government purchases.

5. Suppose economists have found that, for every $5 billion increase in government purchases, the aggregate demand curve shifts by $10 billion (assuming the same price level).
   a) Calculate the multiplier for this economy.
   b) Sketch aggregate demand and supply curves to illustrate the effect of this increase in spending.
   c) On your graph, demonstrate the likely effect of an additional government action: an increase in corporate taxes.

6. Calculate the spending multiplier in an economy in which an initial $6.7 billion change in consumption of domestic items results in an increase in real GDP of $10 billion.

Economic Problem To Be Solved	Type of Policy To Be Used	Description of Discretionary Fiscal Policies	Description of Automatic Stabilizers
Recessionary gap			
Inflationary gap			

Situation	Initial Change in Spending	Multiplier	MPC	MPW	Resulting Shift in AD Curve
A	+$12 billion	———	———	0.8	———
B	–$1 billion	———	———	0.6	———

7. Copy and complete the chart below, which outlines two possible fiscal policies. Then, explain for each policy the economic situation that would cause such a policy to be implemented, the possible outcomes, and the possible tradeoffs.

8. Assume that Canada's public debt stands at $530 billion.

   a) Calculate how many years it would take for Canada's public debt to reach $1 trillion if budget deficits equal $30 billion a year.

   b) Calculate how many years it would take to reduce the public debt to $100 billion if budget surpluses equal $30 billion a year.

9. Research and compare the actual public debts for the last 10 years of the nations that are members of the G7. Draw conclusions about Canada's debt in relation to that of other industrialized countries.

10. a) Study the causal loop diagram on this page and explain the dynamics of the relationships illustrated.

   b) According to the diagram, what factors would reinforce the growth process shown? Sketch a graph that illustrates this growth process over time.

   c) Over time, what factors would balance or limit the growth process shown?

   d) What dangers of high government spending and public debt are suggested by the diagram?

   e) What solutions for these problems are suggested by the diagram?

11. a) Research Canada's current public debt and public debt charges.

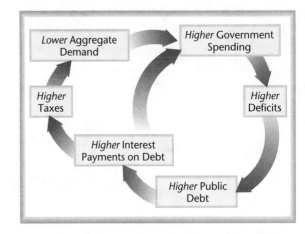

   b) Suggest specific opportunity costs of the public debt charges (for example, spending on health care or youth work programs).

12. For the most recent budget for one level of government, identify at least three spending and taxation changes. Note for each of these changes the specific implications for you, your family, peers, or other members of your community.

13. Examine the most recent federal budget and one from 10 years ago. In a research essay, evaluate and compare the two budgets. Make sure you consider both the economic and the political context of each.

14. Suppose your school's budget had to be cut by 15 percent. In groups, consider how you would cut 15 percent. Identify budget priorities and analyze the opportunity costs of each possible cut, and then present your budget reduction proposals to the other groups. Finally, discuss as the class the issues involved in the process.

CHAPTER 14

Money and Monetary Policy

The fact that the world I inhabited could change so dramatically was entirely a result of money, or, more politely, of the economy. The economy is the soup we live in, and when it is going well, it forms a backdrop as invisible as air. When it starts to fail, we notice as quickly as we notice a lack of oxygen.

—NORA GALLAGHER, AMERICAN WRITER

Money talks, and, depending on who is listening, it can say a variety of things. Money's allure is undeniable. However, it is neither static nor easy to define; it has taken many forms and continues to evolve today. This chapter highlights three main issues: the functions money performs in modern economies, how banks help create money, and the role of Canada's central bank, the Bank of Canada, in stabilizing the economy.

CHAPTER FOCUS

This chapter focuses on the following:
- the functions of money, its components, and the various definitions of money
- the Canadian financial system, types of deposits, cash reserves, and reserve ratios
- the demand for and supply of money, and equilibrium in the money market
- how money is created, and the money multiplier
- the Bank of Canada, its functions, and the tools it uses to conduct monetary policy

SKILLS FOCUS

After studying this chapter, you will be able to:
- explain the functions of money and apply your understanding by proposing a currency
- analyze the functions of financial institutions and the role of the Bank of Canada
- assess holdings for their liquidity, and calculate the money supply according to various definitions
- construct money demand and supply curves, and explain how interest rates determine bond prices
- demonstrate the concept of the money multiplier and the impact of monetary policy
- evaluate and compare the effectiveness of monetary policy and fiscal policy in the business cycle

Money and Its Uses

The Functions of Money

Money serves three separate functions in any economy. It provides a means of exchange, a store of purchasing power, and a measure of value.

Means of Exchange

The most important function of money is that it acts as a means of payment whenever items are bought and sold. Without money, market participants must trade one product for another product, a transaction known as **barter**.

Barter is an unwieldy method of exchanging products. Someone purchasing an item must find a seller who wants what the purchaser is offering in return. In other words, there must be a **coincidence of wants** between both parties. For example, a barber who wants to buy a clock must find a clockmaker who wants a haircut. Because a coincidence of wants is usually difficult to achieve, trade is discouraged, so most people living in a barter system produce many items for themselves.

Money overcomes these problems. The barber can deal with any clockmaker and pay in money, which the clockmaker can then use to purchase a wide range of items.

The benefits of money as a means of exchange are far-reaching. People can minimize the time they spend finding others with whom they can buy and sell. They can also focus their productive activity by devoting themselves to economic pursuits in which they are most adept. The barber can stick to cutting hair and the clockmaker to making clocks. Specialization promotes the division of labour and allows an economy to achieve higher levels of output. Therefore, the use of money not only facilitates transactions of goods and services—it also raises living standards.

Store of Purchasing Power

Money's second function is providing a safe and accessible store of wealth. Money is an attractive store of purchasing power during the period between the time it is earned and the time it is spent.

There are both benefits and drawbacks associated with holding wealth as money. Money's major advantage is its **liquidity**, or the ease with which it can be turned into a means of payment. Assets are most liquid when they can be quickly turned into money with little loss in value. All financial assets are liquid to some degree, but none as much as money, which is perfectly liquid by its very nature.

Recall, however, that for any economic choice there is an opportunity cost. In this case, the cost of holding wealth in the form of money is the income sacrificed by not holding it in some other form. For example, someone who holds wealth by stashing a thousand-dollar bill in a cookie

barter: a system of trading one product for another

coincidence of wants: the situation where someone purchasing an item finds a seller who wants what the purchaser is offering in return

liquidity: the ease with which an asset can be converted into a means of payment

jar is sacrificing the income the wealth could earn if it were converted into a stock or bond. As a result, people hold wealth as money when the benefits of liquidity outweigh the income that could be earned by holding it in another form.

Measure of Value

Money also provides buyers and sellers with a **unit of account**, or pricing standard. The unit of account allows all products to be valued consistently against a common measure—in other words, it provides a point of comparison between, for example, apples and oranges. So, if apples cost $2 per kilogram and oranges cost $4 per kilogram, it is easy to see that oranges cost twice as much as apples. Recall from Chapter 10 that the unit of account does the same on a grander scale; expressing Gross Domestic Product (GDP) as a dollar value simplifies the picture by allowing a wide range of products to be quantified and combined.

In contrast, a barter economy requires many measures of value. The question, "How much does this cost?" would bring the inevitable reply, "It depends on what you've got." A clock, for example, might be exchanged for 100 apples, 50 oranges, 20 loaves of bread, 2 haircuts, or some number of any other product a market participant is offering. As well as creating a confusion of prices, a barter economy is difficult to measure.

The Canadian Financial System

Now that we've defined the functions money serves, we will consider the system in which it operates as well as the supply of money. The supply of money is closely associated with institutions known as **deposit-takers**, which accept funds provided by savers and lend these funds to borrowers. For the deposit-taker, the deposits it accepts and owes back to savers are its liabilities; the funds it lends to borrowers, and which borrowers owe the deposit-taker, are its assets. These institutions make a profit by paying lower interest rates on deposits than they charge on loans.

Not all funds flowing into the institution flow out. Deposit-takers also keep on hand some amount, known as **cash reserves**, so that depositors can withdraw funds when they request them. Because deposit-takers make no income from these cash reserves, they hold only the minimum of their assets in the form of cash reserves.

Deposit-takers fall into two categories: chartered banks and near banks.

Chartered Banks

Chartered banks—often simply called banks—form the backbone of Canada's financial system. Unlike other deposit-takers, these institutions are allowed, through a charter they receive from the federal government, to sell a wide range of financial services.

unit of account: a pricing standard that allows all products to be valued consistently

deposit-takers: institutions or businesses that accept funds provided by savers and lend these funds to borrowers

cash reserves: funds kept on hand by deposit-takers to meet the needs of depositors withdrawing funds

chartered banks: deposit-takers allowed by federal charter to offer a wide range of financial services

SIDELINE

LETS Trade

Barter Canadian-Style

What can a community with little currency but lots of skills do? One answer, which has been adopted by communities around the world, is a new form of barter.

In Britain, you can use acorns to get your hair cut, cockles to mend your roof and stones to paint your house—all thanks to an idea from Vancouver Island.

Acorns, stones and cockles are just three of the nearly 200 alternative currencies that have sprung up in towns and villages throughout Britain. Although each of these currencies is used locally—acorns in Totnes, cockles in Exmouth and stones in Sheffield—none actually exists. They are names given to units of exchange used by members of barter schemes or LETS—Local Exchange Trading Systems.

LETS, alternative economies based on local currencies, originated in Canada in 1982. Michael Linton, of Courtenay, devised the scheme to deal with the immediate problems in his area caused by high unemployment and poverty.

Linton watched his client base shrivel because people in the community had no money. "I started local money in the community because there wasn't any of the other stuff. The initial reason was that simple." said Scottish-born Linton. "I wanted bread on the table, firewood in the stove and a job."

It wasn't until he'd started the system that he realized he was onto something much bigger than his own—or even his community's—needs. The need for LETS is universal because all communities have a dependency on external money. There is a human, a social and an ecological imperative to the system, Linton said.

LETS are local, independent, nonprofit organizations that operate extended barter systems allowing hundreds of people to exchange goods and services throughout a community.

Through LETS and its use of a local currency, members can transcend the limits of conventional one-to-one barter. For a fee of about $20 to cover administrative costs, traders join the scheme, list the goods and services they can provide, and are given an account at zero balance and, in many systems, a chequebook with which to record transactions.

Members are provided with directories that list, like the Yellow Pages, goods and services offered within the local network. In Totnes, Devon, for example, the local LETS directory offers members dozens of services such as baby-sitting, dog-walking, car repair, typing, decorating, language instruction, massage and acupuncture.

Accounts are both interest- and penalty-free and are updated centrally, like those in a bank or credit union. Members are free to divide their charges between cash and LETS units, so that they can cover their monetary costs.

An organic farmer, for example, may be happy to sell his produce for green dollars as long as he can cover his costs for seed in ordinary dollars, since the seed comes from outside the community.

In LETS a unit of local currency is equivalent to one unit of the national currency. In Canada, the name used for most local currencies is "green dollar."

Liz Shepherd is co-ordinator of LETSLink UK, a British national network set up in April 1991, at a time when there were just five systems in Britain, all struggling.

Just more than two years later, there are nearly 200 systems up and running, with more in the pipeline. More than 1,500 starter packs explaining the system have been sold and Liz Shepherd is besieged by inquiries.

Shepherd is full of praise for the Canadian invention. "There are advantages to LETS on many levels," she said. "At the most basic level, with a small system of perhaps 50 people, LETS produces a sort of extended family that helps people out of crisis situations. It starts to rebuild the community spirit."

If your roof needs fixing and you don't have enough money to pay for it, rather than going into debt with the bank or waiting until the hole in your roof gets bigger, you can get someone within the system to do the job and work off that debt using your skills. It is this "stitch-in-time" approach to economics that is a key to the appeal and success of LETS.

Although the growth of LETS has been slow in Canada, with just 12 systems developed in almost as many years, the idea has also been exported to Australia, New Zealand and the U.S., and is now poised to sweep across Europe. Communities in Germany, France, Holland and Denmark have all expressed strong interest in the Canadian model.

Even so, Linton said he feels frustrated that it has taken his idea so long to catch on.

One common accusation levelled against LETS is that it is nothing but a form of underground economy aimed at avoiding taxation. But Linton said: "This is not a moneyless exchange. The fact that it is a local currency does not change our relationship to our national law. A dollar that is green is just as taxable as an ordinary dollar."

"Here, with LETS, we have an answer to poverty, social decline, community disintegration and many of our environmental problems. It's a stunningly simple and creative answer," says Linton.

SOURCE: Abridged from Heather Wardle, "Haircut will cost you 3 acorns," in *The Montreal Gazette*, 15 January 1994, p. 16.

While there are over 60 chartered banks in Canada, 6 big banks dominate the sector—the Royal Bank of Canada, the Canadian Imperial Bank of Commerce, the Bank of Montreal, the Bank of Nova Scotia, the Toronto-Dominion Bank, and the National Bank. Each of these banks has many branches, following what is known as a branch banking system. Together, the "big six" control about 90 percent of Canada's chartered bank deposits and assets. Most of the remaining chartered banks are relatively small foreign-owned banks. Apart from American banks, which are exempt because of recent trade agreements, these banks are limited by law to 12 percent of Canadian chartered bank assets.

The Canadian chartered banking system is therefore an oligopoly. While the reduced competition may lead to some market inefficiencies, it also enhances the financial soundness of the Canadian system. By comparison, in the United States there are well over 10 000 commercial banks. About a third of them operate under federal law and are known as national banks. The others, called state banks, are controlled by state governments. Many of these state banks are relatively small and have few branches. While competition is enhanced by the number of players, the modest size of each bank can increase the chance of financial difficulties.

near banks: deposit-takers that are not chartered and have more specialized services; mainly trust companies, mortgage loan companies, and credit unions

Near Banks

In contrast to chartered banks, **near banks** are not chartered and have more specialized services. The most important are trust companies, mortgage loan companies, and credit unions.

Trust companies administer various types of accounts, including estates and trust funds. They also compete with chartered banks by taking deposits and granting loans, mainly to households.

As their name suggests, mortgage loan companies specialize in granting mortgages, and raise some of their funds through deposit-taking. Recall from Chapter 8 that a mortgage is a loan whose collateral is in the form of land and buildings.

Credit unions (called *caisses populaires* in Quebec, where they are particularly prevalent) are nonprofit institutions that take deposits and grant loans to their members.

Figure 14.1: Chartered Banks and Near Banks in Canada

(total assets, $ billions, 31 October 1993)

Chartered Banks		**Near Banks**	
Royal Bank	$164.9	Trust and mortgage loan companies	$248.4
CIBC	141.3	Credit unions and *caisses populaires*	89.8
Montreal	116.9	Total	$338.2
Scotiabank	107.6		
Toronto-Dominion	85.0		
National	42.7		
Others	73.9		
Total	$732.3		

The "big six" chartered banks dominate the financial services market. These banks hold about 90 percent of all chartered bank assets, and their combined assets are more than double that of near banks.

SOURCE: Bank of Canada, *Bank of Canada Review* (Spring 1994), Tables DI-D3; Canadian Bankers Association, Domestic Banks' Financial Results Detailed Statistics (First Quarter, 1994), p.22.

Other Financial Institutions

In addition to deposit-takers—especially chartered banks—there are other types of financial institutions: insurance companies and investment dealers. Insurance companies offer insurance policies to their clients and use the funds to buy various types of income-producing financial assets. Investment dealers buy and sell financial securities such as stocks and bonds for their customers.

The Financial System

Traditionally, chartered banks, trust companies, insurance companies, and investment dealers have formed the four pillars of the financial system.

Each group had its specialized functions. Now, however, regulations governing financial institutions in Canada and in other countries are gradually being loosened. Financial deregulation, as it is called, allows each institution to perform a wider range of functions.

Now, for example, other financial institutions are taking on some of the functions of chartered banks. "Financial supermarkets" have sprung up to give a complete range of financial services under one corporate roof. While deregulation has promoted competition and efficiency, some critics fear it will lead to several giant companies controlling most of the Canadian financial system.

The Supply of Money

The supply of money is made up of currency and some deposits.

Currency

Currency includes paper notes, such as twenty-dollar bills, issued by Canada's central bank, the Bank of Canada. It also includes coinage produced by the Royal Mint.

currency: paper money and coins

Deposits

Recall that deposits are made to deposit-takers and lent out to borrowers, who pay interest. In this way, chartered banks and near banks make their profits. Deposits can be classified according to the conditions of the deposits. In general, the access the depositor has to his or her funds determines the interest rates paid on deposits. The longer a deposit-taker can make use of the funds, and the fewer the services the deposit-taker provides, the higher the interest rate.

Demand Deposits   In some cases, depositors can demand immediate access to their money. Such deposits are called **demand deposits**, and take the form of current and personal chequing accounts. Depositors can withdraw money directly from the bank or can write cheques, which are a convenient way for depositors to authorize banks to pay a certain sum to a named person or institution. In return for easy access to their deposits and because processing cheques is a relatively expensive operation, depositors receive a lower interest rate, or no interest, on their money.

demand deposits: accounts of funds to which depositors have immediate access

Notice Deposits   Deposit-takers can require notice before depositors withdraw funds in certain cases. **Notice deposits**, as these are called, pay substantial rates of interest but limit or exclude cheque-writing. Traditionally, both chartered banks and near banks accept notice deposits.

notice deposits: accounts of funds for which deposit-takers may require notice before withdrawals can be made

Term Deposits   When depositors guarantee that they will not withdraw their funds for a fixed period of time, deposit-takers can pay a higher

term deposits: accounts of funds to which depositors have no access for a fixed period of time

foreign currency deposits: accounts of funds held by Canadian residents that are valued in foreign currency

M1: the narrowest definition of money, consisting of publicly held currency and publicly held demand deposits at chartered banks

interest rate. **Term deposits,** as these are called, are traditionally accepted by chartered banks and near banks. Term deposits made by households are called personal term deposits, and those made by businesses are known as nonpersonal term deposits.

Foreign Currency Deposits

Some deposits provided by chartered banks in Canada are valued in terms of a foreign currency—usually the U.S. dollar. These **foreign currency deposits,** which are held by Canadian residents, are treated as a separate class of deposit.

Money Defined

What *is* money? The definitions range from the very narrow to the broad. In the following sections and in Figure 14.2, we'll examine the four most common definitions used by economists and government decision-makers: M1, M2, M3, and M2+.

M1

The narrowest definition of money is **M1.** Its two components—publicly held currency and publicly held demand deposits at chartered banks—are the two most intensively used forms of money. Note that only currency

Figure 14.2:   The Canadian Money Supply

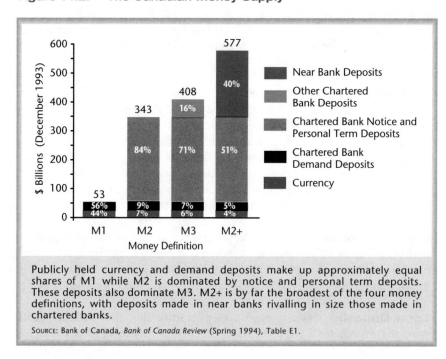

Publicly held currency and demand deposits make up approximately equal shares of M1 while M2 is dominated by notice and personal term deposits. These deposits also dominate M3. M2+ is by far the broadest of the four money definitions, with deposits made in near banks rivalling in size those made in chartered banks.

SOURCE: Bank of Canada, *Bank of Canada Review* (Spring 1994), Table E1.

circulating among the public is part of M1; cash reserves held by chartered banks are not included. Also note that only demand deposits held by the public at chartered banks are included; government-owned deposits are left out. Because of their importance, publicly held currency and demand deposits appear in all other money definitions also.

M2

M2 is a broader definition of money that includes not only publicly held currency and demand deposits at chartered banks (M1), but also funds from notice deposits and personal term deposits at chartered banks. While currency and demand deposits are perfectly liquid, notice deposits and personal term deposits must be converted into another form before being used as a means of payment.

M3

An even broader definition of the money supply is **M3**. M3 includes the components of M2 (publicly held currency, demand deposits, notice deposits, and personal term deposits at chartered banks), plus nonpersonal term deposits and foreign currency deposits at chartered banks. These additional types of deposits are relatively liquid, although less so than those included in M2.

M2+

With the growing importance of near banks in the Canadian financial system, economists have been paying more attention to a fourth definition of the money supply. **M2+** includes publicly held currency, plus demand deposits, notice deposits, and personal term deposits at both chartered banks and near banks. It does not however, include any non-personal term deposits or foreign currency deposits.

Note how the definitions build on one another, all including the most narrow definition, M1. In contrast to M1, other definitions of money include what is sometimes called **near money**. Near money includes all deposits at chartered banks except publicly held demand deposits (which are included in M1), all deposits at near banks, and some highly liquid assets such as Canada Savings Bonds. While relatively easily converted to a means of payment, near money is less frequently used than money as defined by M1.

Choosing a Definition

Since currency and demand deposits are used solely as means of payment, they seem to fit best the definition of money. Therefore, many economists view M1 as the most accurate measure of the money supply. Others believe that M1 is too narrow; these economists prefer broader definitions—especially M2 and M2+. They point to recent innovations in payment methods that have made the accounts included in M2 and M2+ more liquid.

M2: a broader definition of money, consisting of M1 plus notice deposits, and personal term deposits at chartered banks

M3: the definition of money consisting of M2 plus nonpersonal term deposits and foreign currency deposits at chartered banks

M2+: the definition of money consisting of M2 plus corresponding deposits at near banks

near money: all deposits not included in M1, plus some highly liquid assets

The Role of Credit Cards

One of the main causes of the increasing liquidity of M2 and M2+ is the ability many consumers now have to pay with "plastic." A **credit card** provides its holder with the opportunity to buy goods and services with instantly borrowed funds. When a credit card is used for a purchase, the lending institution makes a loan or "credit" to the user equal to the amount of the sale. This loan lasts as long as it takes the credit card user to pay off the monthly bill.

Contrary to popular perception, credit cards are *not* money. They are simply an easy way for buyers to borrow funds for short periods. However, credit cards do have an indirect effect on the money supply by altering the way depositors use their deposit accounts.

Well-timed purchases made with credit cards do not have to be settled for over a month. So, for example, a person making a $50 purchase with a credit card is essentially taking out a short-term loan for the same amount. As long as this loan is paid back promptly, the purchaser is charged no interest. If credit card balances are not cleared monthly, however, the interest rate charged is higher than on most other consumer loans.

About half of all credit card users pay off their outstanding balances each month. Rather than paying currency for purchases throughout a month, card users can keep their funds in their deposit accounts until credit card payments are due. Because they can maintain their deposit accounts longer, they can accumulate more interest. If card users pay off their balance monthly (and so incur no interest charges), they can profit by using credit cards effectively. This trend to use deposit accounts in combination with credit cards has led some economists to suggest that M2 and M2+ are increasingly accurate measures of the money supply.

The Introduction of Debit Cards

Some buyers are now experimenting with a new way of paying with plastic. A **debit card** allows a payment to be made through an instantaneous transfer of funds. While similar in appearance to credit cards, debit cards represent a different type of transaction, because the buyer's account is instantly reduced or "debited" by the amount of the purchase.

Debit cards are part of a widespread financial revolution that also includes the use of automated teller machines. This revolution is based on the ability of computers to move information electronically. For example, a supermarket customer might settle her $30 grocery bill with a debit card. With the use of a cash register linked electronically to financial institutions, the amount of $30 is automatically moved from her account to the supermarket's account.

Unlike credit cards, which are issued only to people who have an acceptable credit history, debit cards can be employed by virtually any depositor. They can be of particular benefit to people who are tempted to

credit card: a means of payment that provides instantly borrowed funds

debit card: a means of payment that instantaneously transfers funds from buyer to seller

overuse the instant spending power provided by credit cards. There are costs associated with debit cards, however. In the short term, the retail sector must pay for a sophisticated computer system. In some cases, this is leading to higher prices for the consumer. However, in the long term, there will be a downward pressure on prices as business costs associated with handling cash are reduced.

Thinking About Economics

Will cash eventually disappear?

Because everyone with a deposit account can use a debit card, it's possible that cash may be phased out. A cashless society would bring with it some significant benefits. Conceivably, consumers would face lower prices as the costs associated with handling cash fall, while the problems of theft would be reduced. Also, since records would exist for all transactions, it would be easier for governments to collect taxes and stamp out illegal activities.

However, a cashless society has potential drawbacks. Critics point out that governments may intervene unduly, that computer records of citizens' transactions and activities would mean a loss of privacy, and that the expense and complexities of cashless business would shut down some businesses and deter others from starting. And, of course, those involved in the underground economy, which depends on cash, would not welcome its demise.

BRIEF REVIEW

1. Money serves as a means of exchange, a store of purchasing power, and a measure of value. In contrast, barter is a cumbersome system of exchange.

2. Canada's financial system includes chartered banks, near banks, insurance companies, and investment dealers. Increasing deregulation is changing the functions of financial institutions.

3. Deposit-takers accept deposits and grant loans. Deposits vary according to their conditions.

4. Money may be defined narrowly as publicly held currency and demand deposits at chartered banks (M1), or it may be defined more broadly to include less liquid assets known as near money.

5. Credit and debit cards are not directly part of the money supply, but are gradually changing the use of money.

The Money Market

The Demand for Money

Recall that money functions as a means of exchange, a store of purchasing power, and a measure of value. In the economy as a whole, money is demanded for reasons related to the first two functions.

Transactions Demand

If real output in the economy rises, transactions increase. If the price level in the economy rises, the quantity of money exchanged increases. Conversely, a fall in real output decreases transactions, and a fall in the price level decreases the quantity of money exchanged. In other words, the change in transactions changes the amount of money demanded. The **transactions demand** for money is connected to money's use as a means of exchange.

Asset Demand

In contrast, the **asset demand** for money is associated with money's function as a store of purchasing power. As discussed earlier, the main cost of holding money is the added income that could have been earned by converting it into a higher-paying liquid asset such as a bond.

Recall that bonds are formal contracts that set out the amount borrowed, by whom, for what period of time, and at what interest rate. Most bonds can be bought and sold among lenders on the open market. When bonds "mature," or reach the end of their term, the bond issuer pays the principal to the bondholder.

On the bond market, prices for bonds are inversely related to the prevailing interest rate. To see why, suppose you purchased a $1000 bond with an interest rate specified as 6 percent per annum. In other words, you expect an annual interest payment of $60 until the bond matures, at which time you, or whoever else holds the bond, will be repaid the $1000 principal. Two years later, you want to sell the bond, but the prevailing interest rate is 12 percent. In other words, newly issued $1000 bonds are promising annual interest payments of $120, while the bond you own promises only a $60 annual interest payment. Because its annual payment is half that of new bonds, your bond will fall in price to about $500, or half of the value of a newly issued $1000 bond. Similarly, if the interest rate declines from its initial value of 6 percent to 3 percent, the price of your bond will double from its original value of $1000 to about $2000, since it provides twice the annual interest payment ($60) than the payment found on a newly issued $1000 bond ($30).

Bonds are the most popular way for governments and large businesses to raise funds. They are also attractive assets. Because they can be easily bought and sold before their term has ended, they offer liquidity as

transactions demand: the demand for money that is related to its use as a means of exchange

asset demand: the demand for money that is related to its use as a store of purchasing power

well as relatively high rates of return. For individuals who hold wealth, therefore, bonds offer the likeliest alternative to holding money.

For these reasons, the asset demand for money is inversely related to the real interest rate on bonds. When this interest rate increases, the prices of bonds fall. Lower bond prices cause some individuals to convert their money into bonds, reducing the asset demand for money. Similarly, a reduction in the real interest rate means that the prices of bonds rise. Higher-priced bonds become a less attractive option for wealthholders, causing more of them to hold money rather than bonds, thus pushing up the asset demand for money.

Money demand is the amounts of money demanded at all possible interest rates. Money demand expressed in a table gives the **money demand schedule**; expressed in a graph, it gives the **money demand curve**, D_m. As Figure 14.3 shows, the money demand curve has a negative slope. This slope is determined by the asset demand for money, which is inversely related to interest rate changes. As we have just seen, a rise in the real interest rate on bonds reduces the asset demand for money, while a fall in the real interest rate increases the asset demand. Therefore, a change in the asset demand causes a change in the quantity of money demanded, or a movement along the money demand curve.

money demand: the amounts of money demanded at all possible interest rates

money demand schedule: money demand expressed in a table

money demand curve: money demand expressed in a graph

Figure 14.3:   The Demand for Money

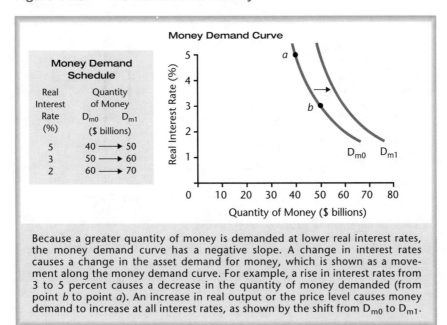

Because a greater quantity of money is demanded at lower real interest rates, the money demand curve has a negative slope. A change in interest rates causes a change in the asset demand for money, which is shown as a movement along the money demand curve. For example, a rise in interest rates from 3 to 5 percent causes a decrease in the quantity of money demanded (from point *b* to point *a*). An increase in real output or the price level causes money demand to increase at all interest rates, as shown by the shift from D_{m0} to D_{m1}.

In contrast, a change in transactions demand changes the amounts demanded at all interest rates—that is, it causes a shift in the money demand curve. An increase in either real output or the price level raises the transactions demand for money at every possible real interest rate. Hence, the money demand curve shifts to the right, from D_{m0} to D_{m1}, as shown in Figure 14.3. Conversely, a decrease in either real output or the price level shifts the money demand curve to the left.

The Supply of Money

money supply: a set amount of money in the economy, as determined by government decision-makers

money supply schedule: money supply expressed in a table

money supply curve: money supply expressed in a graph

While money demanded is inversely related to interest rates, the **money supply** is a set amount determined by government decision-makers. As Figure 14.4 shows, money supply can be expressed in a table, giving the **money supply schedule**, or in a graph, giving the **money supply curve**, S_m. No matter what the real interest rate, the amount of money supplied is a constant value, as depicted by the vertical supply curve, S_{m0}. Only when government decision-makers decide to change the money supply does the supply curve shift. Therefore, the supply curve shifts to the right, from S_{m0} to S_{m1}, only when the government increases the money supply. Likewise, the money supply curve shifts to the left only when the government decreases the money supply.

Figure 14.4:   The Supply of Money

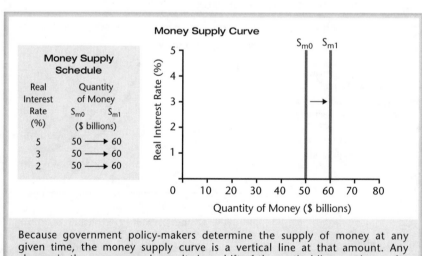

Because government policy-makers determine the supply of money at any given time, the money supply curve is a vertical line at that amount. Any change in the money supply results in a shift of the vertical line, as shown, for example, by the shift from S_{m0} to S_{m1}.

Equilibrium in the Money Market

The demand and supply of money interact in the money market to bring about a state of equilibrium. As shown in Figure 14.5, the equilibrium level of the real interest rate is found at the intersection of the money demand and money supply curves. As usual, surpluses and shortages help bring about equilibrium in the market.

Figure 14.5:   Equilibrium in the Money Market

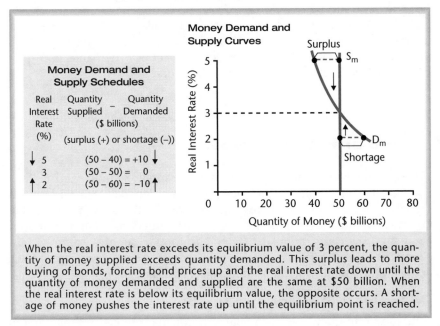

When the real interest rate exceeds its equilibrium value of 3 percent, the quantity of money supplied exceeds quantity demanded. This surplus leads to more buying of bonds, forcing bond prices up and the real interest rate down until the quantity of money demanded and supplied are the same at $50 billion. When the real interest rate is below its equilibrium value, the opposite occurs. A shortage of money pushes the interest rate up until the equilibrium point is reached.

When the interest rate is above its equilibrium level—for example, at 5 percent as opposed to 3 percent in Figure 14.5—there is a surplus of money. In other words, more money is supplied than is demanded. As people try to rid themselves of money and buy assets that will provide high earnings, the demand for these assets rises, pushing up their price and causing the real interest rate to fall. This trend of falling interest rates continues until the discrepancy between the demand and supply of money is eliminated.

In the opposite case, the interest rate falls short of the equilibrium value, as at 2 percent on the graph, causing a shortage of money. In other words, more money is demanded than is supplied. As people try to sell assets such as bonds in order to acquire money, the price of these assets falls, causing the real interest rate to rise until the equilibrium point is attained.

BRIEF REVIEW

1. Demand for money is of two types, each of which is related to a function of money. Transactions demand relates to the function of money as a means of exchange; asset demand relates to the function of money as a store of purchasing power.

2. Money demand is the amounts of money demanded at all possible interest rates, which can be expressed in a table or a graph. The money demand curve has a negative slope because of the inverse relationship of money demanded to interest rates.

3. Money supply is a set amount that is determined by government decision-makers. As a result, the money supply curve is a vertical line at this set amount.

4. The economy's equilibrium interest rate and money supply occur at the intersection of the money demand and money supply curves.

 ## The Bank of Canada

The moving force behind adjustments in the supply of money is the Bank of Canada, which since 1935 has served as Canada's central bank. A wholly government-owned institution, the "Bank" as it is known has been given a mandate to perform four basic functions relating to money and the financial system: managing the money supply, acting as "the bankers' bank," acting as the federal government's fiscal agent, and ensuring the stable operation of financial markets.

Managing the Money Supply

The most important role of the Bank of Canada is to control the amount of money circulating in the economy. That is, the Bank decides and implements monetary policy. Not only does it issue paper currency, but more importantly it affects the activities of chartered banks so that it can vary the supply of money and interest rates. In managing the money supply, the Bank is concerned with three goals: minimizing inflation in order to preserve the purchasing power of the dollar; maintaining real output as close as possible to its potential level, and regulating the external value of the Canadian dollar on foreign exchange markets.

Acting as the Bankers' Bank

The Bank of Canada holds the deposits of financial institutions that are members of the Canadian Payments Association (CPA). The association includes the chartered banks and some near banks—in particular, the larger trust companies and representatives of credit unions and *caisses populaires*. The deposits kept at the Bank of Canada are used for several purposes.

The Canadian Payments Association acts as a clearing house for cheques of both chartered banks and near banks. Suppose, for example, that Depositor A has a chequing account with Tecumseh Trust. He writes a $50 cheque to Depositor B, who deposits this cheque in her account at Elgin Bank, increasing her deposit balance by $50. Elgin Bank delivers the cheque to Tecumseh Trust, and receives $50 in return. This payment between the two banks is actually made by using the accounts kept by both institutions (or larger banks acting as their representatives) at the Bank of Canada. The $50 is transferred from Tecumseh Trust's account to Elgin Bank's account at the Bank of Canada. To complete the entire exchange, Tecumseh then cancels the cheque it has received and reduces Depositor A's deposit account by $50. Each day, every cheque transaction like this is added up by the Bank of Canada, and the accounts of members of the Canadian Payments Association are all "cleared" at once. This procedure vastly simplifies the transactions that are made necessary by the use of cheques among various deposit-takers.

The accounts held at the Bank of Canada by chartered banks are a part of their cash reserves. Recall that these cash reserves—which also include currency sitting in bank vaults—are kept so that sufficient funds are available to meet withdrawal requests from depositors.

On those infrequent occasions when a chartered bank finds that its cash reserves are too low, it can borrow from the Bank of Canada. The Bank provides a short-term loan, or an "advance" as it is usually known, by depositing the required funds in the chartered bank's account at the Bank of Canada. The interest rate charged on these advances is called the **bank rate**. Because the bank rate is higher than the interest rates on other available sources of loans, chartered banks rarely take out Bank of Canada advances. Nonetheless, they are a necessary backup to guarantee that chartered banks do not run out of cash reserves.

bank rate: the interest rate chartered banks are charged on advances from the Bank of Canada

Acting as the Federal Government's Fiscal Agent

In Chapter 13, we discussed the fiscal, or budgetary, policy that Canadian governments institute in order to level out the business cycle. In order to conduct the business of spending, taxing, and so on, the federal government needs a bank to manage its transactions and financial assets. In its role as the government's fiscal agent, the Bank of Canada engages in three main tasks: the Bank holds some of the government's bank deposits and decides where the other deposits should be held, it acts as the government's banker by clearing federal government cheques, and it handles the financing of the federal government's debt by issuing bonds. Government bonds fall into various categories, the most notable being Canada Savings Bonds and treasury bills.

Canada Savings Bonds are popular with household savers. These bonds differ from others in that they are not bought and sold after they

Canada Savings Bonds: federal government bonds that have a set value throughout their term

have first been issued. Instead, holders of Canada Savings Bonds who want their funds back before the bonds have matured must "cash in" the bonds with the Bank of Canada at a set price. Since savers know exactly how much they will receive for the bond during its entire term, this feature of Canada Savings Bonds increases their attractiveness. Recall that ordinary bonds, in contrast, fluctuate in price before their maturity date depending on the value of interest rates in the economy. Hence, they are somewhat riskier than Canada Savings Bonds.

treasury bills: short-term federal government bonds that provide no interest, but are sold at a discount

Treasury bills are an important type of short-term federal government bond. They have terms of three months to a year, and are usually issued in large denominations. Unlike other government bonds, treasury bills provide no interest payments. Rather, they are sold at a marked down price. For example, a treasury bill worth $100 000 might be bought—usually by banks and other financial institutions—for $95 000. Once the treasury bill matures, the holder receives the face value of $100 000, thereby earning an income of $5000 ($100 000 – $95 000). Viewed in another way, the $5000 earned at maturity can be seen as interest on the original purchase price, or as a nominal rate of interest of 5.3 percent [($5000 ÷ $95 000) × 100%]. The price for federal treasury bills is decided at an auction conducted each Tuesday by the Bank of Canada.

Thinking About Economics

How is the auction of treasury bills conducted?

The main buyers in the treasury bill market are the chartered banks, the large near banks, and investment dealers. The Bank of Canada also buys treasury bills to become part of its bond holdings. Buyers provide written bids, which outline the price they are willing to pay and the number of bills they want. As in any auction, the bills go to the highest bidders; those who bid highest have their orders filled first. The average price per week is therefore determined by the supply of bills and the expectations of buyers.

Ensuring the Stability of Financial Markets

In tandem with other agencies, the Bank of Canada supervises the operation of financial markets to ensure their stability. The Bank has a particular responsibility in overseeing the activity of chartered banks. By doing so, it helps protect the safety of depositors' funds and the soundness of the financial system.

The Domino Effect

The Danger of Bank Failure

Both chartered banks and near banks are especially susceptible to financial risk. During a downturn in the economy, a high percentage of a bank's borrowers may no longer be able to pay off their loans. Without the participation of governments, this situation could turn into a crisis, causing depositors to wonder whether their funds are safe.

When many depositors try to make withdrawals from their accounts at the same time, they create a bank run. This occurs whenever a bank loses a large portion of its cash reserves because of depositors' worries over financial security.

Like many situations that cause people to panic, a bank run feeds on itself. Because a bank holds only a fraction of its deposits as reserves, it soon exhausts its cash holdings when faced with a stampede of depositors trying to withdraw their money. A bank's inability to pay off depositors only adds to the chance that it will be forced to declare bankruptcy. It is also likely that other financial institutions will feel the impact as the "domino effect" extends. Not only the financial sector will be affected, but the entire economy can be harmed by widespread bank failures. As households find their financial wealth reduced, they respond by consuming less, pushing down aggregate demand and real output.

Such a crisis occurred in the United States during the early 1930s, when over 9000 banks were forced to declare bankruptcy. Luckily, because of Canada's much more centralized system, no Canadian banks failed during these years.

Since then, several measures have been introduced to make bank runs less likely. One of the most important is depositor insurance, which in Canada is administered by the Canada Deposit Insurance Corporation (CDIC). The bulk of deposits at chartered banks and near banks are covered by this insurance. Depositors are guaranteed to receive funds, if a bank fails, for any amount up to $60 000.

Knowing that these measures are in place makes depositors less likely to react to bad news by withdrawing funds. Still, bank runs have not been entirely eliminated. In 1985, two small Alberta-based chartered banks—the Northlands Bank and the Canadian Commercial Bank—were forced to declare bankruptcy. Despite heavy borrowing from the Bank of Canada and other financial institutions, these banks faced cash drains because most of their deposits were over the $60 000 insurance limit. Not surprisingly, many of these deposit-holders fled when the extent of the banks' bad loans was publicized. Luckily, because of the small size and regional focus of these two banks, their failure caused little harm to the rest of the Canadian financial system.

In an essay, evaluate the following assertion: "The banking system is stable only to the extent of its depositors' faith in the system."

Monetary Policy

Recall that monetary policy involves the Bank of Canada changing interest rates, altering the money supply, or both, in order to stabilize the economy. Our analysis of money and deposit-takers allows us to examine the way in which monetary policy is conducted.

Expansionary Monetary Policy

When real output falls short of its potential level, a recessionary gap is created. In order to stimulate output and increase employment, the Bank of Canada can use **expansionary monetary policy**. Such action is referred to informally as an "easy money policy."

The Bank of Canada applies an easy money policy by expanding the money supply. As shown on the left in Figure 14.6, increasing the money supply shifts the money supply curve, S_m, to the right, causing a drop in the equilibrium interest rate.

To see how this lower interest rate affects aggregate demand, remember that a fall in interest rates makes borrowing funds cheaper. Businesses respond by increasing their investment spending, and households purchase

expansionary monetary policy: a policy of increasing the money supply and reducing interest rates to stimulate the economy

Figure 14.6: An Expansionary Monetary Policy

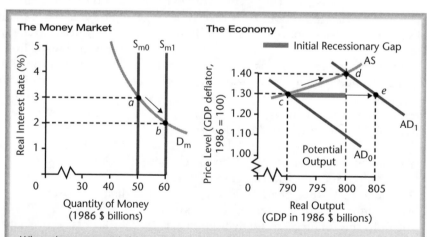

When the economy is in a recession, the Bank of Canada can increase the supply of money, shown by the shift from S_{m0} to S_{m1} on the left, thereby pushing down the interest rate from 3 percent to 2 percent (point *a* to point *b*). Because of the initial spending increase and the spending multiplier, the result in the economy as a whole is an increase in aggregate demand, as shown on the right as the $15 billion shift from AD_0 to AD_1. Output does not rise by $15 billion (from point *c* to point *e*); rather, the price level and output both rise to give a new equilibrium at point *d*, with output at the potential level of $800 billion and the recessionary gap eliminated.

more durable goods, raising consumption. Both adjustments spur an initial increase in spending that is then magnified by the same successive cycles of new spending as seen in the case of an expansionary fiscal policy, as discussed in Chapter 13.

The effect is the same as when government purchases increase. The change in aggregate demand, or total spending, is found by calculating the product of the spending multiplier and the initial spending change. Suppose, for example, that the initial increase in investment and consumption totalled $9 billion and the value of the economy's spending multiplier is 1.67. The total change in aggregate demand is then $15 billion:

$$\text{Total change in output (shift in AD curve)} = \text{initial change in spending} \times \text{spending multiplier}$$

$$\$15 \text{ billion} = \$9 \text{ billion} \times 1.67$$

As shown on the right in Figure 14.6, the $15 billion shift in the aggregate demand curve causes equilibrium output to rise by a smaller amount—$10 billion—because of the accompanying price level rise.

Contractionary Monetary Policy

Conversely, during an economic boom, the Bank of Canada can inhibit spending and inflation with a **contractionary monetary policy**. Such action, also known as a "tight money policy," decreases the money supply. The result, as shown on the left in Figure 14.7, is that the money supply curve, S_m, shifts to the left, driving up the equilibrium interest rate.

The higher interest rate discourages investment spending by businesses as well as consumption spending on durable items by households, so it influences aggregate demand. Both trends cause an initial reduction of spending that is then magnified by the spending multiplier. Suppose, for example, that investment and consumption spending decline initially by $10 billion, and the spending multiplier is 1.5. As a result, the total decrease in aggregate demand is $15 billion:

contractionary monetary policy: a policy of decreasing the money supply and increasing interest rates to dampen the economy

$$\text{Total change in output (shift in AD curve)} = \text{initial change in spending} \times \text{spending multiplier}$$

$$\$15 \text{ billion} = \$9 \text{ billion} \times 1.5$$

Once again, the change in output causes a lesser change in actual spending because of the change in price level at the same time. In this case, as shown on the right in Figure 14.7, the $15 billion decrease in aggregate demand causes a $5 billion decrease in equilibrium output.

Figure 14.7:   A Contractionary Monetary Policy

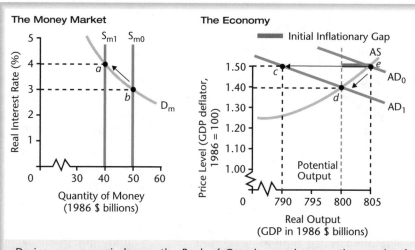

The Money Market

The Economy

During an economic boom, the Bank of Canada can decrease the supply of money, shown by the shift from S_{m0} to S_{m1} on the left, thereby pushing up the interest rate from 3 percent to 4 percent (point *b* to point *a*). Because of the initial spending increase and the spending multiplier, the result in the economy as a whole is a decrease in aggregate demand, as shown on the right as the $15 billion shift from AD_0 to AD_1. Output does not fall by $15 billion (from point *e* to point *c*); rather, the price level and output both fall to give a new equilibrium at point *d*, with output at the potential level of $800 billion and the inflationary gap eliminated.

BRIEF REVIEW

1. Canada's central bank—the Bank of Canada—manages the money supply, serves as a bank for chartered banks and some near banks, acts as the federal government's fiscal agent, and helps to ensure the stability of financial markets.

2. An expansionary monetary policy raises real output toward its potential level by increasing the money supply and decreasing interest rates. The resulting increase in investment and consump-

tion are magnified by the spending multiplier to give an even greater increase in aggregate demand.

3. A contractionary monetary policy reduces real output toward its potential level by decreasing the money supply and increasing interest rates. The resulting decrease in investment and consumption are magnified by the spending multiplier to give an even greater decrease in aggregate demand.

Money Creation

So monetary policy changes the money supply—but by how much? To answer this question, we must look again at the actions of deposit-takers. This is because a substantial portion of money in the economy is held in the form of deposits.

Recall that deposit-takers receive deposits from savers and lend to borrowers, while keeping some cash reserves on hand for withdrawals by depositors. By charging higher interest rates to lenders than they pay to depositors, deposit-takers make profits. In a sense, through this process of receiving deposits and lending funds, chartered banks and near banks *create* deposit money. This is not by some trick of magic, but by the roles played by cash reserves and the profit motive.

Desired Reserves

Until 1994, chartered banks were legally required to hold certain levels of cash reserves, more than near banks were required to hold. After 1994, both chartered banks and near banks have kept only **desired reserves**, which are the minimum amounts of cash necessary to satisfy anticipated withdrawal demands.

desired reserves: minimum cash reserves that deposit-takers hold to satisfy anticipated withdrawal demands

The Reserve Ratio

In general, the more money a deposit-taker holds in deposits, the greater the withdrawals it can expect. Therefore, the best way to deal with anticipated withdrawals is for the deposit-taker to hold a certain portion of deposits in the form of cash reserves. This portion, which can be expressed as a percentage or in decimal terms, is the **reserve ratio**. Suppose, for example, that a bank has a reserve ratio of 0.10. If the bank has deposits of $100 million, then it will hold 10 percent of this dollar value as desired reserves ($100 million × 0.10):

reserve ratio: desired reserves expressed as a percentage of deposits or as a decimal

$$\text{Reserve ratio} = \frac{\text{desired reserves}}{\text{deposits}}$$

$$0.10 = \frac{\$10 \text{ million}}{\$100 \text{ million}}$$

Different types of deposits have different reserve ratios. For example, demand deposits require a higher reserve ratio than do other types of deposits. However, to examine the process of money creation, we'll simplify matters by assuming a uniform reserve ratio.

Excess Reserves

At times, deposit-takers find that their cash reserves exceed desired levels, or they have **excess reserves**. For example, a chartered bank with

excess reserves: cash reserves that are in excess of desired reserves

deposits of $100 million and desired reserves of $10 million may find itself holding $14 million in actual cash reserves:

$$\text{Excess reserves} = \text{cash reserves} - \text{desired reserves}$$
$$\$4 \text{ million} = \$14 \text{ million} - \$10 \text{ million}$$

Because idle cash reserves earn no profit, deposit-takers will try to transform any excess reserves into income-producing assets as quickly as possible. They therefore lend out the full amount of excess reserves. In our example, the bank will lend out the $4 million excess to borrowers.

The Money Creation Process

To see how lending out excess reserves "creates" money, let's consider an example. For the time being, we will make two key assumptions. First, the public holds money in the form of deposits and only uses cheques for transactions. Second, all deposits are made to one sort of deposit-taker, which we'll simply call banks, and all deposits are of one type, which allows cheques to be written against them. We'll also assume the banks' reserve ratio for their deposits to be 0.10, or 10 percent.

First Transaction

At the outset, Cabot Bank has cash reserves equal to desired reserves. However, Saver A receives $1000 in currency and immediately deposits it in Cabot Bank. As shown in Figure 14.8, Cabot Bank has a new cash asset as well as a new deposit liability to Saver A, each equalling $1000. So far, there has been no change in the amount of money in the economy, only in who holds it. Because the $1000 in currency is transformed into $1000 held in a deposit, no money is added to the money supply. (Recall that the $1000 in currency sitting in the vault of Cabot Bank is *not* considered part of the money supply.)

Figure 14.8:   Opening a Deposit

Cabot Bank			
Assets		**Liabilities**	
Cash Reserves	+*$1000*	Saver A's Deposit	+*$1000*

Saver A deposits $1000 at Cabot Bank. As a result, Cabot Bank has new cash assets and deposit liabilities of $1000.

Second Transaction

Because of Saver A's deposit, Cabot Bank's total deposits increase by $1000. At the same time, the actual cash reserves increase by $1000 as well. However, with a reserve ratio of 0.10, Cabot Bank really only wants to keep $100 of the newly deposited $1000 on hand as desired reserves ($1000 × 0.10). As a result of this new deposit, Cabot Bank has excess reserves of $900 ($1000 − $100).

The bank responds by lending $900 to Borrower X. As Figure 14.9 demonstrates, the new loan increases Cabot Bank's deposit liabilities by $900. In other words, by lending out its excess reserves, Cabot Bank creates $900 in new money.

Figure 14.9:   Granting a Loan

Cabot Bank			
Assets		**Liabilities**	
Cash Reserves	$1000	Saver A's Deposit	$1000
Loan to Borrower X	+*$900*	Borrower X's Deposit	+*$900*

Cabot Bank lends out its $900 in excess reserves to Borrower X, creating new loan assets and deposit liabilities of $900. Since Borrower X's new deposit is money, the money supply has risen by $900.

Third Transaction

Now that he has the money, Borrower X uses his $900 loan to purchase goods or services. Figure 14.10 shows the resulting changes in both Cabot Bank's cash assets and the new deposit to Borrower X—they are both reduced by $900.

Figure 14.10:   Withdrawing a Deposit

Cabot Bank			
Assets		**Liabilities**	
Cash Reserves	$100 ($1000 − *$900*)	Saver A's Deposit	$1000
Loan to Borrower X	$900	Borrower X's Deposit	$0 ($900 − *$900*)

When Borrower X withdraws the $900 from his deposit, Cabot Bank's cash assets and deposit liabilities each fall by $900.

Fourth Transaction

So, does reducing Cabot Bank's deposits mean the newly created money suddenly disappears? It doesn't if we take into account Borrower X's $900 purchase. Suppose Borrower X bought something for $900 from Saver B. Saver B, in turn, deposits the $900 from the sale in her account at Fraser Bank. As a result, Fraser Bank's cash assets and deposit liabilities increase by $900, as shown in Figure 14.11. This means that the $900 deposit originally created by Cabot Bank has simply moved to Fraser Bank. As a result of this transaction, there is no change in the money supply.

Figure 14.11:   Accepting Deposit Funds

Fraser Bank			
Assets		**Liabilities**	
Cash Reserves	+$900	Saver B's Deposit	+$900

Saver B deposits the $900 from Borrower X's purchase in her account at Fraser Bank. The bank's cash assets and deposit liabilities both rise by $900.

Fifth Transaction

Now, let's consider Fraser Bank. Because Saver B's deposit to Fraser Bank increases the total deposits of the bank, desired reserves should increase by $90 ($900 × 0.10). Once again, however, the deposit of $900 also increases the cash reserves, thereby giving excess reserves of $810 ($900 – $90).

Because the excess reserves can be put to use to earn profits, Fraser Bank lends the $810 to Borrower Y. As a result, Fraser Bank's cash assets and deposit liabilities have jumped by $810, as shown in Figure 14.12. Because of this rise in deposits, more new money has been created, so the money supply has been boosted by another $810.

Figure 14.12:   Granting a Loan

Fraser Bank			
Assets		**Liabilities**	
Cash Reserves	$900	Saver B's Deposit	$900
Loan to Borrower Y	+$810	Borrower Y's Deposit	+$810

Fraser Bank lends out its $810 in excess reserves to Borrower Y. This creates added cash assets and deposit liabilities of $810. Since Borrower Y's new deposit is money, the money supply increases by $810.

The Money Multiplier

The possible transactions are endless. However, we can see the process of money creation in the few transactions outlined. Recall that the quantity of money increased once, when Cabot Bank lent out its $900 in excess reserves to Borrower X, and again, when Fraser Bank lent out its excess reserves of $810 to Borrower Y. In other words, the money supply increases $1710 in these few transactions. Money will continue to be created as long as banks find they have excess cash reserves to lend out.

Notice how the process of money creation is similar to the process of the spending multiplier, as outlined in Chapter 13. In this money creation process, an initial change in money has a magnified effect on the money supply. The **money multiplier** is the value by which the initial change is multiplied to give the maximum total change in money supply. Suppose, for example, that the initial change in excess reserves is $900 and the final change in the money supply is $4500; the money multiplier therefore has a value of 5:

> **money multiplier:** the value by which the amount of excess reserves is multiplied to give the maximum total change in money supply

$$\text{Change in money supply} = \text{change in excess reserves} \times \text{money multiplier}$$

$$\$4500 = \$900 \times 5$$

The Multiplier Formula

The value of the money multiplier is determined in the same way as the size of the spending multiplier. Recall that the spending multiplier is the reciprocal of the marginal propensity to withdraw (MPW), which indicates how much is taken out of the income-spending stream with each spending cycle.

In the case of the money creation process, deposit-takers hold back a certain portion of the funds in each lending cycle. As we've seen, this portion is determined by the reserve ratio. So, in money creation, the multiplier is the reciprocal of the reserve ratio. In our example, with banks reserving 10 percent (or 0.10) of deposits, the money multiplier is 10 ($1.00 \div 0.10$). In other words, the initial change in the money supply ($900) eventually causes an increase in the money supply of $9000:

$$\text{Money multiplier} = \frac{1}{\text{reserve ratio}}$$

$$10 = \frac{1}{0.10}$$

$$\text{Change in money supply} = \text{change in excess reserves} \times \text{money multiplier}$$
$$\$9000 = \$900 \times 10$$

Adjustments to the Money Multiplier

In order to see how money is created, we temporarily assumed that all money is in the form of deposits, and all deposits are made to one sort of deposit-taker offering only a single type of deposit. However, these assumptions don't hold true in reality. Let's consider the implications in turn.

Publicly Held Currency

The public, of course, does use currency, and currency is a part of all definitions of money. So, rather than all money going to deposit-takers, who then keep some as reserves and lend the rest, some money does circulate and is unaffected by the money multiplier. Thus, in our example, the money supply would not increase by $9000 but by a lesser amount.

Differences in Deposits

As we've noted, there is a wide range of deposit types, and not all types are represented in the narrowest definition of money, M1. Therefore, as deposit money expands in the succession of transactions, not all of it will be reflected as an increase in money supply defined as M1. So, the money supply in our example would increase by an amount less than $9000.

Thinking About Economics

How relevant is the money multiplier in the Canadian monetary system?

The money multiplier represents the *maximum* possible effect of money creation. Returning to our example, the money multiplier formula allows us to specify the maximum amount ($9000) by which the quantity of money rises as a result of the infusion of $900 in new excess cash reserves into the economy. Because of the various factors that influence this increase, the exact size of the money multiplier can vary significantly.

BRIEF REVIEW

1. Deposit-takers reserve a certain percentage of deposits to satisfy withdrawal requests from depositors. This percentage is known as the reserve ratio, and the resulting dollar amount equals the desired reserves.

2. Cash reserves in excess of desired reserves are lent out to borrowers in order to create profit.

3. In the same way that spending is magnified, lending excess reserves magnifies deposits.

4. The money multiplier is the reciprocal of the reserve ratio *and* the maximum value by which an initial change in money changes the money supply.

Tools of Monetary Policy

The Bank of Canada has four different tools it can use to conduct monetary policy: open market operations, the bank rate, government deposits, and moral suasion.

Open Market Operations

Recall that the Bank of Canada sells and buys back federal government bonds. Its role in the bond market is the major tool with which the Bank of Canada conducts monetary policy. Through selling and buying back federal bonds, the Bank of Canada can use deposit-takers' cash reserves as a lever to influence both the money supply and interest rates. Because these transactions take place in the open bond market, they are called **open market operations**.

open market operations: the buying and selling of federal government bonds by the Bank of Canada

Bond Sales

Consider the sale by the Bank of Canada of a $1000 bond to Bondholder A. When the sale takes place, Bondholder A pays for the bond with a cheque written against his deposit account at Cartier Bank. The Bank of Canada sends the cheque to Cartier Bank, which then cancels the cheque and reduces Bondholder A's account by $1000. Most importantly, Cartier Bank pays the Bank of Canada for the cheque by having $1000 taken out of its Bank of Canada account, as shown in Figure 14.13.

Figure 14.13:   A Bond Sale

Bank of Canada			
Assets		**Liabilities**	
Bonds	–$1000	Cartier Bank's Deposit	–$1000

Cartier Bank			
Assets		**Liabilities**	
Reserves at Bank of Canada	–$1000	Bondholder A's Deposit	–$1000

When the Bank of Canada sells a federal government bond to Bondholder A, its bond assets fall, as do its deposit liabilities to Cartier Bank. Meanwhile, Cartier Bank's cash assets at the Bank of Canada decrease, as do its deposit liabilities to Bondholder A. The drop in Bondholder A's deposit immediately reduces the money supply by $1000. With a reserve ratio of 10 percent, Cartier Bank's excess reserves fall by $900 and the money multiplier has a value of 10. Because reductions to deposits are magnified, the money supply drops by as much as an extra $9000 (the $900 decrease in excess reserves multiplied by the money multiplier).

The money supply immediately falls by $1000 due to the loss of the deposit previously held by Bondholder A. Assuming that the reserve ratio is 0.10, Cartier Bank's excess reserves are cut by $900, causing a multiple reduction of the money supply. Cartier Bank has less money available to lend. With a reserve ratio of 0.10 and a maximum money multiplier of 10, the further decline in the supply of money could be as much as $9000 ($900 × 10).

Therefore, the sale of federal government bonds reduces the cash reserves of deposit-takers, which, in turn, cuts back on lending, and finally decreases the supply of money. By selling bonds, the Bank of Canada engages in contractionary monetary policy.

Bond Purchases

Now, consider the implications of the Bank of Canada buying back bonds from members of the public in the open market. Suppose the Bank of Canada buys back a $1000 bond from Bondholder B. Bondholder B receives a cheque from the Bank of Canada, which she deposits in her account at Cartier Bank. On acquiring the cheque, Cartier Bank delivers it to the Bank of Canada, and receives in return a $1000 addition to its Bank of Canada deposit.

As Figure 14.14 shows, both the money supply and Cartier Bank's cash reserves increase by $1000 due to the new deposit held by Bondholder B. However, the bank, with a reserve ratio of 0.10, need only hold back

Figure 14.14:   A Bond Purchase

Bank of Canada			
Assets		**Liabilities**	
Bonds	+$1000	Cartier Bank's Deposit	+$1000

Cartier Bank			
Assets		**Liabilities**	
Reserves at Bank of Canada	+$1000	Bondholder B's Deposit	+$1000

If the Bank of Canada purchases a federal government bond from Bondholder B, its bond assets rise, as do its deposit liabilities to Cartier Bank. From Cartier Bank's perspective, its cash assets at the Bank of Canada increase, as do its deposit liabilities to Bondholder B. The new deposit from Bondholder B immediately adds $1000 to the money supply. With a reserve ratio of 0.10, Cartier Bank's excess reserves increase by $900, while the money multiplier has a value of 10. Because deposits expand, the money supply increases by as much as an extra $9000 (the $900 increase in excess reserves multiplied by the money multiplier).

$100. Therefore, the bank has excess reserves of $900 ($1000 − $100). Cartier Bank will lend this money, which in turn will increase the money supply in a series of transactions similar to those outlined earlier in this chapter. Assuming a uniform reserve ratio of 0.10, we can see that the money multiplier (10, or the reciprocal of 0.10), creates a further increase in the money supply of up to $9000 ($900 × 10).

Therefore, buying back federal government bonds allows the Bank of Canada to practise expansionary monetary policy. Cash reserves increase, resulting in increased lending, which causes the money supply to expand.

The Bank Rate

As we have noted, the bank rate is the interest rate paid by chartered banks when they receive Bank of Canada advances. While the Bank of Canada makes these advances infrequently, the bank rate plays an important role in monetary policy.

The bank rate is tied to the auction of federal treasury bills. Each Tuesday, the rate is adjusted so it is one-quarter of a percentage point above the average return on treasury bills with a term of three months. If treasury bills give a return to buyers of 5.5 percent, for example, chartered banks pay 5.75 percent when borrowing from the Bank of Canada during the next week.

By supplying more or less treasury bills to sell at the weekly auction and by adjusting its own bid for treasury bills, the Bank of Canada can affect the bank rate. This action is a signal of where monetary policy is heading in the near future. A rise in the bank rate signifies that the Bank of Canada will pursue a tighter monetary policy, by lowering the money supply and raising interest rates, in order to dampen spending. A fall in the bank rate indicates an expansionary monetary policy.

If the change in the bank rate is substantial, chartered banks may decide to alter their own interest rates in the same direction. In particular, they adjust their **prime rate**, which is the lowest possible rate charged by chartered banks on loans to their best corporate customers. When the prime rate varies, so do all other rates for depositors and borrowers.

prime rate: the lowest possible interest rate charged by chartered banks on loans to their best corporate customers

Government Deposits

Recall that the Bank of Canada acts as the federal government's banker. However, the federal government's deposits are held in both the Bank of Canada and in chartered banks. The Bank conducts monetary policy by moving some deposits from the Bank of Canada to chartered banks, or vice versa.

Suppose, for example, that the Bank of Canada moves a $1000 government deposit to Cartier Bank. As shown in Figure 14.15, Cartier Bank receives payment by having $1000 added to its account at the Bank of Canada. As a result, Cartier Bank's reserves increase by $1000. While the new government deposit is not held by the public, and so is not included in the definition of money, it does affect Cartier Bank's dealings. If Cartier Bank has a reserve ratio of 0.10, then only $100 of the $1000 new deposit need be kept as cash reserves; the remaining $900 can be lent out. Given the money multiplier of 10 (the reciprocal of 0.10), these excess reserves may be magnified to increase the money supply by a maximum of $9000 ($900 × 10).

Figure 14.15:   Movements of Government Deposits

Bank of Canada

Assets	Liabilities	
	Government Deposits	−$1000
	Cartier Bank's Deposits	+$1000

Cartier Bank

Assets		Liabilities	
Reserves at Bank of Canada	+$1000	Government Deposits	+$1000

When the Bank of Canada moves a federal government deposit from itself to Cartier Bank, Cartier Bank's deposits increase. Cartier Bank's cash assets at the Bank of Canada rise, as do its deposit liabilities to the government. Meanwhile, the Bank of Canada's deposit liabilities to the federal government fall, while the Bank of Canada's deposit liabilities to Cartier Bank rise. With a reserve ratio of 10 percent, excess reserves increase by $900 and the money multiplier has a value of 10. Because of the movement of government deposits, the money supply can increase by as much as $9000.

Therefore, by moving federal government deposits from the Bank of Canada to chartered banks, the Bank of Canada conducts expansionary monetary policy. Conversely, by moving deposits from chartered banks back to the Bank of Canada by calling in deposits, the Bank of Canada conducts contractionary monetary policy.

Moral Suasion

In some cases, the Bank of Canada may choose to intervene more directly in the ways that chartered banks conduct their business. Requests to chartered banks to follow a particular lending policy (for example, to lend out excess cash reserves in a time when deposit growth is needed) are known as **moral suasion**. While the oligopolistic nature of the Canadian chartered banking system makes such requests possible, moral suasion tends to be used only in unusual circumstances.

moral suasion: direct influence by the Bank of Canada on chartered banks' lending policies

Benefits of Monetary Policy

Monetary policy has two main benefits: its separation from politics, and the speed with which it can be applied. These benefits have made monetary policy the most important stabilization tool in recent years.

Separation From Politics

Unlike fiscal policy, which is usually a well-publicized element of the political process, monetary policy is detached from political influence. While the Bank of Canada is under the control of Parliament, as represented by the Prime Minister and cabinet, in practice the Bank of Canada is controlled by appointed officials—the most important being its governor, who serves a seven-year term—and its operations are veiled from public view. Thus, monetary policy tends to be focused on economic rather than political goals.

Speed

Recall that fiscal policy suffers from recognition, decision, and impact lags. While recognizing a problem can also cause a delay in monetary policy and the impact of any policy may also be delayed, decisions regarding monetary policy can be made speedily.

Drawbacks of Monetary Policy

Monetary policy does have two major drawbacks: its relative weakness as an expansionary tool, and its broad impact.

Weakness as an Expansionary Tool

The Bank of Canada is quite capable of restraining an overheated economy during a boom period. By squeezing the chartered banks' excess reserves through open market sales of bonds and shifts of government deposits to the Bank of Canada, it can be assured that the money supply will fall, pushing up interest rates and reducing spending and output.

However, matters are not necessarily so straightforward during a severe recession or depression. While the Bank can increase banks' cash reserves through open market purchases of bonds and shifts of government deposits to chartered banks, there is no guarantee that this will translate into more bank loans and an expansion of the money supply. If banks hold on to their extra cash reserves, the desired increase in the money supply will not occur.

Broad Impact

Unlike fiscal policy, which can be focused on particular regions, monetary policy affects every region of the country uniformly. When the Bank of Canada raises interest rates during a boom, for example, the impact is felt not only in those parts of the economy with overheated economies, but also in areas that have been relatively unaffected by the upswing. As a result, regions already enduring high rates of unemployment experience even more.

BRIEF REVIEW

1. The Bank of Canada pursues monetary policy mainly through open market operations. Buying government bonds from the public is an expansionary policy that increases chartered bank reserves, leading to a magnified increase in the money supply. In contrast, selling bonds reduces the money supply.

2. The Bank of Canada can also influence interest rates through its auctions of treasury bills, which in turn affect the bank rate, which in turn influences the prime rate. A rise in the bank rate signals contractionary policy. A fall in the bank rate signals expansionary policy.

3. By moving government deposits from its own holdings to chartered banks, the Bank of Canada increases chartered banks' excess reserves, which increases the money supply and thus expands the economy. In contrast, the Bank of Canada can reverse the process to conduct contractionary policy.

4. At the rare times it uses moral suasion, the Bank of Canada might try to direct chartered banks to vary interest rates or their lending policies.

5. While monetary policy has the benefits of its isolation from politics and the speed with which decisions can be made, it is less effective for expansion than for contraction, and it cannot be focused on particular regions as can fiscal policy.

ADVANCING ECONOMIC THOUGHT

Lender With a Mission

Muhammad Yunus and Micro-Lending

Lending policies tend to follow a "top-down" approach: they are set by managers of banks and near banks, who determine which individual players in the economy—businesses and households—are elegible to receive loans. In some cases, another stage is added. As we will see in Part 4, the World Bank (known officially as the International Bank for Reconstruction and Development) has traditionally lent funds to nonindustrialized nations for large projects such as hydro-electric dams. However, this is not the only approach that can be taken. By asking the questions, "What function does money have for the most needy, how is it lent, and to whom?" Muhammad Yunus, a Bangladeshi economist, offers a grass-roots alternative.

Yunus is the founder of Grameen Bank, a Bangladeshi credit organisation that has pioneered lending to the rural poor—and in the process stood normal banking conventions on their head.

The customers of Grameen (whose name means rural in Bengali) are almost exclusively those who have no collateral to offer against their loans. Yet defaults are so low its repayment rates would be the envy of most mainstream lenders. "Compared to Grameen Bank," says Yunus, "other banks look like charity outfits for the rich."

Two other things are immediately striking about Grameen. First, the vast majority of its customers are women—a fact not unconnected with the low number of defaults—and, second, its vision extends beyond mere finance. Grameen is perhaps the only bank in the world that encourages birth control, sanitation and a clean environment as part of its lending policy.

As a pioneer in the growing field of "micro-lending," Grameen has shown that the rural poor—even in a country virtually synonymous with deprivation—can make productive use of credit. To many, this approach is a more effective antidote to poverty than traditional giveaways.

The bank's success since it was set up in 1983 has spawned Grameen-type institutions in 30 countries. A group of US politicians recently urged President Bill Clinton to make micro-enterprise development efforts, modelled specifically on Grameen, the "hallmark" of his foreign-aid programme. Yunus already has the admiration of Clinton, who once met Yunus in Washington and deems him worthy of a Nobel prize. "He made enterprise work. He promoted discipline, not dependence," Clinton says.

That, in a nutshell, was the idea. It began 17 years ago, when Yunus, an economics professor at Chittagong University, found himself frustrated at the irrelevance of textbook development theory to the poverty all around him. What bedevilled even the diligent poor around Chittagong, he could see, was the absence of cheap credit. Aside from loan sharks, they could turn to commercial banks, but they demanded collateral.

How, then, to direct credit to those who most need it: the assetless poor? Yunus' answer was to channel loans through wealthier intermediaries like himself. While shunning the peasant farmer and the bamboo-stool maker, the banks happily lend to the more affluent. In turn, Yunus reasoned, these borrowers could lend to the poor, in effect assuming risk that banks would not.

The risk, it turned out, was minimal. Experimenting initially on his own, Yunus acted as guarantor for loans to impoverished village-dwellers, who responded with a surprisingly high repayment rate. Encouraged, but eventually tired of running to the banks, Yunus decided to start his own. The government initially owned 60% of Grameen and the borrowers the rest. Today, its 1.4 million borrowers, each with a mandatory share (Taka 100, or US$2.50 each), own 88%.

Grameen's average loan size is US$75, its maximum except for housing loans. It charges simple interest at a rate of 20% a year, compared with compound interest of 13–16% at Bangladesh's commercial banks. Principal is repaid first, so that a borrower of Taka 2,500 would typically repay Taka 50 a week over 50 weeks. Interest, calculated weekly on the diminishing principal, is repaid only after the principal is paid off, making for an effective interest rate of 10–12%, Grameen sources say.

Home loans are repayable over 10 years at the same weekly rates. The maximum home loan is Taka 12,000, which will build a tin-roofed house.

Muhammad Yunus

SOURCE: *Far Eastern Economic Review*
Hong Kong

Borrowers are formed into groups of five—the basic unit—and are indoctrinated in Grameen social values, known as the "sixteen decisions." Borrowers vow to observe the bank's four basic principles: discipline, unity, courage and hard work "in all walks of life." They also pledge to "keep our families small," shun child marriage and the "curse" of wedding dowries, "build and use pit-latrines," and "plant as many seedlings as possible during the plantation seasons."

Grameen is effective partly because it is self-policing. Rather than bank officials, it is the assetless themselves, meeting weekly, who approve the loans. Group members are residents of the same village, perhaps next-door neighbours. It is this familiarity that provides transparency, guaranteeing that the recipients are truly those who need it most. A bank official attends the meeting, but group members decide who receives a loan, and they assume responsibility for ensuring its repayment.

A typical case: Sahera Khatun, 25, with a six-month-old baby, receives a loan through Grameen Gazipur-Sripur branch, about 95 kilometres north of Dhaka. She receives only Taka 2,375 of the Taka 2,500 approved. Taka 125 is deducted as a 5% contribution to her group fund, and a further Taka 1 per week to her own emergency savings fund. The loan is repaid over a year.

Shaheen Ara Begum became manager of Gazipur-Sripur branch in 1990, since when its lending has increased manyfold. The branch currently has about 1,900 members and has disbursed about Taka 16.6 million (about Taka 5.6 million is outstanding). By year's end, Shaheen expects membership of the branch to reach about 2,100.

A stroll through the village is instructive. Amid an otherwise depressing landscape there stand out some obvious improvements, brought about since the Grameen branch was established in December 1988. Houses are small but immaculate; families, too, are small and the children relatively healthy; and confident-looking women are busy at work in various cottage industries.

Grameen Bank's default rate is about 2%, astonishingly low compared with what Bangladesh's commercial banks suffer: about 70% for agricultural loans and 90% for industrial loans.

The difference, Yunus says, lies in the psychology of the borrowers. The rich can evade the consequences of non-payment; the poor cannot. They value access to credit so highly, and dislike the loan sharks so much, that they are only too grateful for a once-in-a-lifetime opportunity to improve themselves. And, by design, 92% of Grameen's borrowers nationwide are women. The bank targets them because it considers them more reliable than men. Children order their priorities, making them less likely to squander funds, and more likely to use them for household or capital improvements. "If being poor is tough, being a poor woman is toughest," says Yunus.

Today, Grameen has more than 1,000 branches conducting operations in about half of Bangladesh's 68,000 villages. It also runs about 18,000 feeder schools preparing children for government primary schools. It disburses about Taka 750 million in loans each month and has paid-up capital of Taka 120 million.

Grameen posted modest profits until government-mandated pay rises for the bank's staff forced losses of Taka 8.3 million in 1991 and 10 million in 1992. It may break even in 1993.

To be sure, the Grameen approach has its detractors. Some say micro-lending takes place on too small a scale to promote economic growth, and does little to teach skills. For the poor in Bangladesh, however, Grameen is delivering in a way that other banks are not.

Grameen, meanwhile, has become the model for micro-lending programmes in countries as diverse as Kenya, Ethiopia and Sri Lanka. Its experience is not unique. In the Philippines, for example, Tagay sa Pagunlad (Bridge to Progress) has provided credit to the poor since 1982, learning in the process that they can make money go a long way, "precisely because they have so little of it," in the words of director Benjamin Montemayor.

Elsewhere, Malaysia's Projek Ikhtiar, uses the Grameen approach too, and has also shown that small loans at affordable terms can greatly reduce extreme rural poverty.

Back in Bangladesh, Yunus wants to put more emphasis on Grameen's housing projects, which have won praise abroad. The bank has helped build more than 153,000 low-cost, tin-roofed houses with built-in latrines, each costing about US$300. Demand for 10-year loans to pay for them is rising fast.

Yunus is also working on a Grameen health project, planning up to four health centres on an experimental basis, each costing Taka 200,000 annually. He plans to charge Taka 5 a week for each Grameen member, whose family would receive free treatment. Non-members would pay more. Yunus believes the programme could eventually become self-financing. The centres could also become crucial to family planning, helping the government toward its goal of zero population growth.

SOURCE: Abridged from S. Kamaluddin, "Lender with a mission," in *Far Eastern Economic Review*, Hong Kong, 18 March 1993, pp. 38, 40.

1. a) Summarize and evaluate the apparent goals and principles of the Grameen Bank.
   b) Summarize the apparent goals and principles of conventional banking.
   c) Compare the goals and principles of conventional banking with those of the Grameen Bank. For each approach, identify possible benefits and drawbacks.

2. To what extent do you think "micro-lending" might be useful and desirable in Canada? Support your answer using specific examples.

Key Concepts

barter	M2	bank rate
coincidence of wants	M3	Canada Savings Bonds
liquidity	M2+	treasury bills
unit of account	near money	expansionary monetary policy
deposit-takers	credit card	contractionary monetary policy
cash reserves	debit card	desired reserves
chartered banks	transactions demand	reserve ratio
near banks	asset demand	excess reserves
currency	money demand	money multiplier
demand deposits	money demand schedule	open market operations
notice deposits	money demand curve	prime rate
term deposits	money supply	moral suasion
foreign currency deposits	money supply schedule	
M1	money supply curve	

Developing Application and Analysis Skills

1. Define money with reference to its three functions, and give examples.

2. Money has taken many forms throughout history. Seashells, salt, cattle, fish, glass beads, cards—even cigarettes, in World War II prisoner-of-war camps—have been used as currency. Suppose you and 10 other people find yourselves stranded in an isolated corner of the world, with no money system and no contact with others. Imagine and then describe in detail your physical setting. Then, consider the currency that your group would develop. Support your choice with reference to the functions of money.

3. Identify and analyze the differences among the various types of financial institutions, how they are regulated, and the financial services they provide. Give examples to support your analysis.

4. a) Rank the holdings shown in the list opposite in the order of their liquidity.

b) Classify each of the holdings as a component of the following:
i) M1
ii) M2
iii) M3
iv) M2+
v) other

Holdings in a Simple Economy

government savings bonds
cash held privately (in socks, stuffed in mattresses)
deposits by Canadian residents in US$ savings accounts at chartered banks
gold bullion (market value)
treasury bills
term deposits at chartered banks
deposits in personal chequing accounts
term deposits held by businesses at credit unions
gold coins
savings accounts at trust companies
line of credit on personal credit cards
cheques not yet cancelled
stocks

5. Explain how credit cards and debit cards can work to the advantage and disadvantage of consumers.

6. In writing or using a diagram, outline what would happen to transactions demand and asset demand for money at each stage in the business cycle. Draw conclusions regarding the relationships between money demand and the business cycle.

7. a) From the following schedules, create a graph showing the money demand and money supply curves.
b) Identify the equilibrium point.
c) If you held bonds, at what interest rate would you sell them? Why?
d) If you held no bonds, at what interest rate would you buy them? Why?
e) Explain how the market achieves equilibrium.

Money Demand and Supply Schedules		
Real Interest Rate	Money Supplied (S_m)	Money Demanded (D_m)
(%)	($ billions)	
7.5	75	60
4.5	75	75
3.0	75	90

8. Suppose the Bank of Canada is attempting to reduce the money supply at the peak of the business cycle. Explain the results of such actions on the following:

a) the purchasing power of the dollar
b) real output
c) the value of the dollar in foreign exchange markets

9. If the money multiplier is 2.375, calculate the maximum effect of the appearance of $7.5 billion in excess cash reserves in the banking system.

10. Suppose Grand Chartered Bank has deposits totalling $76 billion and a reserve ratio of 9.5 percent.
a) Calculate the desired reserves.
b) Outline and explain the results of deposits increasing by $12 million.

11. Suggest reasons why the reserve requirements for various types of bank accounts differ.

12. Suppose the Bank of Canada issues Canada Savings Bonds valued at $20 million. What is the maximum possible effect if the money multiplier is 2.4?

13. The Bank of Canada issues hundreds of millions of dollars worth of bonds each year, even during a recession. Given that bond selling is a contractionary measure, why do bond sales not further slow the economy?

14. Write an essay in which you compare the benefits and drawbacks of fiscal and monetary policy. In your essay, comment on the relative usefulness of each policy at particular stages in the business cycle.

CHAPTER 15

Debates on Macroeconomic Policy

There were warnings of apprehension
from economists. There always are;
apprehension is their business.

—STEPHEN LEACOCK, CANADIAN WRITER
AND ECONOMIST

According to an old joke, ask two economists the same question and
you'll get three answers. Economists—like any social scientists—do
disagree and, more often than not, their disagreements revolve around
stabilization policy. Because stabilization policy so profoundly affects our
lives—affecting whether we work and what our wages will buy—the
debate over economic stability and the means to reach it heats up most
during times of instability. In this chapter, we explore some of the issues
that are key to macroeconomics; we revisit classical, neoclassical, and
Keynesian economics; and we examine two additional theoretical perspectives: monetarism and supply-side economics.

CHAPTER FOCUS

This chapter focuses on the following:
- demand-pull inflation, and the tradeoffs between inflation and unemployment as expressed by the Phillips curve
- cost-push inflation and stagflation
- wage and price controls, and wage and price guidelines
- the theory of monetarism, the velocity of money, and the equation of exchange
- the theory of supply-side economics, its implementation, and how it has been criticized

SKILLS FOCUS

After studying this chapter, you will be able to:
- analyze the economic perspectives presented in macroeconomic statements
- construct a Phillips curve to demonstrate tradeoffs between the goals of stabilization policies
- demonstrate cost-push and demand-pull inflation
- outline and evaluate wage and price policies implemented in Canada
- demonstrate graphically the causes and effects of various types of inflation
- calculate inflation using the equation of exchange, and apply the monetary rule to an economy
- summarize, evaluate, and propose macro-economic policy from a variety of economic perspectives

Inflation and Unemployment

The relationship between inflation and unemployment is usually an inverse one. So, for example, an increase in aggregate demand during an economic expansion means that equilibrium between aggregate demand and aggregate supply is found at a higher price level and higher output, as shown in Figure 15.1. The increase in price level translates into inflation, and the increase in output translates into lower unemployment. In other words, there is a tradeoff—higher prices for more jobs. Because increased demand pulls up prices, economic expansion that causes inflation is known as **demand-pull inflation**.

demand-pull inflation: inflation that occurs as increased aggregate demand pulls up prices

Figure 15.1:   Demand-Pull Inflation

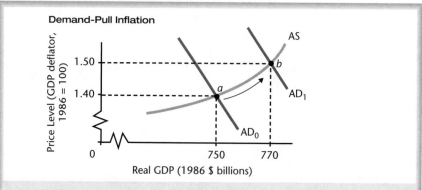

During expansionary times, aggregate demand increases, shifting the aggregate demand curve from AD_0 to AD_1. The result is that the price level rises from point *a* to point *b*. In other words, increased demand *pulls* up prices.

The Phillips Curve

Recall from Chapter 13 that Keynesian economics stresses the inverse relationship between inflation and unemployment as found in demand-pull inflation. Based on the assumption that there is a fixed and predictable inverse relationship between unemployment and inflation, one Keynesian economist—A.W.H. Phillips—created a curve that expresses this relationship. This **Phillips curve** is shown in Figure 15.2.

Phillips curve: a curve expressing the assumed fixed and predictable inverse relationship between unemployment and inflation

According to the Keynesian perspective, if an economy with an inflation rate of 2 percent and an unemployment rate of 8 percent (point *b* in Figure 15.2) experiences demand-pull inflation, the inflation rate will rise at the same time that unemployment decreases to, for example, point *a*. Increased aggregate demand creates shortages in labour markets, which put upward pressure on wages, thereby boosting inflation. In the same way, decreased aggregate demand increases unemployment, which puts

Figure 15.2:   The Phillips Curve

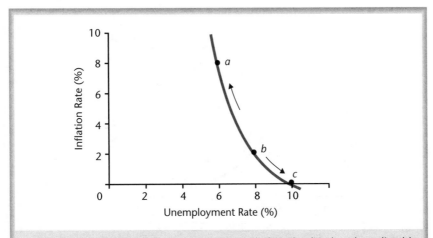

The Phillips curve expresses the Keynesian belief in the fixed and predictable inverse relationship between unemployment and inflation that occurs with demand-pull inflation. When the economy moves from point *b* to point *a*—which may happen as a result of expansionary stabilization policies—inflation increases and unemployment decreases. In contrast, contractionary policies cause the economy to move from point *b* to point *c*.

downward pressure on wages, thereby reducing the rate of inflation. We see this in the shift from point *b* to point *c*.

In the past, the Phillips curve was often treated by governments as a "policy menu." Governments using expansionary fiscal or monetary policies would anticipate a move up the curve, for example from point *b* to point *a*; governments using contractionary fiscal or monetary policies would expect a move down the curve, for example from point *b* to point *c*.

The extent to which Phillips curves are applicable can be seen using historical data for Canada. Figure 15.3 plots annual unemployment and inflation rates for 1960 to 1993. Let's consider the relevance of the Phillips curve to three periods.

From 1960 to 1972

For the years 1960 to 1972, in general, higher inflation accompanied lower unemployment, and vice versa. In other words, inflation during this period was of the demand-pull variety. Therefore, the points indicating inflation and unemployment rates fall in a broad band from which we can draw a Phillips curve, shown in Figure 15.3 with a solid line. Because inflation and unemployment had a predictable inverse relationship, Canadian federal governments were able to use the curve when trying to predict how their stabilization policies would affect the economy.

Figure 15.3:   Shifts in the Phillips Curve

During the years 1960 to 1972, inflation and unemployment rates fell in a broad band, from which a Phillips curve can be drawn (shown as a solid line). In the period from 1973 to 1982, the predictable relationship broke down. However, it seems that the Phillips curve moved to the right (shown as a dashed line) as both inflation rates and unemployment rates were above those in the previous period. In the period from 1983 to 1993, the trend was to lower inflation, but unemployment rates remained high. As a result, the new position of the Phillips curve was not clear for this period.

SOURCES: Adapted from Statistics Canada, *National Income and Expenditure Accounts, Annual Estimates 1926–1986* (June 1988), cat. no. 13-531, p. 214–15; *Canadian Economic Observer, Historical Statistical Supplement, 1993/94* (July 1994), cat. no. 11-210, vol. 8, pp. 36, 48. Reproduced by authority of the Minister of Industry, 1994.

From 1973 to 1982

In the years between 1973 and 1982, the previously predictable relationship between inflation and unemployment in Canada broke down. Most notably, inflation rose from 1973 to 1974 while unemployment remained about the same. This trend was repeated in the years 1979 to 1981. The Phillips curve for the Canadian economy during this period, shown as a dashed line in Figure 15.3, demonstrates that inflation and unemployment overall were greater in this period than in the last.

As this period illustrates, sometimes unemployment and inflation have a direct relationship rather than an inverse relationship. When rising rates of inflation are associated with constant or expanding unemployment, this combination of *stag*nation—that is, consistently low output—and in*flation* is known as **stagflation**.

Stagflation can be caused by a decrease in aggregate supply. During the period from 1973 to 1982, for example, businesses faced rising prices for inputs, largely due to rising oil prices. Oil prices were ten times higher in 1981 than they were at the start of 1973 because of the cartel behaviour

stagflation: a combination of consistently low output (and so constant or expanding unemployment) and rising inflation

of OPEC—the Organization of Petroleum Exporting Countries. In response to increases in input prices, businesses decrease their output, thus reducing aggregate supply. The result, shown in Figure 15.4, is a fall in equilibrium output and a rise in the price level. Because the increased costs push price levels up, this situation is known as **cost-push inflation**. During the 1970s, demands for increased wages further decreased aggregate supply and worsened cost-push inflation.

cost-push inflation:
inflation that occurs as increased production costs decrease aggregate supply, which then pushes up prices

Figure 15.4:   Cost-Push Inflation

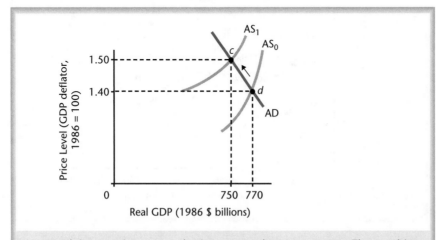

Increased input prices cause businesses to decrease output. The resulting decrease in aggregate supply shifts the supply curve from AS_0 to AS_1. The result is that the price level is pushed up from point d to point c. In other words, increased costs *push* up prices.

From 1983 to 1993

From 1983 to 1993, the stagflation of the previous period was partly reversed. While unemployment rates remained stubbornly high in Canada through most of the 1980s and 1990s, by the early 1990s inflation had fallen to levels not seen since the early 1970s. Note, however, that there was no consistent relationship between inflation and unemployment during this period. While the new Phillips curve was presumably below the Phillips curve for the previous period, its position was not apparent from the behaviour of the economy between 1983 and 1993, as illustrated in Figure 15.3.

Two main factors account for Canada's lower inflation since 1983. Oil prices fell dramatically in the mid-1980s, increasing aggregate supply and restraining increases in the price level. In addition, the recessions of 1981–82 and 1990–91 had a major impact on reducing inflation rates by decreasing aggregate demand. This impact was especially strong given the contractionary monetary policies conducted by the Bank of Canada during both recessions.

Canada was not alone in its troubles. As Figure 15.5 demonstrates, over the period from 1974 to 1991, many countries faced both high inflation and high unemployment.

Figure 15.5:   It Costs Jobs

Wage and Price Policies

In the 1970s and early 1980s, macroeconomic policy-makers faced both increased inflation and rising unemployment. Because fiscal and monetary policies can reduce *either* inflation *or* unemployment but not both at the same time, policy-makers had to find new solutions to stagflation.

By the late 1960s, there was widespread concern that wage demands by trade unions had become unreasonable and that large businesses were increasing prices unjustifiably, thus fuelling inflation. As a result, governments in Canada and various other countries tried to intervene in the form of **wage and price controls** and **wage and price guidelines**. Wage and price *controls* involve governments passing laws that impose maximum allowable increases in wages and prices. Wage and price *guidelines* involve governments encouraging voluntary caps on wages and prices. Canadian governments tried both policies.

Wage and Price Guidelines

In 1969, a federal Prices and Incomes Commission was formed. Its mandate, from 1969 to 1975, was to co-operate with businesses and private-sector labour unions to limit wage and price increases. However, because

wage and price controls: government-imposed restrictions on wage and price increases

wage and price guidelines: voluntary restrictions on wage and price increases

of a lack of support from businesses and labour unions, the Commission had little success. Inflation, which had been 5 percent in 1969, rose to 10 percent by 1975.

Wage and Price Controls

In late 1975, the federal government introduced another, harsher policy. It legislated wage and price controls and created the Anti-Inflation Board to enforce them. By law, wages and salaries were allowed to increase by a maximum of 8 percent in 1976, 6 percent in 1977, and 4 percent in 1978. Workers in industries where productivity was rising rapidly or where previous wage increases had been lower than average were allowed an extra 2 percent. Also by law, businesses were allowed to increase prices only to cover increased costs, and restrictions were placed on profits. To save on the administrative costs of the program, small businesses—including those in farming and fishing—were exempt from the controls.

Inflation did subside in the years 1976 to 1978, during the time the controls were in place. While the inflation rate in 1975 had been over 10 percent, in the next three years it varied between 7.5 percent and 9 percent. However, this fall in the inflation rate was largely the result of changes in food prices, which were not included in the control program. By 1980, two years after the controls were lifted, inflation was again above 10 percent.

"Six and Five" Guidelines

In 1982, the federal government applied wage and price restrictions again. This time, however, the government attempted to limit wages and prices it controlled *directly* while making the restrictions voluntary for the rest of the economy. Six percent was the limit in the 1982–83 fiscal year, and 5 percent in the 1983–84 fiscal year. Provincial governments and the private sector were encouraged to follow the federal lead. While inflation fell dramatically between 1982 and 1984, the consensus among economists is that this was due to the dampening effect of the 1981–82 recession as well as the contractionary monetary policies of the Bank of Canada, rather than the "six and five" guidelines.

The Debate Over Wage and Price Policies

Many economists oppose policies that restrict wage and price levels on the basis of effectiveness, fairness, and efficiency.

"There's nothing wrong with unemployment that a lot of money couldn't fix."

Effectiveness

Voluntary guidelines have shown little success in decreasing inflation in the private sector, because businesses and unions are reluctant to follow them. Also, although legislated wage and price controls may reduce inflation in the short run, Canadian experience shows that inflation rises again after the controls have been removed.

Fairness

Because some sectors are easier to regulate than others, wage and price restrictions are unfairly applied. For example, workers in the public sector and in large regulated businesses bear the brunt of government restrictions, while workers in less easily regulated sectors enjoy higher wage increases. Price restrictions, and the shortages they bring, can also lead to inequities, with output in some markets being distributed in unfair and arbitrary ways. For example, product shortages tempt some buyers to offer "under-the-table" incentives in addition to the product's legal price to assure that purchases are made.

Efficiency

Wage and price restrictions disrupt the functioning of free markets. Since the direct link between labour productivity and income is broken with wage restrictions, workers have less incentive to maximize the amount of real output they produce. Because restricted prices cannot operate as signals of changes in demand and supply, resources may be inefficiently distributed among different sectors. Hence, the long-term growth of the economy may be harmed.

BRIEF REVIEW

1. Inflation and unemployment have often had an inverse relationship. In periods of expansion, the result is demand-pull inflation.

2. The Phillips curve represents the Keynesian assumption of an inverse and predictable relationship between inflation and unemployment. While the Phillips curve applied to Canada in the period from 1960 to 1972, it has been less relevant since.

3. Since the 1970s, inflation and unemployment in Canada have frequently had a direct relationship. Stagflation has been caused largely by decreases in aggregate supply due to price increases of inputs. The result is cost-push inflation.

4. Overall inflation and unemployment rates in Canada increased in the period from 1973 to 1982, shifting the Phillips curve to the right. From 1983 to 1993, unemployment continued to be high but inflation lowered.

5. Various types of wage and price restrictions have been applied in Canada since 1969. Critics suggest that these programs show little success, while fostering inequities and inefficiency.

Monetarism

At the same time as the Canadian government was introducing wage and price controls to combat inflation, the Bank of Canada was following its own anti-inflationary policy. Its strategy was based on an economic perspective known as **monetarism**, which emphasizes the influence of money on the economy and the ability of private markets to accommodate change.

Monetarists Versus Keynesians

We have discussed how Keynesian economists believe private markets to be unsteady and occasional government intervention to be necessary. For Keynesians, fiscal and monetary policies perform a beneficial role by smoothing the ups and downs of the business cycle. Of the two policy options, Keynesians tend to see fiscal policy as more powerful.

Monetarism is a recent extension of the theories that dominated macroeconomics before John Maynard Keynes. Like the neoclassical economists, such as William Stanley Jevons and Alfred Marshall, monetarists believe that the economy is able to adjust to shocks *without* government intervention. While admitting that the economy can be temporarily set off course, monetarists argue that, usually, misguided government intervention just makes economic fluctuations worse. Because they stress the importance of money, monetarists blame unwise use of monetary policies in particular.

The Velocity of Money

Central to monetarism is the concept known as the **velocity of money** (V), or the number of times, on average, that money is spent on final goods and services during a given year. Suppose, for example, that a one-dollar coin changes hands once each month to buy final goods and services, for a total of 12 times in the year. This coin's annual velocity of money is 12.

For the economy as a whole, the velocity of money can be calculated by dividing the nominal GDP by the money supply (M). Suppose, for example, that Canada's nominal GDP is $800 billion and M1 (recalling the definitions of money from Chapter 14) is $50 billion. Each of the dollars in the stock of money must then have been used 16 times to finance this level of activity:

$$\text{Velocity of money (V)} = \frac{\text{nominal GDP}}{M}$$

$$16 = \frac{\$800 \text{ billion}}{\$50 \text{ billion}}$$

monetarism: an economic perspective that emphasizes the influence of money on the economy and the ability of private markets to accommodate change

velocity of money: the number of times, on average, that money is spent on final goods and services during a given year (a concept that is central to monetarism)

The Equation of Exchange

These calculations lead us to another cornerstone of monetarism. Recall that nominal GDP is the total dollar value of all final goods and services produced in the economy over a given period. So, GDP expresses both the price level (P) and real output (Q). In other words, the $800 billion in nominal GDP may be broken down into a price level of 2.0 and a real output of $400 billion:

$$\text{Nominal GDP} = P \times Q$$
$$\$800 \text{ billion} = 2.0 \times \$400 \text{ billion}$$

equation of exchange: the money supply multiplied by the velocity of money equals the price level multiplied by real output

The two formulas above can be combined to form the **equation of exchange**, which is central to monetarism. The equation states that the money supply multiplied by the velocity of money (M × V) equals the price level multiplied by real output (P × Q):

$$M \times V = P \times Q$$
$$\$50 \text{ billion} \times 16 = 2.0 \times \$400 \text{ billion}$$

The Quantity of Money

quantity theory of money: a theory stating that the velocity of money and real output are relatively stable over short periods

According to the **quantity theory of money**, which is generally accepted by monetarists, both the velocity of money and real output are relatively stable over short periods.

As indicated in Figure 15.6, the velocity of money can change over time. For example, the velocity of the Canadian money supply (defined as M1) rose from about 10 in 1970 to about 16 in 1992. One reason for this gradual increase is the growing popularity of credit and debit cards that allow money holdings to be minimized. If buyers hold less money, they must be passing it on from hand to hand more quickly. Monetarists believe that changes in velocity are primarily due to long-run factors, such as the move to credit and debit cards. In the short run, however, the velocity of money is roughly constant.

According to monetarists, real output varies only slightly from its potential level. The neoclassical economists—those before Keynes—thought that wages are fully flexible and, because of this, the economy returns quickly to its potential output after a shock. Monetarists have updated the neoclassical view to accommodate Keynes' criticism of this belief. Wages *can* be inflexible, monetarists say, but only briefly, as economic participants soon adjust to any changes in prices or unemployment.

If both the velocity of money and real output are fairly stable, as is assumed in the quantity theory of money, then there is a straightforward relationship between money and prices. This is shown by the equation of exchange, when both velocity and real output are set at constant values, V* and Q*:

$$M \times V^* = P \times Q^*$$

Figure 15.6: The Velocity of Money

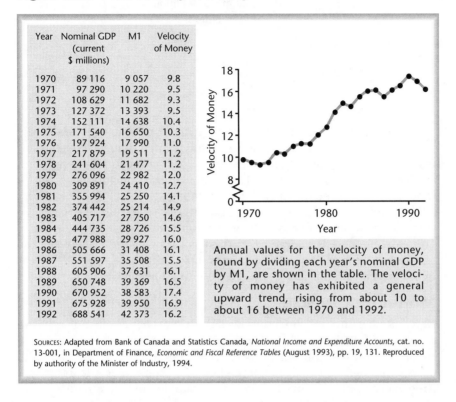

Year	Nominal GDP (current $ millions)	M1	Velocity of Money
1970	89 116	9 057	9.8
1971	97 290	10 220	9.5
1972	108 629	11 682	9.3
1973	127 372	13 393	9.5
1974	152 111	14 638	10.4
1975	171 540	16 650	10.3
1976	197 924	17 990	11.0
1977	217 879	19 511	11.2
1978	241 604	21 477	11.2
1979	276 096	22 982	12.0
1980	309 891	24 410	12.7
1981	355 994	25 250	14.1
1982	374 442	25 214	14.9
1983	405 717	27 750	14.6
1984	444 735	28 726	15.5
1985	477 988	29 927	16.0
1986	505 666	31 408	16.1
1987	551 597	35 508	15.5
1988	605 906	37 631	16.1
1989	650 748	39 369	16.5
1990	670 952	38 583	17.4
1991	675 928	39 950	16.9
1992	688 541	42 373	16.2

Annual values for the velocity of money, found by dividing each year's nominal GDP by M1, are shown in the table. The velocity of money has exhibited a general upward trend, rising from about 10 to about 16 between 1970 and 1992.

SOURCES: Adapted from Bank of Canada and Statistics Canada, *National Income and Expenditure Accounts*, cat. no. 13-001, in Department of Finance, *Economic and Fiscal Reference Tables* (August 1993), pp. 19, 131. Reproduced by authority of the Minister of Industry, 1994.

Adjustments in the price level (P) must then be due to changes in the money supply (M). In other words, according to monetarists, inflation is primarily caused by too much money chasing the products available for purchase in an economy.

Inflation Rates and Monetary Growth

The quantity theory of money can be extended further to propose a close relationship between inflation rates and growth in the money supply. Suppose, for example, that the velocity of money has a constant value of 16, and real output remains at its potential level of $400 billion. What happens to prices when the supply of money (M1) rises from $50 billion to $55 billion? Using the equation of exchange, the price level increases from 2.0 to 2.2:

$$M \times V^* = P \times Q^*$$
$$\text{First } \$50 \text{ billion} \times 16 = 2.0 \times \$400 \text{ billion,}$$
$$\text{then } \$55 \text{ billion} \times 16 = 2.2 \times \$400 \text{ billion.}$$

As is always the case when both velocity and real output are constant, the percentage changes in the money supply and the price level equal one another:

$$\% \ \Delta \ \text{in} \ M \ = \ \frac{(\$55 \ \text{billion} - \$50 \ \text{billion})}{\$50 \ \text{billion}} \times 100\%$$
$$= \ 10\%$$

$$\% \ \Delta \ \text{in} \ P \ = \ \frac{(2.2 - 2.0)}{2.0} \times 100\%$$
$$= \ 10\%$$

Remember that the percentage change in the price level is simply the rate of inflation. Hence, the above result shows that, given constant velocity and real output, the percentage growth in the money supply and the rate of inflation are equal. This is the central conclusion drawn by monetarists from the quantity theory of money.

However, the velocity of money and real output are *not* perfectly constant, so inflation is not always identical to the rate of monetary growth. Therefore, monetarists suggest that there is a rough equality between the two rates. If, for example, the money supply is increased year after year by 10 percent, then inflation will be close to 10 percent as well.

Monetarist Policies

Unlike Keynesians, who treat money as only one element that determines output and inflation levels, monetarists consider variations in the money supply the most significant factor in the economy. For Keynesians, the process through which money influences the economy is a lengthy one. An expansion in the money supply, for example, must first reduce interest rates, then boost investment spending, and finally change aggregate demand, thereby shifting the aggregate demand curve to the right. If any of these links in the chain is weak, then the process of change breaks down. In contrast, monetarists see the impact of monetary changes as being more straightforward and predictable. According to monetarists, assuming a stable velocity of money, adjustments in the money supply translate immediately into higher nominal GDP and increased prices.

On the issue of fiscal policy, Keynesians and monetarists again conflict. While Keynesians regard fiscal policy as a powerful stabilization tool, monetarists argue that it has little influence because of the **crowding-out effect**, which suggests that more government borrowing raises interest rates, which reduces or "crowds out" private investment spending. For example, an expansionary fiscal policy that includes either tax cuts or hikes in government spending will likely prove ineffective, according to monetarists. In their view, any stimulus provided by the policy is largely counteracted by the effects of higher government deficits, as more borrowing leads to higher interest rates and lower private investment.

Even monetary policy can do little to move output from its potential level, monetarists say. So policy-makers should concentrate instead on

crowding-out effect:
the effect of more government borrowing raising interest rates, which reduces or "crowds out" private investment spending

minimizing the harmful effects of inflation. This is achieved when the Bank of Canada minimizes the rate of growth of the money supply.

The Monetary Rule

While most monetarists consider monetary policy to be a powerful instrument, most judge it too strong for central banks to apply wisely. Fluctuations in real output will be lessened, they suggest, if no discretionary monetary policy is used at all. Instead, governments should impose a **monetary rule** that forces the central bank to increase the money supply by a constant rate each year. The rate that monetarists recommend—usually in the range of 3 percent—is based on the long-term real growth in the economy.

monetary rule: a law that forces the central bank to increase the money supply by a constant rate each year

Thinking About Economics

What is the proper macroeconomic role for governments, according to monetarists?

If monetarist guidelines are followed, governments should not attempt to smooth the business cycle. According to monetarists, governments should avoid using fiscal policy because it is ineffective and monetary policy because it is too easily misused. These conclusions are exactly opposite to Keynesian thinking, which considers stabilization policy to be a key function of government.

BRIEF REVIEW

1. In contrast to Keynesians, monetarists believe that the economy has an ability to adjust itself, that government intervention can harm rather than help the economy, and that the money supply is of central importance to the economy.

2. The equation of exchange states that the money supply (M) multiplied by the velocity of money (V) equals the price level (P) multiplied by real output (Q), or nominal GDP.

3. According to the quantity theory of money, both the velocity of money and real output are relatively stable over short periods. A certain percentage change in the money supply causes about the same rate of inflation.

4. Keynesians see the influence of money as indirect and fragile, and fiscal policy as an important stabilization tool. In contrast, monetarists see the influence of money as direct, fiscal policy as ineffective, and monetary policy as effective but easily misused.

5. Monetarists recommend a monetary rule, whereby the money supply is raised by a set annual rate based on the economy's real growth.

Money Matters

Milton Friedman and Monetarism

Friedman and His Influence

The leading supporter of monetarism has been the American economist, Milton Friedman (born in 1912). He was both a student and a long-time professor at the University of Chicago, an institution where the ideas of the neoclassical economists lived on despite the Keynesian revolution of the 1930s and 1940s.

Friedman is perhaps most famous as a promoter of *laissez-faire* capitalism in the tradition of Adam Smith. He has popularized his views in his books *Capitalism and Freedom* (1962) and *Free to Choose* (1980) as well as in numerous magazine articles and TV appearances. Friedman's pro-market outlook stems from his belief that wages and prices in private markets are fairly close to their most efficient perfectly competitive values, while externalities such as pollution can best be dealt with through private lobbying and negotiation, rather than through government intervention. Since governments are inefficient by their very nature, says Friedman, and because they hinder individual freedom, their intervention in private markets should be minimized.

Friedman would replace income-support programs such as welfare and unemployment insurance with a single guaranteed annual income system (as outlined in Chapter 9). He also argues that many functions currently performed by governments could be performed more efficiently by the private sector, if businesses are chosen to fulfil each specified task at the lowest possible cost.

Milton Friedman

The Role of Money   Friedman has contributed to various aspects of macroeconomics, but his most wide-ranging work is associated with the role of money. His belief in the quantity theory has led him to stress the equation of exchange, and he claims that his own empirical research shows the velocity of money to be quite stable in the short run. (Keynesian economists, however, have disputed this conclusion.)

Monetarist policies implemented in Canada and other countries during the 1970s and 1980s have not provided convincing support for Friedman's assertion that the velocity of money is constant. As a result, most economists do not support the quantity theory.

The Self-Stabilizing Economy

However, an important element of Friedman's argument has made its way into mainstream economic theory. This is his description of the economy's capacity to stabilize itself in the long run. According to Friedman, forces push the economy toward its potential output, where unemployment is at its natural level. While the economy may rarely reach this long-run equilibrium, economic fluctuations can be fully understood only if this self-stabilizing tendency is taken into account.[1]

The figure below illustrates a simplified version of Friedman's argument for a hypothetical economy. The short-run tradeoff between output and the price level is shown by the aggregate supply curve. But only at point *b*, which is associated with the economy's potential output, is the economy stationary in the long run. At any other point on the curve, the economy will sooner or later display its built-in tendency to stabilize.

The Self-Stabilizing Economy

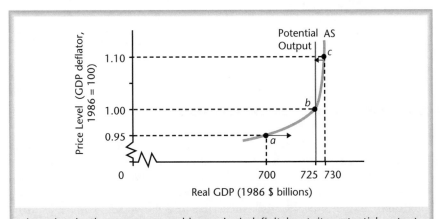

At point *b*, the economy could remain indefinitely at its potential output. However, when equilibrium is at point *c* in a boom, the economy's self-stabilizing tendency will push the aggregate supply curve to the left, so that the potential output can be resumed. The same is true if the economy's equilibrium is at point *a* in a recession. The self-stabilizing tendency will push the aggregate supply curve to the right.

During an economic boom, the economy's equilibrium may be at a point such as *c*, where output is above its potential level. Because unemployment is below its natural rate, tight labour markets allow workers to bargain for higher nominal wages. These wage hikes raise business costs, leading to a decrease in aggregate supply. Equilibrium therefore moves back toward the economy's potential output, and unemployment rises toward its natural rate.

According to Friedman, the opposite occurs during a recession. The economy's equilibrium now drops below its potential output, as at point *a* on the graph, with a high unemployment rate. Workers initially resist any attempts to reduce their nominal wages, as was pointed out originally by Keynes. However, over time, unemployment puts downward pressure on nominal wages. This causes an increase in aggregate supply, boosting output back toward its potential level and lowering unemployment toward its natural rate.

The Long-Run Supply Curve   In either case, the vertical line shown on the graph at the potential output level can be interpreted as this hypothetical economy's long-run aggregate supply curve, since it shows all those points consistent with stable equilibrium in the long run. The presence of this curve, and the self-stabilizing process that underlies it, are now accepted by most economists, although its importance is disputed. Those such as monetarists who see little need for government stabilization policy believe the economy adjusts quickly by itself toward its potential output level. In contrast, Keynesian economists see the self-adjusting process as a slow one, which means government stabilization policy can still play an important role in reducing the severity of ups and downs in the business cycle.

NOTE

[1]Milton Friedman, "The Role of Monetary Policy," *The American Economic Review*, March 1968, pp. 1–17. The modern theory of the self-stabilizing economy also owes its roots to Edmund S. Phelps, "Phillips Curves, Expectations of Inflation and Optimal Unemployment Over Time," *Economica*, August 1967, pp. 254–81.

 ## Supply-Side Economics

Most economists—both Keynesian and monetarist—stress how fiscal and monetary policies influence the economy through shifts in aggregate demand. This follows from their view that any effects on aggregate supply are quite minor.

supply-side economics: the view that adjustments in aggregate supply are the most critical element of government activity

However, other economists subscribe to a viewpoint known as **supply-side economics**. According to supporters of this perspective, adjustments in aggregate supply are the most critical element of government activity and, because the effects are gradual and often hidden, they are usually ignored by policy-makers. Supply-side economists owe a large debt to the theories of early classical economists, such as Adam Smith and David Ricardo. Unlike Keynesians, with their emphasis on changes in aggregate demand, and neoclassical economists, with their stress on the economy's self-adjusting capacity, the early classical economists concentrated on the influence of production costs on prices and incomes.

Reduction in Incentives

Supply-side economists believe increased government intervention in recent decades has dampened productive economic activity. Recall from previous chapters that government intervention takes a variety of forms. According to supply-siders, as economists with this perspective are known, government activity can affect aggregate supply by reducing incentives to engage in productive activity.

Personal Income and Business Taxes

Any time marginal tax rates on personal income and business profits increase, the disposable incomes of income earners fall, making it less worthwhile for them to engage in income-generating pursuits.

Sales Taxes

Hikes in sales taxes also discourage productive activity by reducing the amount of products that can be bought with a given disposable income.

Transfers and Subsidies

Supply-siders criticize more generous transfer payment programs, such as Unemployment Insurance and welfare, as well as subsidy programs, such as farm subsidies. According to the economists, such programs diminish incentives to generate private income.

Regulation

Governments have also played a greater role in regulating private businesses. Whatever their other merits, controls associated with environmental concerns, worker safety, product standards, and workplace equity have all raised business costs and reduced incentives to invest.

Focus on Aggregate Supply

The supply-side effects of more taxes and government regulation can be shown using aggregate demand and supply. Supply-side economists contend that the effects of government activity on aggregate demand are quite minor. In contrast, government activity has a considerable impact on aggregate supply. For the sake of this argument, we will ignore aggregate demand effects to focus on aggregate supply in Figure 15.7.

Figure 15.7: Effect of Government Intervention

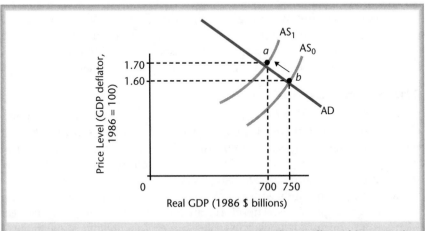

Supply-side economists contend that the most significant effect of increases in taxes and government regulation has been a decrease in aggregate supply, shifting the curve from AS$_0$ to AS$_1$. As a result, the economy is pushed to a higher price level and lower real output (from point *b* to point *a*), and cost-push inflation occurs.

According to the argument, high taxes and increased regulation create cost-push inflation. In other words, increased costs push up prices at the same time that unemployment rises. So, in Figure 15.7, aggregate supply decreases from AS_0 to AS_1 and the equilibrium point moves from *b* to *a*. Therefore, say supply-side economists, the main culprit in causing the stagflation of the 1970s was none other than government itself. By intervening more and more in the affairs of private citizens—often with the best intentions—government policy-makers harmed the economy.

Based on this understanding of economic events, supply-siders call for tax cuts and deregulation, or reduced regulation. In other words, if high taxes and too many regulatory laws cause cost-push inflation, then tax cuts and the loosening of government regulation should improve economic conditions. Increasing the incentives to work, save, and invest should cause an increase in aggregate supply, shifting the aggregate curve to the right. Real output would be boosted and the price level would be pushed down. Supply-siders therefore call for a *laissez-faire* approach by governments—just as Adam Smith and other classical economists had done.

Reaganomics

In the early 1980s, supply-side economics came to be associated with the Reagan presidency in the United States, and was dubbed "Reaganomics." Many supply-side proposals were legislated. Most importantly, personal and business taxes were reduced and the American economy underwent a wave of deregulation.

Critics of these measures suggested that cutting tax rates without also reducing government purchases would cause a harmful increase in the U.S. deficit. However, supply-side economists suggested that reducing tax *rates* would actually lead to an increase in total tax *revenues*.

The Laffer Curve

Laffer curve: a curve that expresses the assumed relationship between tax rates and tax revenues

This startling proposition was based on the most famous element of supply-side economics. The theory is expressed with the **Laffer curve**, which is named after the supply-side economist Arthur Laffer, who popularized it. As Figure 15.8 shows with a hypothetical example, the Laffer curve demonstrates an assumed relationship between tax rates and tax revenues.

According to the theory, tax rates and tax revenues have a direct relationship at low tax rates. Therefore, an increase at lower tax rates also increases tax revenues. Thus, the Laffer curve has a positive slope *at lower tax rates*. In Figure 15.8, a rise in the tax rate from 0 percent to 20 percent raises tax revenues from $0 to $300 billion (from points *a* to *b*).

However, tax rates and tax revenues have an indirect relationship at high tax rates. Therefore, an increase at higher tax rates decreases tax

Figure 15.8:   The Laffer Curve

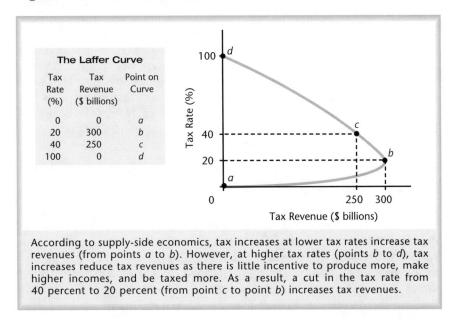

The Laffer Curve		
Tax Rate (%)	Tax Revenue ($ billions)	Point on Curve
0	0	a
20	300	b
40	250	c
100	0	d

According to supply-side economics, tax increases at lower tax rates increase tax revenues (from points *a* to *b*). However, at higher tax rates (points *b* to *d*), tax increases reduce tax revenues as there is little incentive to produce more, make higher incomes, and be taxed more. As a result, a cut in the tax rate from 40 percent to 20 percent (from point *c* to point *b*) increases tax revenues.

revenues. Any rise in tax rates now has a significant dampening effect on economic activity. Income and output levels fall so far that tax revenues drop. Thus, the Laffer curve has a negative slope *at higher tax rates*. As illustrated in Figure 15.8, a further rise in the tax rate from 20 percent to 40 percent reduces tax revenues from $300 to $250 billion (points *b* to *c*). In the extreme case where tax rates are 100 percent, total tax revenues drop to zero (point *d*). At this point, since all income is paid to the government in taxes, there is no incentive at all for economic activity.

Applying the Laffer Curve

There is no doubt that the Laffer Curve contains a kernel of truth—at *very* high tax rates there will be a decrease in revenues if rates are raised even more. Where supply-side economists raised controversy was in applying this concept. According to supply-siders, the economies of countries such as Canada and the United States had already reached or surpassed the tax rate at which revenues are maximized. Therefore, cutting tax rates—as from 40 percent to 20 percent in Figure 15.8 (from point *c* to point *b*)— would lead to an increase in revenues.

This belief was not borne out in the aftermath of the Reagan administration. The U.S. economy enjoyed a long boom during the late 1980s, and some of the stagflation of the 1970s was reversed, largely due to lower oil prices. Between 1981 and 1988, when Reagan was president, the American unemployment rate dropped from 7.5 to 5.4 percent, while the rate of inflation fell from 10.3 to 4.1 percent. However, tax revenues did note rise as supply-side economists predicted they would. Faltering tax revenues, coupled with continual rises in government purchases, led to a ballooning of U.S. government deficits, just as critics of the Laffer curve had predicted. While the deficit of the U.S. government had been less than $80 billion in 1981, during most of the 1980s it remained in the range of $200 billion each year, leading to a jump in gross federal debt from under $1 trillion in 1981 to almost $3 trillion by the end of the decade.

The Influence of Supply-Side Theories

The argument that the Reagan tax cuts would lead to higher tax revenues is now widely seen as an expensive mistake. While some supporters of supply-side economics point to the 1980s boom in the United States as evidence that these cuts stimulated the economy by increasing aggregate supply, the majority of economists believe that this trend can just as easily be explained using mainstream theory. In their view, the United States' large government deficits served as an expansionary fiscal policy that increased aggregate demand, and so caused the boom.

Most economists reject supply-side economics. The general view remains that stabilization policies have their greatest impact on aggregate demand, not on aggregate supply. However, supply-side theories have had some influence. The effects of government activity on aggregate supply—although often limited or only visible in the long run—are now more likely to be acknowledged by all economists.

Thinking About Economics

Does the upper portion of the Laffer curve have any contemporary relevance?

The Laffer curve cannot be completely discounted. While the upper portion, which shows a negative slope, does not appear to be relevant for countries such as Canada or the United States, there is some evidence that it has applied to countries such as Sweden, where tax rates are much higher. The concern that very high tax rates may in fact reduce tax revenues has had one important effect on tax policy: top tax rates on high-income earners in many of these high-taxing countries are lower than they once were.

DEVELOPING
INTERPRETATION SKILLS

Less Work for More People

The Benefits of Job-Sharing

With a trend of increasingly higher and persistent unemployment rates, many interested groups—politicians, employers, and union leaders—have proposed rethinking how we work. One suggestion, outlined in this article, involves sharing out the work among a greater number of people.

Long a cherished dream of union leaders and other social activists, the four-day work week is becoming a reality for thousands of Canadians. But unlike the shift from the five-and-a-half-day to five-day week in the boom decade that followed the Second World War, most Canadians now working reduced hours are also earning less as a result. Many of them are under economic pressure from employers who are threatening layoffs unless they work shorter hours for less pay. Others, particularly young parents who cannot afford to raise a family on just one salary, are cutting back or rearranging their work week to spend more time with their children. Some experts argue that shortening the work week for those who have jobs might at least provide some work for Canada's unemployed.

Certainly, the unemployment problem in Canada is severe—and so far, traditional tactics for combating it have not succeeded. As well, many companies are still slashing their payrolls in response to technological change and intensifying domestic and international competition. However, Ottawa and the provinces are all weighed down with budget deficits and are in no position to stimulate job creation either by increasing spending or cutting taxes.

Yet at the same time as Canadians are looking for work, many of the people with jobs are working harder than ever. Officially, the length of the average scheduled work week for Canadians employed in manufacturing—which traditionally has set the pattern for other sectors—is just over 38 hours, and has changed lit-

SOURCE: Photo by Grant Black.

tle since the late 1960s. But a Statistics Canada survey published in 1993 estimated that in any given week, 800,000 Canadians work overtime for pay, putting in an average of eight extra hours.

So far, efforts by governments to save jobs by reducing costs through a shorter work week, both among their own employees and in the private sector, have proved to be controversial at best. In the largest such initiative, Ontario's NDP government provoked a storm of protest from more than 950,000 unionized provincial and municipal civil servants by passing its Social Contract Act in 1993. It called for a three-year wage freeze and required employees earning more than $30,000 annually to take up to 12 unpaid days off each year. The alternative, Premier Rae argued, would have been to lay off up to 40,000 people.

In Ottawa, one option being considered is expanding a small federal work-sharing program that pays workers unemployment insurance benefits for one day each week if they voluntarily cut back to four days from five. Aimed at small employers facing temporary financial problems, the program was introduced in 1982. It pays workers benefits totalling 55 per cent of their insurable earnings, to a maximum of $85, for the fifth day of the week. But even in 1991, the low point of the recession, payouts totalled only $160 million. In 1993, that declined to $60 million. Both employers and employees enrolled in the program have consistently rated it highly. However, the department's study of the 177,800 workers who passed through the program from 1989 to 1991, revealed some flaws. For 29 per cent of those workers, it only delayed permanent layoffs for a few weeks or months.

Regardless of the approach, the idea of shortening the work week to alleviate unemployment is hardly new. Union leaders have argued for a shorter work week without any reduction in pay, in both good times and bad times, since the late 19th century. During the Great Depression

of the 1930s and other slowdowns, they billed it as a job creation strategy. But according to Desmond Morton, a labor historian and principal of University of Toronto's Erindale College, unions have only won shorter work weeks during economic booms, not slowdowns. "Good things happen in good times," says Morton. "In bad times, people get meaner." Morton adds that in the early stages of a recovery, employers tend to work their existing staff longer hours, rather than hire more workers, because they are uncertain that the upswing will last. Only when they are feeling more secure about their prospects do they reduce hours and begin hiring again.

That is precisely what happened at Chrysler Canada Ltd.'s booming minivan plant in Windsor, Ont. Under a new contract signed with the Canadian Auto Workers union in 1993, Chrysler agreed to reduced hours—and wage increases—for the 4,200 unionized workers in the plant. It also added a third daily shift of more than 800 new assembly-line workers. In recent years, many employees in the plant have been working up to seven days a week as Chrysler struggled to fill orders.

Quite apart from whether reducing or rearranging the work week will make a dent on their bottom line, many employers are at least studying the issue because of employee stress in raising a family. Like many large companies, the Bank of Montreal now has 2,500 of 28,000 employees participating in its flexible work arrangements program. Johanne Totta, the bank's vice-president of workplace equality, says the plan grew out of a 1991 survey of employees that revealed that many were having trouble juggling the demands on their time. Under the program, any employee can propose alternative work arrangements to a supervisor—such as a four-day work week, job sharing or working at home.

Despite the growing popularity of four-day or other rearranged work weeks, many employers caution that there are large hurdles that they must overcome to implement them. The most costly, according to Jayson Myers, chief economist of the Canadian Manufacturers' Association, are so-called payroll taxes that include employer's unemployment insurance premiums, contributions to the Canada Pension Plan and provincial worker's compensation plans, plus contributions to their own company employee benefit plans. Myers says those taxes now make up about one-fifth of an average manufacturing worker's wage and benefit package. While those contributions are to some extent geared to wages and salaries, they are almost like fixed costs incurred the moment an employer hires another worker. And they are rising. Myers says payroll taxes have increased by almost 45 per cent over the past five years. As a result, he says, it is no wonder that many employers prefer to work existing staff overtime, rather than hire another worker and pay both a new employee's wages and another set of payroll taxes.

But advocates of work-sharing, including Frank Reid, a professor of economics at the University of Toronto, say that employers and governments can tie both the premiums and benefits in those programs more closely to hourly earnings, and remove some of the technical obstacles to work-sharing. Regardless of those costs, at least some employers and workers are prepared to experiment with a four-day week in the hope that it will reduce unemployment.

SOURCE: Abridged from John Daly, "The four-day week," in *Maclean's*, 14 March 1994, pp. 36–38.

1. Outline the possible effects—positive and negative—of job-sharing and the shorter work week.

2. How would the following groups view the idea of the shorter work week as a means to alleviate unemployment? Support your answers.

   a) supply-side economists
   b) monetarists
   c) Keynesians

BRIEF REVIEW

1. Supply-side economists focus on the effect of changes in aggregate supply on the economy. They contend that increased government intervention—in the form of higher taxes, greater regulation, and so on—reduces the incentive to engage in productive activity, and so decreases aggregate supply.

2. Supply-side economists argue that tax hikes and added regulation were the main cause of the stagflation of the 1970s.

3. The Laffer curve represents the supply-side economic belief that, if tax rates are high enough, tax hikes lead to reduced tax revenues.

4. Supply-side theories were not borne out by their application in the United States during the Reagan administration.

Key Concepts

demand-pull inflation
Phillips curve
stagflation
cost-push inflation
wage and price controls
wage and price guidelines
monetarism

velocity of money
equation of exchange
quantity theory of money
crowding-out effect
monetary rule
supply-side economics
Laffer curve

Developing Application and Analysis Skills

1. Indicate and explain whether each of the following statements would be supported by economists from the Keynesian, monetarist, or supply-side schools of thought, or a combination of these.

   a) The economy is essentially a self-regulating entity that requires minimal assistance from the government.
   b) Higher taxes and increased regulation are responsible for cost-push pressures in the economy.
   c) Monetary policy as exercised by the government is a potentially destabilizing factor in the economy.
   d) For the most part, government intervention in the economy is counterproductive, if not harmful.
   e) Over time, wages are flexible and adjust to changing economic conditions.
   f) The economy is usually at or near its potential level of output, and stabilization policy can do little to move it.
   g) Variations in the money supply and inflation are directly related.
   h) Government intervention in the economy has a limited effect on aggregate demand, but a substantial effect on aggregate supply.
   i) The money supply has an influence on the economy; however, the connection between money supply, interest rates,

   investment spending, and aggregate demand is fragile.
   j) The tradeoff for increased employment is inflation.

2. a) From the table that follows, draw a Phillips curve.
   b) What is the opportunity cost of an economy moving from Situation A to Situation F?
   c) Describe stabilization policies that would result in this movement from Situation A to Situation F.
   d) On your graph, demonstrate an alternative situation—one of stagflation.

Economic Options for Phillipsville		
Situation	Inflation Rate (% per year)	Unemployment Rate (% of labour force)
A	10	4.0
B	8	4.5
C	6	5.5
D	4	7.0
E	2	9.0
F	1	12.0

3. Create a graph on which you demonstrate and label demand-pull inflation and cost-push inflation, and then explain each situation.

4. Differentiate between wage and price controls and wage and price guidelines. Evaluate the effectiveness of each in controlling inflation.

5. a) Study the causal loop diagram that follows, and explain the cause-and-effect relationships on the diagram.

b) Copy the diagram. Make additions to your copy to show how wage and price controls and/or wage and price guidelines could be used to reduce inflationary pressure in the economy.

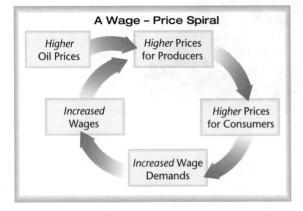

A Wage – Price Spiral

Higher Oil Prices → Higher Prices for Producers → Higher Prices for Consumers → Increased Wage Demands → Increased Wages → (back to Higher Prices for Producers)

6. During times of high inflation, consumers may assume that increased prices will continue to increase, and so will purchase products immediately before the anticipated increases take place. This combination of expectation and action is known as "inflationary psychology," and can be self-fulfilling. That is, consumer purchases due to expected price increases actually cause the price increases.

a) Using a graph or a causal loop diagram, demonstrate inflationary psychology and the possible effects on aggregate demand, real output, and the price level.

b) Suggest and explain policies that could be implemented to deal with the problem of inflationary psychology.

7. Suppose the velocity of money has a constant value of 15 and real output remains constant in the short run at $300 billion. The money supply is $60 billion.

a) Using the equation of exchange, demonstrate the change in price level if the money supply rises to $66 billion.

b) According to monetarists, what change in money supply *should* have been made? Using the equation of exchange, calculate the changes in money supply and in the price level that monetarists would have considered ideal.

8. a) As a class, identify one macroeconomic issue currently being debated in the media and by politicians. Discuss the issue briefly to clarify the relevant problems.

b) Form groups, with each taking one economic perspective: classical, neoclassical, Keynesian, monetarist, or supply-side. (You may need to research the perspectives further.)

c) In your groups, develop policies appropriate to your economic perspective to address the macroeconomic issue you've identified.

d) Present your policies in a class forum, or in writing to be included in a series of policy statements.

9. Write an essay in which you summarize and evaluate a present or recent government intervention in the Canadian economy.

10. Although the Reagan administration was considered by many to support supply-side economics, some critics described Reagan as a Keynesian in disguise. Research the economic policies of the Reagan administration. In an essay, examine the details of each policy and identify the economic perspective(s) they support. Lastly, evaluate the effectiveness of the policies.

PART 4

Canada in the Global Economy

Like other animals, we find and pick up what we can use, and appropriate territories. But unlike the other animals, we also trade and produce for trade.

—JANE JACOBS, AMERICAN URBAN AFFAIRS
EXPERT AND AUTHOR

Products used to move relatively slowly in the world—Canadian lumber was transported by sailing ships to Britain, for example. Now goods are often flown by aircraft and services are delivered by satellite or optical cable. Just as innovations in telecommunications have broken down barriers of geographical distance to create a "global village"—a term coined by Canadian communication theorist Marshall McLuhan—a unified world marketplace also has developed. Never before have national economies been so open to foreign influence, multinational transactions been so common and numerous, and economic actions been so immediately felt worldwide. These final three chapters consider Canada in the global economy, first looking at the foreign sector in Canada, then examining international trade, and finally exploring some of the contentious issues connected with economic growth and Canada's role in the global economy.

CHAPTER 16

The Foreign Sector

That knowledge has become the key
resource means that there is a world economy, and that the world economy, rather
than the national economy, is in control.
—PETER F. DRUCKER, AMERICAN SOCIAL PHILOSOPHER

For all nations, including Canada, the move toward a global economy
is bringing about changes in living standards, employment patterns,
and prospects for growth. In this chapter, we examine how foreign transactions are summarized in the balance-of-payments accounts, and we
study the influence of currency exchange rates. We will also see how
international financial investment has affected Canada's external debt
and levels of foreign ownership in the Canadian economy.

CHAPTER FOCUS

This chapter focuses on the following:
- the balance-of-payments accounts, which include the current account and the capital account
- exchange rates and how they're determined
- demand and supply for Canadian dollars, how equilibrium is reached in the foreign exchange market, and the factors that change demand and supply for currencies
- trends in balance-of-payment accounts and exchange rate systems
- the variety of exchange rate systems and policies

SKILLS FOCUS

After studying this chapter, you will be able to:
- explain the function of the balance-of-payments accounts, and suggest reasons for historical trends
- classify various transactions according to their place in the balance-of-payments accounts
- identify and evaluate direct and portfolio investment
- calculate, using exchange rates, the values of certain currencies, and consider the impact of exchange rates on individuals
- construct demand and supply curves for Canadian dollars in foreign exchange markets, and demonstrate the effects of economic and political changes on exchange rates
- evaluate exchange rate systems for current use
- track exchange rates and analyze factors that are responsible for changes in these rates

The Balance of Payments

As seen in earlier chapters, foreign economies are linked with the Canadian economy through trade. Foreigners enter Canadian product markets by buying Canadian exports. In turn, Canadians buy foreign imports. Foreign spending on Canadian exports represents a monetary inflow for Canada's product markets, while Canadian spending on imports represents a monetary outflow from the Canadian economy.

Recall also that the same principles apply to trading financial assets, such as stocks and bonds. Foreigners enter Canadian financial markets by buying Canadian stocks and bonds, therefore creating an inflow of funds to Canadian financial markets. Of course, foreigners also sell foreign stocks and bonds to Canadians, thereby creating an outflow of funds from the Canadian financial market.

The Balance-of-Payments Accounts

The connections between the Canadian economy and foreign markets are shown in detail using Canada's balance-of-payments accounts. Recall from Chapter 1 that these accounts provide a summary of all transactions between residents of Canada and those of foreign countries that involve exchanging Canadian dollars for some other international currency. At any given time, a statement of the accounts will show how the inflows and outflows "balance."

Receipts and Payments

Transactions in the accounts are divided into receipts and payments. The receipts represent monetary inflows to the Canadian economy, including both foreign purchases of Canadian exports and financing by foreigners when they buy Canadian stocks and bonds. Receipts are considered positive, so they are given a plus sign (+) in the accounts.

Payments, on the other hand, represent monetary outflows from the Canadian economy. They include outlays by Canadians for foreign imports and foreign stocks and bonds. Payments are considered negative, so they are given a minus sign (–) in the accounts.

The Current Account

current account: the summary of all foreign transactions associated with current economic activity in Canada and involving Canadian dollars

Figure 16.1 shows the portion of the balance-of-payments statement that is called the **current account**. This account summarizes all foreign transactions associated with current economic activity in Canada and involving Canadian dollars. The current account includes four types of transactions: trade in merchandise (in other words, tangible goods) as well as in three "invisible" items—trade in services, flows of investment income, and transfers.

Figure 16.1:   Canada's Current Account (1993)

	Receipts (+) (Canadian $ inflows)		Payments (–) (Canadian $ outflows)		Balance (net) (Canadian $ inflows – outflows)
			(Canadian $ billions)		
Merchandise trade	181.0	–	169.3	=	+11.7
Trade in services	27.3	–	39.8	=	–12.5
Balance of trade (net exports)				=	– 0.8
Investment income	9.0	–	33.7	=	–24.7
Transfers	4.3	–	4.0	=	+ 0.3
Current account surplus (+) or deficit (–)					–25.2

The current account details receipts (Canadian dollar inflows) and payments (Canadian dollar outflows) for merchandise trade and nonmerchandise transactions (trade in services, investment income, and transfers). In contrast to the +$11.7 billion 1993 merchandise balance of trade, Canada had a –$0.8 billion 1993 balance of trade (net exports). Overall, for 1993, the difference between total receipts and total payments gave a current account deficit of $25.2 billion.

SOURCE: Adapted from Statistics Canada, *Canada's Balance of International Payments, Fourth Quarter 1993* (March 1994), cat. no. 67-001, vol. 41, no. 4, p. 77. Reproduced by authority of the Minister of Industry, 1994.

Trade in Merchandise

The most significant and obvious components of the current account are Canadian exports and imports of goods, or "visibles" as they are known. Canadians sell a broad range of merchandise exports and buy an equally broad range of merchandise imports. In years when the dollar value of Canadian exports of visibles outweighs that of Canadian imports of visibles, the current account shows a positive **merchandise balance of trade**. For example, in 1993, payments for Canadian exports of merchandise were $181.0 billion and payments for Canadian imports of merchandise were $169.3 billion, giving a positive merchandise balance of trade of $11.7 billion. In contrast, in years when imports of goods outweigh exports, the current account shows a negative merchandise balance of trade.

$$\text{Merchandise balance of trade} = \text{merchandise export receipts} - \text{merchandise import payments}$$

$$+\$11.7 \text{ billion} = +\$181.0 \text{ billion} - \$169.3 \text{ billion}$$

merchandise balance of trade: merchandise export receipts minus merchandise import payments

Nonmerchandise Transactions

The three remaining "invisible" components of the current account—trade in services, investment income, and transfers—are known collectively as nonmerchandise transactions.

Services   Not only do Canadians import and export goods, but they also exchange services with foreigners. One important type of traded service is tourism. Spending by foreign tourists travelling in Canada represents a service export that creates an inflow of funds from foreign countries. Conversely, when Canadians travel outside Canada, their spending in foreign countries is considered a service import that causes an outflow of Canadian funds to foreign hands.

Canadians also import services when they pay foreigners to provide freight and shipping for goods. Likewise, Canadians export services when they transport goods on behalf of foreigners. In addition, a host of other invisible service items, such as insurance and telecommunications, are traded between Canadians and other countries. In 1993, the service account had a net balance of –$12.5 billion, showing that more services were imported by Canadians than were exported.

Investment Income   Dividends to owners of company stocks appear as investment income in the current account, as do interest payments to owners of bonds. An American company's dividends received by a Canadian stockholder, for example, are treated as a receipt in the current account, or a positive figure. In contrast, payments to a German owner of a Canadian government bond are shown as a payment in the accounts, or a negative figure.

Because of extensive foreign ownership of Canadian stocks and bonds, payments of investment income usually overwhelm receipts, giving Canada a large negative balance on its investment income account. This is illustrated by the 1993 balance of –$24.7 billion.

Transfers   Funds entering and leaving Canada as gifts and inheritances, as well as government foreign aid to low-income countries, are considered to be transfers. When new immigrants to Canada bring funds with them, these funds are considered an inflow to the Canadian economy. In contrast, federal government spending on foreign aid is considered an outflow. In 1993, transfers showed a net balance of +$0.3 billion.

Current Account Balance

The receipts represented in Canada's current account are usually lower than the payments. This results in a negative net balance, which is known as a **current account deficit**. In 1993, this shortfall totalled –$25.2 billion. In the unlikely event that receipts on the current account outweighed payments, Canada would have a **current account surplus**.

The Balance of Trade

Two of the four components of the current accounts can be viewed in another way. Canada's **balance of trade** represents both goods *and* services, so it is identical to net exports (X – M), which was discussed in previous chapters.

current account deficit: a negative net balance in the current account resulting from lower receipts than payments for merchandise and nonmerchandise transactions

current account surplus: a positive net balance in the current account resulting from higher receipts than payments for merchandise and nonmerchandise transactions

balance of trade: for both goods and services, receipts (inflows of Canadian dollars) less payments (outflows of Canadian dollars)

In recent years, Canada's surplus in merchandise trade has been more than offset by trade in services, giving a slight deficit in the balance of trade of *all* products. Note that the two terms, "balance of trade" and "merchandise balance of trade" are quite different; despite this, the terms are frequently and inaccurately interchanged by the media, leading to some confusion.

The Capital Account

Figure 16.2 shows another portion of the balance-of-payments statement called the **capital account**. This account summarizes the international transactions of financial assets involving Canadian dollars. Suppose a foreigner buys a Canadian government bond and holds bank deposits valued in Canadian dollars. This ownership of financial assets is being *exported* from Canada, so an inflow of receipts is shown on the capital account. Note, however, that the interest paid on bonds or deposits appears as an outflow on the current account.

Suppose also that a Canadian purchases stock in a foreign company. In this case, the Canadian's ownership is seen as an import of ownership, so the transaction is considered to be an outflow from the capital account. Once again, note that any payment on the financial asset—in this case, a dividend—would appear as an inflow on the current account.

capital account: the summary of all international transactions of financial assets involving Canadian dollars

Short-Term Capital Flows

Most of the movement of financial assets in and out of Canada is connected with day-to-day fluctuations in bank deposits. The associated monetary

Figure 16.2:   Canada's Capital Account (1993)

	Receipts (+) (Canadian $ inflows)		Payments (–) (Canadian $ outflows)		Balance (net) (Canadian $ inflows – outflows)
	(Canadian $ billions)				
Short-term capital flows					+11.5
Long-term capital flows					
Portfolio investment	38.9	–	12.8	=	+26.1
Direct investment	3.2	–	9.2	=	– 6.0
					+20.1
Capital account surplus (+) or deficit (–) (excl. official reserves)					+31.6

The capital account details receipts and payments for short-term and long-term capital flows (portfolio and direct investment). In 1993, there were positive balances for each main category, giving a capital account surplus of +$31.6 billion.

SOURCE: Adapted from Statistics Canada, *Canada's Balance of International Payments, Fourth Quarter 1993* (March 1994), cat. no. 67-001, vol. 41, no. 4, p. 77. Reproduced by authority of the Minister of Industry, 1994.

transactions are referred to as short-term capital flows. If, for example, a foreigner puts funds into a Canadian-dollar bank account, a positive receipt is created in Canada's capital account. Likewise, a negative payment on the account can be caused by a Canadian adding more to a U.S.-dollar bank account.

Long-Term Capital Flows

The remaining transactions on the capital account are associated with the buying and selling of long-term financial assets, in particular stocks and bonds. These long-term capital flows are often referred to as financial investment, and can be divided into portfolio investment and direct investment.

When the investment does *not* give the buyer a controlling interest in the institution issuing the assets, it is called **portfolio investment**. Suppose, for example, a Japanese resident buys a Canadian federal government bond. This would be shown as a receipt, or positive entry, on the capital account. Conversely, if a Canadian investor purchases a few hundred shares in a large American corporation that trades on the New York Stock Exchange, the transaction would be shown as a payment, or negative entry, on the capital account. Portfolio investment in and out of Canada usually produces a positive balance. This is primarily because of the substantial receipts that arise from foreign purchases of Canadian bonds. In 1993, for example, there was a net balance of +$26.1 billion.

In contrast to portfolio investment, **direct investment** is investment that gives the buyer of the financial assets a controlling interest in a company. In the case of a corporation, this may be 50 percent of the company's voting shares, or even less if ownership of the other shares is widely scattered. For example, an inflow of direct investment would occur if an Australian financier gained control of a Canadian goldmining company. An outflow would arise if a Canadian retailer acquired majority ownership of a British competitor.

Canada's net balance of direct investment varies widely from year to year. If Canada is viewed as an attractive place in which to do business, heavy inflows of direct investment lead to an overall positive balance. If other countries seem more appealing to foreign and Canadian investors, there can be an overall negative balance, as was the case in 1993 when direct investment totalled –$6.0 billion.

Capital Account Balance

Typically, receipts on Canada's capital account exceed payments, giving a **capital account surplus**, which in 1993 totalled $31.6 billion. Such a surplus means that there are lower investments by Canadians in foreign markets than by foreigners in the Canadian market. It is also possible for countries to show a **capital account deficit**, meaning that capital outflows exceed inflows. Such a deficit means that there are higher investments by Canadians in foreign markets than by foreigners in the Canadian market.

---

portfolio investment: long-term financial investment (e.g., purchases of stocks and bonds) that does not give the buyer a controlling interest in the institution issuing the assets

direct investment: long-term financial investment (e.g., purchases of stocks) that gives the buyer of the financial assets a controlling interest in the institution issuing the assets

capital account surplus: a positive net balance in the capital account, demonstrating lower investments by Canadians in foreign markets than by foreigners in the Canadian economy

capital account deficit: a negative net balance in the capital account, demonstrating higher investments by Canadians in foreign markets than by foreigners in the Canadian economy

Thinking About Economics

What causes Canada's habitual current account deficits and capital account surpluses?

The frequency of deficits in Canada's current account is closely tied to the high degree of foreign ownership in the Canadian economy. To compensate for this outflow of interest and dividend payments, there has to be a sizable inflow of investment funds from foreigners on the capital account, which means *more* foreign ownership of Canadian financial assets and higher investment outflows in the future. Capital account inflows are achieved by making Canadian bonds especially attractive to foreign buyers. This is accomplished through higher real interest rates than in other countries—particularly the United States.

Balance-of-Payments Surpluses and Deficits

Adding Canada's current and capital account balances (as well as a statistical discrepancy, which accounts for hidden transactions that are impossible to measure) gives a relatively small figure known as a **balance-of-payments surplus** if it is positive and a **balance-of-payments deficit** if it is negative. This surplus or deficit shows whether or not inflows are higher than outflows on all foreign transactions involving trade and financial assets. In 1993, for example, Canada had a balance-of-payments deficit of $0.6 billion, as shown by the negative balance in Figure 16.3. In other words, for that year, outflows exceeded inflows on the combined current and capital accounts.

balance-of-payments surplus: a positive net balance on the balance-of-payments statement, demonstrating greater receipts than payments for the current and capital accounts combined; balanced with changes in official reserves

balance-of-payments deficit: a negative net balance on the balance-of-payments statement, demonstrating lower receipts than payments for the current and capital accounts combined; balanced with changes in official reserves

Figure 16.3:   Canada's Balance of Payments (1993)

(Canadian $ billions)	**Balance (net)**
1. Current account	−25.2
2. Capital account	+31.6
3. Statistical discrepancy	− 7.0
Balance of payments surplus (+) or deficit (−)	− 0.6
4. Changes in official reserves	+ 0.6

The sum of the current and capital accounts, adjusted for the statistical discrepancy, gives Canada's balance of payments. In 1993, the result was a balance of payments deficit of $0.6 billion. Because there must be change in the official reserves of foreign currency to balance any deficit or surplus, the 1993 balance of payments shows a +$0.6 billion change to the reserves.

SOURCE: Statistics Canada, *Canada's Balance of International Payments, Fourth Quarter 1993* (March 1994), cat. no. 67-001, vol. 41, no. 4, p. 77. Reproduced by authority of the Minister of Industry, 1994.

SIDELINE

Going Global

International Finance in Canada

Foreign Liabilities and Assets

The typical capital account surplus and current account deficit shown on the balance-of-payments accounts demonstrate a key characteristic of the Canadian economy: foreigners own more financial assets in Canada than Canadians own in foreign markets. For the Canadian economy as a whole, the financial assets that Canadians hold in other nations, such as stocks and bonds, are considered "foreign assets," while those that foreigners hold in Canada are considered "foreign liabilities."

As Figure A shows, foreign assets equalled $275 billion in contrast to foreign liabilities of $587 billion in 1993. Of the financial assets that Canadians held in other countries, the majority (60.0 percent) were stocks held in foreign corporations. In contrast, the largest percentage of financial assets that foreigners held in

Canada (45.3 percent) were various types of bonds. Another 28.3 percent of foreign liabilities took the form of corporate stocks.

Note that the two concepts—foreign assets and foreign liabilities—can be consolidated. "Net foreign assets" are foreign liabilities subtracted from foreign assets to give a positive or negative figure. If foreign assets outweigh foreign liabilities, the number is positive; if the reverse is true, the number is negative. So, for Canada in 1993, the net foreign assets were –$312 billion ($275 billion – $587 billion):

Net foreign assets = foreign assets – foreign liabilities
–$312 billion = $275 billion – $587 billion

Foreign Ownership

How does Canada compare with other countries? To answer this, we have to con-

Figure A: Canada's Foreign Assets and Liabilities (1993)

Foreign Assets	$ Billions	% Foreign Assets	Foreign Liabilities	$ Billions	% Foreign Liabilities
Stocks	165	60.0	Stocks	166	28.3
Bonds	17	6.2	Corporate bonds	61	10.4
Government reserves and loans	44	16.0	Federal bonds	72	12.3
Other	49	17.8	Provincial bonds	84	14.3
			Municipal and government enterprise bonds	49	8.3
			Other	155	26.4
Total foreign assets	275	100.0	Total foreign liabilities	587	100.0

Of the foreign assets owned by Canadians—split among stocks, bonds, government reserves and loans, and other short-term assets such as bank accounts—stocks in corporations make up the majority (60 percent). In contrast, of the liabilities that Canadians owe to foreigners—in other words, the financial assets in Canada owned by foreigners—45.3 percent are bonds of various types.

SOURCE: Adapted from Statistics Canada, Canada's International Investment Position, 1993 (March 1994), cat. no. 67-202, pp. 25–26, 48–49. Reproduced by authority of the Minister of Industry, 1994.

sider foreign ownership—summarized by net foreign assets—in the context of each country's economy. To do this, we use GDP. As Figure B shows, net foreign assets, expressed as a proportion of the country's GDP, range for seven countries from Germany's *positive* net foreign assets equalling just over 20 percent of its GDP to Canada's *negative* net foreign assets equalling over 40 percent. The United Kingdom, Japan, and Germany all have positive net foreign assets—in other words, residents of these countries own more assets internationally than they owe to foreigners. As a result, these three countries are net foreign lenders.

Many economists see Canada's foreign liabilities as a source of concern. The result of Canada's negative net foreign assets is twofold. While great amounts of foreign investment are made in the Canadian economy (giving a capital account surplus), income from this investment leaves Canada (contributing to a current account deficit).

This large outflow of investment income from Canada each year means that funds that could have stayed in the country to produce and buy domestic products or that could have left the country to purchase foreign goods and services are instead being used to make payments to foreigners. Since this outflow is a loss of Canadian purchasing power, it represents a drain on the Canadian economy. This is especially true for the foreign debts of Canadian governments, since annual outflows of interest payments on these debts are not tied to profitable capital assets, as with most corporate liabilities.

Foreign Control of the Canadian Economy
Much of the controversy surrounding Canada's foreign liabilities has focused on foreign direct investment, which involves controlling interests in Canadian companies.

Figure B: Net Foreign Assets as a Percentage of GDP (1992)

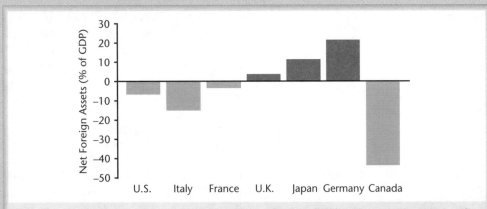

Comparing net foreign assets (foreign assets – foreign liabilities) as a percentage of a country's GDP demonstrates the degree to which foreign ownership in Canada exceeds that in many other nations. For example, while Canada's foreign assets are negative and account for over 40 percent of Canada's GDP, Germany's net foreign assets are positive and account for 20 percent of Germany's GDP.

SOURCE: Department of Finance, Canada, *The Budget 1993* (April 26, 1993), p. 26.

Figure C: **Share of Foreign Control of Capital Employed in Nonfinancial Industries in Canada**

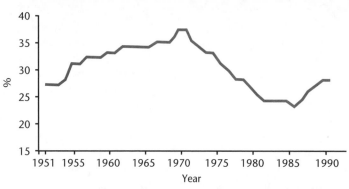

SOURCE: *Statistics Canada, Canadian Economic Observer, cat. no. 11-010, vol. 6, no 4, April 1993. Reproduced by authority of the Minister of Industry, 1994.*

Figure D: **Foreign Control in Nonfinancial Industries (1988)**

	Industry Assets That Are Foreign-Controlled (%)
Manufacturing	44.0
Mining	41.9
Wholesale trade	34.2
Services	13.3
Retail trade	12.1
Construction	5.3
Utilities	3.3
Agriculture, forestry, and fishing	3.0
Nonfinancial industries as a whole	26.2

Overall, 26.2 percent of nonfinancial industries in Canada are foreign-controlled. Of these industries, manufacturing and mining have the highest proportions of foreign control, while utilities and agriculture, forestry, and fishing have the lowest.

SOURCE: Adapted from Statistics Canada, *Annual Report of the Ministry of Industry, Science and Technology under the Corporations and Labour Unions Return Act, Part 1—Corporations 1988* (October 1991), cat. no. 61-210, p. 53. Reproduced by authority of the Minister of Industry, 1994.

Because of past high rates of foreign direct investment in Canada, a relatively high percentage of the country's economy is controlled by outsiders. As depicted in Figure C, the percentage of nonfinancial industries dominated by foreigners rose during the 1950s and 1960s, reaching a high of 37 percent in the early 1970s. After falling to 23 percent by 1986, the figure has been increasing gradually, reaching 27 percent by 1990.

Direct investment by foreigners has been particularly significant in some sectors of the Canadian economy. Figure D shows that foreign control is most prevalent in such industries as manufacturing (44.0 percent) and mining (41.9 percent). In contrast, foreign control is relatively insignificant in such areas as utilities (3.3 percent) and agriculture, forestry, and fishing (3.0 percent).

The debate over foreign direct investment in the Canadian economy is closely tied to the role of so-called *transnational corporations,* such as General Motors and IBM, which have operations in many countries.

Figure E: Largest Foreign-Owned Companies in Canada, 1992

Company	Revenue ($ millions)	% Foreign-Owned	Parent
General Motors of Canada Ltd.	18 347	100	General Motors (U.S.)
Ford Motor Co. of Canada	14 443	96	Ford Motor (U.S.)
Chrysler Canada Ltd.	9 453	100	Chrysler (U.S.)
Imperial Oil Ltd.	7 968	73	Exxon (U.S.)
IBM Canada Ltd.	6 760	100	IBM (U.S.)
Shell Canada Ltd.	4 492	78	Shell Petroleum (Netherlands)
Canada Safeway	4 357	100	Safeway (U.S.)
Sears Canada Inc.	3 957	61	Sears Roebuck (U.S.)
Amoco Canada Petroleum Co.	3 826	100	Amoco (U.S.)
Total Petroleum (N.A.) Ltd.	3 476	74	Total S.A. (France)

SOURCE: *The Financial Post 500 Magazine*, 1993.

Benefits and Drawbacks

Supporters of foreign ownership point to two potential benefits: overall benefits to the Canadian economy, and efficiency.

Overall Benefits to the Canadian Economy

Supporters argue that direct investment by foreign companies in Canada benefits the Canadian economy by increasing the stock of capital assets, thereby raising the productivity and living standards of Canadian workers.

Efficiency

To the extent that transnational corporations concentrate particular types of production in countries where they can be carried out most efficiently, these businesses also help to cut production costs and prices not just for Canadians but for consumers in all countries.

However, critics of direct foreign investment point to the drawbacks of increased foreign liabilities of the Canadian economy, loss of Canadian economic sovereignty, and low levels of research and development expenditures in Canada.

Increased Foreign Liabilities

The first criticism is quite obvious: a high level of any foreign investment increases Canada's debt to foreigners.

Canadian Economic Sovereignty

Canadian governments lose some of their power to govern when foreign-controlled companies are forced to comply with foreign legislation. The most publicized cases have involved U.S. laws that forbid American-owned companies—no matter where they operate—from trading with communist countries such as Cuba.

Decreased Research and Development

Expenditures on research and development by Canadian businesses tend to be lower than in most other industrial countries. Critics of foreign ownership claim that this is so because foreign-owned businesses conduct such activities at their international head offices rather than in Canada. The result is fewer jobs for Canadian scientists and technicians as well as a lower rate of technological progress in the Canadian economy.

Government Policy

Over the past few decades, Canadian policies regarding direct investment by foreigners have undergone an important shift. During the 1970s, the potential drawbacks of foreign control were stressed. In 1974, the federal government established the Foreign Investment Review Agency (FIRA), which was able to stop foreign direct investment it decided was not in the best interests of Canadians. While FIRA turned down a relatively small proportion of the cases it reviewed, it often set conditions on foreign investors relating to such matters as trade and employment that had to be met before a proposal could be approved. Partly because of FIRA's intervention, and its impact on the environment for foreign investment in Canada, foreign control of the Canadian economy declined in percentage terms during the last half of the 1970s and early 1980s, as previously seen in Figure D.

By 1984, changing attitudes led to FIRA being replaced by Investment Canada. This agency can still review much of the foreign direct investment in Canada. In practice, the agency rarely turns down the proposals that come before it, although it sometimes sets conditions that foreign investors must meet in order to gain approval. Partly as a result of this looser policy, foreign control in the Canadian economy has increased, as Figure C shows.

A new trend has been increased Canadian investment in foreign countries, especially in the United States. Of course, given the relative size of the two economies, Canadian investment in the United States will never be as significant to Americans as foreign (especially American) investment is to Canadians.

Now, with the trend toward a "global economy," most countries are facing higher levels of foreign investment than ever before. Given Canada's history of high foreign ownership and the related policies that go with it, Canada's experience will provide lessons for the many countries that are "going global."

Changes in Official Reserves

change in official reserves: use of the government's reserves of foreign currency to influence the international value of the Canadian dollar, as shown on the balance-of-payments statement

To influence the international value of the Canadian dollar (as we'll discuss later), the Bank of Canada sometimes buys and sells foreign currencies, using the government's reserves of foreign currency. The effect of these operations on the flow of Canadian dollars is known as the **change in official reserves**. As shown in Figure 16.3, the change in official reserves is equal in value (and opposite in sign) to the surplus or deficit noted in the balance of payments. In 1993, for example, the +$0.6 billion change in reserves matches the –$0.6 billion balance-of-payments deficit. This positive change in official reserves indicates that the Bank of Canada *bought* Canadian dollars (creating an inflow) by selling some of the government's official foreign currency reserves. In the same way, if there were a balance-of-payments surplus, there would be a negative change in official reserves equal to that amount. This negative change in official reserves would indicate that the Bank of Canada *sold* Canadian dollars (causing an outflow) and bought foreign currency.

Once the change in official reserves is added to the balance-of-payments surplus or deficit, the balance-of-payments accounts sum to zero. In other words, the inflow of funds from foreigners matches the outflow of funds from Canadians, ensuring that the accounts balance. This balance occurs because holders of Canadian dollars who buy foreign currency must engage in transactions of equal value with holders of foreign currency buying Canadian dollars. For example, $1 in Canadian currency can be sold for Japanese yen only if someone is willing to purchase this Canadian dollar in return for yen.

BRIEF REVIEW

1. Because products and financial assets are exchanged between Canadians and foreigners, foreigners participate in the Canadian economy.

2. The current account summarizes all receipts and payments from international trade in merchandise, trade in services, flows of investment income, and transfers of funds. The current account typically shows payments exceeding receipts, giving a current account deficit.

3. Because Canada's balance of trade is the exports of goods and services less imports of goods and services, it is the same as net exports (X – M).

4. The capital account summarizes all international transactions related to the buying and selling of financial assets. Large inflows of funds from foreigners buying Canadian bonds mean that Canada typically has a capital account surplus.

5. The current account (which usually shows a deficit) and the capital account (which usually shows a surplus) are adjusted for statistical discrepancy, but balanced by changes in the official reserves. The Bank of Canada either sells or buys Canadian dollars to adjust the monetary flows.

Exchange Rates

Any transaction that appears in the balance-of-payments accounts involves trading Canadian dollars for another currency. Transactions that are classified as receipts involve foreign currency being sold to buy Canadian dollars. For example, a company that purchases Canadian paper sold in France trades French francs for Canadian dollars to pay the Canadian paper company. In contrast, transactions that are classified as payments involve Canadian dollars being sold to buy foreign currency. A Canadian buying the services of a German architect, for example, exchanges Canadian dollars for German marks to pay the architect.

Currencies are traded in the global **foreign exchange market**. In the Canadian sector of this market, which is run by the chartered banks,

foreign exchange market: the global market in which national currencies are traded

Canadian dollars are exchanged for U.S. dollars, Japanese yen, French francs, and other international currencies. The recent revolution in communications technology has made the foreign exchange market a truly global one, with currency prices internationally consistent and immediately available. For example, if the Canadian dollar is trading at a price of 80 cents in Toronto, then the same price applies in London and Tokyo.

Recall from Chapter 12 that the *exchange rate* is the value of one nation's currency in terms of another currency, and it becomes the price at any location where the two currencies are being exchanged. There are many exchange rates for a certain currency. For example, at any given moment one Canadian dollar may trade for 80 U.S. cents, 130 Japanese yen, or 1200 Italian lire. Because most of Canada's trade is with the United States, the price of the Canadian dollar is commonly related to U.S. dollars. We'll be using the example of Canadian and U.S. dollars in the rest of the chapter, although the same principles apply to all currencies.

Two exchange rates can be used to compare any two currencies—for example, a Canadian dollar with its U.S. counterpart. The first tells us how many U.S. dollars it takes to buy one Canadian dollar—for example, one Canadian dollar may cost 80 U.S. cents. The other way to express the exchange rate is to ask how many Canadian dollars are needed to purchase one U.S. dollar. This amount can be calculated from the first exchange rate using the following formula:

$$\text{Canadian dollars to buy US\$1} = \frac{1}{\text{U.S. dollars to buy CDN\$1}}$$

$$\text{CDN\$1.25} = \frac{1}{\text{US\$0.80}}$$

In other words, the second exchange rate—CDN$1.25 buys US$1—is the reciprocal of the first exchange rate.

Exchange Rates and Prices

One important application of exchange rates is to determine prices of products in terms of a foreign currency—either the U.S. dollar price of a Canadian product, for example, or the Canadian dollar price of an American item.

Foreign prices of Canadian products are calculated by applying the exchange rate to the goods' Canadian dollar prices. For example, when a Canadian export with a Canadian price of $20.00 is sold in the United States, its U.S. dollar price is found by multiplying its Canadian price by the exchange rate expressed as the number of U.S. dollars it takes to buy one Canadian dollar. When the exchange rate has a value of US$0.80 for each Canadian dollar, the American price of this product is therefore US$16.00:

$$\text{U.S. dollar price} = \text{Canadian dollar price} \times \text{U.S. dollars to buy CDN\$1.00}$$
$$\text{US\$16.00} = \text{CDN\$20.00} \times \$0.80$$

Canadian prices of foreign goods are calculated in reverse. As an example, an American product imported to Canada has a U.S. price of $40.00. The import's Canadian dollar price is found by multiplying the American price by the exchange rate expressed as the number of Canadian dollars it takes to buy one U.S. dollar. When the exchange rate has a value of CDN$1.25 for each U.S. dollar, the item's Canadian price is CDN$50.00:

$$\text{Canadian dollar price} = \text{U.S. dollar price} \times \text{Canadian dollars to buy US\$1.00}$$
$$\text{CDN\$50.00} = \text{US\$40.00} \times \$1.25$$

The Foreign Exchange Market

To see how exchange rates are set, we must look at the demand for and supply of Canadian currency in the foreign exchange market. In doing so, we concentrate on the number of U.S. dollars needed to purchase a Canadian dollar.

Demand for Canadian Dollars
The **demand for Canadian dollars** is the relationship between the price of a Canadian dollar and the quantity of Canadian dollars demanded on

demand for Canadian dollars: the relationship between the price of a Canadian dollar and the quantity demanded on the foreign exchange market

Figure 16.4:   The Foreign Exchange Market

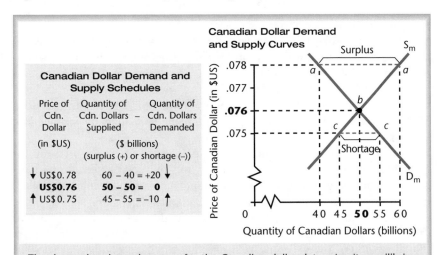

Canadian Dollar Demand and Supply Schedules		
Price of Cdn. Dollar (in $US)	Quantity of Cdn. Dollars Supplied	Quantity of Cdn. Dollars Demanded
	($ billions) (surplus (+) or shortage (–))	
↓ US$0.78	60 – 40 = +20 ↓	
US$0.76	**50 – 50 = 0**	
↑ US$0.75	45 – 55 = –10 ↑	

The demand and supply curves for the Canadian dollar determine its equilibrium value, which equals its exchange rate. If the price falls (to points *c*) below the equilibrium value (point *b*), a shortage of Canadian dollars results. Without government intervention, the forces of demand and supply push the price up to equilibrium (point *b*), causing the Canadian dollar to appreciate. A price above the equilibrium value (at points *a*) causes a surplus of Canadian dollars. Without government intervention, the Canadian dollar would depreciate, returning to its equilibrium value.

the foreign exchange market. The relationship can be expressed in a schedule and a curve. As Figure 16.4 shows, this relationship is inverse, so the curve has a negative slope. For example, a jump in the price of the Canadian dollar in terms of the U.S. dollar reduces the quantity of Canadian dollars demanded.

Canadian dollars are demanded on the foreign exchange market to finance foreign purchases of either Canadian exports or Canadian financial assets. Foreigners buying Canadian exports of goods and services exchange their own currencies for Canadian dollars in order to pay Canadian producers. Likewise, foreigners acquiring Canadian stocks and bonds buy Canadian dollars to settle their purchases.

The negative slope of the demand curve is determined by the first of these two groups—foreign export buyers. A higher Canadian dollar means that Canadian goods and services have higher American prices. Suppose, for example, the exchange rate for Canadian dollars is US$0.75. As a result, a Canadian export with a price of CDN$2.00 originally has an American price of US$1.50 ($2.00 × $0.75). If the value of the Canadian dollar increases from US$0.75 to US$0.80, the American price of this export rises to US$1.60 ($2.00 × $0.80). Because American buyers find Canadian exports more expensive, they purchase fewer of them, decreasing both Canadian export receipts and the quantity of Canadian dollars demanded in foreign exchange markets.

Supply of Canadian Dollars

supply of Canadian dollars: the relationship between the price of a Canadian dollar and the quantity supplied on the foreign exchange market

In contrast, the **supply of Canadian dollars** is the relationship between the price of the Canadian dollar and the quantity of Canadian dollars supplied on the foreign exchange market. Once again, the relationship can be expressed in a schedule or a curve. As Figure 16.4 shows, the relationship is direct, as is typical in supply relationships. A rise in the price of the Canadian dollar causes an increase in the quantity supplied of Canadian dollars.

Canadian dollars are supplied in the foreign exchange market for Canadian purchases of foreign products and financial assets. Canadians buying imported products or foreign financial assets sell Canadian dollars for another currency to complete their transactions.

The positive slope of the supply curve is determined by the first of these two groups—Canadian import buyers. For example, a higher Canadian dollar lowers domestic prices of imported goods and services from the United States. If the Canadian dollar rises from US$0.75 to US$0.80, the U.S. dollar *falls* in terms of the Canadian dollar from CDN$1.33 ($1.00 ÷ $0.75) to CDN$1.25 ($1.00 ÷ $0.80). An American import that costs $3.00 in the United States therefore drops from CDN$4.00 ($3.00 × $1.33) to CDN$3.75 ($3.00 × $1.25). Canadians respond to these lower prices by purchasing more imports, increasing both Canadian import payments and the quantity of Canadian dollars supplied in foreign exchange markets.

Market Equilibrium

Recall that, in competitive markets, the forces of demand and supply bring the market to an equilibrium point, where demand and supply intersect. The same is true of the currency markets. So, when a government allows the value of its currency to vary, the foreign exchange market will move toward an equilibrium point where any discrepancy between amounts demanded and supplied is eliminated. Figure 16.4 provides a hypothetical example.

If (at points *c*) the Canadian dollar exchange rate is below its equilibrium price of US$0.76 (point *b*), the quantity demanded of Canadian dollars on the foreign exchange market is greater than the quantity supplied of Canadian dollars. This causes a $10 billion shortage of Canadian currency, as shown at the exchange rate of US$0.75 ($55 billion – $45 billion). When exchange rates are allowed to vary, the price of the Canadian dollar is forced up to its equilibrium value. In this case, when one currency's price increases against another, the increased currency is said to **appreciate**. The movement to equilibrium is very rapid because foreign exchange markets are highly competitive and involve large numbers of price-conscious buyers and sellers.

appreciate: to increase, as when a currency's price rises in comparison to the price of another currency

In contrast, if (at points *a*) the Canadian dollar is above its equilibrium price, the quantity supplied of Canadian dollars exceeds the quantity demanded on the foreign exchange market. The result is a $20 billion surplus of Canadian currency as shown at the exchange rate of US$0.78 ($60 billion – $40 billion). When exchange rates are allowed to vary, this excess soon pushes down the price of the Canadian dollar until it reaches its equilibrium value. In this case, the Canadian dollar is said to **depreciate** when compared to the U.S. dollar. Again, the movement toward equilibrium happens very quickly.

depreciate: to decrease, as when a currency's price falls in comparison to the price of another currency

Note that both preceding examples involve the variations in the exchange rates that bring about changes in quantities demanded or supplied. In other words, the examples demonstrate movements *along* the Canadian dollar demand and supply curves.

Changes in Demand and Supply

Of course, other factors can cause the Canadian dollar demand and supply curves to *shift*. Demand and supply shifts in the foreign exchange market are related either to trade or to financial conditions. As a result of shifts in the curves, the equilibrium exchange rate changes. Four main factors affect the equilibrium value of the exchange rate: price differences, product demand, interest rates, and speculation.

Price Differences

A country's price level may rise more rapidly than price levels in other countries, so that its own products become more expensive than foreign products. The left graph in Figure 16.5 illustrates a hypothetical example of what happens when Canada's rate of inflation outpaces inflation in the United States.

Figure 16.5:   Exchange Rate Changes

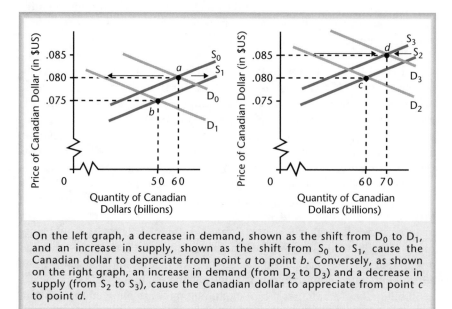

On the left graph, a decrease in demand, shown as the shift from D_0 to D_1, and an increase in supply, shown as the shift from S_0 to S_1, cause the Canadian dollar to depreciate from point *a* to point *b*. Conversely, as shown on the right graph, an increase in demand (from D_2 to D_3) and a decrease in supply (from S_2 to S_3), cause the Canadian dollar to appreciate from point *c* to point *d*.

At any given exchange rate between the two currencies, increases in the prices of Canadian products mean that Americans will purchase fewer Canadian exports, reducing the amount of Canadian currency demanded on the foreign exchange market. This reduces the demand for Canadian dollars, shown as a shift in the demand curve for Canadian dollars from D_0 to D_1. A lower U.S. inflation rate also means that American products become cheaper relative to Canadian products. As a result, Canadian buyers purchase more American imports at any given exchange rate. This increases the supply of Canadian dollars, thereby shifting the supply curve from S_0 to S_1. As a result of these demand and supply changes, the Canadian dollar depreciates, or falls in value, from point *a* to point *b*.

Product Demand

The appeal of a country's products to prospective buyers can also affect exchange rates. Suppose, for example, the quality of Canadian products improves tremendously. As a result, the demand for Canadian products in both foreign and domestic markets increases. The result is shown on the right graph in Figure 16.5.

In this case, Americans increase their purchases of Canadian products, thereby shifting the demand curve for Canadian dollars from D_2 to D_3 in the foreign exchange market. Also, Canadians buy more domestic products and fewer American imports. This reduces the sale of Canadian dollars on the foreign exchange market and so shifts the supply curve to the left, from S_2 to S_3. Both trends cause the Canadian dollar to appreciate, or rise in value, from point c to point d.

Interest Rates

Recall that, in general, Canadian interest rates tend to be higher than American interest rates. If the Bank of Canada implements an expansionary monetary policy, causing Canadian interest rates overall to fall, the gap between Canadian and American rates will shrink. As shown in Figure 16.5, on the left, this has implications for the Canadian dollar.

With the drop in the Canadian interest rate, Canadian bonds become less appealing to financial investors in both Canada and the United States. Fewer American purchases of Canadian bonds mean that the demand for Canadian dollars decreases, thereby shifting the demand curve from D_0 to D_1. Meanwhile, Canadians also reduce their purchases of domestic bonds *and* are more likely to buy foreign financial assets. In order to buy the foreign financial assets, Canadians must sell additional Canadian dollars on the foreign exchange market. The result is an increase in the supply of Canadian dollars, shown as a shift to the right of the supply curve from S_0 to S_1. The movements in demand and supply both cause the Canadian dollar to depreciate.

Speculation

Some individuals, but more often financial institutions, buy and sell on the foreign exchange markets simply in order to profit from short-run changes in currency values. The activities of these profit-seekers, known as **speculators**, affect the demand and supply of particular currencies, and so lead to changes in exchange rates.

For example, if there are signs that the Canadian dollar will soon rise in value against the U.S. dollar, speculators enter the market in such a way as to make this expectation a reality. Figure 16.5, on the right, shows the effects. Lured by potential profits, American speculators demand the currency that is expected to rise in value, so they purchase Canadian dollars by selling their holdings of U.S. dollars. As a result, the demand curve for Canadian dollars shifts from D_2 to D_3. At the same time, Canadian speculators hold onto, and perhaps buy more, Canadian dollars rather than buying U.S. dollars. As a result, the supply curve for Canadian dol-

speculators: individuals or organizations that buy and sell currencies for profit

lars shifts from S_2 to S_3. As a result of both trends, the Canadian dollar appreciates and speculators make a tidy profit.

Thinking About Economics

What factors prompt speculators to enter the foreign exchange market?

Speculators respond to three factors: interest rates, inflation rates, and the political climate. Because of the influence of interest rates on exchange rates, speculators pay particular attention to monetary policy. Any indication that the Bank of Canada is following a contractionary policy, for example, leads speculators to forecast a rise in Canadian interest rates and a resulting increase in the value of the Canadian dollar. Speculation therefore hastens the Canadian dollar's appreciation in the foreign currency market. Speculators also act on the basis of expectations about inflation. For example, they may expect that the Canadian inflation rate will fall compared to inflation rates in other countries. As a result, speculators expect a future rise in the Canadian dollar's value. This prediction again causes intervention in the foreign exchange market that immediately raises the value of the Canadian dollar. Finally, speculators pay attention to political factors—especially their possible impact on foreign-held debt. Suppose, for example, there is a risk that Canada will become politically unstable. Speculators will expect that instability to make Canadian bonds less attractive to foreign investors, thereby reducing the demand for Canadian dollars on the foreign exchange market. In anticipation of the possible fall in the Canadian dollar's value, speculators will sell Canadian dollars immediately, thus hastening the change they predict.

BRIEF REVIEW

1. Exchange rates are prices of currencies in terms of other currencies. They are determined in a global foreign exchange market.

2. The demand for Canadian dollars is the relationship between the price of a Canadian dollar and the quantity of Canadian dollars demanded in the foreign exchange market. The relationship is inverse, so, for example, an increase in price causes a decrease in quantity demanded. This is shown as a movement along the demand curve. Demand for Canadian dollars is created by foreigners' purchases of Canadian exports and financial assets.

3. The supply of Canadian dollars is the relationship between the price of the

Canadian dollar and the quantity of Canadian dollars supplied in the foreign exchange market. The relationship is direct; so, for example, an increase in price causes an increase in quantity supplied. This is shown as a movement along the supply curve. Canadian dollars are supplied in the foreign exchange market for Canadian purchases of foreign products and financial assets.

4. When currency values are allowed to vary, a currency's exchange rate will move toward its equilibrium value, the point of intersection of the demand and supply curves for the currency.

5. Factors that shift the demand and supply curves for a particular currency, and so the equilibrium point as well, are price differences, product demand, interest rates, and speculation.

Exchange Rate Systems

Flexible Exchange Rates

Governments that allow the exchange rate of their currency to vary freely, as assumed in Figures 16.4 and 16.5, are following a system of **flexible exchange rates**, or floating rates as they are sometimes known.

Flexible exchange rates offer one main advantage: market forces quickly eliminate shortages or surpluses so that inflows and outflows soon match each other. However, flexible rates also have an important disadvantage. Dramatic changes in exchange rates mean considerable risks for businesses involved in importing or exporting.

Consider, for example, a Canadian importer of American-made products. If the Canadian dollar depreciates suddenly, the price of the products is pushed up to the point that the products become too expensive for Canadian consumers and quantity demanded decreases. Canadian exporters and their suppliers face similar uncertainty. Suppose, for example, the Canadian dollar jumps in value in comparison to the American dollar. The exporter who exports Canadian products to the U.S. market finds that they become too expensive for the American market and quantity demanded decreases. Because of these fluctuations, incomes and employment in the import and export industries are harmed.

flexible exchange rates: currency exchange rates that are allowed to move freely to their equilibrium levels; also called floating rates

Fixed Exchange Rates

To avoid the uncertainty caused by flexible exchange rates, governments often intervene directly in the foreign exchange market. **Fixed exchange rates** offer the most striking alternative to floating rates. When a government establishes a fixed exchange rate, it sets or "pegs" the value of the country's currency at a certain price in terms of another currency.

fixed exchange rates: currency exchange rates set or "pegged" to a certain value by each country's government

Figure 16.6:   Fixed Exchange Rates

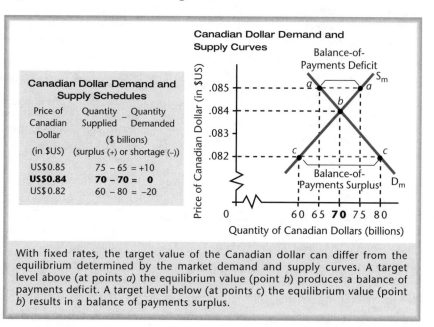

Canadian Dollar Demand and Supply Curves

Canadian Dollar Demand and Supply Schedules

Price of Canadian Dollar (in $US)	Quantity Supplied	–	Quantity Demanded
	($ billions)		
	(surplus (+) or shortage (–))		
US$0.85	75 – 65 = +10		
US$0.84	**70 – 70 = 0**		
US$0.82	60 – 80 = –20		

With fixed rates, the target value of the Canadian dollar can differ from the equilibrium determined by the market demand and supply curves. A target level above (at points *a*) the equilibrium value (point *b*) produces a balance of payments deficit. A target level below (at points *c*) the equilibrium value (point *b*) results in a balance of payments surplus.

Impact of Market Intervention

The effects of fixed exchange rates on the foreign exchange market are illustrated by the hypothetical example in Figure 16.6. This shows that whenever the government's target rate differs from the equilibrium level, either a balance-of-payments surplus or deficit is created.

Suppose the federal government sets a target exchange rate of 82 cents (at points *c*). Because this rate is below its equilibrium level of 84 cents in U.S. currency (point *b*), it creates excess demand for Canadian dollars, with more sought than are available on the market. This means that the inflows represented on the current and capital accounts, which are associated with buying Canadian dollars, exceed the outflows represented on these accounts, which are tied to sales of Canadian dollars. The result is a shortage, and a resulting balance-of-payments surplus, of CDN$20 billion. This surplus is then noted in the balance-of-payments accounts.

To make up for the excess demand of Canadian currency in the foreign exchange market, the Bank of Canada intervenes by selling CDN$20 billion and purchasing U.S. currency in return. In doing so, the Bank is able to curb any rise in the value of the Canadian dollar above the desired level of US$0.82.

Suppose, instead, the federal government set the target level of the Canadian dollar at 85 cents in U.S. currency (points *a*), above the market equilibrium price (point b). As a result, a \$10 billion surplus of Canadian dollars translates into a \$10 billion balance-of-payments deficit. To prop up the Canadian dollar at this preferred rate of US\$0.85, the Bank of Canada intervenes by selling CDN\$10 billion and purchasing American currency in return. In this way, it eliminates the excess supply of Canadian dollars.

Exchange Rate Policy

Sometimes governments use fixed exchange rates to affect domestic output and prices. To see how policy-makers can use exchange rate policy to different ends, let's consider the impact of low exchange rates, high exchange rates, and monetary policy.

Low Exchange Rates

A low target rate for the Canadian dollar, such as US\$0.82 in Figure 16.6, makes Canadian exports cheap and imports of American products expensive. This policy stimulates export revenues and inhibits import spending, thereby increasing net exports. Recall from the discussion of aggregate demand and supply in Chapter 12 that a rise in net exports increases aggregate demand. Hence, lowering the exchange rate serves as an expansionary policy. Both real output and employment are boosted, and any recessionary gap that exists is reduced.

However, there are several problems in setting a low exchange rate. First, there is the danger of inflation. This hazard is especially acute if the economy is near its potential output, when shifts in the aggregate demand curve primarily affect prices. Second, there is a chance that a country's trading partners may respond by reducing *their* exchange rates to maintain their own export markets. When this happens, currencies return to their original relative values, and the original policy achieves nothing.

Despite these risks, a policy of low exchange rates has sometimes been pursued with success. For example, Pacific Rim countries such as Taiwan and South Korea have depressed the values of their currencies as a way of encouraging export-driven growth. Evidence of this strategy is found in their large holdings of foreign currency, which have resulted from the balance-of-payments surpluses associated with a low exchange rate policy.

High Exchange Rates

Setting a high target for the Canadian dollar, such as US\$0.85 in Figure 16.6, has the opposite effect: high exchange rates make imports cheaper and boost the prices of Canadian exports. Therefore, raising the exchange rate serves as a contractionary policy by reducing net exports and decreasing aggregate demand. This puts downward pressure on inflation as well as on real output and employment.

Using a high exchange rate as an anti-inflationary tool has its problems, however. Not only is there a reduction in output and employment—

especially in exporting industries—but also a reduction in the government's foreign currency holdings. Sooner or later, through continual balance-of-payments deficits, the holdings are depleted. In this situation, countries sometimes attempt to bolster their currency reserves by such measures as forcing citizens to sell their foreign currency to the government rather than allowing them to trade it privately. These laws produce underground foreign exchange markets, with prices set at equilibrium levels determined by demand and supply.

Monetary Policy and Exchange Rates

The Bank of Canada can use monetary policy to back its intervention in the foreign exchange market. Recall that interest rates and the price of the Canadian dollar move in the same direction. If the Bank wishes to raise the exchange rate without incurring a balance-of-payments deficit, it can force up interest rates using contractionary monetary policy. Conversely, an easy money policy of low interest rates can be applied to depreciate the exchange rate. In either case, the Bank of Canada influences the Canadian dollar by adjusting its equilibrium value.

Unfortunately, applying monetary policy in this way can complicate stabilization policy. If the Bank of Canada focuses its monetary policy excessively on maintaining a certain target exchange rate, it may end up worsening the business cycle. Therefore, the Bank must make sure its target value for the Canadian dollar allows the economy to move toward its potential output.

Evolution of Exchange Rate Systems

During the past century, there have been three major exchange rate systems used by industrialized countries: a fixed gold standard, a structure of adjustable fixed rates, and the widespread use of the managed float, which offers a middle ground between the extremes of fully flexible and fixed exchange rates.

The Gold Standard (1879–1934)

Except for a brief time connected with the financial turmoil caused by World War I, the international gold standard was in place for over five decades. With this system, each country set the value of its currency in terms of an amount of gold. (For example, the Canadian dollar traded for 23.22 grains of gold.) Because these standards were not adjustable, maintaining a constant exchange rate took precedence over stabilization policy. The gold standard finally broke down under the strains of the Great Depression of the 1930s as governments unsuccessfully attempted to stimulate their exports and domestic employment levels by depreciating their currencies.

The Bretton Woods System (1945–1971)

The disarray caused by exchange rate movements in the latter half of the 1930s led to the creation of the Bretton Woods system after World War II.

(Bretton Woods is the name of the place in the United States where the conference to establish an international monetary system was held.) This system was based on adjustable fixed exchange rates. Governments set an official exchange rate for their currency until persistent surpluses or shortages in the foreign exchange market forced an adjustment. The currency then underwent a **devaluation** (reduction in value) when there were surpluses, or a **revaluation** (an increase in value) when there were shortages.

The organization known as the International Monetary Fund (IMF) was also established at this time. Among other tasks, it promotes the stability of exchange rates through loans to countries that are running out of foreign currency reserves to stabilize their currencies.

From 1950 to 1962, the Canadian government chose to diverge from the international Bretton Woods system and adopted floating rates instead. Substantial inflows of foreign financial investment kept the value of the Canadian dollar high during these years. During most of this period, the Canadian dollar traded above the price of US$1.

Canada returned to a fixed exchange rate system from 1962 to 1970, pegging its dollar at a relatively low value of US$0.925. This action was prompted by speculators who were driving down the Canadian dollar's value. The Canadian experience in the 1960s points out an interesting problem with fixed exchange rates. With such a system, it is difficult for a country to shield itself from foreign inflation. In Canada's case, rising inflation experienced by the United States during this period was automatically "imported" to Canada as prices for American items sold in Canada increased.

Managed Float (1971–1994)

The stability provided by the Bretton Woods system helped promote the high growth rates experienced by most countries in the postwar period. However, the system fell apart in 1971 when the United States—whose dollar had come to serve as an "international currency"—was forced to adopt a **managed float**. Under this system, the foreign value of a currency is allowed to vary over time, but the effects of short-run demand and supply movements in the foreign exchange market are sometimes lessened through government intervention. The move to a partially floating exchange rate provided the American government with the leeway needed to deal with imbalances in the foreign exchange market. By 1974, most other major economies had also switched away from fixed exchange rates.

Canada preceded most other countries in adopting a managed float in 1970. During the early 1970s, high prices for many of Canada's resource exports boosted the demand for Canadian currency. As a result, the Canadian dollar traded above US$1.00. Relatively rapid inflation in Canada during the late 1970s and early 1980s, however, caused the Canadian dollar to decline to an all-time annual low of US$0.72 by 1986. In the late

devaluation: a reduction in the value of a currency by the government that sets the exchange rate

revaluation: an increase in the value of a currency by the government that sets the exchange rate

managed float: a flexible exchange rate system that sometimes involves short-term government intervention

Figure 16.7:   Canadian Exchange Rates

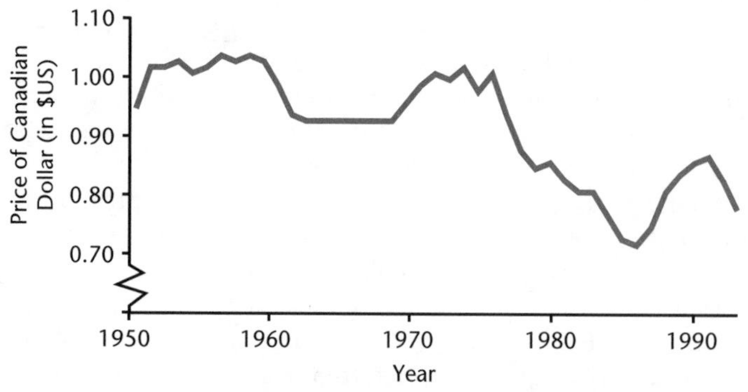

With floating rates, the Canadian dollar rose above US$1.00 in the 1950s. Between 1962 and 1970, it remained close to its fixed value of US$0.925. With a managed float in place since 1970, the Canadian dollar has fluctuated widely.

SOURCES: Adapted from Statistics Canada, *Canadian Economic Observer, Historical Statistical Supplement, 1992/93* (July 1993), cat. no. 11-210, vol. 7, p. 91; *Canadian Economic Observer, Statistical Summary* (May 1994), cat. no. 11-010, p. 52. Reproduced by authority of the Minister of Industry, 1994.

1980s and early 1990s, the dollar rose and then fell in response to interest rate adjustments by the Bank of Canada. The behaviour of the U.S. price of the Canadian dollar in the last few decades is indicated in Figure 16.7.

Thinking About Economics

What are the trends in exchange rate systems?

Because of two factors—the uncertainty of fluctuating currency prices and multinational trade arrangements—some countries started moving back to pegged exchange rates in the 1990s. For example, various member nations of the European Union (EU), including Germany and France, synchronized their currencies through a system of adjustable fixed exchange rates. With the growing integration of national economies, these types of regional exchange rate arrangements will probably become more common. Many economists have predicted that the integration of national economies will bring about a single international currency. While it would simplify the financing of international trade and investment, critics point out that individual countries would lose the ability to conduct their own monetary policies.

Competition Is All

Sylvia Ostry and Canada's Role in the Global Economy

Sylvia Ostry, chair of the Centre for International Studies, University of Toronto, is a leading Canadian economist. She has served as Ambassador of Canada for Multilateral Trade Negotiations, and has represented Canada's prime minister at the Economic Summit. In the following interview with Irene J. Matthews, Ostry evaluates Canadian international competitiveness and the prospects for the North American Free Trade Agreement (NAFTA, which we'll examine in Chapter 17) and gives her prescription for Canada's success in the global economy.

Irene J. Matthews: How do you think Canadian business could improve its competitiveness internationally?

Sylvia Ostry: The enormous increase in international investment from about the mid-1980s has tapered off a bit, largely because of the recession, but will revive. The implications for Canadian business—of investment flows largely concentrated among the corporations of Europe, the United States and Japan (the triad)—are important.

Recent developments in Europe and the United States (and, to a lesser extent, in Japan) show that effective competition in a market means getting inside that market rather than simply exporting into it.

To insure our competitiveness we have to look not just at trade, but at the investment behaviour of Canadian business. The figures for the second half of the '80s show an increased flow of Canadian investment but that flow was still heavily concentrated in the American market. If we want to compete, we need to replicate (at a smaller rate because we are a smaller country) the transnational investment behaviour of our competitors.

More recently, there has been an enormous increase in the investment flows into Mexico and Latin America. This means another magnet attracting investment capital that Canada also needs to attract.

There was an increase in investment in Canada in the second half of the 1980s, but government policy is definitely affecting our ability to lure investment money.

Canadian business has to think in terms of strategic investment in various markets and of investment flows into the country. This will increase competition in a more active way than the flow of goods can. It's not the behaviour of firms, but the behaviour of governments that is crucial.

The recent debate on the constitution has overshadowed the crucial issue of the competitiveness of the Canadian economy. Even the federal government proposal that, after 125 years, Canada should have a barrier-free common market, has been rejected. Provincial desires to erect and maintain barriers and different regulatory regimes suggests that the advan-

ADVANCING ECONOMIC THOUGHT

Sylvia Ostry
SOURCE: Office of Dr. Sylvia Ostry

tage of the common market (which was created by the British North America Act) is not considered important. The impediments presented by our government's policy—rejection of the common market and any mechanisms to cope with the challenges of globalization—are really astonishing.

I.J.M.: What would make us more competitive?

S.O.: I think there are two issues.

The first is the macroeconomic conditions, largely determined by monetary policy and fiscal policy.

We have a rather tight monetary policy (in my view, correctly), because the credibility of our entire policy has rested very strongly on monetary policy to compensate for a weak fiscal policy. Although the federal government has made an effort to try, over the medium term, to reduce the fiscal deficit, that effort has been offset by provincial policy. But monetary policy alone, without an adequate fiscal policy, can't do the job. In a federal state, what's required is a co-ordinating mechanism. Monetary policy alone can only give high real interest rates, relative to the rest of the world, and a high dollar. The macroeconomic situation requires, in a federal state, the kind of mechanism which has been scuttled in the debates.

Second, the microeconomic conditions reveal very serious problems. Our education system shows a high rate of illiteracy and innumeracy, high-dropout rates (much higher than in the past) and low R & D expenditure (low not only in comparison to other industrialized countries but also to Korea, Taiwan, India and even Mexico).

Business must do its part, but it cannot succeed alone.

I.J.M.: What further opportunities could result from the North American Free Trade Agreement?

S.O.: The Free Trade Agreement with the United States provided us with preferential access to the American market. With the NAFTA, one of the issues will be how much will the Mexicans erode that preferential access in the American market.

Secondly, there is the question of what opportunities will exist in Mexico if, in fact, Mexico is into a major take-off in growth. The same question applies to Latin America.

Thirdly, the primary concern for Mexico and Latin America is not really trade. The NAFTA and the Enterprise For The Americas are basically not about trade.

The NAFTA or some agreement is important in order to ensure that the current domestic reforms, both macroeconomic and microeconomic, in Mexico and Latin America seem credible to the outside world. It is important that these countries are seen to be creating stable, highly competitive economies where investment would be well placed. It is hoped that a trade agreement will create the essential element of credibility that these reforms will continue. Mexico and the other countries also assume that a trade agreement will ensure reasonably certain access to the market.

I.J.M.: What is the bottom line?

S.O.: The bottom line of all this, then, is that Mexico and Latin America want investment. The real issue to NAFTA is creation of a magnet for investment.

This takes us back to the question of Canadian policy. Can we be more attractive than Mexico in terms of investment? The answer will depend on our domestic policies.

Our real problems are at home, not abroad. If we can get our own house in order, then we can be a very attractive place for investment capital. If we can't, then the new world of competition for investment will have a very serious effect. I have spoken to many Japanese, for example, who say, "We don't understand how a country your size can have 11 different sets of regulations. We don't find that very efficient." All you can say is: "We've had 125 years, but we don't have the mechanism for an internal common market." This is a serious problem.

I.J.M.: What impact do you see on the financial services sector under trade agreements?

S.O.: Traditionally, we've concentrated heavily on manufacturing, even though world trade in services is now half a trillion dollars. In fact, in Canada we may be more efficient in the service sector than we are in many manufacturing sectors. Our primary resource sectors are in deep trouble: we lag behind in advanced technology, and we are threatened with enormous outside competition. The comparative advantage built on resources is rapidly eroding: people now talk of the "curse" of comparative advantage.

We are really quite competitive in financial services, in consulting engineering services, and in software as a result of a lot of spin-off from the IBM global mandate. The University of Waterloo, where I serve as chancellor, is at a leading edge in software. We should think about how, in very specific terms, we can build on that advantage. I don't mean government subsidies, intervention and so on. (We need to stop bailing out our industries that cannot compete.) What I mean is the supply of information on foreign markets by government, making sure that the money which the government invests in R & D spins off into developing or enhancing new firms.

Apart from the financial services sector and the banks, which are large and can look after themselves, in many other areas of the service sector we can make inroads into other countries and counterbalance the other problems we have.

SOURCE: Interview of Dr. Sylvia Ostry by Dr. Irene J. Matthews for *Canadian Banker*, January/February 1993.

1. Summarize Ostry's assessment of Canada's economic state and her opinion of what Canada should do.

2. In your opinion, what actions of business and government would improve Canada's competitiveness? Support your opinions.

3. a) Why, according to Ostry, is NAFTA both an opportunity and a risk for Canada?
   b) Ostry presents the investment implications of NAFTA for Mexico. Suggest what the investment implications of NAFTA might be for Canada. Explain your answer.

BRIEF REVIEW

1. While flexible exchange rates allow the foreign exchange market to correct imbalances automatically, this system can create instability in the domestic economy, especially for businesses involved in importing or exporting.

2. By fixing, or pegging, an exchange rate, a government can create balance-of-payments surpluses and deficits.

3. Governments can use exchange rate policy as a means of influencing output and price levels. A lower exchange rate fosters more domestic output and employment, while a higher exchange rate reduces inflation. Governments can also use monetary policy to influence exchange rates by adjusting interest rates.

4. Three main exchange rate systems have prevailed worldwide over the past century: the fixed gold standard, the Bretton Woods system of adjustable fixed rates, and the recent preference for the managed float.

Key Concepts

current account
merchandise balance of trade
current account deficit
current account surplus
balance of trade
capital account
portfolio investment
direct investment
capital account surplus
capital account deficit
balance-of-payments surplus
balance-of-payments deficit

change in official reserves
foreign exchange market
demand for Canadian dollars
supply of Canadian dollars
appreciate
depreciate
speculators
flexible exchange rates
fixed exchange rates
revaluation
devaluation
managed float

Developing Application and Analysis Skills

1. a) Explain the function of the balance-of-payments accounts.
   b) Suggest reasons for Canada's historical surplus in merchandise trade and its deficit in the trade in services portion of the current account.
   c) Suppose Canada's merchandise exports are $15 billion and the merchandise balance of trade is +$10 billion. What is the value of Canada's merchandise imports?

2. For each of the transactions described below, note the following:
   • whether the transaction appears in Canada's current or capital account
   • whether the transaction would be classified as a receipt or a payment
   • the category under which the transaction would appear
   a) A Canadian merchant purchases crystal from a supplier in Austria.
   b) A Canadian investor purchases 1000 shares issued by an electronics corporation in Japan.
   c) American investors receive dividend income from shares of Canadian corporations.

   d) Canadian athletes use a British airline to get to the Olympics in Europe.
   e) The Canadian federal government sends financial aid to a country experiencing a cholera epidemic.
   f) Foreign investors purchase Government of Canada bonds.
   g) New Canadians transfer their savings to Canadian banks.
   h) A Canadian investor receives dividends from an American company.
   i) A Canadian manufacturer sells new animation software worldwide.

3. From the newspaper, identify three examples each of portfolio and direct investment in Canada. For each example, state the possible costs and benefits to the Canadian economy.

4. a) Copy and complete the tables that follow, which show accounts for the hypothetical country of Atlantis.
   b) Identify the "visible" components of the current account. What is their net value?
   c) What is the net value of the "invisible" components of the current account?
   d) How would the change to Canada's official reserves be made?

Atlantis's Current Account (Atlantis $ millions)			
	Receipts	Payments	Balance
Merchandise trade	57 890	47 050	_____
Trade in services	8 055	10 500	_____
Balance of trade (net exports)			_____
Investment income	2 800	8 432	_____
Transfers	1 115	850	_____
Current account surplus or deficit			_____

Atlantis's Capital Account
(Atlantis $ millions)

	Receipts	Payments	Balance
1. Short-term capital flows	5 456	7 564	_____
2. Long-term capital flows			
portfolio investment	2 870	5 680	_____
direct investment	1 900	1 100	_____
Capital account surplus or deficit			_____

Atlantis's Balance-of-Payments Accounts
(Atlantis $ millions)

	Balance
1. Current account	_____
2. Capital account	_____
3. Statistical discrepancy	−50
Balance-of-payments surplus or deficit	_____
4. Changes in official reserves	_____

5. a) Draw a causal loop diagram that shows how high levels of foreign ownership in Canada and higher current account deficits have been perpetuated.

b) By making changes or additions to your diagram, demonstrate how this process could be stopped.

6. Calculate the following:

a) the value of US$75 000 in Canadian dollars when the exchange rate is US$1.00 = CDN$1.325

b) the value of CDN$40 000 in American dollars if the exchange rate in (a) applies

c) the value in Canadian dollars of 125 000 Italian lire (L) if the exchange rates are

US$1.00 = L924 and
US$1.00 = CDN$1.325

7. Identify and explain the effect that a decrease in the value of the Canadian dollar would have on each of the following:

a) a Canadian company that exports pulp and paper to Japan

b) the owner of a small Canadian retail business that imports merchandise from Europe

c) a Canadian corporation that wants to raise funds in the world capital markets by selling shares abroad

d) a Canadian corporation paying dividends to foreign shareholders

e) a Canadian student planning to attend university in another country

f) a Canadian making mortgage payments to an American bank for a winter home in Arizona

g) the owner of a Canadian ski resort that is close to the American border

8. For each of the following situations, sketch a graph showing demand and supply curves for the Canadian dollar, and indicate the likely effect of the change described.

a) After the Bank of Canada pursues a zero-inflation policy for three years, Statistics Canada reports the lowest rates of inflation in a decade.

b) The election of a separatist party troubles international observers.

c) Central banking authorities in the United States raise interest rates well above those in Canada.

d) Foreign investors are attracted to Canadian stock markets.

e) The Bank of Canada sells large quantities of Canadian dollars on the foreign exchange market.

f) The federal government announces in its budget that the deficit will be $5 billion higher than expected.

g) A global economic boom creates an unprecedented demand for Canadian resources.

9. What advantages and disadvantages does a managed float system offer to Canada as far as its current and future needs are concerned? In your opinion, would it be possible and beneficial for Canada to adopt a fixed system of exchange rates? Explain your answers.

10. a) With a group, research the exchange rates of one currency over the last five years, and summarize your findings.

b) Research the country whose currency you have tracked to find possible reasons for the changes or trends in the currency's value.

CHAPTER 17

Foreign Trade

It is very odd that, enjoying one of the highest living standards in the world, Canadians in all walks of life should nevertheless believe that their economy is a frail, hothouse creation.

—JOHN H. DALES, CANADIAN ECONOMIC HISTORIAN

Foreign trade is an everyday part of our lives. Consider, for example, what you are wearing or what you ate today. It's likely that many of these products come from outside Canada's borders. The role of exports in our lives is less obvious, but still significant, through the effect that export industries have on Canada's economic activity and employment. In this chapter, we will see why nations exchange goods and services and how governments influence foreign trade. We will also study how the trend toward freer trade is affecting Canada's economy and the well-being of individual Canadians.

CHAPTER FOCUS

This chapter focuses on the following:
- globalization and its effects on trade
- Canada's foreign trade, trade relationships, and trading patterns
- the factors that determine what is traded among countries
- the gains from trade, including product variety, competition, and specialization
- absolute and comparative advantage, and the terms of trade
- forms of trade protection and the arguments for and against it
- Canada's trade policies from its beginnings as a country
- recent international trade arrangements, including the Auto Pact, the European Union, GATT, the FTA, and NAFTA

SKILLS FOCUS

After studying this chapter, you will be able to:
- weigh the costs and benefits of Canada's trading relationship with the United States
- apply the concepts of absolute and comparative advantage and explain the gains from trade
- demonstrate using a graph and explain the effects of free trade, tariffs, and import quotas on particular markets
- explain and illustrate cause-and-effect relationships between trade and employment
- collect, summarize, examine for bias, and compare current articles about international trade
- research and evaluate the implications of recent trade agreements between Canada and the United States
- research and report on Canada's trade relationship with another country
- propose and explain a trade solution to an economy's problems

Canada's Foreign Trade

The Importance of Trade

globalization: the trend of growing foreign trade and investment and the spread of international businesses and markets

The rapid growth of foreign trade and investment flows and the resulting spread of international businesses and markets are all part of a trend known as **globalization**. In recent decades, reductions in transportation costs have helped increase the worldwide importance of foreign trade. Between 1970 and 1991, for example, exports rose from an average of 14 percent of GDP for countries throughout the world to an average of 21 percent. Since the early 1980s, the revolution in communications technology has caused a considerable increase in foreign investment flows. For example, bank loans that crossed national borders or were made in one country but valued in another country's currency rose worldwide from $324 billion in 1980 to $7.5 billion by 1991. Similarly, the sum of all bonds that had been issued internationally increased from $259 billion to $1.65 trillion between 1982 and 1991.

Because of these changes, markets are no longer contained within national boundaries and businesses are more likely to buy resources and sell products internationally. For example, a business with its headquarters in Canada may choose to borrow from Japanese savers, purchase German-made machinery, employ Mexican workers, and sell the bulk of its output in the United States. In both its resource markets and product markets, this Canadian company probably competes with businesses from all over the world.

Within this international trend, Canada has shown a heavy reliance on trade. Figure 17.1 compares the value of exports of various countries as a percentage of their GDP. Canada's exports have a value equal to 25 percent of its GDP, above the world average of 21 percent and considerably higher than the United States' 11 percent and Japan's 10 percent, whose large and diversified economies allow them to be less dependent on exports and imports. However, Canada's reliance on foreign trade is not so great as that of some small industrialized countries, such as Belgium (73 percent) and Switzerland (35 percent).

Canada's Trading Partners

With whom is Canada trading? As Figure 17.2 demonstrates, the United States is Canada's principle trading partner. In 1993, 80 percent of Canada's merchandise exports went to the United States and 73 percent of its merchandise imports came from the United States. The remaining merchandise trade was shared among nations that are part of the European Union (a group of European nations we'll discuss later in the chapter), Japan, other countries in the Organization for Economic Co-operation and Development (which we'll discuss in the next chapter), and all other nations.

Figure 17.1: **The Importance of Trade**

(exports as a percentage of GDP, 1991)

	Percent
Belgium	73
Switzerland	35
Germany	34
Canada	25
United Kingdom	24
France	23
China	20
United States	11
Japan	10
World average	21

The exports of small countries such as Belgium and Switzerland are high in comparison to their levels of GDP. In contrast, the exports of large countries such as China and the United States are lower as a proportion of overall economic activity. When compared to the world average of 21 percent, Canada's exports account for a fairly high proportion of its GDP.

SOURCE: From *World Development Report 1993,* by the World Bank. Copyright © 1993 by The International Bank for Reconstruction and Development/The World Bank. Table 9, "Structure of Demand," pp. 254–55.

Figure 17.2: **Canada's Merchandise Trade by Region (1993)**

	Merchandise Exports		Merchandise Imports	
	($ millions)			
United States	145 331	(80%)	123 533	(73%)
European Union (EU)	10 798	(6%)	13 737	(8%)
Japan	7 940	(4%)	8 363	(5%)
Other OECD countries	3 095	(2%)	4 549	(3%)
All others	13 863	(8%)	19 134	(11%)
Total	181 027	(100%)	169 316	(100%)

The bulk of Canada's merchandise trade is with the United States. The remaining merchandise trade is shared among the member countries of the European Union, Japan, other countries in the Organization for Economic Co-operation and Development, and all other nations.

SOURCE: Adapted from Statistics Canada, *Canadian Economic Observer, Statistical Summary* (March 1994), cat. no. 11-010, pp. 31–32. Reproduced by authority of the Minister of Industry, 1994.

Canada's Trade Patterns

Canada's merchandise trade is made up of exports and imports of both natural resources and manufactured products. As Figure 17.3 shows, Canada's 1993 merchandise exports included almost equal portions of raw or processed natural resources (agricultural and fish products, energy products, forest products, and industrial goods such as minerals and metals) and manufactured products (machines and equipment, automobile products, consumer goods, and other). In contrast, merchandise imports of manufactured goods are more than double that of natural resources. In total, Canada had merchandise exports of about $181 billion and merchandise imports of $169 billion.

Figure 17.3: Canada's Merchandise Trade by Type of Product (1993)

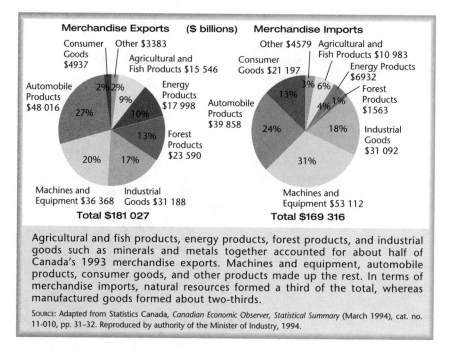

Agricultural and fish products, energy products, forest products, and industrial goods such as minerals and metals together accounted for about half of Canada's 1993 merchandise exports. Machines and equipment, automobile products, consumer goods, and other products made up the rest. In terms of merchandise imports, natural resources formed a third of the total, whereas manufactured goods formed about two-thirds.

SOURCE: Adapted from Statistics Canada, *Canadian Economic Observer, Statistical Summary* (March 1994), cat. no. 11-010, pp. 31–32. Reproduced by authority of the Minister of Industry, 1994.

However, this isn't the whole picture. Recall from Chapter 16 that Canada trades not only merchandise but also services. Of these—involving, for example, tourism, freight, and telecommunications—Canada exported $27.3 billion but imported $39.8 billion in 1993.

Historically, Canada has been considered a significant exporter of natural resources. Recently, though, the proportion of natural resources in Canada's merchandise exports has decreased while the proportion of manufactured goods has increased. For example, in comparison to the roughly equal proportions of manufactured and natural resource exports in 1993, just over a third of Canada's merchandise exports were manufactured goods in 1971. In the same period, the ratio of natural resources to manufactured goods in Canada's imports has varied only slightly, with manufactured goods expanding.

Within Canada's service trade, business services such as insurance, management services, and research and development have increased most quickly as a proportion of both imports and exports. Overall, Canada's trade in services has not grown as quickly as its merchandise trade. Between 1971 and 1993, service exports as a percentage of total exports fell from 15 to 13 percent, while service imports fell from 21 to 19 percent of total imports. These figures are surprising given the recent growth in Canada's service sector. Between 1967 and 1989, for example, Canada's service sector grew from 55 to 64 percent of Canada's real GDP while the goods sector fell from 45 to 36 percent. Employment growth in the service sector has been even more rapid. Service sector employment now represents over 70 percent of all jobs in the Canadian economy.

Thinking About Economics

Why hasn't the rise of a service-based economy been reflected in Canada's international trade?

One reason is that services are usually bought and sold within national borders. For example, in 1989 less than 10 percent of services produced in Canada were exported. In comparison, almost a third of all Canadian-made goods were destined for foreign markets. Another reason for the apparent slow growth in service trade relates to measurement problems. Because services are intangible, foreign trade in these products often escapes detection, especially in the common case where services are traded within a single company. Furthermore, goods and services are often sold in "bundles," and it is the merchandise part of the bundle that is counted. For example, new computer software is usually exchanged in physical form, and is therefore counted as a good rather than as a service. These problems make it difficult to collect trade statistics that adequately reflect the importance of services.

What Is Traded

In general, countries export the commodities they produce most efficiently and import those they would produce least efficiently. Whether or not a country can produce a particular product efficiently is determined by the country's resources, market size, and climate.

Resources

A country's pool of resources is the main factor affecting what it exports and imports. For example, Canada has been endowed with plentiful and rich natural resources that have allowed it to be a major exporter of such products as paper, wheat, and natural gas. As well, Canada has developed its human resources and capital resources in such a way that it can export capital-intensive goods. In contrast, countries with less abundant natural resources, such as Belgium, tend to be major importers of unprocessed products, and countries with a huge pool of labour and relatively few capital resources, such as Bangladesh, tend to be major exporters of labour-intensive goods. For example, almost two-thirds of Bangladesh's exports in 1991 consisted of textiles and clothing, whose production tends to be labour-intensive.

Market Size

Recall that some products exhibit economies of scale—that is, the cost of inputs per unit of output decreases as production increases. As a result, these products tend to be produced in markets where businesses can take advantage of economies of scale. So, for example, cars tend to be produced in countries with large markets of car buyers rather than in small countries or those where few people own cars.

Climate

Climate plays a key role in determining where some goods are produced, especially agricultural products. While tropical fruit could be grown in Canada—in climate-controlled greenhouses, for example—it makes little sense to do so, since tropical fruit can be imported cheaply from countries that are internationally competitive in producing them.

 ## The Case for Trade

Gains From Trade

Having determined what Canada trades and with whom, the question of "Why trade?" still remains. International trade brings significant economic gains: it increases product variety for consumers, promotes competition in each country's markets, and adds to output by allowing countries to specialize in commodities in which they are internationally competitive.

Product Variety

When countries trade, the number of products available to consumers expands. Consider one category of products you purchase regularly—for example, clothing, CDs, or magazines. You will probably notice that many of your purchases were produced in other countries. Adding imports to domestic products gives you greater choice.

Competition

International trade increases the number of businesses selling in a country's product markets. Added competition encourages all businesses to produce goods as efficiently as possible. This results in lower prices for consumers.

DEVELOPING
INTERPRETATION SKILLS

SOURCE: Reprinted with permission — The Toronto Star Syndicate. Copyright Tribune Media Services.

1. Summarize the trade situation identified in the cartoon. According to the cartoon, what factors are contributing to this situation? Support your answers.

2. What strategy does one character suggest to change the situation?

3. In your opinion, what is the message of the cartoon? Support your answer.

Specialization

The most important gain from trade comes from specialization. Without international trade, a country would have to produce everything its citizens need. With international trade, however, a country can use its resources to specialize in the products it makes most efficiently, allowing it to compete in the expanded market. The income from exporting the products that the country has made so efficiently can then pay for imported products that would be more expensive to make domestically. By increasing the output gained from various countries' resources, specialization raises world living standards. In the next sections, we will see how these gains from specialization can be quantified using two related economic concepts: absolute advantage and comparative advantage.

Absolute Advantage

Specialization is easiest to see in the case of two trading partners, each of whom is better than the other at one activity. Suppose a lawyer wants custom-made wooden furniture. At the same time a carpenter wants to prepare a will. As shown in Figure 17.4, the lawyer could build the furniture herself in 20 hours or she could hire the carpenter to do the job in 5 hours. Similarly, the carpenter could prepare the will for himself in 10 hours or hire the lawyer to do it for him in 2 hours. If the two were to trade their products, each product would be produced in the most efficient way possible.

Figure 17.4: **Gains From Trade Based on Absolute Advantage**

	Time Spent Building Furniture	**Time Spent Preparing a Will**	**Time Saved Through Specialization**
Lawyer	20 hours	2 hours	20 – 2 = 18 hours
Carpenter	5 hours	10 hours	10 – 5 = 5 hours

A carpenter can build furniture in less time than it would take a lawyer, while the lawyer can draw up a will in less time than it would take the carpenter. Each has an absolute advantage in one task. To use the resources most efficiently, the carpenter should specialize in building the furniture, while the lawyer should specialize in preparing the will. The carpenter works for 5 hours rather than 10 hours, saving 5 hours. Meanwhile, the lawyer works for 2 hours instead of 20 hours, saving 18 hours.

absolute advantage:

the benefit enjoyed by a producer who can supply a certain quantity of an item more efficiently than can other producers

In the example, the lawyer and the carpenter each have an **absolute advantage**. That is, each trading partner is able to produce one product using fewer resources than would other producers. The resources—in this case, time—saved by trading partners specializing in what they each do most efficiently is summarized in the third column of Figure 17.4.

The same principle applies to countries that engage in trade. For example, Canada may be more efficient than Japan in producing wheat, while Japan is more efficient than Canada in producing stereos. Canadians should therefore specialize in wheat production, leaving the Japanese to concentrate on stereo production. Through trade, both Canada and Japan can use their economic resources to produce the greatest possible output of each commodity. As a result, living standards in both countries increase.

Comparative Advantage

Because of the varying strengths of countries, trade advantages are sometimes not so clear-cut as in the case of absolute advantage. Let's consider a hypothetical case. Both Canada and Mexico can produce paper and computers, but Canada has an absolute advantage over Mexico in *both* products. As shown in Figure 17.5, using equal resources, Canada can produce 12 t of paper compared with Mexico's 3 t or 12 computers to Mexico's 9.

Figure 17.5: Gains From Trade Based on Comparative Advantage

	Hypothetical Output per Worker		Opportunity Cost	
	Paper	**Computers**	**of 1 t of paper**	**of 1 computer**
Canada	12 t	12 computers	1 computer	1.0 t paper
Mexico	3 t	9 computers	3 computers	0.33 t paper

Although a Canadian worker can produce more paper than a Mexican worker (12 versus 3 t) and can make more computers than a Mexican worker (12 versus 9 computers), paper has a lower opportunity cost in Canada (1 computer versus Mexico's 3 computers). Thus, Canadians have a comparative advantage in producing paper while Mexicans have a comparative advantage in making computers. In other words, each has the lower opportunity cost of producing one product.

For the sake of efficiency, it would seem that both paper products and computers should be produced in Canada. However, trade is a two-way street. So, each of the two trading partners must produce and trade a product. To determine what each trading partner should produce, they must determine the opportunity cost of each product, and then produce the product for which they have the lowest opportunity cost. The trading partner with the lowest opportunity cost for a given product has the **comparative advantage**.

comparative advantage: the benefit enjoyed by a producer who can supply a certain item with a lower opportunity cost than can other producers

In our example, the opportunity cost of producing 12 t of paper in Canada is 12 computers, and the opportunity cost of 12 computers is 12 t of paper. This gives a cost ratio of one to one between paper and computers, so that the opportunity cost of 1 t of paper is 1 computer. In Mexico, the cost of producing 3 t of paper is 9 computers, and the opportunity cost of producing 9 computers is 3 t of paper. This gives a cost ratio of one to three between paper and computers in Mexico, so that the opportunity cost of 1 t of paper is 3 computers and the opportunity cost of 1 computer is only 0.33 t of paper. Because paper has a lower opportunity cost in Canada than in Mexico, Canada has a comparative advantage in paper production. Conversely, since each computer has a lower opportunity cost in Mexico than in Canada, Mexico has a comparative advantage in computer production.

Given the comparative advantages in our hypothetical example, the opportunity costs would be lowest if Canada produced paper and Mexico produced computers. This conclusion follows the **law of comparative advantage**, which states that output is maximized when producers specialize in what they can make at a lower opportunity cost than can other producers.

law of comparative advantage: states that maximum output is achieved when producers specialize in what they can make at a lower opportunity cost than can other producers

Let's assume that there are twice as many workers in Mexico as in Canada. The gains from each country fully specializing in the product in which it has a comparative advantage are shown in Figure 17.6. If there is a total of 10 workers in Canada and 20 workers in Mexico, then before trade each country may devote half of its labour force to each product. The combined paper output of both countries is therefore 90 t—60 t from Canada (5 workers × 12 t per worker) and 30 t from Mexico (10 workers × 3 t per worker). At the same time, the combined computer production of both countries is 150 computers, with 60 from Canada (5 workers × 12 computers per worker) and 90 from Mexico (10 workers × 9 computers per worker).

Figure 17.6:   Total Gains From Specialization

	Before Trade		After Trade	
	Paper	**Computers**	**Paper**	**Computers**
Canada	60 t	60 computers	120 t	0 computers
Mexico	30 t	90 computers	0 t	180 computers
	90 t	150 computers	120 t	180 computers

Supposing that there are twice as many workers in Mexico as in Canada, and supposing that production in both Mexico and Canada were equally split between paper and computers before they began to trade, the combined countries would produce 90 t of paper and 150 computers. By specializing through trade, combined production would rise to 120 t of paper and 180 computers.

When both countries specialize completely in the product in which they have a comparative advantage, Canada produces 120 t of paper (10 workers × 12 t per worker) and Mexico makes 180 computers (20 workers × 9 computers per worker). World paper production has therefore risen by 30 t and world computer production by 30 computers. By specializing on the basis of comparative advantage, the two countries are therefore able to raise their total output of both items, with this added production being shared through trade.

Terms of Trade

The benefits of specialization are distributed between trading partners on the basis of the **terms of trade**, or the international price of one product in terms of another product. This price depends partly on the opportunity costs of the products in each country, since producers must get at least the opportunity cost that applies in domestic transactions if they are to engage in foreign trade.

Returning to our hypothetical example, recall that in Canada tonnes of paper and units of computers have a cost ratio of one to one. In order to make trading with Mexico worthwhile, Canadian paper producers demand one or more computers for each unit of paper they sell to Mexico. At the same time, in Mexico the cost ratio of tonnes of paper and units of computers is one to three. To make trading with Canada worthwhile, Mexican computer producers demand 1 t of paper for every 3 or fewer computers they sell to Canada. As a result, the international price of one product in terms of the other must fall somewhere between these limits in order for the two countries to trade:

> Limits to terms of trade   1 t of paper : 1 computer
>
> 1 t of paper : 3 computers

terms of trade: the international price of one product in terms of another

The actual terms of trade are then set by the international demand for each product. So, for example, when the demand for paper is high in both countries, the international price of paper in terms of computers will be close to the limit of 3 computers for 1 t of paper. If instead the demand for computers is high in both countries, the international price of computers will be pushed to the limit of 1 computer for 1 t of paper.

Since Canadians export paper to purchase Mexican computers, they will be best off when paper has the highest possible international price in terms of computers—in other words, when 1 t of paper has its maximum value of 3 computers. In contrast, Mexicans are best off when the terms of trade have reached their lowest limit. In this case, each 1 t of paper imported by Mexicans has an international price of 1 computer, which is the minimum possible value for paper in terms of computers.

BRIEF REVIEW

1. With the recent trend toward globalization, there has been substantial growth in foreign trade and investment and international businesses and markets.

2. In comparison with other countries, Canada depends extensively on international trade. Its most significant trading partner is the United States.

3. Canada's merchandise exports include almost equal portions of natural resources and manufactured products. In contrast, its merchandise imports of manufactured products are double that of natural resources. In addition to merchandise, Canada also has significant trade in services.

4. Canada's exports of natural resources are becoming less significant than they used to be. Since the early 1970s, manufactured goods have grown considerably as a proportion of merchandise exports and slightly as a proportion of merchandise imports. While the service sector has been growing in Canada, international trade in services has not grown as much as international trade in

merchandise. This is because services tend to be bought and sold within national economies and because of problems in measuring service trade.

5. What specific products a country produces for trade depends on what it produces most efficiently. Three factors affect efficiency: resources, market size, and climate.

6. Trade among nations brings significant gains: product variety, increased competition, and specialization.

7. The gains of specialization can best be seen in the cases of absolute advantage and comparative advantage. The law of comparative advantage states that output is maximized when producers specialize in what they can make at a lower opportunity cost than can other producers.

8. The terms of trade are the international price of a product in terms of another product. The terms of trade are determined by both the opportunity costs of the products for the trading partners and the international demand for the products.

 **The Impact of Trade Protection**

Despite the benefits of international trade, countries often try to block imports or subsidize domestic industries. First we'll examine how governments intervene in international trade. Later, we'll consider the arguments against trade that motivate such intervention.

Tariffs

To see the role that foreign trade plays in markets for a specific product, let's consider a hypothetical competitive market for bicycles in Canada. The left graph in Figure 17.7 shows the demand (D) and domestic supply curves (S_{d0}) for bicycles in the unlikely case where there is no foreign

Figure 17.7: The Impact of Import Barriers

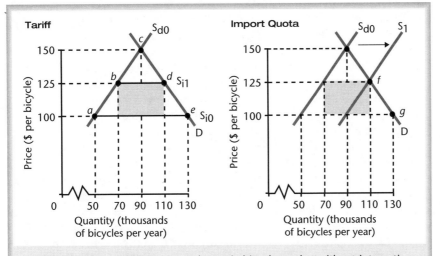

The graph on the left illustrates a domestic bicycle market without international trade, with unrestricted trade, and with tariffs. Without trade, equilibrium price in the market for bicycles is at $150 (point c), the intersection of the domestic demand curve (D) and the domestic supply curve (S_{d0}). With unrestricted imports of bicycles priced at $100, as shown by the import supply curve (S_{i0}), consumers demand 130 000 bicycles (point e), but domestic producers will supply only 50 000 bicycles (point a). Imports make up the 80 000 difference. With a $25 tariff, the price rises to $125 (shown by S_{i1}) at which consumers demand 110 000 bicycles (point d), but domestic producers will supply only 70 000 bicycles at this price (point b). Imports make up the 40 000 difference and the government gains extra revenue shown by the shaded rectangle.

The graph on the right illustrates the same market with an import quota. With an import quota of 40 000 bicycles, supply shifts from S_{d0} to S_1. Compared with the case of unrestricted trade, the change in price and the quantity of imports (from point g to point f) is identical to those resulting from tariffs, but now the shaded rectangle indicates extra revenue to foreign producers. This extra revenue from a higher price at least partially offsets the loss that is due to fewer sales.

trade. Market equilibrium would occur at a price of $150 and a quantity of 90 000 (point c).

If international trade in bicycles existed and this trade were unrestricted, then Canadian consumers would have the opportunity to buy either domestic or imported bicycles. Assuming for our example that the cost of transporting the product is zero, Canadians would be able to purchase foreign-made bicycles for $100, which is the prevailing world price. Since Canadian consumers make up a small proportion of the world bicycle market, their purchases do not affect equilibrium in this market. Hence, an unlimited quantity supplied is available from foreign bicycle producers at $100, as shown by the horizontal line (S_{i0}) at this price.

As shown on the left in Figure 17.7, at a price of $100 Canadian consumers would demand 130 000 bicycles (point *e*). However, Canadian suppliers are only willing to supply 50 000 bicycles at this price (point *a*). The 80 000 difference between domestic supply (S_{d0}) and domestic demand (D) represents the quantity foreign producers could sell in this market. As a result of the international trade, the price has fallen and a significant number of consumers are buying foreign-produced bicycles.

tariff: an excise tax on imported goods

Governments may respond to such a situation by imposing a **tariff**, which is an excise tax on imported goods. Until recent years, tariffs were a major tool of trade protection in Canada as well as in many other countries, especially against foreign manufactured goods. In our example, if a $25 tariff is applied on foreign-made bicycles, Canadian consumers must pay an additional $25—or a total price of $125. The result of this price increase is again shown on the left in Figure 17.7. The supply of imported bicycles is now depicted by a horizontal line (S_{i1}) at a price of $125. At this price, Canadian consumers demand 110 000 bicycles (point *d*). Since Canadian suppliers are willing to supply 70 000 bicycles at this price (point *b*), the difference between domestic demand and domestic supply at this price is 40 000, which foreign producers supply.

When compared to the case of unrestricted trade, tariffs affect consumers and the government in opposite ways. Consumers pay a higher price ($125 instead of $100) and buy fewer bicycles (110 000 instead of 130 000) than they did before the tariff was introduced. However, the government benefits from the tariff through the additional tax revenue it is able to raise. With a $25 tariff per bicycle and 40 000 bicycles imported, the government's extra revenue is $1 million ($25 × 40 000). This is shown on the left graph by the area of the shaded rectangle, whose height represents the tariff per bicycle and whose width indicates the quantity of imports once the tariff is in place.

Domestic and foreign producers are also affected in opposite ways by the tariff. Canadian bicycle producers and their resource suppliers benefit because of the extra earnings tied to the increase in price from $100 to $125 and the rise in domestic production from 50 000 to 70 000 bicycles. Foreign bicycle producers, however, are harmed by the tariff. They face an unchanged after-tax price for each bicycle they sell ($100) while accepting a reduction in imports—from 80 000 to 40 000 bicycles.

non-tariff barriers (NTBs): trade barriers other than tariffs that are used to restrict imports; include import quotas, voluntary export restraints, and domestic regulations

Import Quotas

If tariffs are not an option, a government may use other trade restrictions, known as **non-tariff barriers (NTBs)**, to limit imports. Recently, these barriers have become more popular since governments find it harder to levy tariffs because of international trade agreements.

import quota: a set limit on the quantity of a good that can be imported in a given year

The most common non-tariff barrier is an **import quota**, which is a set limit on the quantity of a good that can be imported in a certain year. Import quotas can work in two ways. A government can impose an import quota itself, or it can use the threat of trade restrictions to force foreign producers to set their own "voluntary" quotas, which are known as **voluntary export restraints (VERs)**. One well-known illustration of a voluntary export restraint involves Canada's imports of Japanese cars. In 1981, an agreement limiting annual Japanese exports of automobiles to Canada was worked out between the two countries. In 1986, when the agreement expired, Japanese automakers continued to limit their exports to Canada voluntarily to stop the Canadian government from taking other types of trade action.

Generally, foreign producers find import quotas preferable to tariffs. To see why, we return to our hypothetical example of the bicycle market in Figure 17.7. The impact of an import quota on this market is portrayed on the right graph, in which the domestic demand and supply curves, D and S_{d0}, as well as the prevailing world price, are identical to those on the left graph. As before, a situation of unrestricted trade (point g) leads to an original $100 price, with consumption exceeding domestic production by 80 000, which represents the initial amount of bicycles imported.

By imposing a maximum level of imports of 40 000, this number of bicycles is added to the domestic supply (S_{d0}) at every price, thereby giving the combined domestic and foreign supply curve S_1. Domestic demand (D) and the new supply (S_1) intersect at the new equilibrium price of $125 and quantity of 110 000 (point f). Again, production is split between domestic and foreign producers. Canadian businesses produce 70 000 bicycles, leaving 40 000 for foreign businesses, shown as the shaded area.

The policy's effect on consumers and domestic producers is the same as with a tariff. The results for the government and foreign producers are different, however. With an import quota, the government no longer receives tax revenue. Instead, the extra revenue indicated by the shaded rectangle on the graph on the right flows to foreign producers in the form of higher prices on the bicycles they still sell in Canada. This extra revenue partly counteracts the loss that foreign producers bear because of the lower quantity they supply in the Canadian market.

Domestic Regulations

Regulations in particular markets can make trade within them expensive for foreign producers, therefore acting as obstacles to trade. For example, Canada requires English and French labelling of products, has certain licensing procedures, and imposes relatively high safety and environmental standards. Also, rules controlling government purchases—known as government procurement policies—may require that, whenever possible, domestic rather than foreign items should be bought by governments. If imports are successfully restricted through these practices, the results are the same as in the case of an import quota.

voluntary export restraints (VERs): import quotas that are voluntarily put in place by the exporting country

Export Subsidies

Export subsidies are payments by a government to domestic exporters so that they can reduce the prices they charge in foreign markets. These programs are intended to raise the amount of exports, thus increasing output and employment in the domestic economy. Besides helping domestic exporters and foreign consumers, an export subsidy imposes a cost on foreign producers, who lose sales to the new low-priced competition, and on the exporting country's own taxpayers, who must foot the bill for the program. Such subsidies have been used by many countries, including Canada, and have been especially common in agricultural markets. Indeed, these programs were a major reason for low prices in global agricultural markets during the 1980s.

 # The Case for Trade Protection

The gains in economic welfare associated with specialization and the law of comparative advantage are generally large enough to make a compelling case for free trade. Consequently, it is common for economists to oppose government policies that protect trade. Nonetheless, particular cases of trade protection can be defended with either economic or noneconomic arguments. We will look at each of these arguments in turn.

Economic Arguments

Six economic arguments can be applied to support various types of trade protection. According to these arguments, trade barriers help to stimulate domestic employment, diversify export-dominated economies, foster infant industries, improve a country's terms of trade, protect a country's environmental and safety standards, and shield domestic workers from imports produced with cheap foreign labour.

Domestic Employment
Because imports are a withdrawal from an economy's circular flow, they have a dampening effect on total spending and output. Thus, a reduction in the level of imports through trade barriers can potentially increase the level of economic activity in the country and provide more jobs for domestic workers.

This argument is legitimate only in certain circumstances, however. Because a strategy of import reduction causes foreign countries' exports to diminish, output and employment levels in these foreign nations will fall. Hence, the new domestic employment in the country imposing trade barriers comes at the expense of jobs elsewhere. The threat of foreign retaliation means that this policy can easily backfire—other nations may try to recapture some of their lost exports and jobs by imposing new trade barriers of their own. Such behaviour makes everyone worse off by limiting the opportunities for each country to specialize based on comparative advantage.

Diversification

Trade barriers can help diversify the economy of a country whose prosperity is closely tied to just a few export products. Examples include Saudi Arabia, which depends on oil, and Barbados, which relies on revenues from tourism. In each case, changes in the international demand for these main exports can lead to wide fluctuations in the economy's total output.

Trade barriers allow for the development of new industries in which the country does not possess a comparative advantage. Traditionally, this reasoning has been used to foster a domestic manufacturing sector. The result, according to supporters of this policy, is an economy that is better able to withstand fluctuations in export markets. Critics point out that the industries created in this fashion represent an inefficient employment of the economy's resources. In the absence of international competition in protected markets, domestic consumers pay high prices for what may be substandard goods.

Infant Industries

Closely related to the argument for diversification is the view that trade barriers should be used to shield infant industries. An **infant industry** is made up of domestic producers that are young in comparison to competitors in foreign countries. Because of their recent origin and small size, domestic producers are not able to take full advantage of economies of scale. Until they are able to, according to supporters, lower-priced foreign imports must be blocked. Such reasoning is valid only if other countries do not retaliate with their own trade barriers. Even if retaliation does not occur, the argument is open to abuse. Once imposed, trade barriers in a given industry are difficult to eliminate. Industry groups—representing both business and labour—tend to fight any reduction in barriers, even once their industry has fully matured.

In recent years, the argument relating to infant industries has gained new importance in high-technology markets, such as the jet aircraft industry, where a few large businesses are able to take advantage of economies of scale. **Strategic trade policy** is the use of programs such as export subsidies to help domestic producers gain a foothold in these industries so they can reap high economic profits in the future. Supporters of this policy suggest that such long-term profits aid the entire country. Also, support of high-technology industries can help prepare the country for structural changes in the global economy. Lastly, the businesses involved can provide spillover benefits to the economy because of their contribution to product development in other industries. As with traditional trade incentives for infant industries, strategic trade policy works only if foreign governments choose not to retaliate with similar policies of their own.

Terms of Trade

If a country's volume of trade is large enough to affect prices in a world product market, then it can use trade barriers to improve its terms of trade.

infant industry: a domestic industry that is young in comparison to its foreign competitors

strategic trade policy: the use of programs such as export subsidies to help domestic producers enter potentially lucrative markets

For example, the United States could impose a tariff on its imports of Canadian lumber. This would decrease the global demand for lumber, pushing down lumber's international price. As a result, Americans would be able to acquire the same amount of Canadian lumber with a smaller quantity of American products. As long as Canada does not retaliate with its own trade barriers, the terms of trade move in the United States' favour.

Environmental and Safety Standards

In order to address spillover costs, in particular those related to the environment and safety, many governments impose standards that can be quite costly to certain businesses. However, standards vary. While some countries may regulate industry either to reduce or to compensate for spillover costs, other countries—especially those with low per capita GDP—may have very lax environmental and safety regulations to allow exporters there to reduce their expenses and product prices.

Critics of lax environmental standards suggest that, without trade protection, increased globalization will be accompanied by an increase in environmental damage. Similarly, critics of lax safety standards believe that without trade protection, workers in all countries are hurt. Those in countries with low safety standards face increased risks of injury on the job, while those in countries with strict standards face a reduction in the demand for labour and therefore fewer available jobs.

According to critics of low environmental and safety standards, countries should maintain high standards and set up trade barriers against exports from countries with lower standards. They argue that, without these two measures, businesses operating in countries with lax standards will continue to profit, other businesses will move their operations to such countries in order to gain a competitive edge, and spillover costs will increase internationally.

Cheap Foreign Labour

A related argument suggests that imports produced by cheap foreign labour need to be blocked from entering an industrialized country in order to protect the jobs of domestic workers. In its basic form, this argument is flawed because it ignores the key reason for the differences among wage rates in various countries. Workers in countries with a higher per capita GDP tend to earn more than workers elsewhere because of their higher productivity, as defined in Chapter 8. Workers in industrialized countries tend to be highly skilled and are employed along with larger amounts of capital per worker. Once average wages in various countries are compared to these different productivity levels, workers in industrialized nations still possess a comparative advantage over low-wage foreign labour in many types of production. Nonetheless, it is likely that certain groups of workers in industrialized countries—especially those in low-productivity sectors—will be hurt by increased trade with less developed countries.

Noneconomic Arguments

The two remaining arguments in favour of trade barriers are based on noneconomic factors: national security and cultural sovereignty.

National Security

The oldest argument for trade barriers relates to national security. A country's citizens may wish to be self-sufficient in producing certain strategic commodities such as basic food items and military equipment. If a war breaks out, supplies of these commodities will then be guaranteed. The way to ensure that domestic industries can develop in these sectors is to insulate them from foreign competition. This argument has been applied in countries such as Israel, where military threats to national security have been a major concern, but its relevance to Canada seems limited.

Cultural Sovereignty

Another noneconomic argument for certain types of trade protection relates to culture. Some countries, including Canada, have felt the need to protect and nurture their own cultural industries by, for example, restricting the imported content of radio and TV programming, limiting broadcast licences, subsidizing "home-grown" authors and visual artists, or purchasing only domestically produced textbooks. In one recent incident, in order to help the French movie industry withstand foreign competition—especially from Hollywood—France blocked American attempts to liberalize international trade in movies. However, critics suggest that, in an age of satellite communications, trade barriers relating to many cultural industries can no longer be enforced.

BRIEF REVIEW

1. Governments may intervene in international markets through a variety of means, including tariffs, non-tariff barriers (import quotas, voluntary export restraints, and domestic regulations), and export subsidies.

2. Tariffs are excise taxes on imported goods. In contrast, import quotas and voluntary export restraints are limits on the quantity of a product that can be imported in a certain year. These barriers result in higher prices, lower consumption, fewer imports, and more domestic production of the item affected. With a tariff, governments gain extra tax revenue; with an import quota or voluntary export restraint, revenues from the resulting higher prices flow to the foreign producers, partly offsetting the effect of the decrease in sales.

3. Domestic regulations can present obstacles to trade. When successful, the results parallel the effects of an import quota.

4. Export subsidies are another form of trade intervention. In this case, govern-

ments make payments to domestic exporters so that exporters can lower the prices they charge in foreign markets. The results are lower sales of foreign products and higher domestic taxes.

5. The economic arguments in favour of trade barriers relate to domestic employment, diversification, infant industries, the terms of trade, environmental and safety standards, and cheap foreign labour.

6. The noneconomic arguments in favour of trade barriers relate to maintaining national security and cultural sovereignty.

 **Trade Policies**

Recall that Canada's most significant trading partner now and throughout much of its history is the United States. As a result, trade between the two countries has played an important role in determining Canadian trade policy.

Early Canadian Trade Policy

In 1854 British and American diplomats signed the Reciprocity Treaty, establishing favourable trade relationships between British North America and the United States. So, for the duration of this treaty, tariff rates were relatively low between the United States and what is now Canada.

This reciprocal trade relationship broke down in 1866 due to a number of political and economic factors. Thereafter, trade between Canada and the United States became increasingly restrictive. As portrayed in Figure 17.8, the average Canadian tariff rate as a percentage of total merchandise imports rose in the years after Confederation.

The National Policy

National Policy: a Canadian policy initiated in 1879 that included high Canadian tariffs on manufactured imports in order to stimulate a domestic manufacturing sector

In 1879, Canada's first prime minister, Sir John A. Macdonald, instituted a wide-ranging tariff policy based on the infant-industry argument for trade protection. The **National Policy** led to high tariffs on manufactured imports to stimulate the development of a domestic manufacturing sector. Without this policy, supporters argued, Canadian manufacturers would be swamped by low-priced American competition produced with the benefits of economies of scale. Due to the National Policy, Canada's average tariff rate in succeeding decades stayed above 15 percent. As a result, many American manufacturers chose to "jump the tariff wall" by setting up branch plants in Canada to allow them to continue selling in Canadian markets.

The Great Depression

While Canada's tariffs gradually fell after World War I, the Great Depression sparked a new round of protectionism. Such a trend is common during economic downturns. With falling output and employment, domestic producers see trade barriers as a way of maintaining their sales despite shrinking markets. In the early 1930s, governments in most industrialized countries raised tariffs—partly for domestic reasons, and partly to retaliate against foreign trade barriers placed on their own exports. Not surprisingly, all countries were made worse off by this move because of the resulting decline in world trade.

Once the damaging effects of this protectionism became evident, Canada and the United States signed two trade-liberalizing agreements in the 1930s, reducing Canada's average tariff rate to below its pre-Depression level.

Figure 17.8:   Average Tariff Rates in Canada

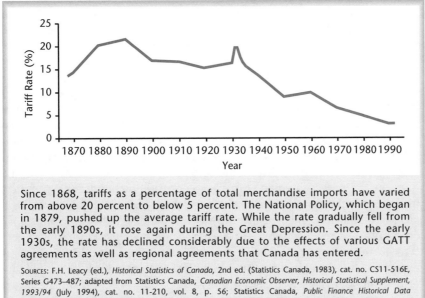

Since 1868, tariffs as a percentage of total merchandise imports have varied from above 20 percent to below 5 percent. The National Policy, which began in 1879, pushed up the average tariff rate. While the rate gradually fell from the early 1890s, it rose again during the Great Depression. Since the early 1930s, the rate has declined considerably due to the effects of various GATT agreements as well as regional agreements that Canada has entered.

Sources: F.H. Leacy (ed.), *Historical Statistics of Canada*, 2nd ed. (Statistics Canada, 1983), cat. no. CS11-516E, Series G473–487; adapted from Statistics Canada, *Canadian Economic Observer, Historical Statistical Supplement, 1993/94* (July 1994), cat. no. 11-210, vol. 8, p. 56; Statistics Canada, *Public Finance Historical Data 1965/66–1991/92*, cat. no. 68-512, pp. 2–3. Reproduced by authority of the Minister of Industry, 1994.

General Agreement on Tariffs and Trade

The liberalizing trend in global trade continued after World War II ended. Canada joined in this movement, partly because many of its manufacturing industries had matured sufficiently to be able to compete against imports without tariffs. In 1947, Canada was one of 22 nations that signed the **General Agreement on Tariffs and Trade (GATT)**. Since then, GATT has grown to include about 100 members and is the most important example of a "multilateral" trade agreement, which involves many countries.

GATT is based on the principle that trade policies of member countries should treat all other members equally. Complaints by one country

General Agreement on Tariffs and Trade (GATT): a multilateral trade agreement that lessens the degree of trade protection among member countries, including Canada

against the trade policies of another are subject to formal rules and judged by impartial panels. If a settlement cannot be reached through compromise, then the complainant country has recourse to limited forms of trade retaliation. GATT has been the most important contemporary cause of liberalized global trade.

Through successive rounds of negotiation among GATT members, both tariff and non-tariff barriers have gradually been reduced. The most important of these negotiations was the Kennedy Round, completed in 1967, which cut average tariffs by about a third, and the Tokyo Round, completed in 1979, which cut tariffs by another third. The result has been a marked reduction of tariffs—especially on manufactured products. Average tariffs for these products in industrialized countries, which were above 50 percent in the 1930s, have since fallen to below 5 percent.

The most recent GATT negotiations, known as the Uruguay Round, were completed in 1993 after seven years of sometimes hostile debate. Remaining tariffs on some manufactured products, such as prescription drugs and medical equipment, are being reduced, while trade in services such as computer software is being liberalized.

Previously protected agricultural products are also affected. Export subsidies to farmers are being cut, while import quotas on agricultural products are being gradually phased out. The agreement will have mixed effects on Canadian farmers. Because other countries must reduce their subsidies on grain exports, Canada's farmers will benefit from higher world prices for grain. At the same time, some Canadian farmers will be hurt. In the past, Canadian prices for eggs, poultry, and dairy products have been maintained above world levels through import quotas on these products. Because such quotas are now disallowed, the Canadian government must replace them with tariffs—some at levels close to 300 percent given the large difference between Canadian and world prices. Over time, the Canadian government will be forced to reduce these tariffs. The result will be increased foreign imports.

Recent Trading Blocs

trading bloc: a relatively small number of countries involved in a trade agreement

A wish to pursue closer economic ties has led some groups of countries to liberalize trade among themselves. A **trading bloc** is a relatively small group of countries involved in a trade agreement. There are three types: free trade area, customs union, and common market. Each type involves increased integration of trade policies.

Free Trade Area

free trade area: an area in which trade is tariff-free, although member countries are able to impose separate trade barriers on outside countries

Trade within a **free trade area** is tariff-free, although member countries are able to impose separate trade barriers on outside countries. A contemporary example of a free trade area is the North American Free Trade Agreement among Canada, the United States, and Mexico.

Thinking About Economics

Why do different regions of Canada develop in different ways and at different times?

This was a question asked by the eminent Canadian economist Harold Innis (1894–1952). The result of his studies, which were later extended by other economists, was the Staples Thesis of Economic Development. According to Innis, several natural resources that have been exploited by Canadians and sold as exports have played crucial roles in Canada's economic and political development and in the development of specific regions. Cod fish drew the earliest European settlers to the east coast of Canada and eventually became the staple industry for much of the east coast. In contrast, central Canada's European settlement centred largely on the highly lucrative fur trade industry. Other staple products followed cod and furs: lumber (from the 1790s to the 1860s), wheat (in the two decades leading up to World War I), and then minerals, oil and gas, and hydro-electric power (after World War I). Not surprisingly, periods in Canadian history without a staple product have tended to coincide with economic downturns. While the staples thesis is difficult to apply to Canada today, it does help explain Canada's economic history and economic conditions in some regions.

Customs Union

A **customs union** is a stronger form of regional integration that includes not only free trade among member countries, but also common trade barriers with the rest of the world. An example is the Caribbean Community and Common Market (CARICOM), which has 12 member countries, including Jamaica, Guyana, and Trinidad and Tobago.

Common Market

A **common market** is a customs union that allows for the free movement of labour and capital among member nations. The best-known example of an emerging common market is the previously mentioned **European Union (EU)**, formerly known as the European Economic Community (EEC), which was first formed in 1956 by six countries—Germany, France, Italy, Holland, Belgium, and Luxembourg. Since then, the European Union has expanded to include a majority of countries in Europe. In 1992, a treaty was signed among member countries that sets them on a path to even closer economic and political integration. Once this process is completed, there will be freer movement of economic resources, standardized economic regulations, and probably a common currency throughout the EU.

customs union: a group of countries with common trade barriers with outside countries as well as a free trade area

common market: a group of countries with not only a free trade area and common trade barriers with outside countries, but also free movement of labour and capital

European Union (EU): an expanding common market of European countries first formed in 1956, formerly known as the European Economic Community (EEC)

DEVELOPING INTERPRETATION SKILLS

A Catalogue of Grievances

GATT and the Environment

Some critics of GATT argue that, by liberalizing trade and applying the same standards to all, standards fall to the lowest common denominator and the environment suffers. The following article, written in 1993, summarizes the fears many environmentalists have about GATT.

Environmentalists object to GATT on the grounds that:

- Trade liberalisation encourages economic growth, and so damages the environment.
- GATT (and the proposed North American Free Trade Agreement), by limiting national sovereignty, limits the rights of countries to apply whatever environmental measures they choose.
- GATT does not allow countries to keep out a product because of the way it's produced or harvested.
- GATT prevents a country imposing countervailing duties on imports produced under lower environmental standards than its own. It also discourages subsidies, which are one way to compensate producers for meeting higher environmental standards than their rivals.
- GATT will—if certain Uruguay-round proposals are agreed—encourage the harmonisation of product standards. This would expose higher standards on, for instance, food additives or pesticide residues, to challenge as trade barriers.
- GATT prevents countries imposing export bans, which they may want to use to protect, say, their own forests or elephants. American environmentalists want to ban the export of certain pesticides that are prohibited in the United States but sold to developing countries.
- GATT frowns on the use of trade measures to influence environmental policy outside a country's territory. Yet increasingly the issues that arouse environmental passion are those affecting what greens call the "global commons"—the oceans and atmosphere, animal and plant species threatened with extinction—that concern all countries.
- GATT may undermine international environmental agreements, through its prohibition of trade measures that discriminate against individual nations. Yet such measures may be the most effective way for countries that play by the rules of an international agreement to penalise others that do not.
- GATT resolves disputes in a secretive way, without allowing environmentalists to put their arguments and without making important papers on a case available to them.

Bow your head, Adam Smith?

SOURCE: © 1993 The Economist Newspaper Group, Inc. Reprinted with permission.

1. Summarize the article's main environmental argument against GATT.

2. a) In 1991, a GATT panel concluded that the United States had to end its import blockade of Mexican tuna that was caught using methods that also killed dolphins. In the role of an environmentalist, argue how this decision demonstrates the negative environmental effects of GATT.

   b) In the role of a GATT supporter, respond to the argument you developed for (a).

3. Some consumer and environmental groups suggest that, if negative effects of a trade policy cannot be combatted by changing the policy, boycotts are an effective option. Research and write a report about boycotts in which you summarize at least one boycott campaign.

Supporters of the EU suggest that the gains from past trade liberalization among members have helped boost recent living standards in West European countries. For example, a 1988 study on the effects of the EU's single market suggested that in its first six years it would reduce prices in member countries by 6 percent, increase real output by 4.5 percent, and create 2 million new jobs. Critics point out the loss of national sovereignty that has accompanied the EU's evolution, and argue that European living standards would have risen with or without freer trade.

The Auto Pact

The Canada–U.S. Automotive Products Agreement, or **Auto Pact**, of 1965 is an example of a free trade area in one class of products—autos and auto parts. Until 1965, high tariffs meant that Canada had an inefficient branch-plant auto industry with high prices for Canadian consumers. The pact eliminated tariffs on both sides of the border for the "Big Three" auto companies as long as their sales in North America had at least 50 percent North American content and their Canadian sales had 60 or more percent of their value added in Canada. The pact was beneficial for the companies involved, allowing them to increase their efficiency. As costs and prices for Canadian-made autos fell, output and employment rose, aiding Canadian workers and the Canadian economy as a whole.

Auto Pact: the 1965 agreement establishing free trade in autos and auto parts between Canada and the United States; formerly known as the Canada–U.S. Automotive Products Agreement

The Free Trade Agreement

Like the Auto Pact, the Canada–U.S. **Free Trade Agreement (FTA)** is an example of a "bilateral" free trade agreement, which involves two partners. Unlike the Auto Pact, the FTA includes trade in virtually all products between the two countries. It was signed by Canada and the United States in 1988 and came into effect in January 1989. Under the terms of the agreement, all remaining tariffs on trade between the two countries will be phased out by 1998, and non-tariff barriers will be reduced. Services are also included, with a national treatment principle being adopted so that service industries in either country can compete in both national markets. Licensing procedures in the two countries are being standardized to help ease this liberalization of services. Canada's ability to screen foreign direct investment has been reduced, while non-North American car companies can trade autos and auto parts freely across the Canada–U.S. border if they meet a revised 50 percent North American manufacturing content rule. There is also greater access for U.S. wine and liquor producers—and, more gradually, for American brewers—in the Canadian market. A continental market for energy has been created. While Canada may still limit its energy exports to the United States during a period of global shortages, Canadians will have to limit their own energy consumption by the same proportion. Of particular note, Canadian cultural policies are largely exempted from the agreement,

Free Trade Agreement (FTA): the 1988 pact between Canada and the United States to form a free trade area allowing Canada to impose policies that affect the trade and ownership of its cultural industries. Finally, a dispute settlement procedure is in place so that when either country retaliates against the other's trade policies, the dispute is judged by an impartial panel using the trade legislation of the retaliating country.

As usual, supporters of free trade point out the potential economic benefits from increased specialization and trade between the two countries. Canadian advocates of the agreement also suggest that it reduces the risk of American protectionist measures directed against Canadian exports. Critics of the deal focus on the possible loss of political sovereignty for Canada, especially because of the restrictions placed on government attempts to screen foreign investment and restrict energy exports. While either country can end the agreement with six months' warning, the gradual strengthening of trade ties between the two countries will make it difficult for any future Canadian government to do so. Critics also stress that Canadian jobs are being lost in previously protected manufacturing industries as foreign companies close their remaining branch plants so they can centralize their production and take advantage of economies of scale. In the important auto industry, the phasing out of tariffs means that there are no longer penalties for companies that do not meet the Auto Pact guidelines, which critics say could work to the disadvantage of Canadian producers.

Effects of the Free Trade Agreement

As expected, in the early years of the Free Trade Agreement Canada and the United States had greater trade flows. From 1989 to 1992, for example, Canadian merchandise exports in sectors liberalized by the agreement increased by 33 percent, while Canadian merchandise imports in the same sectors rose by 28 percent. The increase in Canada's exports was most pronounced in manufacturing industries such as office and telecommunications equipment, as well as in resource-based industries such as chemical products and paper. Meanwhile, Canada's merchandise imports grew most in industries such as processed food, clothing, and furniture. So far, the impartial dispute settlement procedure has tended to work in Canada's favour, although the American government has shown a tendency to reintroduce trade complaints if a panel decision goes against its perceived interests.

There also have been costs associated with the agreement, which it is hoped are only the short-term costs of adjustment. The bulk of these costs fell on workers who lost their jobs in formerly protected industries. It is important to remember that other factors were also causing unemployment to rise during the years immediately after the FTA took effect. The first was the continuing shift of Canadian jobs away from manufacturing and toward the service sector. Second, the agreement came into effect just before the start of a significant worldwide recession. In the long run, trade theory suggests, jobs lost in declining industries hurt by free trade should be replaced by employment in expanding export industries.

The North American Free Trade Agreement

The **North American Free Trade Agreement (NAFTA)**, which was settled in 1993 and came into effect in January 1994, is an illustration of a "trilateral" trade accord, which is among three countries. It extends most of the provisions of the Free Trade Agreement to include Mexico. If we consider only trade with this new partner, it seems that NAFTA will not have a significant impact on either Canada or Mexico because their trade relationship has never been significant. For example, in 1992 trade with Mexico made up only 0.5 percent of Canada's exports and 2 percent of its imports, and much of this trade was virtually tariff-free even before NAFTA.

However, critics of NAFTA suggest possible problems of including a country with a lower GDP per capita in the same free trade area as wealthier, more industrialized countries. They point to the loss of Canadian jobs that could occur if businesses move to Mexico to take

North American Free Trade Agreement (NAFTA): the 1993 pact among Canada, the United States, and Mexico to form a free trade area

Figure 17.9:   NAFTA Economies and Trade

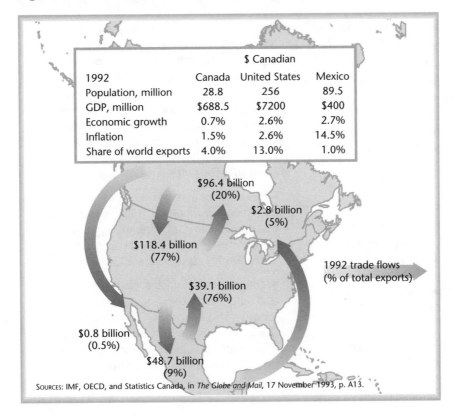

	$ Canadian		
1992	Canada	United States	Mexico
Population, million	28.8	256	89.5
GDP, million	$688.5	$7200	$400
Economic growth	0.7%	2.6%	2.7%
Inflation	1.5%	2.6%	14.5%
Share of world exports	4.0%	13.0%	1.0%

$96.4 billion
(20%)

$2.8 billion
(5%)

$118.4 billion
(77%)

1992 trade flows
(% of total exports)

$39.1 billion
(76%)

$0.8 billion
(0.5%)

$48.7 billion
(9%)

SOURCES: IMF, OECD, and Statistics Canada, in *The Globe and Mail*, 17 November 1993, p. A13.

SOURCE: Mike Constable, Union Art Services

advantage of low-wage labour. Concern has also been expressed over Mexico's lax enforcement of labour and environmental standards. This last concern prompted the addition of two side-agreements to NAFTA. Under the side-agreements, two NAFTA members can set penalties on the third member if that country is not enforcing its labour and environmental laws. So far, it is too early to assess the usefulness of these provisions, or the relevance of the criticisms made against NAFTA.

BRIEF REVIEW

1. Up until the 1860s, Canada had a favourable trade agreement with the United States with low tariff rates.

2. Canada became increasingly restrictive after 1866, particularly with the adoption of the National Policy in 1879. The National Policy raised tariffs to stimulate Canada's own manufacturing sector.

3. High tariff rates continued to the Great Depression, at which point this approach to trade was reassessed.

4. The General Agreement on Tariffs and Trade (GATT) is a multilateral trade agreement created in 1947 and based on the principle that member countries should treat all other members equally. GATT has been a major force in liberalizing international trade.

5. Trading blocs, which are trade agreements among a small number of countries, take a variety of forms: free trade areas, customs unions, and common markets.

6. Trade within a free trade area is tariff-free, although member countries can impose separate trade barriers on outside countries. The Free Trade Agreement (FTA) and its extension, the North American Free Trade Agreement (NAFTA), are examples of free trade areas. Another example of such an area is the Auto Pact between Canada and the United States, which deals only with certain products.

7. A customs union is an even stronger form of regional integration. Not only is the free trade area tariff-free, but members have common trade barriers with the rest of the world. An example is CARICOM.

8. A common market is a customs union that allows for the free movement of labour and capital. The European Union (EU) is an example of a common market. The EU is moving toward even closer economic and political integration.

No Small Change

Dian Cohen and Stabilization Policy in the Face of Globalization

Globalization not only influences trade and investment, it also has an impact on governments by making stabilization policy more difficult to conduct and predict. Dian Cohen is a well-known Canadian economic commentator who is a recognized expert on the rapid changes associated with the rise of the new knowledge-based economy. Besides her work as a journalist and writer, she sits on the boards of several of Canada's major corporations. In the following excerpt from No Small Change, *a book she co-wrote with Guy Stanley, Cohen discusses Canadians' response to recent economic trends as well as the role of stabilization policy in today's global environment.*

Canadians are cranky. Not all, but many. And angry. And feeling betrayed. By their governments, by their employers, perhaps even by themselves. Many business people are baffled, too. A great many are hunkering down and waiting for things to get back to normal, like the characters in Samuel Beckett's *Waiting for Godot*, a play about hope that paralyzes constructive action.

Basically, Canada is held back by a rather large cherished illusion. (A cherished illusion is one that is held even more firmly when we know it's contrary to fact because we find it comforting.) The illusion is that we can deal with challenge by just saying no. In too many places in our powerful society, we have evolved a Canadian culture that is a culture of refusal.

Our discouraged and tentative embrace of globalization is one example of this. In fact, globalization is a tremendous opportunity for every region of Canada. But lukewarm is as enthusiastic as our policy makers can get. Yves Guérard, chairman and chief executive officer of the Montreal-based management consulting firm Sobeco, Inc., says, "There are many forces of change working on the economy and the Canadian reaction has been to negate them or do nothing, hoping they'd go away." Nancy Riche, Canadian Labor Congress vice president, echoes the sentiment: "There really is a sense of helplessness in the country and people don't seem to know where they're going." Here's how William Dimma, chairman of Royal Lepage, Canada's largest real estate broker, understands the paradigm shift that many people talk about when they talk about the "new economy": "It means that the comfortable pew this country has been living in for perhaps a hundred years or more isn't so comfortable any more. We used to sell our resources at reasonable prices. We imported finished goods. And now, in the past ten or fifteen years, it's a different ball game. Our resources aren't in particular demand these days: other people can supply them. And conservation means those resources won't be used as much anyway. Prices are certainly less than satisfactory. And unless we

Dian Cohen

find some other way as a trading nation, we're out in the cold. There's no point in casting blame…we're all guilty. But governments, businesses, the educational system, the media, all of them together have failed either to anticipate, or to do anything about it."

The world's changing, but Canada doesn't seem to be making the transition. Okay, you might ask, why can't we just ask the government to put a "transition" or "adjustment" program in place. After all, they're in charge, aren't they? Sorry, not really. The new economy has ushered in substantial changes in the ability of any government to pursue domestic policy objectives. Here's how it works: the new economy allows firms to increase in size beyond what one country can support, thus removing them from complete control of any national economy. And, the new economy frees up capital markets so that every government's fiscal and monetary policy can be guessed in advance and allowed for.

Probably the most significant consequence of the combination of globalization and linking of computers and communications is that it snatches away from governments the power to do very much about the pace of economic activity within the boundaries of a single country. Ask yourself, for example, why government economic forecasts and policies are so often wrong. If you're the finance minister in a typical advanced country, you're served by hundreds of economists and analysts whose job each year is to put together a national economic plan. That plan is announced in Canada in the finance minister's budget speech. In the United States, the president's annual State of the Union address serves to signal the nation's economic course.

All the economists are very bright people who've taken lots of courses in economics. Fewer have significant experience of the economy. Generally, the government gets its way and gets its measures through the legislature. (The United States is the exception.) Yet every year the run-up to the budget speech is spent in part promising to avoid the errors of the previous year. For generally, despite all the intellectually high-powered inputs, the predictions—economic growth, public sector borrowing requirement, revenue collected or spent—turn out to be wrong. And of course the unemployment rate is generally not correctly identified and the inflation rate is typically wide of the mark.

Why are all these highly paid men and women apparently unable to come to grips with what's happening? Because the trick can't be done. For one thing, you can't produce sensible economic forecasts for a single country when there are no free-standing national economies any more. As forecasters pointed out in the mid-sixties and later: national economic models are irrelevant. Only international analysis is adequate as a basis for decision making.

Second, and related, international markets know more than national forecasters. In the old, nationally based economies, governments were supposed to control the business cycle by taxing away "excess" demand in good times (collecting a surplus) and running deficits to "stimulate demand" in bad times. The combination of globalization and computerization has completely destroyed these policy instruments. For, if a government gives signs that it will increase taxes, then international business shifts its investments to a place where profits will be better.

You don't have to be a rocket scientist to understand the results: when governments go to the companies for the tax, the level of business expansion has dropped. But the existing business base still needs the extra money to pay the higher taxes, so prices and wages are bid upward and the tax provokes the inflation it was intended to reduce. And if a government suggests it will run a deficit, that means it will increase the amount of money it seeks to borrow. International lenders will withhold money until interest rates become attractive enough to offset the increased inflation risks of the deficit. The higher interest rates demanded by lenders choke off the extra economic activity the deficits were intended to stimulate.

These international lenders aren't just big conglomerates. "They" are us and others like us—lots of individuals who've put our money into offshore mutual funds, or opened bank accounts in the States that we operate through computer programs such as Checkfree, or simply with a Citibank card. Big operators and little, the international economy churns around some $500 billion a day on foreign exchange markets. Decisions taken in the international capital markets are the terminator for state economic power.

SOURCE: From *No Small Change* by Dian Cohen with Guy Stanley © 1993. Reprinted by permission of Macmillan Canada.

1. a) Identify the main points raised in the excerpt.
   b) Consult newspapers and magazines. To what extent do economic events support Cohen's main points? Present your findings to the class.

2. What impact has NAFTA had—and will it have—on the situation Cohen describes?

3. In an essay, predict how the relationship between business and government in Canada will evolve in the new global economy.

Key Concepts

globalization

absolute advantage

comparative advantage

law of comparative advantage

terms of trade

tariff

non-tariff barriers

import quota

voluntary export restraints

export subsidies

infant industry

strategic trade policy

National Policy

General Agreement on Tariffs and Trade

trading bloc

free trade area

customs union

common market

European Union

Auto Pact

Free Trade Agreement

North American Free Trade Agreement

Developing Application and Analysis Skills

1. Imagine that you are a Canadian politician who is concerned about Canada's reliance on trade with the United States. Write a speech in which you present the benefits and costs to the Canadian economy of reducing Canada's trade with the United States.

2. a) Suppose the lawyer in the hypothetical example in Figure 17.4 worked at preparing wills for 20 hours, while the carpenter worked at making furniture for the same amount of time. What would be their output?

b) Calculate the upper and lower limits for the terms of trade. Will trade occur if one will is prepared in exchange for four units of furniture? Explain.

3. Using the table opposite, answer the following questions:

a) Which nation has the absolute advantage in producing each product?

b) Which nation has the comparative advantage in producing each product? Which should specialize in which product? Support your answer.

c) Under what circumstances will the countries trade with each other?

Hypothetical Production Table		
	Output per Worker per Hour	
	Skateboards	**In-Line Skates**
Nation A	20	10
Nation B	40	40

4. a) Using the table that follows, draw domestic market demand and supply curves for shoes.

b) Indicate the equilibrium point assuming that no shoes are imported.

c) Assuming that this domestic market has no impact on the world market, indicate the following separate scenarios and their effects on your graph:

i) Unrestricted imports of shoes flood the domestic market at a prevailing world price of $40 per pair.

ii) The government imposes a tariff of $20 per pair of shoes.

iii) An import quota is established at 30 000 pairs of shoes.

d) For each of the scenarios in 4(c), outline the possible concerns and actions of the government, domestic producers, and foreign producers.

Domestic Demand and Supply Schedules for Shoes

Price ($ per pair)	Quantity Demanded (D$_d$)	Quantity Supplied (S$_d$)
	(thousands of pairs)	
10	220	15
20	210	30
30	195	45
40	180	60
50	165	75
60	150	90
70	135	105
80	120	120
90	105	135
100	90	150
110	75	165

5. Explain the relationship shown in this causal loop diagram, and then title the diagram.

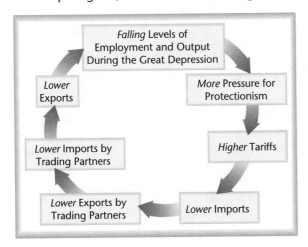

6. Draw a causal loop diagram that reflects how trade-liberalizing agreements signed between Canada and the United States in the 1930s would have affected the output and employment levels of the time.

7. Research one significant event now in the news that relates to international trade, and analyze the treatment of the event in various newspaper and magazine articles. Present your findings in a report.

8. Shortly after the Free Trade Agreement between Canada and the United States came into effect, there were trade disputes over pork, beer, and cedar shingles. Research one of these disputes and report on the following:

a) the background and causes of the dispute
b) the details of the dispute
c) how the dispute was settled

9. Write a research paper that answers the following question: "To date, to what extent has NAFTA been in the best interests of the Canadian economy?"

10. Research Canada's trading relationship with a country other than the United States. In a report, analyze the following:

a) what is traded and the relative importance to each country of this trading relationship
b) absolute and comparative advantages
c) trade policies that affect the trading relationship, any disputes, and the history of the trading relationship

11. Malthusville, a hypothetical town in Canada, once boomed because of its aluminum production. Now, however, strong international competition in the aluminum market means harder times for Malthusville. As Minister of Economic Affairs, you have decided that this community needs help to boost its economic activity. Suggest a range of policies. For each, weigh the costs and benefits. Based on your analysis, choose the most desirable policy and explain your choice.

Economic Growth

I'm a trader.... In word and in deed, I support expanded trade. But I am concerned about quality in trade, not just quantity.... If we do not build economic growth that helps sustain communities, cultures and families, the results will be harsh.

—ANITA RODDICK, ENGLISH ENTREPRENEUR

The distinguishing feature of life in present-day Canada, compared with many other parts of the world, is the prosperity that most Canadians enjoy. Economic growth has transformed Canadian living standards in just a few generations, with real GDP per Canadian about five times higher in the 1990s than it was in the 1920s. Can this trend continue? Why are there such vast differences between rich countries such as Canada and poor countries? How can these differences be addressed? What are the implications of growth and development? These questions are explored in this final chapter.

CHAPTER FOCUS

This chapter focuses on the following:
- economic growth, as indicated by both national output and national output per capita
- a country's production choices and the implications for growth
- economic growth in Canada
- sources of economic growth and the debate over growth
- high-, middle-, and low-income countries and the economic circumstances that characterize each category
- the gap between the rich and the poor countries
- economic development, its dynamics, the vicious circle of poverty, and the strategies used to break the circle

SKILLS FOCUS

After studying this chapter, you will be able to:
- graph economic growth and the effects of particular production choices
- explain the main causes of economic growth and predict its social implications
- apply the Rule of 72
- outline the costs and benefits of economic growth
- summarize obstacles to economic growth and strategies to overcome them
- evaluate an example of foreign aid and research the situation of a low-income country
- explore perspectives of high-, middle-, and low-income countries in a class forum
- assess the human and environmental costs of overconsumption and poverty

 # Economic Growth

Recall from Chapter 1 that economic growth is an increase in the total output of goods and services. The term can refer to the percentage increase in an economy's total output, usually measured by real GDP, or it can refer to a percentage increase in the per capita real GDP. For example, Canada's real GDP, valued in 1986 dollars, was $558.1 billion in 1992 and $570.5 billion in 1993, while the country's population expanded from 28.4356 to 28.7530 million during the same period. Using the first definition, Canada's annual rate of economic growth was 2.2 percent [($570.5 billion – $558.1 billion) ÷ $558.1 billion). Since per capita real GDP rose from $19 627 ($558.1 billion ÷ 28.4356 million) to $19 841 ($570.5 billion ÷ 28.7530 million), economic growth using the second definition was 1.1 percent. The first definition of economic growth is most appropriate when measuring an economy's overall productive capacity, while the second definition better indicates long-term changes in living standards, since more output per capita means an average individual is better off than before.

Economic Growth and Its Impact

In Chapter 1, we saw that the production possibilities curve demonstrates the combination of outputs that an economy *can* produce, assuming constant economic resources and technology. Consider the hypothetical economy illustrated in Figure 18.1. This economy produces consumer goods (loaves of bread) and capital goods (saws). Initially, its production is limited to the combinations of consumer goods and capital goods demonstrated by the curve PPC_0. The economy chooses to produce 40 loaves and 2 saws (point *a*).

Figure 18.1:   The Process of Economic Growth

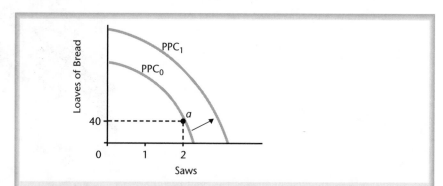

Initially the economy has production possibilities as shown by the curve PPC_0 and chooses to produce 40 loaves of bread and 2 saws (point *a*). Only by increasing economic resources and/or improving the productivity of these resources can the economy grow. By doing so, the economy can expand the production possibilities from PPC_0 to PPC_1.

Because the curve represents all production combinations that are attainable, this hypothetical economy is producing the most it can. Only by increasing economic resources and/or improving the state of technology to use the resources more efficiently can the production possibilities be increased. In Figure 18.1, the shift from PPC_0 to PPC_1 demonstrates an increase in the production possibilities. Now, the economy is able to produce more of either good and economic growth can take place.

Note that the production possibilities model highlights not only the limits of any economy but also the tradeoffs between various goods. Expanding our example in Figure 18.2, a country can choose to produce 40 loaves of bread and 2 saws (point *a*) on the left graph. Alternatively, it can choose to produce 100 loaves of bread and 1 saw (point *c*) on the right graph.

Although a simplification, the two options demonstrate that economies can focus their resources on the production of consumer goods (bread) or the production of capital goods (saws). In contrast to consumer goods, which are simply consumed, capital goods can be used to produce

Figure 18.2:   Production Options and Their Implications

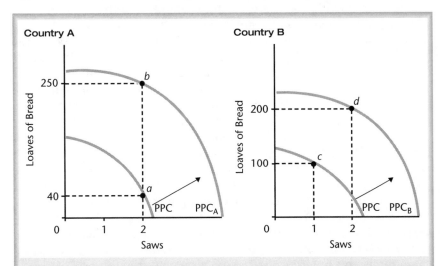

Suppose Countries A and B have the same initial production possibilities (PPC). However, Country A chooses to produce 40 loaves of bread and 2 saws (point *a* on the left) and Country B chooses to produce 100 loaves of bread and 1 saw (point *c* on the right). Because Country A focuses more of its resources on producing a capital good (saws) than does Country B, which focuses on a consumer good (bread), Country A encourages greater growth. Within the same time period, Country A's production possibilities expand to PPC_A, so that it may choose to produce 250 loaves of bread and 2 saws (point *b*). Country B's production possibilities expand less so, to PPC_B, so that it may produce 200 loaves of bread and 2 saws (point *d*).

more products. As such, capital goods are an investment in further production. Because of this, the choices that an economy makes between the production possibilities affect its future growth.

To demonstrate this, let's consider the hypothetical Countries A and B in Figure 18.2, which initially have identical production possibilities curves. By producing 40 loaves of bread and 2 saws (point *a* on the left graph), Country A adds to its economic resources, which in turn fuels economic growth and can mean that more of both consumer and capital goods will be produced in the future. As shown on the left, the production possibilities curve shifts from PPC to PPC$_A$. While the opportunity cost of focusing on capital goods is fewer consumer goods, production of both consumer and capital goods is enhanced in a year. So, for example, Country A can have an output of 250 loaves of bread and 2 saws (point *b*).

In contrast, Country B produces 100 loaves of bread and 1 saw (point *c* on the right graph). Because of this choice the country has more consumer goods for its citizens immediately. However, the opportunity cost of more consumer goods is fewer capital goods, which means that the economy grows considerably less than Country A's. As shown on the right, the production possibilities curve shifts—from PPC to PPC$_B$—but less so than Country A's curve. So, for example, Country B can have an output of 200 loaves of bread and 2 saws (point *d*).

By consuming fewer loaves of bread in the first year, Country A's citizens have gained an advantage in the second year. If they wish, they can now consume more loaves of bread and match the production of saws in Country B. Moreover, Country A now starts from a position of even greater production possibilities as it seeks further economic growth in future years.

The benefits of a high-growth strategy multiply over time. To see why, imagine what happens if, instead of choosing point *b*, the citizens of Country A continue their emphasis on capital goods by again choosing a point on PPC$_A$ with fewer loaves of bread and more saws produced. The longer they follow this policy, the more their production possibilities curve expands and the greater their future potential consumption compared to consumption in Country B. With the passage of time, Country A reaps increasing benefits from high-growth strategy, while Country B's policy of favouring current over future consumption has an increasing opportunity cost in terms of sacrificed economic growth.

Even small differences in growth rates can have a major long-run effect on a country's prosperity and living standards. This is because economic growth, like population growth, builds on itself, thereby showing a pattern of **exponential growth**. To see the effects, we can use a handy mathematical rule, the **Rule of 72**, which states that the number of years it takes a variable to double can be estimated by dividing 72 by the variable's annual percentage growth rate. A variable that grows exponentially at 4 percent a year therefore doubles its value in 18 years:

exponential growth: growth that is based on a percentage change and that builds on itself

Rule of 72: states that the number of years it takes a variable to double can be estimated by dividing 72 by the variable's annual percentage growth rate

$$\text{Rule of 72: Number of years for variable to double} = \frac{72}{\text{annual percentage growth rate}}$$

$$18 \text{ years} = \frac{72}{4\%}$$

Because of their long-term impact, small discrepancies in growth rates are treated seriously by economists and government policy-makers. Consider the hypothetical example in Figure 18.3. Two countries both have a 1995 output of $100 billion, but different growth rates (2 and 4 percent). After only 10 years, the difference between Country X's and Country Y's output is $26.12 billion.

Figure 18.3:   GDP and Growth Rates

	Real GDP in Country X (2% annual growth in real GDP)	Real GDP in Country Y (4% annual growth in real GDP)
1995	$100.00 billion	$100.00 billion
1996	102.00 billion	104.00 billion
1997	104.04 billion	108.16 billion
1998	106.12 billion	112.49 billion
1999	108.24 billion	116.99 billion
2000	110.41 billion	121.67 billion
2001	112.62 billion	126.53 billion
2002	114.87 billion	131.59 billion
2003	117.17 billion	136.86 billion
2004	119.51 billion	142.33 billion
2005	121.90 billion	148.02 billion

Two countries, X and Y, have the same initial GDP in 1995, but different growth rates. Because growth is exponential, Country X's GDP falls behind Country Y's by an increasing margin. For example, while Country X's GDP rises from $100.00 billion to $102.00 billion [($100.00 billion × 0.02) + $100.00 billion] to $104.04 billion [($102.00 billion × 0.02) + $102.00 billion], Country Y's rises from $100.00 billion to $104.00 billion [($100.00 billion × 0.04) + $100.00 billion] to 108.16 billion [($104.00 billion × 0.04) + $104.00 billion].

Economic Growth in Canada

Historically, Canada has had high rates of economic growth. As a result, Canada had the fifth-highest per capita output of any country in the world in 1992 (after the United States, Switzerland, Germany, and Japan). However, while Canada's long-term growth has been impressive, Figure 18.4 shows that increases in per capita real output have varied widely since Confederation.

Figure 18.4: Canada's Economic Growth

In terms of real output per capita, Canada's growth was gradual between 1870 and 1914. There were steep upswings in both the 1920s and early 1940s, but an abrupt decline in the early 1930s. Until 1973, there was steady growth in per capita income, averaging about 2 percent per year. Since then, the average rate of growth has declined. Note that the scale on the vertical axis is *logarithmic* to highlight change.

SOURCES: Adapted from A.G. Green and M.C. Urquhart, "New Estimates of Output Growth in Canada: Measurement and Interpretation," in Douglas McCalla and Michael Huberman (eds.), *Perspectives on Canadian Economic History* (Toronto: Copp Clark Longman, 1994), pp. 160–61; adapted from Statistics Canada, *Canadian Economic Observer, Historical Statistical Supplement, 1993/94* (July 1994), cat. no. 11-210, vol. 8, pp. 7–8, 27. Reproduced by authority of the Minister of Industry, 1994.

Before World War I (1870–1914)

In the 44 years from just after Confederation to World War I, Canada's per capita output, measured in 1986 dollars, rose from $1713 to $3917. The economy's lacklustre growth record in the 1870s was followed by a more rapid rise in per capita real output in the 1880s and 1890s—sometimes attributed to Prime Minister John A. Macdonald's National Policy, which stimulated Canadian manufacturing through high tariffs on imports. The gradual increase in growth rates during these decades was also a part of the worldwide trend toward greater prosperity, as well as a rapid expansion of staple exports, such as wheat, that accompanied the settlement of the Canadian West.

The Interwar Period (1914–1945)

World War I ushered in a period of more unstable growth, with a lower long-term growth trend than in the previous period. After a period of negative growth just after World War I, Canada's per capita real output rose and then fell sharply during the 1920s and early 1930s, before increasing rapidly during the latter part of the 1930s and World War II. Overall, between 1914 and 1945, per capita real output almost doubled from $3917 to $7291.

The Postwar Period (1945–)

Between 1945 and 1973, Canada shared in the worldwide rise in prosperity, achieving a fairly steady growth in living standards of about 2 percent annually. Since the OPEC-spurred oil crisis of 1973, however, there has been a worrisome decrease in the rate of Canadian growth, except between 1983 and 1989, when growth in per capita real output again exceeded 2 percent. Overall, since 1945, per capita real output in Canada has increased over two and a half times to $19 084 by 1993.

Sources of Economic Growth

The production possibilities model shows that the main causes of growth in an economy's total real output are the stock of economic resources and how productively these resources are used. One of the most important causes of growth in Canada's total output—accounting for an estimated 35 percent of the growth in Canada's real GDP between 1961 and 1989—has been the increase in the quantity of labour. Some of this increase is due to higher participation rates for women and young people in the labour force. However, most of it arises from population growth, which now runs at just over 1 percent annually.

Figure 18.5:   The Growth Performance of Selected Countries (1961–1990)

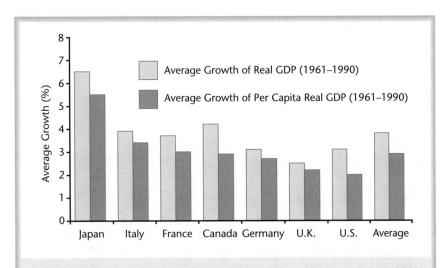

In terms of the average growth rate of real GDP for the years 1961 to 1990, Canada's growth rate of 4.2 percent bettered the average of the seven large industrialized economies selected. Only Japan had a higher growth rate of 6.5 percent. However, in terms of the average growth rate of real per capita GDP, Canada's growth rate was only average, at 2.9 percent.

SOURCE: Adapted from Department of Finance, *Quarterly Economic Review: Special Report* (June 1991), pp. 42–43.

Because of its close association with population growth, an increase in the quantity of labour has a significant impact on the percentage rise in Canada's real GDP, but not on Canadian growth defined in terms of per capita real GDP. Canadian growth performance over the last 30 years compared to other major industrial countries is shown in Figure 18.5 using both definitions of economic growth. While Canada's 4.2 percent growth in real GDP was relatively high, its 2.9 percent growth in per capita real GDP was only average for the group. In contrast, Japan's high growth in per capita real GDP has meant that its citizens, who 30 years ago had significantly lower living standards than Canadians, have been able to catch up since then.

Hence the long-term growth in Canada's living standards is determined by the other main source of growth, labour productivity. Recall from Chapter 7 that labour productivity is the quantity of output produced per worker in a certain period of time. Labour productivity can be applied not only to businesses and industries but also to countries' economies. Consider, for example, a hypothetical economy with a labour force of 5 workers who are employed for 2000 hours annually. In other words, the economy uses 10 000 hours of labour per year (5 × 2000). If real GDP in the economy is $200 000, labour productivity is $20 ($200 000 ÷ 10 000):

$$\text{Labour productivity} = \frac{\text{real output}}{\text{total hours worked}}$$

$$\$20 = \frac{\$200\ 000}{10\ 000}$$

If real GDP in this economy rises to $202 000 in the following year and the number of labour hours remains constant, then the new level of labour productivity is $20.20 ($202 000 ÷ 10 000 hours), representing an increase of 1 percent [($20.20 − $20.00) ÷ 20.00) × 100%].

The source of changes in Canada's living standards, as measured by per capita real output, is dependent on the determinants of labour productivity: the quantity of capital, technological progress, the quality of labour, efficiency in production, the quantity of natural resources, and social and political factors.

Quantity of Capital

As indicated by the production possibilities model, an economy's supply of capital resources plays a central role in enhancing economic growth. By saving a higher proportion of their disposable incomes, Canadians can increase investment and accelerate the accumulation of capital resources, which, in turn, fuel economic growth. On average, the rates of Canadian saving and investment as a proportion of GDP have been higher than in the United States, but lower than in high-growth countries such as Japan and Germany.

Nonetheless, increases in the quantity of capital goods in Canada were high enough to account for an estimated 40 percent of total growth in its real GDP between 1961 and 1989. Because capital inputs have risen more quickly than labour inputs in the Canadian economy, each Canadian worker is employed with a gradually increasing amount of capital. Since 1961, for example, it is estimated that the ratio of capital to labour in Canada has risen by over 80 percent.

Technological Progress

Technological progress is a broader term than the technological innovation discussed in Chapter 7 and encompasses scientific discoveries and their application, advances in production methods, and the development of new types of products. Technological progress—in all its forms—can cause economic growth. Over the long term it plays an important role in increasing labour productivity, often by raising the quality of capital resources with which labour is employed.

Some technological advances occur because of the ingenuity of individuals. Nonetheless, most technological progress is closely tied to **research and development expenditures (R&D)**, or spending that is meant to accelerate the pace of technological progress. Canadians have been relatively successful in taking advantage of international technological progress, but R&D expenditures by Canadian businesses have historically been relatively low compared to those of other countries. For example, R&D expenditures in 1991 represented 2.2 percent of GDP in Japan and 1.9 percent in the United States, but only 0.8 percent in Canada. It has been argued that, because of a small national market, the potential benefits of R&D expenditures are lower in Canada than in other countries. To the extent that freer trade is creating larger product markets for Canadian businesses, however, this argument is no longer relevant. Predictably, Canadian R&D expenditures have shown an upward trend in recent years.

Quality of Labour

The productivity of labour is tied not only to investment in capital goods but also to investment in human capital through education and training. Since the 1950s, a growing proportion of young people have been completing high school and then pursuing postsecondary education. While 62 percent of those 15 years and older had finished high school in 1991, just over 20 percent of the comparable age group had done so in 1960. During the same period, the percentage of those between the ages of 18 and 24 enrolled full-time in universities and community colleges increased from 10 to 33 percent. To the extent that these trends augment the quality of Canada's labour force, they are raising its productivity as well as the economy's rate of growth.

Efficiency in Production

Economic growth is also influenced by changes in the efficiency of production through economies of scale and the reallocation of resources among

technological progress: consists of scientific discoveries and their application, advances in production methods, and the development of new types of products

research and development expenditures (R&D): spending that is meant to accelerate the pace of technological progress

different sectors. Canadian businesses—especially those in manufacturing—have traditionally been unable to take full advantage of economies of scale due to the small size of the Canadian market. Recent moves to freer trade are gradually removing this disadvantage, stimulating both labour productivity and the rate of economic growth—especially since the recession of the early 1990s. However, the shift of Canadian workers from the higher-productivity manufacturing sector to the lower-productivity service sector has, at least in the short run, dampened the rate of economic growth.

Quantity of Natural Resources

Canada's rich supplies of natural resources have doubtless contributed to its past economic growth, as during the boom period of rapidly expanding Western settlement between 1896 and 1914. During most periods, however, the stock of exploitable natural resources in a country remains constant, so that their impact on economic growth is minimal—especially in the modern Canadian economy, which is no longer dominated by primary sectors.

Social and Political Factors

There are a variety of social and political factors that can affect economic growth. Growth will be enhanced in a society that promotes competition, innovation, and entrepreneurship, and by social institutions geared toward enterprise and profit-making. In the political sphere, government regulations and taxes sometimes inhibit economic growth, especially through their impact on levels of saving and investment in the economy.

Thinking About Economics

What factors have led to lower average growth rates in per capita real income since 1973?

The lacklustre growth performance of the Canadian economy since 1973 stems from lower rises in labour productivity. While averaging 3.9 percent between 1961 and 1973, the average annual growth in labour productivity fell to 1.5 percent between 1973 and 1989. The exact cause of this lower productivity—also experienced by other industrialized countries—has not been determined, but it is probably related to lower rates of investment and technological progress (due to higher oil prices and contractionary government policies to combat inflation during much of this period) and shifts of workers from the manufacturing to the service sector. Whatever its exact causes, this productivity slowdown has had important long-term consequences for the prosperity of Canadians.

The Debate Over Growth

Is economic growth necessarily desirable? There are arguments both for and against the emphasis placed on economic growth.

Arguments for Economic Growth

Supporters of economic growth point to three main advantages: its effect on living standards, the opportunities it provides for social improvements, and its psychological benefits.

Living Standards   The main benefit of economic growth is its positive effect on living standards. With rising incomes and output, more wants can be satisfied, both for individuals and for society as a whole. Indeed, the main reason life for most Canadians today is more pleasant than for Canadians of three generations ago is due to the tremendous material benefits that economic growth has provided.

Social Improvements   Economic growth can be channelled not only into more consumption and investment by private households and businesses, but also into higher government spending, allowing for greater expenditures in such areas as health, education, and the promotion of income equity. Such programs are easier to implement when they can be funded from the proceeds of growth rather than through reductions in existing incomes.

Supporters of growth point out that the supposed tradeoff between income equity and economic growth has often been broken in recent decades. In the period between 1965 and 1989, countries with high growth rates tended to have a *more* equal distribution of income than poor countries. For example, the ratio of income shares of the richest and poorest 20 percent of the population was just under 10 to 1 in Singapore, while the average annual growth rate in the country's per capita real GDP was 7 percent. In contrast, Brazil's ratio of richest to poorest income shares was almost 35 to 1, while its comparable growth rate was a much lower 4 percent.

Psychological Benefits   Some people suggest that there are intangible psychological benefits of economic growth as well. A growing economy helps create a mood of optimism and a sense of expanding opportunities.

Arguments Against Economic Growth

Critics of the emphasis on economic growth point to its direct opportunity cost, and to its indirect environmental and social costs.

Opportunity Cost of Growth   Economic growth has a direct opportunity cost, as indicated by the production possibilities model. To promote growth, a country must devote more of its scarce resources to investment in capital goods rather than to current consumption. While this cost is not an overwhelming one for a rich country such as Canada, it is far more significant for citizens of poor countries as they choose an appropriate growth strategy.

Environmental Costs   One of the main indirect costs of economic growth is damage to the environment. Higher levels of economic activity lead to greater exploitation of the world's limited supply of natural resources, as well as causing higher levels of pollution and waste. Supporters of growth suggest that environmental damage is the result of flaws in private markets rather than of economic growth itself. Proper government programs, they contend, can create the conditions for sustainable growth in the future. Critics argue that the dynamics of growth tend to swamp the impact of government regulations and controls. Environmental damage cannot be corrected through tinkering with the market system, they say, but only by a shift in values to end the quest for never-ending increases in living standards.

Social Costs   The social costs of growth are related to the insecurity and risks that come with technological progress. While the general quality of life may be enhanced by technological advances, some resource suppliers will be hurt, and these individuals are often the members of society who are least able to adapt easily to change. At the same time, the pursuit of economic growth may not allow for traditional methods and lifestyles to be maintained. For some, the losses far outweigh any economic benefits.

BRIEF REVIEW

1. Economic growth refers to either increases in an economy's real output or increases in its real output per capita.

2. Economic growth expands the production possibilities, so this growth can be expressed as a shift to the right of the production possibilities curve. Such growth is caused by an increase in economic resources or by technological progress, which increases the efficiency of production.

3. An economy might choose to focus on producing consumer or capital goods. A high-growth strategy involves focusing production on capital goods at the expense of consumer goods in the short run.

4. Because economic growth is exponential growth, the Rule of 72 applies. Even small differences in percentage rates of growth make a significant difference over time.

5. Overall, Canada's rates of economic growth have been high, giving Canada the fifth-highest per capita GDP world-wide in 1992.

6. Population growth and labour productivity have been the sources of Canada's economic growth. In turn, labour productivity is determined by the quantity and quality of capital, technological progress, efficiency, and social and political factors.

7. Arguments for growth concern living standards, social improvements, and psychological benefits. Arguments against growth concern its direct opportunity cost, and the indirect environmental and social costs.

Economic Development

The World's Rich and Poor

Most Canadians live in relative comfort. In contrast, one-fifth of the world's population—about 1 billion people who live mainly in Southeast Asia and sub-Saharan Africa (meaning African countries south of the Sahara desert)—must live on US$370 or less each year.

To consider the disparities between rich and poor countries, the **World Bank** (known officially as the International Bank for Reconstruction and Development) classifies nations into three groups based on their annual per capita GNP: high-income, middle-income, and low-income countries.

High-Income Countries

High-income countries are nations with per capita incomes substantial enough to provide their citizens with widespread prosperity. In 1991, the World Bank classified as high-income countries those with a per capita GNP of US$7911 or more. All of these nations have modern mixed economies based on capital-intensive production and the use of skilled labour. In 1992, there were 22 countries in this "rich club" of nations.

Middle-Income Countries

Middle-income countries are those in which a sizable minority of the population no longer lives in acute poverty. In 1991, this category was composed of nations with per capita GNP between US$636 and US$7910. Included are the former members of the Soviet Bloc—those countries in Eastern Europe and the former Soviet Union that until recently were command economies—as well as other countries primarily in Latin America, the Middle East, and the extreme northern and southern parts of Africa.

World Bank: an international lending institution known officially as the International Bank for Reconstruction and Development

high-income countries: countries with per capita incomes substantial enough to provide their citizens with widespread prosperity

middle-income countries: countries in which a sizable minority of the population no longer lives in acute poverty

Low-Income Countries

Finally, the **low-income countries** include the 40 poorest countries
of the world. In 1991, this group included all nations with per capita
GNP of US$635 or less. Along with China and India—the two most
populous countries in the world—this category includes countries in
sub-Saharan Africa and some nations in Latin America and Southeast
Asia. These countries tend to have low levels of capital resources and
use labour-intensive processes. Their economies tend to emphasize
agriculture and other primary resource industries. Many of these countries share a history as colonies. In some cases, the national boundaries
devised and the economies developed under colonialism have made
the development of modern national economies difficult and full of strife.

In addition to high-, middle-, and low-income countries, other terms are
used to identify categories of countries with similar economies. For example, countries in Western Europe and North America (with the exception
of Mexico), plus Japan, Australia, and New Zealand, are considered **industrially advanced countries (IACs)** because of their degree of industrialization. Hong Kong, Singapore, Thailand, Indonesia, South Korea,
Malaysia, and Taiwan are sometimes called **newly industrializing countries (NICs)**—or, more colourfully, the "little dragons"—because of their
recent strong economic growth and rapid industrialization. Another term,
less-developed countries (LDC), is sometimes used to describe countries
with traditional mixed economies and low per capita incomes.

Points of Comparison

Figure 18.7 presents some points of comparison that together indicate the living standards in selected countries that are high-, middle-, and low-income.

Per Capita Income
The average per capita GNP for high-income countries is over US$21 000.
In contrast, the corresponding figure for low-income countries is US$350,
or about $1 a day.

Health and Social Indicators
Not surprisingly, there are wide disparities in health and social indicators,
such as life expectancy and infant mortality. While average life expectancy in high-income countries is 77 years, it is 62 years in low-income countries and close to 50 years in the poorest countries, such as Madagascar.
Similarly, less than 5 percent of adults in high-income countries are illit-
erate, compared to an average 40 percent in low-income countries.

Energy Consumption
The world's poor use less energy. Average per capita consumption in
high-income countries is about 14 times that in low-income countries,
with Canadians (who have the highest per capita energy use in the

Figure 18.6: Countries Classified by Per Capita Income

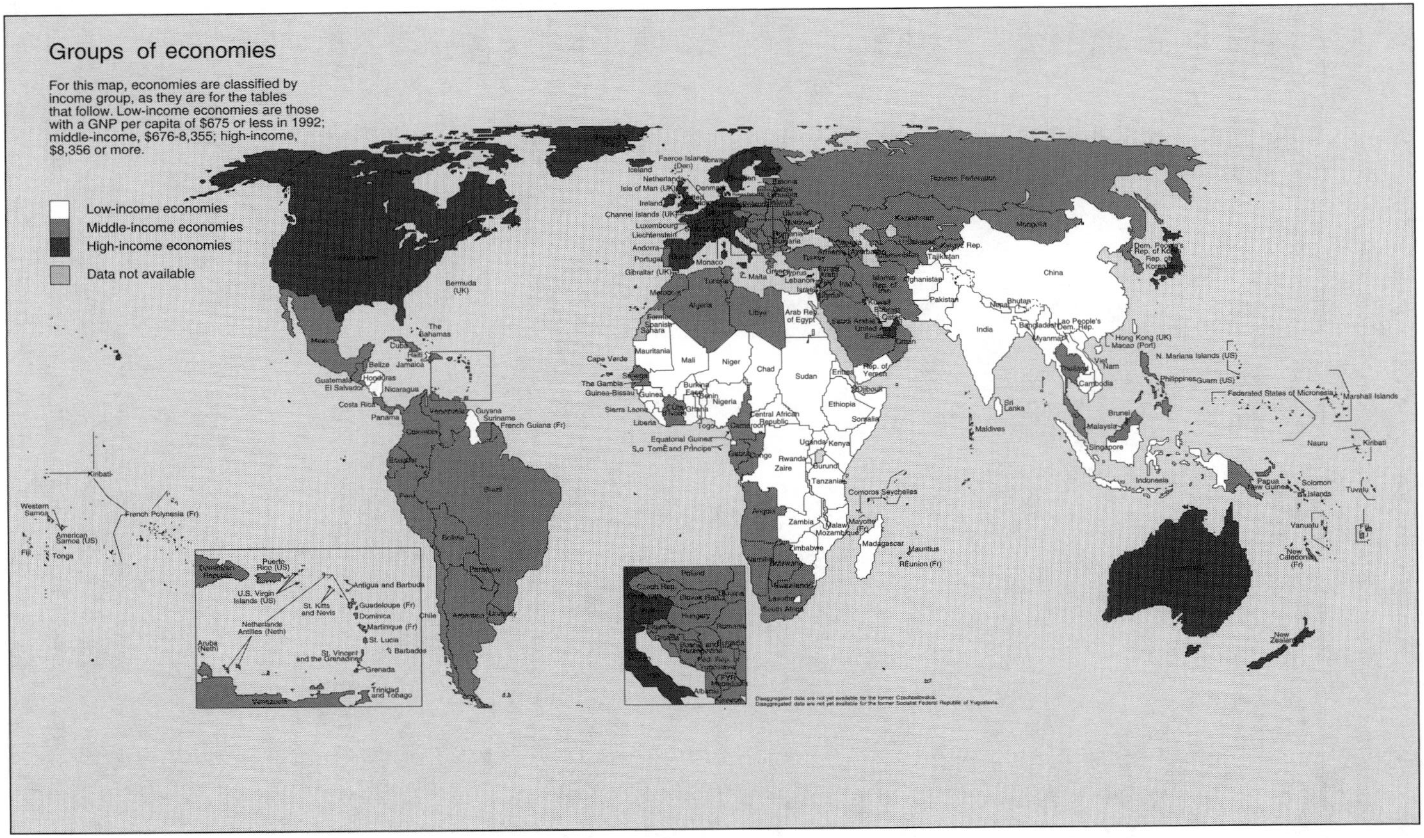

Groups of economies

For this map, economies are classified by income group, as they are for the tables that follow. Low-income economies are those with a GNP per capita of $675 or less in 1992; middle-income, $676–8,355; high-income, $8,356 or more.

Low-income economies
Middle-income economies
High-income economies

Data not available

SOURCE: From *World Development Report 1993*, by The World Bank. Copyright © 1993 by The International Bank for Reconstruction and Development/The World Bank. "Groups of Economies," pp. 234–35.

Figure 18.7:   Indicators of Living Standards for Selected Countries (1991)

	Per Capita GNP (1991 $ US)	Average Annual Growth Rate (%) (1980–1991)	Population (millions) (1991)	Average Annual Growth Rate of Population (%) (1980–1991)	Life Expectancy at Birth (years)	Infant Mortality (per 1000 live births, 1991)	Adult Illiteracy (%) (1990)	Per Capita Daily Calorie Supply (1989)	Per Capita Energy Consumption (kg of oil equivalent)
High-Income Countries									
1. Japan	26 930	3.6	124	0.5	79	5	<5	2 956	3 552
2. Sweden	25 110	1.7	9	0.3	78	6	<5	2 960	5 901
3. U.S.	22 240	1.7	253	0.9	76	9	<5	3 671	7 681
4. Canada	20 440	2.0	27	1.2	77	7	<5	3 482	9 390
All high-income countries	21 050	2.3		0.6	77	8	<5	3 409	5 106
Middle-Income Countries									
5. Brazil	2 940	0.5	151	2.0	66	58	19	2 751	908
6. Hungary	2 720	0.7	10	-0.2	70	16	n.a.	3 644	2 830
7. Iran	2 170	-1.3	58	3.6	65	68	46	3 181	1 078
8. Thailand	1 570	5.9	57	1.9	69	27	7	2 316	438
All middle-income countries	2 480	0.3		1.8	68	38	21	2 860	1 351
Low-Income Countries									
9. Honduras	580	-0.5	5	3.3	65	49	27	2 247	181
10. China	370	7.8	1150	1.5	69	38	27	2 639	602
11. India	330	3.2	867	2.1	60	90	52	2 229	337
12. Madagascar	210	-2.5	12	3.0	51	114	20	2 158	39
All low-income countries	350	3.9		2.0	62	71	40	2 406	376
World	4010	1.2		1.7	66	53	35	2 642	1343

While the average per capita real GDP of high-income countries is about 60 times that for low-income countries, the average growth rates per capita are about the same for high- and low-income countries, above the world average. Whereas overall middle- and low-income countries have population growth rates higher than the world average, high-income countries have lower population growth rates. Overall, life expectancy, daily calorie supply, and energy consumption rise with per capita income, while infant mortality and adult illiteracy fall with per capita income.

Sources: From *World Development Report 1993*, by The World Bank. Copyright © 1993 by The International Bank for Reconstruction and Development/The World Bank.

Table 1, "Basic Indicators," pp. 238–39; Table 5, "Commercial Energy," pp. 246–47; Table 26, "Population Growth and Projections," pp. 288–89; Table 28, "Health and Nutrition," pp. 292–93.

From *World Development Report 1992*, by The World Bank. Copyright © 1992 by The International Bank for Reconstruction and Development/The World Bank.

Table 28, figures from last column of "Health and Nutrition," pp. 272–73.

world) each consuming more than 25 times what citizens of low-income countries consume.

The Gap Between Rich and Poor

When measured by increases in per capita income, recent average rates of economic growth in poorer countries have exceeded those in rich countries. Between 1950 and 1989, for example, the average annual growth rate of per capita GDP for all low-income and middle-income countries was 2.7 percent, compared with the 2.3 percent average for high-income countries.

However, there was a tremendous range of growth rates. Asian nations not included in the high-income category achieved an average growth rate of 3.6 percent in their per capita GDP between 1950 and 1989, largely due to the performance of Asia's "little dragons" and, more recently, China. In contrast, per capita incomes grew by only 1.2 percent on average in Latin American countries and by only 0.8 percent in sub-Saharan African countries. In fact, some incomes in Latin America and sub-Saharan countries fell during the 1980s—a period often called the "lost decade" for the poor.

Despite higher average growth rates in poor countries since 1950, per capita incomes in most of these countries have risen less quickly in dollar terms than in industrially advanced countries. This apparent paradox stems from the relative size of per capita incomes in each group of countries and the fact that growth is exponential. So, for example, a hypothetical country with a per capita income of $1000 growing at 6 percent annually adds $60 to this figure in one year. In contrast, a rich country like Canada with a $20 000 per capita income can add a much higher amount of $200 simply by growing at 1 percent a year.

Thinking About Economics

Is expressing a country's per capita GDP or GNP in American dollars enough to indicate the average income of the country's citizens?

Not necessarily, for two reasons. Recall from Chapter 10 that these statistics have limitations—both quantitative and qualitative—when used as indicators of living standards. For example, neither GDP nor GNP reflect certain nonmarket activities, the quality of products, the distribution of income, and the various environmental consequences of growth. While expressing various countries' incomes in U.S. dollars allows us to compare their value on international markets, this does not tell us what an income will buy within the domestic economy. As any traveller knows, the equivalent in local currency to US$1 can buy significantly different products in one country than in another; for example, the United States and India. So that incomes can be compared more effectively, economists have developed the concept of purchasing-power parity (PPP), which is a method of adjusting for these differences in domestic prices. As a result, the incomes of most low-income countries are adjusted upward. Using this method, it is estimated that in 1990 the industrially advanced countries, with 15 percent of the world's population, accounted for 54 percent of world GDP, while countries of the former Soviet Bloc accounted for 11 percent, and other countries made up the remaining 34 percent. Based on these estimates, the role of poorer countries in the world economy is gradually increasing.

The Dynamics of Development

economic development: an increase in a country's per capita income that is accompanied by a general rise in living standards

Economic development is an increase in a country's per capita income that is accompanied by a rise in living standards for the bulk of its population. In other words, it requires both economic growth *and* a widespread improvement in living standards. For most economists and planners, economic development is desirable and is associated with a structural change from a traditional mixed economy to a modern mixed economy. However, not everyone embraces economic development or the modernization that accompanies it—especially those people who wish to maintain tradition and who oppose the upheaval caused by social and economic change. People who are concerned about the environmental effects of rapid industrialization may also oppose certain aspects of economic development.

vicious circle of poverty: a cycle whereby low standards of living lead to slow growth, thus keeping standards of living low in the future

Low-income countries face a daunting task in attempting to foster economic development. Many of these countries find themselves trapped in a **vicious circle of poverty**—a cycle whereby low standards of living lead to slow growth, thus keeping standards of living low in the future. As Figure 18.8 illustrates, low per capita incomes tend to cause both low investment and rapid population growth. These, in turn, perpetuate the focus on labour-intensive production, which restrains productivity, which dampens economic growth and keeps incomes low.

Low Investment

Low incomes mean that households must use most of their earnings for consumption. Thus only a minor proportion of income is saved in most low-income countries, which makes the financing of investment projects

Figure 18.8: The Vicious Circle of Poverty

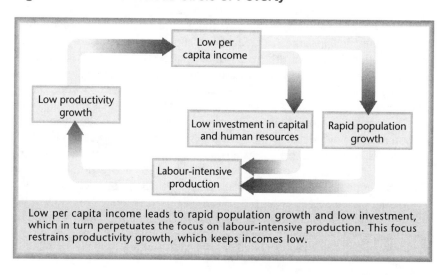

Low per capita income leads to rapid population growth and low investment, which in turn perpetuates the focus on labour-intensive production. This focus restrains productivity growth, which keeps incomes low.

difficult. Widespread poverty also means that product markets in most low-income countries are relatively small, reducing the means for business to engage in profitable investment.

Economic and social conditions in most low-income countries constrain investment in other, more subtle ways as well. Traditions that do not encourage competition or profit-making, for example, can inhibit entrepreneurship.

Rapid Population Growth

Not only are population levels in most low-income countries high relative to supplies of capital and natural resources, but current rates of population growth are increasing this discrepancy. Figure 18.9 outlines population levels in various parts of the world, along with estimates of how these levels will change in coming decades. Among the poorer countries, those in Africa and the Middle East have the highest estimated growth rates between 1990 and 2000, while those in Europe and Central Asia have the lowest. With only one exception, these rates are higher than the expected average growth rates in high-income countries.

As these data suggest, low incomes and rapid population growth tend to go together. They are linked for a number of reasons. To some extent, large families are seen as an economic necessity in low-income countries: given that poor families in these countries tend to have no income security nor pension, more children can provide more labour now to help the

Figure 18.9:   Global Population Trends

	Population (millions)			Estimated Annual Growth Rate (%)	
	1990	**2000 (estimated)**	**2030 (estimated)**	**1990–2000**	**2000–2030**
Low and Middle-Income Countries	4445	5294	7736	1.8	1.3
Sub-Saharan Africa	474	635	1313	3.0	2.4
East Asia and Pacific	1641	1891	2442	1.4	0.9
South Asia	1128	1368	2004	1.9	1.3
Europe and Central Asia	489	517	566	0.6	0.5
Middle East and Northern Africa	236	315	600	2.9	2.2
Latin America and the Caribbean	438	516	721	1.7	1.1
High-Income Countries	817	864	920	0.6	0.2
World	5262	6157	8664	1.6	1.2

According to estimates, the world's population will increase at an average annual rate of 1.6 percent to 6.157 billion in the year 2000, then at an average annual rate of 1.2 percent to 8.664 billion in the year 2030. Most of this growth will take place in the low- and middle-income countries, with estimated average annual growth rates of 1.8 percent (years 1990 to 2000) and 1.3 percent (years 2000 to 2030) and the highest rates in Africa and the Middle East.

SOURCE: From *World Development Report 1993*, by The World Bank. Copyright © 1993 by The International Bank for Reconstruction and Development/The World Bank.

Table A.1, "Population (midyear) and average annual growth," p. 199.

family and later to give the parents some security in old age. At the same time, high infant mortality encourages greater birth rates. These factors, combined with little birth control (due to economic and social factors), result in rapid population growth.

The combination of higher incomes and government-sponsored birth control programs is gradually reducing population growth in many low-income countries, and this trend should continue, as shown in Figure 18.9. However, the projected increases in world population levels over the next few decades are still staggeringly high. The global population is expected to grow from 5.2 billion in 1990 to 8.7 billion by 2030, of which 7.7 billion will live in poorer countries.

Labour-Intensive Production

Low investment means that capital accumulates slowly, while rapid population growth leads to large increases in the supply of labour. Both factors are jointly responsible for creating large supplies of labour in relation to capital resources, thereby causing production in most low-income countries to be labour-intensive.

Low Productivity Growth

Because of labour-intensive production, it is difficult for producers to make use of technological innovations or to achieve the high levels of output needed to take advantage of economies of scale. Production remains less efficient, constraining growth in productivity. Without productivity growth, higher per capita incomes are impossible.

Strategies for Development

While difficult, it is possible to break the vicious circle of poverty, as the recent success of the "little dragons" shows. Breaking the cycle involves three domestic strategies: ensuring a stable political and economic system, investing in resources, and controlling population growth. At the same time that low-income countries are using such domestic strategies, other, higher-income countries can assist with two international strategies: trade liberalization and foreign aid.

Political and Economic Stability

A stable political system and economy are preconditions for development, since political turmoil and wide swings in output and prices both inhibit saving and investment. One of the most important development tasks of governments in low-income countries therefore is to ensure a stable political system and a smoothly running economy. Frequent changes in the country's laws discourage business activity, as do "quick-fix" schemes by governments that involve public spending financed through persistent budget deficits or inflationary monetary policy. In some countries, such as China, economic development has been associated with political repression. However, some recent studies suggest that, in general, economic development is enhanced if it is accompanied by political freedom and democracy. This is because a democratic political system tends to contribute to long-run political and economic stability.

Investing in Resources

For all low-income countries, government investment in human capital through education, health, and social programs is an important component of development. For example, greater education increases the supply of trained labour, which leads to long-term improvements in productivity. As a start, ensuring basic literacy through universal primary education enhances the opportunities for citizens to improve their own living standards.

Many governments in low-income countries also employ programs to stimulate investment in capital goods by trying to encourage the saving that is needed to finance this investment. In market economies, public policy-makers can impose taxes that promote private saving and discourage consumption. These savings can then be made available through financial markets to domestic businesses for investment. However, there is no guarantee that private saving will flow to domestic businesses. All too frequently, these savings leave the country. This problem, known as capital flight, is most acute in countries where internal conditions hinder the potential for profitable investment. While this problem diminished in the early 1990s, the estimated flight of private savings from poorer countries in the 1980s sometimes exceeded $100 billion annually. The total stock of savings that flowed out of these countries is estimated to have reached $700 billion by 1990.

In command economies, the investment process is carried out by public authorities themselves, who channel government revenues to public enterprises for investment. Again, these programs have possible drawbacks, since public investment projects can be chosen for political reasons rather than for their potential economic benefits.

Population Control

Governments in low-income countries can use several approaches to limit population growth. One way is to introduce voluntary birth control programs, which operate by providing incentives for those who participate. Such programs have been used in many low-income countries with varying degrees of success. In India, for example, where such programs have been common for several decades, the annual rate of population growth between 1980 and 1991 remained at a relatively high 2.1 percent. A more stringent approach is illustrated by China's "one-child" policy, which imposes financial penalties on parents who have more than one child. This program has successfully reduced the country's annual rate of population growth between 1980 and 1991 to 1.5 percent. However, the success of this type of compulsory approach must be weighed against the loss of freedom for citizens to make their own decisions regarding family size.

Additional policies and programs can indirectly affect population growth. For example, governments can provide basic social services to the poor involving health care, nutrition, and primary education, as well as family planning. These—alongside other policies and programs that develop new markets, enhance employment opportunities, stimulate investment, generate higher incomes, and improve income distribution—tend to encourage smaller families. Although powerful, such policies and programs can be difficult to implement when they clash with traditions.

Trade Liberalization

The export-driven growth of the "little dragons" shows that self-sustaining development in most low-income countries depends on making efficient use of their own resources, especially labour, to gain the benefits that flow from international trade. Therefore, one of the most important forms of assistance that industrially advanced countries can provide is to make their own markets more open to the exports of low-income countries—especially manufactured goods, which are often subject to trade barriers. This causes short-run adjustment costs for higher-income countries, but economists generally believe that the long-term benefits to low-income countries of such freer trade—as well as to the higher-income countries themselves—far outweigh the costs.

Foreign Aid

While liberalized trade has important long-term implications for international development, direct aid from higher-income countries is essential to breaking the vicious circle of poverty, especially for the poorest of the low-income countries. Most high-income countries run aid programs through their own national agencies; in Canada, government aid is administered by the Canadian International Development Agency (CIDA). A co-ordinated program of development assistance is also provided by two important international lending institutions: the International Monetary Fund (IMF) and the World Bank. While the IMF concentrates on short-term loans to governments, the World Bank uses its financial support from high-income countries to make loans to low-income countries for long-term investment projects that would otherwise not be funded. In particular, it focuses on basic health and education programs as well as on projects that provide utilities such as electrical power and running water. Nongovernmental organizations (NGOs) in high-income countries also provide aid. Recently, governments have begun to fund the work of several NGOs.

Despite the benefits that foreign aid programs can bring, certain programs have been criticized for being misdirected and badly implemented. Another criticism is that the aid is sometimes biased toward certain political aims or development paths, given for the political or commercial ends of the donor country, or designed to favour future markets. For example, in the past, donors tended to favour industry over agriculture, and showed a bias toward large-scale projects rather than more basic, but essential, assistance to small-scale producers.

The IMF and the World Bank have been criticized for such large-scale bias. Also, both commonly require recipient countries to cut back on government spending, reduce their trade barriers, and promote competition within their domestic product markets before they can receive further loans. These organizations believe that these types of constraints are necessary to ensure that aid is effectively used. However, critics argue that these requirements often hurt the poorest groups within the low-income countries and represent interference in the internal affairs of independent nations.

BRIEF REVIEW

1. Countries may be classified as high-income, middle-income, and low-income. At one extreme, high-income countries have modern mixed market economies based on capital-intensive production and the use of skilled labour. At the other extreme, low-income countries tend to have traditional mixed economies, use labour-intensive processes, and may have a history of colonialism.

2. Other classifications used are industrially advanced countries, newly industrializing countries, and less-developed countries.

3. While, on average, the economic growth rates of middle- and low-income countries is high, the gap between rich and poor countries continues to widen in real dollar terms.

4. Economic development occurs when there is a rise in a country's per capita income accompanied by a general improvement in living standards. It is associated with a structural change from a traditional mixed to a modern mixed economy.

5. In the vicious circle of poverty, low incomes, low investment, and rapid population growth tend to perpetuate labour-intensive processes, which restrains productivity and economic growth and keeps incomes low.

6. Strategies for breaking the circle of poverty include domestic strategies ensuring political and economic stability, investing in resources, and controlling population and international strategies (liberalizing trade and foreign aid).

DEVELOPING INTERPRETATION SKILLS

Superstars of Development

The East Asian Miracle

Despite the obstacles, countries can spur development. This editorial describes the example of outstanding growth in the Pacific Rim region.

Average Growth of GNP Per Capita, 1965–90

*High Performing Asian Economies: Hong Kong, Indonesia, Japan, Malaysia, Republic of Korea, Singapore, Taiwan–Province of China , and Thailand

SOURCES: From *The East Asian Miracle*, by The World Bank. Copyright © 1993 by The International Bank for Reconstruction and Development/The World Bank. Figure 1, p. 2. Reprinted by permission of Oxford University Press Inc.

The Asian "tigers" or the "little dragons." However you group them, the handful of countries strung along the western edge of the Pacific Rim are, quite simply, the biggest economic success story the world has ever seen. Since 1965 the eight leading economies of the region—Japan, Hong Kong, Singapore, Thailand, Indonesia, Republic of Korea, Malaysia and Taiwan–Province of China—have grown twice as fast, on average, as the wealthy West and three times as fast as Latin America and the Middle East. In the same period, their share of world trade has grown from nine per cent to 21 per cent.

Nor have the proceeds of this boom flowed exclusively to the rich. Rapid growth has been accompanied by a rapid decline in economic inequality. In the Republic of Korea, the richest fifth of the population now has about seven times as much income as the poorest fifth, about the same ratio as in Australia or France. In Kenya, by contrast the income of the richest fifth is about 22 times that of the poorest.

Living standards have improved as income inequality has fallen. The proportion of Indonesians living in absolute poverty has dropped from 58 per cent to 17 per cent in the span of one generation. In 1960, the average resident of the Republic of Korea had a life

expectancy of 53 years. The figure today is 72 years.

What is behind this remarkable success? Outsiders have tended to credit the "Confucian values" of the region—a high regard for education, a solid work ethic—and these undoubtedly played a role. But this explanation does not account for the Asian countries, such as Burma [or Myanmar] and the Philippines, that have failed to take off. Just a few decades ago, scholars were blaming other "Confucian values"—a fixation with hierarchy and tradition, for example—for the area's backwardness. So the answer must lie beyond culture. But where?

The World Bank recently published what is perhaps the most thorough study yet on the issue. *The East Asian Miracle* methodically dissects the methods of each of the eight high-performing Asian economies to find out what worked, and why. The answers are surprisingly commonplace. The Asian superstars advanced because they excelled at the "accumulation of physical and human capital." That meant getting the basics right in a few areas.

Education

Governments focused their education spending on the crucial lower grades, first by providing universal primary education and later by increasing the availability of secondary education. In contrast to other developing countries, which lavished public funds on expensive university facilities, their spending on post-secondary systems was limited, and the money went mainly toward technical and vocational programs. These measures produced the richest form of human capital: a highly educated workforce.

Savings and Investment

The eight superstars have phenomenally high rates of savings and investment. Savings, lower than Latin America's in 1965, now run at 36 per cent of gross domestic product, twice as high as the Latin American figure. The investment rate is also double Latin America's. Governments encouraged savings by creating secure, bank-based financial systems and, in some cases, by requiring citizens to make high pension fund contributions throughout their working lives. Investment was encouraged by establishing investment-friendly tax regimes and keeping tariffs on imported capital goods low, thus encouraging domestic industries to invest in new plant and equipment.

Fiscal and Monetary Management

All eight governments studied by the Bank were careful to prevent running up high budget deficits that would fuel inflation. In the past 30 years, inflation in the eight has averaged about nine per cent a year, compared with 18 per cent in other low- and middle-income economies.

In addition to these basic strategies, some of the eight have used various forms of active government intervention to guide their economies. This fact has often been waved about by left-leaning economists as evidence that government-directed economies can work. If Japan Inc. and Malaysia Inc. are successful, they say, Brazil Inc., Canada Inc. or Quebec Inc. can be too.

The World Bank is not so sure. It concedes that the eight have often intervened in the market to promote growth—for instance, by subsidizing credit to certain industries and protecting domestic manufacturers with high tariffs. But such interventions, such as Singapore's attempt to drive out labour-intensive industry by arbitrarily raising wages, were spectacular flops. Others made little difference.

The Bank says the one type of intervention that has clearly succeeded is export promotion—the use of subsidies and other policies to sell more goods abroad. But that strategy succeeded only because the East Asian countries had trained, professional bureaucracies to carry it out. Many other developing countries do not have that advantage. And even if they did, the Bank questions whether export promotion can work in the 1990s, now that many export-subsidy and export-credit programs are prohibited under the General Agreement on Tariffs and Trade (GATT).

That leaves the fundamentals. While some types of market intervention may work some of the time, the lesson of East Asia is that governments of developing countries are generally best to concentrate on the things they do best: investing in education, enacting policies that encourage savings and investment, and controlling inflation through firm control of their finances.

These are the humdrum "secrets" of the East Asian miracle. They worked in Japan, Hong Kong, Singapore, Thailand, Indonesia, Republic of Korea, Malaysia and Taiwan–Province of China. They are beginning to work in Chile, Argentina and Mexico. They will even work in the still-developing Dominion of Canada.

SOURCE: Abridged from "The ordinary secrets of the East Asian miracle," (editorial), in *The Globe and Mail*, 22 November 1993, p. A14.

1. What lesson does the "East Asian Miracle" have for Canada?

2. What opinion of the "East Asian Miracle" is the editorial offering? Support your answer.

3. Suggest some of the opportunity costs of the economic growth described in the article.

ADVANCING

ECONOMIC

THOUGHT

Labour Without Limit

W. Arthur Lewis and the Dynamics of Economic Development

Lewis and His Influence

The well-known contemporary economist, W. Arthur Lewis (born 1915), has added considerably to understanding economic growth in low-income countries. Born on the Caribbean island of St. Lucia, he pursued his university education in Britain. Lewis then taught at the University of Manchester and the University of the West Indies before moving to Princeton University in the United States. During his academic career, he has been able to draw on wide-ranging practical experience as an economic adviser to several African governments and to the United Nations. Knighted by the British government in 1963, Lewis won a Nobel Prize in 1979 for his contributions to the study of economic development.

Lewis's Model of Development

In his best-known paper, "Economic Development With Unlimited Supplies of Labour," Lewis created a model to explain development in traditional mixed economies that combine an urban industrial sector with a much larger rural traditional sector. According to Lewis, this situation leads to a distinctive type of labour market. The traditional sector is dominated by family farming and is heavily oversupplied with workers. Because wages for this agricultural work provide only the minimum necessities of life and because many workers are surplus, these workers are easily attracted to the urban industrial sector. As a result of these factors, the urban industrial sector—which Lewis referred to as the capitalist sector—has an unlimited supply of labour at a constant wage.

As Lewis recognized, this model applies more to some countries than to others:

> It is obviously not true of the United Kingdom, or of Northwest Europe. It is not true either of some of the countries usually now lumped together as underdeveloped; for example there is an acute shortage of male labour in some parts of Africa and of Latin America. On the other hand it is obviously the relevant assumption for the economies of Egypt, of India, or of Jamaica.[1]

W. Arthur Lewis

SOURCE: The Bettmann Archive

The Labour Market in the Industrial Sector   Because the supply of labour is unlimited, the labour supply curve in the industrial sector is perfectly elastic—in other words, it is a horizontal line. Lewis assumed the industrial sector wage to be 30 percent above the wage received in the agricultural sector. The figure shows a hypothetical example. If we assume that the agricultural wage is $10 per hour, then the industrial wage will be $13 per hour [$10 + (10 × 0.30)]. This gives a labour supply curve (S) at the wage of $13. Given the demand for labour expressed in the curve D_0, the initial equilibrium in this labour market occurs at an employment level of 100 000 workers (point *a*).

Growth and Employment in the Industrial Sector

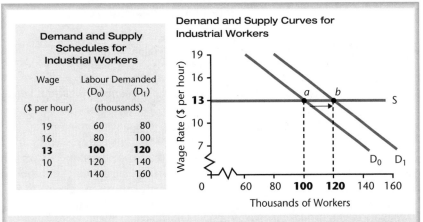

Demand and Supply Schedules for Industrial Workers

Wage	Labour Demanded	
	(D_0)	(D_1)
($ per hour)	(thousands)	
19	60	80
16	80	100
13	**100**	**120**
10	120	140
7	140	160

Initially, equilibrium in the labour market for industrial workers occurs at a wage of $13 per hour and 100 000 workers (point *a*). As more capital is used in the industrial sector, the demand for labour increases, shifting the demand from D_0 to D_1. The new equilibrium occurs at the constant wage of $13 per hour and 120 000 workers (point *b*).

Lewis assumed that most saving in low-income countries is carried out by employers in the industrial sector as they reinvest their profits. Rather than attributing low levels of saving to low standards of living, he suggested that the main problem in these countries is the small size of their industrial sectors, and the consequent lack of profits for reinvestment:

> This model...helps us to face squarely the nature of the economic problem of backward countries. If we ask, "Why do they save so little?", the truthful answer is not "Because they are so poor," as we might be tempted to conclude.... The truthful answer is "Because their capitalist sector is so small" (remembering that "capitalist" here does not mean private capitalist, but would apply equally to state capitalist). If they had a larger capitalist sector, profits would be a greater part of their national income, and saving and investment would also be relatively larger.[2]

The quickest way to counteract low saving, according to Lewis, is to focus investment on the industrial sector. As more capital is used in this sector, the demand for labour increases, shown in the figure by the shift from D_0 to D_1, which increases employment in the sector to 120 000 workers at the fixed wage of $13 (point *b*). Because increased demand does not mean increased labour costs, profits and output can expand quickly in the industrial sector. By increasing profits over what they could have been, this strategy of focusing investment on the industrial sector means that capitalists can reinvest their larger profits to push up production and profits even further. As a result, the industrial sector expands. At the same time, the traditional sector remains unchanged, since labour resources that had shifted to the industrial sector had been surplus agricultural labour.

Relevance for Today

With its stress on industrial expansion as the key to fostering economic growth, Lewis's model has influenced development strategies in many countries. Supporters of the model say that it explains the pivotal role of the industrial sector in promoting economic development. However, critics question the underlying assumption that the increased use of capital in the industrial sector leads to higher employment. These critics argue that technological progress might mean instead that employers invest in labour-saving machinery, which decreases the employment of labour. Critics also point out that many of the countries most successful in raising living standards over the past few decades have initially stressed investment in agriculture rather than in industry.[3]

NOTES

[1] W. Arthur Lewis, "Economic development with unlimited supplies of labour," in A.N. Agarwala and S.P. Singh (eds.), *The Economics of Underdevelopment* (New Delhi: Oxford University Press, 1958), p.401.
[2] *Ibid.*, p. 419.
[3] Criticisms of Lewis's model can be found in Michael P. Todaro, *Economic Development*, 5th ed. (New York: Longman, 1994), pp. 74–79; A.P. Thirlwall, *Growth and Development* (London: Macmillan, 1982), pp. 80–87.

1. Suggest what kinds of activities domestic governments and foreign aid agencies would encourage in countries where Lewis's model is considered relevant. Explain your responses.

2. a) Research the economic history of one of the following nations: Nigeria, El Salvador, Cuba, Nicaragua, Mexico, Indonesia, or Brazil. Then write a report in which you analyze the extent to which the nation's economic history illustrates Lewis's model.
   b) Compare your findings with those of a classmate.

Key Concepts

exponential growth
Rule of 72
technological progress
research and development expenditures
World Bank
high-income countries
middle-income countries

low-income countries
industrially advanced countries
newly industrializing countries
less-developed countries
economic development
vicious circle of poverty

Developing Application and Analysis Skills

1. a) Suppose a hypothetical country called Alpha produces only oil-drilling equipment and petroleum products. Sketch Alpha's initial production possibilities curve.

b) Demonstrate on your graph the effect of each of the following events:
   i) Robotic technology to produce oil-drilling equipment is introduced.
   ii) Next, war is declared on Petrolia, a neighbouring country. Soon after, Petrolia's oil fields are seized by the enemy country.
   iii) Then, despite its neutrality, 65 percent of Alpha's infrastructure is destroyed by air attacks.
   iv) Finally, at the war's end, Alpha's Minister of the Economy dictates a reconstruction policy focusing on the production of capital goods.

2. Use the Rule of 72 to answer the following questions:

a) What annual rate of economic growth does a country need to double its per capita GDP in 12 years?

b) If a student buys a $1000 Canada Savings Bond that pays compound interest at a rate of 8 percent per year, how many years will it take for the interest paid to equal the value of the bond?

c) If the current rate of inflation is 4 percent, how many years will it take for money to lose half of its purchasing power?

3. To what extent does growth in the quantity of labour available to a nation have a significant impact on the following? Explain each answer.

a) the nation's real GDP

b) the nation's standard of living

4. Draw causal loop diagrams to demonstrate the following:

a) the positive results of economic growth

b) the negative results of economic growth

5. a) Explain the vicious circle of poverty.

b) Create a causal loop diagram demonstrating how certain strategies can be used to break the circle.

6. a) Using a wide range of material—newspapers, TV news broadcasts, magazines, computer databases, and so on—research and analyze the current circumstances and concerns of one low-income country, plus current policies and programs affecting it.

b) Present your findings in a research essay.

7. a) Form three groups, each to assume the role of either low-income countries, middle-income countries, or high-income countries.

b) In role, discuss in your group your economic and political circumstances, and your perspective.

c) Suppose there is an international call for a renewed effort to have all countries achieve economic growth and high living standards. In your group, consider your response to this call.

d) In a class forum, present your group's circumstances, perspectives, and responses.

 # Notes

Part 1

p. 3   Burke quoted in Paul A. Samuelson et al., *Economics*, 6th Cdn. ed. (Toronto: McGraw-Hill Ryerson, 1988), p. 2.

Chapter 1
p. 4   Shaw quoted in Paul Wonnacott et al., *Economics*, 3rd Cdn. ed. (Toronto: McGraw-Hill Ryerson, 1990), p. 3.

p. 6   Ghandi quoted in Robert Andrews, *The Concise Columbia Dictionary of Quotations* (New York: Columbia University Press, 1987), p. 130.

p. 30   Economic Council of Canada, *First Annual Review* (Ottawa: Queen's Printer, 1964).

p. 31   John Robert Colombo, ed., *The 1994 Canadian Global Almanac* (Toronto: Macmillan, 1993), p. 84.

p. 32   *Ibid.*, p. 180.

p. 33   World Resources Institute, *The 1993 Information Please Environmental Almanac* (New York: Houghton Mifflin, 1992), pp. 303–5, 314–15, 329.

Chapter 2
p. 42   H. Liebenstein, "Bandwagon, Snob, and Veblen Effects in the Theory of Consumer Demand," in *The Quarterly Journal of Economics*, vol. 64 (1950), pp. 203–4.

p. 60   Kenneth Kidd, "Root Awakening," in *The Globe and Mail Report on Business Magazine* (December 1993), pp. 72–79.

Chapter 3
p. 72   Publilius Syrus quoted in John Bartlett, *Familiar Quotations* (Boston: Little, Brown and Company, 1980), p. 112.

p. 82   Ingrid A. Bryan, *Economic Policies in Canada*, 2nd ed. (Toronto: Butterworths, 1986), p. 27; Richard R. Barichello, *Technical Report No. E/I 2: The Economics of Canadian Dairy Industry Regulation* (Ottawa: Economic Council of Canada, 1981), pp. 21, 24.

p. 86   Denton Marks, *Housing Affordability and Rent Regulation*, Research Study No. 8 by the Commission of Inquiry into Residential Tenancies (1984), p. 98.

Part 2

p. 93   Hutcheson quoted in *Familiar Quotations*, p. 305.

Chapter 4
p. 94   Clark quoted in Samuelson, *Economics*, p. 590.

p. 96   Statistics Canada, *Small Business in Canada: A Statistical Profile 1984–1986*, (April 1989), cat. no. 61-231, pp. 8, 13; *Annual Report of the Minister of Industry, Science and Technology under the Corporations and Labour Unions*

Return Act, Part 1—Corporations, 1988 (October 1991), cat. no. 61-210, pp. 85, 188.

Chapter 5
p. 124 Surplis quoted in Robert M. Hamilton and Dorothy Shields, *The Dictionary of Canadian Quotations and Phrases*, revised and enlarged edition (Toronto: McClelland and Stewart, 1979), p. 134.

p. 128 *The Economist* (12 September 1992), p. 76.

p. 128 *Marketshare* (11 December 1993), p. 3.

p. 138 C.G. McFetridge (research co-ordinator), *Canadian Industry in Transition* (Toronto: University of Toronto Press, 1986), pp. 139–42.

p. 140 John Jewkes, David Sawers, and Richard Stillerman, *The Sources of Invention*, rev. ed. (New York: St. Martin's Press, 1968).

Chapter 6
p. 148 Adam Smith, *The Wealth of Nations, Books I—III* (Harmondsworth, UK: Penguin Books, 1983), p. 119.

Chapter 7
p. 182 Ostry quoted in "Canada Inc.," in *The Globe and Mail Report on Business Magazine* (June 1993), p. 56.

p. 195 Richard G. Harris, "Who Gets the Jobs: Computers or Imports?" in *Policy Options* (July–August 1994), pp. 41–42.

Chapter 8
p. 206 Jean Howarth, "Treasure Island," in Elspeth Hannan, et al., *Environment in Perspective* (Toronto: Harcourt Brace & Company, 1993), p. 64.

p. 209 Statistics Canada, *Income Distributions by Size in Canada, 1992* (December 1993), cat. 13-207, p. 34.

p. 212 Ontario Minister Responsible for Women's Issues, *Green Paper on Pay Equity* (November 1985) pp. 9–10.

p. 217 *The 1994 Canadian Global Almanac*, p. 200; Labour Canada, *Directory of Labour Organizations in Canada, 1992–93*, cat. no. 2-2-1992, p. xv.

p. 222 Morley Gunderson and W. Craig Riddell, *Labour Market Economics*, 3rd ed. (Toronto: McGraw-Hill Ryerson, 1993), pp. 401–2.

p. 224 *The 1994 Canadian Global Almanac*, p. 31.

p. 241 Brenda Daglish, "Are They Worth It?" in *Maclean's* (9 May 1994), pp. 34–37; Helen Cordes, "How Much Dough for the Big Cheese?" in *Utne Reader* (March/April 1992), pp. 17–18.

Chapter 9
p. 242 By permission of the Estate of Donald Creighton.

p. 250 Statistics Canada, *Income Distributions by Size in Canada, 1992* (December 1993), cat. no. 13-207, p. 42.

p. 251 *Ibid.*, pp. 16–18, 181, 186–87. Francois Vaillancourt, *Income Distribution and Economic Security in Canada* (Toronto: University of Toronto Press, 1985), p. 18.

p. 253 *Income Distributions by Size in Canada, 1992*, pp. 170, 172.

p. 256 Canadian Tax Foundation, *The National Finances: An Analysis of the Revenues and Expenditures of the Government of Canada 1993; The 1994 Canadian Global Almanac*, pp. 164–70.

p. 258   *The 1994 Canadian Global Almanac*, p. 166.

p. 264   *The National Finances*, p. 7:34.

p. 265   Richard A. Musgrave, et al., *Public Finance in Theory and Practice*, First Cdn. Ed. (Toronto: McGraw-Hill Ryerson, 1987), pp. 297, 384–85, 444.

p. 276   Ontario Fair Tax Commision, *Wealth Tax Working Group Report* (March 1993), p. 40.

Part 3

p. 279   John Maynard Keynes, *The Collected Writing of John Maynard Keynes: Vol. IV, A Tract on Monetary Reform* (London: Macmillan, 1971), p. 65.

Chapter 10

p. 280   Martin Luther King, Jr., *Strength to Love* (New York: Harper & Row, 1963), p. 64.

p. 288   Statistics Canada, *National Income and Expenditure Accounts, Quarterly Estimates, Fourth Quarter 1993* (March 1994), cat. no. 13-001, pp. 4–5.

p. 290   *The National Finances*, p. 3:2.

p. 291   *National Income and Expenditure Accounts*, pp. 4–5.

p. 293   Statistics Canada, *Demographic Statistics*, 1993, cat. no. 91-213, p. 66, and *see* Figure 11-4.

p. 293   *See* Chapter 12 and Figure 11-4.

p. 293   OECD, *The OECD Observer*, no. 188 (June/July 1994), pp. 24–25.

p. 294   Statistics Canada, *Canadian Economic Observer* (May 1994), cat. no. 11-010, p. 3.16.

Chapter 11

p. 306   Tobin quoted in Samuelson, *Economics*, p. 72.

p. 317   Statistics Canada, *Labour Force Annual Averages 1993* (February 1994), cat. no. 71-220, p. C-2.

p. 319   *See* Developing Interpretation Skills—The Age of the Part-Timer: The Shift From Full-Time Work.

p. 320   Economic Council of Canada, *First Annual Review*, p. 38.

p. 323   *See* Chapter 15, Developing Interpretation Skills—Debates Over Full Employment: How Should It Be Defined?

p. 324   *Labour Market Economics*, pp. 212, 544.

p. 326   Bernard Fortin and André Bernier, "The Welfare Cost of Unemployment in Quebec: Harberger's Triangle Meets Okun's Gap," in *Canadian Journal of Economics*, vol. 21 (1) (February 1988), p. 162; A. Okun, "Potential GNP: Its Measurement and Significance," Proceedings of the Business and Economic Statistical Association, 1962.

p. 326   Statistics Canada, *Canadian Economic Observer, Historical Statistical Supplement, 1992/93* (July 1993), cat. no. 11-210, p. 12, and *see* Figures 10.3 and 11.4.

Chapter 12

p. 334   Truman quoted in Augarde, ed., *The Oxford Dictionary of Modern Quotations* (Oxford: Oxford University Press, 1991), p. 218.

p. 334   *Canadian Economic Observer, Historical Statistical Supplement, 1992/93* (July 1993), cat. no. 11-210, p. 7.

p. 352   *Ibid.*

Chapter 13

p. 370   Innis quoted in *The Dictionary of Canadian Quotations and Phrases*, p. 299.

p. 382   John F. Helliwell, et al., "Comparing the Dynamics of Canadian Macro Models" in Canadian Journal of Economics, vol. 12 (February–November 1979), p. 186.

p. 384   *See* Developing Interpretation Skills—Mountain or Mirage? The Debate Over Public Debt. *The Budget Plan* (Department of Finance, Canada: February 1994) p. 50.

p. 385   *Quarterly Economic Review: Special Report—Fiscal Indicators and Reference Tables* (Department of Finance, Canada: March 1992), p. 25.

p. 386   *The Budget Plan* (February 1994), table 14, and *see* Figure 13.6.

p. 388   *See* Figure 11.5.

Chapter 14

p. 402   This quotation first appeared in the *Family Therapy Networker*. The author is Nora Gallagher and is copied here with permission.

p. 407   Canadian Bankers Association, *Bank Facts 1994*, p. 1. Canadian Bankers Association, *Bank Financial Results 1992/93 Fiscal Year, Domestic Banks*, (December 1993), p. 22. H.H. Binhammer, *Money, Banking and the Canadian Financial System*, 6th ed. (Toronto: Nelson, 1993), p. 187.

p. 407   U.S. Bureau of the Census, *Statistical Abstract of the United States 1992*, 112th ed. (Washington, DC: 1992), p. 496.

p. 421   Ronald A. Shearer, et al., *The Economics of the Canadian Financial System*, 2nd ed. (Scarborough: Prentice-Hall, 1984), p. 333.

p. 425   *Money, Banking and the Canadian Financial System*, p. 268.

Chapter 15

p. 442   Leacock quoted in John Robert Colombo, ed., *Colombo's Canadian Quotations* (Edmonton: Hurtig, 1974), p. 342.

p. 448   John Saywell, *Canadian Annual Review for 1969* (Toronto: University of Toronto Press, 1970), p. 316; Margot J. Fawcett, *The 1976 Corpus Almanac of Canada* (Toronto: Corpus Publishers Services, 1976), pp. 10–36.

p. 455   Milton Friedman, "The Role of Monetary Policy" in *The American Economic Review*, vol. 58 (1) (March 1968), p. 16.

p. 461   U.S. Bureau of the Census, *Statistical Abstract of the United States 1992* (Washington: U.S. Department of Commerce, 1992), pp. 315, 381, 473.

p. 462   Charles E. Stuart, "Swedish Tax Rates, Labor Supply, and Tax Revenues" in *Journal of Political Economy*, vol. 89 (5) (October 1981), p. 1020.

Part 4

p. 469   Jane Jacobs, *Systems of Survival* (New York: Random House, 1994), p. i.

Chapter 16

p. 470   Peter F. Drucker, "The Age of Social Transformation" in *The Atlantic Monthly*, vol. 274 no. 5, November 1994, p. 76.

p. 494   *The Canadian Encyclopedia* (Edmonton: Hurtig, 1985), p. 602.

Chapter 17

p. 504   Dales quoted in *The Dictionary of Canadian Quotations and Phrases*, p. 302.

p. 506   World Bank, *World Development Report 1993* (Oxford: Oxford University Press, 1993), p. 255. *The Economist* (19 September 1992), p. 6.

p. 508   *Canadian Economic Observer, Historical Statistical Supplement, 1993/94*, cat. no. 11–210, p. 60. Economic Council of Canada, *Employment in the Service Economy* (Ottawa: Ministry of Supply and Services, 1991), pp. 8, 15–17, 58; Statistics Canada, *Canadian Economic Observer* (October 1993), cat. no. 11-010, Table 3; *Canadian Economic Observer, Historical Statistical Supplement, 1993/94*, cat. no. 11-210, pp. 56–57; *Canada's International Transactions in Services 1992 and 1993* (July 1994), cat. no. 67-203, pp. 17–18, 23, 28.

p. 510   *World Development Report 1993*, p. 268.

p. 519   Ingrid A. Bryan, *Canada in the New Global Economy* (Toronto: John Wiley & Sons, 1994), p. 303.

p. 523   *The Economist* (9 April 1994), p. 52.

p. 526   *The Globe and Mail* (21 January 1993), p. B1.

p. 527   Richard Pomfret, *The Economic Development of Canada*, 2nd ed. (Toronto: Nelson, 1993), pp. 42–49.

p. 527   Instituto del Tercer Mundo, *Third World Guide 93/94* (Toronto: Garamond Press, 1984), p. 81.

p. 527   *The Economist* (26 March 1994), p. 58; (21 May 1994), p. 69.

p. 530   Daniel Schwanen, "A Growing Success: Canada's Performance Under Free Trade," in *C.D. Howe Institute Commentary*, no. 52 (September 1993).

Chapter 18

p. 538   Roddick quoted in *The Globe and Mail* (17 February 1994), p. B7.

p. 540   *Canadian Economic Observer, Historical Statistical Supplement, 1993/94*, p. 7.

p. 543   *See* Chapter 10 Sideline—Canadians Live Best.

p. 545   Statistics Canada, *Aggregate Productivity Measures* (July 1991), cat. no. 15-204E, p. 85.

p. 545   *See* Figure 18-7.

p. 546   *Aggregate Productivity Measures*, p. 85.

p. 547   Statistics Canada, *Industrial Research and Development 1993 Intentions* (September 1993), cat. no. 88-202, p. 14.

p. 547   Statistics Canada, *Education in Canada* (November 1993), cat. no. 81-229, pp. 117, 245; *1973 Education in Canada*, cat. no. 4-2200-501, pp. 403, 508.

p. 548   *Aggregate Productivity Measures*, p. 19.

p. 549   *World Development Report 1991*, p. 137.

p. 551   *World Development Report 1990*, p. 1.

p. 551   *World Development Report 1993*, p. 234.

p. 554   *World Development Report 1991*, p. 14.

p. 555   *The Economist* (15 May 1993), p. 15.

p. 559   *Ibid.* (27 August 1994), pp. 15–17.

p. 559   *Ibid.* (25 September 1993), pp. 33–34.

p. 559   *See* Figure 18.7.

Glossary

ability to pay: the principle applied to taxation whereby taxes vary in proportion to a taxpayer's financial resources

absolute advantage: the benefit enjoyed by a producer who can supply a certain quantity of an item more efficiently than can other producers

accounting-profit rate: a measure of a business's profitability, calculated as its accounting profit divided by owner's equity

aggregate demand: the relationship between the general price level and total spending in the economy

aggregate demand curve: the relationship between the general price level and total spending in the economy expressed on a graph

aggregate demand factors: variables that cause changes in total expenditures at all price levels

aggregate demand schedule: the relationship between the general price level and total spending in the economy expressed in a table

aggregate supply: the relationship between the general price level and real output produced in the economy

aggregate supply curve: the relationship between the general price level and real output expressed on a graph

aggregate supply factors: variables that change total output at all price levels

aggregate supply schedule: the relationship between the general price level and real output expressed in a table

annually balanced budget: the principle that government revenues and expenditures should balance each year

appreciate: to increase, as when a currency's price rises in comparison to the price of another currency

arbitration: the process of having an outside party determine and dictate a settlement to employers and unions

asset demand: the demand for money that is related to its use as a store of purchasing power

Auto Pact: the 1965 agreement establishing free trade in autos and auto parts between Canada and the United States; formerly known as the Canada–U.S. Automotive Products Agreement

automatic stabilizers: built-in measures, such as

taxation and transfer payment programs, that lessen the effects of the business cycle

average cost: the sum of average fixed cost and average variable cost at each quantity of output

average-cost pricing: the practice of setting price where it equals average cost

average fixed cost: the fixed cost per unit of output

average product: the quantity of output produced per worker

average revenue: a business's total revenue per unit of output

average variable cost: the variable cost per unit of output

balance-of-payments accounts: a summary of all transactions between Canadians and foreigners that involve exchanging Canadian dollars for other currencies

balance-of-payments deficit: a negative net balance on the balance-of-payments statement, demonstrating lower receipts than payments for the current and capital accounts combined; balanced with changes in official reserves

balance-of-payments surplus: a positive net balance on the balance-of-payments statement, demonstrating greater receipts than payments for the current and capital accounts combined; balanced with changes in official reserves

balance of trade: for both goods and services, receipts (inflows of Canadian dollars) less payments (outflows of Canadian dollars)

balanced budget: the situation where a government's expenditures and revenues are equal

bank rate: the interest rate chartered banks are charged on advances from the Bank of Canada

barter: a system of trading one product for another

base year: the survey year used as a point of comparison in subsequent years

benefits received: the principle applied to taxation whereby taxes are geared to the benefits each taxpayer gains from government activity

bond: a contract between a borrower and the holder of the contract that entitles the holder to interest plus repayment at the maturity date

breakeven point: the level of output where price

(or average revenue) equals average cost

budget deficit: the situation where a government's expenditures exceed its revenues

budget surplus: the situation where a government's revenues exceed its expenditures

business: an enterprise that brings individuals, financial resources, and economic resources together to produce a good or service for economic gain

business cycle: the cycle of expansions and contractions in the economy

business's demand curve: the demand curve faced by an individual business, as opposed to an entire market

business's labour demand curve: a graph showing the possible combinations of workers demanded by a business at each possible wage

business's labour supply curve: a graph showing the possible combinations of workers supplied to a business at each possible wage

business's supply curve: a curve that shows the quantity of output supplied by a business at every possible price

Canada Savings Bonds: federal government bonds that have a set value throughout their term

capital account: the summary of all international transactions of financial assets involving Canadian dollars

capital account deficit: a negative net balance in the capital account, demonstrating higher investments by Canadians in foreign markets than by foreigners in the Canadian economy

capital account surplus: a positive net balance in the capital account, demonstrating lower investments by Canadians in foreign markets than by foreigners in the Canadian economy

capital gains: earnings from selling an asset, such as land, at a higher price than it was purchased for

capital good: an item that is used to produce other products

capital-intensive process: a production process that employs more capital and less labour

capital resources: the processed materials, equipment, and buildings used in production; also known as capital

capital stock: the total value of productive assets that provide a flow of revenue

cartel: a union of oligopolists who have a formal market-sharing agreement

cash reserves: funds kept on hand by deposit-takers to meet the needs of depositors withdrawing funds

ceteris paribus: the assumption that all other things remain the same

change in official reserves: use of the government's reserves of foreign currency to influence the international value of the Canadian dollar, as shown on the balance-of-payments statement

change in quantity demanded: the effect of a price change on quantity demanded

change in quantity supplied: the effect of a price change on quantity supplied

chartered banks: deposit-takers allowed by federal charter to offer a wide range of financial services

circular flows: the circulation of money and the circulation of consumer products and economic resources in the economy

closed shop: a specific labour market in which all workers covered by a collective agreement must be union members

coincidence of wants: the situation where someone purchasing an item finds a seller who wants what the purchaser is offering in return

collateral: assets pledged by a borrower as security against a loan; these assets can be seized by the lender if the loan is not repaid

collective bargaining: the process of union representatives negotiating with employers over workers' wages, hours, and working conditions

collusion: oligopolists acting together as if they are a monopoly

command economy: an economic system based on public ownership and central planning

common market: a group of countries with not only a free trade area and common trade barriers with outside countries, but also free movement of labour and capital

comparative advantage: the benefit enjoyed by a producer who can supply a certain item with a lower opportunity cost than can other producers

complementary goods: products that are consumed together

complementary resources: resources that are used together

concentration ratio: the percentage of total sales revenue in a market earned by the largest businesses

constant-cost industry: an industry that is not a major user of any single resource

constant returns to scale: a situation in which a percentage increase in all inputs results in an equal percentage increase in output

consumer price index: a measure of price changes for a typical basket of consumer products

consumer product: an item that gratifies people's needs and wants

consumer sovereignty: the effect of consumer needs and wants on production decisions

contraction: a sustained fall in real output of an economy

contractionary fiscal policy: government policy that involves decreasing government purchases, increasing taxes, or both to restrain spending and output

contractionary monetary policy: a policy of decreasing the money supply and increasing interest rates to dampen the economy

contractionary policies: government policies designed to stabilize prices and reduce output

corporation: a company that has a legal status independent of its owners

cost of living: the amount consumers must spend on the entire range of goods and services they buy

cost-of-living adjustment clauses: provisions for income adjustments to accommodate changes in price levels, which are included in wage contracts

cost-push inflation: inflation that occurs as increased production costs decrease aggregate supply, which then pushes up prices

craft union: a labour union of workers in a particular occupation

credit card: a means of payment that provides instantly borrowed funds

credit risk: the assessed likelihood of a borrower not repaying a loan

crowding-out effect: the effect of more government borrowing raising interest rates, which reduces or "crowds out" private investment spending

currency: paper money and coins

current account: the summary of all foreign transactions associated with current economic activity in Canada and involving Canadian dollars

current account deficit: a negative net balance in the current account resulting from lower receipts than payments for merchandise and nonmerchandise transactions

current account surplus: a positive net balance in the current account resulting from higher receipts than payments for merchandise and nonmerchandise transactions

customs union: a group of countries with common trade barriers with outside countries as well as a free trade area

cyclical unemployment: unemployment due to the ups and downs of economies and businesses

cyclically balanced budget: the principle that government revenues and expenditures should balance over the course of one business cycle

debit card: a means of payment that instantaneously transfers funds from buyer to seller

decision lag: the amount of time needed to formulate and implement an appropriate policy

decrease in aggregate demand: a decrease in total expenditures at all price levels

decrease in demand: a decrease in the quantity demanded of a product at all prices

decrease in supply: a decrease in the quantity supplied of a product at all prices

deduction: a type of reasoning in which one states a hypothesis before examining the facts

deflation: a general decrease in the level of prices

demand: the relationship between the various possible prices of a product and the quantities of that product consumers are willing to purchase

demand curve: a graph that expresses possible combinations of prices and quantities demanded of a product

demand deposits: accounts of funds to which depositors have immediate access

demand determinants: factors that can cause an increase or a decrease in a product's demand

demand for Canadian dollars: the relationship between the price of a Canadian dollar and the quantity demanded on the foreign exchange market

demand-pull inflation: inflation that occurs as increased aggregate demand pulls up prices

demand schedule: a table that shows possible combinations of prices and quantities demanded of a product

dependent variable: the variable in a causal relationship that is affected by another variable

deposit-takers: institutions or businesses that accept funds provided by savers and lend these funds to borrowers

depreciate: to decrease, as when a currency's price falls in comparison to the price of another currency

depreciation: the decrease in value of durable real assets over time

depression: a particularly long and harsh period of reduced real output

desired reserves: minimum cash reserves that deposit-takers hold to satisfy anticipated withdrawal demands

devaluation: a reduction in the value of a currency by the government that sets the exchange rate

direct investment: long-term financial investment (e.g., purchases of stocks) that gives the buyer of the financial assets a controlling interest in the institution issuing the assets

direct relationship: a relationship in which a change in the independent variable causes a change in the same direction of the dependent variable

discouraged workers: unemployed workers who have given up looking for work

discretionary income: disposable income minus purchases of necessities

discretionary policy: intentional government intervention in the economy, such as budgeted changes in spending or taxation

diseconomies of scale: a situation in which a percentage increase in all inputs causes a smaller percentage increase in output

disposable income: household income minus personal taxes and other personal transfers to government

division of labour: the extent to which jobs of different workers are specialized into separate tasks

double counting: the problem of adding to GDP the same item at different stages in its production

durable goods: goods that are consumed repeatedly over time

economic costs: a business's total explicit and implicit costs

economic development: an increase in a country's per capita income that is accompanied by a general rise in living standards

economic efficiency: employing scarce resources in such a way as to derive the highest benefit

economic growth: an increase in an economy's total output of goods and services

economic models: generalizations about or simplifications of economic reality; also known as laws, principles, or theories

economic problem: the problem of having needs and unlimited wants, but limited resources with which to satisfy them

economic profit: the excess of a business's total revenue over its economic costs

economic resources: basic items that are used in all types of production, including natural, capital, and human resources

economic system: the organization of an economy, which represents a country's distinct set of social customs, political institutions, and economic practices

economic value: the opportunity cost of a product

economics: the study of how to distribute scarce resources among alternative ends

economies of scale: a situation in which a per-

centage increase in all inputs causes a larger percentage increase in output

elastic demand: demand for which a percentage change in a product's price causes a larger percentage change in quantity demanded

elastic supply: supply for which a percentage change in a product's price causes a larger percentage change in quantity supplied

entry barriers: economic or institutional obstacles to businesses entering an industry

equation of exchange: the money supply multiplied by the velocity of money equals the price level multiplied by real output

European Union (EU): an expanding common market of European countries first formed in 1956, formerly known as the European Economic Community (EEC)

excess reserves: cash reserves that are in excess of desired reserves

exchange rate: the value of one nation's currency in terms of another currency

excise taxes: taxes that are charged on particular products, and often expressed as a dollar amount per unit of quantity

expansion: a sustained rise in real output of an economy

expansionary fiscal policy: government policy

that involves increasing government purchases, decreasing taxes, or both to stimulate spending and output

expansionary monetary policy: a policy of increasing the money supply and reducing interest rates to stimulate the economy

expansionary policies: government policies designed to reduce unemployment and stimulate output

expenditure approach: a method of calculating Gross Domestic Product by adding together all spending in the economy

expenditure equation: the equation that states that GDP is the sum of personal consumption (C), gross investment (I), government purchases (G), and net exports (X – M)

explicit costs: payments made by a business to businesses or people outside of it

exponential growth: growth that is based on a percentage change and that builds on itself

export subsidies: payments by a government to domestic exporters so that these exporters can reduce the prices they charge in foreign markets

exports: foreign purchases of Canadian goods and services

fair rate of return: the maximum accounting-profit rate allowed for a regulated monopoly

final products: products that will not be processed further and will not be resold

financial capital: assets in the form of cash, bonds, and shares

fiscal policy: government stabilization policy that uses taxes and government purchases as its tools; budgetary policy

fiscal year: the twelve-month period to which a budget applies

fixed costs: economic costs for inputs that remain fixed at all quantities of output

fixed exchange rates: currency exchange rates set or "pegged" to a certain value by each country's government

fixed incomes: nominal incomes that remain fixed at some dollar amount regardless of the rate of inflation

fixed inputs: inputs whose quantities cannot be adjusted in the short run

flexible exchange rates: currency exchange rates that are allowed to move freely to their equilibrium levels; also called floating rates

foreign currency deposits: accounts of funds held by Canadian residents that are valued in foreign currency

foreign exchange market: the global market in which national currencies are traded

foreign trade effect: with changes in the price level, expenditures on imports change in the same direction, while expenditures on exports change in the opposite direction

free goods: items that are so plentiful that they do not have any cost

Free Trade Agreement (FTA): the 1988 pact between Canada and the United States to form a free trade area

free trade area: an area in which trade is tariff-free, although member countries are able to impose separate trade barriers on outside countries

frictional unemployment: unemployment due to being temporarily between jobs or looking for a first job

full employment: the highest reasonable expectation of employment for the economy as a whole

fully indexed incomes: nominal incomes that automatically increase by the rate of inflation

functional finance: the principle that government budgets should be geared to the yearly needs of the economy

GDP deflator: an indicator of price changes for all goods and services produced in the economy

GDP gap: the difference between potential and actual real output, or Gross Domestic Product, of an economy

GDP identity: Gross Domestic Product calculated as total income is identical to Gross Domestic Product calculated as total spending

General Agreement on Tariffs and Trade (GATT): a multilateral trade agreement that lessens the degree of trade protection among member countries, including Canada

globalization: the trend of growing foreign trade and investment and the spread of international businesses and markets

government purchases: current government spending on goods and services

Gross Domestic Product: the total dollar value at current prices of all final goods and services produced in Canada over a given period

gross investment: purchases of assets that are intended to produce revenue

Gross National Product: the total income acquired by Canadians both within Canada and elsewhere

high-income countries: countries with per capita incomes substantial enough to provide their citizens with widespread prosperity

human capital: the income-earning potential of a person's skills and knowledge

human resources: the efforts of people involved in production, including labour and entrepreneurship

hypothesis: a formal statement of a tentative observation or insight, to be tested for its validity

immediate run: the production period during which none of the resources required to make a product can be varied

impact lag: the amount of time between a policy's implementation and its having an effect on the economy

implicit costs: the owner's opportunity costs of being involved with a business

import quota: a set limit on the quantity of a good that can be imported in a given year

imports: Canadian purchases of foreign goods and services

income approach: a method of calculating Gross Domestic Product by adding together all incomes in the economy

increase in aggregate demand: an increase in total expenditures at all price levels

increase in demand: an increase in the quantity demanded of a product at all prices

increase in supply: an increase in the quantity supplied of a product at all prices

increasing-cost industry: an industry that is a major user of at least one resource

independent variable: the variable in a causal relationship that causes change in another variable

induction: a type of reasoning in which one states a hypothesis after examining the facts

industrial concentration: market domination by one or a few large businesses

industrial union: a labour union of workers in a certain industry, no matter what their occupations

industrially advanced countries (IACs): countries that have a high degree of industrialization

inelastic demand: demand for which a percentage change in a product's price causes a smaller percentage change in quantity demanded

inelastic supply: supply for which the percentage change in a product's price causes a smaller percentage change in quantity supplied

infant industry: a domestic industry that is young in comparison to its foreign competitors

inferior goods: products whose demand changes inversely with income

inflation: a general rise in prices

inflation premium: a percentage built into a nominal interest rate to anticipate the rate of inflation for the loan period

inflationary gap: the amount by which equilibri-

um output exceeds potential output

injections: additions to an economy's income-spending stream

inputs: the resources used in production

interest: the payment to a lender for use of money loaned

interest rate: the percentage rate with which interest on loans is determined

intermediate products: products that will be processed further or will be resold

inventories: stocks of unsold goods and materials

inverse relationship: a relationship in which a change in the independent variable causes a change in the opposite direction of the dependent variable

investment demand: the relationship between interest rates and investment

investment demand curve: the relationship between interest rates and investment expressed on a graph

investment demand schedule: the relationship between interest rates and investment expressed in a table

invisible hand: the tendency for competitive markets to turn self-interested behaviour into socially beneficial activity

item weights: the proportions of each good in

the total cost of the basket of consumer goods used to calculate CPI

job discrimination: hiring, wage, and promotion decisions based on criteria other than a worker's credentials or performance

job segregation: the discriminatory division of occupations

kinked demand curve: a demand curve with two segments, one fairly flat and one steep, that is typical of rival oligopolists

labour force: all people who either have a job or are actively seeking employment

labour force population: the population, with specific exclusions, from which Statistics Canada takes a random sample for the labour force survey

labour-intensive process: a production process that employs more labour and less capital

labour market demand curve: a graph showing the possible combinations of workers demanded in a certain labour market at each possible wage

labour market supply curve: a graph showing the possible combinations of workers supplying their labour in a certain labour market at each possible wage

labour productivity: the quantity of output produced per worker in a given period of time; the average product of labour

labour unions: workers' organizations that negotiate with employers about wages, working conditions, and job benefits

Laffer curve: a curve that expresses the assumed relationship between tax rates and tax revenues

laissez faire: the principle that governments benefit society the most by not interfering in economic activity

law of comparative advantage: states that maximum output is achieved when producers specialize in what they can make at a lower opportunity cost than can other producers

law of demand: states that there is an inverse relationship between a product's quantity demanded and its price

law of diminishing marginal returns: at some point, as more units of a variable input are added to a fixed input, the marginal product will start to decrease

law of increasing opportunity costs: the concept that as more of one item is produced by an economy, the opportunity cost of additional units of that product rises

law of supply: states that there is a direct relationship between a product's quantity supplied and its price

less-developed countries (LDCs): countries

with traditional mixed economies and low per capita incomes

liquidity: the ease with which an asset can be converted into a means of payment

loanable funds: all the monies made available to lenders by borrowers

lockout: the employer tactic of barring workers from the workplace

long run: the production period during which all resources required to make a product can be varied, and businesses may either enter or leave the industry

long-run average cost: the minimum short-run average cost at each possible level of output

long-run decrease in aggregate supply: a decrease in total and potential output at all price levels

long-run increase in aggregate supply: an increase in total and potential output at all price levels

Lorenz curve: a graph showing the cumulative distribution of income among a country's households

low-income countries: the poorest countries in the world, as defined by per capita incomes

M1: the narrowest definition of money, consisting of publicly held currency and publicly held demand deposits at chartered banks

M2: a broader definition of money, consisting of M1

plus notice deposits, and personal term deposits at chartered banks

M2+: the definition of money consisting of M2 plus corresponding deposits at near banks

M3: the definition of money consisting of M2 plus non-personal term deposits and foreign currency deposits at chartered banks

macroeconomics: the branch of economics that takes a wide-ranging view of the economy, studying the behaviour of economic sectors

managed float: a flexible exchange rate system that sometimes involves short-term government intervention

marginal cost: the extra cost of producing an additional unit of output

marginal-cost pricing: the practice of setting price where it equals marginal cost

marginal product: the extra output produced by an additional worker

marginal productivity theory: the theory that businesses use resources based on how much extra profit these resources provide

marginal propensity to consume: the effect on domestic consumption of a change in income

marginal propensity to withdraw: the effect on withdrawals—saving, imports, and taxes— of a change in income

marginal resource cost: the extra cost of each additional unit of a resource

marginal revenue: the extra total revenue earned from an additional unit of output

marginal revenue product: the change in total revenue associated with employing each new unit of a resource

marginal tax rates: tax rates that are calculated as percentages of each extra dollar of taxable income

market: a set of arrangements between buyers and sellers of a certain item

market demand: the sum of all consumers' quantity demanded for a product at each price

market economy: an economic system based on private ownership and the use of markets in economic decision-making

market equilibrium: the stable point at which demand and supply curves intersect

market power: a business's ability to affect the price of the product it sells

market share: a business's proportion of total market sales

market supply: the sum of all producers' quantity supplied at each price

means testing: a procedure whereby transfer payments vary according to a recipient's income

mediation: the process of

having an outside party determine and propose a settlement to employers and unions

merchandise balance of trade: merchandise export receipts minus merchandise import payments

microeconomics: the branch of economics that focuses on the behaviour of individual participants in various markets

middle-income countries: countries in which a sizable minority of the population no longer lives in acute poverty

minimum-cost pricing: the practice of setting price where it equals minimum average cost

modern mixed economy: an economic system that combines aspects of a market economy and a command economy; production decisions are made both in private markets and by government

monetarism: an economic perspective that emphasizes the influence of money on the economy and the ability of private markets to accommodate change

monetary policy: government stabilization policy that uses interest rates and the money supply as its tools

monetary rule: a law that forces the central bank to increase the money supply by a constant rate each year

money demand: the amounts of money

demanded at all possible interest rates

money demand curve: money demand expressed in a graph

money demand schedule: money demand expressed in a table

money multiplier: the value by which the amount of excess reserves is multiplied to give the maximum total change in money supply

money supply: a set amount of money in the economy, as determined by government decision-makers

money supply curve: money supply expressed in a graph

money supply schedule: money supply expressed in a table

monopolistic competition: a market structure characterized by many buyers and sellers of slightly different products and easy entry to, and exit from, the industry

monopoly: a market structure characterized by only one business supplying a product with no close substitutes and restricted entry to the industry

moral suasion: direct influence by the Bank of Canada on chartered banks' lending policies

multiplier effect: the magnified impact of a spending change on aggregate demand

mutual interdependence: the relationship between oligopolists, in which the actions of each business affect the other businesses

national income accounts: accounts showing the levels of total income and spending in the Canadian economy

National Policy: a Canadian policy initiated in 1879 that included high Canadian tariffs on manufactured imports in order to stimulate a domestic manufacturing sector

natural monopoly: a market in which only one business is economically viable because of economies of scale

natural resources: the resources from nature that are used in production, including land, raw materials, and natural processes

natural unemployment rate: the unemployment rate that defines full employment

near banks: deposit-takers that are not chartered and have more specialized services; mainly trust companies, mortgage loan companies, and credit unions

near money: all deposits not included in M1, plus some highly liquid assets

needs: the essentials of life, such as food and shelter

negative unplanned investment: an unintended decrease in inventories; a shortage

net domestic income: the total income earned by Canada's households

net exports: exports minus imports

net investment: gross investment minus depreciation

net tax revenues: taxes collected, minus transfers and subsidies

newly industrializing countries (NICs): countries that recently have exhibited strong economic growth and rapid industrialization

nominal GDP: Gross Domestic Product expressed in current dollars

nominal income: income expressed in current dollars

nominal interest rate: the interest rate expressed in money terms

nondurable goods: goods that are consumed just once

nonmarket activities: productive activities that take place outside the marketplace

nonprice competition: efforts to increase demand through product differentiation, advertising, or both

non-tariff barriers (NTBs): trade barriers other than tariffs that are used to restrict imports; include import quotas, voluntary export restraints, and domestic regulations

normal goods: products whose demand changes directly with income

normal profit: the minimum return necessary for

owners to keep funds in their business

normative economics: the study of how the economy ought to operate

North American Free Trade Agreement (NAFTA): the 1993 pact among Canada, the United States, and Mexico to form a free trade area

notice deposits: accounts of funds for which deposit-takers may require notice before withdrawals can be made

oligopoly: a market structure characterized by only a few businesses offering standard or similar products and restricted entry to the industry

open market operations: the buying and selling of federal government bonds by the Bank of Canada

open shop: a specific labour market in which union membership is not compulsory

opportunity cost: the utility that could have been gained by choosing an action's best alternative

output: the quantity of a good or service that results from production

partially indexed incomes: nominal incomes that increase by less than the rate of inflation

participation rate: the percentage of the entire labour force population that makes up the labour force

partnership: an unincorporated business that is owned by two or more people

peak: the point in the business cycle at which real output is at its highest

per capita GDP: GDP per person, calculated as GDP divided by population

per capita real GDP: GDP per person, expressed in constant dollars from a given year

perfect competition: a market structure characterized by many buyers and sellers of a standard product and easy entry to and exit from the industry

perfectly elastic demand: demand for which a product's price remains constant regardless of quantity demanded

perfectly elastic supply: supply for which a product's price remains constant regardless of quantity supplied

perfectly inelastic demand: demand for which a product's quantity demanded remains constant regardless of price

perfectly inelastic supply: supply for which a product's quantity supplied remains constant regardless of price

personal consumption: household spending on goods and services

personal income: the income actually received by households

personal saving: funds saved by households

Phillips curve: a curve expressing the assumed fixed and predictable inverse relationship between unemployment and inflation

picketing: the practice of striking workers taking positions around the outside of the workplace, usually with signs, to publicize their cause to others

portfolio investment: long-term financial investment (e.g., purchases of stocks and bonds) that does not give the buyer a controlling interest in the institution issuing the assets

positive economics: the study of economic facts and how the economy operates as it does

positive unplanned investment: an unintended increase in inventories; a surplus

potential output: the real output, or Gross Domestic Product, associated with full employment

poverty: a situation in which a person's income is inadequate to provide the necessities of life

poverty line: an income level below which a household is classified as poor

predatory pricing: an unfair business practice of temporarily lowering prices to drive out competitors in an industry

price ceiling: a maximum price set below equilibrium

price elasticity of demand: the responsiveness of a product's quantity demanded to a change in its price

price elasticity of supply: the responsiveness of a product's quantity supplied to a change in price

price floor: a minimum price set above equilibrium

price leadership: an understanding among oligopolists that one business will initiate all price changes in the market and the others will follow by adjusting their prices and output accordingly

prime rate: the lowest possible interest rate charged by chartered banks on loans to their best corporate customers

principal: the amount of a loan, excluding interest

private sector: the part of an economy in which private markets dominate

product differentiation: efforts to make a product distinct from that of competitors

product markets: markets in which consumer, or final, products are traded

production: the process of transforming a set of resources into a good or service that has economic value

production possibilities curve: a graph that illustrates the possible output combinations for an economy

production possibilities schedule: a table that shows the possible output combinations for an economy

productive efficiency: making a given quantity of output at the lowest cost

profit-maximizing employment rule: states that a business should use a resource up to the point where the resource's marginal revenue product equals its marginal resource cost

profit-maximizing rule: produce at the level of output where marginal revenue and marginal cost intersect

progressive tax: a tax that increases as a proportion of income as income increases

proportional tax: a tax that remains constant as a proportion of income for all incomes

public debt: the total amount owed by the federal government as a result of its past borrowing

public debt charges: the amounts paid out each year by the federal government to cover the interest charges on its public debt

public good: a product whose benefits cannot be restricted to certain individuals

public sector: the part of an economy in which governments dominate

quantity demanded: the amount of a product consumers are willing to purchase at each price

quantity supplied: the amount of a product businesses are willing to supply at each price

quantity theory of money: a theory stating that the velocity of money and real output are relatively stable over short periods

real capital: assets such as buildings, equipment, and materials used by businesses to produce goods and services

real expenditures: total spending in an economy, adjusted for changes in the general price level

real GDP: GDP expressed in constant dollars from a given year

real income: income expressed in constant base-year dollars

real interest rate: the nominal interest rate minus the rate of inflation

real rate of return: constant-dollar extra profit provided by a project each year stated as a percentage of the project's initial cost

recession: a decline in real output that lasts for six months or more

recessionary gap: the amount by which equilibrium output falls short of potential output

recognition lag: the amount of time it takes policy-makers to realize that a policy is needed

regressive tax: a tax that decreases as a proportion of income as income increases

rent: the payment for use of a productive resource that is available only in a fixed amount

research and development expenditures (R&D): spending that is meant to accelerate the pace of technological progress

reserve ratio: desired reserves expressed as a percentage of deposits or as a decimal

resource markets: markets in which economic resources are traded

retained earnings: profits kept by businesses for new investment

revaluation: an increase in the value of a currency by the government that sets the exchange rate

Rule of 72: states that the number of years it takes a variable to double can be estimated by dividing 72 by the variable's annual percentage growth rate

sales taxes: taxes that are charged on a wide range of products, and calculated as a percentage of their prices

scarcity: the limited nature of resources, which underlies the basic economic problem

seasonal unemployment: unemployment due to the seasonal nature of some occupations and industries

self-interest motive: the assumption that people act to maximize their own welfare

seniority rights: the workplace privileges provided to workers who have the longest experience with their employer

share: partial ownership of a corporation, which entitles the shareholder to dividends and, hopefully, a profit once the share is sold; also called a stock

short run: the production period during which at least one of the resources required to make a product cannot be varied

short-run decrease in aggregate supply: a decrease in total output at all price levels, with no change in potential output

short-run increase in aggregate supply: an increase in total output at all price levels, with no change in potential output

shortage: an excess of quantity demanded over quantity supplied

shutdown point: the level of output where price (or average revenue) equals average variable cost

sole proprietorship: an unincorporated business that is owned by a single person

speculators: individuals or organizations that buy and sell currencies for profit

spending multiplier: the value by which an initial spending change is multiplied to give the total change in real output

spillover benefits: positive external effects of pro-

ducing or consuming a product

spillover costs: negative external effects of producing or consuming a product

spillover effects: external effects of economic activity, which have an impact on outsiders who are not producing or consuming a product

stabilization policy: government policy designed to lessen the effects of the business cycle

stagflation: a combination of consistently low output (and so constant or expanding unemployment) and rising inflation

strategic trade policy: the use of programs such as export subsidies to help domestic producers enter potentially lucrative markets

strike: the union tactic of members ceasing to work

structural unemployment: unemployment due to a mismatch between people and jobs

substitute goods: products that can be consumed in place of one another

substitute resources: resources that can be used in place of one another without affecting output

supply: the relationship between the various possible prices of a product and the quantities of the product that businesses are willing to supply

supply curve: a graph that expresses possible

combinations of prices and quantities supplied of a product

supply determinants: factors that can cause an increase or a decrease in a product's supply

supply of Canadian dollars: the relationship between the price of a Canadian dollar and the quantity supplied on the foreign exchange market

supply schedule: a table that shows possible combinations of prices and quantities supplied of a product

supply-side economics: the view that adjustments in aggregate supply are the most critical element of government activity

surplus: an excess of quantity supplied over quantity demanded

tariff: an excise tax on imported goods

tax: a payment required by government from individuals or businesses, with no direct good or service being provided in return

technological progress: consists of scientific discoveries and their application, advances in production methods, and the development of new types of products

term deposits: accounts of funds to which depositors have no access for a fixed period of time

terms of trade: the international price of one product in terms of another

total cost: the sum of all fixed and variable costs at each quantity of output

total product: the overall quantity of output produced with a given workforce

total revenue: the total income earned from a product, calculated by multiplying the product's price by its quantity demanded

trading bloc: a relatively small number of countries involved in a trade agreement

traditional economy: an economic system in which economic decisions are made on the basis of custom

traditional mixed economies: economic systems in which a traditional sector co-exists with modern sectors

traditional sector: the part of an economy in which custom and traditional production techniques dominate

transactions demand: the demand for money that is related to its use as a means of exchange

transfer payments: government payments to households or other levels of government

treasury bills: short-term federal government bonds that provide no interest, but are sold at a discount

trough: the point in the business cycle at which real output is at its lowest

underemployment: the problem of workers being underutilized, either as part-time workers or by working at jobs not appropriate to their skills or education

underground economy: all the productive transactions that go unreported

unemployment rate: the percentage of a labour force that is involuntarily unemployed

union shop: a specific labour market in which all workers covered by a collective agreement must become union members after a certain period of employment

unit-elastic demand: demand for which a percentage change in price causes an equal change in quantity demanded

unit of account: a pricing standard that allows all products to be valued consistently

universality: the principle applied to transfer payments whereby benefits are provided to all, regardless of income

utility: the satisfaction gained from any action

value added: the extra worth of a product at each stage in its production; a concept used to avoid double counting in calculating GDP

variable costs: economic costs for inputs that vary at each quantity of output

variable inputs: inputs whose quantities can be adjusted in the short run

variables: factors that have measurable values

velocity of money: the number of times, on average, that money is spent on final goods and services during a given year (a concept that is central to monetarism)

vicious circle of poverty: a cycle whereby low standards of living lead to slow growth, thus keeping standards of living low in the future

voluntary export restraints (VERs): import quotas that are voluntarily put in place by the exporting country

wage: the amount earned by a worker for providing labour for a certain period of time; sometimes known as salary

wage and price controls: government-imposed restrictions on wage and price increases

wage and price guidelines: voluntary restrictions on wage and price increases

wants: desires for nonessential items

wealth: ownership of financial assets, such as stocks and bonds, or real assets, such as buildings and land

wealth effect: with changes in the price level, the real value of households' financial assets changes, causing households to adjust their spending

welfare society: a society in which the government plays a major role in attempting to ensure the economic well-being of its citizens

withdrawals: deductions from an economy's income-spending stream

working to rule: the union tactic of members slowing down work by adhering strictly to their job descriptions

World Bank: an international lending institution known officially as the International Bank for Reconstruction and Development

Index